# TCHAIKOVSKY

# TCHAIKOVSKY

## ANTHONY HOLDEN

BANTAM PRESS

LONDON · NEW YORK · TORONTO · SYDNEY · AUCKLAND

TRANSWORLD PUBLISHERS LTD
61–63 Uxbridge Road, London W5 5SA

TRANSWORLD PUBLISHERS (AUSTRALIA) PTY LTD
15–25 Helles Avenue, Moorebank, NSW 2170

TRANSWORLD PUBLISHERS (NZ) LTD
3 William Pickering Drive, Albany, Auckland

Published 1995 by Bantam Press
a division of Transworld Publishers Ltd
Copyright © Anthony Holden Limited 1995

The right of Anthony Holden to be identified
as the author of this work has been asserted in accordance
with sections 77 and 78 of the Copyright Designs and Patents
Act 1988.

A catalogue record for this book is available
from the British Library

ISBN 0593 024680

Typeset in 10½ on 12½pt ITC Garamond Light by
Phoenix Typesetting, Ilkley, West Yorkshire.

Printed in Great Britain by
Mackays of Chatham, plc, Chatham, Kent.

*For*

RICHARD HOLDEN
LISA HARRISON
BECKY WALSH
DOMINIC GIBBERD
MATTHEW JOHNSON
*and*
ISABEL EVANS

# ACKNOWLEDGEMENTS

THE AUTHOR OF THIS NEW STUDY OF TCHAIKOVSKY – THE PRODUCT of four years' research around Russia, the United States and Europe – is a biographer, not a musicologist. Academics and professional musicians already know that the standard survey of Tchaikovsky's work will long remain David Brown's monumental 'critical and biographical study', written over fifteen years and published in four volumes between 1978 and 1991. Professor Brown has also played an important role in alerting a wider audience to the work of Alexandra Orlova, whose pioneering researches have led to, among many other volumes, her invaluable 'self-portrait' of the composer, in which she tells Tchaikovsky's story in his own words. The most significant recent contribution has come from Alexander Poznansky, a Russian cultural scholar now based at Yale University, whose 'quest for the inner man', published in 1991, offers a fresh and vivid psychological profile.

In recent years, Tchaikovsky studies have seen Orlova and Poznansky locked in mortal combat over the composer's attitude to his sexuality, and above all the mystery surrounding his death, with David Brown acting as a genial referee. All three have been extremely gracious, in their very different ways, to this *parvenu* usurper who suddenly arrived in their midst in 1991, proving brash enough to join the debate with lectures at the 1992 Edinburgh Festival and the 1993 International Tchaikovsky Conference at the University of Tübingen, Germany, as well as conducting an investigation into the composer's death for BBC Television.

David Brown has been particularly generous with his time and expertise, welcoming rather than resenting my sudden decision to pitch my tent on his turf; Alexandra Orlova has also proved a cherished ally, sharing much of her own original research; Alexander Poznansky will disagree strenuously with some of the conclusions reached in this book, but he too engaged in a vigorous exchange of views.

Another renowned Tchaikovsky scholar, Henry Zajaczkowski, imparted freely of his wisdom while I was working on the text. He and David Brown were each kind enough to read the book in manuscript, and make many helpful suggestions, but this should not be taken as any endorsement of my own opinions or conclusions. Other Tchaikovsky *cognoscenti* whom I have reason to thank for their time and expertise include: Boris Nikitin, Yuri Nagibin and Valery Sokolov (Moscow); Arkady Klimovitsky and Georgy Abramovsky (St Petersburg); Vladimir Ashkenazy, Peter Donohoe, Leslie Howard, Nicholas Kenyon, Colin Nears, Ken Russell, Robert Tear and Stephen Walsh (UK).

In three visits to the Tchaikovsky Archive at Klin, north of Moscow, I was warmly welcomed by the director, Galina Belonovich, and deputy director, Marina Turcheva. I was allowed to inspect Tchaikovsky's house, wield his baton, examine his death-mask; but I was refused permission to join the approved Russian scholars at work in the documentary archive itself. The archivist at Klin, Polina Vaidman, herself a noted Tchaikovsky scholar, was extremely patient, and as helpful as current practice permits, in answering my many questions, some of them oft-repeated.

At the St Petersburg Conservatoire, whose first intake of students in 1862 included the twenty-two-year-old Pyotr Ilyich Tchaikovsky, I am grateful for the kind assistance of the director, Vladislav Chernushenko, and deputy director, Alexander Belonenko; Anna Abramovskaya, librarian; Professors Ilya Musin and Ludmila Kovnatskaya; Tatyana Broslavskaya and Natalia Grigorieva.

Also in St Petersburg, I received invaluable help from Inna Voitova, widow of Alexander Voitov, historian and archivist of the School of Jurisprudence; and Boris Mezyas, one of the current occupants of the apartment in which Tchaikovsky died. Chief among others in St Petersburg who offered help, friendship and distinctively Russian hospitality were the actress Tamara Abrosimova, the sculptor Mikhail Annikushin and the television journalist Irina Taimanova. The photographs of St Petersburg in this book were commissioned by the author from Andrey Usov.

The writer Catriona Bass, who happened to be living and working in St Petersburg throughout my research period, led a team of researchers and translators responding to my requests, notably Inessa Lomakhina, Alexander Andreyev and Ekaterina Boyarskaya. Academic institutions where we received assistance include the St Petersburg (formerly, of course, Leningrad) Historical Archive, the St Petersburg Public Library, the Museum of Music and the Arts and the Theatre Museum.

Also in St Petersburg, Elena Budyakovskaya was good enough to share with me some of the work of her father, Andrey Budyakovsky, whose five-volume life of Tchaikovsky was banned from publication by Soviet censors in 1942 – less than a year after his death, aged thirty-six, in besieged Leningrad. Budyakovsky's *Tchaikovsky: the Symphonic Music* had been published in the Soviet Union in 1935; his work on four further volumes, including a biographical study highly candid for its time, was almost complete when the war intervened. Despite the subsequent efforts of his wife and now his daughter, Budyakovsky's pioneering *Tchaikovsky: Life, Musical Activity, Works* has yet to find a publisher, in Russia or elsewhere.

Slava Zelenin was my researcher and interpreter in Moscow, where I also received help and hospitality from Peter Pringle of *The Independent*, Eleanor Randolph of the *Washington Post*, Marcus Warren of the *Daily Telegraph* and David Chater of Sky News (formerly of ITN). Honourable mention should also go to the novelist and entrepreneur Eddy Shah, with whom I managed to cause something of a furore back home by inadvertently spilling the secrets of the Goebbels Diaries after a chance meeting on the ramparts of the Kremlin.

During my travels, my inadequate Russian necessitated the help of Melanie Anstey, Irina Mishina, Yana Goichman and Jane Quigley, who also undertook the translation of various documents back in London, as did Neil Stratton and Charles Earle of Babel Translations, Chiswick, and Emily Matthews. Joe Holden unearthed numerous useful documents in the Central Music Library, Victoria, London. The final responsibility for all translations in the text remains mine, unless otherwise stated in the notes.

I am indebted to the director of the Edinburgh Festival, Brian McMaster, for an invitation to lecture, chair a seminar and otherwise take part in the Tchaikovsky commemoration at the 1992 Edinburgh Festival, where I was kindly housed by Mark and Colette Douglas-Home. It was thanks to Neil Billen, and with the help of Stephen Walsh, that I edited a Festival supplement on Tchaikovsky for *Scotland on Sunday*.

I am also grateful to Prof. Dr Thomas Kohlhase of the University of Tübingen, Germany, for an invitation to lecture on Tchaikovsky's death to a distinguished gathering of scholars from around the world at the 1993 International Tchaikovsky Conference. My interpreter on this occasion was John David Morley, who also helped me run a crucial witness to earth in Niedernhausen, Germany: Mrs Natalya Kuznetsova-Vladimova, younger sister of Tchaikovsky's sister-in-law, who was at first helpful, then decidedly unhelpful, in a series of telephone interviews.

Expert advice on the medical aspects of the composer's death was offered in Moscow by the cholera specialist Valentin Pokrovsky, President of the Russian Academy of Medical Sciences; and in London by Dr David O'Connell and Dr Tom Stuttaford of *The Times*. For other assistance I am indebted to James Burkitt; the Revd Dr Ian Bradley; David Chesterman; George Darby; Raymond Gubbay; Ron Hall; Nicholas Morgan and Susann Smith of BBC Radio 3 and Anna Gregory of Classic FM.

My third and last research trip to Russia was made under the auspices of BBC Television, to make an *Omnibus* film entitled *Who Killed Tchaikovsky?* to mark the centenary of the composer's death. No praise can be too high for the superb team with whom I worked for two months in Russia and six in London: John Purdie, producer/director; Nigel Williams, executive producer; Allen Charlton, editor; Fyodor Popov and Yusuf Baig, production managers; Anne Hampsey, production secretary; and the MosFilm crew of Boris Kocherov, Georgy Gegshidze and Alexander Solomotov, temporarily assisted by Sam Holden.

Of my many friends at Bantam Press in London I am especially grateful for the unfailing support of Ursula Mackenzie, Paul Scherer and Mark Barty-King; the editorial skills of Jennie Bull; the picture research of Celia Dearing; the indexing wizardry of David Lee; and the publicity expertise of Patsy Irwin. In Toronto Cynthia Good of Penguin (Canada) remains an indispensible champion of every diverse project I come up with. In the United States Harold Evans, president and publisher of Random House, has continued to maintain the steadfast support of my work which he has now shown, through various metamorphoses for both of us, over more than twenty years. Straddling the Atlantic between them, with her characteristic efficacy and elegance, has been my literary agent, Gill Coleridge, aided and abetted by Clare Roberts, Penny Liechti and Ros Ramsey.

This time around, new standards of tolerance and understanding have been set by my wife Cindy, my sons Sam, Joe and Ben, and my stepchildren Benj and Siena, not least about living in a house filled with Tchaikovsky's music for four long years. They join me in dedicating this book, with love and respect, to my godchildren.

## A Note on Transliteration of Russian Names

To have followed the recent international guidelines on transliteration of Russian names would have been to write a biography of Čajkovskij rather than Tchaikovsky. So transliteration of names from the Cyrillic alphabet is based throughout on Library of Congress practice, with modifications where it simplifies pronunciation, e.g. Pyotr for Petr, Andreyevna for Andreevna, etc. Non-Russian names have largely been preserved in their original language, e.g. Laroche (not Larosh). Common sense and the quest for consistency have dictated occasional exceptions even to these rules; on the same principle as Marya, Yulya and Lidya, for example, the oft-quoted volume of *Recollections* becomes *Vospominanya* rather than the more familiar *Vospominaniya*. Contemporary names have been left as they were found on books or record-sleeves. I am grateful to Catriona Bass for her expert guidance through this minefield.

## A Note on Dates

Throughout Tchaikovsky's lifetime the Julian calendar was still in use in Russia, twelve days behind the Gregorian calendar already adopted throughout the Western world. To clarify the narrative chronology of this book, Gregorian dates are used throughout – the composer's birthday, for instance, being 7 May rather than 25 April. This has involved adding twelve days to the dates of all letters, diaries and other documents written in Russia at the time. The sole exceptions come in the source notes, where I have felt it necessary to exempt articles in Russian newspapers and journals of the day, and adopt the more familiar practice of giving both dates, as in *Novoe Vremya (New Times)*, 14/26 August 1878.

*The notion that one day people will try to
probe into the private world of my thoughts
and feelings, into everything that I have
so carefully hidden throughout my life . . .
is very sad and unpleasant.*

PYOTR ILYICH TCHAIKOVSKY, 1880

# CONTENTS

# PROLOGUE

## 'The most Russian of us all'

ON THE MORNING OF SUNDAY 29 OCTOBER 1893, MODEST ILYICH Tchaikovsky arose early to find that his house guest had already been up for some hours. At the breakfast table of his St Petersburg apartment, the indigent playwright found his eminent older brother poring over the score of his new symphony, due to be sent the next day to his publisher in Moscow.

At the age of fifty-three, Pyotr Ilyich Tchaikovsky looked seventy. But his careworn features belied an undiminished inner energy, with that October Sunday morning marking the high point of his professional life. The previous evening, Tchaikovsky had conducted the first performance of his Sixth Symphony, the *Pathétique*, in the Assembly Hall of the Nobility (now St Petersburg's Symphony Hall). Though the reception had been more respectful than rapturous, the composer was unperturbed. He knew from long experience that his devoted public often took a few performances to warm to his music; and, more importantly, he himself was pleased with the piece, which seemed to represent a fitting climax to his musical life.

'Something strange seems to be happening with this symphony,' he wrote that day in a covering note to his publisher in Moscow, Pyotr Yurgenson. 'It's not that people don't like it, more that they seem puzzled by it. As for myself, I am prouder of this symphony than of anything else I have ever written.' It was a familiar paradox – the juxtaposition of public and private responses – for which Tchaikovsky could expect a sympathetic hearing from his old friend Yurgenson. 'Never mind,' the composer closed, 'we'll soon be able to talk all this over, as I'll see you in Moscow on Saturday.'[1]

Unlike most artists destined to be honoured by posterity, Tchaikovsky could feel confident of immortality while still alive to savour it. Growing international renown had recently seen him heaped with as many public honours abroad as in his native Russia. At last, thanks to a relatively new career as a conductor, he was financially secure. Still full of physical energy and musical imagination, he found his life richer in fulfilment and promise than a man of his melancholy disposition had long allowed himself to expect.

Just a week before, Tchaikovsky had told his friend Nikolay Kashkin that he had never felt better, never more content.[2] Apart from several European conducting engagements, there were plans afoot for an ambitious concert tour of the Russian provinces – as far afield as the Black Sea, the Caucasus and a chain of towns along the Volga. The very next day held satisfying prospects, with meetings with the directors of the Kononov and Mariinsky opera companies to discuss overdue revivals of two of his less successful works, *The Oprichnik* and *The Maid of Orleans*. Both companies were also currently restaging one of his two great operatic masterpieces, *Eugene Onegin*.

Yet Tchaikovsky would never enjoy that conversation with Yurgenson in Moscow the following Saturday. By then he would be lying mortally ill in this very room. Within a week of this last optimistic moment, Russia's beloved national composer would be dead.

Like his mother before him, if his brother Modest is to be believed, Tchaikovsky succumbed to cholera, contracted that week after carelessly drinking a glass of unboiled water. Posterity has naturally accepted this as truth for most of the subsequent century. In this as in so much else, however, Modest is *not* to be believed. His three-volume biography of Tchaikovsky, published within a decade of his brother's death, has stood for almost a century as the standard sourcebook on the composer's life. But close scrutiny of Modest's account shows it to be riddled with errors and omissions. Just as his quotations from his brother's letters and diaries are highly selective, so his account of the composer's private life is heavily censored – with one clear object in mind. As Tchaikovsky had devoutly hoped, Modest goes to great pains to conceal from posterity that his celebrated brother was a homosexual.

As was Modest himself. His last service to his revered sibling, an act of self-interest as much as loyalty, was to hide from the world the true facts of his death. It was a conspiracy subsequently joined by several generations of Soviet censors, anxious to preserve the pristine reputation of a composer so close to all Russian hearts. For a century this fiction has been further compounded by the loyalists guarding the Tchaikovsky Archive in Klin, sixty miles north-west of Moscow, controlled from the composer's death until 1992 by members of his family and their direct descendants. The archive is still in the hands of Tchaikovsky *apparatchiks*, unwilling to allow Western scholars free run of its documents, as if Gorbachov and glasnost, Yeltsin and the collapse of Communism had never happened.

Only since the flight to the West of one Klin-trained scholar has the world become aware of the apparent truth which, at the composer's request, Modest conspired with the doctors at his deathbed to conceal: that Tchaikovsky in fact committed suicide, on orders.

'I have a very strong feeling that people die at the right moment,' Benjamin Britten, a great admirer of Tchaikovsky, once told his friend Imogen Holst. 'The greatness of a person includes the time when he was born and the time he endures.'[3]

The manner of Tchaikovsky's death, to paraphrase Britten, is inextricably linked with the day-to-day details of his life. Death comes not merely as the end, but as a natural climax to the short- or long-term chain of events preceding it. Even death, so to speak, can carry a logic which the bare facts of the preceding narrative too often distort or deny.

In Tchaikovsky's case, it is more than plausible to see his medium-length but very full life as a slow, tortured progress towards a bizarre but wholly inevitable demise. The milestones along that route are, moreover, marked by great musical works brimming with self-reference, in the shape of dark and highly emotional introspection. To link the work of composers to the concurrent events of their lives is usually a glib, populist mistake; in the case of Tchaikovsky, however, it is often as great a mistake not to. 'It is a terrible irony', in the words of one of the most distinguished of contemporary Tchaikovsky exponents, Vladimir Ashkenazy, 'that so much suffering and torment bequeathed us so much wonderful music.'[4]

This is not a truth contemporary Russians care to acknowledge. Today, as always, Moscow and St Petersburg intellectuals believe that biographies of great artists should concentrate only on their work. To the current intelligentsia, living symbols of the word their country has given to the English language, the examination of private, offstage lives remains a decadent Western habit, offensive to the Russian sensibility, especially when the life under scrutiny happens to be that of a great Russian.

'Who cares how he died?' as one musical historian put it to me in the interval of a St Petersburg performance of *Swan Lake*, raising his glass of vodka in yet another toast to Pyotr Ilyich: 'Just listen to his music!' It is an attitude which, like so much else in modern Russia, is fast changing.

'Is it true? Tchaikovsky was a *blue man*?' My St Petersburg taxi driver had heard me mention the composer's name, and asked his heartfelt question as we bounced through yet another pothole, crunching my head painfully into the roof of his battered Lada. *Goluboy*, which translates literally as 'blue one', was the current Russian slang for a homosexual. 'I am shocked. I love music. Tchaikovsky was my hero. Like Freddie Mercury. Another *blue man*.'

In October 1992, during my second research trip to Russia, the authorities were gingerly introducing the populace to certain historical facts known to the rest of the world for as many as seventy-five years. One of them – first broadcast on television, according to my musical cabbie, that very week – was the devastating news that Tchaikovsky, still the revered national composer, had been gay.

Knowledge and understanding of homosexuality was at that time, and still remains, in very rudimentary shape in the former Soviet Union. But contemporary Russians are now slowly awakening from their long Communist sleep not merely to a better understanding of male homosexuality (which was at last legalized by Boris Yeltsin in June 1993), but to its central role in Tchaikovsky's life and work.

In the St Petersburg of the mid-1990s, now as always the 'gay capital' of Russia, armed security men are needed to keep murderously prejudiced mafiosi clear of a sudden spate of transvestite cabaret shows, redolent of Isherwood's 1930s Berlin. In the vanguard of reform, and the struggle to lead openly homosexual lives with as much freedom as their Western confréres, are the members of a group calling itself the Tchaikovsky Society for the Promotion of Sexual Minorities.

As an epitaph, this would certainly have the composer shuddering in his ornate grave in 'Musicians Row', just around the corner from Dostoevsky, in the cemetery of the Alexandr Nevsky monastery. In these difficult days for his motherland, Tchaikovsky's music is performed as much as ever, symbolizing Russia's character and aspirations more eloquently than at any time since it was officially out of favour in the 1920s. But Tchaikovsky himself, of course, shared his countrymen's distaste for prurient curiosity about the private lives of great men. It was a 'sad and unpleasant' price of fame, he complained to his friend and patron Nadezhda von Meck, to think that 'one day people will try to probe into the private world of my thoughts and feelings, into everything that I have so carefully hidden throughout my life.'⁵ In his own case, he went to the ultimate lengths – in death, as in life – to conceal the true nature of his sexuality from all but his most intimate friends. Although it shaped and informed his music, through his own guilty sense that it was essentially 'unnatural', Tchaikovsky's homosexuality was to him a secret worth taking to the grave – prematurely, if need be.

That is the key to the mystery at the heart of this book, and the essential irony in any retrospective assessment of Tchaikovsky. But Britten's remark also refers to the periods of history through which great artists live. In retrospect, Tchaikovsky's times were shaped by two events little more than a decade before his birth and two after his death: the execution of the 1825 Decembrist rebels, and the October 1917 revolution which was its natural long-term consequence. The intervening period was one in which Russia, as so often throughout its history, turned inward upon itself, treating all things Western, or European, with aggressive suspicion.

To the socialist philosopher Alexandr Herzen, the Russian 'Slavophiles' and 'Westernizers' of the period were like the imperial eagle, 'whose two heads faced in opposite directions but in whose breast there beat one heart.' As a consequence, in the words of one musicologist, 'few questions have concerned Russia during the last two hundred years as much as the problem of her relationship with the rest of Europe . . . None of her important writers or composers has failed to reflect it.'⁶

This was the subtext of Tchaikovsky's professional life: the musical argument between the 'nationalist' and 'Western' styles, in the shape of the 'radicals' versus the 'traditionalists'. His central achievement is to have defied the prevailing orthodoxy with such steadfast vision, becoming the first truly full-time, professional composer in his country's history, and the only one of his day to look (and travel) west, cross-fertilizing with his European predecessors and counterparts. The very name Tchaikovsky, in Russian, means 'like a seagull' – highly appropriate in view of the time he spent travelling: a restless, rootless wanderer, forever migrating between his beloved Russian landscape and the less ethereal attractions of Western Europe.

Before Tchaikovsky's birth in 1840, there had been no indigenous tradition of Russian music beyond its folk tunes and the unaccompanied choral singing at the heart of its religious worship. By 1913, only twenty years after his death, the première of Stravinsky's *The Rite of Spring* signified Russia's arrival in the very vanguard of twentieth-century music. Tchaikovsky was the sole bridge between these two remarkable eras.

And yet, for all his Western sophistication, Tchaikovsky's voice remains quintessentially Russian – to Stravinsky, 'the most Russian of us all' – with his own character so uncannily reflecting the introspective, darkly brood-ing, richly emotional qualities which have come to characterize Russian music, however crudely, to Western ears. If it has long been fashionable to deride Tchaikovsky, because of the sheer popularity of so much of his music, the current revival of his reputation is at last granting due ac-knowledgement to his gifts not only as a supreme melodist and a master orchestrator, but an artist remarkably bold and original in his thinking – 'a genius', in Alexander Poznansky's apt phrase, 'of the emotions'.

That his greatest work should so largely have been forged from his own suffering in itself justifies a 'Western' approach to his life, as indeed does his own espousal of all things European. That he lived in an age when he felt it necessary to hide his true, 'unnatural' character was the source of both his private tragedy and his public success. If, in the end, it drove him to suicide at the age of only fifty-three, depriving posterity of more Tchaikovsky, it is hard to see where he intended to go – where, indeed, any composer could have gone – after those last, dying notes of the *Pathétique*, consigning himself and his anguish to *morendo* oblivion.

# PART I

## 1840–65
## MUSICIAN IN THE MAKING

*I began to compose as soon as I knew what music was.*

# CHAPTER I

## 'A child of glass'

TOWARDS THE END OF THE COLD WAR, THE REMOTE RUSSIAN TOWN OF Votkinsk found itself at the heart of US–Soviet nuclear arms negotiations. In the early 1970s the Soviet military machine had chosen this tranquil eighteenth-century lakeside settlement, 600 miles east of Moscow in the foothills of the Urals, as the site of one of its most notorious production plants. Amid the century-old smokestacks – left in place, it would seem, to confuse Western satellite spy cameras – there arose a new factory known simply as the Votkinsk Machine Building Plant, geared to produce the SS-20 missile, the latest mobile middle-range rocket to supplement the nuclear forces of the Warsaw Pact.

More powerful, more accurate and more reliable than any weapon previously made in Europe, the SS-20 in time became a symbol of the last gasp of Soviet nuclear expansion. Under the terms of the 1987 Inter-mediate Nuclear Forces treaty, the first US–Soviet pact to reduce nuclear weapons, Moscow eventually agreed to destroy the 650 missiles built in Votkinsk and close the production lines. By the early 1990s, United Nations inspectors were on hand to check that the plant was manu-facturing nothing more sinister than prams and washing machines.[1]

During its two decades as the SS-20's birthplace, Votkinsk was of-ficially declared one of the Soviet Union's 'closed' cities, rendering inaccessible another, less contentious, birthplace on its ancient south side, redolent of an earlier age. In this bright yellow mansion at the

3

water's edge, on 7 May 1840, Pyotr Ilyich Tchaikovsky was born, the second son of Ilya Petrovich Tchaikovsky, chief inspector of the local mines and metallurgical works.

At a time of simmering social unrest in Russia, Ilya Petrovich was a typical product of the middle-class gentry who formed the backbone of the civil service, holding the line between the landowning aristocracy and the enslaved masses in the stagnant decades before reform and upheaval. A kindly, industrious but wholly unremarkable man, rarely without an optimistic smile on his face, Tchaikovsky's father had risen to his well-heeled status more through effort than distinction. The chief characteristic of this 'sympathetic, jovial and straightforward character', according to his son Modest, was 'benevolence, or, more specifically, an affection for everyone he met.'

> In youth, manhood and old age he loved his neighbour, and his faith in him remained unshaken. His trustfulness knew no limits . . . to the end of his days, everyone he met was 'an excellent, honourable, good fellow' . . . Disillusionment was to cut him to the quick, but had no power to obscure his rosy view of human nature. It would be hard to find another man possessed of so many devoted friends.[2]

A lieutenant colonel in the Department of Mines, forty-two-year-old Ilya Petrovich was the son of another civil servant, Pyotr Fyodorovich Tchaikovsky, who had risen to the rank of Chief of Police in Slobodsk and Glazov, both towns in the province of Vyatka, on whose border Votkinsk stood. The police chief also had something of a reputation as a faith healer. Before his death in 1818, his wife, Anastasia Stepanova Posokhova, had borne him no fewer than twenty children, of whom Ilya Petrovich was the youngest.

During Tchaikovsky's years of fame, his more pretentious relatives would speak proudly (if vaguely) of their aristocratic Polish ancestry; but the composer himself preferred to take pride in the knowledge that his Cossack great-grandfather had died as a result of wounds sustained at the Battle of Poltava, in the service of Peter the Great, and his great-great-grandfather had served as a deacon in a St Petersburg church. 'Love of Russia and all things Russian was so deeply rooted in him,' wrote Modest, 'that while he cared nothing for pedigree, he rejoiced to discover among his earliest ancestors on his father's side one Orthodox Russian from the district of Kermenshchug.'

Of himself, late in life, Tchaikovsky would say, 'I have never come across anyone more in love than I with Mother Russia and Great Russia especially . . . I love passionately Russian people, the Russian language,

the Russian way of thinking, the beauty of Russian faces, Russian customs. Lermontov says he is unmoved by "the sacred legends of the dim
and distant past", but I love even these . . .'[3] To this extent he remained
much more of a 'populist' than a proto-Marxist in the ideological struggles
ahead, from which he in fact chose to remain largely aloof. But this
deeply rooted Russian sensibility was to combine with a feeling for
Western culture unique among artists of his age. Politically, Tchaikovsky's
views may have reflected his country's decaying feudal past; musically,
meanwhile, they heralded the only significant way forward. This paradox
lies at the heart of his lasting importance not merely to Russian but to
European culture; and its roots lie deep in these childhood years in the
provincial Russian countryside, which were to leave an indelible mark
that all the subsequent years of metropolitan sophistication could never
erase.

Amid the barren wastes of the east Russian steppes, as much of a cultural as an industrial wilderness, his well-bred parents also shaped their
son's artistic inclinations much more than has hitherto been recognized.
After graduating from the School of Mining Engineers, Tchaikovsky's
father had followed his own into the civil service, where he had made
steady upward progress through the ranks of the Department of Mines.
Modest Tchaikovsky is archly dismissive of their father's abilities – 'his
career cannot have been brilliant, since it took him twenty years to rise
to the rank of lieutenant colonel' – but Ilya Petrovich was evidently
an honest, incorruptible man, a rare enough figure in the Russian civil
service of his day.

By the time of Pyotr Ilyich's birth, moreover, his post at Votkinsk made
Ilya the unofficial squire of the town, with responsibility for a large estate
and the serfs who worked it, powers of punishment and patronage, a
seat on the magistrates' bench – even his own private Cossack army,
one hundred strong. In an otherwise unremittingly philistine outpost
– seen from the capital for what it was, a God-forsaken exile halfway
to Siberia – the large and amply staffed Tchaikovsky house was the
scene of frequent musical soirées and other elegant gatherings, presided
over by the moustachioed patriarch and his formidable wife, Alexandra
Andreyevna.

Tchaikovsky's mother was Ilya Petrovich's second wife. In 1827, at
the age of thirty-two, he had married Maria Karlovna Keiser, a Russian
of German descent, who bore him a daughter, Zinaida, but died only
two years later. Anxious to give his daughter a family upbringing, and
always something of a ladies' man, Ilya had remarried within two years
– this time a Russian of French descent, eighteen years his junior.
Twenty-year-old Alexandra was the daughter of the Marquis André

d'Assier, whose family had fled to Russia in 1685, upon the revocation of the Edict of Nantes. Her mother had died when she was three. An elegant and cultured figure, and a young widower, the Marquis had ensured that music played a central part in his daughters' upbringing at a St Petersburg orphanage – so much so that Alexandra's sister, Ekaterina, later enjoyed some renown as an opera singer. Although herself less naturally gifted, Tchaikovsky's mother sang and played the piano with all the refinement expected of young society ladies. In the capital this would have been taken for granted; in remote Votkinsk, it caused something of a sensation.

It was pure coincidence that his promotion in 1836 took Ilya Petrovich back to Vyatka province, scene of the high points of his own father's career in the public service. By the time they arrived in Votkinsk in 1837, Ilya and Alexandra had already been married four years and lost one child, a girl, at birth; within a year of their arrival she bore him their first son, Nikolay Ilyich, and two years later their second, Pyotr. An expansive hostess, described by her contemporaries as 'tall and distinguished-looking, with wonderfully expressive eyes', Tchaikovsky's mother was also considered 'not exactly handsome' – by all, it seems, but her second son, who thought her radiant. All his life he was haunted especially by the memory of his mother's large but beautiful hands. 'Such hands', he used to say, 'do not exist nowadays, and never will again.'[4]

Those hands at the piano were the first obvious influence on the later course of Pyotr Ilyich's life, there being no musical talent at all in the Tchaikovsky genes. His Assier forebears also bequeathed him a mild form of epilepsy, which had plagued his maternal grandfather. A nervous, highly strung child, in contrast to his stolid, unexceptional older brother, Pyotr seems to have decided at a remarkably early age that the way to his mother's heart was via the keys of her piano.

A cold, unhappily distant parent, not given to displays of physical affection, Alexandra Andreyevna was usually too absorbed in her own concerns, and her star status in small-town society, to take much notice; while relishing the respect her modest talents won her in Votkinsk, her true self seems to have been lost in Chekhovian longings to get back to the big city. These feelings were shared by her stepdaughter, Zinaida – with whom Alexandra, a woman herself denied mothering, developed a closer bond. The inevitability of an eventual return to the sophistication of St Petersburg was the assumption on which she based her children's early upbringing, designed to equip them for life in a society far smarter and more civilized than that into which they had unavoidably been born.

Freudians would no doubt suggest that Tchaikovsky's early dealings with his mother – struggling up a one-way street, only to find a cul-de-sac

– sewed the early seeds of his homosexuality, the particular nature of which would finally prove his undoing. At the same time, for all her faults, Alexandra inadvertently etched another motif of lifelong significance to her son and his talents: a sympathetic fascination with deprived, suffering or otherwise doomed women, which would find musical shape in works from *Romeo and Juliet* to *Francesca da Rimini*, *Swan Lake* to *The Queen of Spades*.[5] Womankind, whether suffering or not, would provide all the pivotal figures in his life, not least because his sexual interests lay elsewhere. When Pyotr Ilyich was only two, his mother inadvertently set this process, too, in train, by providing him with a younger sister, another Alexandra ('Sasha'), who was to become one of his life's mainstays.

A third son, Ippolit, followed a year later in 1843, giving Alexandra senior an excuse to escape to the imperial capital, St Petersburg, in search of a governess for her growing brood (the local school being beneath consideration). Contemporary accounts suggest that a professional young woman of the right calibre would have taken some persuading to leave the capital for the unlovely remoteness of Votkinsk, enduring an arduous three-week journey for the privilege. But it seems to have been their mutual love of all things French – a shaping spirit for Pyotr Ilyich – which helped Tchaikovsky's mother win over the figure of Fanny Dürbach, a demure and warm-hearted twenty-two-year-old French Protestant from Alsace, who now became the next female to make a significant contribution to the moulding of the young Tchaikovsky.

Though she warmed to Alexandra and Nikolay during their long journey together to Votkinsk, Fanny became increasingly nervous as its end approached. 'My concern and uneasiness grew', she recalled, as she wondered what kind of life she had landed herself with, what sort of people would be sharing her eastern exile. The governess's memories of her arrival at Votkinsk, conveyed years later to Modest, paint a vivid portrait of the Tchaikovsky household and its genial paterfamilias:

> When at last we reached the house, one moment was enough to show that all my fears were groundless. A crowd of people ran out to greet us; there were joyous embraces and kisses; amid the throng, it was hard to tell family from servants. All were united by a universal, infectious happiness. Everyone greeted the return of the mistress of the house with equal warmth and affection. Monsieur Tchaikovsky himself came up to me and, without a word, embraced and kissed me like a daughter. The straightforwardness of this patriarchical gesture immediately gave me his public stamp of approval, confirming me as one of the family. It was not as if I had just arrived – more as if, like Mme Tchaikovskaya and her son,

I too had returned home. Next day I went about my duties without the slightest concern or fear for the future.[6]

It is a commonplace at this early point in the biographies of composers to paint a picture of the young genius at the piano night and day, eschewing the outdoor games of his contemporaries, preferring to sight-read symphonies and pick out fledgling melodies before his feet can even reach the pedals. If Tchaikovsky is an exception, it is only insofar as he displayed no outstanding talent at this age, more a growing obsession with music, not entirely natural in one so young.

He himself was to contribute to this kind of mythology by declaring, 'I started to compose as soon as I knew what music was.' Like his mother, the four-year-old boy showed an easy aptitude – with no especial measure, as yet, of skill or fluency – for a pastime which was soon to grow into his prime preoccupation. But he was still only four when family history does record that, during Alexandra's absence in the capital, Pyotr Ilyich produced his first composition, generously acknowledging a little help from his two-year-old sister Sasha. It was a song called 'Our Mama in St Petersburg'; and the pair of them could not wait, wrote Ilya to his wife, to perform it for her upon her return. The piece, of course, does not survive; but it seems unlikely to have rivalled the first musical steps of the boy Mozart.

Fanny Dürbach had been hired primarily to look after Nikolay, now nearly seven, and a Tchaikovsky niece, Lidya Vladimirovna, whom Ilya had all but adopted. Sasha and Pyotr (given the affectionate diminutive 'Petya' within the family) were considered still too young to need a governess; but the boy was too inquisitive to abide such fascinating things going on in the house without him. Gradually, with a wide-eyed Sasha in tow, he wormed his way into Fanny Dürbach's affections, and thus her classes – which the governess in fact welcomed, for Nikolay was a somewhat dull and lazy pupil, and Lidya 'difficult'. Fanny found Petya, by contrast, absorbing. While concerned by the child's acute sensitivity, to which his mother remained oblivious, she could immediately see that he was unusually gifted. Her attempts to avoid patronizing him, and thus to treat him on a par with his older brother, were well-intentioned but doomed. When she scolded them both one day, for failing to solve a problem she had set, Fanny chose to berate them for ingratitude to their father, who 'worked so hard and made such sacrifices' to provide them with an education.

Nikolay heard me out to the end with utter indifference, then carried on with his games as if nothing had happened. Petya remained sombre until supper. By the time he was undressing for bed, and I had completely forgotten about the episode, he suddenly burst into tears, proceeded to insist how desperately he loved his father; that he was filled with gratitude to both his parents; and that I had been unjust to reproach him. I had the greatest difficulty in calming him down, for his sensitiveness in every aspect of life passed all imagining . . . Truly he was *un enfant de verre*.[7]

The one area in which the otherwise vigilant Fanny could offer Petya no help or encouragement was music. His governess in fact did her best to prevent her charge rushing to the piano as soon as the day's lessons were over; she preferred him to read a book or join in a storytelling session. To her, music had become an almost unhealthy obsession to the boy, especially now that he had the added inspiration of an orchestrion, brought home by his father from a visit to St Petersburg. A superior form of barrel-organ, with stops capable of adding orchestral effects to the melody line, the Tchaikovsky family orchestrion could play airs from Bellini and Donizetti, Weber, Rossini and Mozart – above all, to young Petya's ears, highlights from *Don Giovanni*, notably Zerlina's aria 'Vedrai, carino'.

As the composer himself later testified, this primitive musical instrument fostered his lifelong adoration of Mozart, particularly his celebrated *dramma giocoso*, and great fellow-feeling with the Italian school. By the age of six, Pyotr Ilyich was in the habit of rushing from orchestrion to piano, and picking out the tunes with increasing fluency. Throughout the house, he would constantly drum his fingers on the nearest available hard surface, his eyes rapt at the tunes taking shape in his head. On one occasion, when an exasperated Fanny protested about the noise, he drummed instead on a nearby window-pane, growing so animated that finally his hand crashed through the glass and was badly cut.

It was soon after this that Tchaikovsky's parents entertained a Polish pianist of their acquaintance, who naturally gave an evening concert for the thin line of local gentry. After the Pole had played two Chopin mazurkas, six-year-old Pyotr Ilyich insisted on taking over at the piano, and repeated the music from memory with sufficient aplomb for the maestro to compliment him as a 'promising' musician. On another such evening the boy fled from the room, to the surprise of Fanny and his parents, who had been expecting pleas to be allowed to stay up late. Two hours later Fanny looked into Petya's bedroom, to find the child still fully dressed, sprawled on his bed in hysterical tears. 'Oh, the music, the music!' he sobbed. 'Save me from it, Fanny, save me! It's here . . . in here!' – he struck his forehead – 'and it won't leave me in peace.'[8]

Apart from this fixation with music, which Fanny found quite alarming, the young Pyotr Ilyich was noted for a soft-heartedness and generosity which merged into vulnerability. Once, when he disappeared from the house long enough for his parents to grow worried, it transpired that he had been knocking on all the doors in the poorer part of town, trying to find a home for the last of a litter of kittens born in the home of one of his father's serfs. On another occasion, Fanny recalled, his love of all things Russian had him kissing the mother country in an atlas, while spitting on all the others to the west of it. When Fanny scolded her Petya, reminding him that those countries too were full of living, breathing human beings, and that she herself came from France, the boy replied 'Oh, but Fanny . . . didn't you see that I was covering France with my arm?'

A wily diplomat, then, at seven, as well as an embryonic nature-lover – but still the boy's overwhelming priority was music. After the incident of the broken window, his parents took his preoccupation seriously enough to engage a piano teacher, a freed serf named Maria Markovna Palchikova; but the boy all too soon outstripped her. Already, thanks to Fanny, he was well-versed in French and German; at the same time, with her encouragement, he was also beginning to write poetry. When Modest visited Fanny in France nearly fifty years later, a year after Tchaikovsky's death, she was able to produce several specimens she still possessed. Even after all that time she would not part with them, but allowed the composer's brother to copy down several examples.

One such was an attempt at a historical essay in verse entitled 'The Heroine of France', evincing the beginnings of a lifelong fascination with Joan of Arc (which would later lead to an opera, *The Maid of Orleans*). Others include the seven-year-old's effusions on his beloved Mother Russia, a boyish threnody on the death of a bird, and an imaginary conversation with his guardian angel. It is a curiosity worth recording, complete with schoolboy errors (italicized by the humourless Modest), to show that the young Tchaikovsky – if not quite the 'little Pushkin' Fanny called him – was already possessed of religious yearnings and a fevered imagination.

> *Tez* ailes dorées ont volé chez moi
> Ta *voi* m'a *parler*
> O! que j'étais heureuse
> *Quant* tu *venait* chez moi
> Tes ailes *son blanc* et pur aussi
> Viens encore une *foix*
> Pour parler de Dieu puissant![9]

With the benefit of hindsight, it is tempting to wonder whether Fanny herself might not have been the young Tchaikovsky's guardian angel; and whether this isolated rural upbringing in the care of his devoted governess might not have proved a safer long-term haven for this highly-strung 'child of glass' than a transplant to city life – which was now his sudden, unexpected and unwelcome fate.

Mindful of his young wife's restlessness – now shared by his growing daughter, Zinaida, who had returned home upon leaving school – Ilya Petrovich had confided to a friend in Votkinsk that he was thinking of retiring from his state post and accepting an attractive offer of private employment in Moscow. Trusting to a fault, he promptly resigned his lucrative eastern sinecure (with the rank of major-general) and transported his household all 600 weary miles, only to find that his false friend had got there ahead of him, and secured the job for himself.

'Even the loss of his entire fortune, due to misplaced confidence,' recalled Modest, 'did not make [Ilya] any more suspicious of his fellow-men.' For the rest of the Tchaikovsky family, however, the consequences were dire. To eight-year-old Pyotr Ilyich, it was all a baffling tragedy, resulting in the sudden disappearance of his beloved Fanny, who had been sneaked out of the household without even a farewell (in the hope of sparing the boy's feelings). Though she had been a part of his life for only four years, his governess had come to occupy a far more substantial niche in it than his mother – not replacing her in his affections, of course, but saving him as yet from the emotional and physical excesses – including, perhaps, his hereditary proneness to epilepsy – to which his unnatural zeal for music appeared to be leading.

At this early stage in his life Tchaikovsky's passion for music seemed simply a curious imbalance, about which Fanny had every right to be concerned. In all other respects, Pyotr was a normal and healthy child, as capable as any of his less well-bred contemporaries of coming home covered in mud, his hair dishevelled. Not so in Moscow, however, where his half-sister Zinaida took over his education. More partial to his brothers than to the precocious Petya, Zinaida gave him less of her time and attention, thus initiating a lifelong coolness between them. This period also witnessed the first signs of a significant change in Pyotr Ilyich's character. From the happy country boy, delighting as much in nature as in his music, he began gradually to turn into a more sullen and fractious child, lazing around the house with no apparent focus to his life.

The Tchaikovsky family's stay in Moscow proved a brief and unhappy interlude. The collapse in Ilya's fortunes happened to coincide with an epidemic of cholera, to which one of the housemaids nearly succumbed

– foreshadowing much more tragic irruptions of the disease in the life of Pyotr Ilyich. After only a month, in mid-November 1848, mother and children followed Ilya to St Petersburg, where Nikolay and Pyotr were enrolled as pupils in the fashionable Schmelling School. After Fanny's congenial regime, Pyotr hated it. There was much catching-up to be done merely to hold his own at a school which drove its pupils very hard. He would leave home at 8 a.m. each morning, not returning until 5 p.m., often working till after midnight to get through the stiff doses of homework.

Both brothers were subject, meanwhile, to the cruel taunts and bullying which so often greet late schoolboy arrivals. Within a month both had developed measles, brought on by their run-down physical condition, and accentuating their already low spirits. 'The children are not the same people they were in Votkinsk,' their mother wrote to Fanny. 'The happiness and gaiety has quite gone from them. Nikolay is constantly pale and thin – and Pyotr too . . . He and the others speak of you every day. Petya says he is trying to persuade himself that life here in St Petersburg is a bad dream, that one day he will wake up and find himself back in Votkinsk, back with his own dear Fanny. Then, he says, he would be the happiest boy on earth!'[10]

While Nikolay made a normal recovery, and was soon back at school, an ever more fragile Pyotr remained ill for weeks – leading the family doctors, in February 1849, to diagnose a disease of the spinal cord (probably spinal meningitis). Though modern science might suspect the problem to be as much psychological as physical, a complete and indefinite rest was ordered. In all, it took the boy six months to make a full recovery, by which time he was spared a return to the Schmelling School. His father had found a new post as manager of an iron works in Alapaevsk, another remote Urals mining town even further east than Votkinsk.

Was it coincidence that an illness which had lasted five months, from December to May, now vanished within a month, once the boy was returned to his beloved Russian countryside, back in the care of a private governess? The one consolation for his wretchedness in St Petersburg had been a steady advance in his musical training, under the sympathetic and apparently expert tuition of a pianist named Filippov. With his parents, both of whom were enthusiastic theatregoers, Petya had also made his first visits to the opera and the ballet, which had brought the enchantments of the orchestrion blazing into theatrical life.

Otherwise, the deep-seated nervous disorders which would characterize both his life and work had already taken hold of the young Tchaikovsky. Ill at ease; lacking in self-confidence; hiding from any kind of unwelcome challenge; clinging to his mother's skirts, the family his bulwark against the world: these were to be the hallmarks of the restless, wandering older man as much as the uprooted nine-year-old. To make matters worse, he was returned to the tutelage of Zinaida, now aided by cousin Lidya; between them these two young women managed further to drain the boy's self-confidence in all but his musical studies. His choice of literature was too sophisticated for them – already he was reading Gogol, Fénelon and Chateaubriand – so the girls took their revenge in easier ways. Constantly taunted, even mocked for his indifferent schoolwork, Pyotr would again seek solace in the piano. 'It is the only thing', he wrote to Fanny, 'that can cheer me up when I feel sad.'

Besides, Alapaevsk was no Votkinsk. Whatever country charms his first home had held for the young Tchaikovsky were absent from this bleak industrial settlement, where the lack of their former status and social life made his parents, too, less ebullient. One rare bright moment came in May 1850, eight days before his tenth birthday, with the birth of two more brothers: Modest and his twin Anatoly. 'I think they are angels come down from heaven,' wrote Pyotr to Fanny, with the excess of sentiment typical of Tchaikovsky family letters, but also with the genuine fellow-feeling inherited from his father. Where other ten-year-olds might have resented the arrival of younger brothers, further distracting the attentions of an already distant mother, the young Tchaikovsky could not contain his delight.

But there were no music teachers in Alapaevsk capable of helping him continue to advance. Zinaida was as unsympathetic a tutor as ever, mortified by the family's return from the bright lights of the capital to a rural wasteland bereft of marriageable men. And Nikolay had been left behind in St Petersburg, to prepare to follow his father into the School of Mining Engineers. The more letters arrived with glowing reports of his athletic and musical prowess, the more Pyotr developed a somewhat unlikely dose of hero-worship for his absent older brother, with whom he had forged a bond during their brief mutual suffering at Schmelling. He missed him, he now declared, 'terribly'.

Alas for Pyotr, he was soon told by his anxious parents that he would not be joining Nikolay, as he had assumed, at the Mining School. Nor could they contemplate an education designed to foster his musical talents. In the Russia of the 1850s a career as a professional musician was quite simply a contradiction in terms. Music-making was merely a parlour refinement of the gentry, predominantly female, with public concerts given almost exclusively by visiting European companies and soloists. Professional musicians had no standing in polite society, not least because there were as yet no music schools to produce them.

On the recommendation of a friend, Modest Alexeyevich Vakar, in whose care he had left Nikolay, Ilya Petrovich had been making enquiries about the Imperial School of Jurisprudence, one of the élite institutions then mass-producing top-flight candidates for the civil service. The school was also renowned for the strict discipline which his increasingly wayward son appeared to need. In his country torpor, the indolent Pyotr was even neglecting his correspondence with Fanny, and was mortified when a letter arrived from France bemoaning his long silence. Unknown to him, Fanny had heard from a friend of the falling-off in her young Pushkin: 'I cannot imagine how his character, which once showed so much promise of noble sentiments, could so completely change.'

Zinaida was clearly inadequate to the task of preparing her brother for the school's challenging entrance exams, so his mother engaged a new governess by the name of Anastasia Petrovna Petrova. Now Pyotr resumed his letters to Fanny, and in rather more cheerful vein, for Anastasia was a warm and sympathetic character who also encouraged his interest in music. In a well-meant but rather hollow gesture, his parents sent for his old piano teacher, Maria Palchikova, from Votkinsk, ostensibly to teach Sasha; Maria rejoined the household more as a musical companion than tutor to Pyotr Ilyich, so far had his talents and indeed his knowledge now outdistanced hers. That summer, however, saw him more contented, less fractious, than at any time since the family's departure from Votkinsk. There was, moreover, the prospect of a trip with his mother back to St Petersburg. Although filled with apprehension at the idea of boarding school, he comforted himself with the thought of an extended period of single-minded attention from the object of all his affections.

Alexandra Andreyevna had become, if anything, even less dutiful a mother since her return to the life of country grandee, and the drawn-out exertions of carrying twins. But the less attention she paid to Pyotr, the more she became the object of his adoration; her reluctance to accept his hugs, especially when wearing her latest dress from the city, naturally served only to increase his aching affection. Now they travelled together to the capital, Alexandra liberated from the tyranny of the infant twins. Although Sasha and Zinaida shared their journey, Pyotr and his schooling were its central purpose, and he enjoyed several blissful weeks of his mother's undivided attention as he prepared for the examinations required to enter the school's preparatory classes.

Not until he was twelve could he enter the School of Jurisprudence proper. Two years as a boarder in its preparatory school, 800 miles from home, thus stretched uneasily ahead of him. But the boy made a confident start, passing the entrance exams with distinction enough to earn a climactic moment of maternal fuss before the shadows behind this trip began to close in on him. His launch into school life signified, he knew all too well, his mother's departure. As the dread day approached, in early October, she promised him one final, farewell treat: an evening at the Mariinsky Theatre, to see Glinka's celebrated opera *A Life for the Tsar*. The outing had been thoughtfully suggested by his father, who had written to his wife reminding her not to neglect their son's love of music; and it left an indelible effect on the ten-year-old Tchaikovsky – his awestruck reverence for Glinka, the 'father of Russian music', exceeded only by that for his mother.

Eventually the day came for her to depart. From the home of Modest Vakar, with whom they had been staying, and in whose care he was to be left, the boy rode with his mother in her carriage as far as the Central Turnpike, the crossroads at which travellers towards Moscow were traditionally waved off. On the way the child shed a few tears; but when the time came for his mother to leave, he lost all his boyish self-control and sobbed inconsolably. At the moment of final farewell, as the carriage door was closed upon her, he refused to let go of the handle. Screaming, he had to be hauled off by force, and dragged away. As the coachman whipped the horses, and the carriage started to move off, he broke free of his captors and chased after it, flinging himself towards the rear wheels. Catching hold of the backboard, in a forlorn attempt to prevent his mother's departure, he was dragged along the muddied, cobbled street until the carriage's increasing speed shook him off. The ten-year-old boy was dumped in the dirt as his mother's carriage sped away.

'To his life's end,' according to his brother, Modest, 'Tchaikovsky could never recall this hour without a shiver of horror . . . Although in later life he went through many tragic experiences, although he knew disappointments and renunciations, he could never forget the sense of resentful despair as the carriage containing his beloved mother disappeared from view.' [11]

Within days another domestic tragedy, of which he was the wholly innocent cause, added cruelly to his woes. During an outbreak of scarlet fever at the school, pupils were given the option of going home or being sequestered within the building throughout the quarantine period. Taking pity on young Pyotr, still inconsolable at his mother's departure, Modest Vakar invited him to stay with his family, despite the risk of infection, rather than being incarcerated at school.

Tchaikovsky had not himself contracted the disease. But he appears to have been a carrier, for the grim consequence was that the elder of the

Vakars' own sons, five-year-old Nikolay, soon developed a serious case, which led to his death on 6 December. Nikolay's parents had protected their young house guest from the gravity of their son's condition; now they also went to great pains to reassure Pyotr that he should not blame himself. This, of course, proved an impossibility. For once, we can take Modest's word for it that Tchaikovsky was 'devastated' by guilt (which, though neither he nor they could realize it, the Vakars' generosity perhaps prevented him working out). He would rather, he wrote his parents, that he had died himself.

Despite the tragedy, the Vakars remained steadfast friends to the boy, offering him the welcome chance to meet up with his brother Nikolay beneath their roof each Sunday. Now there was more than merely 'the shadow of his parting from his mother', in Modest's words, to 'darken the first year of his school life.' An aching homesickness 'overcame all other emotions, colouring his every interest, every wish, every thought. For two whole years, as is evident from his letters, he lived only for the moment he would see his parents again. He knew no other preoccupation, nourished no other hope.'

Among the letters preserved from that first year at school is one sent to his parents on his father's nameday, 1851 – a document forlorn enough to rival anything Tchaikovsky ever wrote, in words or even in music:

> I congratulate you, my saintly Papa, on your Saint's Day, and wish you all good things on earth; I also send you good wishes, my lovely, precious Mama, for this dear anniversary. I like to remember this day last year. I remember we went out on a boat trip the next day. I remember the tent, I remember the boat, I remember the peasant choir, I remember the Ekaterinburg orchestra, I remember the illuminated monogram, I remember the dancing, I remember Sasha, Malya, Polya and me. I remember all the visitors, I remember lovely Zinusha and her lovely dance with lovely Lidusha, I remember everybody, and finally I remember that poor creature which has flown from its little nest, which has said farewell to all that it will never see again – I remember Pyotr Tchaikovsky.[12]

Nor did life much improve over the next two years, which saw his letters home become as florid in their terms of endearment – his parents are 'blessed', 'adored', 'beautiful angels' – as they were self-pitying in tone and content. Though surrounded by kindly souls in his brother, the Vakar family and his form teacher, a sympathetic French master named Joseph Berrard, the young Tchaikovsky could not master his sense of loneliness and isolation. Even Christmas, birthdays and vacations had to be endured without his family, who made matters no better by constantly promising to visit him soon, and constantly failing to do so.

Not until September 1851, almost a year after his mother's traumatic departure, did Tchaikovsky's father arrive in St Petersburg on an oft-postponed three-week visit. Ilya took Pyotr to live with him during his stay, and held out hope that the family might at last return to his side, as he had fallen out with the management of the Alapaevsk metal works and was again looking for new employment.

Tchaikovsky senior had reason to be delighted with his son's progress at the preparatory school; he had come third in the annual examinations, and received high grades for conduct, despite the forfeit of one Sunday off for 'laziness', and a rare rebuke from Berrard: for failing to name some boys who had broken school rules by dancing a noisy polka to his piano-playing. One of the few references to any musical activity throughout these two years – apart from nostalgic renditions of his mother's favourite song, Alyabiev's *The Nightingale* – the episode became the subject of yet another contrite letter home, pleading for news of his family's departure for St Petersburg, which again seemed subject to interminable delays. At first it was to be December, then January, then the spring, then May. Easter 1852 found Tchaikovsky in rising spirits as the day of the great reunion approached – and threatening, not for the first time, to 'smother my darling angels with kisses':

> But soon, *so soon*, I shall no longer be writing you letters, but talking with my beloved angels in person. Ah, how wonderful it will be to come home from school for the first time in my life, to see you, to kiss you. I believe this will give me greater happiness than anything in my life so far.[13]

Tchaikovsky's parents at last returned to St Petersburg in the early summer of 1852, and reunited the ecstatic Pyotr with his siblings for an extended country summer at a rented dacha north of the city, on the Black River. From Modest's rather weary account, it seems that he and his twin were the victims of numerous practical jokes symbolizing their brother's rediscovered *joie de vivre*. Joining the immediate family were Ilya's nieces, Lidya and Anna Merkling, the latter of whom was to become one of the composer's lasting friends. Looking back on this idyllic summer, Anna later recalled the young Tchaikovsky as a 'thin, nervous, highly sensitive boy . . . notable for his affectionate sensibility, especially towards his mother.'[14]

The vacation proved a happy prelude to a greater challenge that autumn, as twelve-year-old Pyotr Ilyich learnt that he had passed the examinations qualifying him to move on as a fully-fledged student to the School of Jurisprudence proper. In his formative years at this Dickensian institution, Tchaikovsky was supposed to find himself drawn to the same bureaucratic calling as his father. Instead he would discover within himself a quite different summons, far from musical, which was in time to torment every day of his adult life and to prove his eventual undoing.

# CHAPTER II

## 'Respice finem'

THE MAGNIFICENT RIVERSIDE BUILDING WHICH ONCE HOUSED ST Petersburg's Imperial School of Jurisprudence still sprawls along one of the city's quasi-Venetian embankments, facing the Summer Garden across the Fontanka River. Today it is a crumbling beehive of scruffy offices comprising the sometime Leningrad Institute of Town Planning. A satellite dish now sits beside the rusting green cupola on its roof, an incongruous modern appendage atop a crumbling institution whose architecture nevertheless bears eloquent witness to its days of corporate pride.

On the corner of the adjacent street was the childhood home of the young Tchaikovsky's schoolgirl sister; from his dormitory window, Pyotr Ilyich would wave excitedly to his mother whenever she came to visit. Today it is a main artery of St Petersburg called Tchaikovsky Boulevard – a tribute to the school's most famous old boy which now carries heavy irony, as the role of his *alma mater* and its pupils in his subsequent life always made him uneasy, and may even have led to his death.

Founded by Prince Pyotr Oldenburg in 1835, St Petersburg's Imperial School of Jurisprudence was an unashamedly élitist institution, designed primarily to staff the upper echelons of the Russian civil service. Throughout the second half of the nineteenth century, the senior state officials of late Tsarist Russia were drawn almost exclusively from this and one other St Petersburg school, the Tsarskoe Selo Lyceum (also known as the

Alexandr Lycée). Between 1840 and 1893, the span of Tchaikovsky's life, 46.3 per cent of the two schools' graduates climbed to the highest four ranks of the civil service. During this period the School of Jurisprudence alone produced eleven ministers of state, forty-three members of the State Council and eighty-one senators.[1]

Tchaikovsky thus attended the School of Jurisprudence, as Soviet historians proved fond of pointing out, at 'an important time in Russian history.'[2] The school brought enormous influence to bear on late Tsarist politics, in an age when Russia had become cripplingly bureaucratized. Even the role of Britain's public schools or America's Ivy League universities in producing senior politicians and civil servants cannot compare with the single-mindedness with which these two Russian lycées – in other respects very like their western counterparts – bred their pupils specifically to run the country. Their admission criteria, too, were even more exclusive. Places were reserved only for sons of the hereditary gentry listed in Book Six of the Genealogical Register, *Rodoslovnaya kniga* (for those, that is, who had gentry status by 1685); for the sons of civil servants above Grade V; and for the sons of the military above the rank of colonel. In Tchaikovsky's case, his father's civil service rank was rather more of a qualification than the pedigree of his forebears.

The school's motto was 'Respice finem' ('Remember your objective'). Its own central objective, as pupils had little chance to forget, was 'love and devotion to God, throne and motherland'. In the summary of one official, the school's purpose was 'not only to educate the rising generation, but to instruct it in the spirit of Christ, of love and devotion to the Tsar and the Motherland, of honour and duty, and to train it for orderly and systematic work.'[3] This creed was indistinguishable from that of the Lycée's first director, E.A. Engelhardt, who wound up its inaugural ceremony with the invocation: 'Go forth, my friends, to your new walk of life! Revere God and his Holy Law; love the Tsar Benefactor and the Motherland; defend justice, and sacrifice everything for it . . . A good name, not wealth, nor rank nor ribbons, brings honour to a man. Above all, keep your conscience undefiled.'[4]

Their upmarket backgrounds combined with the powerful patriotism bred in them to lend an intense sense of élitism to the school's pupils and graduates, all of whom had joined an exclusive club for life*. Slightly larger than the Lycée, the School of Jurisprudence admitted some 250 twelve-year-old pupils each year, for a seven-year course of studies. The fees in Tchaikovsky's day were 600 roubles per

---

*Although the School of Jurisprudence closed in 1917, its former pupils were still holding reunions as late as the 1960s.

annum, fifteen times more than the University of St Petersburg itself.

For the first four of their seven years in the school's distinctive green uniform and cocked hat, pupils worked on a general curriculum ranging from mathematics, physics and natural history to geography, languages and literature. Not until their last three years did they begin to specialize in legal studies, taking in everything from Roman, state, financial and criminal law to forensic medicine, comparative legal practice and practical law. The school's daily routine was extremely rigorous, lasting from 6 a.m. to 10 p.m. six days a week, during which seven hours of classwork and three of preparation left two hours for meals, two for religious services and two for extra-curricular activities. There were annual exams, with bi-annual reviews, and a heavy work programme imposed during school holidays. With parental visiting severely restricted – one afternoon a week, and that for a very short period – pupils were under the most relentless pressure, in a harshly competitive atmosphere fostered by strict and often unsympathetic instructors.

For thirty years from 1849, the year before Tchaikovsky's arrival, the school's director was Alexandr Yazykov, formerly chief of police at Riga, and a martinet who turned the college into a fledgling version of a military barracks. If the school's sacrosanct 'code of honour' was breached, sanctions ranged from public humiliation to incarceration in the 'prison room', or corporal punishment for more serious misdemeanours.

Public floggings were nothing unusual. Vladimir Taneyev (elder brother of the pianist and composer Sergey), who was two classes below Tchaikovsky, has left vivid accounts of staff inflicting as many as sixty lashes on a naked boy as his peers watched queasily, with growing and lasting resentment. 'Even forty years later,' he wrote, 'I cannot forget that disgusting experience.' Ippolit Tchaikovsky, the composer's brother, also described his feelings while forced to watch a boy lashed half to death after being caught smoking. 'When I had to watch and hear the swish of the huge, supple birches, brandished with a run-up by strong soldiers straining one after the other to strike the strongest blow across the boy's ravaged body, my legs grew weak, my head swam, and, I would close my eyes, close to fainting.'[5]

Small wonder, in the face of such austere and violent authority, that the boys bonded together into groups which would last for life. The harshness of the regime inevitably brutalized even less sensitive souls than Tchaikovsky's, and Taneyev vividly describes the hounding of weaker brethren by nascent thugs who hunted in packs. So remorseless was the persecution of some poor boys that 'to kill any of their persecutors would have been too mild a punishment for their sufferings at their hands. They lived in a permanent state of nervous tension, and must clearly have been psychologically damaged for the rest of their lives.'[6]

The young Tchaikovsky appears to have been lucky. There is no evidence that he was ever himself lashed, or singled out for bullying, despite an apparently 'kind, gentle and thoughtful' exterior which must have tempted the uglier spirits. He was also fortunate in his class-teachers, a succession of the more understanding and sympathetic instructors, who appreciated his good behaviour (although he had already, it seems, taken up his lifelong habit of smoking) and his musical talents, rare in so remorselessly philistine an institution.

Though the senior and junior schools were carefully divided, occupying different parts of the building, even eating at separate times, a strong sense of solidarity developed between the older and younger boys in the face of so harsh and authoritarian a regime. Far from relying on any system like 'fagging' – the divisive brand of junior servitude practised in British public schools, often involving physical punishment – the school's hierarchical nature led the older boys to devise their own, private methods of dealing with miscreants. In this way, they could often avoid news of misdemeanours reaching the ears of the staff, let alone involving them in the passing of judgement and pronouncing of sentence. For a school created to turn out lawyers, this was indeed a display of considerable youthful initiative.

There were, of course, other motives, other consequences. Not unnaturally, in so monastic a hothouse society, this senior–junior 'solidarity' (blithely encouraged by the school authorities) led in turn to a wide variety of homosexual experiment – practised quite openly, with no stigma attached. After two years at the school, it would seem, the handsome young Tchaikovsky was already embarked on one activity which would forever shape both his character and his work, when suddenly he was overcome by a calamity which would leave a permanent scar on both.

The year of 1854 began joyfully for the Tchaikovsky family – especially, if for the wrong reasons, in Pyotr's eyes – with the marriage of Zinaida to Colonel Evgeny Olkhovsky, to be followed in the autumn by that of cousin Lidya to his older brother. But that June, barely a month after Pyotr's fourteenth birthday, his mother contracted cholera. For a few days the woman for whom Tchaikovsky bore, in his own words, 'a kind of morbidly passionate love', appeared to be making a normal recovery. But on 25 June, at the age of only forty-one, she died.

The children were elsewhere, housed with an aunt, when Alexandra Andreyevna suffered a relapse so severe that, by her son's own evidence, 'she died without having time to say farewell to all those around her'. This would seem to give the lie to those who suggest that the fourteen-year-old Tchaikovsky heard his mother's screams (or was even, as in the film director Ken Russell's vivid imaginings, a traumatized eyewitness[7])as she was lowered into the scalding hot bath – then the last-resort treatment for cholera victims, designed to reactivate the kidneys – as he himself would be nearly forty years later. Pyotr and Sasha were hurried to her deathbed, Ippolit tells us, too late to witness the administering of the last rites.

For the rest of his days Tchaikovsky would bemoan his mother's premature departure from his life, which had 'a huge influence on the way things turned out for me.' It was more than two years before he could bring himself to pass the news to Fanny Dürbach, ending a letter in 1856 with the startling postscript: 'Finally, I must tell you of a terrible tragedy that occurred two and a half years ago . . .' In another letter, two decades later, he was still telling another trusted confidante that he had never managed, and never would, to reconcile himself to the fact that 'my mother, whom I loved so much and who was such a beautiful person, is gone for ever; and that I shall never have the chance to tell her that after twenty-three years of separation I still love her as much as ever.' In his fortieth year, he marked the twenty-fifth anniversary of his mother's death by telling the same friend: 'Every moment of that appalling day is as vivid to me as though it was yesterday.'[8]

All his life, according to Modest, Tchaikovsky could not mention his mother without weeping. However sentimental his feelings about her in later life, like so many men deprived at a young age of mothers colder and remoter than they remember, the fourteen-year-old Tchaikovsky's sense of loss and isolation was undoubtedly traumatic. On the day of his mother's funeral his father too succumbed to cholera, but made a full recovery after a week. The best way for his fragile son to cope with all this, Ilya determined, was to send him straight back to school, where the daunting daily workload would occupy his mind.

His sense of isolation now stronger than ever, the adolescent Tchaikovsky began to forge schoolboy friendships intense enough to compensate for the loss of his mother and the absence of the rest of his family. Some of them were to last his lifetime: with Alexey Apukhtin, for instance, whose poems he would later set to music, and with Vladimir Gerard, to become a celebrated forensic orator who would one day deliver the funeral oration beside Tchaikovsky's grave. The one would soon become his longstanding lover, the other the object of his unrequited sexual desire. Other lifelong friends from this period include Prince Vladimir Meshchersky, later to provoke a series of high-society scandals, and to earn the sobriquet 'Prince of Sodom and citizen of Gomorrah'; and one

Vladimir Adamov, who remained a keen amateur musician while rising to the top of the Ministry of Justice. 'The mutual attraction [with Adamov] was so strong,' writes an unusually candid Modest, 'that they remained intimate friends until death severed the connection.' Already Tchaikovsky's sexual tastes were settled. Where other pupils indulged in homosexual by-play as a passing rite of puberty, the fledgling composer had found his lifelong vocation. In his graduation photograph he is the only boy in his class brazen enough to be seen holding his neighbour's hand.

Music was scarcely a high priority on the curriculum of the School of Jurisprudence, but boys were taken on regular visits to the theatre and the opera, where Tchaikovsky broadened his acquaintance with the work of Rossini, Bellini, Verdi and Mozart. The only musical instruction he enjoyed at school was some piano tuition from Franz Becker, a piano manufacturer who made occasional visits as a token music teacher. At this early stage of his life Tchaikovsky also enjoyed singing, with the notable support of his kindly aunt, Ekaterina, who had encouraged him during one summer vacation by praising his voice, especially his ability to trill, when they joined forces for the coloratura duet from Rossini's *Semiramide*. She also took him through Mozart's *Don Giovanni* at the piano – an experience he later recalled as crucial to his musical development:

> This was the first music to make an overwhelming impression on me . . . Through it I penetrated into that sphere of artistic beauty in which soar only the greatest of geniuses . . . It is entirely thanks to Mozart that I chose to dedicate my life to music. He it was who inspired my first efforts, and made me love music above anything else in this world.

At school the young Tchaikovsky also sang in the choir, years later recalling that he had 'a splendid treble voice'. Evidently it broke rather late, for he was chosen three years running to sing the treble solo in the annual service conducted by the Metropolitan of St Petersburg himself. It was his first experience of the liturgy, which made 'the most profound, poetic impression' upon him.

At fifteen he took extra-curricular music lessons, on Sundays, from a twenty-three-year-old German pianist newly arrived in St Petersburg, Rudolph Kündinger, who would later become a professor at the Conservatoire. Kündinger, by his own confession, saw no particular evidence of any unusual talent. Interviewed by Modest after Tchaikovsky's death, he recalled that Ilya Petrovich had asked him whether it was worth his son's thinking in terms of a career in music. 'I replied in the negative, because I did not then see in Pyotr Ilyich the genius that would later make itself manifest.' Kündinger also had first-hand experience of 'just how difficult was the life of the professional musician in Russia at that time.' It required an outstanding talent even to contemplate such an unorthodox career. 'He had certain undeniable skills: a good ear, a sure memory, a fine touch. But none of this gave me reason to predict that he could become even a fine performer, let alone a composer.'[9]

One thing that did strike Kündinger was Tchaikovsky's ability to improvise at the piano: 'In this, certainly, one could sense something beyond the ordinary.' His schoolfriend Gerard also describes how, after choir practice, Tchaikovsky would sit at the harmonium of the school's White Hall and improvise on whatever themes they had just been singing. 'We were amused,' said Gerard, 'but not imbued with any expectations of his future glory.'[10] Other contemporaries describe Tchaikovsky's musical 'tricks', one of which was playing the piano with the keyboard covered by a towel; but again there were no presentiments of his future distinction. His skills at the piano did not even command much respect among either staff or fellow-pupils. More musical kudos was enjoyed, it seems, by his classmate Avgust Gerke, the son of a celebrated pianist of the day, and himself a talented amateur pianist who was to become a distinguished lawyer.

Other recollections of the schoolboy Tchaikovsky may be less reliable. Like most memories of subsequently great men, collected in volumes reeking of hindsight, they appear to be coloured by the contributor's own immortal yearnings. There emerges, however, a reliable enough consensus that Tchaikovsky was among the best-liked boys of his year by both staff and fellow-pupils, for qualities such as 'honesty', 'openness' and 'generosity'. His friend Fyodor Maslov told tales about his untidiness and forgetfulness; absent-mindedness and 'only moderate diligence' were also the chief characteristics remembered by Gerard. Together these young friends all worked on the college journal, *The School Messenger*, for which Tchaikovsky wrote a solemn 'History of Literature in Our Class'. He also kept a private diary, which he called 'Everything', and (according to Maslov) trustingly left lying in his schooldesk, rather than locking it safely away.[11]

Like his father, the young Tchaikovsky does not seem yet to have developed the slightest capacity for malice. Though in later life his judgements of his fellow-men would become selectively harsher, he would always remain a kindly, thoughtful soul amid peer groups such as his family and his changing coteries. With no marked streak of independence, the schoolboy Tchaikovsky managed the unusual feat of remaining popular while seemingly somewhat precious. He was also, as photographs now begin to testify, something of a pretty face.

'Both the fact of its being an all-male institution, and the transitional age of its students,' writes Alexander Poznansky, the most indefatigable researcher into Tchaikovsky's sexual habits, 'contributed to the homoerotically charged atmosphere at the School of Jurisprudence.' In his exhaustive 'quest for the inner man', Poznansky amply documents his conclusion that the seeds sown in Tchaikovsky's childhood took firm root here at school, amid an atmosphere of male bonding to which women were creatures of distant derision.

At the weekly dancing classes, for instance, the young men were 'naturally obliged to dance with each other, one taking the role of the gentleman and the other that of the lady.' Communal bathing gave the adolescents 'an opportunity to study attentively all the physical changes going on in their own bodies and those of their schoolmates.' As to the public floggings: 'That practice could only stimulate the students' interest in, and perhaps morbid fixation on, the male buttocks . . . Both the deep motivation and the ultimate consequences of the act may lead to sado-masochistic or homosexual gratification.'[12]

The widespread practice of mutual masturbation, even buggery, seems to have been tolerated by the authorities as part of natural daily life. Only in the 1840s, before Tchaikovsky's arrival, is there evidence of one expulsion for sexual reasons, apparently on the insistence of the victim's horrified parents, perhaps *pour encourager les autres*. There was baffled outrage among the students. Graduates of the British public school system may well muster a wry smile at the meditations of one former student, the critic Vladimir Stasov: 'What if the whole world were to take it into its head to act in this way? Half Russia would probably have to be expelled from schools, universities, regiments, monasteries, anywhere you care to name, all in the name of the most pure and perfect morality.'[13]

But most graduates of those monastic British institutions, like those from the 1850s School of Jurisprudence, emerged as orthodox heterosexuals, however damaged their attitudes toward women. What made Tchaikovsky different? Poznansky cites his father's reputation as a ladies' man, which 'may have provoked in the boy, possibly at a subconscious level, a reverse reaction – if only by virtue of a child's rebellion against paternal authority and example.'[14]

Rather more likely, as has been seen, it was his mother who played the dominant role in the development of his sexuality, with his genial father merely adding another dimension of femininity to the formula. His mother's abrupt disappearance from his life, moreover, at this crucial stage of his sexual development, left him open to schoolboy practices which became his norm – and, as they diversified into an exotic range of homosexual tastes, supplied the subtext of a lifetime of psychosexual torment, expiable only in his music.

Already the boy had suffered misfortunes enough to offer ominous portents for the future: the abrupt removal of his childhood mainstay, Fanny Dürbach; his sense of responsibility, at ten, for another boy's death; two years of separation from the family he worshipped (and always would) as the paradigm of a happy life; and his adored mother's two brutally symbolic departures, the one temporary, the other permanent. Now, as he advanced timidly through his teens, there emerged the catalyst for a lifelong sequence of further such traumas. As Tchaikovsky himself would eventually confess: 'My whole life has been a chain of misfortunes because of my sexuality.'[15]

# CHAPTER III

## 'I can be *somebody*'

EIGHTEEN-FIFTY-NINE, THE YEAR WHICH SAW TCHAIKOVSKY LEAVE school and reluctantly join the civil service, also happened to be that in which a failed civil servant named Ivan Goncharov published his second novel, *Oblomov*, that immortal satire on the collective inertia which has dogged Russian society throughout its history. A decent enough fellow, if something of a dreamer, Oblomov is first encountered lying in bed, where he remains for most of the first chapter. As emblematic a character as any in Dostoevsky, rapidly to achieve the status of myth, Goncharov's eponymous hero soon lent his name to that peculiarly Russian failing which has seen this vast potential superpower stagnate for decades between sudden spasms of violent action, such as the failed revolutions of 1825 and 1905 between which Tchaikovsky lived and died.

The decade immediately ahead, as it happened, was to be the one such period in the composer's lifetime: an era of major reforms which would yet again fall prey to 'oblomovism', this time sowing the long-term seeds of the successful revolution half a century later. Although his delicate irony pierced deep into the Russian soul, Goncharov's prime target was the complacent middle-class gentry typified by the civil service, with its nostalgia for a provincial Russian Arcadia which had never really existed – as, perhaps, in the provincial childhood of the civil servant's son who graduated from the School of Jurisprudence, a respectable third in his class, in May 1859, the month of his nineteenth birthday. Before he too disappeared into the ossified layers of the Russian bureaucracy, Pyotr Ilyich Tchaikovsky was determined to enjoy what was left of his youth.

As his brother's childhood ends, and he embarks on adult life, Modest is anxious to reassure posterity that Pyotr Ilyich had formed some lively friendships with members of the opposite sex; his cousin Anna Merkling, for instance, had become a confidante close enough to share 'intimate secrets of the heart'. But Anna was half again as old as Pyotr, more a valued friend than an object of passion, as she remained throughout his life; and however valued her friendship, it is highly unlikely that he shared with her the true secrets of his heart.

At school, for some years, it had already belonged to a boy named Sergey Kireyev, whose name is conspicuous by its absence from Modest's pages. Modest makes no mention of a letter he himself received from his brother upon his own graduation from the School of Jurisprudence eleven years later, recalling the day Pyotr Ilyich had himself left the school, when his 'vivid joy' had been 'mixed with bitterness' at his parting from 'my genius, my angel, my friend' Kireyev (evidently the inspiration for the song of that name, to words by Fet).[1] But the relationship had apparently continued. In 1861, two years after leaving school, Tchaikovsky wrote to his sister Sasha that his heart was 'still in the same place'; to him, the Kireyevs are 'the Holy Family'. Typically, however, he follows the news of Sergey's rapid recovery from illness with a reference to his sister Sofia – 'she has grown very pretty' – as if trying to persuade Sasha, and perhaps himself, that here lay the true object his affections.

As Tchaikovsky embarks on his civil service career, as a clerk (first-class) in the Ministry of Justice, Modest and his other Russian biographers grow anxious to move on as swiftly as possible to the next chapter, where they can return to the respectable subject of his development as a musician. There are obvious reasons to draw a decent veil over the one period of Tchaikovsky's life in which music appears to have come a distant second to more carnal interests. Still in the thrall of Gerard, his longing for whom appears never to have been requited, he was also the constant companion of Apukhtin, already a precocious poetic talent attracting the praise of Turgenev and Fet, and already an open and unabashed homosexual. In 1859, soon after their graduation, the death of Apukhtin's own mother deepened a bond between him and Tchaikovsky which would survive decades of distance and occasional disagreement.

The initial bond between them, as schoolboys, had been a Wildean reverence for 'art for art's sake', which united these two young aesthetes against all that the boors of the School of Jurisprudence could throw at them. Even in his mid-teens, amid the homoerotic pranks of his peers, Apukhtin made no secret of the fact that his own sexual preference was no transitional experiment. Already it was clear to him, for all his plump, ungainly lack of physical charm, that this was his true nature. There was no reason for Tchaikovsky, by far the weaker partner, to hear in this anything other than an echo of his own emergent self.

Any unease about his own nature had yet to make itself felt. Homosexuality was not merely illegal in Russia, punishable by public disgrace, loss of civil rights and exile to Siberia; it was widely regarded, even in the most liberal of circles, as a 'vice'. Like Victorian England, late Tsarist Russia affected a strict public morality while indulging itself in all sorts of private passions; even in this atmosphere, however, homosexuality was never exactly fashionable, always something of a taboo. But these first few years of post-school euphoria, unencumbered by any creative preoccupations, form the period when Tchaikovsky appears to have been least uncomfortable with his own sexuality. Before long, it would be the cause of torment slowly escalating to catastrophe.

For now, Tchaikovsky was content to resign himself to the dreary, Oblomovish routine of a junior recruit to the civil service, expected to set his sights on a steady climb up the bureaucratic ladder. If his daily routine was stultifying, there were compensations enough after hours. His social life was, to say the least, lively for one so fundamentally shy and retiring; to his brother Anatoly, he confessed that he would 'lose a night or two's sleep' from nerves about a forthcoming dinner party. Adopting his most disapproving tone of voice, Modest describes how at this stage his brother, even after leaving school, seemed to him to remain a schoolboy: 'The same insatiable thirst for laughter, the same continual pursuit of pleasure at all costs, the same superficial view of the serious aspects of life, all remained as much a part of him in his newfound freedom as they had been at school.' The young Pyotr Tchaikovsky was 'a drifter', doing the minimum work necessary to hold down his job, with no real interest in his new profession or much else beyond his social life.

> With the change from youth to manhood came also the desire to taste the pleasures and excitements of life. The future appeared to him an endless carnival, and, with nothing in his young life as yet to disabuse him, he surrendered himself to this seductive illusion. With his impulsive temperament, he took life easy: a good-natured, carefree young man, unencumbered by serious interests or aspirations.[2]

Tchaikovsky's close friend Herman Laroche, soon to become an important early champion of his music, describes the young civil servant as 'a dashing young man-about-town', clean-shaven (in defiance of fashion), smartly dressed despite a meagre budget, and a favourite among his growing circle of fashionable friends. The dashing young man himself seems surprised, in letters of the period, by his ability to conquer his shyness, and his lifelong dread of crowded rooms, in pursuit of an active social life. With its almost complete absence of musical activity, this was, in short, a wholly uncharacteristic period of his life. Only his pursuit of sexual adventure was to remain a constant. 'The Tchaikovsky of the 1860s and the Tchaikovsky of the 1880s,' wrote Laroche, 'were two very different people.'[3]

For some time the Tchaikovsky family had pooled its fortunes with those of Ilya's brother, himself called Pyotr. To the composer's father, in enforced retirement, sharing a house with his brother's family was the only way to make ends meet. Then another case of misplaced faith, this time entrusting his fortune to a friend's widow, cost Ilya his life savings – and Pyotr Ilyich his piano lessons with Kündinger. Forced to look for work again, at the age of sixty-three, Tchaikovsky's endearingly Micawber-like father did indeed see something turn up, thanks again to one of the many friendships he had made. This time it was the directorship of the St Petersburg Technological Institute which he secured with the assistance of an acquaintance who owed him a favour. With the job came a decent salary and a handsome apartment, in which a married sister-in-law, Elizabeth Schobert, was installed as housekeeper.

She it was who introduced Tchaikovsky to the curious figure of Luigi Piccioli, a Neapolitan voice coach who had lived and worked in St Petersburg for ten years. Estimates of Piccioli's age, as he formed what Modest calls 'an intimate friendship' with the teenage Tchaikovsky, ranged from fifty to seventy-plus; apart from dyeing his hair and rougeing his cheeks, he concealed in his collar a bizarre precursor of the modern facelift, a primitive device to stretch his skin and smooth out the wrinkles. For all his eccentricities, however, Piccioli was a good musician, and a forthright one; no lover of Bach or Beethoven, or even Glinka's sacred *Life for the Tsar*, he admitted the greatness only of his fellow-Italians, Rossini and Bellini, Donizetti and Verdi. The youthful Tchaikovsky would enjoy arguing with this Italian grotesque; but his mind was at least temporarily elsewhere. Nor was he much at home.

For a while, Tchaikovsky had uncharacteristically lost interest in his family's fortunes. Even his beloved sister Sasha's marriage in 1860 to a wealthy landowner, Lev Davidov, enforcing her departure to the Ukraine, did not prompt the outpourings of grief which were his wont before and after this period of idle self-indulgence. After six months at the Ministry of Justice, he had been promoted to personal assistant to his department head, despite a complete lack of any apparent effort on his part. Asked soon after he left the Ministry what his duties had been, he confessed himself 'unable to remember'. The only anecdote to survive his three years there has him stopping to talk to a colleague while delivering an important document signed by his chief; as he chats, Tchaikovsky absent-mindedly tears strips off the paper and eats them. Modest relates the tale with a certain scepticism, while attesting that his brother did indeed have a lifelong habit of tearing up theatre or concert programmes and nibbling them throughout the performance. Less convincing, perhaps, is the nonchalance apparently displayed by the bored civil servant about returning to his boss with an explanation as to why he required a second signature on a replacement document.

Music had hitherto been the only subject which could rouse Tchaikovsky to any enthusiasm, any original opinion, any display of individualism. In contrast to his 'general docility, and compliance in the opinions of others', on musical questions he would 'brook no disagreement'. In all other matters, according to Modest, he was 'as malleable as a piece of wax'. Now, with little or no music to rouse him from his torpor, Tchaikovsky was enjoying the life of a popular young dandy. To Sasha he wrote of his love of St Petersburg, where a stroll down Nevsky Prospekt could cheer him up even when 'broke' and 'unhappily in love'. Most of the time he was far from broke – a salaried civil servant with no financial obligations – but confessed to squandering his money on 'idle pleasures'. Though he was less than frank with her, Sasha was perhaps among the few able to guess what those pleasures entailed.

Under the ample wing of Apukhtin, 'my court jester and best friend', Tchaikovsky was fast becoming an active member of St Petersburg's homosexual underground. Though Modest remains silent on the subject, the letters and diaries of the composer and his contemporaries suggest a sybaritic life amid an exotic demi-monde of the idle rich. The flamboyant Apukhtin himself makes an irresistible Russian counterpart to Oscar Wilde: not as fecund a poet, perhaps, but equally outrageous in his behaviour, papering the walls of his apartment with portraits of young officers, and enlivening the dizzy round of balls and parties with his glittering wit and camp midnight pranks. The other centre of Tchaikovsky's sexual gravity was Prince Alexey Golitsyn, another high-society homosexual brazen enough to live openly with a male partner, and to organize lively gatherings of the like-minded.

At this stage in his life, it seems clear, Tchaikovsky was happy to take the chance of indulging his sexual appetite with no mixed feelings. Noted for his enthusiastic impersonations (in whatever company) of female dancers – 'he had a gift', as Modest puts it, 'for making the unacceptable acceptable' – the guilt-ridden public figure was still a phantom beyond Tchaikovsky's personal horizon. It is unclear whether he yet felt his homosexuality irreversible, more than a passing phase, though the lack of all his subsequent *angst* would suggest that he did at this stage foresee an eventual return to what he would always call 'normality'.

Against this backdrop of unabashed sexual abandon, it was music which was to prove the ineluctable bridge from one Tchaikovsky to the other – from the idle, self-indulgent libertine to the dedicated, hard-working professional, and thus from the carefree, rampant homosexual to the tortured, self-loathing misfit. Given the apparent absence of anything but party tricks in his musical repertoire at this time, and the composition of a few waltzes and polkas he did not even bother to commit to paper, it is hard to track this transition from dilettante to committed, serious-minded musician. Though he clearly deserves considerable credit, it cannot have been entirely due to Piccioli, the one professional musician in his life, constantly carrying him off to the theatre to hear the Italian masters. Still his knowledge of music was woefully limited, not least because of Piccioli's prejudices.

At a time of great social ferment in Russia, the youthful Tchaikovsky took little interest in politics. Following Russia's defeat in the Crimean War, Tsar Alexandr II had embarked on a historic programme of liberal reform, in marked contrast to the rigid autocracy of his father, Nikolay I. Persuaded that liberalism was the best route to modernization (while also the best way to keep the peasantry in check), Alexandr overhauled the legal system, liberated the universities, and drastically reduced censorship. Bliss should it have been in that dawn to be alive, let alone young; yet the twenty-one-year-old civil servant makes only passing mention in one letter even of the most momentous reform of them all: the Emancipation of the Serfs in 1861, at much the same time as the abolition of American slavery.

Nor is there any evidence that he read the cult book of the year among rebellious Russian youth, Turgenev's *Fathers and Sons*, though his lifestyle had so far verged on near-orthodox nihilism. It was during that same year, however, that a distinct change overcame the dissolute young aesthete, who began once again to talk of a career in music, and to re-enter the close-knit life of his family. To Modest, it seemed that his brother had 'grown weary of a life of idle dissipation, and felt a desire to start afresh.' But there is a casuistic note in his brother's assumption that Tchaikovsky 'had grown afraid that he would be overwhelmed in this slough of a petty, useless and vicious existence'; and there is less than meets the eye in Modest's suggestion that 'some unknown event' had led to Tchaikovsky's feeling of 'satiety'. The reluctant civil servant might well have remained relaxed about his non-conformist private life, had his working hours offered greater fulfilment.

One figure undoubtedly given less than his due for Tchaikovsky's conversion is his father – a man largely bereft of musical knowledge or experience, yet loving enough to change his mind and countenance his son giving up a civil service career for music. 'For shame, Petya,' exclaimed Ilya's brother, Pyotr, on hearing the mere idea under discussion. 'How could you exchange Jurisprudence for a hooter?'[4] Yet Ilya Petrovich himself could not have been more encouraging, however much he may have had to suppress his own instincts. Indeed, the only documentation for this turning-point comes in a letter from Tchaikovsky to his sister Sasha, written in March 1861, after his father had raised the matter over dinner one evening. Ilya Petrovich had apparently given his blessing, in principle, to the notion of a career as a musician. Now it was Tchaikovsky himself who became dubious. 'If I do have any talent, it is probably too late to develop it,' he complained to Sasha. 'They've turned me into a civil servant, and a lousy one at that.' In a postscript he adds that he was studying musical theory – specifically, thoroughbass. 'Who knows, maybe in a few years you'll be going to my operas and singing my arias?'[5]

But as soon as music was back on his agenda, there was an immediate, if welcome diversion: his first chance to travel abroad. When an old friend of his father, an engineer named Vasily Pisarev, offered him a trip to Europe as his secretary-cum-interpreter, Tchaikovsky jumped at it, securing leave of absence from the Ministry for the summer of 1861. In excited letters home he conveyed his distaste for Berlin, a 'gloomier' version of St Petersburg. He much preferred Hamburg, where he and his employer evidently attended dances with 'women of dubious reputation – this place is full of them!' and frequented the 'inferior' parts of town. Via Cologne they proceeded to Antwerp, Brussels and Ostend, where the 'roar of the sea' delighted him as much as the unexpected sight of mixed bathing.

In August they arrived in London, where the constant rain dampened his spirits, although he took to English food – 'simple, unfussy and tasty, it comes in generous portions' – and was 'overwhelmed' by a performance of Handel's *Messiah* at the Crystal Palace, though he appreciated the singing of eighteen-year-old Adelina Patti (then first capturing the British audiences she would hold for twenty-five years) less than the jugglers and trapeze artists in Chelsea's Cremorne pleasure gardens. They toured the Houses of Parliament and Westminster Abbey, and even ventured underground into Brunel's Thames Tunnel (now the Rotherhithe Tunnel), where Tchaikovsky found it 'so stuffy I was nearly sick.'

A week later they were in Paris, the destination Tchaikovsky had most eagerly awaited, when suddenly the trip went terribly wrong. For reasons he never disclosed, the young secretary fell out with his employer, and they parted on extremely bad terms. The problem, it would seem, was more than merely that Tchaikovsky had run up debts to Pisarev of some 300 roubles, despite his wages and a travel allowance from his father. 'What can I tell you about my trip abroad? It's better to draw a veil over it' was all he would say to his sister that autumn. 'If ever I made an enormous mistake at any time in my life, this was it. You think you know Pisarev? Well, beneath that veneer of *bonhomie*, that outward show of decent, if unpolished manners, there lurks the most bestial of minds. Never before had I realized that so vile a creature could walk the earth. You cannot conceive what it was like to be tied inseparably to so charming a companion for three whole months . . .'[6]

From the violence of his language, and that last resort to sarcasm, it has naturally been assumed that the older man made unwelcome sexual advances to his twenty-one-year-old travelling companion.[7] If so, Tchaikovsky is guilty of more than mere hypocrisy in responding with such venom. By one account, he capitalized on Pisarev's departure by renting an apartment with an old friend from the School of Jurisprudence, Vladimir Yuferov – with whom, according to letters home soon restored to their usual high spirits, he was soon having 'a high old time'.[8] Perhaps Pisarev, with his obvious taste for the low life, had appalled his young friend with some outrageous proposals for *heterosexual* adventures.

On his return home, the juxtaposition of these two experiences – his falling-out with Pisarev and his falling-in with Yuferov – seems to have brought on his first real spasm of unease over his sexuality. 'How shall I wind up?' he asks Sasha later in the same letter. 'What does the future hold for me? I can't bear to think about it. All I know is that sooner or later (and probably sooner) I shan't have the strength to cope with the "problem" side of my life, and it will smash me into tiny pieces.'[9]

The dawn of 1862 saw Tchaikovsky in determined mood. With a possible promotion in the offing, he was buckling down to his work, and had already determined to stay in St Petersburg, stationed at his Ministry desk, throughout the summer. At the same time he embarked on a more structured approach to his musical education, all too aware of the embarrassing gaps in his knowledge. Though well-versed in the operatic repertoire, he scarcely knew what a symphony was – nor even, according to Modest, how many Beethoven had written. Six weeks after his last letter to his sister, Pyotr was again writing in much more optimistic terms:

> I think I told you that I'd begun studying musical theory. Well, it's going very well. I don't want to sound boastful, but I'm sure you'd agree that it would be a pity to waste my modest talents, not even to chance my arm . . . But the one thing I dread is my lack of will-power. Maybe my laziness will win the day, and I'll pack it all in. But if only I can keep at it, and prove everyone wrong, then I'll show you: I can be *somebody*.[10]

It would no doubt have come to pass sooner or later, by whatever means, but Tchaikovsky's initiation into formal musical training happened to take place by accident. The dilettante musician had a music-loving cousin, an officer in the Horse Grenadiers, with whom he enjoyed a genial rivalry. According to Tchaikovsky's friend Nikolay Kashkin, this cousin one day boasted that he could make the transition from one key to any other in no more than three chords. Taking up the challenge, Tchaikovsky came up with various ingenious improvisations, but could not match his cousin's feat. Considering himself the superior musician, he asked the young officer where he had learnt such a thing. Thus did the future composer hear for the first time of the public classes held by the newly formed Russkoe Muzykalnoe Obshchestvo, the Russian Musical Society.

Founded in 1859 under the dynamic leadership of Anton Rubinstein, already a celebrated virtuoso pianist and a prolific composer, the RMS owed its existence to the energies of the Tsar's German-born aunt, the Grand Duchess Elena, who persuaded Alexandr II himself to become its patron. Established 'to encourage indigenous talent by offering formal education in music, and to develop a taste for music in Russians,' it promoted public concerts at the Assembly Hall of the Nobility, and held free public classes in the Grand Duchess's own home, the Mikhailovsky Palace. The first organization to provide any framework for musical instruction in Russia, it was to prove the forerunner of the country's two great Conservatoires.

Rubinstein had been inspired to 'define the status of the musician in Russian society', according to his memoirs, by an incident at the Kazan Cathedral in St Petersburg, where he was fulfilling his statutory obligation to go to confession at least once every three years. When he presented himself for registration, the deacon was not prepared to recognize 'musician', nor even 'artist', as an acceptable profession. Asked his father's profession, after several minutes of questioning, Rubinstein answered 'Merchant of the second guild.' The deacon, 'greatly relieved', exclaimed 'At last! You are the son of a merchant of the second guild, and as such we shall inscribe your name.'

The incident, said Rubinstein, left 'an indelible impression on my mind. Evidently the name and estate of musician, universally acknowledged in other lands, had in Russia no clearly defined meaning. What was Glinka, after all? A landowner, a nobleman in the government of Smolensk. And Serov? An official in the Post Office Department . . .'[11] Borodin, he might have added, was a professor of chemistry, Balakirev a mathematician, Rimsky-Korsakov a naval officer and Musorgsky a civil servant.

There is no underestimating the significance of Rubinstein's revolution in the Russian attitude to professional music-making, and Tchaikovsky's good fortune in being the right age in the right place at the right time. Music tuition had previously been the preserve of private schools and aristocratic salons; public performances had largely been confined to the work of contemporary Russian composers and the Italian school of opera, performed by European visitors. Now a much wider public was introduced to the full gamut of works by Handel and Bach, Schumann and Schubert, and standards of performance began to improve immeasurably.

Even historians of the Soviet era felt obliged to concede that 'the country's nineteenth-century social development had demanded a systematic musical education to match the already efficient systems for learning the humanities and engineering.'[12] Now, at last, Rubinstein and St Petersburg had shown the way, and this first batch of pupils was to produce musicians quite as varied and distinguished as their teachers. Among Tchaikovsky's intake, some of them to become his friends for life, were Laroche and Vasily Bessel, who would later become his St Petersburg publisher. Both watched with wide eyes as the young dandy metamorphosed into a dedicated musician, determined to make a name for himself.

The society's tutor in musical theory was Nikolay Zaremba, a controversial figure among the musicians of the day, but just the man to impose the discipline Tchaikovsky so sorely needed. Though Russian himself, Zaremba was a disciple of the German school of composition; under his own teacher, Adolph Marx of Berlin, he had come to revere Beethoven to the exclusion of other, more recent Europeans such as Berlioz and Schumann. Criminally, in the view of the Russian school, he attached little importance to Glinka. Not much of a composer himself – he once showed Tchaikovsky a string quartet, which he described to Laroche as 'OK, in the style of Haydn' – Zaremba even had a low opinion of Mozart. Mocked by Balakirev, and derided by Musorgsky, he was undoubtedly narrow-minded, acknowledging no composer later than Mendelssohn. But Tchaikovsky's rough-and-ready technique was transformed by the rigorous regime he imposed. Though he would later rebel against Zaremba's strictures, Tchaikovsky always acknowledged the significance of his first real teacher's role in his development as a composer.

In Tchaikovsky, for all his slapdash approach to his work, Zaremba was the first to sense an unusual talent, and to encourage it. The young man was surprised, and touched, when his tutor called him aside one day and urged him to apply himself to his work more seriously; showing unwonted warmth, Zaremba assured Tchaikovsky of his 'unquestionable' talent. 'From that moment,' says Laroche, our source for this story, 'Pyotr Ilyich decided to cast off his idleness, and took to his work with an energy that never failed him.'[13]

On 20 September 1862 Pyotr Ilyich Tchaikovsky was among the first intake of students, albeit part-time, to enrol at the newly opened St Petersburg Conservatoire, the first institution of its kind in Russia. His application, preserved in the Tchaikovsky archive at Klin, shows that he wanted to study 'mostly theory'.[14] Growing as it did from the Russian Musical Society, the Conservatoire opened with Anton Rubinstein as its founder-director, and Zaremba as professor of composition. Housed in a handsome building beside the River Neva, it boasted a distinguished international staff, with eminent performers such as the pianist Fyodr Leshetitsky, the violinist Henryk Wieniawsky, the harpist Albert Zabel and the flautist Cesare Ciardi establishing a long and distinguished tradition of teaching.

Out of his own slender means, Rubinstein himself provided funds for pupils to learn wind instruments in sufficient numbers to form the nucleus of a student orchestra; for two years Tchaikovsky took flute lessons with Ciardi, eventually becoming proficient enough to take part in chamber music and symphony concerts. His studies at the Lutheran Church's majestic organ with Heinrich Stiehl proved less inspirational. Where the flute would always play a highly distinctive role in all his orchestral writings, Tchaikovsky was never to compose a single piece for organ solo.

'Sooner or later, I am now thoroughly convinced, I shall give up my job and devote myself exclusively to music,' he wrote to his sister just two days after the Conservatoire had opened. 'Don't suppose that I am convinced I shall become a great artist. It's just that I feel a deep sense of vocation. Whether I turn out to be a celebrated composer or a humble pedagogue, my conscience will be clear – and I will have no grounds for bitterness or remorse about the quirks of fate.'[15]

Of course, he added, he would not be giving up his day-job 'until

I am quite certain that I am destined to be a musician rather than a civil servant.' For now, he continued his work at the Ministry, but with less enthusiasm than ever. Even after his diligence the previous summer, when he had astonished his family by bringing work home in the evenings, he had failed to win that prized promotion – a setback as much for his finances as his ego. His indignation at being passed over 'knew no bounds', according to Modest, who for once is surely right to conclude that 'this incident undoubtedly precipitated his eventual decision to devote himself wholly to music.'[16]

Now he was back at home full-time, living alone with his father, the dutiful son felt the need for a gradual campaign to reassure the kindly, indulgent old man. With Nikolay pursuing his career as a mining engineer in the provinces, Ippolit away in the Navy, and the twins at school all week, Pyotr virtually mothered Ilya Petrovich, arranging each day's menus with the family cook, and organizing each evening's enter-tainment. 'You won't believe me,' he told Sasha, 'but living alone with Papa is not in the least dull. I have lunch with him at home every day, and we spend the evenings playing cards or going out to the theatre . . .'

To the twelve-year-old twins, Anatoly and Modest, he had quite consciously become a surrogate mother. 'My love for these two,' he told Sasha, 'and especially (keep this to yourself) Tolya, grows by the day. Deep in myself I cherish this feeling, and think it the best part of me. When things get me down, I have only to think of them and my heart lifts, remembering that my life has a purpose. I am doing my best to substitute my own affection for the mother's love they can never now know – nor, alas, much remember. It appears, moreover, that I am proving successful.'[17]

To Alexander Poznansky, there is a darker side to Tchaikovsky's relations with his younger brothers – 'a dimension beyond that of ordinary fraternal affection'. It seems 'indisputable', he concludes, 'that the relationship of the three Tchaikovsky brothers was saturated with eroticism, including its physical manifestations, to an extraordinary degree.'[18] It was nothing unusual, in so physically warm a family, for brothers to share beds, however disparate their ages. But the sheer lavishness of Tchaikovsky's affection for the twins – and, to be fair, the twins' hero-worship of their fun-loving older brother – makes the modern reader distinctly uneasy when he writes letters authorizing one to 'smother' the other with kisses on his behalf, and climbs into bed with them to play 'lively games'.

At this stage, as he told Sasha, Pyotr Ilyich nurtured a secret preference for Anatoly, the more self-contained of the two twelve-year-olds. In the wide-eyed Modest, it seems clear, he saw too much of himself

– a problem which he was not as deft as he thought at concealing. That Anatoly should turn out to be a heterosexual adult and Modest a homosexual is not in itself too remarkable; modern studies of twins reveal differing orientation, to a surprising degree, in sexual as much as other characteristics. With the twenty-two-year-old Pyotr Ilyich as his surrogate mother, however, clearly favouring his twin brother over him, Modest's fate was probably already sealed. When he too developed artistic aspirations, with conspicuously less success, it was to make a highly combustible combination with their common sexuality – casting Modest, in life as in art, as Boswell to his brother's Johnson.

On 25 April 1863, after six months as a part-time student, Tchaikovsky resigned his post at the Ministry of Justice and entered the Conservatoire as a fully-fledged musician-in-the-making. Although he had won his father's approval, his timing could not have been worse. That same month Ilya Petrovich retired from the Institute of Technology, depriving the family of its main source of income.

In a show of determination about his new career, the hard-working music student took it upon himself to boost the household budget with extra teaching by day and evening work as an accompanist. He told his sister that he had 'completely renounced all luxuries and amusements' – ostensibly to reduce his expenditure, but also as another token of his single-minded devotion to music, even at the expense of his sex life. It was time, he also decided, to look the part. By the autumn, his friends scarcely recognized the long-haired figure in the shabby old coat as the dapper dandy they had once known.

As his studies with Zaremba progressed from harmony to counterpoint, the young Tchaikovsky was far more heavily influenced by Rubinstein, with whom he worked on orchestration. An immensely powerful presence – 'he inspired us students', says Laroche, 'with unbounded affection, and not inconsiderable awe' – Rubinstein ran the school like a benevolent despot, setting his pupils fiendishly challenging exercises and quickly losing patience with those who did not adhere to his own conservative musical tastes. Although Tchaikovsky benefited enormously from the single-minded enthusiasm of Rubinstein's approach, a debt he was always swift to acknowledge, he felt his way towards his own distinctive style despite his teacher rather than because of him.

Among contemporary evidence for this are the recollections of a student named Alexandr Rubets, who described Rubinstein's habit of beginning a class by reciting some verses, then requiring his pupils to come up overnight with some music inspired by them, in such forms as rondo, polonaise or minuet. One day Rubinstein assigned Tchaikovsky a poem by Zhukovsky called 'Midnight Review', already the subject of a celebrated romance by Glinka; so amused was Rubinstein by this piece of mischief that he could not resist interrupting Zaremba's class to share the joke with both teacher and pupils. Seeing things from Tchaikovsky's point of view, and 'unable to bear the thought of it', Rubets protested to Rubinstein, who shrugged his shoulders and said 'So what? Glinka wrote his own music – and Tchaikovsky will write his.' Two days later, Tchaikovsky's 'Midnight Review' turned out to be a completely different animal from Glinka's: no mere romance, but 'a full-scale, complex tone poem, with a varied and intricate accompaniment to each verse.'[19]

Rubinstein's creative approach – designed, despite his insistence on classical orthodoxy, to encourage individuality – was in direct contrast to Zaremba's doctrinaire rigour, thus making the ideal combination to help the young Tchaikovsky begin to find his own voice. For these first two years, his musical education was further broadened by many hours at the piano with Laroche, playing adaptations for four hands of great works to which they had no other means of access. Together they explored Beethoven's ninth symphony and Schumann's third, the symphonic poems of Liszt and Wagner – who himself visited St Petersburg in 1862, and was to remain something of a *bête noire* for Tchaikovsky, always more impressed by his instrumentation than by his musical voice. An unlikely early enthusiasm for the music of Henri Litolff, notably his overtures *Robespierre* and *Les Girondistes*, awakened his interest in 'programmatic' music – works which consciously represent specific ideas or feelings on the composer's part. Laroche, whose evidence for all this Modest reproduces at length, also records Tchaikovsky's early aversion to the combination of piano and orchestra, and to the timbre of a string quartet – mental blocks which he would soon overcome to spectacular effect.

Laroche also introduced Tchaikovsky to one of the grand musical figures of the day, Alexandr Serov, a critic and composer for whose opera, *Judith*, he retained a somewhat unlikely admiration all his life. But so violently did Tchaikovsky disagree with Serov's musical opinions, not least his disregard for Anton Rubinstein as a composer, that he only once accepted an invitation to the great man's regular Tuesday soirées. That particular Tuesday, as it happened, the other guests included Dostoevsky, who spent the whole evening talking 'complete rubbish, as literary men do about music.'[20]

At home, Tchaikovsky could also enjoy an acquaintanceship at only one remove with his great literary hero, Pushkin, three of whose works he would turn into operas. His sister Sasha's mother-in-law, Alexandra Ivanovna Davidova, had now settled in St Petersburg with five of her children. The senior Davidovs had known Pushkin well. He had been a frequent guest at their country estate in Kamenka, where Tchaikovsky too was to spend many a fruitful summer. Alexandra's oldest daughter, Elizaveta, also regaled the young composer with memories of Pushkin and Gogol, and tantalizing tales of happier adventures around Europe than he had himself so far enjoyed.

The family entertained hopes that Tchaikovsky might take some romantic interest in her younger sister, Vera – as, it appears, did Vera herself. This was, in time, to cause the young homosexual considerable problems; as yet, however, these nostalgic evenings were the foundation for Tchaikovsky of an honorary membership of the Davidov family, which over the years compensated for the lack of his own. They were to share his rise to fame, and to support him through his many moments of crisis, to a far greater degree than most of his friends. It was to a Davidov, the youngest and to him the most significant of them all, that he would dedicate his last and greatest work, the *Pathétique* symphony; and it was at the Davidov estate at Kamenka, now reigned over by his sister, that he would write his first really mature work.

First, however, there was the diversion of a summer as the guest of his less reputable friend, Prince Alexey Golitsyn, who laid on a veritable 'fairy tale' at his ancestral estate at Trostinets, in the Ukraine. Despite other invitations, including one to Kamenka from his sister, Tchaikovsky opted for the luxurious magnificence of princely hospitality, climaxing in a day-long party in his honour, on his Name Day, 11 July. It began after church with a celebratory alfresco breakfast, and ended that evening with 'a walk through torch-lit woods to a clearing, where a banquet in [Tchaikovsky's] honour was served in a splendid marquee for guests and serfs alike.' Small wonder he wrote somewhat guiltily to his sister that he was 'rather enjoying' himself – enough, it seems, to postpone for several more weeks his return to the Conservatoire, sending word that he was suffering from a toothache.

Small wonder, too, that Rubinstein did not think much of the composition exercise with which he returned, an overture to Alexandr Ostrovsky's play *The Storm*. Even the supportive Laroche described it as 'a museum of anti-musical curiosities'. The summer, it seems, had been too full of the distractions Tchaikovsky had vowed to put behind him. Had the dandy-turned-aesthete so irrevocably foresworn his old ways? There is no documentation of the companions who might have diverted him that summer, beyond the prince himself, eight years the composer's senior, and already well on his way to a notoriety that would scandalize St Petersburg. Ranged against Sasha Davidova – the Snow White sister hovering in the sidelines, issuing constant invitations to work in equally congenial summer surroundings – Golitsyn becomes a Faustian figure, symbolizing temptations which Tchaikovsky could never quite master.

History, however, has judged *The Storm* more generously. To David Brown it shows 'a fabulous talent' at which Tchaikovsky's earlier Conservatoire exercises had only hinted. Written four years earlier, in 1860, and today better-known as the inspiration for Janáček's opera, *Katya Kabanova*, Ostrovsky's play was then regarded as the finest work of the leading playwright of the day. Tchaikovsky had previously considered basing an opera on the story of the tragic Katerina, who confesses her infidelity to her husband and, amid the eponymous storm, drowns herself in the Volga. Hearing of other, more senior composers' interest in operatic versions, he scaled his plans down in a precise synopsis which ends with the storm itself as 'a climax of desperate struggle and death' – and the first example of his long musical infatuation with 'fallen' women. Tchaikovsky sent the piece to Rubinstein via Laroche, who received a dressing-down as severe as if he had written it himself. His mentor's vehement objections to the ideas and inventions in the piece, as well as to aspects of its orchestration, persuaded the crestfallen Tchaikovsky never to publish it, though it would certainly have made a more than worthy Opus 1.

Having spent the summers of 1863 and 1864 *chez* Apukhtin and Golitsyn, he stiffened his resolve and spent that of 1865 at Kamenka. Though less exotic than the prince's Trostinets, it was an estate with inspiriting associations. Here Pushkin had written his poem 'The Prisoner of the Caucasus' and enjoyed an affair with Alexandra Davidova's sister-in-law; here in 1820 the poet had been privy to the revolutionary talk which led five years later to the Decembrist uprisings and saw Alexandra's husband exiled to Siberia.

Sasha's husband, Lev Davidov, had not inherited his father's revolutionary instincts; in conversation with him, as brother-in-law and host, the largely apolitical composer rested content to see things Lev's way. Anything for the quiet life Kamenka was so well-equipped to provide, leaving him in peace all day to work on his summer assignments from Rubinstein, and to relax by night in the bosom of the only family he would ever have. By the time he left, at the end of August, Tchaikovsky had finished translating into Russian (at Rubinstein's behest) the Belgian musicologist François-Auguste Gevaert's treatise on instrumentation. More significantly, he had also sketched out an Overture in C minor and noted down the theme of a Ukrainian folk song then in vogue among the Davidov gardeners. Initially incorporated into the B flat movement for a string quartet, it later resurfaced in his *Scherzo à la Russe* for piano, which eventually became his Opus 1 no.1.

After an eventful journey back to St Petersburg, combining a near-fatal carriage crash with a shortage of food along the route, Tchaikovsky arrived back in the capital to find he had nowhere to live. His father had married again, this time an elderly widow named Elizaveta Mikhailovna Lipport; but shortage of funds had forced Ilya Petrovich to take refuge, without his wife, in the care of his elder daughter, Zinaida. Fond though he was of his new stepmother, Tchaikovsky had no particular wish to live alone with her, and accepted the offer of free accommodation with Apukhtin. According to one visitor, poet and musician lived together that autumn 'like husband and wife . . . Tchaikovsky would stroll over to Apukhtin (stretched, as always, on the sofa) and say he was going to bed. Apukhtin would kiss his hand and say "Run along, my darling, I'll join you in a moment."'21

After two consecutive free summers, that autumn saw Tchaikovsky's first experience of real poverty, compounded by recurring eye trouble and piles. Whatever consolations there might be, scrounging off friends like Apukhtin did not come easily to him; and he had yet more reason to be grateful for the kindness of his stepmother, Elizaveta, and his old singing teacher, Picciolo, both of whom frequently fed him. His father's new wife also spared him considerable embarrassment by paying off a tailor threatening public trouble over an unpaid bill. 'I don't know', he wrote to Sasha of their stepmother, 'how I'd have survived without her.'

But Tchaikovsky's return to the capital had also brought the most satisfying moment of his musical life so far – although, thanks to his slow progress home from Kamenka, he had missed it. On 11 September, the day before he and the twins finally got back, no less a figure than Johann Strauss the younger, the 'Waltz King' of Vienna, had conducted the first public performance of the young Tchaikovsky's *Characteristic Dances* at an open-air concert in the Pavlovsk Park. The piece had begun life as another exercise for Rubinstein – who must, in his contradictory way, have recommended it to Strauss. Tchaikovsky later immortalized this, his first publicly performed work, by building it into his opera *The Voevoda* as the 'Dances of the Hay Maidens'.

A month later, on 12 November, followed the first public performance of his B flat string quartet movement, by student players including Vasily Bessel, one of his future publishers. Two more weeks, and Tchaikovsky himself conducted his Overture in F at another Conservatoire concert. The composer showed an extremely nervous reluctance about conducting – even his own work. To Laroche he confided, apparently with a straight face, his fear that his head would fall off. The critic-to-be, who was in the audience, describes how Tchaikovsky duly kept a firm hold on his chin with one hand, throughout the piece, while conducting with the other. 'He could not rid himself of this phobia for years.'22

That autumn, Rubinstein had set Tchaikovsky a truly fiendish task for his graduation exercise: a cantata on Schiller's 'An die Freude' ('Ode to Joy'). Given the renown of Beethoven's setting of the same text in the finale of his Ninth Symphony (the 'Choral'), the task before the young composer was daunting enough to be a black joke even by Rubinstein's standards. Having been given the assignment in late October, moreover, he had little more than two months to have it ready for performance at the graduation examinations on 12 January 1866 (New Year's Eve, 1865, by the old calendar).*

The task completed, Tchaikovsky grew so nervous at the prospect of the performance, and of the intense public spotlight under which his first work would inevitably be compared to that of the mature Beethoven, that he could not bring himself to obey the school rubric and attend his graduation concert. Furious at this display of indifference to his authority, an outraged Rubinstein gave serious consideration to denying Tchaikovsky his diploma. But this was the star pupil of the first class to graduate in the Conservatoire's young history; Tchaikovsky's final report adjudged him 'excellent' in composition theory, 'good' at orchestration, 'extremely good' as a pianist and 'satisfactory' as a conductor.[23] This was the school's first Silver Medal graduate, whose name would be immortalized in marble on the Conservatoire's grand staircase (where it can still be seen today, at the head of a list of largely forgotten successors) as the year's most outstanding graduate. Rubinstein was obliged to relent, and allowed the concert to go ahead in his absence.

Verdicts on the cantata were mixed. That of the fearsome critic César Cui, the most articulate voice of the nationalist composers grouped around Balakirev, was withering – and typical of the unsparing attitude he would take to Tchaikovsky, whether as fledgling or mature (and rival) composer:

> The Conservatoire composer, Mr Tchaikovsky, is utterly feeble. His composition was written under the most difficult circumstances it is true: to order, to a deadline, on a pre-ordained theme, and with strict adherence to familiar forms. If he had any talent at all, nonetheless, it would surely at some point in the piece have broken free of the chains imposed by the Conservatoire. To avoid wasting more space on him, let me say merely that Messrs Reinthaler

* The 115-page manuscript score of Tchaikovsky's 'An die Freude' is lovingly preserved to this day in the library of the St Petersburg Conservatoire. Like many historic documents in latter-day Russia, the original is readily handed over for inspection to the surprised Western visitor, accustomed to poring over such treasures beneath glass, under close scrutiny.

and Volkmann will no doubt rejoice over his cantata, delighted that their numbers are increased.[24]

To offset this dispiriting abuse, Tchaikovsky could rely on the re-assuring figure of Herman Laroche, whose long and invaluable support of the composer now began with some characteristic (but more than welcome) overstatement. Although couched as yet in a private letter, Laroche's praise for Tchaikovsky would soon be coming from a critical pulpit almost as influential as Cui's:

> This cantata is the greatest musical event in Russia since [Serov's] *Judith*. I will tell you frankly that I consider yours the greatest talent to which Russia can look for its musical future at present. More powerful and original than Balakirev, more lofty and inventive than Serov, far more refined than Rimsky-Korsakov. In you I see the greatest – perhaps the only – hope for our musical future.

Shrewder than he may sound, Laroche was at pains to emphasize that it was Tchaikovsky's future promise which excited him as much as his youthful accomplishments:

> Your own really distinctive voice will probably not emerge for another five years or more. But these ripe and classic works will surpass everything we have heard since Glinka. To sum up, I honour you not so much for what you *have* achieved, as for what you soon *will*. The proofs you have offered us so far are but solemn pledges to outshine all your contemporaries.[25]

Although Anton Rubinstein was less impressed, considering Tchai-kovsky's instrumentation 'heretical', his brother Nikolay was intrigued. Also a virtuoso pianist, and a well-established conductor, he had founded the Moscow branch of the Russian Musical Society in 1860. Six years later, in a mirror-image of his brother's achievements in St Petersburg, Nikolay had been appointed the first director of the Moscow Conservatoire, which was due to open its doors to its first students that September.

Where Anton Rubinstein had declined to give Tchaikovsky's cantata a second St Petersburg performance unless he agreed to substantial changes, Nikolay now offered the Overture in F a public performance in Moscow, under his baton, if the composer would make wholesale revisions. The first offer Tchaikovsky rejected; and for all its ambitious youthful promise, the cantata was never again performed. To the second, however, he responded enthusiastically. Under Nikolay's guidance, he added considerable muscle to the piece, plus a completely new coda, and was rewarded by a standing ovation after its Moscow première three months later.

Why had Tchaikovsky succumbed to Nikolay Rubinstein's blandishments rather than those of Anton – who, for all his volatility, had done so much to launch his musical career? It was more than merely the scale of the work required on each piece that swayed the composer towards Moscow. Nikolay Rubinstein had offered the twenty-five-year-old failed civil servant a salary of fifty roubles a month and the imposing title of Professor of Musical Theory at the new Moscow Conservatoire.

# PART II

---

## *1866–76*
## THE COMPOSER

*Have I really nowhere else to go?*
*It's unspeakably sad.*

# CHAPTER IV

# 'You are needed here'

IN OCTOBER 1921, ALMOST THIRTY YEARS AFTER TCHAIKOVSKY'S DEATH, Igor Stravinsky had occasion to write to *The Times* of London about his 'great and beloved' compatriot. Although the composer of *The Rite of Spring* might have seemed an unlikely champion of the composer of *Swan Lake*, Stravinsky owed a great deal more to Tchaikovsky than merely the fact that his father had sung in some of his operas. To those who could (or would) not hear Tchaikovsky's music as 'specifically Russian', he replied that, on the contrary, it was 'more often profoundly Russian than music which has long since been awarded the facile label of Muscovite picturesqueness.' Of Tchaikovsky's ballet, *The Sleeping Beauty*, he wrote:

> This music is quite as Russian as Pushkin's verse or Glinka's song. Whilst not specifically cultivating in his art 'the soul of the Russian peasant', Tchaikovsky drew unconsciously from the true, popular sources of our race.[1]

Stravinsky was prolonging an internecine Russian argument which had then raged some sixty years, and was rising to the boil as Tchaikovsky left his beloved St Petersburg in January 1866 for the less sophisticated, very provincial city of Moscow. Behind him he left not merely Anton Rubinstein, to whom his music was too independent of the great Western masters, but an increasingly powerful group of composers who would consider it not independent enough.

Under the leadership of Balakirev, the natural heir of Glinka, such composers as Musorgsky, Borodin, Rimsky-Korsakov and Cui vehemently opposed Rubinstein and all his works, accusing him of using his Conservatoire to promote reactionary Western musical habits, in defiance of their own proud and rigorous nationalism. The '*Moguchaya Kuchka*', as they became known – the 'Mighty Five', or 'Mighty Handful' – even founded their own rival music college, the Free Music School, under the patronage of the then Tsarevich, Nikolay.

As Rubinstein's best-known student, Tchaikovsky was a natural target for the Five, as witnessed by Cui's savage assault on his student cantata. It would now be only another two years before the performance and publication of his first mature works saw him more deeply embroiled in this debate, which would continue to simmer throughout his working life and beyond. Ultimately, Tchaikovsky's independence of the 'Mighty Five' would be the measure of his reputation; so it was, for once, a kindly stroke of the 'Fatum' which he so dreaded that saw him off to Moscow, away from their influence, to lay its foundations.

There was considerable irony in Tchaikovsky's surrender of the sophistication of the Russian capital for the rank provincialism of its ancient predecessor. Mid-nineteenth-century Moscow remained an isolated, introspective symbol of Russia's stagnant past, in stark contrast to the dynamic, westernized, boulevard life of the St Petersburg he had come to love, symbol of Alexandr II's great liberal reforms. Moscow's musical life, for instance, was rudimentary; beyond the pit of the Bolshoi, the city could boast not one symphony orchestra approaching professional standards. This was emblematic of the ancient Russian capital's view of the world. Scuttling down the dark alleyways which characterized their life, beyond the trademark onion-domes of the Kremlin and its environs, Muscovites remained profoundly suspicious of the Western influences which had in their view colonized St Petersburg and seduced their Tsar – all of which, to the young Tchaikovsky, seemed the only way forward. For all his own innate conservatism, he would never completely surrender his heart to Moscow, his base for the next twelve years.

> Yes, he revered Moscow's ancient monuments, and he enjoyed the picturesque views of the Kremlin and other historic parts of the city. But he couldn't stand the dirty, swampy pavements, and the lack of facilities for citizens of very limited means . . . In all his truest sympathies he remained a son of St Petersburg, which had long since surpassed Moscow in these elementary amenities.[2]

This fundamental paradox would haunt the beginnings of the young Tchaikovsky's new career, deepening the nervous anxiety which was anyway his natural state. All the deep psychological problems which would plague his life – and profoundly enrich his music – can be seen in stark relief as he takes the first, faltering steps of his professional life. Already there are tensions between creativity and self-doubt, between his place in orthodox society and his secret sexual longings. The hypersensitivity evident since his childhood, and the tendency towards morbid introspection, are both in these early years aggravated by the conflict between teaching and composing, between his fondness for women as social companions and his dread of them as sexual predators, between his love of louche metropolitan life and his respect for Muscovite traditionalism. In his first few months in Moscow, as he ambitiously embarked upon writing a symphony, these simmering self-doubts erupted in a tetchy, rather adolescent outburst of misanthropy. It was, as yet, the best way Tchaikovsky could find of masking his chronic insecurities, as much from himself as from the world in which he felt so ill at ease.

Even before leaving St Petersburg, he had compensated by telling his sister that he was suffering from 'a disease of the spirit', which manifested itself in 'incredible depression' and 'hatred of the human race'. Now, as his nerves jangled their way through his first forays into Moscow society, a letter to Apukhtin, denouncing his former friends in St Petersburg, earned a justly acerbic rebuke. 'You call me Golitsyn's court rhymester,' fumed his old friend, in the tones of a rejected Falstaff. 'Well, you have definitely gone mad – running away from here and peppering me with abusive letters . . . !' Then, in a more serious voice, he chided his friend for such self-indulgence:

> You continue to believe, like a naïve schoolgirl, in 'labour' and 'struggle'. Odd that you don't mention 'progress' as well. Why should we labour? Against whom or what should we struggle? My dear, sweet, spoilt little schoolgirl, it is time for you to grasp once and for all that labour is sometimes an unwelcome necessity, always the worst punishment to befall mankind; it is *not* an occupation chosen by preference, according to personal inclination and taste.[3]

Apukhtin was one of the few who knew both Tchaikovskys within the confused twenty-five-year-old: the serious-minded musician and the decadent hedonist, constantly at odds over appearances and priorities. In Nikolay Rubinstein's Moscow, moreover, this internal conflict had plenty to feed on.

To Tchaikovsky, Nikolay Rubinstein was 'a very kind and sympathetic man, more approachable than his brother, but not to be compared to him as an artist.' To Modest, 'all Moscow was personified in Rubinstein . . . of whom it is no exaggeration to say that he was the greatest and most lasting influence on Tchaikovsky's career. No-one, artist or friend, did so much for the advancement of his fame, gave him greater support and appreciation, or helped him more to conquer his initial nervousness and timidity.'

Though he was only five years older than Tchaikovsky, Rubinstein's distinction made the gap seem much wider. Known as 'the Moscow Rubinstein', to distinguish him from his brother, Nikolay was a figure quite as commanding as Anton, full of obsessive energy and blazing with diverse talent. 'He could represent all branches of musical society in his own person,' testified Laroche. 'Although he spent all his nights at the English Club, playing cards for high stakes, he managed to take part in every social event, and was acquainted with all circles of Moscow society, commercial, official, artistic, scientific and aristocratic.'[4]

Like his brother, Nikolay Rubinstein surrounded himself with a musical 'court' to whom he was generous beyond his means. From the day Tchaikovsky arrived in Moscow, for instance, Nikolay took him into his home. But Rubinstein's lavish hospitality was to prove a mixed blessing. Although it saved the impecunious young composer money – his host would also feed him, even buy him clothes – the price of admission to Rubinstein's lively social circle proved a high one for Tchaikovsky to pay. So gregarious was his host that the house was always full of people, not all of whom the eclectic young Tchaikovsky found agreeable.

Amid those his young snobbishness rejected, however, he rejoiced in three new friendships, which would last his lifetime: with the music publisher, Pyotr Yurgenson, and two fellow professors at the Conservatoire, the critic Nikolay Kashkin, and the cellist and chorus-master Karl Albrecht. Later, to Tchaikovsky's delight, Herman Laroche also arrived from St Petersburg to take up a teaching post. In the months before the formal opening of the Conservatoire, when the preliminary classes were relatively undemanding, there was plenty of time for both work and play. With the high-spirited Rubinstein and Kashkin, Tchaikovsky shared a taste for carousing and card-playing deep into the night; with the more austere Albrecht, whom Rubinstein called his 'right-hand man', he preferred to talk music while accepting many a welcome free meal in the bosom of his family. Even in his friendships, especially during his years of comparative poverty, were reflected the ominous contradictions in his private world.

So tense was he under Rubinstein's roof that he was nervous about working late at night, for fear that the scratching of his quill pen would keep his boss awake through the thin partition-wall. Equally nervous at first about lecturing, he quickly grew in confidence, despite the unnerving presence of so many females. For the first (if not the last) time in his life, Tchaikovsky was surrounded by adoring women – both at the Conservatoire, where they tended to be dilettante students, seeking accomplishment rather than distinction, and in the extra-curricular life of its lustily heterosexual director. Only to his stepmother did Tchaikovsky confess his 'terror' at the sight of 'such a high proportion of crinolines, chignons etc.'

As well as introducing Tchaikovsky to fashionable clubs, where he read Dickens's *Pickwick Papers* and played cards with the great playwright Ostrovsky, Rubinstein insisted on dragging his reluctant young protégé along to society balls. A handsome young man, increasingly described by his contemporaries as one of the city's most eligible bachelors, Tchaikovsky constantly found himself having to deal with unwelcome female advances. Still persuaded by his love of family life that he cherished feminine company, and would surely one day marry, he embarked on a number of flirtations which all went sour with curious abruptness. Why was it that women became 'less interesting', 'tedious', even 'nightmarish' on closer acquaintance? Tchaikovsky mused over the problem in letters to his family – not least to his somewhat prurient father, forever egging him on towards marriage – without yet acknowledging the obvious answer.

A chronic insomniac, he increasingly sought solace in coffee and card-games, liquor and cigarettes – four 'vices' he would indulge all his life, often chiding himself in his diaries. Yet his working days were none too demanding. Only twice a week, on Tuesdays and Fridays, was he required to lecture at the Conservatoire; even then, there was no need to rise until nine or ten, as a late lunch, usually around 4 p.m., would allow him four hours' work, whether teaching or composing, from 11 a.m. until 3 p.m. Then he would take his main meal of the day, usually at the homes of friends, before a few more hours' work, usually refreshed by an afternoon stroll. After an adventurous evening amid Moscow's many pleasures, he would write letters and read into the small hours before attempting to sleep.

His first musical task in Moscow was to complete the orchestration of his Overture in C minor, which he duly submitted to Rubinstein for performance by the Russian Musical Society's Moscow branch. Never one to let friendship affect his judgement, the maestro declared it 'unsuitable'. Tchaikovsky duly sent it on to St Petersburg, and to the other Rubinstein – who received it, reported Laroche, 'with a deep, ironical bow'. But Anton shared his brother's low opinion of the piece, as did several other conductors to whom Laroche loyally argued its merits. In time, Tchaikovsky came to agree; years later, he scribbled the words '*Awful rubbish*' across the manuscript score. At the time, with the persistence of youth, he proceeded instead with his Overture in F. Amid continuing work on his symphony, he even toyed with the idea of writing an opera.

Increasingly homesick, Tchaikovsky took the chance of the Easter vacation to slip back to St Petersburg. After a restorative break with his family, he reluctantly returned to Moscow on 16 April – which also happened to be the day on which the first of several attempts was made on the life of the Tsar, Alexandr II.

The honeymoon period for Alexandr's reforms was over. In St Petersburg's Summer Gardens a lone gunman from the growing ranks of the non-conformist, proto-revolutionary nihilists took several vain potshots at him. Caught up in the patriotic backlash, Rubinstein led a group of students around Moscow, repeatedly performing the National Anthem. That evening, all were due to attend a performance of Glinka's *A Life for the Tsar*, whose libretto now took on new meaning. The opera concerns the rescue of the first Romanov Tsar from the hands of Polish soldiers in 1613, and the word was that this latest would-be assassin was himself a Pole. Amid feverish excitement at the Bolshoi, Tchaikovsky obliviously kept his nose buried in the score – to the consternation of those around him, who could not believe that any true Russian could, on a night like this, be more interested in the opera's music than its political reverberations. At last their patience snapped, and they demanded that this heretical member of the audience leave forthwith. A startled Tchaikovsky, quite unaware of what had been happening, sensed that he was in genuine danger. He took to his heels and ran.

Typically, he made no mention of the incident in his flow of letters home, which always avoided setbacks and embarrassments. Increasingly, he mentioned his health, which was beginning to concern him. To sixteen-year-old Modest, with whom he was already developing a confessional relationship, he speaks of 'little fits', even 'apoplectic fits' which were punctuating his sleepless nights. Dr Vasily Bertenson, the family doctor who would attend him on his deathbed, later testified that Tchaikovsky had been afflicted by such fits 'since childhood', though there is no other reliable evidence for this. Tchaikovsky's 'fits', if fits they were, sound like a mild form of his hereditary epilepsy. They tended to occur, by his own evidence, around bedtime; so their likely cause was the effect on his habitual nervous tension of some particular anxiety, arising either from the events of the day, or those ahead of him the next day. So much did he dread these attacks, he told Modest, that he would quite often go without sleep altogether.

He was therefore in no frame of mind to cope with Cui's devastating indictment of his cantata, published in early April, three months after the St Petersburg concert. 'When I read his terrible verdict,' he told a friend, 'I don't know quite what I did with myself. My eyes grew dark, my head swam, and I ran out into the street like a madman, without knowing where I was, or what I was doing.' All day, by his own account, he wandered around the city in a daze, telling himself 'I'm barren, ungifted, insignificant, good for nothing . . .'[5]

Never had he been so much in need of the undaunted support of Rubinstein and his circle, who continued to take him seriously as a composer, offering a seasoned blend of encouragement and criticism. Though Rubinstein still refused to conduct his Overture in C minor, describing it as 'too uneven', he now fulfilled his promise to perform the Overture in F. In May 1866, five months after his arrival in Moscow, the fuss made of Tchaikovsky after the concert signalled the true launch of his career as a composer. Even more flattering than his first ovation from an audience was his reception afterwards, at a dinner given by Rubinstein in his honour:

> When I walked into the room, the last to arrive, it was to the sound of prolonged applause, during which I could only blush and bow clumsily in all directions. At the end of the meal, a toast was drunk to Rubinstein, after which he himself proposed another to me, and applause again broke out. I tell you all this in such detail because the evening amounted to my first real public success, and was therefore a very special one for me. (Another detail: the orchestra too applauded me, at rehearsal.) I will not pretend that this has done anything but raise my regard for Moscow and all its charms.[6]

In spite (or perhaps because) of the charms of Moscow, work on his symphony proceeded 'sluggishly'. When writing ever more homesick letters to his family, he preferred to distract them with social news, knowing that his fond old father was longing to hear about his amorous adventures. By the summer, he was duly delighting Ilya Petrovich with enthusiastic reports of a certain 'Mufka', his neighbour Tarkovsky's nickname for his niece, Elizaveta Dmitrieva. To Modest he wrote of his 'preoccupation' with the girl, apparently the cause of much tiresome teasing from Rubinstein (who had himself, it seems, already enjoyed her favours[7]). This phrase is the furthest Tchaikovsky goes; yet it is typical of his father to reply that 'the niece' was his favourite detail from his son's letter: 'She must be so pretty, so lovely, and of course so clever. I have quite fallen in love with her myself, and can't wait to meet her when I come to Moscow.' It is not hard to imagine Tchaikovsky's reaction. Within six weeks, old Ilya's hopes are predictably dashed: 'My feelings for Mufka have completely cooled. I am very disillusioned with her.'

Was it purely coincidence that his sister Sasha suddenly announced that the roads to Kamenka were 'impassable' that summer, frustrating Tchaikovsky's plans to work on his symphony there in her care? Or that she and their father arranged instead for him to summer with her sister-in-law Vera, near St Petersburg, chaperoned by Modest and Vera's mother? All the family knew that Vera fancied herself in love with Pyotr Ilyich; apparently they now decided it was time to get them back together before some Muscovite *femme fatale* stole him away. The result, again predictably, was disaster. Already Tchaikovsky blamed his 'fits' on the symphony, and the long, painful hours of labour its composition had caused him; now, with the strain accentuated by Vera's menacing presence, those fits returned with a vengeance.

Having finished sketching the symphony in May, he spent June on the orchestration, often working through the night, finally undermining what was left of his mental and physical health. By the end of what was meant to be a restorative summer, his doctors pronounced that he was on the verge of a nervous breakdown. Only narrowly, according to the medics, had he avoided a complete collapse into insanity. So terrifying were his hallucinations, and so alarming the numbness in the extremities of his body, that Tchaikovsky vowed never to work through the night again.

Due back in Moscow for the formal opening of the Conservatoire on 13 September, he lingered in St Petersburg to regain his strength. His recovery was not helped by a rash decision to submit his symphony, even in its unfinished form, to Anton Rubinstein and Zaremba, with a view to possible performance. Both men criticized it ferociously. No details of their strictures survive, beyond Zaremba's disapproval of the second subject of the first movement, with which Tchaikovsky was particularly pleased (though he would later relent and rewrite it).

On his return to Moscow, amid all the demands of the Conservatoire's opening ceremonies, he was commissioned by Nikolay Rubinstein to write a Festival Overture on the Danish National Anthem, to mark the new Tsarevich's marriage to the Danish Princess Dagmar. With the Conservatoire rehoused in a new building, in which he and Rubinstein took up residence, he took to working in an inn called 'The Great Britain', where there was more peace during daytime hours. He finished the Overture by late November – an early indication of how fast he could work when things were going well – but the celebrations were eventually postponed until the following April, by which time there was no room for Tchaikovsky's piece (which became his Op.15). The heir to the throne, who as Alexandr III would become one of Tchaikovsky's warmest supporters, never actually heard the overture performed; but he rewarded its composer with a pair of gold and turquoise cuff-links, which the hard-up young reprobate promptly sold.

Now he could return to his symphony with renewed motivation, for Nikolay Rubinstein agreed to conduct the *scherzo* in Moscow that December, and again in St Petersburg two months later (despite his brother Anton's continuing disapproval of the work). But the reception on both occasions was lukewarm; and it was not until February 1868 that Tchaikovsky's first symphony, which he called 'Winter Daydreams', would be performed in its entirety. Although the reception was much more enthusiastic, the symphony would be revised substantially in 1874 before its publication the following year, and would not receive another public performance until 1883.

Fifteen years on, having always retained 'a soft spot' for his first major composition, he still argued that 'although it is full of the sins of youth, yet it contains more of fundamental substance and quality than many of my subsequent works.' He subtitled the first two movements 'Reveries of a Winter Journey' and 'Land of Desolation, Land of Mists', but the programmes are by no means as accessible to the listener as in his later symphonic writing. The piece abounds, however, with the freshness, lyrical melodies and stylish orchestration which were to endear Tchaikovsky to posterity, so it seems harsh that it has not won a secure place in the modern repertoire. All too readily is it forgotten that symphonies were still very much a western phenomenon, a European measure of excellence, and that this was one of the first ever written by a Russian composer.

The main effect of Anton Rubinstein's continuing criticism, and the reception of his symphony in the capital, was to alienate Tchaikovsky from the St Petersburg he had once loved, and swing his affections increasingly towards Moscow. Pyotr Ilyich, as Modest attests, was always a great bearer of grudges. 'He hardly ever forgot a slight to his artistic pride. Even if it came from someone he loved, he would immediately grow cold towards them – and stay that way for ever. Not just for months or years, but for decades he would carry the wound unhealed in his heart. No inconsiderate word or unfriendly deed was ever forgotten.'[8]

To Tchaikovsky's brother, this was 'no doubt the result of having been spoilt as a child'. After years of being sheltered from the slightest unpleasantness, or even indifference, 'what would to others have seemed a pinprick became to him a mortal blow.' Perhaps so; but this decidedly mean streak in a man so often hailed for his 'universal kindness', his 'unfailing generosity', also betokens both fierce pride and woeful insecurity. Throughout the next, important stage of his development as a composer, it would manifest itself in resentment, at times contempt, of fellow-composers offering no more than a constructive exchange of ideas – carefully balanced with treacly respect to those who might prove useful to him.

As he turned inward to his Moscow coterie, his growing friendship with Ostrovsky led to their collaboration on an opera based on the playwright's *The Voevoda* ('The Provincial Governor'). The partnership did not get off to a good start. After Ostrovsky sent him the first part of the libretto, in April 1867, Tchaikovsky promptly lost it, obliging the most distinguished playwright of the day to write it again from memory. Four months later the composer told his brother Anatoly, with no trace of penitence, of the trouble he had 'dragging' the rewrite out of him. When he then wrote to Ostrovsky with plans for a complete revision of Act II (which the playwright blandly ignored), the eager young composer seems to have had no sense of the chaos he was causing in the life of this busy public figure; it is scarcely surprising that Ostrovsky soon lost patience with the project, and Tchaikovsky was obliged to finish the libretto himself.

He had spent that summer with Anatoly, in what was planned as an extended visit to Finland. Modest tartly observes that his brother took 'one of the twins, his funds not being sufficient for him to take both'. It is thus with some satisfaction that he proceeds to record the chaos that ensued. Pyotr Ilyich's 'usual naiveté about money' finds them penniless after only a few days; they return to St Petersburg to cadge some funds from their father, only to find that he has decamped to the Urals; en route to Hapsal, and salvation with the Davidovs, they are obliged to travel 'between decks' on the steamer, 'suffering terribly from the cold'. Once there, Tchaikovsky was back in misanthropic mode, working by day on *The Voevoda* and by night, in a stream of letters to trusted friends, denouncing his hosts and the company they kept. In a rare tranquil moment he also composed the now celebrated 'Chant sans paroles', which he later united with two other piano pieces under the title *Souvenir de Hapsal*, and dedicated to Vera Davidova.

'Vera may have told you', he wrote to Sasha, by way of explanation, 'how we often joked about the farm at which we would end our days together. Well, I can tell you that, as far as I was concerned, it was no joke.' What Tchaikovsky meant was that he was serious about the farm – 'I long passionately for the kind of quiet, peaceful life one leads in the country' – rather than about poor, patient Vera. There follows more world-weary misanthropy before the nub of this striking letter: 'I am too *lazy* to form new ties, too *lazy* to start a family, too *lazy* to take on the responsibility of a wife and children. In short, marriage is to me inconceivable.'9

An apparent attempt to assuage his guilt, the dedication of these charming piano pieces to Vera can only have worsened her plight. In a long series of heart-searching letters to his sister that autumn, amid whose convoluted arguments he is clearly in search of a facesaving escape route, Tchaikovsky protested that he could regard Vera only as a cherished friend. Any thoughts of deeper feelings which might lead to marriage, he insisted, were in her head alone; for his part, he had done nothing to raise her hopes. 'As regards my coldness, which so upsets her,' he went on, 'it derives from many things, chief among which is that I love her only as a sister . . .'10

It is a phrase which will recur, at similar but more dramatic moments, in the composer's star-crossed relations with the opposite sex. For the present, Vera herself appears to have made the heroic self-sacrifice of swallowing her hopes of marrying Tchaikovsky – hopes shared, it would seem, by the entire family, whom he had made a very botched job of disabusing – while remaining, as he wished, his loyal friend.

For his part, the composer continued to persuade himself that his neurosis about marriage was nothing to do with his sexuality, and everything to do with his work. This self-deception now had him drowning his sorrows with increasing regularity, the beginning of a lifetime of heavy drinking. Despite a chronic lack of funds – which prevented him, to his chagrin, joining the select coterie of the English Club – he seems to have been able to afford enough liquor to end most evenings drunk, as he confessed to Anatoly. 'But do not think I am not getting on with anything,' he added defensively. 'From morning till dinner I am hard at work.'11

This also seems, for once, to have been the truth. Capitalizing on his careless loss of Ostrovsky, by taking the welcome chance to fashion his own words to suit his music, he was nearing completion of the opera by the end of the year. That December, at a Russian Musical Society concert in Moscow, Nikolay Rubinstein conducted an extract from *The Voevoda*, the 'Dances of the Hay Maidens' (in fact a reworking of those 'Characteristic Dances' written in 1865, and first conducted by Johann Strauss at Pavlovsk). The response was so enthusiastic that Yurgenson, who had already published his *Scherzo à la Russe*, now made plans to publish the Dances in an arrangement for piano duet. Soon, to Tchaikovsky's malicious delight, a request for a score arrived from

St Petersburg. This was his chance to dictate terms to his old employers, who had been so scathing about his work. He refused to hand over the music until he received 'a letter signed by all the directors', to which Zaremba agreed via Nikolay Rubinstein. 'I can't let these villains give me such off-hand treatment,' he wrote to Modest. 'They must be spat on, so they appreciate my true worth.'

Such self-confidence was not to become a Tchaikovsky hallmark. For most of his working life he revelled in his own music while he was writing it, then fretted about it once it was finished. This would prove true, indeed, of *The Voevoda* – for which, as yet, he was displaying merely the rash enthusiasm of youth.

At the end of December 1867, meanwhile, Tchaikovsky was assigned by Rubinstein to look after Berlioz during a visit to Moscow in which the revered Frenchman conducted two extremely successful concerts (one of them attended by an audience estimated at 12,000). Glinka had called Berlioz 'the greatest of contemporary musicians,' but the young Tchaikovsky admired him without warming to his music. Envisioning, perhaps, his own old age – though he was still only twenty-seven – he was moved by the sight of this great musician as 'an old and broken man, persecuted alike by fate and his fellow-creatures'. At a banquet in Berlioz' honour, Tchaikovsky delivered an elegant tribute in French, showing due respect more than heartfelt admiration in a decent attempt to redress the balance. It was his first encounter with one of the great musicians of his time. But the episode proved more significant for his first meeting with Balakirev, the sometime mathematician then regarded as one of Russia's leading composers.

This momentous rendezvous took place against a background of radical change in the Russian musical scene. That year, 1867, had seen Anton Rubinstein's retirement not only from the Conservatoire (of which Zaremba became director) but from the conductorship of the highly influential RMS concerts, to be succeeded by Balakirev himself. The powers of patronage which went with the job – the choice of repertoire, the advancement or otherwise of his fellow-composers – saw Balakirev take over from Rubinstein as the most influential musical figure in the capital. Naturally, it was seen as a victory for the nationalists, with whom Tchaikovsky's first dealings were highly cautious.

His letter demanding the directorship's signatures, endorsing his 'Dances of the Hay Maidens', now returned to haunt him. Given the new regime, he was obliged to write a duly respectful missive to the potential conductor, Balakirev, requesting his personal endorsement for the work. The diplomat in Tchaikovsky also solicited 'a word of encouragement if you feel able', adding that 'coming from you, such encouragement would be extremely welcome.' Alas, Balakirev did not feel able to offer encouragement as easily as Tchaikovsky had hoped. He too wrote courteously, but disappointingly. He would not be conducting the work, nor did he think it 'appropriate' to offer encouragement.

But the older man, seeing that Tchaikovsky could become a figure useful to his cause, softened the blow with some deft flattery:

> Encouragement, in your case, would be both inappropriate and dishonest. Encouragement is for artistic infants, whereas I can tell from the orchestration and technique in your score that you are already a fully-grown artist, to whom *strict criticism* is more fitting than encouragement . . . I will be delighted to give you my opinion when we meet in Moscow. It will be much more useful to play through the piece together at the piano and examine it bar by bar. Criticism is a poor substitute for lively argument![12]

Tentatively though it had begun, the relationship between Tchaikovsky and Balakirev would swiftly grow into an important if as yet somewhat one-sided one, enabling the younger man to realize his true musical maturity. In the meantime, 1868 saw his public career beginning to build momentum. As he completed *The Voevoda* and readied it for performance, February saw the première of his first symphony win a warm reception in Moscow, where the following month he himself conducted his 'Dances of the Hay Maidens'. Again, according to Kashkin, Tchaikovsky felt obliged to hold his head on while wielding the baton; and this time he made a complete exhibition of himself.

> I could see from the moment Pyotr Ilyich appeared that he was a nervous wreck . . . He walked on between the orchestra's desks hunched up, as if he didn't want anyone to see him. When he finally made it to the podium, he looked like a man who would rather be anywhere else. He forgot every note of his own piece, was blind to the notes in his own score, and failed to give the players their cues at all the most crucial moments. Luckily, the orchestra knew the piece so well that they took no notice of their inept conductor and all his incorrect instructions. They performed the piece perfectly well, occasionally looking up at the composer with big grins on their faces.[13]

Despite its conductor, the piece was well enough received; so its composer merely vowed never to pick up a baton again, and returned to his work. On the side, he began to earn some welcome extra income as an occasional music critic, offering cautious praise for Balakirev and Rimsky-Korsakov in a Moscow journal called *The Contemporary Chronicle (Sovremennaya letopis)*. This led to a warm reception from the 'Mighty Handful' when he visited St Petersburg in April. Received *chez* Balakirev, and at the home of the dying Dargomyzhsky, the group's patron saint, he was flattered by their attentions but determined to maintain his musical independence.

Rimsky-Korsakov, who first met him at the Balakirev soirée, recalled the young Tchaikosvky in terms characteristic of the envy he would later feel for his success: 'He proved a pleasing and sympathetic man to talk with, one who knew how to be simple of manner and always speak with evident sincerity and heartiness . . . As a product of the St Petersburg Conservatoire, Tchaikovsky was viewed rather negligently if not haughtily by our circle and, owing to his being away from St Petersburg [in Moscow], personal acquaintanceship was impossible.'[14] Given the patronizing note in Rimsky's voice, it is not surprising that Tchaikovsky saw his Moscow base as offering a safe haven from the Five's potentially overpowering influence. He could maintain cordial relations, acting as the group's unofficial 'ambassador' in Moscow, while keeping his distance and going his own way.

David Brown has expressed regret that the terms 'nationalist' and 'Western' are commonly used to characterize the civil war in late nineteenth-century Russian music, suggesting 'radical' and 'traditionalist' as preferable alternatives. Either way, it is an easy mistake for the layman to overlook the radicalism of the nationalists, who, in Professor Brown's summary, were 'eager to explore further the new musical territories being opened up by contemporary innovators, and to incorporate into their new revelations a full exploitation of their national musical resources, not as incidental embellishment but as a formative factor in their style and technique.' Anton Rubinstein and his followers, by contrast, were 'suspicious or hostile to the new trends in music, wishing instead to preserve in their own works what they saw as the best in the Western tradition of the immediate past.'[15]

Tchaikovsky 'laughed at [the Five's] ultra-radical tendencies,' according to Modest, and was 'contemptuous of their naïve and crude efforts, especially those of Musorgsky.' At the same time, while angered by their brash attacks on his idol, Mozart, he was nevertheless impressed by the 'force and vitality' in some of their work. To his brother, Tchaikovsky's relations with the St Petersburg group were 'like those between two friendly neighbouring states . . . cautiously prepared to meet on common ground, but jealously guarding their separate interests.'[16]

Educated in the 'traditional' school, but duly respectful of the 'radical', Tchaikovsky was thus beginning a long struggle to remain independent of both, while rejected by neither. At this seminal moment in the development of Russian music, his great achievement was the highly distinctive compromise so appreciated by Stravinsky: bringing the best of Western influences to bear on his rich Russian heritage.

At the same time, whether he knew it or not, he was embarked upon a vain struggle towards another compromise – between his love of company and his self-styled misanthropy, his need for solitude and his longing for a family, his sexual tastes and his desire to make a respectable marriage.

Still tormented by the patient Vera, he poured out his confusion in letters to Sasha, begging her to tear them up. To Modest, at the same time, he was penning extraordinary lectures on the 'shameful' and 'abominable' habit of masturbation: 'It is better to endure some slight discomfort, and preserve your self-esteem, than to slide towards ruin.' With his limitless capacity for self-deception, Tchaikovsky might as well have been writing these letters to himself. Certainly, they amount to the equivalent of a spiritual diary, a form of thinking aloud which revealed his state of mind to all listeners but himself. Even now, it is clear, he regarded his homosexuality as a 'correctable' abnormality, a natural extension of his first sexual experiences which could surely be redeemed by the right woman. We do not yet hear the expressions of regret, the tortured vacillation between sexual relish and self-disgust, which would overcome him in later years. But the portents are clear in his violent strictures to Modest, in whom Tchaikovsky can already see an unwelcome replica of himself. If he was urging his brother, ten years his junior, to 'cure' himself of his homosexual leanings 'before it is too late', what was he meanwhile telling himself?

For two years he had been giving lessons in music (and quite possibly other pursuits) to a talented teenager named Vladimir Shilovsky, stepson of the colourful Vladimir Begichev, repertory director of the Moscow Imperial Theatres. Tchaikovsky had been introduced to Begichev by a baritone in the Bolshoi company, Konstantin de Lazari. Soon they had all become firm friends, and Tchaikovsky's relationship with young Vladimir, then fourteen, had swiftly become one of those for which Modest employs the word 'intimate'. That summer, all four set off together on an extended tour of Europe, with Begichev paying Tchaikovsky's way in return for continuing Vladimir's tuition.

As with his previous foray into Europe, however, the trip was not a great success. Already uneasy at accepting such largesse, Tchaikovsky was also troubled by acute homesickness, which would become habitual during his frequent travels. 'I am sick with longing for my homeland,' he wrote to Sasha, 'especially because of so many loved ones there, whom the summer is my only chance to see.' There was a minor drama in the Zoological Gardens of Berlin, where the sight of a boa constrictor eating a live rabbit hugely entertained Begichev, but reduced Tchaikovsky to sobbing hysterics for the rest of the day. In Paris his pupil was taken ill, thwarting their plans to tour 'the most picturesque places in Europe', but giving the three adults the chance to take in several operas, at one of which Tchaikovsky was excited to find himself sitting near the celebrated French composer Daniel François Auber.

It was at the Begichevs, that spring, that he had first met the Belgian soprano Désirée Artôt, one of the most lustrous opera stars of the day, whose beguiling voice and histrionic charms had all men she met at her feet. Back in Moscow that autumn, when Artôt returned to sing Desdemona in Rossini's *Otello*, Tchaikovsky proved no exception. 'She sang so beautifully,' he wrote to Anatoly that September. 'She is a wonderful woman. We are becoming close.' By October they were 'very friendly . . . Rarely have I met so good-natured, intelligent and sensible a woman.' By November he had made her a musical gift, the dedication of a *Romance* in F minor, his Op. 5, which Rubinstein played publicly in her honour. Artôt was five years older than Tchaikovsky; she was, according to Laroche, 'a plain if passionate spinster in her thirties, with a waistline beginning to thicken'; and she was constantly on the move, being much in demand all over Europe. Yet by Christmas, to the horror of his friends, Tchaikovsky had decided he wanted to marry her.

Born Marguerite Joséphine Montagney, the daughter of a professor of horn at the Brussels Conservatoire, Désirée Artôt had studied with Pauline Viardot in London and made her professional début, at the age of twenty-two, at a state concert in the presence of Queen Victoria. Her career had blossomed in Paris, where she won praise from Meyerbeer and Berlioz, before she moved south to become the main attraction of a succession of Italian companies, winning a huge following in roles from Rosina and Angelina (*La Cenerentola*) to Leonora (*Il Trovatore*). It was thus at the height of her international fame, fresh from a triumph at Covent Garden, that she arrived in Russia in 1868 with the Italian company of one Eugenio Merelli. In the spring, according to Tchaikovsky, she had made no particular impact on him; he had looked on with some disdain as Begichev's wife Marya, herself an amateur singer, went on bended knee to kiss Artôt's hand in front of her dinner guests.

The autumn, however, was a different story. He was captivated by her powerful stage presence and remarkable range; to Tchaikovsky, as Laroche saw it, Artôt was 'dramatic singing personified, an opera goddess fusing numerous gifts which would normally be shared among several different artists.' To Modest, Tchaikovsky himself sighed: 'Ah! If you knew what an actress and singer she is! Never before has any artist had me under such a spell. What a shame that you cannot hear or see her. How you would appreciate her gestures and the grace of her movements!' Fond of impersonating female dancers, Tchaikovsky gazed upon Artôt with an unusually expert eye.

It is significant that so much of Tchaikovsky's praise was reserved for the professional rather than the private Artôt. For it was, of course, the glamorous yet talented diva, rather than the real woman behind the top billing, with whom he had fallen in love. She was undoubtedly a formidable character, both gifted and accomplished; yet her hold over men was evidently little to do with her looks – beginning, at thirty-three, to show her age – or the ubiquity of her pushy mother, anxious to marry her off. By December, however, Tchaikovsky's infatuation with Artôt was common knowledge. The gossip had even reached St Petersburg, whence Anatoly wrote his brother an inquisitive note, having heard that 'all anyone talks about in Moscow is your marrying Artôt.' To Modest, by way of reply, Tchaikovsky apologized for having been out of touch so long. 'All my spare time has been devoted to one special person . . . with whom I am very, very smitten.'

Like lovelorn teenagers, as de Lazari looked on, they 'gazed at one another with shining eyes, blushing with mutual embarrassment as they talked.' He and Tchaikovsky's other friends, especially Rubinstein, strongly disapproved. If he married a celebrated singer, they told him, he would play the 'pitiful' role of his wife's husband, a mere appendage to her fame – living off her earnings, trudging round Europe in her wake, losing both the opportunity and the inclination to work. 'In a word,' as Tchaikovsky himself summarized Rubinstein's verdict, 'when my passion cools, I will be left only with hurt pride, despair and ruin.'[17]

Artôt, for her part, appears to have made no offer to give up her career for his. Booked up for months ahead, she thrived on the limelight her talents had won her, and was not about to surrender it for an idle Russian exile as the wife of an impoverished composer with no immediate prospects of fame or fortune. Besides, her mother disapproved of the match, regarding Tchaikovsky as too young and insignificant for her distinguished daughter, and swallowing the gossip about his drinking and gambling. By some accounts, this information was furnished by a rival suitor. But according to Tchaikovsky's future sister-in-law, Praskovya (not always a reliable witness), it was Nikolay Rubinstein himself who made a point of going round to tell Artôt's mother that Tchaikovsky 'was not fitted for the part of husband' – in other words, that he was a homosexual. Tchaikovsky, by her account, 'never suspected the dirty trick that Rubinstein had played on him.'[18]

Either way, by the time he confided in his father at New Year, having apologized for taking so long over a letter he knew Ilya Petrovich was eagerly awaiting, Artôt's mother had taken her off to Warsaw without him.

In her absence, the inner Tchaikovsky appears to have returned to cool his alter ego's ardour. As he details the development of the relationship, in a curiously matter-of-fact tone of voice, he strongly implies that it was Artôt who made all the running, which is not at all the story told by his friends. Although implying the marriage was still on – they planned to meet at her estate near Paris that summer, he told his father, to make a final decision – his long and typically convoluted letter seems to be preparing the old man for another disappointment.

> I am, dear Papa, in a very difficult position. On the one hand, I am devoted to her with my whole heart, and cannot envisage living my life without her; on the other, cold reason obliges me to take very seriously the grim picture painted by my friends . . .[19]

Nonsense, came the prompt reply from his ever optimistic father.

> With such a woman as your 'Desired One' [Désirée], you will enhance rather than squander your talent . . . Why assume that you will lose the chance to pursue your own work if you follow her? Can this mean that you are not your own man? That you would be no more than a hanger-on, carrying her train and then merging into the crowd like a humble footman? No, my friend, be a servant, but an independent-minded one . . .[20]

For all his father's well-meaning enthusiasm, Tchaikovsky was still wallowing in self-doubt when his dilemma was suddenly resolved for him. From Warsaw came the announcement – it arrived, brutally, in a letter to Nikolay Rubinstein – that Artôt had abruptly married a Spanish baritone in Merelli's company, Mariano Padilla y Ramos. Rubinstein showed no mercy as he broke the humiliating news, openly exulting as he cried: 'Thank God, thank God! . . . You are needed here by us, by Russia, not wasted at the beck and call of some famous foreigner.' Tchaikovsky, according to Kashkin, 'turned white, and walked out without a word.'[21]

Within days, however, he was making light of it all in a letter to Modest, and was reported by de Lazari to be 'himself again, quite calm and back to work'. It has been well observed that Tchaikovsky was 'not so much suffering the pain of a lost love as smarting from a sense of humiliation and betrayal'; and it does indeed seem highly likely that 'Tchaikovsky's homosexuality must have been somehow related to what happened.'[22] The very fact that this apparently decent woman did not contact her fiancé before marrying someone else – at the very least, a gross breach of etiquette – suggests that she felt justified in treating him with contempt. That he, for his part, offered no complaint – appearing, on the contrary, to sigh with relief – further implies that he had no particular wish for her motives to be too deeply explored; and that he himself had realized, in his own recoil from the prospect of sexual domesticity, that the marriage could never have worked.

Later that year, in November 1869, the Merelli roadshow inevitably passed through Moscow again, complete with Artôt. Tchaikovsky was well aware that he could not avoid her; he had reworked choruses and recitatives for Auber's opera Le Domino Noir, which would require them to rehearse together. 'This woman has done me great harm,' he told Anatoly ruefully, but offered no further details of their enforced reunion. The only evidence comes again from Kashkin, who happened to be sitting near Tchaikovsky at the opening night: 'He seemed very tense. When Artôt appeared onstage, he hid his face behind his opera glasses, where they remained until the end of the act. Yet he could not have seen much, for tears were streaming down his face, behind the glasses, which he made no attempt to conceal.'[23] It is hard to agree with Poznansky that Tchaikovsky was moved to tears by the music.[24]

Over the years, which would hold much worse horrors for him, Tchaikovsky seemed to become reconciled to his treatment at Artôt's hands – perhaps grateful that she, unlike other women with axes to grind, had not broadcast his homosexuality as his fame grew. They were to meet again briefly, and accidentally, six years later, when she emerged from Rubinstein's office to find him next in the queue. Some twenty years after she had rejected him, however, in 1888, they were able to meet in Berlin as old friends, reminiscing with wry smiles about what had passed between them; in a gracious gesture, perhaps also a grateful one, Tchaikovsky dedicated to her his Six French Songs, Op. 65, to add to the ironically named Romance of 1868.

At the start of the new academic year which followed this drama, Rubinstein had increased Tchaikovsky's workload at the Conservatoire, with a consequent rise in pay. To his dismay, it was still not enough for him to afford an apartment of his own – primarily to escape from the circus surrounding Rubinstein, who would anyway not hear of it.

For all his hard work in finishing The Voevoda, his involvement with

Artôt that autumn had seen him request a postponement of its first performance. Now, on 11 February 1869, it was finally premièred to considerable acclaim, with the composer taking no fewer than fifteen curtain-calls. Though favourably reviewed, and praised by his coterie, the work never found favour with the public, and received only five performances before vanishing for ever from the repertoire. The only dissenting note at the time came from, of all people, Laroche – whose faint praise appeared to Tchaikovsky to amount to damnation; where others criticized the work for slavish submission to Western, especially German, influences, Laroche accused its composer of watering down his Russian folk sources. It was the first time his loyal old friend, the only one spanning both the St Petersburg and Moscow years, had offered anything but the most enthusiastic support, dating right back to his praise of the graduation cantata. Yet Tchaikovsky immediately broke off all relations.

The following month saw the first performance of his symphonic fantasia, *Fatum* – an ironic choice of title in view of Tchaikovsky's perennial preoccupation with 'Fate', or destiny, and its recent brutality in solving his Artôt dilemma for him. Although it too was well received, and he wrote to Anatoly that he thought it 'the best thing I've written so far,' Tchaikovsky was soon to become disenchanted with the piece. Still to find his true voice as a composer, he would soon destroy the manuscript scores of both *The Voevoda* and *Fatum** – though not without preserving their more successful passages, for recycling into later works, as was his habit throughout his life. One reason may well have been some stern criticism from Balakirev, his relations with whom were becoming increasingly central to his work.

The previous year, to signal his approval of Tchaikovsky's use of Russian folk themes in so much of his work so far, Yurgenson had commissioned him to make piano arrangements for *50 Russian Folk Songs*. This had involved Tchaikovsky in borrowing from Balakirev's own reworkings – with due acknowledgement, involving a protracted correspondence. Now he dedicated *Fatum* to Balakirev, and anxiously sought his reaction. When it came, it was devastating:

> Your *Fatum* has been performed [in St Petersburg] reasonably well . . .
> There wasn't much applause, probably because of the appalling
> cacophony at the end of the piece, which I don't like at all. It
> is not properly gestated, and seems to have been written in a
> very slapdash manner. The seams show, as does all your clumsy

* Both were reconstructed, after his death, from surviving orchestral parts.

stitching. Above all, the form itself just does not work. The whole thing is completely unco-ordinated.[25]

Where Laroche had urged Tchaikovsky to delve deeper into the classics, Balakirev now begged him to make a closer study of the 'moderns'. Citing Liszt and Glinka, he bemoaned Zaremba's influence on his protégé, damning even the 'Byronic' text he had added as an epigraph. 'If you must indulge in such slush, at least choose something suitable from a good Russian, like Lermontov . . .' Then, in almost the same breath, the great man calmed Tchaikovsky's wrath with an unexpected grace-note: 'I have written with total candour, as I am sure you won't change your mind about dedicating *Fatum* to me. It means a lot to me, as a sign of your respect for my work. And I have a very soft spot for you . . .'

Although he made no mention of them, Balakirev was having problems of his own. His bold choice of modern repertoire for the RMS concerts had, it transpired, earned him the enmity of the Grand Duchess Elena. That May she fired him from the job of conductor. A week later, an impassioned article in his defence appeared in *The Contemporary Chronicle* – written by none other than Tchaikovsky.

This sequence of events was to prove crucial to his career. He had not yet brought himself to reply to Balakirev's dispiriting letter (even though the senior composer's detailed criticisms were 'right on the mark'[26], as Tchaikovsky himself would later agree). By goading him into supporting his critic, however, the Grand Duchess earned Tchaikovsky an important long-term friend. It was a considerable risk for him to take, as the influential lady herself was due in Moscow the very day the article appeared. And Tchaikovsky was canny enough to make sure Balakirev realized this, by writing him a simultaneous note confirming the dedication of *Fatum*, and drawing his attention to his newspaper article about 'la belle Hélène'. Stoically thanking Balakirev for his candour – 'I was not at all offended,' he says unconvincingly – he forlornly confesses that 'it would have cheered me enormously if you had found *just one thing in it* you could praise . . .'

Balakirev's immediate response was 'utter delight . . . I admit that I thought you had taken umbrage at my strictures. Forgive me for even suspecting this of you. Now I love and respect you all the more.' From this exchange of letters was to grow a collaboration, under Balakirev's enlightened despotism, which would produce Tchaikovsky's first mature masterpiece.

# CHAPTER V

# 'What is the point?'

IN MARCH 1869 TCHAIKOVSKY ATTENDED A MASKED BALL IN MOSCOW dressed as a woman. This was nothing too unusual, it seems, as the evening is remembered less for his disguise than for the comical misunderstandings it prompted. Skirt-chasing as usual, Vladimir Begichev pointed out the latest object of his affections to a masked woman he assumed to be his friend Tchaikovsky, wearing clothes borrowed from his wife. Only later did Begichev discover, no doubt to his cost, that the exotic creature in whom he had confided *was* his wife.[1]

At the time Tchaikovsky was deeply in love with a pupil named Eduard Zak, then fifteen – the age at which, all his life, he found young men at the height of their sexual allure. Four years later, Zak would take his own life. That the boy was one of the great loves of Tchaikovsky's life seems clear from two entries in his diary for consecutive days in September 1887, fourteen years later, when he still recalls with poignant clarity 'the sound of his voice, the way he moved, but above all the way he used to look at me . . . The death of this boy, the fact that he no longer exists, is beyond my understanding. I believe I have never loved anyone as much as him . . .'

But why does Tchaikovsky go on to speak of his 'guilt' about Zak?

> My God! No matter what they told me at the time, and how I have
> since tried to console myself, my guilt about him is unbearable! Yet

72

despite it all I loved him – that is, not loved [in the past tense], but love him still. His memory is sacred to me![2]

Could the composer have felt that he was somehow responsible for Zak's suicide? No details of the boy's death survive. What does seem likely, however, is that it was Zak – not, as Modest suggested, his schoolfriend Vladimir Gerard[3] – who inspired the sublime love theme in Tchaikovsky's first mature masterpiece, the fantasy overture *Romeo and Juliet.*

Could the knowledge of this, combined with some unknown misfortune, have driven this apparently romantic young man to have chosen the same fate as Romeo? We are now unlikely ever to know. But it is striking that the first of Tchaikovsky's regular injunctions to Modest to shun homosexuality, to avoid the 'tragedies' to which it can lead, comes at precisely this period. 'If there is the remotest possibility,' he wrote to his brother in January 1870, 'try to be normal'.* The fact that Modest shared his own sexual orientation, he continued, had him very depressed. 'At your age you can still force yourself to love [the opposite sex]. Try it at least once. Maybe it will work.' All was not going well, it would appear, with Eduard Zak.

Zak's name does not appear anywhere in Modest's narrative, even though Tchaikovsky's letters show that he persuaded their brother Nikolay to give his former pupil a job in 1871, then pleaded that he be transferred nearer Moscow: 'It's absolutely *essential* that I see him. For God's sake arrange it!' Modest's suggestion that the *Romeo and Juliet* love theme was inspired by Gerard, the heterosexual object of the schoolboy composer's unrequited love, looks very like a smokescreen, to hide a more complex truth. Although the claim is made in Modest's (still unpublished) memoirs, reputedly much more candid about his and his brother's homosexuality than the earlier biography, he would still have been concerned to conceal the precise nature of the composer's sexual tastes, let alone any tragic episodes arising from them.[4]

So it was the unlikely combination of Zak and Balakirev who were between them responsible, like musical midwives, for wringing from Tchaikovsky the first authentic expression of his true musical voice. The one, perhaps, symbolizes the tortured sensibility, the other the technical mastery, which would henceforth unite in Tchaikovsky's most characteristic and successful work.

It was during a walk with Kashkin in August 1869 that Balakirev suggested to Tchaikovsky the notion of an overture based on Shakespeare's

---

* The adjective has been deleted by Soviet censors, but is assumed by most commentators, working on the evidence of other letters, to have been 'normal'.

romantic tragedy. The twenty-nine-year-old composer was finding his would-be mentor 'tiresome' during his extended visit to Moscow that summer; though his advice was 'of some use', as he grudgingly conceded, Balakirev made excessive demands on his time and 'would weigh heavily upon me' if he lived permanently in the same city. 'He is a good man, and kindly disposed towards me, but for some reason I never feel at home in his company. It is the narrowness of his musical views and the persistence with which he clings to them which I find especially irksome.'[5]

At the time Tchaikovsky was wrestling with a doomed project, an opera entitled *Undine*, sparked by his bizarre fondness for a German folk-tale concerning a lovelorn nymph who turns into a fountain. Given a ready-made libretto (already used in a mediocre setting by Alexey Lvov), he worked on it single-mindedly enough to complete the piece in six months, including two summer months at Kamenka marked by Ippolit's wedding. That autumn, after delivering his manuscript to the Imperial Theatres ahead of the agreed date, he encountered at first procrastination, then rejection. As he had with *Fatum*, the downcast composer eventually destroyed the manuscript score. The only surviving fragments are parts of Act One, which received a lukewarm reception when performed in Moscow the following March: an Introduction, Undine's aria, a chorus, wedding march and duet. All were duly recycled in his incidental music for Ostrovsky's *The Snow Maiden*, his second symphony, and the celebrated G flat *Pas d'action* in Act II of *Swan Lake*.

Against this background, Tchaikovsky at first made heavy weather of *Romeo and Juliet*. 'I'm completely burnt out,' he wrote to Balakirev. 'I didn't want to write until I had sketched out at least something, but my mind is utterly bereft of even one tolerable musical thought. I'm beginning to fear that my Muse has flown away. Perhaps she's gone to visit Zaremba!' Though fearful that he 'might have to wait a long time for her return', Tchaikovsky had not bargained for Balakirev *becoming* his Muse, though that is more or less what ensued. From St Petersburg arrived an enormous letter, setting out Balakirev's own approach, ten years before, to the composition of an overture to *King Lear*. There followed a detailed plan for a *Romeo and Juliet* overture, complete with suggestions for the key scheme. Balakirev even set down the first four bars as they would sound if he were writing the piece. Then, more endearingly, he turned amateur psychiatrist: 'Now don your galoshes, take up your walking-stick and set out for a walk along the boulevards, starting up the Nikitsky. Steep yourself in your musical plan, and I am confident that by the time you reach Sretensky Boulevard some theme or episode will have suggested itself!'[6]

Though never prone to underestimating himself, Balakirev could not have realized quite how apt was his choice of subject for Tchaikovsky, or how effective his methods to rouse the composer from his post-*Undine* torpor. The theme of tragic love, centring around a doomed young woman, could not have been more likely to provide the kind of stimulus on which his musical imagination thrived, however resistant he remained (as yet) to overtly programmatic music. Previous failures had resulted from too slavish an adherence to a story-line, as in *The Storm*, or too vague a response to a general atmosphere, as in *Fatum*. The tragic ingredients of *Romeo and Juliet*, by contrast, offered precisely the right blend of changing moods and moments to move him to both lyrical and intensely dramatic heights. Far from trying to reflect the dramatic progression of the play, Tchaikovsky merely takes its highlights as inspiration for, above all, the thrillingly violent clashes of the feud motif; one of the most ravishing love themes he ever wrote; and a coda depicting death as 'mere oblivion' (rather than 'Wagnerian transfiguration'7) – thus pre-echoing the fourth movement of the Sixth Symphony, often seen as a vision of his own demise.

Balakirev would reject some of his early drafts – the opening, for instance, sounded more like a Haydn quartet than the Liszt chorale he had cited – and the piece would become something of a shuttlecock between the two before assuming its final, familiar shape with Tchaikovsky's last revisions ten years later. The first performance, conducted by Nikolay Rubinstein in Moscow on 28 March 1870, was not a success; and Balakirev regretted Tchaikovsky's decision, with Rubinstein's encouragement, to rush the piece into print. So much did Balakirev admire certain passages, however, that he was soon able to play the entire work through on the piano, from memory, while still insisting that the beginning and end needed 'completely rewriting'.

It was thanks largely to his enthusiasm that the St Petersburg première won unexpected praise from Cui, for which Tchaikovsky wrote a note of surprised thanks. 'You used to be five. Now you are six!' Balakirev was told by the mighty critic Vladimir Stasov, and Tchaikovsky suddenly found himself in danger of acceptance by the St Petersburg musical mafia. Swallowing Balakirev's strictures, he set to work on a first full revision that summer, leaving all but the ending (to be rewritten in 1880) as we know it today.

By then he was also at work on another opera. Undeterred by the failure of *The Voevoda* and *Undine*, Tchaikovsky was at first tempted by a libretto entitled *Mandragora*, offered him by a botanist friend, clearly familiar with his weakness for story-lines about fantastical, lovelorn females rendered immortal as natural objects (in this case, a flower). Tchaikovsky had composed a 'Chorus of Flowers and Insects' before

Kashkin, mercifully, persuaded him of the libretto's inadequacies, and he turned instead to a play by the historical novelist Ivan Lazhechnikov, *The Oprichnik*, about the doomed love for a princess of Andrey, one of Ivan the Terrible's bodyguard. This time the composer would be his own librettist.

After completing the first version of *Romeo and Juliet* in 1869, Tchaikovsky had celebrated by writing his first set of songs since his childhood piece, 'Our Mama in St Petersburg': the Six Songs, Op. 6. Grossly underrated as a composer of songs, many of which are achingly tender, he managed in this first set to produce, to a text by Goethe, that which remains to this day the best-known of the hundred or so he would write: literally translated as 'No, only he who has known', it is better known as 'None but the Lonely Heart'. No modern recital or recording of Tchaikovsky's songs is complete without this touching complaint.

Now he followed up with the equally poignant 'To forget so soon' – to words by his old friend Alexey Apukhtin. For all the volatility of their relationship, which lurched from violent row to emollient embrace all their lives, the two artistic homosexuals shared a *contra mundum* solidarity which formed a unique bond from their schooldays to the grave. This was the bond Tchaikovsky also shared with the notorious Prince Vladimir Meshchersky, who continued to weave in and out of his life in the role of lugubrious patron and protector. Of the passing figures who became his prime preoccupations, however briefly, amid disconcerting visits to Moscow by both Artôt and Vera Davidova, the current favourite was a minor courtier named Vladimir Bibikov, who worked in the Office of Petitions to the Tsar. As always, the erotic nature of the relationship can be measured in direct proportion to the number of cuts made by Soviet censors in letters referring to Bibikov. Even these moral watchdogs, however, could not crack all Tchaikovsky's codes, and some details inevitably slip past them. When telling Modest in late 1869 that he is out on the town with this new friend 'almost every night', for instance, the composer betrays their mutual secret by signing off: 'Bibikov sends you a kiss'.

Another continuing presence in his life was the wayward and now rather sickly Vladimir Shilovsky, who was constantly attempting to seduce him away from the Conservatoire. So bored was Tchaikovsky with his college routine, and so anxious to become a full-time composer, that Shilovsky might have succeeded, were it not for the sheer scale of the domestic drama which seemed to follow him around. Now he was going abroad for two years, for the sake of his failing health, and begged Tchaikovsky to accompany him. It was an impossible notion, not only because of the composer's reluctance to become a rich man's dependant, and his perennial fear of illness and death, but because of his work. The composer felt he owed it to his pupil at least to escort him to St Petersburg to see him off, with the promise of a visit during the summer. Even this brief absence from Moscow got him into trouble, as was always the way with Shilovsky; hearing that he had been in town without contacting them, his numerous relatives in the capital were mightily offended. Again, it was his sister Sasha who came to the rescue – interceding with them, at his request, on his behalf.

News of Shilovsky's worsening condition forced Tchaikovsky to bring forward his travel plans, and the end of May saw him heading through Germany to Paris, where he met up with a 'very weak' but 'overjoyed' Shilovsky and proceeded to the spa resort of Bad Soden, near Frankfurt. Though not, as the composer had feared, dying, Shilovsky was 'hanging by a thread', as Tchaikovsky put it to Anatoly. In weak but scarcely terminal condition, it was his proneness to wild excesses 'which could lead any day to consumption' that were worrying Shilovsky's doctors and indeed Tchaikovsky. He took some satisfaction in nursing the young man, to whom he was 'an Argus, the saviour of his life'; but he also took the opportunity to slip off to nearby Mannheim for concerts in honour of the centenary of Beethoven's birth. Here he was deeply impressed by his first hearing of the *Missa Solemnis* – 'music of the greatest genius' – before travelling on to Wiesbaden to see Nikolay Rubinstein, who was spending his vacation locked in determined but vain combat with the roulette wheel.

In an uncharacteristically idle summer, depressed by his string of failures as much as by the sight of so many invalids, Tchaikovsky was considering his options when his next move was decided for him, in mid-July, by the outbreak of war between Prussia and France. To avoid the throng of refugees along Germany's western border, he and Shilovsky diverted via Stuttgart and Ulm to the Swiss border, which they reached after five days' uncomfortable and relatively dangerous travel. Now, amid the glories of the Swiss countryside, the composer's spirits lifted. They settled at Interlaken, where Tchaikovsky began to improve his health with regular walks, and returned to the revision of *Romeo and Juliet*.

Advised by his own doctors to remain at least six weeks in the Swiss mountain air, his patience with his wayward young companion began to wear thin. Shilovsky had become 'so disgustingly vulgar', he complained, 'so empty and abandoned', that throughout August the composer's daily walks became longer and longer: 'I have seen such splendours as cannot be imagined, but the constant company of this trivial, petty tyrant has me at my wits' end.' As soon as the six weeks were up, he was on his way home in renewed health and high spirits, diverting via Munich for a day with his old schoolfriend, Prince Alexey Golitsyn, and Vienna to meet up with his brother Nikolay.

With work on *The Oprichnik* proceeding sluggishly, and readily set aside for the revisions to *Romeo and Juliet*, Tchaikovsky was delighted early in 1871 to be asked by Rubinstein to prepare a concert of his own work for performance at the Assembly of the Nobility. In the past five years, since his arrival in Moscow, he had composed almost thirty works; though some had proved more successful than others, he could choose from a symphony, two symphonic fantasias, an overture and a quartet movement, not to mention several pieces of incidental music for the stage, twelve pieces for piano, fifty Russian folk-song arrangements, a dozen 'romances' (or songs) and the two operas he had destroyed. But it was more than a year since the last public performance of any of his music; his career was in danger of faltering before it had gathered momentum. He needed such a concert; and such a concert needed a new work.

When Rubinstein told him that his funds could not run to a large orchestra, it turned out to prove a blessing in disguise. At the suggestion that he instead attempt a string quartet, Tchaikovsky's mind went back to a tune he had heard at Kamenka two summers before. While scoring the ill-fated *Undine*, he had noted down a folk-song, 'Sidel Vanya', which a peasant had been singing outside his open window. Within six weeks it now became the centre-piece of his String Quartet no. 1 in D major (Op. 11) – the main theme of its second movement, the celebrated *andante cantabile*, which proved so popular that Tchaikovsky himself would later make a separate arrangement of it for cello and string orchestra.

Five years later, at a private performance of the quartet, Tchaikovsky would be moved to find Tolstoy, sitting beside him, reduced to tears by the *andante cantabile*: 'Never have I been so flattered in my life, nor felt so proud of my work.' Over the years the sheer popularity of the piece would come to haunt him. Many arrangements were made, besides his own; and too many audiences, he complained to Modest from Germany in 1884, 'don't want to hear anything else!' At the time, the quartet was the first piece he had written to gain wide public popularity, giving his career just the boost it needed. He dedicated it to Sergey Rachinsky, his botanist friend and would-be librettist, who presciently exclaimed: '*C'est un brevet d'immortalité que j'ai reçu!*'

After a period in the professional doldrums, Tchaikovsky was suddenly relaunched upon the world by a programme consisting of this new quartet, some songs ('None but the Lonely Heart' was reprised by its first performer, the contralto Elizaveta Lavrovskaya) and some piano pieces (Rubinstein himself played the *Rêverie* and *Mazurka* from Three Piano Pieces, Op. 9). Among the audience was another literary hero, Turgenev, whose presence in itself also served to bolster Tchaikovsky's public standing.

So it was with renewed confidence that he returned to his work on *The Oprichnik*, of which he wrote to Balakirev in June: 'I have now surrendered myself whole-heartedly to composing this opera.' That month he took his work with him to Kamenka, where Sasha had organized him a greater degree of privacy, with his own separate entrance to the attic room where he composed.

She now had an infant son, Vladimir, as well as an older son and four daughters, and was well aware of their capacity to interfere with her brother's work. But she was also aware of her brother's delight in her children, as was further evidenced that summer when he wrote, directed and even choreographed for them a miniature ballet called *Swan Lake*. Family memories of this momentous event naturally vary, but Yuri Davidov's memoirs maintain that at least one of the Dances for Swans in this light-hearted Kamenka entertainment eventually found its way into the legendary ballet which his uncle would compose five years later. (If so, it seems likely to have been the duet rejected from *Undine*.)[8]

By the time he left Kamenka that August, Tchaikovsky had completed and scored the first act of *The Oprichnik*. Now he was forced to set it aside, as he travelled to Nizy in the nearby Kharkov province, to the estate of his friend Nikolay Kondratiev, to work on a textbook on harmony commissioned by Yurgenson. So productive was he that summer that it was written and despatched to the publisher within three weeks. He even braved a few days *chez* Shilovsky, at Usovo, near Kiev, after tiring of Kondratiev's noisy house-guests and 'insubordinate' servants. In coded letters to Modest, Tchaikovsky seems to imply that Kondratiev exercised droit de seigneur over his male as well as his female serfs – a habit which might well result in their insubordination, but could scarcely merit the indignation of a friend now about to plunge deeper than ever into the sexual morass of the Moscow underworld.

Back in Moscow for the new academic year, Tchaikovsky was finally able to make the long-awaited break with Rubinstein and move into a place of his own. It was a modest three-room apartment vacated by Laroche, who had returned to St Petersburg as professor of the theory of composition. His replacement in Moscow was another old friend of Tchaikovsky's, Nikolay Hubert, until recently deputy conductor of the Kiev Opera – who was delighted to take Tchaikovsky's place in Rubinstein's apartment, thus easing the composer's conscience at deserting the employer and friend who had been so good to him.

'His delight at finding himself the sole master of his own little flat of three rooms was', says Modest, 'indescribable.' Thoroughly liberated by having his own home for the first time in his life, at the age of thirty-one, Tchaikovsky promptly engaged a manservant, one Mikhail Sofronov, from the country town of Klin, sixty miles north of Moscow. Bequeathed to him by another Conservatoire professor, twenty-one-year-old Sofronov was a country-loving peasant who insisted on returning home to Klin each summer. He effectively silenced his master's protests by sending down as his replacement his younger brother, Alexey, just twelve years old when he arrived as Tchaikovsky's servant for that first summer of 1871.

Despite his obvious lack of domestic experience, young Alexey was rather more to Tchaikovsky's taste than Mikhail. Gradually the brothers became dual servants all year round. Within five years the composer had dismissed the older in favour of the younger, who would remain in Tchaikovsky's service to his dying day (and indeed play a central role in the events following his death).

At first, however, Mikhail appears to have satisfied his master in quite as many and various departments as eventually would his brother. There is no doubt that Alexey performed sexual services for Tchaikovsky[9]; and that Mikhail was sexually attractive to Modest, if too old for the composer himself. In a letter to Modest of December 1872, Tchaikovsky refers to 'Mikhailo' as 'the object of your affections' and indeed as a 'Leporello' in his own life, suggesting that Mikhail might well have proved willing to procure for his master boys a few years younger than himself. 'I am very satisfied with him,' Tchaikovsky tells Modest, 'and even more so with his younger brother.' Five years later, after Mikhail has departed the scene, he is writing that Alexey 'well understands all my needs, and more than satisfies all my demands.' (The passage was deleted, needless to say, by the Soviet censors.) By then, Alexey was eighteen, and had 'lost his looks', in Tchaikovsky's eyes, to an 'inexpressible' degree. But he remained 'as dear to my heart as ever . . . Whatever may befall us, I will never let him go.'[10]

In its early years, this bizarre *ménage à trois* was often supplemented by the presence, in this two-bedroom apartment, of a lodger named Nikolay Bochechkarov – one of Shilovsky's less savoury friends, whose hold over Tchaikovsky baffled such other friends as Kashkin, who saw him as no more than an effete freeloader. It is curious that the composer's musical friends could not see this 'parasite' for the pimp he obviously was, earning his keep by catering to his landlord's exotic needs.

Tchaikovsky's independence of Rubinstein evidently enabled him, for the first time since his arrival in Moscow five years before, to indulge himself freely in the paedophiliac demi-monde of 'rough trade' and 'rent boys' so much to his taste. The role of Pandarus was played by *tyotki*, or 'aunties' – the scornful slang for passive homosexuals (exemplified by Bochechkarov), who now began to make regular appearances in Tchaikovsky's letters to those few correspondents, primarily Modest and Anatoly, privy to his secret life. Although he would always remain ambivalent about their seedy underworld, affecting distaste for its ambience while sampling its wares, his own penchant for drag costumes was a typical 'auntie' hallmark.

Another early lodger in the crowded Tchaikovsky apartment was an architect named Ivan Klimenko, whose own word for it we have that he 'succumbed to Pyotr Ilyich's seductive invitation and lived with him for some time'.[11] Though Klimenko would later marry and father children, it seems likely that he too was Tchaikovsky's lover at this time. Soviet censors removed all trace of him from the composer's correspondence, but this time they were foiled by Klimenko's own reminiscences, which quote letters from the composer feminizing his name to 'Klimenka' and its affectionate diminutive 'Klimenochka' – a regular habit of Tchaikovsky's when writing to fellow homosexuals, usually during love affairs.* In one such letter comes a 'seductive invitation', with Tchaikovsky playing the voluptuous 'Sultan' addressing his 'favourite concubine' on behalf of his 'divan', newly upholstered, and 'longing for you to come back to Moscow and rest your weary limbs on its rejuvenated shoulders'. Speaking further for his 'divan' (which, in Russian as in English, carried a double meaning as the Turkish 'government'), the 'Sultan' expresses the hope that he will 'not be forced to turn our requests into demands, disobedience of which entails the penalty of death by impalement . . .'[12]

In other letters of the period, Bochechkarov's patronymic is feminized by Tchaikovsky to 'Lvovna' (changed back by Modest to the masculine patronymic 'Lvovich'). This elderly Pandarus seems to have been responsible for all sorts of late-night disruptions in the new Tchaikovsky household, and for constant provision of sexual gossip about *'tutti quanti'*. His relationship with his host was stormy, but the composer could at least rely on his discretion about his numerous sexual adventures during this period, which was to prove a crucial one for his evolving self-perception.

At this stage of his development, Tchaikovsky seems to have shared the

---

* This period also saw Tchaikovsky addressing Modest as 'Modestina' in letters signed 'Petrolina'.

exterior world's distaste for the camp behaviour of the 'aunties', even for some of their more arcane practices, while continuing to indulge his own similar sexual needs. As Alexander Poznansky argues, this was not so much hypocrisy as 'an inability to reconcile an intellectual position with instinctual demands'. Tchaikovsky's personality, as Poznansky points out, was at root very traditional, and 'the rigorous moral education he had received from his parents was only enhanced by his highly idealistic view of art and the artist and by his habitual religious reverence.' As a result, he considered his homosexuality 'natural, and no doubt resented the social stigma it carried', while at the same time he 'never related it in his mind to the rest of the ethical standards of the culture to which he belonged.'[13]

As an increasingly well-known and popular figure in Moscow society, the composer naturally dreaded any word of his secret life reaching the public arena and tarnishing his reputation. His fear of such gossip would haunt him all his life, and drive him at times to desperate remedies. Such secrets, nevertheless, are hard to hide, especially in the life of an apparently eligible bachelor in his early thirties, living by day in high-society circles and by night in their notoriously indiscreet antithesis.

These were the years during which his dread of public exposure as a homosexual began to take deep root in Tchaikovsky's psyche. As yet, with the resilience of youth, he could weather the occasional storm, flinch with passing pain at the odd piece of gossip to reach his ears, knowing that it was the price he must pay for his irresistible desires. In time, however, as his fame grew with his reputation, the strain would take an ever heavier toll.

But these Moscow years, for all that, were among the most care-free lived by a perennially careworn man. On top of his double life, Tchaikovsky took upon himself certain burdens which should really have been his father's, notably the welfare of the twins, now leaving school and embarked upon their careers. With Ilya Petrovich still in a state of penury, Tchaikovsky's letters are peppered with constant requests to friends to find them gainful employment, transfer them nearer to him, and pardon their youthful excess. This was especially true of Modest, of whom Tchaikovsky wrote to their brother-in-law, Lev Davidov: 'I am very worried about Modest. I can't adjust to the notion that he will now have to survive pretty much on his own. Just as I am convinced that Tolya [Anatoly] will work hard and attain a respectable position, I am equally alarmed about Modest. I suspect he will wind up as some sort of failure, though an interesting one . . .'[14] When Modest accused his brother of coldness, Tchaikovsky asked Anatoly to intervene: 'There wasn't any coldness. It was just that, when he was in Moscow, it was upsetting for me to realize that he is *the same as me*'[15] (author's italics).

Along with Bochechkarov, and occasionally their older brother Nikolay, the twins also became another drain on Tchaikovsky's already stretched finances. Never too careful with his money, and always generous to a fault, he was still a low-paid Conservatoire professor whose salary would barely accommodate his own needs, let alone those of sundry hangers-on. The income from his musical activities – concert performances, publications and newspaper criticism – should have proved a welcome bonus; but it was largely dissipated on his expanding coterie and indigent relations.

To maintain this unruly entourage, Tchaikovsky took on extra work for *The Contemporary Chronicle*, for whom he reviewed concerts of music by Wagner, Beethoven, Schumann and Mozart, plus a continual flow of Italian opera. But he never felt comfortable in the role of critic, and the arrangement soon petered out. Constant money worries now combined with a growing boredom with his teaching, mounting irritation with the Conservatoire and all its works, and increasingly pent-up frustration at the lost time and energy which he longed to devote to composition. As he continued to work on *The Oprichnik* – 'It has to be ready,' he told Nikolay on 10 October, 'by the end of the year' – he again grew downhearted. 'I expect that this wretched opera will suffer the same fate as my poor *Undine*,' he wrote to Balakirev. 'Despite it all, I do want to get it finished, as I'm in no fit state to tackle any other work with much enthusiasm.'[16]

Balancing his work with his social life, not to mention his Conservatoire commitments, was becoming something of a problem, not eased by Shilovsky's insistence that he join him in the South of France for Christmas and New Year. Tchaikovsky had never before spent the festive season outside Russia; but he agreed to go, telling Anatoly that the trip must remain secret from everyone except Rubinstein: 'I want them all to think I've gone to stay with our sister.'

Only one letter survives from this excursion, which seems to have had the composer in melancholy mode: 'On the very day I left Moscow I was gripped by an all-consuming depression which stayed with me right through the journey and has not left me even now.' After a week in Nice he was writing again to Anatoly (Modest, significantly, was receiving no letters from his brother at this time): 'How curious it is to arrive from the depths of the Russian winter in a climate where I can step outside without an overcoat, where oranges, roses and lilacs are in bloom, and the trees are covered in leaves.' Amid a 'taxing' social life, he enjoyed 'many pleasant hours, especially those in the early morning, when I sit alone by the sea in the warm, but not too warm, sunshine.'

Aged only thirty-one, Tchaikovsky puts the reader in mind of Thomas Mann's Aschenbach, forlornly watching the boys playing on the beach, as he continues:

> But even these moments are not without sadness. What is the point of it all? Old age has set in, and I have nothing more to look forward to. All I have to live on are my memories and my hopes. But what have I to hope for?[17]

This time there is no mention of any wayward behaviour from Shilovsky, who even persuaded his reluctant companion – handsomely paid, as usual, for his services – to return by way of Genoa, Venice and Vienna. These annual trips to Europe, fast becoming a habit with Tchaikovsky, were also becoming a need. Thanks to Shilovsky, however, they were also a profit-making enterprise. So the composer was really protesting too much when he wrote to his father that 'my idleness was upsetting me, and in the end I was very glad to get home to Moscow.' All he had to show for the trip were the Two Piano Pieces (Op.10), one of them the popular *Humoresque*, which he dedicated to Shilovsky. Upon his return, galvanized by an idle winter, he swiftly turned out a song for the character of Count Almaviva, to the accompaniment of two violins, for a Conservatoire production of Beaumarchais' original stage play of *Le Barbier de Séville*.

Perhaps through guilt about the slow progress of his work, perhaps through discretion about his private life, there followed a rare three months in which Tchaikovsky wrote no letters at all. *The Oprichnik*, by no coincidence, was finished by April and delivered in early May – not to the Moscow authorities who had rejected *Undine*, but to Eduard Napravnik at the directorate of the Imperial Theatres in St Petersburg. This was to prove a happy choice, even though production of the opera would be subject to interminable delays. A Czech only a year older than the composer, Napravnik had been appointed chief conductor of the Mariinsky in 1869, and was to reign supreme there for forty-seven years, during which the house enjoyed the highest international reputation. Already Napravnik had conducted the first performance of the revised *Romeo and Juliet*; in time he would supervise the first performances of five of Tchaikovsky's operas; and the long working partnership between them would prove of enormous benefit to both.

During the same period, Tchaikovsky also found time to accept and fulfil a commission for a cantata, to celebrate the bicentenary of the birth of Peter the Great. On 13 June it was performed alfresco on the Troitsky Bridge, at the opening of a Polytechnic exhibition to mark the occasion. So hurriedly had he written the piece that its opening and closing sections turn out to be reworked borrowings from the finale of his First Symphony. 'Pompous anonymity allies itself with pedantry,' mutters a disapproving David Brown, 'to manufacture as dull a piece as Tchaikovsky ever wrote.'[18]

Later that same day, Tchaikovsky left Moscow for his sister's estate at Kamenka. The summer of 1872 was again to prove peripatetic. After a month with the Davidovs, made all the merrier by his father's presence, he moved on to Kiev, to meet Modest, in the company of a new friend named Sergey Donaurov. A civil-servant-turned-composer, like himself, Donaurov had a facility for writing popular romances; a steadfast friend to Tchaikovsky, he would later supervise the translation of his songs into French. So well did they all get on that summer, when Tchaikovsky seems to have patched up his rocky relations with Modest, that Donaurov was invited to join the brothers as they moved on to Kondratiev's estate at Nizy and Shilovsky's at Usovo.

An eloquent witness to Tchaikovsky's uncomplicated happiness that summer is his Second Symphony, sketched in three weeks at Sasha's, and entirely free from his characteristic melancholy, not to mention the self-doubt which would nag the work of the mature composer. Its unwonted *joie de vivre* may also have something to do with an apparent disaster which overtook Tchaikovsky between sketching and orchestration, eventually to metamorphose into a lasting belly-laugh.

At the start of the long journey home, after changing from coach to train at Vorozhba, the composer realized that he had left behind all his baggage, including his money and the sketches for his new symphony, at the last staging-post. This apparent carelessness was in fact the result of some drunken high spirits, after he and Modest had wined and dined well enough to move Tchaikovsky to one of his regular practical jokes. Upon calling for the horses to be harnessed for the final leg to Vorozhba, he was told none too politely by the postmaster that he would have to wait overnight. At the climax of the ensuing argument, the composer demanded the complaints book, which he signed 'Prince Volkonsky, Gentleman of the Emperor's Bedchamber'. The signature had the desired effect. Within minutes the carriage was ready, and a penitent postmaster bowed and scraped the brothers off to Vorozhba. Not until they arrived there did Tchaikovsky realize that, amid the confusion, he had left all his baggage behind. Returning to collect it was not, thanks to his drunken ruse, a happy prospect.

A sober Modest handed over his few remaining roubles and blithely proceeded on his way, leaving his brother to sort out his self-inflicted problems. Not wishing to confront the postmaster, assuming that he would have examined the baggage and discovered the owner's true identity, Tchaikovsky sent another hapless emissary back in his place and settled down for an uneasy night's sleep in a rat-infested attic. Next morning saw his problems worsen, with the return of his messenger empty-handed. The postmaster had refused to release the belongings of so eminent a figure to anyone but His Royal Highness himself, in person. Tchaikovsky had no choice but to return himself, unsure whether the price of retrieving his belongings would be an impersonation of royalty, or a craven apology. To his relief, he discovered that the postmaster was none the wiser, having respectfully left the baggage untouched.

Warming to the role of the gracious prince, Tchaikovsky thanked the official profusely, fell into conversation and finally asked his name. 'Tchaikovsky', replied the delighted postmaster, throwing the composer back into confusion. Had the fellow unmasked him? Was this his idea of revenge? He took his leave sharply, still unsure of the answer. Once Kondratiev's enquiries revealed that the official's name was indeed Tchaikovsky, the episode afforded the composer one of his favourite anecdotes for the rest of his life.

Beneath this outwardly contented summer lurked two long-running worries for Tchaikovsky: the financial difficulties of the Moscow Conservatoire, which had for some time threatened even his meagre income, and the unknown fate awaiting *The Oprichnik* at the hands of the directorate of the St Petersburg Imperial Theatres.

The first was now resolved swiftly, to satisfaction all round, by a government grant which not only secured the Conservatoire for five years but enabled Rubinstein to increase Tchaikovsky's salary by more than 50 per cent. With another burst of journalism, he soon had enough money to move to a larger apartment. 'I have spent a mountain of money and set myself up in great luxury,' he told Anatoly, by way of apology that he could not help him pay off some medical bills. Their older brother, Nikolay, came to Anatoly's rescue, and also treated a surprised Pyotr Ilyich to a splendid dinner while passing through Moscow, without choosing to inform him that he was about to get married.

But Tchaikovsky did not read too much into this. Throughout that autumn, on top of his Conservatoire and newspaper duties, he was obsessed with his Second Symphony. 'It so preoccupies me that I'm in no fit state for anything else,' he wrote to Modest in mid-November. 'This work of genius (as Kondratiev calls my symphony) is nearing completion . . . I think it's my best work yet in terms of polished form, not hitherto my strong suit.'

Typically, Tchaikovsky was to revise this opinion, and indeed the symphony, before becoming jaded with it. Throughout his working life he tended to have enormous faith in a piece while he was writing it, then become disenchanted with it all too soon after its completion or first performance, regardless of the public or critical reaction. If the work was a public success, as this symphony was to prove, the process of discovering its faults would merely take a little longer.

By the end of November he told Klimenko that he was 'frenziedly' busy with the scoring, despite simultaneous work on a gift for Nikolay Rubinstein, a short serenade for his Name Day, and six more songs, the Six Romances (Op. 16). By early December the symphony was finished in time to take with him to St Petersburg – where he had been summoned, rather to his annoyance, to play through *The Oprichnik* for the Imperial Theatres' directorate. There were other operas, it seems, vying for the committee's favours; while dismissive of them all in letters to friends and colleagues, he confessed to Sasha that his own audition was 'a terrible ordeal . . . I was convinced that I would be rejected, so much so that I resolved in advance not to go round to see Papa, for fear that my distraught demeanour would upset him.'[19]

In fact, he scored notable triumphs on both fronts. The directorate warmly approved *The Oprichnik*, which was scheduled for performance the following spring, in both St Petersburg and Moscow. While in the capital awaiting this verdict, he played through the final movement of his new symphony for the '*Kuchka*', assembled at Rimsky-Korsakov's home, to find this daunting group 'almost tearing me to bits with rapture'. Rimsky's wife, Nadezhda, 'begged me in tears' to let her arrange the movement for piano duet. Already his old schoolfriend and St Petersburg publisher, Vasily Bessel, had contracted to publish the vocal score of the opera; now he also negotiated the rights to Rimskaya-Korsakova's piano version of 'Zhuravl' ('The Crane'), as the final movement of the symphony was known, after the Russian folk song which ran through it.

Tchaikovsky himself eventually made the piano arrangement, when Rimskaya-Korsakova's work was delayed by illness; and he was glad, eight years later, that for this and other reasons Bessel had not got around to publishing the full score. In 1880 Tchaikovsky made a thorough revision, before publication, of the symphony by then known as the 'Little Russian'. So thoroughly did his structural approach meet with the nationalists' approval, and such effective use did he make of three folk tunes from the Ukraine, or 'Little Russia', that Kashkin came up with the nickname which has stuck to the symphony to this day.

At the time, in January 1873, Tchaikovsky solemnly sought permission to dedicate the symphony to the Moscow branch of the Russian Musical Society, by way of gratitude for their support since his arrival from

St Petersburg seven years before. It was a move which proved as shrewd as generous; the society promptly rewarded him with a handsome financial grant, and the promise of almost immediate performance. Postponed because of the sudden death of their founder-patroness, the Grand Duchess Elena, the first performance was finally given in Moscow on 7 February, with such success that Rubinstein promptly arranged another hearing for 9 April. After the first performance his old sparring-partner Laroche, who had come down from St Petersburg for the occasion, wrote in the *Moscow Register*: 'Not for a long time have I encountered a work whose thematic ideas are so powerfully developed and whose musical contrasts so well planned and executed.' After the second, Tchaikovsky was applauded after each movement, garlanded with laurels, and presented with a commemorative silver cup.

In between these two Moscow triumphs, the symphony's St Petersburg première, on 7 March under Napravnik, won only marginally less acclaim. Tchaikovsky's delight could not be marred even by a sour review from the ever curmudgeonly Cui. Writing ten years later, in 1883, Vladimir Stasov was to call the finale of this symphony 'one of the most important creations of the entire Russian school' – no mean tribute in view of Stasov's verdict on the rest of Tchaikovsky's work: 'The Conservatoire, academic training, eclecticism and overworking of musical materials laid its dread, destructive hand on him. Of his total output, a few works [*Romeo and Juliet*, *The Tempest*, *Francesca da Rimini*, and the String Quartets Nos 2 and 3] are first-rate and highly original; the remainder are mediocre or weak.'[20]

'I have only one interest in life: success as a composer,' Tchaikovsky had written to Klimenko the previous autumn, urging him to come and visit his new Moscow apartment. The letter is full of the melancholy which had come to characterize the composer (and so much of his music), though there are moments when it sounds affected.

> Day after day I go to the Conservatoire, day after day we meet
> up to get drunk, Yurgenson above all, and day by day I grow
> more depressed . . . On the whole, depression gnaws away at
> me largely because I am growing older, all too aware that every
> passing day brings me closer to the grave.

This letter to Klimenko was written at much the same time as he reported good progress on the symphony hailed as a 'work of genius' by their friend Kondratiev. After its successful première, he is writing to Modest:

The day is approaching when Kolya, Tolya, Ippolit and Modya will
no longer be 'the Tchaikovsky brothers', but 'the brothers of *the
Tchaikovsky*.' I make no secret of the fact that this is the most
cherished goal of all my hard work. To grind everything around
one into dust simply by one's own greatness – would not that be the
ultimate pleasure?! So tremble, for soon my fame will crush you.

Even between intimate brothers, these are not the words of a depressed
man, or indeed one lacking in self-confidence. Tchaikovsky's change of
mood can partly be attributed to the transition from his characteristic
anxiety while finishing a piece to his predictable elation when it proves
successful. Even then, however, the elation soon fades, as indeed does
the confidence in his work. These are the words, in short, of a highly
neurotic man prone to the wildest mood-swings.

But 1873 was proving a good year for a composer in need of one.
That March he scored another success with some instrumental music
commissioned by his old friend Begichev, for a Bolshoi production of
Ostrovsky's new play *The Snow Maiden*, a reworking of an old Russian
fairy tale about a girl of snow who comes to life; warned that her
heart must never be warmed by love, she inevitably falls for another
girl's fiancé, and finally melts beneath the spring sunshine. Though
written in only three weeks – 'at incredible speed', wrote Kashkin
(and Brown is not alone in finding 'signs of haste') – Tchaikovsky's
work was rather better received than Ostrovsky's. It earned him more
violent invective from Cui: 'The ideas are banal, the harmony trite,
the finish (or absence of finish) rough and clumsy.' But the steadfast
Rubinstein preferred to respond to public opinion by mounting an RMS
concert of the music in its own right. *The Snow Maiden* was one of
the few of Tchaikovsky's earlier works which the composer himself
never disowned. His subsequent plans to expand it into an opera
were abandoned only when Rimsky-Korsakov beat him to it in 1882;
Tchaikovsky was so annoyed that it was some years before he could
bring himself to look at his rival's now celebrated version.

Despite its short run, his music for the play earned him enough to
decide to return to Switzerland that summer, this time on his own. He
began his journey at Nizy, where Apukhtin was another of Kondratiev's
house guests. While swimming Tchaikovsky caught a chill severe enough
to oblige him to move on to Kamenka for ten days' recuperation in his
sister Sasha's care. Here he contemplated another symphony, all too
soon aborted, though the theme which roused him to action survives
in the *Capriccioso* for piano (Op. 19, no. 5).

With Yurgenson, whose advance on *The Oprichnik* had helped finance the trip, he entered Europe by way of Breslau and Dresden before moving on via Cologne to Zurich. Travelling alone, and keeping a journal for the first time in his life, Tchaikovsky spent ten days roving Switzerland – Zurich, Lucerne, Geneva – before embarking on an ambitious plan to explore the length and breadth of Italy. As early as Milan, however, the heat had proved too much for him, and he turned back to Paris, still his favourite destination. Running out of funds after only a week, he headed back towards Usovo, knowing Shilovsky was absent, with his next project very much in mind.

A new and important convert to Tchaikovsky's cause, since that evening in St Petersburg when he had played through the finale of the Second Symphony for 'The Five', was their new leading light, Vladimir Stasov. The foremost critic of the day, with no pretensions as a composer (unlike the rest, Cui included), Stasov was as generous with his advice as Balakirev. A few days after warming to Tchaikovsky at the Rimsky-Korsakovs', Stasov had written him a long and detailed letter suggesting three works of literature suitable for programme music: Sir Walter Scott's *Ivanhoe*, Gogol's *Taras Bulba* and Shakespeare's last play, *The Tempest*: 'You'd be able to write the most wonderful overture on this subject.' It was this last idea which intrigued the composer in the early months of 1873.

First, he needed more advice from his new mentor. Did there, for instance, need to be a tempest in *The Tempest*? 'By which I mean, is it essential to portray the elements in all their fury in an overture based on a piece in which they are merely the prelude to the real drama? If you say a tempest *is* necessary, where should it go: at the beginning or the end? If not, could I perhaps call the overture *Miranda*?' Again it was the plight of the only woman in the piece by which Tchaikovsky's imagination was fired.

Stasov was in no doubt. 'Yes, yes, yes,' he replied almost immediately. '*Of course* there must be a tempest. Without it the overture wouldn't be an overture, and the whole programme would be quite different.' There followed lengthy, detailed proposals for the structure of the piece, including the intriguing suggestion that 'the storm should be different from every previous one by *beginning suddenly*, at full strength, in violent turmoil, not emerging or growing stronger *by degrees*, as usually happens . . .' Scene by scene Stasov laid out Tchaikovsky's musical plan for him, incorporating the characters of Miranda and Ferdinand, Caliban and Ariel, and ending with Prospero renouncing his power beside 'a calm and tranquil sea, lapping the shore of the now deserted island, whence all have sailed away to the distant pleasures of Italy'. If Tchaikovsky followed his plan, Stasov concluded, it would be 'quite impossible to omit the sea at the beginning and end, and to call the overture *Miranda*.'[21]

Tchaikovsky did indeed follow his plan, with such enthusiasm that the piece was written in ten days – 'as if,' he later recalled, 'I was moved by some supernatural force.' In Shilovsky's absence, Usovo was the perfect place to work. 'I was in an exalted, ecstatic frame of mind, wandering alone through the woods by day, over the boundless steppes in the evening, and sitting by night at an open window, listening to the solemn silence of this remotest of places . . . During these two weeks I sketched out *The Tempest* with no effort at all.' Then Shilovsky returned, and this reverie was shattered: 'All the charms of my intimate communion with nature immediately disappeared. My little corner of Paradise turned back into a commonplace country estate.'[22] After only 'two or three more tedious days', Tchaikovsky returned to Moscow to complete scoring the overture. As soon as December the piece was premièred there under Rubinstein, though Stasov himself had to wait almost a year to hear it (conducted by Napravnik) in St Petersburg. After attending its first rehearsal, *The Tempest*'s 'only begetter' was delighted, tempering his enthusiasm with just a few rather brutal reservations:

> What an incomparable work! The storm itself is of course trite and unoriginal, Prospero very ordinary, and near the end there is a very banal cadence straight out of some awful Italian opera finale – but these are minor quibbles. All the rest is wonder piled on wonder! . . . What languor, what passion! . . . The orchestration is superb . . . Rimsky-Korsakov and I both send you our heartiest, our very heartiest congratulations, and warmly shake you by the hand.[23]

As usual, there had to be one dissenting voice. If it was not Cui, who for once went overboard in Tchaikovsky's praise – 'such passion, such talent, so exquisitely sonorous a score!' – it had to be Laroche, who found the piece 'unoriginal', accusing his sometime friend of too closely echoing Schumann, Glinka and Litolff. 'I don't care whether he likes *The Tempest* or not,' Tchaikovsky raged to Modest. 'I didn't really expect him to . . . But what does gall me beyond belief is his insinuation that I have stolen from every living composer.'

He would not be pleased to know that twentieth-century musicologists are surprised to find Mendelssohn's name missing from Laroche's list, citing the 'Bottom-as-ass' theme from *Midsummer Night's Dream*, a work avowedly admired by Tchaikovsky, as the inspiration for *The Tempest*'s Caliban. But almost all critics, at the time and since, are agreed that the lovers' music, after its deliberately wide-eyed opening (often dismissed as trivial), grows to 'one of the most perfectly wrought passages in all Tchaikovsky's music.'[24] Characteristically, the composer's own feelings about the piece vacillated for years; by the time he heard a Paris performance in 1879, he had become wholly disenchanted with it.

The same autumn, despite recurring illnesses, he had already turned out two poignant romances, 'Take my heart away' and 'Blue eyes of spring', as well as twelve short piano pieces, the Six Pieces (Op. 19), and Six Pieces on a Single Theme (Op. 21). The second of these he dedicated to Anton Rubinstein, by way of thanks for a recent dedication he himself had received from his first employer. True to form, the curmudgeonly Rubinstein neither acknowledged the gesture nor ever performed the pieces in public. But the success of *The Tempest* now spurred Tchaikovsky to write his second string quartet, which he completed with remarkable speed in January 1874. 'Never has music flowed from me so easily and simply,' he told Modest. 'I wrote it in virtually a single sitting.' Anton Rubinstein, who happened to be in town, was the only guest at his brother Nikolay's to disapprove of the piece when the F major quartet (Op. 22) was privately performed in mid-February, prior to its public première in Moscow on 22 March. 'We liked the quartet very much,' testified Rimsky-Korsakov, who was present. 'At this time, Tchaikovsky was charming to talk to, and a man of the world in the best sense of the term, always animating the company he was in.'[25]

'If I have written anything in my life that is truly heartfelt, and flows straight from deep inside me, it is the first movement of this quartet,' said Tchaikovsky, goaded by Laroche's comment that it was 'too cold'. Again, twentieth-century verdicts on the Second String Quartet have been mixed, and it has never found as secure a place in the repertoire as its predecessor.

Anton Rubinstein's continuing resistance to his work had now begun to rattle Tchaikovsky. That night at Nikolay's, when the Second String Quartet had been played, his criticism could not have been more graceless. 'Throughout the piece,' according to Kashkin, 'Anton Grigorievich listened with a dark, disapproving look on his face. As soon as it was over, with his usual ruthless candour, he declared that stylistically this was not a chamber piece, that he didn't comprehend a note of it, etc.' Everyone else present was 'in ecstasies'.[26]

A few days later, Tchaikovsky told Vasily Bessel that he found himself 'in a darker mood than ever before'. So easily swayed by others in his own feelings about his work, Tchaikovsky's self-confidence was ebbing again. His private life at this time also seems to have been becalmed in some rare doldrums; in his letters there are references to few friends around him other than the old gossip Bochechkarov, the unruly Shilovsky and the peripatetic Kondratiev. It was during the winter of 1873–74, according to Modest, that his brother's spasms of depression became noticeably 'longer, stronger and more frequent'. In December, Tchaikovsky wrote Modest a long letter confiding his own sense of growing personal isolation. His friendships were reliable, but somehow unfulfilling: did the fault lie in his friends, or in him?

The little-known Second String Quartet holds a lasting place in any psychological profile of Tchaikovsky, for it is the first piece in which his contemporaneous personal dilemmas are clearly evident in the music. The piece contains much material, as Brown points out, 'which shows a rigorous determination to exclude anything of himself.' At the same time, however, its slow movement 'is a most naked exposure of his stress-filled personality – less brutally emotional than some that were to come later, perhaps, but the most self-declaring piece he had yet composed.'[27]

This was not true of his next work to be offered for public scrutiny, for it had, of course, been completed two years before. The first few months of 1874 saw Tchaikovsky shuttling back and forth to St Petersburg for consultation with Napravnik over the long-delayed première of his opera *The Oprichnik*, which finally took place at the Mariinsky on 24 April. To Tchaikovsky's profound anxiety, a proud Nikolay Rubinstein brought the entire Conservatoire staff up from Moscow for the occasion; and they were not disappointed. The evening proved an unqualified success for Tchaikovsky, who was awarded a handsome monetary prize at the first-night dinner. While duly grateful, he was never comfortable at such moments, and could not wait to get out of town. A commission from the *Russian Register* to review a Milan production of Glinka's *Life for the Tsar* was excuse enough to leave for Italy within forty-eight hours. He thus missed Cui's latest tirade against his 'barren' work, which was 'bereft of ideas', 'lacking a single distinguished passage, a single happy inspiration'.[28] Laroche, of course, this time took quite the opposite view.

*The Oprichnik* was Tchaikovsky's first real public triumph, yet within a fortnight he was disowning it in a letter to Modest.

> *The Oprichnik* torments me. This piece is so bad that I fled from all the rehearsals to avoid hearing a single note. At the performance itself, I wished that the earth would swallow me up . . . Isn't it odd that, when I finished it, at first I thought it utterly delight-ful. But then, from the very first rehearsal, what disappointment! There's no *style*, no *action*, without which the public will reject any opera.[29]

He was wrong. *The Oprichnik* enjoyed fourteen sold-out performances in St Petersburg, prompting productions later that year in Odessa and Kiev. Its public popularity remained high throughout his lifetime, though with posterity it has been eclipsed by his later operas.* To one twentieth-century critic, '*The Oprichnik* is not a great opera; neither is it a bad one. At times it's third-rate, sometimes cheap, yet it is a good deal better than either Cui's or the composer's own damnation would suggest.'[30] To another, 'Tchaikovsky has not yet found his individual touch with *The Oprichnik*, but in the handling of [specific motifs] and in the effective pacing of a few scenes, as well as the beauty and dramatic potency of certain moments, we can see the seeds of the characteristics that were to flower in *Eugene Onegin*.'[31]

Part of the opera's appeal to the public was the somewhat risqué quality of its subject-matter. For its negative depiction of a Tsar, in this case Ivan the Terrible, Lazhechnikov's play had been banned by the censor since the 1840s (as indeed had Pushkin's *Boris Godunov*). Only since the accession of the more enlightened Alexandr II in 1855 had a more indulgent attitude been taken to musical adaptations, the sung word being deemed *less* powerful than the spoken. The two plays were finally allowed onto the stage in the late 1860s, enabling Musorgsky to set about his version of Pushkin, and Tchaikovsky his of Lazhechnikov. The resulting operas reached the stage of the Mariinsky within two months of each other, and it will come as a surprise to latter-day opera-goers that, while both were well received, Tchaikovsky's proved the more popular.

On reaching Italy, he discovered that Milan's Glinka production had been postponed till late May, so changed course to pay his first visit to Venice. Perhaps, like Aschenbach, he should have headed for the Lido. 'Were I obliged to spend an entire week here, I should kill myself in despair on the fifth day,' he told Modest. 'No matter where you walk, you end up lost in a maze of stinking alleyways leading nowhere.' Not even his delight in the city's art treasures could overcome his sense of desolation: 'This is a gloomy place, dead and deserted. Not merely are there no horses. I haven't even seen a single dog.' After one more day he escaped on the round-Italy tour he had planned the previous summer, wandering via Rome to Naples and Pompeii to Florence – growing increasingly homesick as he went, and still in low spirits about *The Oprichnik*. 'You are thinking what a good time I must be having,' he wrote to Modest, 'sending you letters first from Venice, then from Rome

---

* A concert performance of *The Oprichnik* at the 1992 Edinburgh Festival, broadcast by BBC Radio 3, was a rare chance to hear it. There is no complete recording currently available.

and Naples, now from Florence. But all this time, Modya, you cannot envisage an unhappier man than me.'[32]

Obliged to return to Moscow in mid-May for the Conservatoire's graduation exams, he was on the road again as soon as they were over, with a very specific purpose in mind. Tchaikovsky was determined that all his brooding about *The Oprichnik* would now bear fruit; he felt that the rehearsal process had helped him learn from his mistakes, and he had to admit how gratifying it was, back in Moscow, that the public success of the piece seemed undimmed by his own private doubts. Furthermore, he had the perfect vehicle for his next attempt.

For some time Tchaikovsky had known about a competition launched by the Russian Musical Society for an opera to a libretto by the poet Yakov Polonsky, loosely based on Gogol's comic fantasy *Christmas Eve*. The text had in fact been commissioned for Serov by the Grand Duchess Elena; but both had died while Polonsky was at work, leaving the RMS to find a good home for the poet's libretto. At one stage the previous year, Tchaikovsky had even been involved in discussions about the terms of the competition. Now he made it clear that he wanted to take part. Apart from a useful sum of money, the winner was guaranteed publication of his work and a production at the Mariinsky in St Petersburg. This was a goal he still very much coveted.

Pausing only to check that neither Balakirev, Rubinstein nor Rimsky-Korsakov were entering the competition, Tchaikovsky took his servant Alexey with him to Kondratiev's estate at Nizy. There he worked on Polonsky's libretto for six weeks, from mid-June to the end of July, when he moved on to Shilovsky's estate at Usovo, anxious to complete his work before the distractions of the new academic year. By the end of August, despite averaging only three hours' work a day amid games of bezique and other country pursuits, he had first sketched and then scored the entire opera. Entitled *Vakula the Smith*, it had come to him so fluently, in such a burst of inspiration, that it retained a special place in his affections for the rest of his life. 'Until his dying day,' according to Modest, 'he remained convinced that it was the best of all his operas.'

Only several weeks after submitting *Vakula the Smith* to the competition judges – anonymously, as the rules required – did Tchaikovsky discover that the deadline for entries was not in fact the end of the year, as he had thought, but the following August. It was an understandable mistake, as the rules had changed several times. But now he was faced with a year's wait for the judges' verdict. As usual, before anyone else had a chance to change his mind, he was pleased with his latest musical offspring, enthusing to Modest as if it were literally that: 'All my thoughts and feelings are now bound up in my beloved child *Vakula* . . . You cannot conceive how much I love him! I'm sure I will go completely mad if he does not prove a success.'

But this very enthusiasm now led him to cause his new love-child almost terminal damage. Upon discovering his mistake about the competition entry date, Tchaikovsky was distraught at the thought of so long a delay in the production of his beloved *Vakula*. Already he had somewhat bent the rules of the competition by writing 'Ars longa, vita brevis' on the title-page of the manuscript, not unaware that his handwriting would be very familiar to some of the judges. Deciding that he simply could not wait a year for their verdict, and arguing that a production was 'of more importance to me than the money', he wrote to the director of productions at the Mariinsky, Gennady Kondratiev (no relation of his friend Nikolay), asking whether *Vakula* might be withdrawn from the competition and submitted right away for more urgent production. Alas for Tchaikovsky, Kondratiev raised the matter not merely with his Mariinsky colleague Napravnik, but with the president of the Russian Musical Society, Grand Duke Konstantin, who took a very dim view of the composer's conduct.

Tchaikovsky was obliged to write a grovelling letter to Napravnik, himself one of the judges, while denying the charge that he had behaved improperly. 'You are unjust to suspect me of double-dealing. Duplicity could not have been further from my thoughts. I beg you to dismiss such suspicions, and to disabuse the Grand Duke, who, according to Rubinstein, is very displeased by what I have done.'[33]

The letter might have saved the day, had not Tchaikovsky promptly proceeded to sabotage his own efforts at damage limitation. He himself persuaded Nikolay Rubinstein, another of the judges (who therefore should also have known better), to conduct the opera's overture at a public concert in Moscow on 4 December 1874. Any remaining pretence of anonymity was thus abandoned. In his recklessness, the composer also spent much of early 1875 trying to persuade Yurgenson and Bessel, his Moscow and Petersburg publishers, to print the opera, thus further flouting the rules of the competition.

All this, he protested, was due simply to his pride in the piece, and his anxiety to place it before a wider audience. He was also, of course, desperately worried that its chances of success would be damaged if it failed to win the first prize. When he offered to play it through for Rimsky-Korsakov, yet another of the judges, it was as if the competition had no rules at all. Rimsky evidently found Tchaikovsky's impatience with such details contagious, for he offered some criticisms a fortnight before the judging, in a letter expressing 'no doubt at all that your opera will win the prize'.

In late October Laroche and three other judges joined Napravnik, Rubinstein and Rimsky-Korsakov in awarding the first prize of 1,500 roubles 'to the composer of the opera with the motto "Ars longa, vita brevis"' – for all the world as if they did not know who he was. This particular composer's version, they added, was not only the best entry, but the *only* entry to meet the artistic standards required.

*Vakula the Smith* was not finally performed until December 1876, when it won only a muted response from the public. Cui and Laroche were at one, for once, in its favour; but the composer himself soon began to feel his habitual post-partum doubts, writing to Taneyev that *Vakula* was 'a triumphant failure . . . It is too choked with detail, too heavily scored, its vocal lines too thin . . . Stylistically, it is wholly unoperatic. There is no breadth or sweep to it.'[34] *Vakula* stayed in the Mariinsky's repertoire for three more seasons, each revival giving its composer greater cause for concern. For all his self-pitying strictures, however, he never lost his soft spot for the piece, nor his faith in its possibilities. In 1885 he embarked upon a wholesale revision, completely rewriting almost half of both music and libretto, and even retitling the opera *Cherevichki* ('The Slippers'). In 1887 he himself conducted its relaunch at the Bolshoi, and was this time undeterred by the continuing lack of public enthusiasm. It was never again performed in his lifetime; but in 1890, three years before his death, he still felt able to tell Yurgenson that he believed 'unreservedly' in *Cherevichki*'s future in the operatic repertoire. 'I consider it musically my best opera,' wrote the composer of *Eugene Onegin* and *The Queen of Spades*.

Back in the autumn of 1874, as Tchaikovsky discovered his mistake over the competition deadline, his hopes for *Vakula the Smith* were unclouded. Then came the apology to Napravnik, the displeasure of the Grand Duke, and all the musical politics which could so swiftly sink his spirits. It was thus on the first slope of another downward curve, acutely aware of his loneliness and his apparently limited talents, that he moved to a larger Moscow apartment, took comfort in revivals of the Second String Quartet and *The Tempest*, and began sketching what was to prove the most popular piano concerto ever written.

# CHAPTER VI

# 'I'm all written out'

'WORTHLESS . . . UNPLAYABLE . . . HACKNEYED . . . CLUMSY . . . AWKWARD
. . . trite . . . vulgar . . .'
Nikolay Rubinstein's scathing assault on Tchaikovsky's First Piano
Concerto must take its place high among the richly ironic moments
in musical history, from the Emperor Joseph II telling Mozart that his
music had 'too many notes' to the hapless impresario who turned
down The Beatles. The Concerto No. 1 in B flat minor (Op. 23) now
ranks among the most popular and frequently heard pieces of music
ever written. Today, 120 years after its composition, some seventy-five
different versions are available on compact disc recordings alone – more
than any other single work, classical or popular, in the CD catalogues.
In both London and New York, it is perennially the concerto most often
performed in any season, most broadcast in any year.

Tchaikovsky leaves no clue as to why, in the wake of *Vakula the Smith*,
he chose the concerto form for his next major composition. What is clear
is that he worked at the piece in an almost obsessive frenzy, completing
his sketches in barely six weeks, and taking it for granted that Rubinstein
himself would give the first performance early in the New Year.

By the end of 1874 Tchaikovsky's public standing as a composer was
fast consolidating. The First Symphony had at last been published; *The
Tempest* was winning praise from his St Petersburg rivals; both his
quartets were also travelling well. Even *The Oprichnik* continued to

defy his own misgivings, its Kiev première being the only interruption
he would allow to his work on the concerto. Aware of his own limitations
as a pianist, he solicited Rubinstein's comments on the piano part before
embarking on the instrumentation. The fateful meeting took place on
Christmas Eve 1874*, in a classroom at the Conservatoire, whence both
were due to go on to a party at Albrecht's.

> I played the first movement. There came not a single word, no
> response of any kind! I began to feel as foolish, as embarrassed
> as a man who has cooked a meal for a friend who proceeds to
> eat it without saying a thing. Say *something*, for God's sake, if only
> to tear it apart with constructive criticism! Just one encouraging
> word, even if it isn't gushing praise!

Rubinstein, he sensed, was 'arming his thunderbolts'. His silence, to
Tchaikovsky, was that of a man thinking 'How can I single out details,
when the very essence of the whole piece disgusts me?' Kashkin and
Hubert, who were also present, seemed to be waiting nervously to see
which way to jump.

Steeling himself, Tchaikovsky played on to the end. 'Again silence. I
got up and asked "Well?"' It was then that, quietly at first, but gradually
assuming the tones of Jupiter the Thunderer, a torrent of abuse poured
forth from the mouth of Nikolay Grigorievich.' The concerto was
'worthless' in every respect. It was 'impossible to play, with passages
so hackneyed, so clumsy, so awkward that it was impossible to put
them right.' The piece as a whole was 'trite and vulgar'. Tchaikovsky
had 'pinched this bit from here and that bit from there'. Only two or
three short sections could possibly be salvaged. The rest had to be
'scrapped or completely rewritten'.

Warming to his task, Rubinstein sat down at the piano and cruelly
began to parody the piece. 'This, for instance,' he yelled over his
clattering, 'what is *this* supposed to be? And *this*? You can't *possibly* have
meant it?' The whole scene both 'stunned' and 'mortified' Tchaikovsky.
What most offended him, however, was the tone of voice in which
Rubinstein's tirade was delivered. 'If a stranger had happened to come
in, he would have assumed I was some lunatic, an untalented and
dim-witted scribbler who was wasting the time of this eminent musician
with his ridiculous rubbish.'

Tchaikovsky walked out of the room without a word. Perhaps encouraged by Hubert and Kashkin, who had been equally stunned by

* January 5 1875, according to the Western calendar.

the force of his remarks, Rubinstein followed him upstairs and, seeing how distraught he was, drew him aside into a quiet room. 'There he told me all over again how impossible my concerto was, how this passage and that passage required radical alteration, and that if I had made wholesale changes along the lines he suggested by such-and-such a date, then he would bestow upon me the honour of including the piece in some concert of his.'

Tchaikovsky replied: 'I will not change a single note. I will publish the piece exactly as it stands.'[1]

In the short run, he seems to have proved as good as his word, changing his mind about dedicating the piece to Rubinstein, and awaiting a more favourable response from another performer. It came, within weeks, from Hans von Bülow, the German pianist and conductor, whose talents Tchaikovsky the music critic happened to have praised after a Moscow concert the previous year.

Hence it came to pass that the first performance anywhere in the world of this highly celebrated piece took place on 25 October 1875 in the unlikely setting of Boston, Massachusetts, during an American tour by von Bülow, to whom the concerto was finally dedicated. The piece, the pianist wrote to Tchaikovsky, had been so successful that the audience demanded an encore of the finale. 'If only', sighed Tchaikovsky to Rimsky-Korsakov, 'that happened here!' The first Russian performance, in St Petersburg on 13 November, with Gustav Kross as soloist, was not a success; Cui and Laroche both wrote lukewarm reviews, and Tchaikovsky himself was unhappy with Napravnik's direction of the orchestra. The first Moscow performance, three weeks later, was much more to his satisfaction, despite the bizarre fact that Rubinstein himself had agreed to conduct. So accomplished was the playing of the nineteen-year-old prodigy, Sergey Taneyev, that Tchaikovsky himself wrote a review of the concert, avowing that he 'could not have hoped for a better performance.'

The following year, before publication of the concerto, he did in fact make some amendments to the piano part following suggestions from the pianist Edward Dannreuther, who gave the first British performance at the Crystal Palace, London, on 23 March 1876. Two more years followed, with the concerto enjoying continued success abroad, before Rubinstein finally swallowed his pride and learnt the piano part, subsequently becoming one of the work's foremost champions.

Had Tchaikovsky, therefore, exaggerated the ugly scene at the Conservatoire in December 1874? The letter from which his account comes was written more than three years after the event, when he again had reason to feel aggrieved with Rubinstein; at the time he seems to have told no-one so vividly of his humiliation, though his self-pity was evident in another letter, suggesting that he had no-one to tell. Two weeks after the event, Tchaikovsky wrote to his brother Anatoly that the holiday season had seen him in the grip of 'a great depression'. His pride had been dealt 'a savage blow' by 'none other than Rubinstein . . . who cannot get out of the habit of seeing me as a beginner in need of advice, candid comments, hard judgements.' Hubert's indecision in the face of Rubinstein's onslaught had also wounded Tchaikovsky.

> Just think: these two are supposed to be my best friends, so there is thus no-one in the whole of Moscow who treats me or my work with tender loving care. You can see how hard this is for me . . . I am very, very lonely here. Without my work, I would fall into a terminal depression.[2]

But which did Tchaikovsky find the more depressing: his professional or his personal life? There was no-one in Moscow, he told Anatoly, whom he could call a friend 'in the true sense of the word'. It was, in his own mind, his homosexuality which had caused 'an unbridgeable gulf' between him and the rest of society. 'It lends my personality an aloofness, a fear of company, excessive shyness, a mistrust of everyone – in sum, a thousand qualities which make me ever more unsociable. Lately, believe it or not, my thoughts have been turning quite seriously to life in a monastery, or some such place.'

Tchaikovsky's determination to leave Moscow dates from this winter, which had seen him 'reach the extremity of disgust with life and yearning for death.' He needed, at the very least, an urgent 'change of scenery'. At present, this was impossible, as he wearily continued his dull Conservatoire routine – enlivened only by the dramatic progress of his star pupil, Taneyev (the younger brother of his schoolfriend Vladimir, who so vividly described those public floggings). In this multi-talented young prodigy, who would become a prominent composer and all-round musician, the self-styled misanthrope had found another lifelong friend – if, in this case, a purely professional and personal one.

Through the self-pity of that spring, he managed to finish the scoring of the piano concerto; write the wistful *Sérénade mélancolique* (Op. 26) for the Hungarian violinist Leopold Auer, professor of violin at the St Petersburg Conservatoire; compose no fewer than eighteen more songs (Op. 25, 27 and 28, this last including the enduring 'The Fearful Minute' and 'Why Did I Dream of You?'); and 'survive' more successful Moscow performances of his 'ugly, ill-starred' opera, *The Oprichnik*.

This might not seem too fallow a season for a man in supposedly terminal decline. For a man without friends, moreover, there was always the country hospitality of Shilovsky and Kondratiev. Bobbing between their estates at Usovo and Nizy that summer, he managed to sketch his third symphony, the *Polish**, in less than two months. The instrumentation was begun in the care of his sister Sasha at Verbovka, another Davidov estate adjoining Kamenka, and finished back at Usovo, care of Shilovsky, to whom the work was eventually inscribed.

Although perhaps the least satisfactory of all Tchaikovsky's symphonies (in part, perhaps, because of the haste with which it was composed), it enjoyed a successful première under the direction of Rubinstein in Moscow that November, just two weeks before the Taneyev–Rubinstein performance of the piano concerto. The same month also brought the news of *Vakula the Smith*'s victory in the RMS opera competition, soon followed by a flattering letter from Rimsky-Korsakov, inviting his comments on some contrapuntal exercises in the style of Bach. Tchaikovsky was delighted enough to return the compliment in lavish terms:

> I prostrate myself reverentially before your noble artistic modesty and extraordinary strength of character . . . No words can do justice to my boundless esteem for your artistic personality. How slight and pallid, how complacent and naïve do my own slight efforts seem beside your achievements . . . I am wholly convinced that, given your great gifts and unfailing conscientiousness, works will come from your pen to dwarf everything written in Russia before them.[3]

After its inauspicious start, 1875 had proved a very fruitful year. Tchaikovsky had even managed to fit in a Russian translation of Lorenzo da Ponte's libretto for Mozart's *Le Nozze di Figaro*, at Rubinstein's request, for a forthcoming Conservatoire production. By the late autumn he could again afford to be seen in high spirits, not least because of a visit to Moscow by Camille Saint-Saëns – a fellow composer of growing renown, but also a fellow homosexual with whom he established an immediate rapport. To his delight, he discovered that the Frenchman even shared his penchant for impersonating female dancers. A wide-eyed Nikolay Rubinstein, at the piano, was thus the sole witness of one of the unlikelier moments in the history of late nineteenth-century music, when Tchaikovsky and Saint-Saëns teamed up to perform, on the stage of the Conservatoire concert hall, a short ballet entitled *Pygmalion and Galatea*.

---

* This somewhat inappropriate nickname was coined by the English conductor Sir August Manns, after the composer's marking *tempo di Polacca* on the symphony's finale.

There are, of course, no reviews of this particular Conservatoire performance. By Modest's account, no doubt based on his brother's, thirty-five-year-old Tchaikovsky danced Pygmalion, while forty-year-old Saint-Saëns undertook the role of Galatea with 'rare dedication'. This promising collaboration was not, alas, to last; when Saint-Saëns reneged on a promise to introduce the *Romeo and Juliet* overture to France the following year, relations between the two composers cooled. As venerable, world-famous composers, however, they would have a chance to laugh over this fond memory together almost twenty years later, when reunited in England to receive honorary degrees at Cambridge University.

Weary of provincial life, and anxious to be nearer his brother, Modest Tchaikovsky had for some time been looking for work in either Moscow or St Petersburg. His quest had only recently ended at the home of a wealthy landowner named Herman Konradi, who, with his wife Alina, was seeking a tutor for their eight-year-old, deaf-mute son, Nikolay. Tchaikovsky encouraged Modest to accept the post – in which, over the next decade and more, he was to show an uncharacteristic blend of conscientiousness and sensitivity. Before formally agreeing a contract, however, the Konradis insisted that Modest undergo a year's training in Lyon, at the private school run by the world's leading specialist in the care of deaf-mutes, Jacques Gugentobler.

Still high on his cavortings with Saint-Saëns, Tchaikovsky agreed to escort Modest as far as Paris, stopping en route in Geneva, where their sister was living in temporary exile while the Kamenka estate was being renovated. The brothers arrived in time for New Year, to find Sasha pregnant again, before proceeding to Paris – where, on 20 January, Tchaikovsky's life was 'for ever altered' by his first hearing of Bizet's *Carmen*. Never, wrote Modest, had he seen his brother so deeply moved by an evening in the theatre. 'Although it does not pretend to be profound,' Tchaikovsky later wrote of *Carmen*, 'this music is so charming and simple, so vigorous, so sincere and uncontrived, that I have committed just about the whole piece to memory, from beginning to end . . . To me, *Carmen* is a masterpiece in the true sense of the word: that is, one of those rare works which uniquely reflect the musical aspirations of an entire era.'[4]

While in Paris, he began work on his Third String Quartet (also to prove his last). Tchaikovsky intended it as a tribute to the memory of Ferdinand Laub, his friend and Conservatoire colleague who had led the first performances of both his previous quartets, and who had died the previous year.

On his return to Russia, leaving a disconsolate Modest to get on with his new life in Europe, there were, as usual, many distractions. In St Petersburg, where he spent ten days attending rehearsals for the first performance in the capital of his Third Symphony, he was sorely tempted by the offer of a bursary to finance two years' work abroad, if only to return to Modest's side; but it came to naught, as did Cui's sudden attempts to win his friendship, despite more savage reviews of his new songs, during rehearsals of the critic's own new opera, *Angelo*.

Back in Moscow, nevertheless, the Third String Quartet, in E flat minor (Op. 30), was finished within a month, and privately performed two weeks later, on 14 March, at another of Nikolay Rubinstein's soirées. This time there was no Anton Rubinstein to spoil the party; if anything, it was the composer himself who blunted the enthusiasm of the other guests. Despite all the successes of the past year, he was sinking towards another crisis of self-confidence. 'I think I'm all written out,' he confided to Modest the next day. 'I've begun to repeat myself, and can't come up with anything new. Can I really have sung my swansong? Have I really nowhere else to go? It's unspeakably sad . . .'

The quartet was in fact warmly approved at the first of three public performances two weeks later, a Conservatoire concert in honour of the visiting Grand Duke Konstantin Nikolayevich. Its brooding, elegiac mood, foreshadowing Tchaikovsky's own musical obituary, has won the Third Quartet a marginally more secure place in the repertory than the composer's own preferred Second. To most critics, the first movement is the finest of all three, 'more complex and subtle in structure'[5]; to the Conservatoire audience at that first performance, the andante was worthy of tears. Given its *funebre e doloroso* tones, however, those tears may have been shed more in memory of the popular Laub. Amid all the sophisticated sentimentality of Tchaikovsky's chamber music, posterity has tended to follow Tolstoy in weeping to the *andante cantabile*, thus ensuring Tchaikovsky's First Quartet a far greater following than either of its successors.

It was around this time that Tchaikovsky heard from von Bülow of the warm reception accorded his First String Quartet in Boston, where interest in his work had grown since the success of the First Piano Concerto. Heartened by von Bülow's support, he took the chance to vent his spleen against his curmudgeonly ex-mentor Anton Rubinstein, who had told Bessel that the quartet was not worth publishing. 'This Olympian God has never shown anything but utter contempt for everything I have written, and it has wounded me grievously,' he wrote to von Bülow – whose support, by contrast, meant so much. Thanks to another champion of his work, Anton Door, a former Conservatoire colleague, to whom he had dedicated his *Valse-Caprice* for piano, Tchaikovsky was also gaining a following in Vienna. Even Liszt was impressed. 'I wish to assure you of the lively interest I take in the works of the new Russian composers – Rimsky-Korsakov, Cui, Tchaikovsky, Balakirev, Borodin,' he wrote to Bessel that summer. 'Next year I shall suggest that other works by these composers be performed. They deserve serious attention in musical Europe.'[6]

Heartened by success abroad, if still regarding himself as a prophet without honour in his own country, Tchaikovsky set to work on a series of twelve piano pieces, each to represent a month of the year (but known, illogically, as *The Seasons*). By the terms of the commission from Nikolay Bernard, editor of *Nouvelliste*, for whom his songs had already comprised four vocal supplements, Tchaikovsky was required to deliver only one short piece a month for publication, by instalments, over a year. Plenty of time was therefore available for the next major project in his sights: a ballet commissioned the previous summer by the Imperial Theatres, with which he had tinkered on and off throughout the busy year behind him.

Although intrigued by the challenge of writing for an entirely new genre, he had accepted the commission, as he later confessed, 'primarily for the money'. It seemed a happy omen that the chosen theme was the same as that on which he had improvised for his sister's children at Kamenka five summers before, *Swan Lake*. But it is one of the supreme ironies of Tchaikovsky's life that he was destined never to see a satisfactory production of *Swan Lake*, let alone appreciate the supreme place it would assume in the pantheon of classical ballet scores. The first production, at the Bolshoi, was an abject failure, thanks to the inadequacy of the choreographer, conductor, dancers and orchestra; and no new production was ever mounted in his lifetime.

Mystery shrouds the genesis of the piece, apparently a blend of folk stories from Russia and Germany. Did Tchaikovsky himself suggest the story, because of the children's entertainment he had devised in 1871? Did the composer himself devise the outline scenario? Some historians have thought so, though his unfamiliarity with the genre would seem to make both assumptions unlikely. The story-line is traditionally assumed to have been developed by Vladimir Begichev, Shilovsky's stepfather, with the aid of the dancer Vasily Heltser, though neither was credited in the programme for the first production. Nor did Tchaikovsky know much about balletic writing; Kashkin tells us that he thought it sufficient 'to take ballet scores out of the library and make a detailed study of this kind of composition.'[7] If he needed technical advice on tempi for the dancers, or the sequence in which scenes for various forces should come, there was no-one able to provide it. The whole project, in short, was a triumph of hope over inexperience. Even when it came to rehearsals, Tchaikovsky could not have been as involved as he habitually was with his operas, knowing nothing of the technicalities involved.

Against this background, it is scarcely surprising that the work became something of a chore, which he again completed with remarkable speed. Having sketched two acts at Usovo the previous summer, adding some instrumentation in spare moments that autumn, March found him with only a month in which to write nearly three whole acts by his deadline of late April. 'I'm up to my neck in scoring the ballet,' he wrote to Anatoly on 29 March, a month after finishing the third quartet. 'I've got to devote the whole of Easter to finishing this endlessly boring, interminable job.' He finished the ballet at Shilovsky's estate at Glebovo on 22 April, with two days to spare.

His letters of the ensuing year, leading up to the Moscow première of *Swan Lake* on 4 March 1877, also reveal little about the genesis of the first production. There are mentions of various private previews of the music – at the Conservatoire, and at his own home – in a piano transcription swiftly accomplished by Kashkin; but very little about progress at the Bolshoi, where he was being asked to drop some numbers and add others in accordance with the personnel available. Tchaikovsky's one letter to Modest from rehearsals sounds almost flippant:

> You wouldn't believe how comical it is to watch the ballet-master creating dances with the most solemn and inspirational air to the sound of one lone violin . . . Yet it fills me with envy to watch the ballerinas and *danseurs* throwing smiles to an imaginary audience, and relishing each opportunity for leaping and spinning about, as if it were their sacred duty.[8]

At least he was able to report that 'everyone at the theatre is raving about my music.' At this stage of his career, however, ballet seems to have been an infinitely less important medium to Tchaikovsky than opera; although apparently satisfied with his work, he appears unusually indifferent to its fortunes. According to Modest, there was a marked absence of 'the nervous tension and other strains' which always accompanied the build-up to an opera première.

So when the first night of this most celebrated of all ballets proved a failure, Tchaikovsky was curiously unmoved. The 'impoverished décor'; the 'absence of any outstanding dancers'; the 'paucity of the choreographer's imagination'; and the inadequacy of the orchestra, under a conductor who 'had never before had to cope with so complex a score'

– all this, says Modest, 'enabled the composer with justification to lay the blame for its failure upon everyone but himself.'[9]

To some extent, Tchaikovsky appears to have been a victim of ballet politics. It was a rigid tradition that new ballets, which were rare enough, became vehicles for the house's prima ballerina, in this case Anna Sobeshchanskaya. But she did not dance the part of Odette until the fourth performance, by which time it was too late to save the reputation of either the composer or his work. The first night of *Swan Lake* went to her much less talented rival Paulina Karpakova – largely, it seems, because of the financial muscle of her husband, a Greek millionaire. Karpakova's limited performance was but one aspect of an indifferent production of a piece which was always going to annoy the Moscow cognoscenti because it drew on a German rather than a Russian source.

> A ballet with subject taken from the life and beliefs of the people would not only be incomparably more interesting for the Russian public, but also incomparably more useful. It could be a representation of the particular mores of Russian life; it could acquaint the audience with traits of the national character; in a word, it could cease being a series of lovely but empty and sometimes absurd scenes.[10]

Amid this nationalistic high seriousness, the critical response was lukewarm. There were complaints about 'a poverty of creative fantasy' and 'thematic and melodic monotony' which might well raise eyebrows today. Thanks to his familiarity with the score, Kashkin's was the most enthusiastic review, though even he considered *Swan Lake* a pale shadow of Tchaikovsky's other work to date. 'The music has many beautiful moments, some of them perhaps even too good for a ballet; but it would be wrong to rank it alongside Tchaikovsky's previous compositions.'[11] We also have Kashkin's word for it that, despite its mediocre début, this production of *Swan Lake* nevertheless 'held the [Bolshoi] stage for many years, until the scenery fell to pieces.'

As with so much of his work, Tchaikovsky himself grew disenchanted with *Swan Lake* following the tepid reception accorded a production which evidently did it scant justice. Only twelve years later, in Prague, would he experience 'one brief moment of unalloyed happiness' during a performance of the second act. But it was not until soon after the composer's death that the work would begin its steady progress toward immortality, as better choreographers brought a more stylish response to its central theme of poignantly doomed young love. This, as always, was Tchaikovsky's main concern, and the driving impulse beneath the work's more haunting melodies. The composer would have been appalled by the subsequent manglings inflicted upon *Swan Lake*, notably the 'happy ending' often imposed after his death. It is central to Tchaikovsky's musical purpose that the ballet ends with the death of both the lovers, Siegfried and Odette. Thanks to its enduring place in the hearts of audiences, however, *Swan Lake* has passed into a realm where the box-office manager has as much say in many modern productions as the choreographer.

While completing the score of *Swan Lake* at Shilovsky's, Tchaikovsky had suffered several bouts of fever. Within a fortnight of his leaving Glebovo they grew much worse, and his doctor feared the onset of typhus. After the frantic activity of the previous eighteen months – not eased now by a flying visit to St Petersburg to deal with mounting production problems on *Vakula* – the composer was ordered to take a summer rest at Vichy before proceeding, as he had long planned, to Richard Wagner's first summer festival at Bayreuth.

The prospect of escaping from Moscow was the only thing which kept him going through the rest of the Conservatoire's spring term, where his lectures were becoming ever more eccentric and ill-prepared. To his growing unease, he was also developing something of a reputation for, at best, favouring his male students over the females – or, at worst, taking some of his male students home with him. Amid the continuing chaos of life under his roof, with Bochechkarov still coming and going, and Kondratiev seeking asylum from a wife who had discovered his affair with his manservant, Tchaikovsky felt himself on the verge of a slide towards terminal scandal. It was all he could do to complete the term without further incident, despite his growing infatuation with a violin student named Yosif Kotek, and escape to Europe, Modest and Vichy.

But the summer of 1876 started badly, and soon grew worse. What should have been a fortnight at Kondratiev's ended after three days, when his host unsurprisingly refused his demand that his still 'insubordinate' servant, another Alexey, be dismissed. 'Every night,' Tchaikovsky told Modest, 'he organized drinking parties in the servants' quarters, which made sleep quite impossible. I was at my wits' end.'

Seeking refuge at Kamenka, he found that Sasha had not yet returned from Geneva. After two weeks in the indifferent company of her husband, he set out in her direction, only to find that she had now herself embarked on the journey home. Hoping to meet her en route, he was not told that she had again changed her plans, and waited in vain for six days in Vienna, where a performance of Rossini's *William Tell* was the only source of light amid an encircling gloom. 'I'm fed up with Vienna, where to be alone for a few days is the height of boredom,' he wrote to Modest, before moving on to join him in Lyon. A last-minute delay in his travel plans, the reasons for which have vanished between the censors' scissors, would seem to indicate that he had found some young man to alleviate the gloom of Vienna. 'After all,' as he wrote pointedly to Modest, 'it seems such a waste to travel the world without getting to know the locals . . .'

Back in Moscow, Tchaikovsky had warmed to the Konradis. Now, in Lyon, he was delighted to find his potential wastrel of a brother fulfilling his end of their bargain. For the last couple of years, Tchaikovsky's copious letters to his brother had combined some generous encouragement of his literary ambitions with ever harsher indictments of his personal conduct. Above all, Tchaikovsky could not forgive what he saw of himself in Modest – the talented young man sure to be doomed by his sexuality. His unease over their shared inclinations seems to have increased during this trip, when the composer's undoubted love for his brother was given cause, for the first time, to blend with respect. The conscientiousness with which Modest cared for young 'Kolya' Konradi was, to Tchaikovsky, the making of his brother. 'There is an affection between master and pupil,' he told Anatoly, 'which I find very touching.' In the process, Kolya himself was becoming 'one of the creatures dearest to my heart in the entire world.'[12] It was a real wrench to move on after only three days, to keep his appointment with the healing powers of Vichy.

Here, within hours of his arrival, it became clear quite how profound was the depression which had been seeping into Tchaikovsky's psyche all year. An enforced period of inactivity was all that was needed to have it bubbling to the surface. On his very first day in Vichy, he wrote to Modest, so frustratingly nearby in Lyon: 'Such an awful, deadly melancholy has overcome me that I doubt I can stay here long. I can't tell you what an awful place this is, nor how total is the absence of anything at all here to divert or console me . . .'[13] This was compounded by having to get up at 5 a.m., which he hated, to take his place in the jostling queue for the precious mineral water, which he hated even more. The rest of the time was spent avoiding 'obnoxious' fellow Russians, while contemplating his acute loneliness, and his complete inability to concentrate on any work. On his second day there, by his own account, he 'dissolved into tears ten times'. In a letter to Anatoly, Vichy was 'accursed, loathsome, revolting! Everything here conspires to make my stay utterly intolerable!'[14]

Tchaikovsky's second letter to Modest was prefaced with a quotation from Dante's *La divina commedia*: 'Nessun maggior dolore\Che ricordarsi del tempo felice\Nella miseria' ('There is no greater misery than to remember happy times in sad').[15] It may have been meant as a touching reference to their few happy days together in Lyon, but to

Modest it signified more. To Tchaikovsky's doting brother, who had for some time been urging an orchestral work based on yet another doomed woman, Francesca da Rimini, this was a clear sign that the composer's depression could surely be cured by a prompt return to work. 'Why don't you try setting *Hamlet?*' he wrote helpfully. 'Or Francesca,' he went on. 'Or *Othello?* Or what about Lermontov's Tamar (. . . the one who drowns her lovers)?' Tchaikovsky was unmoved. His replies spoke only of his obsession with getting out of Vichy.

This he finally achieved after only eleven days, on the pretext of a sudden domestic crisis in Moscow, and by agreeing to take with him a large stock of Vichy water to complete his cure. At least he admitted to feeling better physically, though mentally he was in turmoil. Rushing straight to Modest's side in Lyon, he proposed a soothing trip through the south of France, taking Kolya and his governess along for the ride. All went smoothly via Avignon and Montpellier to the small coastal resort of Palavas-les-Flots, where all four members of the party were struck down by the local water. Tchaikovsky's distress at his own discomfiture was made much worse by the sight of poor little Kolya's. 'Kiss that divine little boy's hands for me,' he later wrote to Modest, 'and kiss his little feet too, but especially his divine little eyes. You've no idea how much I adore him. He is not out of my mind for a minute.'[16] To the 'divine' little Kolya himself, it was not enough for Tchaikovsky to sign his letters Uncle Pyotr, even Uncle Petya. 'I kiss you warmly a thousand million times' was how one letter ended, suggesting that even a nine-year-old deaf-mute boy was not beyond the range of the composer's sexual aspirations.[17]

Just as well, perhaps, that Tchaikovsky was due in Germany, to fulfil his last commission for the *Russian Register* with an account of Wagner's first Bayreuth Festival. En route, he confessed that he was spending money lavishly, on presents for his servants Mikhail and Alexey ('Alyosha'). 'What the hell. The main thing is to have a good time.'[18] Arriving in Bayreuth on 12 August, he was dismayed to find a bevy of Russian colleagues, including (Nikolay) Rubinstein, Laroche, Hubert, Cui and Albrecht, among the thousands who had been drawn there for the first complete performance of Wagner's *Ring* cycle. Gratified to find that his reputation had preceded him, Tchaikovsky enjoyed a cordial meeting with Liszt, but was somewhat put out when Wagner himself proved 'too busy' to receive him.

Given Tchaikovsky's ability to bear grudges, and to err on the side of harshness in his verdicts on fellow composers, Wagner's behaviour was scarcely conducive to a warm review of his mighty work. To be fair, Tchaikovsky had already declared his antipathy to Wagner's previous style, and *The Ring* was unlikely to have been any more to his taste.

He recognized the scale of Wagner's achievement, but the music itself left him cold. His first impression, he wrote after seeing *Das Rheingold*, was of 'bewildering confusion amid which one can occasionally catch fleeting glimpses of striking and beautiful detail.'

When the final performance had to be postponed by twenty-four hours, because of the illness of one of the singers, Tchaikovsky and Laroche took the chance of a carriage ride into the country, 'to enjoy the silence'. With the last chords of *Götterdämmerung*, Tchaikovsky declared that he felt as if he had been 'released from captivity'.

> *Nibelungen* may perhaps be a very great work, but there has certainly never been anything as long-winded and boring as this interminable piece. The accumulation of the most complex and arcane harmonies, the colourlessness of the vocal lines, the endlessly long dialogues, the absence of anything of the slightest interest or poetic quality in the subject-matter – all this stretches the nerves almost beyond endurance . . . Once music was intended to give audiences pleasure; now, thanks to Wagner, its purpose is to torture and exhaust them. There are, of course, some wonderful moments. But the cumulative effect is to bore people to death.[19]

Tchaikovsky could not get out of Bayreuth fast enough. Pausing briefly in Nuremberg to finish his articles for the *Russian Register*, and finding himself overwhelmed by homesickness, he cancelled plans for a few days at the seaside and headed straight for Verbovka and Sasha. Having arrived in a highly agitated state, he calmed down within days. As well as his sister and her growing brood, nearly all his family was there: his father and stepmother, his brothers Anatoly and Ippolit (the last of whom he had not seen for several years). Lamenting Modest's absence, he wrote to tell him that those summer days passed in 'great, great happiness'. Only his father's frailty worried him, aggravated by the recurring illnesses of Elizaveta Mikhailovna. Sasha, too, seemed rather too preoccupied for her brother's taste with the health of the local peasants, 'with whom she busies herself from morning to night'. It may not have been evident to his family, but Tchaikovsky's return to its bosom after a tense and irritable summer abroad had helped crystallize the dilemma which had seen him so depressed all year.

That July, while they had all been ill in the south of France, Modest had been very struck by his brother's solicitude to young Kolya while briefly *in loco parentis*. Thanks to the Vichy water in his baggage, the composer had been less afflicted by the dire effects of the local water than had his travelling companions; as Modest and the governess suffered, Tchaikovsky had taken charge of young Kolya Konradi, and had obviously loved every minute of it. 'There was a sudden chance for the deep, untapped vein of parental feeling in my brother's soul to show itself,' wrote the watching Modest. 'Nervous and irritable after his confinement at Vichy, still disturbed by the lingering depression which had gripped him there, Pyotr Ilyich was all attentiveness, patience and gentleness itself in his dealings with this deaf and dumb child, himself nervous and fidgety, and capable only with extreme difficulty of making himself understood.' The 'mutual adoration' between man and boy became even stronger. To Modest, this unexpected responsibility for a boy entirely dependent upon him, this sudden and brief assumption of the role of paterfamilias, 'showed Pyotr Ilyich a way out of the melancholy that was tormenting him, out of the loneliness which had so afflicted him in recent years.'[20]

Modest was right; but he had overlooked another consequence of these sudden longings in his brother's heart. Tchaikovsky had been well aware that his deep affection for Kolya Konradi was at least partly erotic. Now, before he revealed the true consequence of this episode, his distaste at his own nature found expression, not for the first time, in an onslaught on his brother – the mirror-image of himself which he had for years been trying to correct. It was almost as if Modest had become Dr Jekyll to his own Mr Hyde. To be tutor to so charming a child, and a homosexual, Tchaikovsky wrote to his brother, was a dangerous combination.

Amid the family life at Kamenka so central to his own peace of mind – so indispensable, indeed, to his mental stability – the composer had evidently been reflecting upon the nature of his own feelings for Kolya. An uneasy mix of genuine avuncular affection and guilty sexual desire had been brought into sharp focus by the sudden intensity of his brief spell as a surrogate father. What if the governess had not been present to keep him and Modest on their best behaviour? To what 'unnatural' temptations might they not have succumbed, especially with a child unable to report them to any authorities, parental or worse?

Shuddering at the thought, Tchaikovsky fired off another salvo to Modest about the need to shed his homosexuality and become 'as other men'. What made it all worse was his brother's evident gift as a special tutor; Tchaikovsky's parting sight of Modest walking away on the beach in France, hand in hand with young Kolya, was an image which had lingered touchingly in the composer's mind. Pending any success as a writer, Modest had found a vocation which brought out the best in his hitherto shiftless character; to make the most of it, and to avoid disaster, it was imperative in Tchaikovsky's eyes that his brother either suppress or alter his sexual proclivities.

Here amid his family, Tchaikovsky saw all this more clearly than ever. Moved by his longing for a family of his own, and by the contradiction at the heart of his brother's way of life, he reached a decision which would astonish all who knew him, and bring him within a year to the brink of ruin.

To Tchaikovsky himself, at that moment, it was a move which would solve his own problems, and usefully concentrate Modest's mind. With due solemnity, after just one week's reflection at Sasha's, he thus wrote to his brother: 'I am now entering a very critical period in my own life. When I get the chance, I shall explain it all to you in greater detail. For now, I shall say just one thing: "I have decided to get married."'[21]

If a way with melody and a gift for orchestration rank high among Tchaikovsky's hallmarks, they are run a close third by his almost lyrical capacity for self-delusion. From mere moodiness via misanthropy to melancholia, he had for nearly twenty years devised a variety of ways of disguising his true problems – effective enough, in both the short and the long run, to hide them more from himself than from others. Now, at the age of thirty-six, the rising composer was embarked upon a course which all who knew him could foresee ending in disaster – for him, certainly, and probably also for whatever unhappy woman he chose to be his bride.

Not until it was too late did those friends make their views known. To be fair to them, Tchaikovsky did not give them much chance. To be fair to him, he thought that he was acting from noble instincts. And to be fair to her – the hapless one, accepted almost at random – she threw herself at him with all the feminine guile at her command.

Which was not much. But Tchaikovsky was no more equipped to recognize feminine guile than he was to become any kind of husband. As blind spots go, his were almost wilfully self-destructive. Even while explaining to Modest his motives for getting married, he was persuading himself quite as much as his brother that he was acting out of the purest altruism. 'It is inevitable that I must do this,' he wrote, 'not only for myself, but for you and Tolya, and for Sasha, and for everyone I love. But for *you* especially! You, Modya, should also think seriously about doing the same thing . . .'

It was not just a momentary whim, of which he would soon think better. Back in Moscow three weeks later, without waiting for Modest's response, Tchaikovsky reaffirmed his intentions – and his instructions to Modest – explaining that he had been 'doing a lot of thinking' in the two months since they had parted in France.

The upshot of all this hard thinking is that I have made a firm decision, starting today, to enter into lawful matrimony with anyone prepared to have me. It seems to me that our *inclinations* are the biggest and most insurmountable obstacle to our happiness, and that we must fight against our natures with all our strength.

This bizarre promise is followed by what sounds very much like a threat:

I love you very much, I love Kolya very much, and for both your sakes I earnestly hope that you are never parted. But you can stay together only on one condition: that you no longer remain *what you are now*.

This was, Tchaikovsky went on, not just 'to silence the gossips' – or, in his own memorable French euphemism, for the sake of *'qu'en dira-t-on'*. It was also 'for you yourself, for your peace of mind.' After yet another passage lost to the censors, Tchaikovsky continues:

You say that it is difficult, at your age, to conquer your passions. To this I say that it is easier, at your age, to turn your tastes in a different direction. In this, I would think, your religious inclinations should prove a strong support.

To warn his brother against the perils of being a homosexual tutor, while he himself enjoyed daily dealing with pupils at the Conservatoire, may have smacked of hypocrisy even to Tchaikovsky himself. For his own part, he repeated, 'I shall do everything within my power to marry this very year. If I should lack the courage to go through with it, I shall anyway abandon for ever my previous habits, and shall endeavour to be numbered no more among the company . . . [of homosexuals].'

'I think of nothing', he concluded, 'but ridding myself of all pernicious passions.'[22] In the interim, of course, he did no such thing. While expressing sudden doubts about the wisdom of marriage in letters to Anatoly, he was soon extolling the virtues of bachelor life to Modest, and confessing to a spate of homosexual adventures. 'It is so wonderfully tranquil – I am *almost* happy! – to come home in the evenings to my small, cosy, peaceful apartment, and settle down to a good book. In moments like these I probably hate as much as you do that unknown, beautiful woman who will force me to change my habits and my friends . . . I am so set in my ways – and my *tastes* – that it is simply impossible just to cast them off like an old glove. Besides, willpower is not one of my stronger points. Since my last letters to you I have already given way some three times to my natural compulsions . . .'

It was less than a month since those 'last letters'. Whatever vows he might make, Tchaikovsky told his brother, 'it is impossible to fight one's weaknesses.' In a crucial passage he attempts to convey to Modest the agonies of 'embarrassing' loved ones, and accepting their 'forgiveness' for his 'sins':

> There are some who cannot despise me for my vices simply because they began to love me before coming to suspect that I am in truth a man with a lost reputation. This applies, for instance, to *Sasha*! I know that she guesses *everything* and *forgives* everything. This is how I am treated by very many of those whom I love or respect. Can you really believe that I am anything other than oppressed by the knowledge that *they pity and forgive me*, when in fact I am guilty of nothing! And is it not a terrible thought that those who love me can sometimes be *ashamed* of me! All this, you see, has happened a hundred times before and will happen a hundred times again . . .

'In a word,' he concluded, the purpose of marriage (or 'an open affair with a woman') was 'to shut the mouths of various contemptible creatures whose opinions don't bother me at all, but can cause pain to my loved ones.'[23]

Amid these torments, Tchaikovsky remained as musically productive as ever, dashing off in five days that October a March that would continue to stir audiences a century later, while continuing work on a romantic overture about yet another fallen woman.

Although no political animal, as he had shown at that 1866 performance of *A Life for the Tsar*, even Tchaikovsky had been stirred ten years later when Turkish massacres of Christians in the Balkans led to a declaration of war by Montenegro and Serbia. With Russian volunteers flocking to their side against the Turks, and the whole nation roused by such attacks on its fellow Slavs, the autumn saw Russia itself on the brink of being drawn into the conflict. The possibility of war drew a rare political comment from Tchaikovsky that autumn: 'It is frightening but also pleasing that our beloved country is ready at last to give proof of her character.'[24] A week later, he happened to be visiting a female acquaintance when her son – 'a pleasant, intelligent young man' – announced that he had enlisted to fight in Serbia. 'His mother fell down in a faint, and lay there a long time incapable of speech. I was very shaken by the scene . . .'[25]

It was soon after this incident that Nikolay Rubinstein, far more of a political activist, asked Tchaikovsky to write a new piece for a RMS concert in support of the charity aiding the Balkan war victims and equipping Russian volunteers. In the first week of October, in just five days, he had written the *Marche Slave* (originally known as the Serbo-Russian March[26]). Unabashedly stirring, using Serbian folk tunes to offset its patriotic bombast, the March was received with rapture at its RMS première on 17 November. 'The uproar that broke out in the hall,' according to one member of the audience, 'was beyond description. The entire audience was on its feet, many standing on their seats and crying *Bravo!* or *Hurrah!*. The March had to be repeated, after which the pandemonium began again . . . It was one of the most stirring moments of 1876. Many of the audience were in tears.'[27] Like Elgar's Pomp and Circumstance March No. l, alias *Land of Hope and Glory*, Tchaikovsky's *Marche Slave* gave more pleasure to audiences than to its composer, uneasily aware that its musical qualities were but a small factor in its popular success. 'Effective' was the highest praise Tchaikovsky himself could find for it.

In three weeks of October, between the composition and performance of the March, he had also written a piece much closer to his heart, of considerably more substance, and directly informed by the growing turmoil in his own private life. It was on the train from Palavas to Paris, musing over the sight of Modest and Kolya on the beach, that Tchaikovsky had first read the fifth canto of Dante's *Inferno*, with its tragic tale of Francesca da Rimini, killed by her hunchback husband for loving his brother, and condemned to eternal orbit in the second circle of Hell. From that moment he had been 'aflame' with desire to write something about Dante's tragic heroine. After rejecting an opera libretto drafted by Modest (who reworked it, after his brother's death, for Rachmaninov), Tchaikovsky decided on a symphonic fantasia on the model of his *Romeo and Juliet*. With its equally powerful love theme (the central *andante cantabile non troppo*), and its swirling evocation of the whirlwinds of hell, *Francesca*'s first St Petersburg performance in March 1878 was to prove Tchaikovsky's greatest public success to date.

But first he had to enter his own private hell, in which he too would be condemned to spin for the rest of his mortal days. In the turbulent year ahead, the reluctant homosexual in search of a bride would adopt as his own spiritual epitaph Dante's famous lines on Francesca:

> *Nessun maggior dolore*
> *Che ricordarsi del tempo felice*
> *Nella miseria.*

# PART III

---

## *1877–78*
## CRISIS

*It seems to me that I am now irretrievably lost*

# CHAPTER VII

## 'To silence the gossips'

IN FEW LIVES CAN A PRECISE MOMENT BE DEFINED WHEN THE FORWARD movement from birth clearly shifts to a long but inevitable descent into death. In Tchaikovsky's case, that moment certainly came in May 1877, when he received an unexpected letter from a former student of the Moscow Conservatoire named Antonina Milyukova.

The year had begun in comparative calm, after a resplendent coda to 1876. At a private Conservatoire soirée in December, Tchaikovsky sat next to the guest of honour: his literary hero since his youth, the great Tolstoy. During the *andante cantabile* of his First String Quartet, the composer noticed that tears were streaming down the writer's face. Years later, and for the rest of his life, he would recall it as his proudest professional moment. Twice that week Tolstoy called on Tchaikovsky at his apartment, and stayed to talk all evening, later writing to him of the concert that he had 'never enjoyed so rich a reward for my literary labours as that wonderful evening.' Tchaikovsky felt 'extraordinarily proud and flattered', he told his sister, by Tolstoy's interest in him. 'His ideal personality has quite enchanted me.'[1]

Now, with work well advanced on his Fourth Symphony, the composer could allow himself to embark on his most ambitious project yet: an opera of Pushkin's masterpiece, *Eugene Onegin*, suggested to him by the operatic contralto Elizaveta Andreyevna Lavrovskaya. At first he thought it a 'crazy' idea.

Then, during dinner on my own at an inn, I fell to brooding about it, began to see the possibilities, got quite carried away and by the end of the meal was determined to take it on. I rushed off in search of a copy, found one with some difficulty, raced home, read it through with rapture and passed a totally sleepless night – the reward for which was the scenario of a wonderful opera on Pushkin's text.[2]

His collaborator on the libretto was Konstantin Shilovsky, brother of the wayward Vladimir, whose sudden marriage now clouded his long and intimate relationship with the composer. For all the satisfactions of Tchaikovsky's work, the realities of his day-to-day life were again crowding in to shoulder them aside. 'Life is horribly empty, boring, *trivial*,' he wrote to a bisexual acquaintance. 'I've been thinking about marriage, or a stable union of *some* sort.'[3]

Into the midst of this gathering gloom came a dramatic profession of undying love. 'It was a longish letter containing a declaration of love for me,' Tchaikovsky later told Kashkin, 'signed by one A. Milyukova, who said she had fallen in love with me some years before when she was a student at the Conservatoire.'[4]

Absorbed in planning *Onegin*, the composer set the letter aside, returning to it only some days later amid a pile of other correspondence. Although his reply is lost, it was evidently somewhat evasive, listing his own 'shortcomings' and gently counselling the girl to 'master her feelings' before she got hurt. It was scarcely, to be sure, the reply of a man openly intent on marriage who had just received what amounted to a proposal. Milyukova's response made this clear:

> It is time, you tell me, to master my feelings. Although you will not see
> me, I comfort myself with the thought that you are now at least in the
> same city as I am, whereas in a month, perhaps less, you will probably
> be gone, and God knows whether I shall ever be fortunate enough to
> see you, as I too plan to leave Moscow. But wherever either of us
> may be, I shall never be able to forget you or master my love for you.
> What appealed to me in you I can no longer see in any other man.
> After you, in short, I no longer wish even to look at another man.[5]

This was Antonina at her most controlled. When her messenger returned empty-handed, with news that the composer had already left town (to work on *Onegin* with Shilovsky at Glebovo), she lost what self-restraint she possessed and dashed off another, much longer letter, this time threatening suicide in the face of Tchaikovsky's apparent indifference:

I've been in agony for a whole week, Pyotr Ilyich, unsure whether or not to write to you. I can tell that you have already begun to find my letters tiresome. But would you really break off this correspondence without even seeing me once? No, surely you cannot be so cruel. Do you take me, perhaps, for a tease, or a gullible young thing, that you attach no weight to my words? How can I convince you that every word I write is true, that I could never lie about something like this?

Since your letter I love you twice as much. What you may think to be your faults mean nothing to me. If you were perfect, I would perhaps not be so in love with you. As it is, I am dying of longing for you. I burn with desire to see you, to sit and talk with you, though I am also terrified that I would be struck dumb. There is no human failing that would cause me to fall out of love with you . . .

All day I stay at home, pacing the room from corner to corner like a lunatic, thinking only of the moment I shall see you, and throw myself on your neck, smothering you with kisses. But what right have I to make such assumptions? Perhaps you do indeed think I am too forward . . . Let me assure you that I am a respectable and honest woman in all senses of the word, and that there is nothing about myself I would wish to hide from you. My first kiss will be the one I give to you, and to no-one else in this world.

Farewell, my beloved. Do not try any more to put me off you, because you are wasting your time. I cannot live without you, so perhaps I shall soon kill myself. Let me see you and kiss you so that I can remember that kiss in the other world.

Farewell. Yours forever, A.M.[6]

It was the simple romantic force of Tatyana's love letter to Eugene Onegin, cruelly spurned by the haughty young gallant, which had first drawn Tchaikovsky to Pushkin's masterpiece as an operatic subject: 'One strong dramatic theme: love, intimacy.' In the absence, as yet, of a libretto, it was thus with Tatyana's 'Letter Song' that he had begun his work on the score. So rapt did he become, succumbing to 'an invincible spiritual need to write the letter music,' that he 'forgot all about Miss Milyukova'. Worse, he 'lost her letter – or, perhaps, hid it so well that I could not find it, and remembered it only when, some time later, I received a second.'[7]

Completely immersed in his work, in his own words, Tchaikovsky 'identified with Tatyana so thoroughly that she became a living person to me, as real as everything around her. I loved Tatyana, and I was furiously angry with Onegin, who seemed to me a cold and heartless cad.' It was at this point, evidently, that Antonina's second letter arrived.

'She complained bitterly that she had received no reply to her first, adding that if this letter too met with the same fate, there would be nothing left for her to do but commit suicide.'

Now, in Tchaikovsky's mind, Antonina took on Tatyana's poignantly heroic status, while he himself was no better than Onegin. 'Indeed, it seemed to me that I had behaved even more shabbily than Onegin. I grew fearfully angry with myself for the heartless way in which I had treated this girl who was in love with me.' The second letter contained an invitation to visit her. 'I set forth at once, to make her acquaintance.'[8]

This first meeting between Tchaikovsky and his admirer took place on 1 June. At their second, a day or two later, the composer proposed marriage. When she accepted, he immediately knew he had made the most cataclysmic mistake. 'I cannot describe the appalling horrors I went through over the next few days.'

How had Tchaikovsky so precipitously wrought such disaster upon himself? His own answer, characteristically, was to blame Fate. 'It seemed to me that some force of fate was driving me towards this girl,' he explained a month later. 'When first we met, I again made it clear to her that I felt for her nothing but sympathy and gratitude for her love. After leaving, however, I began to think I had behaved thoughtlessly. If I did not wish to encourage her feelings, why had I gone to see her? And where would it all lead? From her second letter I could only conclude that, having taken this step, were I now to reject her, I would be making her desperately unhappy, and driving her to a tragic end.'[9]

Back home, making a list of pros and cons, and well aware of his recent declaration to various family members that he intended to marry, Tchaikovsky reflected what pleasure the match would give his eighty-two-year-old father. The pleasure it would also afford his other relatives, or so he persuaded himself, was about as genuine as his own. Those closest to him knew as well as he did why his plans for marriage were so misconceived; yet he had now landed himself on the horns of a dangerous dilemma: 'To preserve my own freedom at the cost of this girl's death (and *death* is not an idle word here; she does indeed love me to distraction)? Or to *marry*?' He was 'obliged', in his own cold phrase, 'to choose the latter option'.[10]

In the same breath as his proposal of marriage, he told Antonina that he did not love her. But he pledged, whatever might befall them, to be her 'staunch and grateful friend'. He gave her a candid self-assessment – 'my irritability, my moodiness, my anti-social nature' – and he told her of his uncertain financial circumstances. 'Then I asked her whether she wanted to be my wife.' The poor wretch leapt at the chance. 'Of course, she answered in the affirmative.'

The one 'shortcoming' Tchaikovsky omitted to mention was, of course, the secret of his sexuality. Even from himself he continued to conceal the true cause of his unease:

> After living thirty-seven years with an innate aversion to marriage, it is very distressing to be drawn by force of circumstance into the role of a *bridegroom*, who, moreover, is not in the least attracted to his bride. I must now alter my entire way of life. I must devote myself to the well-being and contentment of this other person whose fate is now conjoined with mine. All this is not going to be easy for a bachelor accustomed to putting himself first.[11]

His first decision did not bode well. It was 'to go off to the country for a month, as planned,' leaving his bride-to-be to fend for herself while her groom took stock of his situation (and got on with composing *Onegin*). 'It will give me a chance to contemplate changing my ways, to grow used to accepting my future with equanimity.' At Konstantin Shilovsky's estate, while working on the libretto of *Onegin*, Tchaikovsky tried to reconcile himself to his decision. He even managed, by some country casuistry, to look on the bright side. 'I know from long experience how often some unknown, menacing prospect can eventually prove a blessing in disguise, just as hard work towards some prospect of happiness can end in disillusion. Well, let things turn out as they may!'[12]

At twenty-eight, Antonina Ivanovna Milyukova was already past the age at which most girls of the day were married. When Tchaikovsky made discreet enquiries about her, all he could elicit was 'an unprintable profanity'[13] from his Conservatoire colleague Eduard Langer, who had taught her piano. A professional seamstress before becoming a music student, she had not seen out the Conservatoire course. From a lack of either talent or money, probably both, she had dropped out in the summer of 1875, two years before she first wrote to Tchaikovsky. How she was earning her living at the time is unknown, as is much else about Antonina's early life (though recent suggestions that she had already re-sorted to prostitution are unsupported by any documentary evidence).

He makes no mention of it in any account of his dealings with her – he may, indeed, genuinely not have realized – but the composer had in fact known Antonina for some years before he received that fateful first letter. They first chanced to meet around 1865, at the Moscow home (now the site of a McDonald's restaurant) of a mutual friend: her brother's sister-in-law, Anastasia Khvostova, a well-known singer and a friend of the visiting Apukhtin.[14] The composer, it seems fair to assume, may well have forgotten the occasion, or at least the face of his friend's sixteen-year-old relative; but Antonina, by contrast, appears to have held a torch for him from that moment. In her own, little-known recollections, she speaks of regular encounters with him around the Conservatoire during her student days in the early 1870s. 'I was always thrilled to see him, and he was very kind to me, even affectionate . . .' Given his indifference to female students, it can be believed that the composer knew Milyukova by sight, if not by name; again, however, he shows no signs of recognition in his own account of that 'first' meeting, the day before he proposed. 'For more than four years,' Antonina confesses, 'I had loved him secretly.' Like a superstitious schoolgirl, she swore an oath that if she went every day for six weeks to pray at a particular Moscow chapel, she would win him. 'Whatever the weather, I went there without fail . . . kneeled in the rain and snow and prayed fervently.'[15]

She is certainly embroidering, forty years on, when she goes on to say: 'I could easily tell that he liked me, but was too shy ever to have proposed.' But Antonina Milyukova was not entirely the crazed half-wit depicted by Modest, and thus by most subsequent chroniclers of her sad saga. She was a simpleton – even, perhaps, 'an incarnation of the commonplace', as she has recently been dismissed[16] – but the responsibility for the ensuing tragedy was much more Tchaikovsky's than hers. Deluded by Modest's undisguised animosity towards Antonina (who remained a living threat to his dead brother's reputation even as he was writing his biography), twentieth-century Tchaikovsky studies have tended to blame the failure of his marriage on his choice of the wrong woman. In truth, Antonina was as much the right woman for Tchaikovsky as any other. It was marriage which was the wrong institution.

By choosing the adoring Antonina, as is clear between the lines of his letters to Modest, he thought he would secure not merely a compliant wife, to run an efficient household for him, but a wife who would afford him a respectable exterior in society while turning a blind eye to his sex life. By her own account, he told her that he had never loved any woman, and felt he was already 'too old to fall passionately in love'. But she, Antonina, was the first woman of whom he could say that he 'liked her very much'. If she could accept a 'quiet, calm kind of love – the love of a brother', then he would be hers. 'Of course,' she recalled unequivocally, 'I agreed to all his conditions.' After chatting together rather awkwardly for a while, in the wake of his proposal, the composer 'very charmingly' offered his cheek as he took his leave of her. 'I threw my arms', she tell us, 'around his neck. I shall never forget that kiss. He then left at once.'

If Tchaikovsky believed he had made his sexual preferences clear in the phrase 'the love of a brother', he was deceiving himself as much as his bride-to-be. No wonder she took the news of his departure to the country with equanimity; he was, after all, going to work on his opera *Eugene Onegin* – and to Antonina, to her dying day, this was 'the best of his operas', because it was 'based on our love.'

> He himself is Onegin, and I am Tatyana His previous and subsequent operas are not fired by love. They are cold and scrappy. They have no consistency. *Onegin* is the only one of his operas that is good from start to finish.[17]

From his country retreat at Glebovo, 'this wonderful, quiet, sweet, beloved corner of the world,' Tchaikovsky wrote to Modest that the opera was progressing well. He had an entire, separate house at his disposal, and saw no-one during his working hours except his servant Alexey. He described in detail his daily routine, his morning and evening strolls, his complete absorption in his work. The one thing he did not mention in his flow of letters to any of his friends or relatives, not even to Modest, was his decision to marry Antonina. The frequent mentions of Alexey, and of visits to Moscow to see his young violinist friend, Yosif Kotek, imply rather that his private life was continuing much as normal. Perhaps, as has been suggested, Tchaikovsky even envisaged a future ménage like that of his married friend Kondratiev, 'with his wife tolerating a male servant in the role of her husband's lover.'[18] Perhaps he thought she would also tolerate ex-pupils other than herself sharing his bed. Or perhaps he simply did not think about her at all.

Not until early July, less than two weeks before his wedding day, did he finally write to inform his 'dear and beloved' father of his plans:

> Your son Pyotr has decided to get married. As he does not wish to do this without your approval, he begs that you give him your blessing for his new life. I am marrying a young woman named Antonina Ivanovna Milyukova. She is poor, but she is a decent and honest girl who loves me very much. You know, my dear Papa, that it is not without careful thought that a man of my age decides to wed. So you must not worry about me. I am sure that my wife-to-be will do everything she can to make my life calm and happy. I beg you not to mention this for the moment to anyone except Lizaveta Mikhailovna. I shall of course be writing to Sasha and my brothers myself.[19]

Ilya Petrovich was of course delighted with this news from his 'most beautiful' son, through whom he spoke directly to Antonina in his reply: 'My dear Antonina Ivanovna, as of yesterday I ask permission to call you my God-given daughter. Love your chosen bridegroom and husband. He is truly worthy of it.' Addressing his son again, he asked to be informed of the date of the wedding, so that he might come, despite his age, to offer his blessing in person. Tchaikovsky evidently wanted no such thing. He knew that his sister and brothers would try to talk him out of it; and he knew in his heart they would be right. Not until the very last minute – 17 July, the day before the appointed date – did he inform Sasha, making his feelings for his bride-to-be pretty clear in the process.

> I won't tell you much about her, apart from the fact that she is thoroughly respectable and desperately in love with me, as I still don't really know her very well . . . And I shan't be bringing her to see you at Kamenka until I get over my sense of shock that my nieces will call her 'Auntie'. As yet it seems to me audacious of her to have become the aunt of your children, whom I love more than any other children in the world.[20]

His sister's reply acknowledges the fact that, by the time she received his letter, the dread deed would already have been done.

> By now you are married, which means there is now another creature for me to love, so I shall not pass on all I have felt over these past few days. May God grant you happiness. If you wish to make me happy, and set my mind at rest, bring your wife to stay. I want to get to know her, so I can love the person lucky enough to have become your lifelong companion.[21]

Modest, too, was left to the last minute. Even if he had decided to attend the wedding – which was, to say the least, unpredictable – his brother left him no chance. This time, Tchaikovsky acknowledged as much in his letter: 'By the time you receive this, I will already be married. I made up my mind at the end of May, but have since kept my decision secret so as not to trouble you and all my loved ones with doubt and uncertainty until the deed was done.' That he had spent the intervening month 'quietly and happily' at Glebovo, where he had already written two-thirds of *Onegin*, Tchaikovsky offered as proof that he was entering into matrimony 'calmly and rationally'. Modest, naturally, was deeply offended at this high-handedness from his adored older brother – the more so because his twin Anatoly *was* invited to the wedding, and did indeed attend.

Where Sasha had been fussing that Tchaikovsky might marry the wrong woman, and Modest arguing that any woman was the wrong one to marry, Anatoly was a rock of stability who could be relied upon not to shake his brother's already fragile self-confidence about the course upon which he was embarked. To Anatoly, therefore, Tchaikovsky adopted a different approach – significant for its lack of any warm remarks about Antonina, whom he depicted more as an accomplice, even a victim, than a partner. 'I am marrying a girl who is not particularly young, but utterly respectable, and who has one main quality: she is in love with me like a cat.'[22] Antonina, in other words, was exploitable.

He told none of his other friends – Kashkin or Rubinstein, Laroche or Albrecht – in advance of the ceremony. Only on the morning of his wedding did he write to break the news to Vladimir Shilovsky. As Tchaikovsky had planned, Anatoly and Kotek were the only witnesses at the hugger-mugger ceremony which took place at St George's Church on Moscow's Malaya Nikitskaya Street, on 18 July 1877. Things got off to an inauspicious start when the happy couple realized they had both forgotten to bring the red satin cloth upon which they were supposed to stand while taking their vows. Someone was sent to fetch one, but it did not arrive until the ceremony was all but over. In the meantime, Tchaikovsky stood on Anatoly's white silk handkerchief, leaving his bride to stand on the bare floor.

In subsequent accounts of the proceedings, the composer praises the 'artistic beauty' with which the service was conducted by his chosen priest, Dmitry Razumovsky, also Professor of the History of Church Music at the Conservatoire, and thus a professional colleague. Otherwise, the groom told Kashkin, he spent the entire service 'in pretty much of a daze'. He felt 'outside of it all, quite uninvolved' until the priest invited him, at the end of the service, to exchange kisses with the bride. 'At this point I felt a stab of pain through my heart, and such anxiety gripped me that I began to weep.' Clearly sensing his brother's distress, Anatoly rushed to his side to offer moral support.[23]

By the bride's own account, the wedding breakfast was more like a wake. After the service, Tchaikovsky went straight back to his bachelor apartment, leaving Anatoly to welcome his bride to the reception at the Hermitage Hotel. 'A great many dishes of all sorts had been prepared,' she recalled, 'but I scarcely touched a thing. Already I felt cold from fearful foreboding that terrible events lay ahead. Later, my cousin told me that the atmosphere was so cold it had been more like a funeral.'[24]

After a token appearance at the dinner Tchaikovsky again returned to his apartment, without his bride. They met up again at 7 p.m. at the railway station, where they boarded the train to St Petersburg. Before it had even left the station, Tchaikovsky felt 'fit to scream from [trying to hide] the sobs that were suffocating me.' He also felt obliged to engage his bride in conversation 'at least as far as Klin' – some sixty miles – in order to 'win the right to settle back in my own seat and be left alone in the darkness'.[25]

But his plan was thwarted by the unexpected arrival in the carriage, after the train's second stop, of his old schoolfriend Prince Meshchersky. The two men left Antonina alone as Tchaikovsky, amid copious tears, poured out his sorrows. Full of tender sympathy, Meshchersky managed to calm him down – to the extent that Tchaikovsky was able to return to Antonina, after the train had passed Klin, feeling 'much restored'. Meshchersky arranged the couple a sleeping compartment, with the result that the composer was able to report that he had 'slept like a log'.

This account of the journey comes from a letter Tchaikovsky wrote to Anatoly the following day, on his arrival in St Petersburg. Its contents appear to suggest that Modest's twin brother was entirely privy to Tchaikovsky's miseries, that he had known the full extent of his sufferings on his wedding day:

> After such a terrible day as 6 [18] July, after all that interminable moral torture, it is hard to make a swift recovery. But all adversity has a positive side: although I suffered intolerably, seeing so clearly your concern for me, your presence nevertheless enabled me to endure my sufferings with some fortitude . . . Tell me, if you please, what meaning is there to all our trials, failures and ordeals alongside the force of my love for you and yours for me? Whatever the future may hold, I take heart that your love will always offer me support and solace.[26]

Having somehow managed to survive the rest of the journey, Tchaikovsky's first act on reaching St Petersburg was to contact Kotek about Anatoly's well-being. This sharing of his suffering was now a way of emphasizing as much as expiating it. Tchaikovsky needed to know that his brother was relaxed and happy, or so he told him, before he could begin to gauge his own peace of mind.

Through it all, Antonina seems to have remained oblivious to her husband's torments. This was a great relief to him. 'Even now she seems quite content,' he reported to Anatoly. *'Elle n'est pas difficile.* She agrees with everything I say, and is happy with whatever I arrange.' Her equanimity appears to have survived even the unseasonably foul weather in the capital, where the newly-weds spent their first evening at a concert, leaving at the interval to return to their suite at the Europa Hotel. There followed what appears to have been a momentous attempt (*pace* the train) at a wedding night.

From Tchaikovsky's account to Anatoly, it seems clear that Antonina must have made some moves towards an attempted consummation of the marriage. We have her husband's word for it that she became very upset about something, and that he had to 'beg her to calm down' before taking his customary sleeping draught, valerian, and retiring on his own for the night. First, however, he evidently felt the need for a long heart-to-heart, 'to clarify further the precise nature of our relationship'. Whatever disappointment she may have been feeling, Antonina remained compliant. *'She agreed whole-heartedly to all my conditions,'* he reported, underlining as he went, *'and says she will never want more than to love me and take care of me.'* The negotiations concluded, he slept 'the sleep of the dead'.

Next day, he further confided to Anatoly that all might yet work out according to plan. There was no need for the usual Tchaikovsky pessimism. 'She may be a very *limited* human being, but even that's to my advantage. A wife of any intelligence might have me afraid of her. With this one, I am so far ahead of her, so superior in every way, that there is no chance of that!'

These were words he would live to regret. But during those first few days, as he later told Kashkin, his main worry was how little he and his wife seemed to have in common. Antonina did 'her level best to be a good wife', but she showed 'no interest at all in everything I hold most dear'. She was capable of mustering an enthusiastic response 'only to the most trivial things'. When it came to music – as Kashkin was to discover for himself, when he later took pity on Antonina and gave her piano lessons – she showed no taste, less appreciation and very little interest.

But Tchaikovsky's most shattering discovery was that his wife did not know a single note of his own music. In this, with some justice, he felt grievously betrayed. Antonina had not bothered to attend any of the RMS concerts at which she might have caught a glimpse (let alone heard the music) of the man with whom she claimed to have been 'in love for four years'. Nor did she seem to think her oversight of much significance.[27]

This desperate revelation seems to have rendered Tchaikovsky speechless. It was certainly where the relationship, if it had ever begun, ended. Already, when alone with Antonina, he began to sense that terminal feeling of claustrophobia familiar to all victims of failing marriages. Friends like Laroche were dragooned into taking him out to dinner, even prevailed upon to offer him their own homes as a sanctuary in which to escape from his wife. Upon chance meetings with other friends or relatives, in the streets or parks of the capital, he could not bring himself to introduce the woman at his side as his wife. Even when he took Antonina to see his father and stepmother, watching with relief as Ilya Petrovich predictably fussed over his new daughter-in-law, he thought he saw tears of sympathy in his stepmother's eyes. 'This sweet and perceptive woman must have guessed that I was living through the most difficult and painful days of my life.'

Between the lines of her own (none too reliable) recollections, which otherwise speak very warmly of Tchaikovsky, even Antonina comes close to admitting that their honeymoon had its problems. 'He liked women in simple dark dresses, but it was summer and I always wore light dresses . . . I bought some false coral [jewellery] and he got angry that his wife should be seen in false coral . . . We went to have our photograph taken together, and he complained that everyone was always pestering him to let them take his photo; now, thanks to me, he was going to have to pay . . .'[28]

Five days after the wedding, Tchaikovsky was reduced to desperate remedies:

> Physically, my wife has become *totally repugnant* to me . . . Yesterday morning, while she was taking a bath, I went to mass at St Isaac's Cathedral. I was feeling an urgent need to pray.[29]

Even the power of prayer, however, could not redeem his profound disillusion with his wife – in his eyes, now, this gauche and ignorant creature. Two days later, with the marriage only a week old, he was clearly approaching crisis point. 'Yesterday', he told Anatoly, 'was probably the most painful of all since [my wedding day]. In the morning I concluded that my life was irreparably ruined, and suffered a bout of the bleakest despair. By three, quite a crowd had come to visit us: Nikolay Rubinstein, his sister Sofia, Malozemova, Karl Davidov, Ivanov, Bessel, Laroche. We all dined together.' He felt unable to hide his true feelings from his friends. 'It was terrible, Tolichka, *terrible, terrible, terrible*. I have reached a real crisis. If it weren't for my love for you, and the comfort that others too continue to love me through these *intolerable spiritual agonies*, I might already be finished – either dead or just gone mad.'[30]

At Tchaikovsky's insistence, the newly-weds returned to Moscow the next day. Apart from anything else, he had run out of money, and needed to borrow some funds to set up house. Soon there followed the ritual excursion to meet his mother-in-law, which only added to his woes, as he found in her 'none of the loving qualities which I had been led to believe she possessed'. Indeed, he disliked Antonina's entire family – though by now, perhaps, predisposed to do so.

He chose this scene as the way to break to his sister the news that his marriage was not all wine and roses. Not until two weeks after the wedding, when Anatoly and Modest had long been put in the picture, did Sasha receive the news that her brother 'would be lying if I said I was swimming in an ocean of ecstasy'. There followed the usual platitudes about Antonina 'doing everything possible to make me happy', being 'content with her lot', regretting nothing, and 'doing everything in her power to show that her whole life revolves around me.'

If he thought he was reassuring Sasha, Tchaikovsky's angst shows through all too clearly in what might otherwise have been portrayed as a routine inspection by his new in-laws. 'Lord, what an unpleasant family!' he told his sister.

> After three days with them in the country, I begin to see that everything I can't stand in my wife derives from her belonging to a completely weird family, where the mother was always arguing with the father – and now, after his death, does not hesitate to malign his memory in every way possible. It's a family in which the mother *hates* (!!!) some of her own children, in which the sisters are constantly squabbling, in which the only son has completely fallen out with his mother and all his sisters, etc etc![31]

Back in Moscow, Tchaikovsky sought refuge in the bottle, desperate for the 'blissful moments of oblivion' alcohol could afford him as he began to consider his alternative escape-routes. 'I need to be alone', he confided to Konstantin Shilovsky, 'to take stock of my situation objectively, and make a judgement as to the wisdom or foolishness of the decision I made.'

As news of his marriage gradually reached Conservatoire friends and colleagues, well aware of his sexual tastes, they reacted with a mixture of puzzlement and concern. 'The news was so unexpected, so bizarre, that at first I did not believe it,' said Kashkin. 'Moscow was always full of wild rumours.' When Albrecht confirmed that the rumours were true, Kashkin worried not so much about the fact of Tchaikovsky's marriage – he was another confidant with whom the composer had occasionally discussed the notion – as about the secrecy which seemed to surround it. Even now he had returned to Moscow, Tchaikovsky kept his wife hidden away, and introduced her to no-one. His constant companion was young Kotek, with whom he also shared the full extent of his misery. 'I cannot begin to tell you', he wrote to a mutual friend, 'how much brotherly support he has shown me. He is a good man in every sense of the word.'[32]

During their week away, Antonina had been cheated out of some money supposedly due for the sale of a forest inherited from her father. As the couple sought out cheaper lodgings, Tchaikovsky's finances became so stretched that he was obliged to fire the older Sofronov brother, Mikhail, and content himself with only one manservant, while hiring a maid and a cook for his wife. 'It was so tedious, so utterly futile, to be in Moscow without getting any work done. (I couldn't work because I didn't have any energy left for it, and it was anyway impossible in our cramped lodgings.) I don't know how I stayed sane.' The death of Vladimir Adamov, a close companion since their schooldays, then plunged him deeper into depression: 'It's just one thing on top of another . . . I feel utterly overwhelmed.'

On 7 August, less than three weeks after their marriage, he left Antonina behind in Moscow and set out to spend the summer at his sister's estate. Behind the relatively brave face he was showing to the world was a man on the brink of spiritual collapse. Within a month, he would be attempting suicide. En route to Kamenka, from Kiev, he wrote a long letter which begins to explain why:

> As I contemplate spending the rest of my life with this woman, I also realize that, far from feeling the slightest fondness for her, I *hate* her in every sense of the word. It seems to me that I am now irretrievably lost – along with the best and only decent part of me, my music. The rest of my life stretches ahead as a long, slow, pathetic process of vegetation, an intolerable black comedy . . . How can I even think about my work? I have fallen into a deep despair, made all the deeper by the lack of anyone to give me hope or consolation. I have begun to long fiercely and hungrily for death, which now seems to me the only solution . . .[33]

If Tchaikovsky lacked 'anyone to give me hope or consolation', to whom was he saying so, while so nakedly baring his soul about his predicament? These outpourings were addressed to a woman he had never met – and never would, though she was to become the mainstay of his life for almost fourteen of the sixteen years left to him.

That year had seen Tchaikovsky's life invaded by two women, one of whom would soon bring him to the brink of self-destruction, while the other was to prove his salvation.

# CHAPTER VIII

# 'My beloved friend'

AT THE TURN OF THE NEW YEAR, FOUR MONTHS BEFORE RECEIVING THAT
fateful first letter from Antonina, Tchaikovsky had received another which
was to have an even more profound impact upon the rest of his life.
Ostensibly, it was simply a thank-you note for a small piece of work,
for which he had anyway been handsomely paid:

> Gracious Sir, Pyotr Ilyich,
> Permit me to express my sincere thanks for the speedy execution of
> my commission. To tell you into what ecstasies your composition sent
> me would be unnecessary and unfitting, because you are accustomed
> to the compliments and homage of those much better qualified to
> speak than a creature so musically insignificant as me. It would only
> make you smile. I have experienced so precious a delight that I could
> not bear to have anyone find it ridiculous, so I shall content myself
> with asking you to believe absolutely that your music makes my
> life easier and pleasanter to live.[1]

Thanks to his young friend Kotek, Tchaikovsky appeared to have
found not just a fan, but a potential patron. Nadezhda Filaretovna von
Meck was the wealthy widow of a Russian railway tycoon, to whom she
had borne no fewer than eighteen children (twelve of whom survived)
before his sudden death the previous year. Married at the age of sixteen,

and widowed at forty-six, Madame von Meck was nine years older than Tchaikovsky; a keen amateur musician, wealthy enough to retain her own private suite of artistes, she was also an ardent admirer of his music. As suspicious as he was of the world at large, she had very little to do with it – preferring to care for her huge brood of children, and manage her equally unwieldy fortune with the aid of a brother and her eldest son.

By the standards of her day, Nadezhda von Meck was a quite remarkable woman, who had already lived a very full life. The daughter of another music-lover, she had known considerable hardship in the early years of her marriage to Karl Fyodorovich von Meck, then a twenty-eight-year-old engineer working for the Moscow–Warsaw railroad. She it was who persuaded her husband to raise the capital to branch out on his own and start building new railways, which he managed to spectacular effect during the rapid expansion of Russia's rail network in the 1860s. Having amassed a fortune of huge proportions, he made it a condition of his will that his wife manage it after his death. As she did so, with considerable acumen, she also began to make a name for herself as a generous public benefactress and a discriminating patron of the arts.

During 1876 Mme von Meck had asked Nikolay Rubinstein for help. She needed a young violinist to work with her on pieces for violin and piano. It was an attractive proposition, as she spent much of her time travelling throughout Russia and Europe, or preoccupied with her family; so the successful applicant could expect to 'see something of the world' as well as enjoying large amounts of free time to devote to his own studies. The salary, furthermore, would be generous.

Rubinstein had recommended the impecunious Kotek, then fast becoming Tchaikovsky's closest friend as well as a passionate admirer of his music. Once the young violinist was installed in von Meck's household, it took little of his advocacy to persuade her to commission the rising musical celebrity to arrange one of his works for violin and piano. The commission had been swiftly executed in December 1876, while Tchaikovsky's main task was his Variations on a Rococo Theme, for cello and orchestra (Op. 33), which he dedicated to the cellist Wilhelm Fitzenhagen. Upon receiving von Meck's note of thanks, the composer replied the same day:

> Gracious lady, Nadezhda Filaretovna,
> I am sincerely grateful for the kind and flattering words that you were good enough to write to me. To a musician, with all the disappointments and failures that obstruct his path, it is a comfort to know there is a small minority of people like yourself who truly and warmly love our art.[2]

Unable to foresee the colossal role she would play in his life, Tchaikovsky briefly forgot his new patron as he busied himself with pressing family matters. Amid a false alarm over his father's health, which had all the siblings converging on St Petersburg, he was also seeing his brother Anatoly through one of his periodic bouts of depression. The financial generosity he had always shown his younger brothers was now, meanwhile, extended to more distant relatives: the pleas of a cousin, an aunt and her son were all answered with roubles he could ill afford.

By late February he felt obliged to steel his nerve to more conducting, purely as a way to earn money; his stewardship of his own *Marche Slave* at a Bolshoi concert was 'very clumsy, nervous and uncertain – but successful'.[3] It was time, he decided, to lay plans to conduct his own music abroad, as much to boost his income as to enlarge his reputation. 'I must master this insane shyness of mine,' he wrote to his sister, 'for my plans for a foreign tour surely depend on my being my own conductor.'[4] The private angst beneath the confident public veneer he meanwhile poured into early sketches of his Fourth Symphony.

One unforeseen consequence of his Bolshoi concert was a second letter from von Meck – dated two days later, 27 February – in which for the first time this apparently demure woman made quite clear her longing for a more intimate relationship, if only by correspondence: 'I should like very much to tell you at length of my fancies and thoughts about you, but I fear to take up your time, of which you have so little to spare. Let me say only that my feeling for you is a thing of the spirit and very dear to me. So, if you will, Pyotr Ilyich, call me erratic, perhaps even crazy, but do not laugh. It could be funny if it were not so sincere and real.'[5] The composer replied the next day, encouraging her to give vent to her feelings:

> Why do you hesitate to tell me all your thoughts? I assure you I should have been most interested and pleased, as I in turn feel deeply sympathetic toward you. These are not mere words. Perhaps I know you better than you imagine. If, some happy day, you will do me the honour of writing me what you have so far withheld, I shall be very grateful.[6]

This was all the encouragement von Meck needed to unleash a sudden and breathless outpouring, to a man she had never met, which abandons all the formality of their previous correspondence, hurtles along in long, disjointed sentences, begins as a nervous fan letter and ends as little less than a passionate declaration of love:

Your generous reply to my letter filled me with joy deeper than I have long known, but you know this common failing of human nature: the more kindness you receive, the more you want, and although I promised never to sink to self-indulgence, I am not sure I have the strength to resist, for I cannot stop myself asking you an enormous favour which you may find unwelcome and inappropriate, though you will perhaps understand that someone who lives as reclusively as I have inevitably decided long ago that what people call social relationships, the conventions of society, etiquette, what you will, are to her but sounds without any meaning. I am not sure how you will respond to this, Pyotr Ilyich, but from all I know of you I suspect that you of all people will be slow to condemn me for asking – if I am wrong, then I humbly beg you to tell me so directly and bluntly, and turn down my request – which is that you give me your photograph . . . I possess two already, but I want to have one from you. I want to search your face for clues as to those sources of inspiration, those feelings which inspire you to compose music which transports me into a realm of sensations, aspirations and desires that life itself can never satisfy . . .

The first work of yours I ever heard was *The Tempest*. I have no words for the impact that it made upon me; for several days I was completely delirious, beyond any hope of salvation. I must tell you that I cannot separate the musician from the man; and in that man, the servant of such high art, even more than in others, I hope and expect to find all the human qualities I adore. For me, the perfect man is definitely a musician, but his talent must be equalled by his human qualities for him to make a profound and lasting impression . . . So, as soon as I had calmed down from my initial response to your music, I immediately wanted to know what kind of man could have written such a work. I began to look for opportunities to find out as much as possible about you, took any chance to hear whatever I could, listened carefully to every aspect of public opinion, to individual judgements, to chance remarks – and here I should tell you that most of the adverse comments I overheard sent me into raptures. *Chacun à son goût!* Just the other day I heard of one of your opinions which so thrilled me, and with which I felt such complete sympathy, that you at once became, as it were, very close to me – or, at any rate, very dear to me. It is my opinion, you see, that it is not only friendship which draws people together, but even more a similarity of outlook, a shared capacity for depth of feeling, and a common range of sympathies, so it becomes possible to be close although far distant.

I am so intent on knowing everything about you that at any time you care to name I can tell where you are and, as often as not, what you are doing . . . There was a time when I was desperate to meet you. But now, the more enamoured I become of you, the more an acquaintanceship frightens me – I am sure I would be in no fit state to make sense as we began a conversation – though if we were to meet by chance, face to face, I would be unable to treat you as a stranger, and I would hold out my hand to yours, if only to press it, without a word being spoken. In short, I prefer to think of you from a distance, to hear you in your music, and to feel at one with you in your work . . .[7]

The closing phrases of this letter were to lay the foundations of a remarkable partnership, unique in the long history of great artists and their patrons. While maintaining an insatiable curiosity, at the very least, about Tchaikovsky and all his works, von Meck would also remain adamant about keeping her distance. Her bond with the composer was dependent upon not meeting him, in the face of the mightiest temptations. There was much more to this than merely her own trembling unease that she would fail to live up to his expectations. She wished to preserve the composer-philosopher as her Platonic ideal of a man – almost, in her world view, the Nietzschean Superman even then in the making – at whatever cost to her own fragile psyche.

As yet, Tchaikovsky could not be expected to sense the scale of the role she would play in his future. For now, despite his unease about her researches into his private life, he too unbuttoned enough to reply in kind:

You are quite right, Nadezhda Filaretovna, to suppose that I am of a disposition sympathetic to your own unusual spiritual feelings, which I understand completely. I dare to think that you are not mistaken in thinking me, as a human being, close to you. Just as you have gone to some lengths to measure public opinion about me, so I for my part have seized every opportunity to glean information about you and the way you live. I have always been drawn to you as a person whose moral and spiritual disposition has so much in common with my own. There is, to be sure, one characteristic which sets us both apart: that we both suffer from the same condition, namely misanthropy – but an unusual type of misanthropy, beneath which there is undoubtedly no hatred or contempt for our fellow human beings. Those who suffer from this condition do not live in dread of the hurt they might suffer from the machinations of mankind; rather, they dread the disenchantment, the yearning for perfection, which follows so hard upon every intimacy. There was a time when I was so weighed down by the yoke of this dread of people that I went all but mad . . . Now, however, I have survived this ordeal with sufficient strength for life to have long ceased to be intolerable. I have been saved by my work, work that is also such a pleasure . . .

[So] you will believe me when I say that I quite understand why, loving my music as you do, you do not wish to make the personal acquaintance of its creator. You are worried that you will not discover in me those attributes with which your imagination, inclined to an ideal portrait, has endowed me. And you are absolutely right. I am quite sure that, on closer acquaintance, you would not find that balance, that perfect harmony between the musician and the man, of which your imagination dreams.[8]

With this letter Tchaikovsky enclosed not merely a photograph (an old one, pending another 'dreaded' session at the photographer's), but a Funeral March on themes from *The Oprichnik*, as requested by von Meck in the coda to her first long letter. She replied at once, boldly enough to send him a photograph of herself – 'not expecting it to give you any pleasure, merely to express to some extent the depth of the feelings I hold for you.' Taken by one of her daughters, it also included her youngest child, five-year-old Ludmila – 'Milochka', as she was called by the family – of whom she allowed herself some fond maternal indulgence to the composer, ending 'I would like you to get to know the little one a bit.'[9]

This almost daily correspondence was becoming too much for Tchaikovsky, who was enjoying a brief flurry of performances in Moscow. Early March saw the first performance there of *Swan Lake* and the Second String Quartet, swiftly followed by *Francesca da Rimini*, which was twice repeated within a fortnight. The small-scale commissions from von Meck were lavishly paid, and took little enough of his time and energy away from his work on the Fourth Symphony, though he felt obliged to defer a commission for arrangements of some children's songs (for which he had little enthusiasm, and never actually completed) and to reject a proposal from Stasov that he base an opera on Alfred de Vigny's historical romance, *Cinq-Mars*. Gounod had recently adapted the same work; and Tchaikovsky was anyway intent upon *Eugene Onegin*. Amid all this activity, von Meck's last letter languished without reply.

Not for six weeks did he hear from her again – by which time he was embarked upon his adventures with Antonina Milyukova. On her return from St Petersburg, von Meck lost no time in writing again, this time ostensibly to commission a work to be entitled *Reproach*, for violin and piano. She already possessed a piece of that name, she explained, by a (now forgotten) composer named Kohne, but could not warm to it as it appeared to concern a specific individual: 'My *Reproach* must be impersonal; it may relate to Nature, or Fate, or yourself, but not to anyone else . . .' In the further details of her commission, unwittingly or otherwise, von Meck paints a dark portrait of her state of mind:

> My *Reproach* must depict an intolerable condition of the soul, that best expressed by the French phrase *'Je n'en peux plus!'* It must convey the impression of a heart broken, of feelings trampled on, ideas betrayed, pride wounded and happiness stolen – everything, everything that is most precious and valued ruthlessly and pitilessly destroyed . . . My *Reproach* must embody an impression of sadness beyond endurance, of suffering which can be no further endured – of death itself, if possible, so as to find in music, at least, the solace and relief that life itself rarely grants when most they are needed . . .[10]

This *cri de coeur* also went unheeded, or so it would seem, by a composer with too much else on his mind. Von Meck made quite clear the source of all her feelings: 'If you have ever lost what most you loved and treasured,' she wrote pointedly, 'you will know what I mean . . . And the recollection of *lost* happiness must also be evident [in the piece]. Nothing can express this condition of the soul more eloquently than music, and no-one is better qualified than you to understand what I mean. That is why I am not afraid to confide all my innermost feelings, thoughts and desires to you, and have every faith that I am right to entrust my very soul into your truly pure hands . . .'

Tchaikovsky's initial reply to these desperate outpourings was a brief note explaining that she would have to wait 'longer than usual' for her piece; he was so 'desperately busy' that he could not predict 'whether I shall be able to find a moment when I am in the right mood'.[11] He may also have felt that the programme which she outlined with such passion was too similar to that he had only recently tackled in *Francesca da Rimini*. That evening, however, he did find the time to write a longer letter which directly tackled the 'ticklish' subtext of their mounting correspondence: money.

> It has already occurred to me that your previous commissions from me had two motives: one, you genuinely wished to possess some compositions of mine, in one form or another; and secondly, that you were aware of my financial difficulties, and wanted to help me

out. Such lavish payments for such meagre efforts persuades me this must be so.

Von Meck's last letter, Tchaikovsky told her, seemed to him 'exclusively, or almost exclusively' governed by her desire to help him financially. This was why he had at first replied so curtly, feeling 'a positive *disinclination*' to execute her commission. 'I don't want there to be one false note in our relationship, which there certainly would have been if I had just dashed off *any old thing* for you, lacking the particular inspiration you crave, and sent it along purely for some disproportionate reward. I trust you would never imagine that I would undertake any musical work purely for the sake of the 100 rouble bill at the end of it?' There was, of course, nothing degrading about an artist accepting money for his efforts, he continued; but a commission such as hers required 'a particular kind of inspiration – a mood that does not always appear to order'. It would be 'artistically dishonest' of him to use his technical skills to present her with 'false metal for true' – much though he needed, he confessed, 'this *hateful* metal'.

How could someone with an income as decent as his sink so deep into debt that it 'poisoned' his life and 'paralysed' his inclination to work? It would, he sighed, take too long to explain. Instead, Tchaikovsky boldly adopted a full-frontal approach.

> I have made up my mind to seek your help. You are the only person in the world I am not ashamed to ask for money. For one thing, you are exceedingly kind and generous; for another, you are very rich. I would much rather concentrate all my debts in the care of one single, generous creditor, and use her help to disentangle myself from the grasp of moneylenders. If you would agree to loan me enough to be rid of them once and for all, I would be eternally grateful to you for an act of kindness beyond measure. You see, my debts total a rather large sum, something like 3,000 roubles. I could repay this amount to you in one of three ways: (1) by undertaking different commissions for you, such as the arrangements I have already done; (2) by assigning to you the royalties due for the performances of my operas; or (3) by sending you a proportion of my salary every month . . .

She should not be embarrassed, he continued somewhat disingenuously, by opting for the first method. 'Thanks to my many years of experience, little tasks like the arrangements you have commissioned are completely effortless for me, so much so that even if you asked for one every day for the next two years, I would not deem it adequate recompense for the assistance I seek.' A composition like *Reproach*, however, was an altogether different proposition. 'It requires a specific mood, a combination of conditions which is not always possible.' Besides, he was engrossed in his new symphony – which, he now announced, he would like to dedicate to her, 'as I think you will find it reflects your innermost feelings and thoughts.' Until it was finished, any other work would be an intolerable burden, especially in his 'anxious, troubled and irritable' frame of mind. With a final promise one day to compose her *Reproach* – a promise he would never keep – Tchaikovsky gingerly returned to the subject of money.

> I would be most upset if you were to be offended by my request. My main reason for making it was to exclude once and for all from our relationship the subject of money, a highly awkward subject when it crops up as often as it has hitherto. I hope our dealings may henceforth be more open and direct. A correspondence in which one side is always offering money, and the other always accepting it, cannot be wholly frank . . . Be that as it may, I feel sure that, whatever your response to this letter, it cannot alter your opinion of my honesty. If I am wrong, and this letter offends you, then I beg your forgiveness. I am not myself these days, very tense and edgy, and I suppose that tomorrow may see me regret sending this letter . . .[12]

That same day, as he surely expected, saw the money duly arrive with a letter which positively thanked him for asking for it – and would hear no talk of repayment. 'I thank you from the bottom of my heart, my most respected friend, for the trust and friendship you have shown me in the directness of your appeal . . . As for methods of repayment, please do not trouble yourself even thinking about it.'[13] Tchaikovsky returned a fulsome note of thanks, and the two went their separate ways for the summer, exchanging addresses and promising to keep up their correspondence.

The next letter Tchaikovsky wrote von Meck was dated 15 July, confiding the circumstances of his betrothal to Antonina. In his letters to relatives on this subject, immediately before the wedding, he adopted a deceptively calm façade. To von Meck, three days before the event, he revealed the true extent of his doubts and fears. Clearly, he had no conception of the profoundly mixed feelings with which his patron would receive news of his impending marriage. So flattered was he by her depiction of this man-musician as her ideal human being, so confident that it accounted for her wish not to meet him, that Tchaikovsky had quite failed to see the implications of some striking phraseology in her next heartfelt missive.

One thing in your charming letter, and one thing only, disturbed me: the conclusion you draw from my reluctance to make your acquaintance in person. You seem to think that I fear disillusion that you are not the ideal combination of man and musician of which I dream. But on that score you need have no fear: I have already found that ideal in you. It is no longer in any doubt. Your conclusion might have been right, if I did not feel increasingly confident that you do indeed personify my ideal, and can make up for all the feelings of disenchantment, regret and melancholy I endure. Yes, if I had happiness in my hands, I would give it over to you. But no, my fear of meeting you now has a quite different cause, an entirely different feeling behind it . . .[14]

So recent a widow, so susceptible to romantic emotions, yet so concerned to maintain a strictly disciplined façade, clearly felt she would lose all self-control if confronted with the presence of her personified ideal. Tchaikovsky could not be expected to see it, but Nadezhda von Meck was in love with him – a Platonic love, of course, to be conducted from a safe distance, but a love which wanted him for its own, purchased and paid for in full, and did not particularly wish to hear of his marriage to another.

In the circumstances, she rose to the occasion magnificently, offering her heartfelt congratulations on his intent to marry: 'always a gamble, of course, but in your case I am delighted because, for someone with such a heart of gold, with such a complex capacity for delicate feeling, it would be a crime to hide so precious a light beneath a bushel.' As soon as possible, however, she changed the subject to Pushkin and Pisarev, over whose respective merits they were having a difference of opinion, before expressing the plaintive (and redundant) hope that his marriage would not affect their friendship. 'I am sure that even in your new circumstances you will not forget that in me you have a friend who feels deeply attached to you, and that, whatever lies and fabrications public opinion may noise abroad, you will always see me only as a very close friend who loves you.' Perhaps sensing the troubles to come, she added: 'You will always write to me with complete candour, won't you, Pyotr Ilyich? Nothing you tell me about yourself can ever embarrass me.'[15]

The letter was sent to the Moscow Conservatoire, to which Tchaikovsky returned a week later, his private world beginning to disintegrate. There was no danger now of his forgetting his new friend because of his new partner; quite the opposite, as his funds grew dangerously low. 'Strange and presumptuous as it may seem,' in his own words, he was already 'obliged to turn to you again for financial assistance.' The money she had already advanced him had seen him off to the Caucasus, as planned, and in some style. 'Then marriage came into the picture. All the rest of the money went on the wedding and the expenses it involved.' He explained about the forest his wife had inherited from her father; how she had been 'swindled' out of the 4,000 roubles it was worth; and how they were now 'surviving hand to mouth, with nowhere to live, nothing to live on' – no funds, even, to enable him to decamp to the countryside and leave it all behind him.

Of the progress of his marriage, and his own frame of mind, he would tell her in his next letter: 'I am so on edge that I am in no fit state to give you a calm and careful account of recent events, and because I am still not quite sure what is happening to me. I still cannot decide whether I am happy or not. All I know is that I am *completely unable to do any work.*'[16]

The money, of course, arrived by special messenger the same day, with the mildest of enquiries as to what might be wrong. 'Why are you so sad, why do you feel so on edge? It is not worth getting yourself so worked up, or sinking into such a depression, which is anyway, surely, easily cured. Go to the country; enjoy nature, peace and quiet, serenity; and think of me sometimes . . .'[17] In a brief acknowledgement, rushing to leave town, Tchaikovsky gave her some hint of the depths of his difficulties: 'If I survive this traumatic spiritual struggle intact, I will have you to thank for it, and you alone. A few more days, and *I swear to you* that I would have gone mad.'[18]

Having fled to Kiev on her money – another 'loan' he would never repay – it was here that Tchaikovsky paused en route to Kamenka and wrote to von Meck the long letter threatening suicide, and giving the most wretched account of his wedding and honeymoon. Only to her, not yet to his relatives (apart from Anatoly) did he spell out his loathing for Antonina – coupling it with his deep-seated fear, which his patron of all people would share, that his wife might cost him his inspiration as a composer.

> My wife bears no guilt for any of this. She did not make the proposal of marriage. So to allow her to sense that I do not love her, that I regard her as an intolerable burden, would be cruel and unworthy. The only solution is to pretend. But to pretend for the whole of one's life is surely a unique form of torture.

Then comes the apparent suicide threat – swiftly if unconvincingly followed by a reassurance that 'a violent end' was 'out of the question', because of his affection for his family and friends. 'To commit suicide would be to deal them a mortal blow.'

Having no doubt caused his adoring patron considerable alarm, Tchaikovsky again changes direction to suggest that his music, too, would keep him alive. 'I am weak enough (if weak is the right word) to love life, to love my work, to love my future successes. Above all, *I have yet to say* all that I can and want to say before the time comes for me to pass on to eternity . . . I have not yet said even one-tenth of what I want to. My heart is full; it bursts to pour itself out in music. Who knows, maybe I can leave behind me something genuinely worthy of praise from an artist of the first rank? I am bold enough to hope that this may come to pass.' After describing his grim visit to meet his wife's family, and the effect upon him of the death of his friend Adamov, Tchaikovsky wonders whether he might not go mad, leaving his anxious correspondent dangling in tantalizing uncertainty:

> I cannot tell what the future holds, but at present I feel as though I am emerging from an appalling, agonizing nightmare, or a long and terrible illness. Like a patient recovering from a fever, I still feel very weak and can think straight only with difficulty . . . Once I have got some rest, and calmed my nerves, perhaps I will be able to resume my normal routine in Moscow and look on my wife in a quite different light. At heart she has many qualities that might eventually combine to make me happy. She loves me most sincerely, and desires nothing but my peace of mind and contentment. I feel very sorry for her . . .[19]

There was one important reason why Tchaikovsky felt able to unburden himself with such candour to an ardent admirer he had never met, far more so than to his equally fond siblings. If some of his family knew that he was homosexual, von Meck, as far as he knew, did not. Therein, of course, lay the fundamental cause of his marital torments, which he felt obliged to portray to his patron (and thus, to a large extent, to himself) as a rather more spiritual problem.

A suspicious or cynical mind might suspect that the composer was not averse to painting as dire a picture as possible to his highly valued new friend, with her financial more than her spiritual assistance in mind. As he settled in at Kamenka, however, abandoning his plans to move on to the Caucasus, he grew more placid, and his letters less dramatic. Within four days he was 'overjoyed' to be among his family, and convinced that 'time can cure me: little by little I will recover.'[20] When von Meck replied sympathetically, concealing her own jealousy to suggest that there were times in life when one just had to '*se résigner*, or make the best of a bad job',[21] he replied in tones of gloomy agreement, seemingly more resigned to a fate he continued to insist was self-inflicted. Refreshed by a combination of family pampering and Essentuki mineral water, he was soon 'immeasurably calmer and better . . . starting a completely new lease of life . . . quite sure that I shall emerge victorious from this awkward situation.'[22] It was time to recognize that there was 'no escaping' the 'new obligation' he had imposed upon himself: 'My only course, as you say, is to *write it off as a bad job* and try to be artificially happy.'[23]

With the conceptual work on his fourth symphony finished, he could ease himself back into composition with its less demanding orchestration. Heartened by Modest's encouragement, he even managed to sketch some new sections of *Onegin*. By the end of August he was much more himself, savouring such country pastimes as hunting, constantly postponing his return to Moscow, and Antonina. Absence made his heart grow no fonder; but the violence of his reaction against her was mellowing to mere distaste. 'Ah, how little I love Antonina Ivanovna Tchaikovskaya!' he confided to Anatoly in September, when his return to Moscow could be postponed no longer, because of the approach of the new Conservatoire term. 'What profound indifference this woman inspires in me! How little am I stirred by the prospect of seeing her again! At least the thought of her no longer instils horror in me, merely boredom . . .'[24]

Within the week, he finally tore himself away from his sister and her family, but proceeded no further than Kiev, where he lingered three last, contemplative days despite a letter from Antonina begging for his return. She was finally able to meet him off the train on 23 September – more than six weeks since his departure – and tell him of all her hard work setting up an apartment fit for his return. She had already hired three cooks, been robbed twice, taken one cook to court, and was now afraid to go out and leave the apartment to the third. 'I am quite satisfied with the arrangements,' he told his brother gloomily. 'It is elegant, comfortable, even quite luxurious . . . As to how I am feeling, Tolya, let me keep my own counsel awhile. All I can say is that I am in a state of some distress. I expect it was inevitable after that overflow of happiness at Kamenka. I have decided that I must simply be patient for a while – and then, who knows, calm, contentment and maybe even happiness will gradually emerge.'[25] To von Meck, meanwhile, he was painting a much bleaker picture. The apartment was 'cosy' and 'nicely furnished', but he looked upon it 'with hatred and anger'. Death, in the end, was 'the greatest of all blessings, and I pray for it with all my soul.'[26]

At the Conservatoire, which reopened the day after his return, Tchaikovsky's closest friends and colleagues could see that he was attempting to put a brave face on deep-seated troubles. During his absence only Albrecht had seen Antonina; because he remembered his friend's wife from her student days, he had offered her his assistance preparing the apartment for her husband's return. Kashkin was not alone in finding Tchaikovsky's bravura exterior 'phoney . . . It was all too clearly a sham. Pyotr Ilyich was a past master at trying to hide his true feelings, but he was never any good at it. Noticing how tense and edgy he seemed, we all handled him with kid gloves, asking no questions and leaving it to him to offer an invitation to meet his wife.'

That invitation, in the end, came from Yurgenson, who within a few days hosted a dinner for Tchaikovsky's friends to meet Antonina. When he tried to engage her in conversation, Kashkin noticed how the composer could not leave them alone, constantly finishing her sentences for her, or changing the subject, 'presumably for fear that her inability to hold a decent conversation would embarrass all concerned.' It was the same all evening, with whomever she met, leaving Kashkin with the anxious impression that there was 'something unnatural' about Tchaikovsky's 'over-protectiveness'. The general impression Antonina made on his friends was 'favourable, if rather colourless'. A few days later, as some of the group gathered for a routine meeting in his office at the Conservatoire, Nikolay Rubinstein summed up their feelings about Antonina Ivanovna: 'She's certainly pretty, and well enough behaved, but she's not particularly *likeable*. It's as if she were not quite a real person, more some sort of synthetic confection.' Kashkin agreed. To him, Antonina was 'not quite real'.[27]

At home, to Tchaikovsky, she was all too real – and all too adept at making conversation, most of it an unending stream of inanities about her family, her childhood, and above all the long procession of men who had thrown themselves at her, from celebrated artists and military men to millionaire bankers and members of the Imperial Family itself. After just a couple of days, Tchaikovsky became terminally claustrophobic. 'During the day I tried to get on with my work, but in the evenings I found her company intolerable. Not daring to visit a friend, or even the theatre, I would set off each evening for a walk, and wander for hours through the far-flung, little-known streets of obscure Moscow.'

To Antonina herself, recollecting it many years later, this was a period of great happiness. 'I would look at him surreptitiously, so he didn't notice, and admire him enormously, especially during morning tea. So handsome, with kindly eyes which melted my heart, he breathed such freshness into my life! I would just sit there looking at him, and think "Thank God he belongs to me and no-one else! Now he is my husband, no-one can take him away from me . . ."'[28]

Tchaikovsky, meanwhile, was falling apart. For his friends, that first meeting with Antonina at Yurgenson's would also prove their last.

Although their colleague went about his Conservatoire duties with his usual conscientiousness, he would disappear the minute they were over and could not be found in his usual out-of-hours haunts. Not even to von Meck could he confide his despair. Far from gradually becoming tolerable, as he had hoped, day-to-day life with Antonina was worse than his direst imaginings. Within a week he could bear no more. As he began to look for a way out, Tchaikovsky's desire for death was not, for once, mere self-dramatization. Incapable of confronting Antonina directly, or of facing public humiliation, he could see no alternative to suicide.

Still concerned for his family's feelings, he cast about for a way to make his death look like an accident; and on one of his evening walks around the city he came up with a strikingly simple solution. As the autumn nights grew colder, he found himself staring into the depths of the chill Moskva River. 'It occurred to me that it would be possible to kill myself by contracting pneumonia. So I waded into the water up to my waist, unseen in the pitch darkness, and stood there until my aching body could no longer endure the freezing cold.' He eventually emerged from the river 'convinced that I would now die from pneumonia or some respiratory illness.' Back home he passed it off as a fishing accident: 'I had been inveigled into a night-time expedition, and had fallen in by mistake.'[29] But there is confirmation that this was a serious suicide attempt in the inscription, in the composer's own handwriting, on the cover-page of the score of the Fourth Symphony: 'In the event of my death, deliver this to Mme von Meck.'[30]

As it transpired, Tchaikovsky's constitution proved so sturdy that he did not catch so much as a cold. This latest embarrassment persuaded him that his need to be free of Antonina was now as urgent as it was absolute. Deprived even of death, the ultimate method of leaving his wife, he now resorted to a simpler form of direct action – cabling Anatoly in St Petersburg, and asking him to send a telegram in Napravnik's name seeking his urgent presence in the capital. The summons arrived the next day.

Tchaikovsky paused only to write a note to Albrecht, explaining that he was needed immediately in St Petersburg in connection with the revival of *Vakula*, and that he would return by the following Tuesday. When Anatoly met him at the station the following day, 7 October, he barely recognized his brother. The last two weeks had taken such a toll on Tchaikovsky that he had to be helped to a nearby hotel, where he immediately suffered a violent nervous attack, then fell into the long and deep sleep of total exhaustion. Anatoly summoned a psychiatrist, who ordered complete rest amid a change of scenery, insisting that under no circumstances must he ever see his wife again, let alone live with her. His loyal brother set off to Moscow to break the news to Antonina.

But first Anatoly went to see Rubinstein, to tell him all. Fearing that Tchaikovsky's brother might be 'too soft' on Antonina, Rubinstein promptly took charge of the situation and accompanied him to the Tchaikovsky apartment, where a surprised Antonina invited them in and ordered the servant to prepare tea. Rubinstein proceeded to spell out the details of her husband's condition, and the psychiatrist's report, with a bluntness which, said Anatoly, 'made me go hot and cold'. To both their surprise, Antonina listened meekly, and announced that she would be pleased to agree to whatever her 'darling Peti' wanted. Then she began to pour tea.

As soon as he decently could, Rubinstein made his excuses and left Anatoly to discuss 'more personal family matters'. The scene which ensued left Anatoly dumbstruck. 'Antonina Ivanovna saw Rubinstein to the door, and returned with a broad smile on her face, saying "Well, who'd have thought I would entertain the famous Rubinstein to tea at my home today!"'[31] She then launched into another litany of the men who had fallen for her, and asked her brother-in-law what he would like for dinner.[32]

A stunned Anatoly followed Rubinstein out of the door as fast as he could, headed straight back to St Petersburg, and made urgent arrangements to take his brother on a prolonged tour of Western Europe. After barely three months, less than half of which he had spent in his wife's company, Tchaikovsky's marriage was over.

# CHAPTER IX

## 'I must hide for a year'

WITHIN A WEEK, BY 17 OCTOBER 1877, THE TCHAIKOVSKY BROTHERS WERE in Switzerland, where they took rooms at a modest pension in the small town of Clarens on Lake Geneva. The only other occupants of the Villa Richelieu were two elderly German women who never left their room, even to eat. 'I must hide for a year,' Pyotr wrote to Modest the next day. From the moment of his arrival he sprayed letters in all directions, each containing a subtly different version of recent events.

In an attempt to contain scandalous gossip, Anatoly had agreed with Rubinstein an official line for the Moscow grapevine: that Tchaikovsky had been taken ill, had been rushed abroad for a rest cure, and would eventually be joined by his wife. Now the composer was concerned not merely to avoid public humiliation – above all, that the failure of his marriage would be put down to his homosexuality – but to minimize domestic damage.

Different people, he had decided, must be told different things. Family in St Petersburg, for instance, should be told that the brothers had left Russia from Moscow, and vice versa, to avoid upsetting anybody. Modest would be given, as yet, only a partial version of events, as the marriage had been designed in part to encourage him to seek the same escape-route from his sexuality. Ilya Petrovich, so delighted by the match, and in such frail health, should be told the most laundered version of all: that Antonina had been due to accompany them, but had been detained in Moscow at the last minute by domestic matters. This deception was assisted by the forlorn fact that, following the fake telegram from St Petersburg, she had insisted on accompanying her husband to the station to wave him off, little realizing that his precipitous departure marked the end of their married life. Years later, there is still a note of surprise in Antonina's voice when she writes of this moment: 'He never came back to me.'[1]

In his first letter from Clarens to Mme von Meck, Tchaikovsky was especially economical with the truth, telling her of his summons to St Petersburg without revealing that it was a sham he had himself engineered. In the same breath he expressed joy at escaping 'the web of lies, deception and intrigue' in which he had become enmeshed. At the root of it all lay his continuing fear of her too discovering his guilty secret – about which it seems highly likely that she already knew, and could not have cared less. But he also had to bear in mind that his patron had herself been in Moscow at the time, and would no doubt have been upset to have heard only from third parties of her trusty friend's departure. Tchaikovsky must also have deemed it wise to remain vague about other details, at least for now, as his most urgent purpose was to ask her for yet more money.

> I need to rest here awhile, calm my nerves, and stop myself going over it all in my mind. I must also organize some provision for my wife, and work out my future relations with her. I am again in need of money, and can turn to no-one but you. It is terrible, it hurts and distresses me deeply, but I am forced to grasp the nettle and appeal again to your inexhaustible generosity . . . My meagre resources are almost exhausted and I have no hope of help but you.[2]

In the same letter, while pleading for time before giving a 'calm' account, Tchaikovsky tells his 'friend and saviour' that his two weeks in Moscow with his wife was a period of 'unbearable torment'. He knew immediately that time would not enable him to make the best of a bad job: 'In despair I sought death, which seemed my only way out.' He was filled with such hatred for his wife that at times he 'wanted to strangle her'. While reiterating that Antonina was in no way to blame, that it was all the fault of his own 'weakness of character, impracticality, naïvety', Tchaikovsky uses ever more violent language about his wife. To von Meck, as to himself, he would remain in the lifelong habit of projecting his own self-hatred onto the hapless creature whose life he had so carelessly ravaged.

Von Meck was quick to reveal the opinion she had previously kept to herself 'lest it sound like advice'. She was 'delighted' that he had fought his way free of a situation requiring deception and intrigue, neither of which were typical or worthy of him. 'You tried to do your *very best* for another human being. You struggled against insuperable odds – in vain, of course, because someone like you will always succumb to such pressures rather than compromise.' Thank God his brother had rescued him in the nick of time. 'How can you think for one moment that you might have fallen in my estimation? I understand everything you have been through, and I myself would have taken exactly the same course – except that I might well have made the break even sooner, as I do not share your capacity for self-sacrifice.'3

As if to deepen the bond between them, or at least its deliciously conspiratorial air, she was careful to explain that her enquiries of Nikolay Rubinstein had been made in a disinterested way – 'as if you were still a stranger' – so as to preserve the secrecy of their friendship. Tchaikovsky was relieved. 'I'm very glad you did not let Rubinstein sense that you know me intimately,' he added in a postscript to his next long letter, written two weeks after his first, evasive plea for funds. He had no wish for Rubinstein, his employer and somewhat inconsistent friend, to know that von Meck had become his primary source of financial support.

Not that he told her so. The main burden of this letter was to give his patron the fuller portrait of Antonina for which she had asked. His only fear was that it would not be objective enough: 'The wound is still too fresh'.

> She is of medium height, blonde, not especially handsome to look at, with a face more pretty than beautiful. Her eyes are a wonderful colour but quite without expression; her lips are too thin, so her smile is not a pleasant one. Her complexion is rosy. Overall she looks young for her age; although in fact twenty-nine, she looks twenty-three or twenty-four. Her manner is full of affectation – not one movement or gesture is quite what it seems – but her general appearance gives a favourable impression. Behind neither her facial expressions nor her movements is there that elusive quality which reflects an inner, spiritual beauty – a gift of nature, which cannot be acquired. All too evident in my wife, constantly, on all occasions, is a conspicuous longing to be liked – an artificiality which tells very much against her. Despite all that, she none the less belongs to that category of attractive women who manage to make men pay attention when they meet them.

So far, so good. But that was 'the easy part' of his task. In proceeding to describe Antonina's character and intellect, Tchaikovsky was, as he put it, 'faced with insurmountable problems'.

Her head and her heart are both completely empty. In neither is there anything worth describing. All I can do is swear to you that never, not once, has she articulated a single idea to me, shown any vestige of feeling. She was capable, it is true, of displays of affection. But it was that particular kind of affection which manifests itself in constant hugging, constant endearments, even at moments when I could not hide from her my (perhaps undeserved) dislike of her, which was growing stronger by the hour. There was no genuine feeling, it seemed to me, behind all the caresses. They appeared merely conventional, something she deemed a necessary duty of married life. Never once did she show the least interest in my work, what I was writing, what my plans were, what I was reading, or my artistic and intellectual tastes . . .

So how could he have chosen to pool his fortunes with so wholly unsuitable a partner? 'I keep asking myself the same question. It was an act of total madness. I was touched by her love for me, which at the time I thought genuine, and imagined that in due course I would come to love her too. Now I am entirely persuaded that *she never really loved me*. But, to be fair, she acted sincerely and honourably: her wish to marry me she herself mistook for love.' The harder she had tried to win his affections, however, the more alienated he had felt. His struggles against his growing feelings of antipathy all proved vain. 'What was I to do with my recalcitrant heart? This antipathy grew not daily, not even hourly, but by the minute, swelling gradually to a hatred stronger than I have ever known before, more ferocious than I would have thought myself capable of. In the end I could no longer contain it. The rest you know . . .'[4]

Antonina had by now been taken in by Sasha, who had fetched her from Odessa to Kamenka, and undertaken to act as intermediary. As Tchaikovsky languished in Switzerland, waiting for funds from von Meck to see him onward to Italy, it must have seemed a cruel irony that the person he so hated was blithely installed in his own favourite place, among the people he most loved. To make matters worse, his sister gamely undertook the wholesale 're-education' of his wife, and was soon reporting a vast improvement, hinting that she was preparing the ground for a reconciliation. Tchaikovsky could only answer with polite caution, thanking his sister for all her efforts but begging: 'For God's own sake, never mention the possibility of our living together again.' Thanks to Sasha, the woman it had been easy to hate – the woman who had told Anatoly from Odessa that she was having a fine old time, with soldiers at her feet – was now turning into a forlorn victim of his cruelty, winning his family to her cause. By November he was writing to Sasha: 'I beseech you on my knees to send her away from Kamenka. Do it for the sake of all that is holy. It is essential for your peace of mind, and for mine.'

Tchaikovsky's exasperation shines clearly through his account of Antonina's next move. His wife, he told von Meck, had resigned herself to her fate quite calmly. But his pride is clearly hurt at her apparent indifference to his abandonment of her. 'She who had me on the verge of suicide has accepted my flight, our separation, the news of my illness with an equanimity I cannot fathom. Oh, how blind and foolish I have been!' From Kamenka she had written Anatoly a letter which, to Tchaikovsky, smacked uncomfortably of blackmail. He withheld the details from von Meck, saying only that his wife had 'suddenly changed from a meek little dove into a very angry, very demanding, very untruthful woman. She makes all sorts of wild accusations against me, the gist of which is that I have unscrupulously deceived her.'[5]

To Modest, however, he listed Antonina's accusations in more detail: 'I am a deceiver who married her in order to hide my true nature . . . I insulted her every day, her sufferings at my hands were great . . . she is appalled by my shameful vice, etc., etc.' For the rest of his life, Tchaikovsky would live in dread of Antonina's power to expose his sexual leanings. For now, he used his wife's threats to justify to his family, those in the know, how right he had been to leave her. He did not want them feeling sorry for her. 'What vileness!' he exclaimed to Modest. 'To hell with her!'

To von Meck, meanwhile, he continued to vacillate between detailing Antonina's shortcomings and shouldering all the blame on himself. This was calculated to add spice to his sufferings as those of a decent and honourable man. Shrewdly, he chose to mention a moment when he supposedly 'tried to gauge her maternal instincts.' Unless he was inventing it, as a ploy to make Antonina even more hateful to von Meck, it must have been a nervous moment for the composer when he asked his wife whether she liked children. 'Yes, when they are clever,' he reports her as replying. To his patron, with her huge brood of children – to her, the main justification of the otherwise dubious institution of marriage – this must have damned Antonina almost as much as her indifference to Tchaikovsky's music.[6]

Tchaikovsky's account of the entire episode, in short, is to be trusted as little as that of Modest, written for (and largely accepted by) posterity on his brother's behalf. Both appear to exaggerate the gravity of the composer's physical and psychological condition. He had been through a severe shock to his system, forcibly reminding him that his ambitions to be 'as other men' were doomed, and that he was capable of inflicting cruel and unusual treatment on another, quite innocent human being to get his way. He had thus also endured a sustained period of guilt, expiated only by thinking himself into a self-righteous hatred of the woman he had wronged. For all the talk of an extended nervous breakdown, however, he seems unlikely to have suffered much more than sustained bouts of neurotic hysteria. Even the tame psychiatrist, with his very convenient prescription of life without Antonina, may well have been a phantom invented by the Tchaikovsky brothers. Although their friends did include one Ivan Balinsky, a highly reputable 'alienist', there is no independent documentation of any meeting at this time.

The much-vaunted interruption to his work, when analysed from his own letters, had in truth been quite brief and much less drastic than he had made it appear. 'I just cannot get down to work,' he had written to Mme von Meck upon his arrival at Kamenka.[7] Just nine days later, he told her he was feeling 'so much better that I have got down to scoring your symphony.'[8] Another week, and he had also written enough of *Eugene Onegin* to be depressed about it.[9] By his return to Moscow six weeks later, according to a letter written the next day, the scoring of the first movement of the symphony had been complete.[10]

So much for Modest's original suggestion that his brother had been 'comatose for two weeks' (later explained away, following some scepticism, as a misprint for 'two *days*'). Tchaikovsky's work evidently suffered some upheavals during this period, but the six months between his engagement to Antonina and his 'rest cure' in Clarens saw him complete two of his mightiest achievements: a symphony, dedicated (anonymously, at her request) to his 'best friend', and an opera closely reflecting the experiences through which he had himself been living. Tatyana's 'Letter Song' may have moved him to accept Antonina's proposal; but the next scene in the opera, as in its composer's own life, sees Onegin tell his admirer to 'master her feelings' for him, as he can offer her only 'the love of a brother'. Far from endangering his work during this period, Tchaikovsky's abortive marriage seems rather to have enhanced it. Were it not for his need to convey the extent of his suffering, relieved by occasional moments of optimism, the Fourth Symphony might be a much less remarkable combination of angst and serenity. And were it not for his confused feelings for Antonina, as she herself poignantly points out, *Eugene Onegin* might not be the affecting imbroglio it is of love lost, promise betrayed.

At the time, the main effect of the episode on Tchaikovsky's life was to secure him a permanent end to his financial problems. In a note slipped in with her last long letter, Mme von Meck suggested that the way to avoid the embarrassment of his constantly asking her for loans was to settle on him an annual subsidy of 6,000 roubles, paid in monthly instalments.

'My God, how kind, generous and tactful this woman is,' Tchaikovsky wrote to Modest (in the same breath as denouncing Antonina as a 'reptile').

> And at the same time how wonderfully clever, for while rendering me
> such unique and immeasurable service, she does it in such a way that
> I cannot doubt for a moment that it gives her enormous pleasure.

Von Meck knew the way to her composer's heart. Now her triumph over her short-lived, ill-starred rival was complete.

It was, for once, with some trepidation that Tchaikovsky awaited the arrival of his brother Modest in Italy at the end of 1877. For Modest's twin brother Anatoly, who had become his brother's mainstay during these long months of crisis, appears also to have replaced Modest in his affections. 'When I came home and your room was empty, my heart was wracked with pain, which grew to an agonizing *crescendo* as the evening wore on,' Tchaikovsky wrote to Anatoly after his eventual return to Russia in December. 'All too soon, as was only to be expected, I suffered a ferocious hysterical fit . . . I lost all control over myself.' There were no words, he went on, to describe how much he missed his brother. 'My love for you is a bottomless pit.' This letter, written the very evening of Anatoly's departure, crossed with one his brother wrote him during his journey home. 'When the train left, it was all I could do to stifle my emotions and prevent myself bursting into tears . . . You can never imagine how much I love you.'[11]

Thanks to the new flow of funds from von Meck, the brothers had been able to move on from Clarens in mid-November – at first to Paris, where Tchaikovsky was dismayed to be told by a doctor that there was nothing wrong with him: 'You can live to be a hundred'. He was happier in Florence, but obliged to move on to Rome to collect his mail (not least among it more money from von Meck). Plunged back into a self-indulgent melancholy, he began to regret leaving Clarens, where at least he had been able to work. 'I really am a very sick man,' he complained to von Meck from Rome. 'I cannot bear the slightest noise. Yesterday in

Florence and now here in Rome every passing carriage drives me mad, every street-shout, every sound has my nerves in shreds. The crowds of people filling the narrow streets unnerve me so much that I regard every stranger I see as a deadly enemy.'[12]

Worst of all, he spent two days in a state of total shock, firing off panicky telegrams, when there was no sign at the Rome post office of von Meck's *lettre chargée*; eventually, after he had ordered the entire building searched, it turned up filed in the wrong place. 'According to the clerk, the misunderstanding arose because there was a "de" before your name!!! If you ask me, it's because these Italians are bone idle. Your letter had been sitting here for five days, yet for two days running they tell me it's not here. Scandalous!'[13] The same thing happened next day with the precious score of his symphony – eventually found, after he had kicked up another fuss, under mail addressed to the letter 'I'.

The money's arrival enabled him to proceed to Venice, where he installed himself in an expensive hotel room overlooking the Grand Canal. After a day's sightseeing, which he enjoyed much more than he had in Rome, he settled back down to work. Within four days he had orchestrated the second act of *Onegin*, interrupted only by a long letter of complaint from Antonina. So tetchy did it make him that his evening walk saw him haranguing a newspaper vendor proclaiming a Turkish victory in the continuing war; the next day, seeing Tchaikovsky approach, the vendor changed his cry to 'Russian victory!'

In his copious correspondence with von Meck, meanwhile, the composer tried to rise above his personal woes in an intense exchange of philosophical views, in which both admitted to abandoning orthodox religion in favour of differing degrees of humanism. Her primary faith, she explained at length, was in 'goodness and truth – sincere, unselfish, incorruptible'; while he, for his part, could only envy people with such ideals: 'I seem to be condemned to a life of doubt, of seeking an escape from conflicting opposites.' In the same letters they reached a polite but fundamental disagreement about the nature of music, in which she found religious, even moral qualities. 'I am convinced', wrote von Meck, 'that if the most heartless robber, at the very moment when his knife is poised above his victim, could suddenly hear some music, he would drop the knife and weep.'[14] None too sure about this, Tchaikovsky was appalled by her suggestion that music could have the same effect upon her as a glass or two of sherry. 'I'm especially offended by your comparison of music with intoxication,' he complained. 'Man has recourse to liquor to deceive himself, to give himself the *illusion* of contentment and well-being . . . [whereas] music is not deception, but *revelation*. Its unique power is to reveal to us elements of beauty which are not accessible by any other means, the contemplation of which reconciles us to our lives not just for that moment, but for ever.'[15]

It was a rare if well-mannered disagreement amid the nearly three hundred letters this unlikely couple exchanged during 1877–78 (not to mention the ones he confessed to tearing up and not sending because of their 'unworthiness'). The detail, at times, is quite extraordinary for two correspondents who had never met, and who knew they could never be lovers. Amid long and heartfelt discussions on the nature of religion and idealism, politics and music, he will suddenly tell her whether or not he left his window open at night; amid all the genuine pressure of his work, he would confess to 'rushing back' from his long afternoon walks because of his need to write to her; to her, the mere sight of one of his letters is 'rose-coloured, aromatic . . . like ether, for inhaling its scent will ease my pain.'[16] She longs to hear the sound of his voice, 'not to my face, of course, but from somewhere you cannot see me.'[17] They marvel at the apparent telepathy which had them thinking the same thoughts while half a continent apart: 'I have long been amazed', says von Meck, 'by the remarkable empathy and almost supernatural affinity of ideas and feelings evident in almost every single one of our letters . . . From your last one I can tell that our thoughts, our perceptions, even our disappointments are linked by the same destiny.'[18] Amid profuse declarations of thanks for her generosity (usually, as in the following example, preceding another request for money), Tchaikovsky tells von Meck that he loves her 'with all the power of my soul . . .'

> There is something so special about our relationship that it often stops me in my tracks with amazement. I have told you more than once, I believe, that you have come to seem to me the hand of Fate itself, watching over me and protecting me. The very fact that I do not know you personally, while feeling so close to you, accords you in my eyes the special status of an unseen but beneficent presence, like a benign Providence . . .[19]

At the end of November, as she reported on the first Moscow performance of his Rococo Variations, he replied that he had writer's block. He had been invited to contribute a piece to an album to mark the unveiling of the Bellini Monument in Naples, but 'for the first time in my life I couldn't squeeze out of myself *a single note*'.[20] Somehow, however, he managed to continue the orchestration of the second act of *Onegin*, including the vocal score which Anatoly was due to take back with him to Russia. Urging Tchaikovsky too to return to Moscow, von Meck offered him the use of a wing of her town house on the Boulevard

Rozhdestvensky; they would not meet, of course, but he would be so fortified from the outside world that no-one need even know he was there. But Tchaikovsky was still too afraid of having to explain the last few months to anyone. After a brief excursion to Vienna, he proposed an extended stay in Venice, where he had found a quiet room overlooking the Lido at the Hotel Beau Rivage.

On 2 December he moved on with Anatoly to Vienna, where they met up again with Kotek, now a pupil of the great Joachim, but fallen out of favour with von Meck. The composer's priorities are clear when he writes to his patron that her former protégé – and his former lover – had become 'a desperate womanizer'. This, he knew, was the reason why the young man had been banished from the von Meck ménage; her disapproval was so strong that she avoided all mention of the subject in her reply to Tchaikovsky, who later discovered she had refused Kotek the mere one hundred roubles he had requested to continue his studies in Berlin.

Tchaikovsky's own von Meck money proved a mixed blessing when it enabled his servant Alexey Sofronov to join him in Vienna, facilitating Anatoly's departure. En route back to Venice, it so happened that Tchaikovsky and his 'Alyosha' travelled from Austria in the same railway compartment in which he and Anatoly had so recently made the same journey. 'This redoubled my grief [at your departure],' he wrote to Anatoly. 'As I wept, I had a vision that you, too, were weeping for me at the selfsame moment, which of course made everything worse . . . Farewell, my darling, my beloved. I kiss you a million times. What would I not give to kiss you in reality!'[21] This was swiftly followed by another, even more intimate Christmas greeting: 'I lie on my bed thinking of you, wishing, dreaming, imagining that I am smothering you with kisses. Ah, how I love you, Tolya!' And, as Modest approached, another: 'Sometimes it feels like my soul simply wants to leave my body and fly to you. When shall I see you again?' Four months later he was still sufficiently exercised to write: 'Apart from the fact that I love you passionately, I have no idea at all what to say to you . . . I kiss you, my little one . . . I kiss your neck. I kiss your eyes. I kiss your lips.' Anatoly, it seems, had become the misplaced recipient of all the emotional energies for which Antonina had hoped.

These four months – five, since Anatoly's departure – had proved eventful ones for Tchaikovsky, still haunted by the spectre of Antonina, but still managing to combine a prolific musical output with an equally active sex life. The prospect of Alexey's arrival had been greeted with a letter so effusive that its innuendoes have not survived the cuts of the Soviet censor.

For the first time in his adult life, Modest had been kept at bay by his adored older brother. During Tchaikovsky's months of torment, the two had exchanged the usual loving effusions, but Modest had been given only a partial account of the Antonina saga. Between the lines, of course, the failure of his brother's marriage was something of a triumph for Modest, who had so strenuously advised against it; but he was not going to make any capital of this, merely seek to return to his brother's side. As Tchaikovsky grew keener on the idea, once Anatoly's departure became inevitable, he even wrote to Kolya Konradi's father, Herman, pleading that Modest be allowed to bring his charge to stay with him in Europe.

Modest's arrival in December coincided with even better news from Kamenka: Sasha had finally 'seen through' Antonina and thrown her out. His sister now realized, she wrote, that 'she was never in love with you, just desperate to land a husband.' The last straw seems to have been a change of heart on Antonina's part about becoming a nurse. The family had warmly approved her plan, which might have given her life a new direction, even led to a new marriage, and thus to the divorce Tchaikovsky so desperately desired – at least in principle if not altogether in practice, given his obsessive fear of gossip. Within a few days, however, Antonina had changed her mind, and announced her intention to return to Moscow – the last place, of course, the composer wanted her to go. 'I pray to God she chooses somewhere else to live before the next academic year,' he wrote to von Meck. 'The prospect of running into her would be highly unnerving.'[22]

The question of divorce had first arisen in his correspondence with his sister when his wife had arrived at Kamenka. He was as yet reluctant, for obvious reasons, to contemplate the publicity attendant on a court case. If Antonina wished to remarry, he would of course let her go – 'but not now. I cannot at present return to Russia. I am sick, and I need to rebuild my strength . . . My nerves are not yet strong enough to cope with all the fuss a divorce would entail.' Three months later, he remained reluctant to return to Russia, for all von Meck's supplications. St Petersburg was out of the question because of his father, who had been told nothing about the collapse of his son's marriage, and who was apparently devastated even by the news that he had travelled abroad without his wife. 'It would be impossible for me to see him,' Tchaikovsky told von Meck. 'I could not bring myself to lie to his face.' As for Moscow: the scars of his recent ordeal there had yet to heal. 'I would have to hide. I still cannot face anyone beyond my immediate family without being unhinged by anxiety . . . I am still so sick. I just can't face it all.'

A letter from Anatoly, now back in Moscow, served only to re-inforce his fears. Already Modest had told him that his illness had been front-page news: 'Only the [Russo-Turkish] war is as heated a topic of conversation, from the drawing rooms of Grand Dukes to the columns of the newspapers, most of whom have published denials of the rumour that you have gone mad . . .' Now Anatoly confirmed that his brother would find it 'very unpleasant' to be back in Moscow. 'There are so many rumours that God have mercy on you! All of them are sympathetic, to be sure, but I quite appreciate that you would find it very awkward and uncomfortable here.'

For the first time in his life, if not the last, Tchaikovsky was having to face up to the fact that his homosexuality might become known beyond the tight circle of his family and intimate friends. It was a prospect which filled him with despair. Although the Antonina experience had finally persuaded him once and for all that he could never be 'as other men', it was not something he cared to acknowledge publicly. Quite the opposite. By now he was all but paranoid on the subject, openly terrified that speculation about the failure of his marriage might lead to the exposure of his guilty secret – that it might even reach the ears of his patron. It became, in his own word, his 'monomania'. To Nikolay Rubinstein, from whom he had few secrets, he wrote that autumn: 'I beg you, for God's sake, not to summon me to Moscow before next September . . . I should die at the prospect of being talked about, pointed at, and so on. In short, my monomania is still with me.'

Now it was Rubinstein, in what was intended as a helpful gesture, who managed to extend his friend's monomania to embrace the whole of Europe. On being invited to lead the Russian musical delegation to the Paris International Exposition of 1878 – intended as a signal honour, and a method of delaying his return to Russia – Tchaikovsky replied in horrified tones: 'You know the cause of my monomania . . . Think of all the people I would meet in Paris, all the countless new acquaintances I would make: every one of them I should soon suspect of knowing about me the one thing I have struggled so long and hard to conceal. This would completely destroy me . . . I cannot face going anywhere where I am required to be conspicuous, to be in the public eye and the centre of attention.' His dogged refusal to go to Paris was incomprehensible to Rubinstein, who grew angry over the embarrassment and inconvenience the episode caused him. Now he became the butt of some cruel exchanges between von Meck and Tchaikovsky, who behind his back cruelly railed against the man to whom he owed so much.

Hitherto Rubinstein had remained entirely supportive, generously re-assuring Tchaikovsky that 'Your reputation as a musician is too high for anything irrelevant to compromise it'. So had other old friends like Apukhtin, whose scarcely concealed glee at the failure of the marriage was softened with a cryptic reminder that his *real* friends 'could not care less what kind of sauce, sweet or oily, you prefer on your asparagus'. With von Meck, again, the debate was conducted in somewhat different terms – with her commending him for refusing, like her, to care about worldly opinion when in fact he was consumed by concern about it. At the turn of the year, when the Christmas holiday saw him go four days without a letter from her, he was terrified that 'she had learnt about *that*, and decided to break off relations.'

From other aspects of Tchaikovsky's letters at this time, it would appear that Modest's return to his brother's life excited him rather less than the reappearance of young Kolya Konradi, the 'angel' whom it was 'such a delight to kiss and caress'. Even a minor crisis involving a protracted stay in San Remo, while his servant Alexey was treated for syphilis, only briefly unsettled Tchaikovsky's ever improving spirits. And the death of his half-sister Zinaida, whom he had scarcely seen since his childhood, moved him to few of his usual laments about mortality; he was, for once, more concerned about the effect on others, notably his father and Zinaida's children, than on himself. So fast was the composer now recovering from his trauma that he was quickly settling back into his old ways.

In Florence the previous autumn, he had been taking an evening stroll with Anatoly when they came upon a crowd gathered around some street musicians. 'It turned out to be a boy of about ten or eleven, singing to the accompaniment of a guitar. He had a wonderfully rich, full voice, with a warmth and polish rarely found even in the most accomplished of artists. Most striking of all was that the song had a tragic strain, which sounded particularly poignant on the lips of a child. I was captivated.' Back in Florence two months later, this time with Modest and Kolya, he mounted a desperate search for the boy, whom he eventually found performing in the annual carnival. Cancelling 'another amorous rendezvous', as he told Anatoly, he invited the child, whose name was Vittorio, to come and sing for him in his hotel room. To von Meck he enthused about the rhythmic charms of Italian folk singing, and especially of Vittorio's song 'Pimpinella' (which he was to set as the last of his Six Songs, Op. 38);[23] to Anatoly he described the boy's 'stunning beauty', and his 'indescribably attractive eyes and smile', before the Soviet censor again intervenes.

'Only now,' he confessed to Anatoly, 'especially after the episode of my marriage, have I finally come to conclude that there is nothing more pointless than wanting to be anything other than what I am by nature.'[24]

# PART IV

---

## *1879–84*
## THE WANDERER

*To regret the past and to hope for the future,*
*never to be satisfied with the present: that is*
*the story of my life.*

# CHAPTER X

# 'A free man'

ON 22 FEBRUARY 1878, WHILE TCHAIKOVSKY WAS STILL RELISHING THE delights of Florence, Nikolay Rubinstein conducted the first performance of his Fourth Symphony in Moscow. Among those present was its covert dedicatee, Mme von Meck, who reported that despite a poor performance from the orchestra, whom she considered under-rehearsed, 'the audience received it very warmly, especially the *scherzo*. At the end there was tremendous applause, with the audience calling for you.'[1]

She was telling him only part of the truth. His closest musical friends, those to whose opinion he attached more importance, were so unsure about parts of the symphony that they left Tchaikovsky to fret for a month, to his mounting distress, without a word of comment, let alone praise. He had certainly been present 'in spirit', as he put it, at the première; from Florence he had calculated 'minute by minute' when the opening bars would ring out, and what the audience would be thinking: 'Probably that the first movement (the most complex, but also the best) was too long – and not, on first hearing, entirely comprehensible. The rest [is] much more straightforward.' A telegram from Rubinstein and the other musicians involved assured him only that his work had been well played, without a word as to its merits. 'Perhaps,' Tchaikovsky wondered aloud to von Meck, 'they are to be taken for granted?'

In his reply to her congratulations – the only word of praise he received, and that from a not impartial party – he described the symphony as 'a faithful echo' of the torments he had undergone during the latter half of 1877. But he was also at pains to emphasize that it was just that, an 'echo', and nothing more. For the most part the work had been conceived and sketched before his marriage to Antonina, though he admitted 'modifying' it during the subsequent months of orchestration. The symphony's alternations between angst and serenity, even joy, throughout each of its four movements clearly reflect the respective effects upon him, as he was writing it, of his wife and his patron. Now he spelt out to von Meck, in detail he had never before imparted (or ever would again), the 'programme' behind the piece, punctuating his remarks with musical quotations from the first movement.

> The introduction is the *seed* of the whole symphony, undoubtedly the central theme. This is *Fate*, i.e. that fateful force which prevents the impulse towards happiness from entirely achieving its goal, forever on jealous guard lest peace and well-being should ever be attained in complete and unclouded form, hanging above us like the Sword of Damocles, constantly and unremittingly poisoning the soul. Its force is invisible, and can never be overcome. Our only choice is to surrender to it, and to languish fruitlessly. Feelings of desolation and hopelessness thus grow stronger and more destructive. Surely it would be better to turn away from reality and wallow in daydreams? What bliss! A sweet and tender daydream appears. A gracious, spellbinding human form flits by and beckons us away. How good it feels! How distant now seems the obsessive first theme of the allegro. Daydreams have gradually taken complete possession of the soul. All things gloomy and joyless are forgotten. Here, at last, here is true happiness! . . . But no, these were but daydreams, and Fate inevitably returns to wake us from them.

'Thus,' he sums up, 'life consists of a constant alternation between harsh reality and fleeting dreams or visions of happiness . . . There is no hiding place . . . We can only drift on this sea until it engulfs us and pulls us down to its depths.'

The programme for the second movement encapsulated 'another phase of depression': that melancholy mood typical of an evening when, 'tired from your day's work, you are sitting alone, and you have picked up a book, but it slips from your hand . . .' Harking back to his favourite Dante dictum from *Francesca da Rimini*, Tchaikovsky distils the feeling at which he was aiming in terms of 'memories crowding in . . . It is sad that so much *has come and gone*, yet pleasant to recall your youth . . .

You feel nostalgia for the past, yet no compulsion to start life over again. Life has wearied you; it is pleasant to pause and weigh things up. Memories abound – of those happy days when your young blood bubbled, and life was good, but also of hard times, moments of pain, irreparable losses. Now it all seems so distant. It is both sad yet somehow sweet to immerse yourself in the past.

The third movement was designed to express 'no definite feeling', more a series of 'capricious arabesques' and other fleeting images of the kind which flash past the imagination after a few drinks, in the first stages of intoxication. 'You are neither happy nor sad. You are thinking of nothing specific, just letting your imagination run free, and somehow it begins to paint strange pictures' – a tableau of drunken peasants, a street song, in the distance a military procession – 'the kind of disjointed images which flash through your head as you are falling asleep. They have nothing to do with reality; they are strange, wild, incoherent.'

In resolving all these elements, the fourth and final movement appears to draw on Tolstoy's recently published (in serial form) *Anna Karenina*, notably the scene in which Levin reconsiders his own values while watching some peasants dancing. 'If you can't find causes for joy within yourself, look at others. Go out among the [common] people. See what a good time they have, utterly surrendering themselves to feelings of joy . . .' The music paints 'a picture of peasants celebrating a festival'. Yet barely has Tchaikovsky's listener managed to drown his own troubles in the joys of others when, inevitably, '*Fate* intervenes again, to bring you back to yourself.' The rest of the world dances on, oblivious to your woes, still finding plenty to enjoy in life, however innocent and unsophisticated. 'So you have only yourself to blame. You cannot say that everything in the world is sad. Learn from the happiness of others, with their simple but potent pleasures. It *is* possible to live.'[2]

As Tchaikovsky's only explicit exegesis of a musical 'programme', this oft-quoted passage has come, over the years, to be taken far too literally. To students of the composer's true character, the incongruously upbeat ending smacks at best of self-deception, more likely of an *ex post facto* casuistry, its elaborate ornamentations tailor-made for his patron's romantic longings. A month later, still having heard nothing from his musical colleagues in Russia, he solicited the views of Taneyev, who replied promptly and all too honestly. In his response to a fellow-musician, painfully grateful for his candour, Tchaikovsky spoke of his Fourth Symphony in much more convincing terms.

You are right to suggest that my symphony is programmatic. What I
don't understand is why you consider this a fault. I live in dread of
the opposite – that is, I should not wish to write symphonic works
which express nothing, which consist only of empty experiments
with chords, rhythms and modulations. Of course my symphony is
programmatic, but its programme is such that it cannot be expressed
in words . . . Shouldn't a symphony – the most lyrical of all musical
forms – be just such a work? Should it not express all those things
for which there are no words, but which the soul wishes to express,
and which needs to be expressed?

Taneyev had found the symphony 'excellent in parts', but less impressive 'overall' than, for instance, *Francesca da Rimini*. Although he
much admired the first movement, he considered it (as the composer had
feared) too long: 'It has the feeling of a symphonic poem to which three
movements have been arbitrarily tacked on to make up a symphony.'
After a critique of the *andantino* and *scherzo*, Taneyev declared his
dislike of the trio, 'which sounds like it comes from a ballet'. Rubinstein,
he reported, had liked the finale 'best of all'. Taneyev could not agree.
Apart from its unconvincing structure, the symphony's principal failing,
to which he could never reconcile himself, was that 'in each movement
there is a passage which smacks of ballet music: the central section
of the *andante*, the trio of the *scherzo*, the march-like passage in the
finale . . .'[3] This stung Tchaikovsky into a memorable riposte:

I simply do not understand what it is that you call ballet music, and
why you 'cannot reconcile yourself' to it. Do you consider as ballet
music every cheerful tune which has a dance rhythm? If so, you must
be unable to reconcile yourself to most of Beethoven's symphonies, in
which you find such passages all over the place . . . It is beyond my
comprehension that you should use 'ballet music' as a term of abuse
. . . I can only assume that the 'ballet-like' sections of my symphony
displease you not because they are 'ballet-like', but because they are
*bad*. You may well be right, but I still can't grasp why dance tunes
may not crop up here and there in a symphony, even if only to
convey a deliberately vulgar strain of coarse humour. Again I must
cite Beethoven, who employed this device more than once . . .

Tchaikovsky further invoked Beethoven under the heading of 'programme' music, citing his Fifth Symphony as having 'inspired, in its
programmatic essentials, the concept of [my] own symphony.' If Taneyev
could not understand what Tchaikovsky had tried to achieve, 'then it

The civil servant turned music student in his early twenties (*Range/Bettmann*).

Tchaikovsky's father, Ilya Petrovich (*Novosti*); his mother, Alexandra
Andreyevna (*Roger-Viollet*); and his childhood home in Votkinsk
(*Lebrecht Collection*).

His governess, Fanny Dürbach (*Novosti*).

BELOW: The Tchaikovsky family in 1848, with his parents surrounded by (left to right) eight-year-old Pyotr Ilyich, his sister Sasha, his half-sister Zinaida and his brothers Nikolay and Ippolit (*Lebrecht Collection*).

ABOVE: The schoolboy Tchaikovsky (front row, in front of bow-tied teacher) holds hands with his neighbour in the 1859 graduation class of the Imperial School of Jurisprudence (*Novosti*) (inset). BELOW: Moscow in the 1860s (*Hulton-Deutsch Collection*).

The brothers Nikolay (left) and
Anton Rubinstein,
Tchaikovsky's mentors
(*Novosti*). His friend
Nikolay Kashkin (below)
(*Novosti*), his publisher
Pyotr Yurgenson (centre)
(*Novosti*) and his fellow-
composers Balakirev
(*Lebrecht Collection*) and
Rimsky-Korsakov.

The soprano Désirée Artôt (*AKG London*), whom Tchaikovsky (here in his mid-twenties) briefly thought of marrying in 1868-69.

An engraving of the first performance of *Swan Lake*, 1877 (*Range/Bettmann*).
BELOW: The composer (right) with his brother Modest (centre) and his deaf-mute pupil, Kolya Konradi, in San Remo, 1878. Standing behind is Tchaikovsky's manservant, Alexey Sofronov.

The newly-weds: Tchaikovsky and his ill-fated bride, Antonina Milyukova, soon after their wedding in 1877.

follows only that I am no Beethoven, something I have never doubted for one moment.' As if to settle both matters once and for all, he concluded emphatically: 'There is not even a single phrase in this symphony, i.e. mine, which I did not feel deeply, and which did not serve as an echo of the sincere impulses of my soul.'[4]

For all his righteous indignation, Tchaikovsky was grateful for Taneyev's careful response, rightly suspecting that his friend was hiding from him a lukewarm reaction to the symphony's first performance. Not until its St Petersburg première, the following November, would the Fourth Symphony begin to receive its due respect, earning its place in the repertoire as the first of his four major symphonic achievements – 'expanding the form', as Laroche put it in his review, 'beyond its traditional boundaries.'

The Fourth Symphony, Tchaikovsky wrote to von Meck, was 'a step forward in my technical development'. In truth, of course, it was a great deal more. The most important step forward, as one biographer has argued, was in the composer's emotional development. 'All the frustrations of his endemic homosexuality and bottled-up emotions, further engendered rather than released by the fiasco of his marriage, are let loose in this symphony – the first and perhaps least important work in a line of masterpieces or near-masterpieces in this vein which included the *Manfred* Symphony and the last two symphonies, the symphonic ballad *The Voevoda* and [the opera] *The Queen of Spades*.'[5]

Taneyev, in the same letter, waxed as enthusiastic about *Eugene Onegin* as he had nit-picking about the symphony. 'A wonderful opera! And yet you say that you're thinking of giving up. On the contrary, it's now more important than ever for you to compose. You are writing better than you ever have before. Put to even more profitable use your attainment of such perfection . . .' With these two works, in other words, both forged largely through suffering, Tchaikovsky had taken his first unambiguous step towards the lasting achievements of his maturity.

After two months of a 'dull but tranquil' daily routine in Florence, the composer felt 'completely recovered from my madness'. All that remained was his personal brand of misanthropy, which he thought he would 'probably never shed'. Otherwise, 'the man who in May decided to marry Antonina Ivanovna, in June (as if nothing had happened) wrote an entire opera, in July got married, in September ran away from his wife . . . was not I, but another Pyotr Ilyich Tchaikovsky.'[6]

To his adoring patron, Tchaikovsky's musical response to the disasters of 1877 had confirmed him as her true stereotype of the romantic artist, sublimating his personal suffering and worldly ennui in sublime, at times even optimistic music. 'How delighted I am', von Meck would confirm, 'to have found in you living proof that my ideal of the composer can exist.'[7] To Tchaikovsky himself, the rest of his life began with some home truths, especially about his sexuality. Never again would he consider marriage a possible smokescreen for, or escape-route from, his 'true nature', to which he could now allow free rein without inhibition. Never again would he delude himself that he was as capable of sexual love for women as for men. He had finally persuaded himself, as much as Anatoly, that there was 'nothing more futile than wanting to be anything other than what I am by nature.'[8]

If the spiritual aftermath of his marriage contained silver linings, the practical consequences were unremittingly bleak. Since January Tchaikovsky had been trying to negotiate a financial settlement with Antonina, who was demanding a monthly allowance of one hundred roubles. His agreement was conditional on her good behaviour; if ever word reached him that she had been abusing his good name, or if any conduct on her part 'tended towards the disturbance of my tranquillity', the subsidy would cease forthwith. This warning apparently did nothing to prevent her striking deep behind Tchaikovsky's defences, by writing hurt letters to his father. They were intercepted by Anatoly, and subsequently returned unopened, but the composer was deeply enraged. Through his brother he warned 'the spawn of hell', as he now referred to his wife, that all subsidies would cease immediately unless she gave a written undertaking never again to contact himself, his father or any other member of his family. In return for said undertaking, on top of the hundred roubles a month, she would receive a once-and-for-all lump sum of 2,500 roubles.

Make it 10,000 roubles, suggested von Meck, if she will agree to a divorce. The eager recipient of all Tchaikovsky's marital complaints, his patron could not understand why the composer appeared so hesitant about the divorce for which she was herself offering to pay. In his letters, he was all bravado: 'If she wants a divorce,' ran his instructions to Anatoly, 'so much the better'. But in private his longstanding fear of scandal, and exposure as a homosexual, reigned supreme.

The divorce laws of the day, moreover, were highly restrictive. The only feasible ground was adultery, which would have to be stage-managed for witnesses. Tchaikovsky's declared willingness to arrange such an event convinced no-one in the know, least of all Anatoly, now acting as his lawyer as well as his chief family confidant. Antonina's growing eccentricity had the composer seriously worried about the threat of exposure, even blackmail. By divorcing her, which entailed a full and final lump-sum settlement, he would lose control over her future conduct. The leverage offered him by the monthly allowance, and thus by procrastinating over the details of divorce, seemed a safer tactic for the foreseeable future.

At the end of February, with Modest, Kolya and Alexey in tow, Tchaikovsky returned to the Villa Richelieu at Clarens, on Lake Geneva, intent on resuming work on a piano sonata he had started sketching in Florence. Over the first few days, he had occasion to complain of noisy interruptions in the next room, as his servant undertook a spirited seduction of his landlady's maid, Marie. His 'Alyosha', he decided, had been treated over-indulgently: 'Henceforth he will be nothing more than a servant to me. The over-spiced affections of old are no more.' This proved doubly true when, to the embarrassment of all concerned, a product of the union emerged nine months later.

Struggling over the sonata, he dabbled each day in lesser piano pieces – the nucleus of what would become his twelve salon pieces (Op. 40) – and was casting around for his next major project when the rearrival in his entourage of young Kotek proved a mixed blessing. On the one hand, his was another mouth to feed; Tchaikovsky saw no irony in complaining to von Meck that her former protégé appeared 'quite happy to live at someone else's expense'. At the same time, the violinist offered 'much-loved' male companionship, a partner for musical diversions in the evenings, and exactly the inspiration he was seeking for his next major composition. With Kotek on hand, himself in need of a new project to divert him, Tchaikovsky began to plan his Violin Concerto in D major (Op. 35).

The change in the composer's spirits evident from the vibrant lyricism of the concerto, in such stark contrast to the hollow dullness of the piano sonata, can only be attributed to the arrival of Kotek, of whom he remained almost inordinately fond. But the high-minded Tchaikovsky's disapproval of the young man's readiness to rely on the financial support of others, especially his father, saw a certain edge enter their relationship, otherwise a model of personal and professional compatibility. This in turn gave the Violin Concerto the sharply conflicting moods which have carried it through to posterity. It was sketched and completely orchestrated in less than a month. The dedication would certainly have been Kotek's, had not Tchaikovsky continued to live in dread of 'malicious gossip'; instead it was offered to the composer's friend Leopold Auer (already the recipient of the *Sérénade mélancolique* three years earlier), whose celebrity, he hoped, would better assist the work's public fortunes.

In the event Auer proved less grateful than troublesome, protesting that the concerto was 'almost impossible' to play, with the long-term result that the première scheduled for 22 March 1879 in St Petersburg was postponed *sine die*. According to Yurgenson, Auer complained that he feared he would 'do himself a mischief' if he attempted the solo part as it stood. In his memoirs, published thirty years after Tchaikovsky's death, a defensive Auer protested that he had merely wished to make 'revisions' to the solo part, and that his busy schedule had prevented him getting around to this for two years. During that time, Tchaikovsky later recalled, he considered his 'poor child' to have been 'cast cruelly into the abyss of eternal oblivion'. Even Kotek had proved reluctant to learn it. Still haunted by the fate of his First Piano Concerto at the hands of Nikolay Rubinstein, Tchaikovsky eventually gave up on Auer and transferred the dedication to another virtuoso, Adolf Brodsky, who gave the concerto its first performance three years after it was written, on 4 December 1881, at a Vienna Philharmonic Society concert conducted by Hans Richter.

As Auer continued to find excuses not to play the piece, Brodsky also gave its first Russian performance at an RMS concert in Moscow on 20 August 1882. Both the piece and Brodsky's performance of it were very well received. This had not been the case at the world première in Vienna, which had provoked violent controversy – drawing huge acclaim for Brodsky but vituperation for the piece and its composer, perhaps explained by Tchaikovsky's well-known antipathy for Brahms. From the eminent Austrian critic Eduard Hanslick, one of Brahms's leading champions, came the most damning remark ever made about Tchaikovsky's work in his lifetime: that this violin concerto was a prime example of those musical compositions which the listener could 'hear stinking'. Hanslick reviled the very hallmarks which have since made the piece so popular: its athletic energy, its robust romanticism and its red-bloodedly Slavonic finale.

> For a while it moves along well enough, musical and not lacking spirit, but soon the roughness gets the upper hand and remains in charge until the end of the first movement. It is no longer a question of whether the violin is being played, but of being yanked about and torn to tatters. Whether it is at all possible to extract a pure sound out of these hair-raising acrobatics I do not know, but I do know that in making the attempt Mr Brodsky tortured his audience no less than he did himself. The adagio, with its gentle Slav melancholy, is well on the way to reconciling us and winning us over. But abruptly it ends, making way for a finale that transports us into the brutish, grim jollity of a Russian church festival. In our mind's eye we see nothing but common, ravaged faces, hear rough oaths and smell cheap liquor.[9]

Tchaikovsky had not been as wounded, according to Modest, since Cui's devastating indictment of his graduation cantata fifteen years earlier. The composer was so affected that he was able to recite Hanslick's remarks in full, in the original German\*, to his dying day.

Among the music Kotek and Tchaikovsky had played through together that summer were Brahms's First Symphony and Lalo's concerto-style *Symphonie espagnole*; both admired the Lalo as much as they disliked the Brahms, and its influence can be heard in the Violin Concerto's opening movement, whose lyrical elegance also shows the continuing influence of Saint-Saëns. As in his First Piano Concerto, Tchaikovsky made an unorthodox start by opening with some striking phrases which are then discarded and never heard again. But the sensuous beauty of the ensuing *allegro moderato* is itself one of the main reasons for the concerto's enduring popularity with soloists and concert audiences, as is the melody sustaining the ensuing *canzonetta andante*. When Tchaikovsky and Kotek had played through the original draft to Modest at Clarens, both soloist and brother had expressed reservations about its slow movement; confirmed in his own doubts, the composer promptly discarded it and sketched this entirely new *andante* in just one day, orchestrating it in four. The result was Tchaikovsky's most sustained piece of melodic writing since the central theme of *Francesca da Rimini*.

Never one to waste his rejects, he reused the original as *Méditation*, the first of the three pieces for violin and piano, *Souvenir d'un lieu cher* (Op. 42), written the following month. The concerto's replacement *canzonetta* leads without pause into the concluding *allegro vivacissimo*, a rondo whose lyrical gipsy rusticism and wild Cossack folk-dance themes call for bravura skills from both soloist and orchestra. As is typical of Tchaikovsky's major works for solo instrument and orchestra, the piece makes exceptional demands upon the soloist, in terms of both virtuosity and stamina; but neither Auer's protests nor Hanslick's sympathy for them have stopped most subsequent concert violinists making it a cornerstone of their repertoire.

By the end of April, another major work accomplished, Tchaikovsky was ready to return to Russia, if not yet to Moscow. First stop was to be Kamenka for the spring, with Modest, Kolya and Alexey.

Bureaucratic heavy-handedness conspired to sour the long-awaited

---

\*'Tschaikowsky's Violin-concert bringt uns zum ersten Mal auf die schauerliche Idee, ob es nicht auch Musikstücke geben könne, die man stinken hört . . .' Hanslick was paraphrasing the German politician, poet and aesthete Friedrich Vischer (1807–87), who had recently argued that there were certain 'lascivious' paintings which the viewer could 'see stinking'.

thrill of his return via Vienna, after more than six months in Europe, to his 'beloved motherland'. Detained for passport irregularities by a 'drunken incompetent' of an immigration officer, then searched by over-zealous customs officials, Tchaikovsky was finally dismayed to find himself seated in a 'filthy dirty' railway compartment. But his complaints to von Meck were soon staunched by an unexpected bonus on his arrival at Kamenka, where Sasha and Lev had prepared for him his own separate cottage, complete with upright piano, detached from the main house and commanding a picturesque view of the nearby village. Able to compose here without fear of interruption, he continued work on his Piano Sonata in G major (Op. 37), and embarked on his popular set of piano pieces, the *Album for Children* (Op. 39).

It would almost have been a return to normality, with Tchaikovsky as content and productive as he had ever been, were it not for an apparent collapse of his critical faculties. The Piano Sonata, to at least one critic, is 'a strong candidate as the dullest piece Tchaikovsky ever wrote'.[10] The trouble was that continuing reminders of Antonina's menacing presence lurked on the margins of his life. Reluctantly allowing Anatoly to pursue the question of divorce, and secretly relieved when his wife proved obstructive, Tchaikovsky prepared himself for more sleepless nights as he entered into a direct correspondence with her. There was no question, he was at pains to stress, of a reconciliation: 'Never, under any circumstances, in any way, or for any reward in the world, will I ever again agree to live with you.' Her reply was understandably bitter, complaining of 'the suffering you have forced upon me since October, cruelly consigning me to the mockery and ridicule of the world.' Where now was the 'faultless demigod' she had married? After sounding off in some style, Antonina finally accepted the von Meck solution, his offer of 10,000 roubles, if he would also pay off debts amounting to another 2,500. Facing the prospect of a divorce, Tchaikovsky was obliged to appear delighted, writing to von Meck that he had 'danced around the garden with joy for an hour and a half'. In other letters to his family, however, his old apprehensions resurface, darkened by a growing unease at his financial dependence on his benefactress.

Von Meck's pecuniary control over his peace of mind, which caused him much heartsearching at this time, was now in uneasy alliance with her own growing need to have him near her. While maintaining her insistence that they never meet, she was offering him the use of her estate at Brailov, near Kamenka, during her continued absence in Moscow. Recalling her dismay when he had ducked her first offer of hospitality, at her Moscow town house, Tchaikovsky this time felt obliged to accept, taking Alexey with him from Kamenka at the end of May.

His ten-day sojourn at Brailov proved none too onerous a courtesy to his patron. Tchaikovsky lived in high style, he told his sister, waited on hand and foot in a 'palace' equipped with every luxury, spared any interruptions from the outside world. He was even able to forget Antonina long enough to add two short pieces for violin and piano to the discarded slow movement from his Violin Concerto, dubbing the finished product *Souvenir d'un lieu cher* (Op. 42) – a title thrillingly cryptic enough to gratify its inevitable dedicatee, his absentee hostess. He left the piece at Brailov as a surprise gift for her return.

This retreat from reality proved all too brief, with the complex mechanics of his divorce demanding his reluctant presence in Moscow by mid-June. Tchaikovsky dreaded his return: to him Moscow now symbolized drudgery (in the shape of the Conservatoire), menace (the threat of malicious gossip) and terror as much of his colleagues and friends as of the lurking presence of Antonina. 'God forbid I should bump into her in Moscow,' he wrote to Modest, 'lest I get fatally carried away with rage.' The composer was now convinced, fairly or unfairly, that his wife was 'deranged'. Her behaviour was certainly inconsistent; all attempts to discuss the practicalities of divorce, whether by Tchaikovsky or his various intermediaries, received confused and illogical, at times hostile replies. All demonstrated to her husband the grim truth that he would never be rid of Antonina's deeply disturbing irruptions into his life. 'It is clear', he told von Meck gloomily, 'that she intends to play the role of some supreme arbiter of my fate.'[11]

He kept the visit as short as possible, struggling through a reunion with his musical colleagues, hosted by his publisher, Yurgenson; enjoying a gossipy dinner with his old friend Bochechkarov; and worrying about Anatoly's capacity to combine overwork with an energetic love life. But it was, of all things, the Russian Orthodox Church which gave him the excuse he needed to scuttle away after just three days. While setting out the byzantine procedures prescribed for divorce, in themselves sufficient to unnerve him, the secretary of the Consistory made it quite clear that large-scale bribery was an integral part of the system. On his relieved return to Kamenka, however, even his outrage at the church and all its works, given splenetic vent in a letter to von Meck, did not prevent Tchaikovsky returning to work on his sketches of a solemn liturgy of St John Chrysostom. Church music, as Yurgenson had told him, could be good for business.

To his recent piano pieces, he now also added some of his most accomplished songs. Of the Six Romances (Op. 38), the best-known is the robust Don Juan's Serenade; but far the most memorable is the haunting 'Amid the din of the ball', to words by the poet Alexey Tolstoy (a distant relative of the novelist). During his 'recovery' period, since the première of the Fourth Symphony, Tchaikovsky had consciously been trying to write 'at least one small piece a day'. Now, in six months, he had completed a piano sonata, two sets of piano pieces (twenty-two in all), a set for violin and piano, six songs and a large mass. Suggesting their respective values to Yurgenson, as was his practice, he reached a combined total of 915 roubles – 'but, seeing I have written so much at one go, I will let you have the lot for 800.' As much as the money, which was marginal in the context of his allowance from his patron, Tchaikovsky was seeking to broaden the range of his published works – essential for the advancement of his international reputation.

An indispensible champion of his music, Yurgenson had also agreed to act as official liaison with his estranged wife. For the rest of his life, Tchaikovsky would henceforth open his publisher's letters with trembling fingers, unsure whether they contained good financial or bad marital news. That summer Antonina was proving at first elusive, then unco-operative. Refusing to go along with the phoney divorce procedures, she had even written to the priest who had married them, Tchaikovsky's Conservatoire colleague, suggesting that it was his responsibility to persuade her husband to return to her. To Yurgenson's assurance that she would not have to perjure herself in a divorce court – that the evidence of her husband's infidelity would be presented by others – she made the ominous reply: 'I will prove the reverse.' Alarmed by this apparent threat to expose him in the most public forum possible, Tchaikovsky instructed Yurgenson to take firm action to get Antonina out of Moscow. She was to be paid (by von Meck, of course) the 2,500 roubles required to clear her debts, and a further advance on monthly allowances, on the strict condition that she leave Moscow at once, and stay away while there was any chance that he might be there. She was also told that she had for ever forfeited the lump sum settlement of 10,000 roubles which had been on offer.

These negotiations disturbed the tranquillity of an idle summer with the Davidovs, first at Kamenka, then at their nearby estate of Verbovka, where Tchaikovsky did not enjoy separate working facilities. Welcoming distractions from his worries, he diverted himself with hunting and playing the fond uncle, directing his extended family in some amateur theatricals. The comings and goings of Modest, Anatoly and, for once, Ippolit, lent light and shade to his pastoral retreat; but as the summer wore on, and the prospect of the new Conservatoire term began to loom, he soon slumped into his familiar melancholy. 'To regret the past and to hope for the future, never to be satisfied with the present: that is the story of my life,' he wrote to the departed Anatoly.[12] Soon his depression began to degenerate into his habitual 'misanthropy', as he called it, and he felt the need to be alone again. Planning a return to Brailov, this time on his own, he diverted via Kiev and Kondratiev's estate at Nizy, to savour a last few days in Modest's company, this time without young Kolya. Then he returned to the absent arms of his patron.

In a summer throughout which he had consciously eschewed more musical work, and greedily devoted himself to reading, Tchaikovsky happily wallowed in von Meck's extensive library at Brailov. Dealing with the proofs of *Eugene Onegin*, his mind naturally rambled around possible subjects for another opera, and de Musset's *Les Caprices de Marianne* temporarily supplanted his long-cherished plans to set *Romeo and Juliet*. After only four days, however, both were forgotten when his inactivity suddenly caught up with him, and he felt a sudden urge to sketch an orchestral scherzo – the impulse for what would become his First Suite for orchestra. Girding his loins for the inevitable return to Moscow, he drafted three movements and sketched a fourth before time finally caught up with him. As if incapable of facing Moscow – fraught with such perils as the Conservatoire, Antonina, even the heavy presence of Mme von Meck – he announced his intention to go to St Petersburg to see Anatoly and their father.

En route, casually picking up an abandoned newspaper, he was devastated to read a gossipy article about the Moscow Conservatoire, licking its lips at the number of love affairs apparently conducted between professors and their female students. As if this were not enough, it continued: 'Love affairs of another kind also go on at the Conservatoire – but of these, for obvious reasons, I shall spare you the details.'[13] Mentioned by name in the article, if under another heading, Tchaikovsky was quite unmanned. The malicious gossip that he had so long feared appeared to be awaiting him on no uncertain scale. Convinced that the journalist could only be referring to him – as he made clear in an alarmed letter to Modest, calling the article 'a foul, base, vile, slanderous philippic' – he promptly made what he felt the only possible decision, if a drastic one: to resign from the Conservatoire as soon as possible. There was no way he could avoid the imminent autumn term; he could not inflict upon Rubinstein, still irritated by his failure to go to Paris, the chaos which would follow a precipitous resignation. But his mind was made up to leave before the end of the year.

In St Petersburg, while tenderly ministering to his family, and renewing his ties with Apukhtin, he spent six days finishing a long, bleak letter to Mme von Meck, ostensibly asking for her advice, but between the lines assuming her support for his bold decision. It was, after all, only her largesse which made it possible for him even to contemplate resignation.

He told her (in carefully guarded terms) of the newspaper article; of his shock at hearing strangers on the train discussing himself, the failure of his marriage and his reported 'insanity'; of the petty tyrannies of the 'intolerable' Rubinstein, and of the monotonous drudgery his teaching work had now become.

The idea of going back to his teaching duties after a year off was 'burdensome, repugnant, depressing, monotonous and appalling.' At times, on the journey north, he had 'even longed for the ultimate in time off, i.e. death . . .'

> What would you say if I were soon to leave the Conservatoire, quietly and without fuss, never to return? What if I were to continue living as far away as possible for another year or two? Until now I have always felt that, as there are so few people capable of teaching my subject, I was somehow morally obliged to stay at the Conservatoire; that I should sacrifice myself, regardless of my own nature and instincts. Recently, I have begun to change my mind. For one thing, I have always been a terrible teacher, not least because I have come to look on all my pupils as deadly enemies, there merely to torture and torment me. For another, should I not be devoting all my time and energy to the work I love, which amounts to the whole purpose, the whole meaning, the whole significance of my life?[14]

This appeal to his patron's sense of his musical worth could not go unheeded. To be doubly sure of an affirmative answer, however, Tchaikovsky hinted that his newfound freedom might enable him to spend more time under her roof, whether at Brailov or elsewhere. It had become impossible for him to live 'anywhere but in the country or abroad'; in short, he would 'like to lead the kind of nomadic life I have for the last year or so'. How much and how well he would compose, with his spirit 'liberated from the terrible squabbles' of his former life as a teacher – and husband! Only in the country or abroad, only when free to move on as he pleased, could he feel completely free from contamination by one whose mere existence would always inhibit or oppress him. 'I speak of *that certain personage*, of that living monument to my madness, whose sole purpose in life is to poison every minute of mine.'

He had not yet, Tchaikovsky lied, made up his mind. He would value von Meck's urgent opinion. 'Nothing in the world would make me do anything against your wishes . . .' It took a week for the expected reply to arrive, from San Remo.

I will tell you at once that I would be *utterly delighted* if you quit the Conservatoire. I have long thought it absurd that a man of your abilities, as intelligent, sophisticated and talented as you are, should be dependent on the whims of a petty tyrant in all particulars your inferior . . . As for the good your teaching would have done the generations to come, you will bless them much more with your *compositions* than by correcting their octaves and fifths. There are countless people who are good for nothing else, but you can build artistic monuments for young people to study and delight in. In short, it is completely to my liking, and in accordance with everything I believe in, everything I live for, that you should resign a position that is not commensurate with your worth and abilities. You have my whole-hearted blessing, my dear friend, for a move which I am sure you won't regret . . .[15]

While still in the capital, Tchaikovsky's uncharitable feelings about Nikolay Rubinstein were redoubled by the offer of a post from the director of the St Petersburg Conservatoire, Karl Davidov, who promised almost twice as much money for half as much work. No wonder he wrote to von Meck and his brothers what a splendid fellow this Davidov was. Even as Rubinstein was singing Tchaikovsky's praises in Paris, still using his influence to advance his music in Europe, the man himself proceeded gloomily on to Moscow, wondering how best to break the news of his departure to a man he had come to regard as a burden, but to whom he in fact had good reason to be very grateful.

When the term finally began, he had clearly talked and thought himself into a corner. There was no way he could see any redeeming feature in his life at the Conservatoire. 'I hate its professors, its students, its very walls,' he complained to Anatoly. 'I escape to the park each evening as if from some loathsome, stinking, suffocating dungeon.' Kashkin, Albrecht, Laroche, even Yurgenson he now found 'intolerable'. Entering and leaving the Conservatoire without a word to anyone, ignoring people's greetings, he increasingly sought the company of garrulous old Bochechkarov, and turned once again to the consoling powers of alcohol.

Disinclined to compose, having persuaded himself that creative work was incompatible with his teaching routine, it was only with the greatest difficulty, and after many evasions, that he fulfilled a contractual obligation to provide a new baritone aria for *The Oprichnik*. Of Antonina, at least, there was no sign; but now a new tormentor quite as alarming surfaced in the shape of her mother, who asked him to act as sponsor at her younger daughter's wedding, earnestly urging him the while to return to the 'complete and utter bliss' still available with Antonina.

Rubinstein's triumphant return from Paris was the chance for which Tchaikovsky had been waiting to beg release from his shackles. So mortified was he by the grand reception accorded the homecoming director, and so reluctant to beg any favours which might leave him in his debt, that he was still hesitating when Rubinstein himself sought him out. How was his old friend Tchaikovsky? Was he pleased to be back among his old friends and colleagues? It was too good a chance to miss. When the composer poured out his feelings, and insisted he could not remain at his post beyond the end of the current term, Rubinstein was most understanding; the two men embraced warmly, and parted 'on the best of terms'.

The director proved an even better friend than Tchaikovsky could have hoped, or perhaps deserved. Within days of his return Rubinstein could see for himself how little point there was in trying to retain the services of a composer fretting to stretch his wings. He suggested that some of Tchaikovsky's duties – all, before long – be taken over by Taneyev. The three agreed that he could slip away to the countryside, then write feigning illness, to avoid another spate of awkward questions. Within the term's first few weeks, by the end of October, Tchaikovsky was bidding farewell to his friends and colleagues of a dozen years.

'Yesterday I gave my last lesson,' he wrote to von Meck on 19 October 1878. 'Today I leave for St Petersburg. And so, at last, I am *a free man*.'[16]

# CHAPTER XI

## 'Things can't get worse'

SIX WEEKS LATER, ON 2 DECEMBER, TCHAIKOVSKY ARRIVED IN FLORENCE
to find an apartment made ready for him in loving detail, right down to
a new grand piano, books to his taste, Russian newspapers and his
favourite cigarettes. It was the doing, of course, of Madame von Meck,
who had begged him to come and live at her expense just two doors
away from the villa she herself had taken on the Viale dei Colli.

On the journey down to Italy, the composer fretted about the likely
constraints imposed by her proximity, and the seeming inevitability that
they would meet. Could it even be a trap to 'lure' him into her arms,
now that his marriage was unequivocally behind him? Was that why
she was so keen to promote (and finance) his divorce? But a reassuring
letter awaited his arrival, and he calmed down enough to settle in quite
happily, convinced that all would be well.

'Whatever may lie ahead this year, it can't be worse than the last,'
he had written to von Meck from this same city at the beginning of
the year. If the ensuing twelve months had brought mixed fortunes,
they had at least proved musically productive; and now they were
ending on a high note, with his liberation from the Conservatoire and
the prospect of open-ended wandering to his favourite haunts around
Europe and rural Russia, living the restless, rootless life he had come to
find so congenial. Florence – in the company, as it were, of his patron
– seemed as good a place as any to start.

It took him a few days to get used to the sheer strangeness of the set-up, with letters flowing back and forth daily – a kind of handwritten conversation – and the sight each morning of his benefactress pausing outside his windows, clearly hoping for a glimpse of her great composer at work. 'What am I supposed to do?' he complained to Modest. 'Go to the window and bow? If so, why not open it and shout "Good morning"?' Von Meck had tactfully given him a copy of her daily itinerary, complete with routes of the walks she proposed to take, so that they could avoid uncomfortable chance encounters. And her long, thoughtful and warm letters, for all their newly bold terms of endearment, betrayed no hint of any attempt to manoeuvre him into a meeting. Catching sight of each other at the theatre, whether by chance or design (on her part), only reinforced the self-restraint she had always shown in avoiding direct conversation. And just as he was relaxing into it all, their mutual joy in this curious, arms-length companionship was heightened by news from home of the successful St Petersburg première of 'her' symphony, the Fourth. It had caused, reported Modest, 'quite a stir'.

But still this Florentine 'idyll', as he tactfully called it in his letters to his hostess, was in truth less than idyllic for Tchaikovsky. There was little music worth hearing in the city, and he could not settle to any prolonged work. His only apparent pleasure came from reading *Little Dorrit*. 'Dickens and Thackeray are about the only people I can forgive for being English,' he told Anatoly, still bitter about Britain's role in the Russo-Turkish war. 'Of course one must add Shakespeare, but he lived in an age when that insufferable nation was less ignoble.'

In a move which made him very uncomfortable, von Meck now invited him to visit her villa while she was out, so that they could each share a picture of the other's daily domestic movements. The composer politely declined, pleading embarrassment at forcing everyone out of the house. Instead, the best she could do was to maintain a proxy presence in his household via the visits of her new protégé, a budding musician named Vladislav Pakhulsky, for twice-weekly lessons in composition. Though less convinced than his patron of Pakhulsky's musical talents, Tchaikovsky felt it was the least he could do, by way of gratitude for all her munificence, to take an interest in the young man and try to bring out the best in him.

He could only hope, meanwhile, that von Meck's eternal vigilance did not extend to the interest he was again taking in other boys around Florence, via a gay pimp of his long acquaintance named Napoleon. At first, he told Modest, he had tried to avoid the man who had so enlivened their last stay here together; but soon, with a certain, Figaro-like inevitability, the old rogue had caught up with him in the street one day, and was promptly leading him back into temptation. As long as the von Meck ménage was around to keep an eye on him, Tchaikovsky manfully resisted. By Christmas, however, she had moved on to Vienna, suggesting that they meet up again in Paris in February.

This parting shot again alarmed the composer, already unnerved by a letter declaring that she hoped 'things might *always* be just as they are now', and that she might '*always* take care of *every* aspect' of his well-being.[1] Von Meck had all but ordered him to move on to Clarens, where he had worked so fruitfully in the past, before proceeding to her side in the French capital. Anxious to track down a copy of the libretto for Auguste Mermet's opera *Jeanne d'Arc*, which he was hoping to use as the basis for his own *The Maid of Orleans*, he himself had planned to go there sooner, and resented his patron's rearranging of his itinerary to suit her needs.

Within a few days of von Meck's departure, however, he was surprised to find himself missing her, lamenting the absence of the daily correspondence which had so recently seemed such a strain, even confessing to Modest to a few tears at the sight of her empty villa. Only now did he realize how much he had in fact enjoyed her morning processions past his window, how flattered he had been by her hopes of a glimpse of him. Guiltily gilding his petty resentments with praise of her unbounded generosity, he finally worked out a compromise over his onward travel arrangements. He would proceed to Clarens, as she wished, but he would do so via Paris.

What he did not tell von Meck was that he had arranged to meet up there with young Kotek, still the object of her contempt. As it turned out, the reunion was not a success. Hoping for musical companionship, perhaps inspiration, Tchaikovsky soon found himself depressed and irritated by his young friend's obsessive womanizing; running short of money, he began to sink back into a depression – exacerbated, it would seem, by an unwonted period of prolonged sexual abstinence. (Alexey, these days, travelled merely as his servant.) Impressed though Tchaikovsky was by Sarah Bernhardt in Racine's *Andromaque*, his repeated visits to the Comédie Française were less for cultural than voyeuristic reasons. He had become obsessed with a dashing young actor by the name of Boucher, who had first caught his eye when in Paris with Modest two years before. Reminding his brother of their joint enthusiasm for the young man, he described how the play's dénouement called for him to slap another character across the face: 'What wouldn't I give to have that precious hand slap me across the face a hundred times!'[2]

For all its cultural and other charms, he found the noise and bustle of Paris a disconcerting contrast to the tranquillity of Florence. Increasingly irritated by Kotek, for whose excesses he was paying, his mood was rapidly worsened by the news of yet more trouble from Antonina. He had managed to keep her at bay while in Florence, angrily rejecting the offer of one of Modest's less savoury friends to pursue his wife with a view to proving *her* guilty of adultery; inevitably, he raged, she would accuse him before all the world of spying on her. Now, in Paris, he heard that she had been sending abusive letters to Yurgenson.

But Anatoly had even more alarming news: he had been approached by a man claiming to be a relative of Antonina, one Simonov, saying that she was now ready for a divorce, and desired to know his terms and conditions. At first Tchaikovsky panicked, interpreting this as a blackmail attempt. He had visions of his wife bringing against him a criminal charge of sodomy: 'I can see myself in the dock, outwitting the prosecution in my closing speech, but collapsing beneath the weight of the shameful indictment,' he wrote to his brother. Censors deleted the even more candid confession: 'I have tried to put a brave face on things, but already I consider myself utterly ruined.' In a few days he had calmed down, and told Anatoly to have nothing to do with so dubious a representative of 'that serpent'. He would deal with the matter whenever he returned to Moscow, in his own time and his own way. 'She can divorce me on the grounds of adultery, impotence, whatever she likes,' he declared boldly, while still in deep dread of the revelations a court case might bring.[3]

Mme Mayor's boarding-house at Clarens came as an oasis of calm amid all the drama. Arriving on 11 January, he was delighted to find the Villa Richelieu all but empty; now almost part of the family, he need not worry about his music disturbing other residents. Determined to proceed with *The Maid of Orleans*, he soon found the Mermet libretto inadequate, and began to write his own from Zhukovsky's translation of Schiller's *Die Jungfrau von Orleans*. Composing by day, and writing in the evenings, he would break off for his habitual afternoon strolls; the persistent deletions from his letters to his brothers suggest that he used them to renew old acquaintanceships. His work rate slowed, and he became involved in an irritating correspondence with Stasov, who refused his request to intervene on Rubinstein's behalf with Alexey Suvorin, the belligerent owner/editor of *Novoe Vremya* (*New Times*). The paper's charges about Rubinstein's management of the Conservatoire, in Stasov's view, were justified. Tchaikovsky was reluctant to intervene himself, for fear of Suvorin turning his guns on himself and the mysteries of his failed marriage.

After five otherwise tranquil weeks, again running short of funds, he reluctantly moved on to Paris. 'In truth I would much rather remain here,' he told Yurgenson, 'but I am obliged to move on. How and why is rather a long story.' Upon his arrival, ten days later than von Meck had expected, there was awkward confusion over the apartment she had rented for him; Tchaikovsky considered it too expensive, and insisted on moving to another, then a third, in the Hotel Meurice on the Rue de Rivoli. The entire atmosphere was markedly different from Florence. With her 'dear, priceless friend' at his most irritable, despite constant apologies for his ingratitude, von Meck succumbed to a series of migraines, begging that the flow of letters between them slow to just one a week. Sequestered across town, Tchaikovsky could see little point in the arrangement. In Florence, at least, there had been a powerful sense of proximity; here in Paris, out of sight and less communicative, his patron might as well have been in Moscow. Only the twice-weekly visits of the lugubrious Pakhulsky signified otherwise.

Where once he had found daily correspondence a strain, he was now offended by the lack of it. Had not von Meck been so slavishly devoted to him, she might have had good reason to resent the impatience, even paranoia, evident in her dependent composer's muttered asides. The whole set-up, he complained to his inner circle, was 'abnormal', a 'charade'. None the less *The Maid of Orleans* proceeded apace, and was finished by early March – short of orchestration, 'mere brainwork'.[4] Four days later, after attending a Paris performance of his own *Tempest* incognito, he left via Berlin for Russia, where his brothers joined him for the première of *Eugene Onegin* at the Moscow Conservatoire on 29 March.

Tchaikovsky had insisted that the first performance be undertaken by Conservatoire students, concerned that the 'anachronisms and absurdities' of a grand opera house production, with professional singers set in their ways, might smother the finely wrought detail of his tableau of 'lyrical scenes'. *Onegin*, he was well aware, was highly unconventional in both form and style. His original phrase for 'lyrical scenes', *Liricheskie stseny*, was carefully chosen, designed to lend his opera a poetic framework as much as to convey his diffidence at setting Russia's best-loved poetic masterpiece. Although he could not hope to mirror all of the many layers of Pushkin's verse novel in music, Tchaikovsky was saying, he might at least admit the listener to the innermost moments of the drama. With his original Russian audience, moreover, he could count on a broad degree of familiarity with both the text and its main characters.

Tchaikovsky has often been accused of 'sentimentalizing' Pushkin's drily ironic, detached style. In his version of the figure of Onegin himself, however, the composer surely did manage to convey Pushkin's classic portrait of the *lishni chelovek*, the 'superfluous man' who haunted so much of nineteenth-century Russian literature, the high-minded 'outsider' who felt his intellect and sensitivity placed him above and apart from the salon society of the day. Like his friend Lensky, who metamorphoses from carefree lover to doomed philosopher, Onegin travels a long musical journey, wringing from Tchaikovsky some of the most affecting, least sentimental melodic developments he would ever write. But as in Bizet's *Carmen* – the contemporary opera which he most admired, and whose influence is so evident in *Onegin* – it is the female lead who is in fact given the two most glorious themes, recurring motifs subtly modulated to reflect her dramatically changing fortunes.

That first performance at the Conservatoire was (as Madame von Meck had feared) a somewhat rough-edged affair. But Tchaikovsky was steadfast in his insistence on chamber-scale productions of a piece which demands theatrical intimacy; in 1885, after he had revised the third act, *Onegin* finally triumphed on the stage of the Mariinsky, under Napravnik. In the ensuing century it has never lost its place in the international repertoire; in the mid-1990s one typical verdict in the many available opera guidebooks called it 'the most popular of all Russian operas' and the creation of Tatyana 'the greatest single achievement of all Tchaikovsky's operas.'[5]

Returning to St Petersburg the morning after the opera's somewhat muted première, Tchaikovsky was plunged straight back into the maelstrom created by his marriage. *Eugene Onegin* seemed to have become the measure of its beginning and now its interminable death throes.

Far from keeping her distance, as promised, Antonina had returned to the capital in search of her errant husband. Now she tracked down Anatoly's apartment, where the composer was staying. On 5 April, having persuaded the concierge to let her in, she awaited Tchaikovsky in his brother's study. Although forewarned by the anxious doorman, the composer was quite unprepared for the 'shattering' scene which followed. The moment he entered the room, as he described it to von Meck, his wife flung her arms around his neck and smothered him in tearful kisses, pleading repeatedly that she could not live without him, and would agree to any conditions if only he would come back to her. As he tried to extricate himself from her embrace, without adding to her mounting hysteria, Tchaikovsky again accepted his share of the blame for what had happened, but protested that he could never again agree to cohabitation. In the face of more sobbing, and more protestations of undying love, he became desperate to get rid of her. Take time to think it all over again, he suggested. If she would return to Moscow at once, he promised to write to her, even to visit her. He gave her a hundred roubles for the journey, and allowed her a brief reunion with his brothers (who had been listening anxiously next door). Somewhat placated, Antonina duly undertook to do as he wished, and slowly took her leave, pausing only to give her husband a full list of her current male admirers.[6]

But she did not go away. Over the next few days Tchaikovsky's wife hovered around the apartment, accosting him in the street, even taking a room in the same building. In the face of his persistent rejections, she protested that she could not bear to be too far from him, and would wait to return to Moscow in his company. Four days after bearding him in Anatoly's study, she sent him another desperate letter, forlorn in its protestations of unconditional love, tragic in its agonized ravings about her state of mind. 'If you cannot love me as I love you, at least show me some compassion,' she pleaded. 'Come to me. I am yours, body and soul. Do with me what you wish.'

Long gone, however, was the guilty penitence which had marked Tchaikovsky's initial reaction to the collapse of his marriage. Hounded into a blind rage, he fled to Moscow, en route to Kamenka, only to find Antonina still in hot pursuit. Again she invaded his apartment, this time in defiant mood. Abandoning her pleas for sympathy, she now returned to the subject of money. Somehow, to his horror, she had learnt about his understanding with von Meck. Fifteen thousand roubles, she announced, was her price for leaving Russia, where he had made her life a misery. Relieved that she was back in bargaining mode, Tchaikovsky told her he would see what he could do.

That night he returned home to a note from Antonina asking for fifty roubles to tide her over. He had the 'weakness', as he put it, to send her twenty-five. A divorce settlement, he argued over his patron's protests, was out of the question. Antonina could not be relied upon to cope with the practical details, nor to stick to the terms of any agreement reached. The only solution open to him was to stay away from Moscow and St Petersburg, visiting only when his musical commitments made it unavoidable, and then as briefly as possible. To eliminate all chance of encountering Antonina, his sole option – also, of course, his dearest wish – was to remain abroad.

First stop, in the meantime, would be Kamenka – where he eventually arrived, with Modest and Kolya Konradi, back on the verge of nervous collapse. Anxious to complete the scoring of his new opera, he wrote his wife the letter he had promised her – a brutal affair refusing her every request and announcing that all future letters from her would be returned unopened.

Antonina's name would continue to haunt him throughout the summer, but he felt he could now rely on Anatoly to keep her at bay. Thus having exorcized his wife, at least for the moment, he was at last able to get back to work, rounding off the First Suite with an extra movement, and revelling in the instrumentation of *The Maid of Orleans*. His next task was a piano transcription of the Suite – an urgent ingredient of the Yurgenson formula for guaranteeing as many performances (and thus royalties) as possible. All these tasks were finished before his thirty-ninth birthday, which was celebrated with an all-day picnic in the woods. Tchaikovsky waited long enough to observe Modest's birthday on 13 May, before moving on alone for a brief break at Brailov.

Although he passed the time in desultory fashion, with only von Meck's household staff for company, his stay proved a valuable investment with his patron. 'Now more than ever, and here more than anywhere, I feel our spiritual closeness and I revel in it,' she wrote upon reaching the estate after his departure. 'The rooms you used have already been renamed "Pyotr Ilyich's bedroom" and "Pyotr Ilyich's sitting-room". The trees in the woods where we have both sipped tea, the benches on the crag where both of us have lingered, those same nightingales we have both heard – all of them, all, *belong to both of us*. My God, what ecstasy this brings!' She begged him to return later in the summer, and take up residence in her nearby cottage at Simaki, in an attempt to recreate the closeness they had known in Florence. As uneasy and reluctant as ever, Tchaikovsky knew it would not be prudent to decline.

Back at Kamenka, he sunk himself in Dostoevsky's *Brothers Karamazov* (then appearing in serial form), despite his patron's worries about its effect on his already troubled nerves. He wallowed in family life all June, enjoying one of his happiest summers for years – clouded only by the illnesses, for once, of others. A mystery ailment was dogging his sister, Sasha, who was euphoric one day, depressed the next. From the capital came the news that their frail old father was also far from well. At Nizy, in Kondratiev's care, Bochechkarov was dying of dropsy; Tchaikovsky paid his old friend a final visit while rushing to finish his opera. So put out was Mme von Meck, still awaiting him at Brailov, that he could postpone Simaki no longer, and agreed to spend the month of August there as her guest.

His habitual discomfort at his patron's proximity was at first quelled by the sheer beauty of the place: an old house with a well-stocked garden, bounded by a river, with a magnificent view extending beyond the village to distant woods. There was a coach and horses at his disposal, but he preferred, as always, to walk, revelling in the surrounding copses where he could wander for hours 'without meeting a soul'. Or so he thought.

There were early portents of the event he would call a disaster. Again von Meck sent him a schedule of her daily movements, so that he could be sure to avoid any chance encounters. Again Pakhulsky

came and went, aggravating his unease, especially when he promised to bring over von Meck's youngest daughter, the oft-mentioned
Milochka, to meet him. Tchaikovsky forestalled this plan in a letter
which plainly, almost bluntly, summarized how highly he prized his
'non-acquaintance' with his benefactress.

> My relations with you *as presently constituted* are quite perfect, a
> necessary condition of my peace of mind. I would not wish to see
> them change one jot. As things are, I think of you as my good
> but unseen angel. All the immeasurable charm and poetry of our
> friendship resides in your being so close to me, so infinitely beloved
> . . . But it also depends on our *not being acquainted* in the usual
> sense of the term, and this *non-acquaintance* must also include all
> those closest to you. I want to love Milochka as I have loved her
> until now. If she were suddenly to appear here before me, the spell
> would be broken. All your family are dear to me, and especially
> Milochka, but for God's sake let everything stay as it is now. What
> would I say to Milochka when she asked *why I did not go to see
> her mama*? I would have to embark on that relationship with a lie
> – a white lie, of course, but still a lie. I would find that intolerable.

Soon after this, as von Meck reluctantly relented, came the critical
moment Tchaikovsky had so feared. It took a chapter of accidents, but for
once – and once only – the inevitable happened. On the fateful afternoon
of 26 August the composer miscalculated the time of his afternoon walk,
setting out earlier than usual; through no fault of her own, meanwhile,
von Meck inadvertently returned home to Brailov later than her usual
4 p.m. For one excruciating moment they came face to face on a track
through the woods – he on foot, she in the vanguard of a fleet of carriages
bearing her entire family. Both were thrown into complete confusion.
Tchaikovsky simply raised his hat, and moved on without a word. 'It
was awful,' he reported to Anatoly and Modest. '*Horribly* embarrassing.'7
He immediately sent round a contrite note of apology, taking the blame
for the 'mishap' entirely upon himself, only to find that his patron was
in ecstasy. 'It was thrilling,' she replied. 'I can't tell you how sweet and
enchanting a moment that was . . . I do not want any personal contact
between us, but silently, passively, to be around you, to be near you . . .
to perceive you not as a phantom but a living, breathing person whom
I so adore, from whom I receive so many blessings, all of which fill me
with rapture.' The more Tchaikovsky drew away from personal contact,
even proximity, the more she seemed to crave his presence. 'There's no
ointment without a fly in it,' as he put it to his brothers. 'The fly in this

instance is N.F. [von Meck] and her family and hangers-on. I'm sure they won't actually bother me, but their proximity is very bothersome . . .'

Soon after, as in Florence, she invited him to visit the main house at Brailov while she was out. This time, of course, he knew the place well, and felt quite comfortable accepting, on the pretext of inspecting her latest art acquisitions. The next evening she arranged for him to mingle with the crowd, unseen and incognito, during a fireworks display in honour of her son's name day. Again he enjoyed himself more than he expected, revelling in the deception. Twice, he told her in an exuberant letter of thanks, von Meck 'passed by very close' to him. 'I was lurking near the gazebo, beside the lake. My delight was tinged with a thrill of fear, lest the watchmen apprehend me as a burglar!' There were other occasions that summer, documented by the von Meck children, when the two came within peering distance of each other. But both were so short-sighted that neither ever knew.

It was during this summer that Mme von Meck obtained a copy of the piano-duet transcription of the Fourth Symphony – 'our symphony' – which had become all but the phantom child of their spiritual union. 'I am worthy of this symphony being mine alone,' she enthused to its composer. 'No-one hears its every nuance as I do, no-one can appreciate it as deeply as I. Musicians may admire it with their intellect, but I feel every note and empathize with my whole soul. If I must die for listening to it, then die I must, but I shall still listen.' In the same letter, Tchaikovsky's patron gets so carried away that she permits herself, for the only time in their fourteen-year relationship, an overt confession of love for the composer:

> I wonder whether you can understand the jealousy with which I regard you, even though there are no personal relations between us. Are you aware that I am jealous of you in the most inexcusable way, as a woman is jealous of a man she loves? Do you realize that when you got married I was in utter despair? I felt as if part of my heart had been torn away. In my agony, I became bitter. The thought of your intimacy with that woman was unbearable. And do you know the full extent of my unworthiness? When you proved to be unhappy with her, I rejoiced. I was full of self-reproach, and hid my feelings from you, but I was powerless to control them. No-one can alter their true feelings. I hated this woman because she made you unhappy, but I would have hated her a hundred times more if she had made you *happy*. As I saw it, she had stolen from me someone who was mine by right, mine and

mine alone, because I love you as no-one else does, and I value
you above all else in this world.[8]

'Forgive me,' the letter ended. 'Forget everything I have said. I am wrong
in the head.' But she still sent the letter, blaming her ardour on the Fourth
Symphony: 'The symphony is why I have blurted all this out.'

A confused and somewhat alarmed Tchaikovsky took more than a week
to pen a reply, written in hesitant instalments at the end of September as he
moved from St Petersburg to Moscow to the Konradi estate at Grankino. It
was not a happy interlude: his visit to the capital, where he stayed with
Anatoly, was primarily to see his increasingly weak father, who could
not have long to live. While dealing with the old man's continuing
disappointment – and bewilderment – at the failure of his marriage, he
was confronted by another pile of 'utterly crazy' letters from Antonina.
In Moscow he went on a three-day drinking binge; reliving the old days
seemed the easiest way to cope with Rubinstein and other Conservatoire
friends. By the time he reached the Konradis, he was obsessed with the
idea of getting out of Russia. It scarcely mattered where.

In his reply to von Meck, all he could do was pour out yet more
gratitude for all her munificence. Avoiding any direct comment on her
declaration of love, let alone any reciprocation, he said simply: 'I owe you
everything.' The only kind of love he could offer her would be expressed
in music. All that autumn, he was more cautious than ever in his replies
to her many suggestions of idylls together around Europe. Naples was
her latest suggestion; the more passionately her letters craved a 'reunion',
the more urgently he found commitments elsewhere and other obstacles
to his joining her. Eventually, however, he saw no alternative. Pausing
only to see his father again in St Petersburg (and to inspect Apukhtin's
new lover), he enjoyed a happy few days with Kotek in Berlin before
yielding to von Meck's desperate pleas that he join her in Paris.

Reluctant as he was to inspire yet more effusions – which could, so
it seemed to him, be leading in awkward directions – Tchaikovsky felt
he had little choice. It would, of course, cost him nothing, his patron
having arranged him the same very comfortable rooms as before. It
would ensure the steady continuance of his annuity, despite his failure
to respond in kind to her declaration of love, however chaste it may
have been. And the added incentive on this occasion was that she had
begun negotiations with Eduard Colonne, resident conductor of one
of Europe's finest orchestras, for a Paris performance of her beloved
Fourth Symphony – which had the same effect on her, she declared
to the composer's tacit disapproval, as opium. The symphony as a
whole was 'matchless', but the first movement in particular was 'the

last word in art, the summit of genius, the crowning triumph, the meaning of God . . . There is nowhere else for music to go. For the sake of this music, one could surrender one's soul or lose one's mind without a moment's regret.'

Colonne it was who had conducted the performance of *The Tempest* attended by the composer in March. Tchaikovsky much admired him, but took the realistic view that a French conductor and his French audience were more likely to champion the French symphonists of the day. Tempted by the large subsidies on offer from von Meck, however, Colonne had agreed to inspect the symphony, and a score had been despatched to him. Tchaikovsky could only wait.

When she arranged for the delivery to his rooms of an outstanding Erard piano, von Meck could not have known how well it suited Tchaikovsky's latest purpose. While in Kamenka, dealing with the proofs of the First Suite, he had grown bored and listless; he was pretending to savour the joys of sewing, hemming towels and marking the Davidov linen, when one morning he awoke with almost missionary zeal. A new theme had suggested itself to him, which took some ten days to become the first movement of his Second Piano Concerto. While in Moscow he was overwhelmed by the mastery with which Nikolay Rubinstein had performed his sonata; despite the contretemps over the First Piano Concerto (to which Rubinstein was now an enthusiastic convert), Tchaikovsky decided that he was the natural dedicatee for his second.

Again it would turn out otherwise; again the concerto would be premièred in the United States rather than Russia; and again there would be a long and bitter squabble over revisions. But Rubinstein's virtuosity was the driving-force behind Tchaikovsky's new purposefulness in Paris as he set about the concerto's finale, sketched in a week, and embarked upon an ambitious and unusual *andante* for the second movement. In only two weeks, by 15 December, the whole piece was ready for orchestration.

Although it has long lain hidden in the overgrown shadow of his first, Tchaikovsky's Second Piano Concerto – and especially its rapturous *andante* – ranks with any piece he wrote for solo instrument and orchestra. The composer himself, as always, vacillated about its merits for the rest of his life; and emendations published after his death, robbing the work of some of its finest passages, have been largely responsible for the undue neglect in which it has too long languished.

The fault, indirectly, was Nikolay Rubinstein's. As sensitive as Tchaikovsky had been to his criticism of the First Piano Concerto, he was equally unnerved by a lack of criticism of his second. Having sent the score to Moscow for appraisal, he eventually heard back from Taneyev that 'not a note need be altered'. The composer naturally assumed that this was also Rubinstein's opinion, only later hearing that his dedicatee thought the piano part 'too episodic', that it did not 'stand out enough' from the orchestra. But Rubinstein would not live to perform the concerto, with or without revisions; it fell to his brother Anton to conduct the first Russian performance, in Moscow on 30 May 1882, with Taneyev as soloist.

A month later, Taneyev came up with some unwelcome reservations. The first two movements were too long; the violin and cello solos in the second movement detracted from the piano part. Tchaikovsky was understandably piqued, wondering why no-one had chosen to make these points before the work's first public airing. He eventually made some amendments of his own before conducting the work himself six years later, in a version with which he finally declared himself satisfied. This did not stop his pupil Alexandr Ziloti continuing to suggest further changes, to an extent which made the composer's 'hair stand on end'. Despite Tchaikovsky's intransigence, supported by Yurgenson, Ziloti's revised version was that published after the composer's death, which stood for many years as the standard performance text, and was no doubt responsible for the work's comparative obscurity. Only in recent years, with the restoration of the string solo parts in the *andante*, has the Second Piano Concerto begun to win back its rightful place in the canon.

Not for some years did Tchaikovsky himself learn that his Second Piano Concerto had in fact received its world première, like his First, in the United States. On 12 November 1881, in New York City, it was used by the English virtuoso Madeleine Schiller as a vehicle for her triumphant return to the concert platform after an enforced absence of three years. The conductor on that occasion, Theodore Thomas, makes no mention of the occasion in his subsequent memoirs, suggesting that he and his soloist were as oblivious as the composer to the fact that this was the first public performance anywhere in the world of what was to prove one of Tchaikovsky's most undervalued works.

Another index of the composer's renewed pleasure in his work, which can be heard in the Second Piano Concerto more than any piece written since the catastrophe of his marriage, was his delight that autumn of 1879 in Paris in returning to the dandyish ways of his youth. 'You should just see me!' he joked to Anatoly. 'It would give you a good laugh.'

I'm quite the French fop, strolling the boulevards in my new grey tailcoat and the toppest of top hats, a silk cravat with a coral

pin at my neck, and lilac gloves on my hands. As I cruise the
mirrored arcades on the Rue de Paix, I pause by the shop windows
to admire the reflection of this remarkably elegant figure. As has
happened before, in short, I'm quite swept away in a fever of
fashion. I'm having a new suit cut, and I've ordered a dozen
shirts. It's costing me a fortune . . .[9]

It was Tchaikovsky's first burst of high spirits for quite some time,
reflecting his utter delight at escaping Russia and the fulfilment of his
first really fine work since *Onegin* two long years before. In Paris, also,
there was much music to relish, not least a craze (ten years after his
death) for Berlioz; and the roguish company of Kondratiev, in town
to take a cure for syphilis. By mid-December he was spared even von
Meck's oppressively brooding presence, as she took her family home
for Christmas. Now, at last, he could lay plans to move on where
he chose – to Rome, perhaps, where Modest and his young charge
had been living since November. The only drawback, as he heard
from Kondratiev, was that two of his less savoury old friends, Prince
Golitsyn and his lover Masalitinov, were also installed in the Italian
capital. Where once he would have relished their louche antics, the
post-marital Tchaikovsky was thoroughly rattled by any spectres from
his past. When the prospect of seeing them made him hesitate – the
mere thought of 'that inseparable pair', he told Modest, filled him with
'horror' – his brother undertook to tell them that he would be too bowed
down by work for any socializing.

When he arrived in Rome on 20 December, they were inevitably among
the first people he saw. Tchaikovsky found himself thoroughly disenchanted. Theirs was still the outrageously camp world of his youth, as if
preserved in aspic, which he had now left far behind; after one evening
struggling to be polite, he pleaded that he would have little more time
to share with them. As a result, Tchaikovsky was soon enjoying Rome
much more than he had expected. The orchestration of his new piano
concerto was punctuated by an enthusiastic sightseeing programme with
Modest, in unseasonably fine weather, during which he concluded that
he was no great judge of the visual arts, but boldly suggested to von
Meck that Michelangelo was their Beethoven and Raphael their Mozart.
His appetite for work became strangely inconsistent; one day he would
complain of a languid torpor, the next he was seized by a sudden urge
to revise his Second Symphony. As with the Fourth Symphony, he was
apprehensive (and not a little put out) to have heard nothing from
Moscow about the first performance of his First Suite, which Rubinstein
had conducted on the day he arrived in Rome.

Through his own fault, meanwhile, he missed Colonne's long-awaited Paris performance of the Fourth Symphony. Having wished to hear it (for the first time) incognito, spared the embarrassments of being known to be present, he had blithely told Colonne that there was no need to give him advance notice of the performance; the conductor had taken him at his word, informing Tchaikovsky only on the morning of the concert. One day's more notice, he sighed, and he would have dashed up to Paris to hide himself in the audience. As he feared, however, the symphony received only a lukewarm reception, moving Colonne to schedule only two movements, the *Andantino* and *scherzo*, for a second hearing that season. Dismayed, Tchaikovsky was quite abrupt with von Meck when he heard of her plans to approach Colonne with sponsorship for performances of the First Suite and *The Maid of Orleans*. Vanity concerts (which, to him, were what her largesse amounted to) were beneath his dignity. Besides, he did not want the musical world knowing, via the inquisitive Colonne, that his growing international reputation was founded on a widow's pension.

His old misanthropy returning, not to mention his sexual appetites, he swallowed his pride and permitted himself some dalliance amid Golitsyn's demi-monde. Then Kondratiev arrived for a month, and embarked upon a programme of debauchery which soon ground down Tchaikovsky's patience. At the beginning of 1880, it was thus in somewhat desultory Roman mood that he began adapting many of the popular tunes of the streets into a suite of popular Italian melodies, which would eventually emerge as the *Capriccio Italien*. Although still a popular favourite, as much a staple workhorse of Tchaikovsky 'gala' evenings as the 1812 Overture and the First Piano Concerto, the *Capriccio* must surely rank among his less inspired works. That he should have been satisfied with it, at the time, is an indication of the low state not just of his morale, but of his self-critical as much as his creative faculties. If the spectre of Antonina was still haunting him, on top of his increasingly mixed feelings about his patron, he had yet more reason early in 1880 to sink back into depression when he learnt from Anatoly that their father had died in St Petersburg on 21 January.

Tchaikovsky was not as grief-stricken as his considerable capacity for self-pity might suggest. Ilya Petrovich, after all, had been ill for some time, and at the age of eighty-four had comfortably exceeded the average life expectancy of the day, even among the upper-middle classes. Although Tchaikovsky 'wept copiously' while reading Anatoly's letter, mourning 'the departure from this world of a thoroughly decent man with the spirit of an angel', he was nothing like as affected as he had been by the death of his mother. Only six months before, in June, he had remarked to von Meck that it was the twenty-fifth anniversary of his mother's death, and he 'still missed her as much as ever'. If von Meck had become a mother-substitute, as much as some bizarre kind of alternative spouse, Tchaikovsky had no more need of a father figure. In recent years, in fact, the sentimental old man's concern about his marriage had made him something of an emotional burden to his son, who already considered himself emotionally burdened enough. His father's death, in truth, had a swiftly cathartic effect; within minutes of folding Anatoly's letter, and accepting that his father was no more, Tchaikovsky felt 'enlightened and reconciled at heart'.

No hint of mourning is evident in the *Capriccio*, on which he worked until May. Its superficiality and lack of invention appears, at root, to be a striking index of Tchaikovsky's need for bouts of emotional turmoil to wring from him the highly wrought musical passions which forged his best work. By so carefully insulating himself from the outside world and all its attendant perils, he was in danger of neutralizing his own creative forces. By the end of the year, when the *Capriccio* met with only moderate enthusiasm in St Petersburg (after a triumphal first performance in Moscow), Tchaikovsky himself had begun to have doubts about the 'musical substance' of the piece, if not its 'orchestral effectiveness'.[10] To David Brown, the composer was paying the price of becoming an almost total recluse. 'The superficiality, even emptiness of the Italian Capriccio suggests, perhaps more than any other work of this phase, the degree to which Tchaikovsky could retreat not only from the people around him (except for the chosen few), but also – paradoxically – detach himself from his environment. His capacity to withdraw into himself was now complete.'[11]

In March, still in Rome, he reluctantly fulfilled a small but significant commission from Karl Davidov at the St Petersburg Conservatoire, to contribute to a series of musical tableaux commemorating the silver jubilee of Tsar Alexandr II. Otherwise, the bulk of 1880 was to prove a somewhat fallow year for Tchaikovsky. He had produced the Second Piano Concerto, the *Capriccio Italien* and the 'Montengrin Tableau' in barely three months, as well as revising the Second Symphony and preparing the vocal score of *The Maid of Orleans*. But his creative juices were not flowing freely; while busying himself with the publishing and performance chores for this ragbag of recent compositions, he was no closer to finding the right vehicle or genre for his next major work. Nor did his heart really seem to be in the search. The bustle of Rome, for all his self-imposed, anti-social isolation, had him in world-weary mood as the time came for him to return to Russia.

He travelled via Paris, where Kondratiev was on a permanent binge, and Berlin, where he found Wagner's *The Flying Dutchman* 'noisy and boring'. In both cities, reading between the lines of his butchered letters home, the composer resumed his lifelong habit of 'cruising' those areas well known to the initiate as homosexual meeting-places. For the thirteen years remaining to him, in which he continued to document his world travels in minute detail to his intimates, it is quite clear what Tchaikovsky often means when he mentions going out for a 'stroll'. In Paris, there was the added bonus of Kondratiev's young servant, Sasha Legoshin, who would visit him each morning before his master awoke, and proved 'most obliging'.[12]

St Petersburg seemed 'oppressive and gloomy' when he arrived on 19 March, to be met by Anatoly and escorted straight from the station to a restaurant dinner with Apukhtin and his lover, Alexandr Zhedrinsky. Did Tchaikovsky ever envy his poet friend's decision to parade his homosexuality so openly, to make no secret of the fact that he shared his life with a live-in lover, very much as husband and wife? The presence at the dinner of Zhedrinsky's father, a provincial governor, would seem to indicate that even stiff-backed Russian officialdom had learnt to live with such arrangements. Members of the royal circle were well known in high society to be flamboyant homosexuals, enjoying outrageous lifestyles. One such, of course, was his old schoolfriend Prince Meshchersky, with whom he now renewed his acquaintance.

To Tchaikovsky, however, even though he moved in the most liberal artistic circles, an atmosphere of social tolerance was little incentive to parade his own sexuality before the world. Not merely did he have a dread of scandal; in his heart, as in his letters and diaries, he continued to wish that he were 'as other men'. Although he indulged his predilections on a recklessly promiscuous scale, he ensured that his 'secret vice' was known only to a like-minded sympathetic circle, to whom the episode of his attempt at marriage was merely an act of misguided folly. For now, he was content to lead a covert, hole-in-corner sex life while devoting his familial instincts to the needs of his loved ones.

And never, it seemed, had they been more in need. Following the death of their father, and unwelcome upheavals in his professional life, Anatoly was undergoing another bout of what would now be recognized as clinical depression. As the composer patiently ministered unto his brother's needs, he wrote with a sigh to von Meck that he was embarked upon 'another of my periodic bouts of martyrdom'.[13] Together the brothers visited Ilya Petrovich's grave, in the capital's Smolensk Cemetery, and called on his grieving widow, Elizaveta.

Swamped with administrative matters requiring his urgent attention, all of them important to his burgeoning reputation, Tchaikovsky was meanwhile caught up in a domestic crisis at the Konradis. Aware that their marriage had been in difficulties for some time, he was nevertheless surprised to find Kolya's mother openly living with her lover, Vladimir Bryullov, and Herman petitioning for divorce. Tchaikovsky and Modest were both concerned about the effect of all this upon vulnerable young Kolya, still only twelve. Feeling it his duty to attempt to effect a reconciliation, Tchaikovsky soon realized that it was a hopeless task. Within weeks the Konradis were indeed divorced, and Alina and Bryullov married.

Like Tchaikovsky's own idealized mother, though he himself was the last to know or admit it, Alina had always been a somewhat cold and distant parent to Kolya. Now she contentedly left the child in the custody of his father, who would slowly begin to resent Modest's role in his son's life, especially their regular disappearances abroad. For the present, however, as Tchaikovsky saw it, his brother would have to become 'both mother and father' to the bewildered boy.

Amid all this, Tchaikovsky's main professional objective was to use his brief visit to St Petersburg to promote the fortunes of *The Maid of Orleans*. He was pleasantly surprised to find that his stock was rising in the capital; while he was there, the RMS devoted an entire concert to his music, featuring the *Romeo and Juliet* overture, the First Suite, and excerpts from *Eugene Onegin* including Lensky's aria and Tatyana's 'Letter Song'. Now the society's president, no less a figure than the Grand Duke Konstantin Nikolayevich, brother of the Tsar, requested a meeting.

Perennially shy of such occasions, Tchaikovsky had to be persuaded by Napravnik of the obvious truth that it was a unique opportunity for advancing his reputation. The potentially stiff atmosphere was eased, however, by a chance meeting with the Grand Duke's son, Konstantin Konstantinovich, at the home of Lev Davidov's sister, Vera Butakova. Himself an amateur musician, and a minor poet published under the name K.R. (for Konstantin Romanov), the younger Grand Duke utterly charmed Tchaikovsky, with whom he talked music deep into the night. Understanding the composer's aversion to formal occasions, Konstantin arranged for the meeting with his father to take the shape of a small, intimate dinner party, again *chez* Butakova, a week later. The encounter with the grand royal personage, long an admirer of his music, was thus made as painless as possible for Tchaikovsky. The Grand Duke 'could not have been more charming'; but the occasion's more lasting consequence was the cementing of Tchaikovsky's friendship with his twenty-two-year-old son. He felt obliged to wriggle out of Konstantin's wildly bold suggestion – terrifyingly akin to a royal command – that the composer accompany him on his forthcoming three-year round-the-world trip as a lieutenant in the Russian Navy; but in time an important friendship was to blossom in other ways, both private and professional.

On Tchaikovsky's arrival in Moscow, on 14 April, a chance encounter with Konstantin's father led to another evening spent in the company of the Tsar's brother. His new acceptance in the highest circles made the predictable reappearance of Antonina even more unnerving than usual. This time it began in the shape of a letter from her mother, always a more canny opponent, who again appeared to be making veiled threats. 'Your good name', she wrote *en passant*, 'must surely be precious to you.' There followed yet more requests for yet more money, in return for yet more promises to take Antonina abroad and bother him no more. Tchaikovsky replied with a token consignment of roubles, as was now his wont, expecting no more than a temporary respite from this infinite source of woe.

He was right. In early July a letter arrived from Antonina herself, more incoherent than ever, but chilling him to the marrow with her most direct threat yet. Apparently, she complained, he had been spreading 'vile rumours' about her in St Petersburg. 'Why don't you start with yourself, and tell [people] about your shameful vice, before passing judgement on me?' In one breath she again linked the issues of money and divorce, in the next she was refusing to sign 'any of your vile and malicious pieces of paper'.[14]

Now he felt certain that her erratic behaviour ruled out all chance of divorce proceedings ever becoming a realistic possibility. While privately relieved, as throughout this tortured saga, at avoiding the threat of court proceedings and public scandal, he again wrote to von Meck in significantly different terms. The mere sight of Antonina's handwriting now made him, he told her, both morally and physically sick. The whole business again depressed and drained him. At each of these eruptions he continued to give an only half-true account of his feelings to his patron – who, for reasons which made him distinctly uneasy, still argued the need for divorce and offered the means to pay for it. For his part, Tchaikovsky knew that Antonina would continue to dog him. But he was prepared to put up with anything rather than provoke her into a public assault, or give her increasingly wandering mind any occasion to mount one.

By now he was at Simaki for the month of July, in von Meck's absence abroad. It was the climax of a rural summer which had so far proved far from tranquil. Arriving at Kamenka in early May, he had just put the final touches to the scoring of the Second Piano Concerto when a sequence of domestic disruptions made further work impossible. First Modest fell ill, obliging Tchaikovsky to take charge of Kolya just as the bewildered and all but helpless creature was reeling from his mother's disappearance and his parents' subsequent divorce. Then Sasha, whose continuing illnesses had been diagnosed as an ominous stomach disorder, left for a recuperative break in Europe with her elder daughters, at the same time that her husband was away on a business trip. This left Tchaikovsky in charge of the entire brood: as well as Kolya, Sasha's twelve-year-old daughter Natalya, and Zinaida's daughter Evgenya (whom Sasha had taken in after her mother's death).

An avuncular adoration of children is by no means a qualification for looking after them, especially argumentative girls on the cusp of puberty. A week of barely controlled chaos ensued before Lev returned to take charge. The main consequence of the episode was to confirm Tchaikovsky's conviction that his eight-year-old nephew Vladimir Davidov, nicknamed 'Bob' within the family, was his pre-eminent favourite among the younger members of his extended family. Eventually to be the dedicatee of his uncle's sixth and last symphony, the *Pathétique*, Bob Davidov was to become a central figure in the composer's final years.

These unexpected domestic duties were a mere subtext, however, to the main worry of Tchaikovsky's summer, temporarily supplanting even Antonina as a cause for urgent concern. Alexey, his manservant, without whom he found life hard to contemplate, was approaching the age of compulsory military service. There was no obvious way of winning him an exemption, but the normal term of six years could be reduced to three if Alexey were to pass a statutory examination.

With this in mind, Tchaikovsky himself had been coaching the lad, and had even enrolled him for the summer in the local school at Kamenka, thus depriving himself of some of the daily ministrations on which he had come to rely. With the exam scheduled for early July, he found himself in an unwonted Kamenka paralysis, unable to live his normal life, and even less to get down to any substantial work. All that emerged during this trying time were a few duets and romances, composed primarily for musical evenings amid the family, but eventually collected as Op. 47.

For once genuinely unable to accept von Meck's invitation to join her at Brailov, Tchaikovsky eventually arrived there after her departure, to find awaiting him a lavish gift which moved him to mixed feelings. It was an elaborate gold watch, no doubt immensely expensive, which she had commissioned in Paris the previous winter. On one side it depicted Joan of Arc, subject of his current preoccupations, on the other Apollo and the Muses. Much though he prized it, Tchaikovsky would have preferred the money. He had, he confessed to Anatoly, been expecting a gift of roubles to be awaiting him; without it, he now faced a bleak and impecunious autumn. Having already begged and spent advances on his patron's annual subsidy, and nevertheless run up debts to the tune of 4,000 roubles, he was forced to appeal to his publisher, and retreat to Simaki to finish the proofs of *The Maid of Orleans*.

Scanning his published compositions in his absent patron's book-shelves, and comparing them with the copious amounts of unpublished sheet music around her piano, he determined mainly for financial reasons to spend the rest of the summer getting his publishing affairs in order. As the proofs of the *Capriccio Italien* and the Second Piano Concerto arrived for correction, and he embarked on the final revision of the *Romeo and Juliet* overture, he enlisted the aid of Taneyev, Kashkin and others with the First and Third Symphonies, as well as *The Tempest*. As Yurgenson dealt with copious requests from his client for scores of his piano works and songs, all with a view to final revision and republication, the publisher felt able to advance Tchaikovsky enough money to ease his immediate worries.

He could only sigh when von Meck wrote from Switzerland asking him to look over some scores by one 'Bussy', the latest addition to her musical entourage, a talented young French pianist with aspirations as a composer. Tchaikovsky's patron had in fact got the name of her latest protégé slightly wrong. It was Claude Debussy.

Back at Kamenka, again working hard amid more family theatricals, Tchaikovsky finally addressed himself to an unexciting commission which he had allowed to languish since June. '[Nikolay] Rubinstein has been appointed head of the musical section of the Exhibition of 1881,' Yurgenson had written.

> He asks you to choose between the following, and compose a formal piece (for which, of course, you will be paid . . .) 1. An overture to open the exhibition. 2. An overture to mark the Tsar's silver jubilee. 3. A cantata in whatever form or style you please, given a dash of church music of an Orthodox nature, for the opening of the Cathedral of Christ the Saviour.[15]

Tchaikovsky found the options pretty dispiriting. Always averse to occasional music, he had no particular fondness for the Tsar nor much enthusiasm for the new cathedral. It took a wheedling letter from Rubinstein, asking for a favour from so valued a friend, to goad him into action four months later. His brief was now to write more or less anything he wanted, so long as it lasted between fifteen and twenty-five minutes and did not require a soloist. Complaining that these formal pieces for anniversaries and consecrations called for little except 'banalities and lots of noise', he grudgingly dashed off what was to become, much to his displeasure, one of his most celebrated compositions.

The *1812 Overture* – formally known as *The Year 1812*, a festival overture to mark the consecration of the Cathedral of Christ the Saviour – took Tchaikovsky less than a week to write. Well aware of its shortcomings, he was undismayed when the exhibition was eventually postponed for a year. In need of the money, however, he ignored his contract to the extent of offering the overture to Napravnik for prior performance in St Petersburg, with an accompanying letter saying: 'I don't think the piece has any serious merits, and I shan't be the slightest bit surprised or offended if you find it unsuitable for concert performance.' Aware that the work ought really to await its première at the time and place for which it had been commissioned, Napravnik politely declined. The *1812 Overture*, Op. 49, was thus first performed on 20 August 1882, under the baton of Ippolit Altani – not, as is popularly supposed, outside the cathedral, but in a concert hall purpose-built for the Exhibition.

The cathedral having been built to commemorate the Russian defeat of Napoleon in 1812, Tchaikovsky naturally chose to give the Marseillaise full rein before silencing it amid the booming of victorious Russian cannons. Add the national anthem, 'God Save the Tsar', and a folk melody cannibalized from his first opera, *The Voevoda*, and you have a formula for the Russian equivalent of 'Land of Hope and Glory'. Its popular success in his lifetime surpassed even that of the *Andante cantabile*; and with posterity, again like Elgar, Tchaikovsky is best remembered for one of his own least favourite compositions.

He had written the *1812 Overture*, Tchaikovsky told von Meck, 'without any warm feelings of love'. At the same time, however, he was writing a quite different piece which was 'entirely heartfelt', and so, he dared to think, 'not entirely without its merits'. He was speaking of the sumptuous *Serenade for Strings* (Op. 48), which had begun life that September as a potential symphony or string quartet; by the time he had finished it six weeks later, in late October, he had compromised on a serenade.

That Tchaikovsky could simultaneously produce two such dissimilar works, poles apart in both spirit and quality, is a continuing index of the turmoil still simmering beneath the surface of his life. Shrugging off the postponement of the *1812*, he knew the *Serenade* was well worthy of him, and was anxious to present it to the world. On 3 December, only three weeks after sending the score to Yurgenson, he was delighted by a surprise performance in his honour at the Conservatoire, under the enthusiastic baton of Nikolay Rubinstein. The *Serenade*'s formal

St Petersburg première under Napravnik in October 1882 was a popular triumph, with the *Valse* receiving an immediate encore.

By its first performance in Moscow, another conductor was waxing lyrical. 'This is the best thing Tchaikovsky had written,' he told Yurgenson. 'It is a work you should be proud to publish.' Now, at last, even Anton Rubinstein was forced to admit Tchaikovsky's greatness.

# CHAPTER XII

## 'I hate to be abroad'

THE EARLY 1880S, TCHAIKOVSKY'S 'YEARS OF WANDERING', WOULD FAST propel him towards an international celebrity. Already, as the decade opened, there were encouraging signs that his reputation was growing rapidly beyond the borders of his native Russia. In London and Wiesbaden, after its triumphant première in Boston, von Bülow had played his First Piano Concerto with great success. From Germany Fitzenhagen also reported a warm reception for the *Rococo Variations*. In Paris, where Colonne was proving an important champion of his music, there were plans to perform his Third String Quartet and *Sérénade mélancolique*.

At home, he had been gratified by (but declined) an invitation to become director of the Kiev branch of the Russian Musical Society. Now the St Petersburg Philharmonic were laying plans for two concerts devoted entirely to his music. The Violin Concerto, *1812 Overture* and Second Piano Concerto had yet to be performed; but his Liturgy of St John Chrysostom was winning acceptance not only in Moscow and St Petersburg, but in Kiev and beyond. At the turn of the year the *Capriccio Italien* was being repeated, by public demand, in both St Petersburg and Moscow. That January 1881 *The Maid of Orleans* was also to be given its first performance in St Petersburg, and *Eugene Onegin* a command performance in Moscow. With the revised version of his Second Symphony scheduled for an RMS concert on 12 February, the close of the 1880–81 Moscow musical season was dubbed 'Tchaikovsky week' by one critic. A year ago he had been merely respected as a composer; now he was developing a popular following. To Taneyev, who had been gently chiding him for coyness, even hypocrisy about his growing reputation, he wrote:

> I compose, i.e. express my moods and feelings via the language of music. So of course, like anyone with something to say, or pretensions to saying something, I need people to listen to me – and the more they do listen, the more gratifying it is. In that sense I love *fame*, naturally, and hope for it with my whole heart . . . But it does not follow that I love the trappings of *fame* as manifested in all those dinners, suppers and musical soirées which I find completely alien, and at which I always suffer mightily.[1]

Yet the same month saw the increasingly distinguished composer spending many of his evenings at an upright piano, patiently accompanying the amateurish warbling of the wife of a Moscow regimental commander.

For all his efforts, which included some shameless attempts at string-pulling, Tchaikovsky had failed to prevent his servant, Alexey, from being drafted into the Army. The young man had passed the exam shortening his military service, but proved unlucky in the ballot which might have delayed his conscription. After ten years living cheek by jowl, as Tchaikovsky lamented in letters to von Meck and Modest, their separation was 'the most terrible wrench' – terrible enough to see the unlikely figure of this eminent composer hanging around the barracks day and night, in the remote hope of an hour or two with Alexey when he came off duty. Such was his devotion to his 'little soldier' that Tchaikovsky not only overcame his distaste for spending any more time in Moscow than was strictly necessary; by way of ingratiating himself with Alexey's commanding officer, he even agreed to take part in his wife's musical soirées. They were, he admitted, a 'terrible ordeal', but worth it if they won him a few extra hours with his beloved 'Alyosha'.

This domestic disaster quite marred his enjoyment of a succession of concerts which marked the high point of his reputation in Russia to date. In swift succession, at the turn of the year, Moscow saw performances of *The Oprichnik*, the First Quartet, the Liturgy of St John, the *Capriccio Italien*, *Eugene Onegin* and *The Maid of Orleans* – this last the first performance of a work which would never, alas, find as much favour with the public as with its composer. Posterity has broadly agreed with the verdict of César Cui at his sourest: '[It is] a weak work from an otherwise gifted composer: dull, monotonous, banal and far too long (it drags on past midnight), its only occasional flashes of bright, vivid music being echoes of his previous operas.'[2]

Through January and beyond Tchaikovsky's mind and heart were in the barracks with Alexey, from whom he took an emotional farewell when he was finally obliged to move on to St Petersburg, for the première of Modest's play *The Benefactor*, at the Alexandrinsky Theatre on 21 February. The first performance also proved the last (although the play was later to enjoy moderate success in revised and retitled form). By modelling his unpleasant protagonist on his pupil's father, Herman Konradi, Modest did little to ease the continuing friction between them, and was forced to abandon his plans to take Kolya to Europe with his brother. The composer moved on alone, his spirits sinking ever lower, via Vienna and Florence to Rome, where he found himself missing everyone – Alexey, Modest, Kolya, even von Meck – and abandoned himself to alcohol and the louche demi-monde of Kondratiev and Golitsyn.

Also in town was the junior Grand Duke, Konstantin Konstantinovich ('K.R.'), partway through his world tour. As always Tchaikovsky revelled in the high-society invitations, pretending it was all a frightful bore while fussing about tail coats and modes of address. Only for such notables would he abandon his usual reserve and consent to play some of his music at social gatherings. So aimless had he become, and so seduced by the flattery of the nobility, that he moved on with the Grand Duke's party to Naples, and was even considering his invitation to continue with him via Athens to Jerusalem, when on 13 March dramatic news from the homeland brought their merry-go-round to an abrupt halt. A terrorist bomb had killed the Grand Duke's uncle, Tsar Alexandr II, plunging Russia into a constitutional crisis.

Only hours before his death, at the hands of a protest group calling itself the Will of the People, Alexandr had approved a draft constitution extending the liberal reforms he had begun twenty years before with the Emancipation of the Serfs. Once the summary execution of his assassins had made them martyrs to the intelligentsia, however, his son Alexandr III revoked all his father's legislation and embarked on a grimly repressive, reactionary regime. Amid the grieving Russian community in Italy, Tchaikovsky was appalled by the Tsar's murder, and more homesick than ever. 'At times like this I hate to be abroad,' he wrote to Anatoly. 'I yearn with my whole soul to be in Russia so that I might keep in close touch with events, take part in the demonstrations of support for the new Tsar, know all the details – and, in short, share the daily life of all my own people.'[3] As the Grand Duke's entourage rushed straight home to St Petersburg, the composer was left in especially dislocated mode, pouring out his patriotic grief and indignation in letters rather than music.

It was not the best time to hear from Yurgenson the latest news of Antonina: that she had borne 'some gentleman' a child, who had been handed over to the Hospital for Foundlings. According to local gossip, she was now living in Moscow with the child's father. At least, Tchaikovsky wrote to von Meck, he finally had 'irrefutable proof' of his wife's infidelity, omitting to mention why he might need it. Divorce was further than ever from his mind, now that he had himself plunged back into his old 'bad habits'. Besides the possibility of scandal, of which he still lived in permanent dread, a divorce would cost him a sizeable sum – and he had for some months been hearing whispers that the von Meck estate was in trouble.

He had naturally said nothing in his letters to his patron about the spate of rumours which had followed him from Moscow to Rome. But he was not slow, in February, to grasp the significance of a brief passage in one of her letters, casually mentioning that she was thinking of leasing Simaki and taking up 'permanent residence' at Brailov, to get the affairs of the estate in 'proper working order'. Von Meck gave no further details, but Tchaikovsky had heard that the debts of her late husband – larger and far more extensive than she had known – had returned to haunt her, and that her affairs had been badly mismanaged by her son Vladimir (who had proved almost as extravagant as his mother).

Now Tchaikovsky took the bull by the horns, offering to spare her the burden of supporting an indigent composer. 'Highly though I value my freedom and my creature comforts,' he wrote, 'I should consider them intolerable if I thought that they in any way diminished the life of my too tactful, too generous friend!'

> If I say I owe you my life, I am not guilty of exaggeration. So for God's sake, my dear friend, do not feel you must spare me the truth. If you are indeed obliged to trim your sails, then let me do the same. I can return to work in one of the Conservatoires, where they would welcome me with open arms . . . Your own well-being is far more important than mine. My own comfort is hateful to me if it comes at the expense of yours.[4]

Couched in such intense, apparently selfless terms, his letter could only evoke a dismissal of equally heartfelt embarrassment. She was appalled at the thought of his worrying on her behalf. 'The sum involved is so paltry beside my million-rouble ruin that it really doesn't tip the scales either way. So I beg you, if you do not wish to distress me, never to mention these matters again. In return, I promise that you will be the first to know if things get so bad that our arrangement becomes a problem.'[5]

This unsettling sequence of events was next overtaken by a completely unexpected tragedy: the death of Nikolay Rubinstein, in Paris, at the age of only forty-five. Hearing that Rubinstein was seriously ill, and had paused in the French capital en route to Nice for urgent treatment for intestinal tuberculosis, Tchaikovsky had immediately rushed to his side. But he arrived too late. Along with such luminaries as Massenet, Lalo and Turgenev, he attended a memorial service in the Russian Orthodox church in Paris on 26 March, then watched his old friend's body placed in a lead coffin for transportation back to Moscow. His mixed feelings about 'the Moscow Rubinstein', sparked almost entirely by his initial rejection of the First Piano Concerto, had long since softened to their original affection, as Rubinstein's last years were clouded by the unceasing attacks of Suvorin's *Novoe Vremya*. Tchaikovsky had been wholly supportive; and now, to von Meck, he wrote with enormous warmth of the man about whom he had so often railed to her. More than any other single figure, after all, the younger Rubinstein had proved a doughty champion of Tchaikovsky's music, and been responsible for his growing renown.

Tchaikovsky was all the more shocked, therefore, by the apparent lack of grief shown by the elder Rubinstein, Anton, who arrived from Spain just in time for the memorial service. 'Far from being crushed by his brother's death, he seems almost *pleased* about it,' he told Anatoly. 'I find his conduct *sickening*.' Tchaikovsky put it down to sibling rivalry, and returned to self-consolation, surprised by the comfort he found in prayer. 'My mind is in darkness,' he wrote to von Meck, 'but how could it be otherwise in the face of such questions, too much for mere mortals, as death, the purpose and the meaning of life, infinity etc . . . I find myself relying more and more on the only bulwark available against such calamities: a love of God, of which I have not hitherto been capable . . .'[6] Amid such self-reassurance – more emotional and sentimental, as always, than intellectual – he penned a tribute to Rubinstein, including a detailed account of his last days, which appeared in both the *Moscow Register* and the *Russian Gazette*.

Rubinstein's death, the Tsar's assassination and Mme von Meck's financial problems combined to fill Tchaikovsky with an ineluctable longing to return home. Unable to face the prospect of Rubinstein's funeral in Moscow, not least because of his contempt for Anton's lack of feeling, he dallied a few days in Paris and Berlin before arriving back in St Petersburg on 6 April. It was to prove a longer stay than he planned, thanks to Sasha's continuing ill-health, which saw her detained in expert care in the capital. Abandoning all thoughts of work, for a while Tchaikovsky thought he might have to escort his sister to a rest cure in Carlsbad. As long as she and her husband were detained in St Petersburg, however, he could better help Sasha by heading down to Kamenka to look after the children again.

He travelled via Moscow, to see Alexey, and was flattered but horrified to find himself invited to succeed Rubinstein as director of the Conservatoire. Declining without hesitation, he proceeded to the barracks, where his worst fears seemed to be confirmed: Army life was hardening his beloved servant, making him 'coarser' both physically and morally. As soon as he had arrived in Kamenka, Tchaikovsky threw all caution to the winds, and braved the prying eyes of military censors in an outpouring of almost crazed grief.

> Each evening, after undressing, I pine for you. I sit at my desk sobbing, once I remember that you are not here beside me . . . No-one could ever replace you . . . Ah, dear, sweet Lyonya! If you were to stay in the Army a hundred years, I would never grow out of the habit of you . . .[7]

So sorely did he miss Alexey that he even shared his sorrows in florid terms with von Meck, breaking his long habit of hiding such feelings from her. Still deeply distressed by the death of Rubinstein, Tchaikovsky was in no mood to compose that summer. As he continued his emotional, self-pitying quest for some form of religious consolation, his half-numb mind turned to the notion of more church music, specifically an All-Night Vigil. After enormous difficulties finalizing the correct text to set, he began sketching the work in the evenings, once his duties with the children were done, and had completed a first draft of all seventeen movements by July.

Disinclined to tackle any more major creative task, but again in need of funds, he had meanwhile asked Yurgenson to come up with some lucrative summer work for him. Capitalizing on this sudden burst of church music – he had recently, after a long legal struggle, acquired publication rights to the Liturgy – Tchaikovsky's publisher prevailed upon his reluctant client to edit the complete church music of an earlier Russian composer, Dmitry Bortnyansky. It was tedious work – Tchaikovsky found Bortnyansky's music 'as monotonous and barren as a steppe'[8] – but sheer boredom had him working at breakneck speed, and by November he had completed what would gradually appear as a ten-volume edition.

In the meantime, anxious to keep his own career on track, he had mapped out the first four numbers of a new opera, eventually to emerge as *Mazeppa*. Largely based on Pushkin's epic poem *Poltava*, the libretto combined its eponymous hero's heroic but vain struggle for Ukrainian independence from Russia with the poignant tale of his doomed love for his god-daughter, Marya.

Tchaikovsky was to have yet another love–hate relationship with his latest brainchild, even more so than with many of his previous works-in-progress. Its composition would take longer and cause him more difficulty than any other major work – so much so that he wondered aloud to von Meck and Taneyev whether his powers were failing – but *Mazeppa* would eventually prove more of a success in his own lifetime than with posterity. Rare revivals still remind the contemporary opera-goer that the piece possesses undeniably great moments – notably the lamentations of Marya's imprisoned father, her tender love duet with Mazeppa, and her ultimate descent into madness. But Tchaikovsky laboured perhaps too long and hard on *Mazeppa*; the difficulties he experienced lend the piece a staginess and inconsistency which have denied it a lasting place in the repertoire.[9]

The composer's spasmodic work on *Mazeppa* proved the backdrop to a difficult summer for the whole Tchaikovsky family. Now addicted to her pain-relieving morphine but otherwise improving from her early summer crisis, Sasha returned to Kamenka in better spirits, only to suffer a relapse upon the return home of her eldest daughter, Tanya, in an almost hysterical state.

In Moscow Tanya had broken off her engagement to an Army officer, Count Vasily Trubetskoy, who had invaded her rooms and made improper advances; at worst, as Tanya claimed to her uncle, he had tried to rape her. Either way, she had fled back to Kamenka in bad shape, smoking heavily, drinking uncontrollably, and injecting herself with large quantities of morphine. With Tanya's wild behaviour disrupting everyday life, Sasha in the doldrums, Lev sinking into a deep depression, and Alexey's absence still weighing heavily upon him, Tchaikovsky yearned to escape. 'As much as I love my family,' he confessed to von Meck, 'there are times I need to get away from them. It's as if some ancestral curse were consigning them all to eternal gloom . . .'[10]

Using the same device as he had to escape Antonina, he asked Yurgenson to send an urgent telegram 'saying something like *Your presence in Moscow urgently required re (something-or-other). Come a.s.a.p.*'[11] His publisher duly obliged, but Tchaikovsky got cold feet. Despite it all, he confided to Anatoly, he would have felt guilty about abandoning his loved ones at the height of their woes. Besides, Kamenka had become his only real home, whether he liked it or not. Here, at least, he could achieve a settled working rhythm, where the interruptions were minimal.

How curious is fate! By courtesy of N.F. [von Meck], I am a totally free man, free to live wherever I feel like. But here is the proof that money can't buy *real* freedom. Of all places on earth I know none less attractive (in terms of natural beauty) than Kamenka; and the greatest charm of the place – living contentedly in the bosom of my family – has now turned into something of a nightmare. But I feel doomed to spend a large proportion of my life here. And this is something about which I have no right to complain . . .[12]

Still the summer upheavals persisted. Now Tchaikovsky found his tranquillity disrupted by the regular and riotous visits of a posse of young Hussars stationed nearby, all with their eyes on the Davidov daughters. With Sasha on a rest cure in Odessa, Lev had gone (at Tchaikovsky's suggestion) to Brailov to scrutinize the running of the estate, with a view to making economies. Dismayed to find von Meck's affairs in very poor shape, Lev's intervention came too late. Just as she was inviting him to take over the running of the place, on the familiar condition that they never meet face-to-face, she suddenly found herself obliged to sell it. Only the previous month she had again been begging Tchaikovsky to join her there, and he himself had begun to entertain the idea, as a restorative interlude from the chaos of Kamenka. His benefactress had told him that her money worries were easing; but now, it appeared, the sale of the estate was essential to her chances of continuing financial stability.

Surrounded by universal woe, Tchaikovsky meanwhile encountered further troubles of his own, in the shape of a young man who had first appeared in his life two years earlier, and now returned to haunt him.

Leonty Grigorievich Tkachenko had first written to Tchaikovsky from Poltava in October 1879, professing himself a great admirer of his music, who wished to study with him but did not possess the means. Could he, perhaps, become the composer's manservant, to be paid in music theory lessons?

It is typical of Tchaikovsky that the 'correctness' of this letter from a complete stranger moved him to respond equally correctly. Rather than dismiss this bold request out of hand, he replied courteously that he could not possibly employ Tkachenko as his servant, but was prepared to help him if he could demonstrate in a second letter that he was young and gifted enough for it 'to lead somewhere'. From Tkachenko's reply, which arrived two weeks later, the composer learnt that he was twenty-two years old, and that his knowledge of music was 'as weak as his desire to become a professional musician is strong'. Although both intelligent and talented, so it seemed from his letter, he had no musical training at all; and Tchaikovsky's harsh but realistic conclusion was that he had 'left it too late'. Full of sympathy for the young man, he replied as kindly as he could that 'the years in which study might bear fruit have passed.'

Tchaikovsky heard nothing for a year. Then, on 28 December 1880, another letter arrived from Tkachenko, this time from Voronezh in Central Russia, returning the composer's letters 'in case they should fall into the wrong hands after my death'. The youth, it seemed, was bent on suicide. He bade Tchaikovsky farewell, saying that a life spent 'labouring solely for a morsel of bread' was not worth living. Deeply alarmed, the composer considered dropping everything and rushing to Voronezh. Even more effective, however, was an immediate cable to a friend of Anatoly's in that part of the world, asking him to raise the alarm in Voronezh and try to find the young man before it was too late. Within twenty-four hours he learnt that Tkachenko, though clearly on the verge of mental collapse, had been run to ground 'in time'. Tchaikovsky at once invited this troubled soul to meet him on his return to Moscow, sending him fifty roubles for the journey. 'What will come of all this I cannot say, but I am mightily relieved to have saved him from self-destruction. Judging by his letters he is a somewhat wild and strange young man, but intelligent enough, virtuous and very honest.'

The composer says nothing to suggest that Tkachenko's suicide threat reminded him of that of Antonina Milyukova, three and a half years before, which had also wrung from him urgent measures to discourage precipitous action, with the direst possible results. In Tkachenko's case, however, the immediate consequences were surprisingly different. Almost a fortnight passed before he received a reply to his long and careful letter, which had offered the youth 'my firm friendship, to try to support you through life's vicissitudes'. He was astonished to find his helping hand brusquely rejected. Far from thanking him for his kindness, Tkachenko bluntly dismissed Tchaikovsky's soothing words and indeed his financial assistance. 'He told me in no uncertain terms that it was *useless* for me to take it upon myself to reassure him about life's silver linings (when in fact I had said nothing of the sort) and that there was no way in which I could persuade him that life in this world is worth living.' Despite rejecting Tchaikovsky's money, saying he could 'manage perfectly well without it', Tkachenko then said he would come to Moscow as requested and 'hear you out'.

To the crestfallen composer, this was 'all very strange' and did 'not bode at all well for the future'. But when he met Tkachenko in Moscow the following month, he found himself agreeably surprised. He was 'nervous, timid, abnormally shy' but 'intelligent and mature . . . if possessed of rather strange views'. Convinced of his own artistic talent, yet forced to eke out a living as a railway guard, he had fallen into a misanthropy with which the composer could only empathize. Tchaikovsky resolved to secure him a place at the Conservatoire for the rest of the academic year, and to support him financially for the foreseeable future.

No sooner had Tkachenko settled to his studies than he demanded a meeting with Tchaikovsky 'for a serious talk'. The composer was then forced to listen as his young protégé denounced his 'moral corruptness'. The composer's generosity, he argued, was entirely self-interested, 'like those ladies who busy themselves with philanthropy because it is *the done thing*, and to win themselves praise.' Not wishing to be 'a victim of your weakness', as he put it, Tkachenko told him to expect no thanks, for he refused to consider him his benefactor. Understandably put out, Tchaikovsky defended himself against Tkachenko's charges, then dismissed the young man, telling him that he would continue to subsidize him at the Conservatoire, but did not wish to see him again. He himself was leaving Moscow for Kamenka, and he encouraged his charge to concentrate on his studies.

That was how things stood six months later, in that summer of 1881, when Tchaikovsky's already unsettled tenancy of Kamenka was further disrupted one August morning by a sudden flap among the Davidov servants. Causing chaos at the railway station, they announced, was an unsavoury-looking young man who refused to reveal his name but demanded to see Tchaikovsky. He had walked all the way from Moscow; rejected all offers of food, though obviously starving; and told the local police to do with him what they pleased. Realizing at once who it must be, Tchaikovsky 'ran to the station in great agitation, half expecting him to be waiting to blow his brains out in front of me.'

He found Tkachenko in a 'desperate' state, so glad to see him that he collapsed in hysterical sobbing. Tchaikovsky organized some tea and spent most of the day calming him down. He had walked all this way, it appeared, to tell the composer that he was unworthy of further subsidy at the Conservatoire. If Tchaikovsky would pay his fare as far as Kharkov, where his sister lived, he would send him his diary for the summer, which would say everything that he felt unable to confess face-to-face. At the end of a traumatic day, as he waved off his unruly charge, Tchaikovsky found he had again warmed to Tkachenko, whom he could only see as possessing 'a good but broken nature, like a character out of Dostoevsky.'

Taking his hint from this phrase, Alexander Poznansky too sees Tkachenko as a romantic figure straight out of the Russian fiction of the day, one of the *raznochintsy* typified by Eugene Onegin, 'socially displaced intellectuals with a keen sense of self-importance who had lost a taste for tradition and could find no place for themselves in their environment'. Tchaikovsky made the same mistake. In Tkachenko's letters, not to mention his erratic behaviour, it might be thought that the composer would have divined ominous echoes of Antonina, pointing to another clear case of clinical neurosis. When the diaries duly arrived, in a fat package which preoccupied Tchaikovsky for more than a week, they offered further evidence of a fundamentally unstable character, riddled with sexual neuroses.

Confronted with a heterosexual obsessionist mirroring his own homosexual promiscuity, the shocked composer found himself at a loss as to how to deal with confessions 'even more candid than Rousseau's'. He was not himself blameless in that department, he told Tkachenko, but it was 'excess' which would prove his undoing. 'The point is this: to be able to rise above one's bodily desires and thus control them. This comes only with training.' Although the diaries have not survived, this sounds very much like a reference to masturbation, about which the composer had chided Modest in his youth. All his life Tchaikovsky took the conventional view that 'self-abuse' was a crude and debilitating practice, leading to all sorts of dire consequences. 'Ah, Leonty Grigorievich,' he sighed, 'you are a good person, a nice person, but morally sick. Not your fault, of course; you are the victim of circumstances . . . or of Fate.'

Although he could not advise him to persist with his musical training, the composer found some literary merit in Tkachenko's diary and offered to continue to subsidize him if he would attempt a career as a writer. Encouraged by a second opinion from Modest (whose own talents Tchaikovsky tended to overestimate), the composer continued to finance Tkachenko throughout 1882. The would-be writer stuck doggedly to his task, regularly despatching autobiographical sketches for the perusal of his patron, who was eventually forced to admit that his confidence had been misplaced. On 20 November Tchaikovsky wrote a long letter which none too artfully concealed his own anxiety about open-ended subsidies to a writer of limited talent whom he did not wish to offend into drastic action:

> Since it is only very recently that you have begun to concentrate on developing your literary talent, and since it will be a long time before your hard work will make up for the inadequacy of your education and turn you into a mature, fully-fledged writer, you face several years, for all the clarity of your personal ambitions, living without the kind of specific employment which brings with it those responsibilities which are necessary to define and adorn a

fulfilled life. What you need are interests and enthusiasms which will make your life worthwhile for the indefinite future until you become an established writer, while not distracting you from the task at hand. After much thought I believe I have identified the perfect occupation for both your temperament and your ambitions. Can you guess what it is? *A village schoolteacher.* In my view, there is no more honourable, no more *holy* role in the service of society than that of a village schoolteacher.

There appears to have been a reply of some sort from Tkachenko before he lapsed into silence for almost a year. He cannot have been too hurt or exasperated by the suggestion of village school-teaching, for Tchaikovsky is writing to him from Paris in January 1883 in the friendliest of voices: 'How are you? Where are you? Let me know how things are going. It's more than two months since I heard from you.' Reply came there none – until October, nine months later, when Tchaikovsky arrived at Verbovka to discover a package from Tkachenko, returning all his letters, without explanation, and asking for more money. The composer duly obliged, and that was that. He never heard from Tkachenko again.

The Russian editors of the entire correspondence, still unavailable to Western scholars, imply that Tkachenko did indeed become a village schoolmaster, with Tchaikovsky's assistance, for at least a part of that year. But nothing more is known of this curious bird of passage, who revealed so much of the composer's confused yet kindly character as he flitted in and out of his life during these somewhat fallow years. 'A pathetic, and rather unsympathetic individual' was Tchaikovsky's final verdict on Tkachenko. In a case such as this, not untypical of the composer's dealings with those waifs and strays who sought his help throughout his life, the first epithet might rebound to haunt him, but certainly not the second.[13]

By the end of that summer of 1881, when Tkachenko's arrival at Kamenka had so compounded the domestic confusion, and his diary so rattled his sexual nerves, Tchaikovsky was faced with yet another addition to his woes. The harsh new Tsar, Alexandr III, suddenly extended all military conscription to six years, thus undermining all the composer's efforts on behalf of his beloved manservant. The only compensation was that Alexey was entitled to a month's leave that summer.

Tchaikovsky had originally planned to take Alexey with him to Simaki, where they could have enjoyed some quiet weeks together at von Meck's expense; now he rushed to his side in Moscow, where he found nothing but gloom and doom. The 'curse' of that summer, it seemed, persisted.

Anatoly was still languishing from a series of broken love affairs; the Conservatoire, despite a new director in Hubert, was still in a state of shock at Rubinstein's death; Alexey could not be roused from morose reflections on his extended military service; and von Meck took the chance to send round his old *bête noire*, Pakhulsky, for more lessons in composition. In three weeks Tchaikovsky ran through all his reserves of money and good humour. Mid-October saw him back at Kamenka in lower spirits than ever, abandoning *Mazeppa* for another stab at an opera of *Romeo and Juliet* – while all the while he knew that there was much work still to be done, against a fast approaching deadline, on his edition of Bortnyansky.

Amid the Davidovs' continuing domestic woes, the only moment of relief came with news from Sasha in Odessa that another daughter, Vera, had become engaged to marry a naval officer with an all too familiar name. Nikolay Rimsky-Korsakov, adjutant to Grand Duke Konstantin Nikolayevich, turned out to be no relation to the composer with whom Vera's uncle was always to enjoy decidedly mixed relations. When his niece brought the young man home for the family's blessing, Tchaikovsky took an immediate liking to him. 'What miserable creatures you and I are!' he wrote to Modest that day. 'We must live out our whole lives without knowing for one moment the true fulfilment of happiness in love.'[14]

Modest, Tchaikovsky's first biographer, explains his brother's creative paralysis throughout that long, difficult summer in terms of Rubinstein's death, Alexey's absence and von Meck's money worries, only touching on the chaos at Kamenka. He makes light of the family problems for obvious reasons, quite apart from the fact that he was not himself there.

But the composer's most recent biographer, David Brown, is surely right to conclude that conditions at Kamenka were perhaps the central factor in Tchaikovsky's creative torpor. In the long term the absence of Alexey, the loss of his havens at Brailov and Simaki, even an unwonted wish to get away from his family were 'blessings in disguise'. The regular patterns of his life in the early 1880s, since the trauma of his marriage, had become 'dangerously protected, even cosy . . . insulated too much from those sometimes painful experiences which were essential if his creative powers were again to be stimulated into full activity.'[15]

The birth of Antonina's lovechild had rendered even her less of a threat to the composer's fragile psyche. As he left Kamenka that November to return to Europe, Tchaikovsky himself seemed to feel his old creative juices beginning to flow more freely again. Only the choice of his next project still frustrated him. Pausing in Kiev for a fortnight, primarily to attend Vera's wedding, he was so struck by a play called *Vanka the Steward*, a dramatization by Luka Antropov of a short story by Dmitri

Averkiev, that he briefly wondered whether it should not supplant both *Mazeppa* and *Romeo and Juliet* as the subject of his next opera. An opera, whichever one of them, it was to be. Of that he felt sure as he arrived in Italy via Vienna – where he seems to have been completely unaware of, and thus to have missed, Brodsky's first performance of his Violin Concerto under Hans Richter.

Via Venice and Florence, where he paid due homage outside the villa rented by von Meck, he at last arrived back in Rome, where Modest, Kolya and Kondratiev were awaiting him. Also in the Italian capital at the time was Franz Liszt, attending a series of concerts to mark his seventieth birthday. 'It was impossible not to be moved as this old man of genius acknowledged, with great feeling, the wild acclaim of the Italian audiences,' Tchaikovsky recorded. 'But I cannot warm to Liszt's music. It contains more poetic embroidery than real creative power, more colour than draughtsmanship.'[16]

Still dithering between his three different opera subjects, he could not settle to any one of them. He wanted to be writing music, not libretti, so asked Yurgenson to see if Averkiev himself might adapt *Vanka the Steward*. As with *Romeo and Juliet*, it was the love scene which really fascinated him. At Kamenka that summer he had already drafted a love-duet for Shakespeare's star-crossed lovers, simply putting words to a pretty straightforward adaptation of the famous love theme from his Fantasy Overture*. Now a love scene between Mazeppa and Marya presented itself as the most enticing possibility, and by mid-December he was able to report to his patron that he had begun composing. 'Who knows? If it fires me, I might even write a whole opera on this theme.'[17]

The reason for this apparent lack of conviction becomes clear two weeks later, when he is apologizing to von Meck for dismissing her suggestion, some time before, that he write a trio for piano, violin and cello. 'Do you remember that I boldly declared how much I hated this combination of instruments? Well, out of the blue, despite it all, I have decided to test my powers in this area, into which I have not so far ventured. I have already written the opening of a trio . . .'[18]

In repeating his distaste for this combination of instruments, going on to gush that his 'act of will' would prove worthwhile just for the pleasure it would give his benefactress, Tchaikovsky was being somewhat disingenuous. What he really had in mind was a posthumous tribute to Nikolay Rubinstein, which clearly had to include a piano part reflecting his old friend's virtuosity. Although written yet again

---

*The incomplete vocal score of this love duet was found after his death, and is occasionally performed (in Taneyev's realization) for its curiosity value.

in trying circumstances, specifically the hostile critical response to his Violin Concerto, Tchaikovsky had finished the sketches in three weeks, and felt growing confidence in the work as he brought it towards its final form. The trio was to prove perhaps his most polished piece (together with the *Serenade for Strings*) since the masterworks of 1877–78, the Fourth Symphony and *Eugene Onegin*; yet he showed an endearing uncertainty about his talents in this uncharted territory. 'Before you print it,' he demanded of Yurgenson, 'it's vital that Taneyev, Hřímalý and Fitzenhagen play it through . . . I would very much like Karlusha [Albrecht], Kashkin, Hubert and his wife and *our whole circle* to be at this run-through. It is *absolutely crucial* that Karlusha or some other expert string player take a close look at my bow markings and make any appropriate corrections.'[19]

Aware of constant accusations that his solo parts were fiendishly difficult, largely because he was not himself a virtuoso instrumentalist, Tchaikovsky wanted to take no chances on a piece whose dedication seemed sure to win it even greater attention than usual. After the trio of his choice had indeed played it through privately in Moscow, in his absence, he was delighted to receive an enthusiastic letter from Taneyev, adding that Hubert had already received requests for repeat performances. Once he had himself heard another dry run, however, he made wholesale revisions before having the confidence to dedicate his Piano Trio in A minor (Op. 50) 'to the memory of a great artist'. It was to enjoy wide popularity within his own lifetime, and to join the *Pathétique* among the obsequies played after his own death.

The Tchaikovsky brothers' tour of Italy, with young Kolya and a fourteen-year-old companion they had hired for him, Grisha Sangursky, continued against a backdrop of mixed news from home. Wintering in Kiev, in the hope of marrying off Tanya, the Davidovs were still plagued by their daughter's wild and erratic behaviour. From Moscow, meanwhile, came the unexpected and much happier news of Anatoly's engagement to the daughter of a wealthy merchant. Tchaikovsky's relief that his brother had at last found a bride, thus relieving him of the recurrent role of amateur psychiatrist, shone through as he passed on the news to von Meck.

Another source of relief was the departure from Italy of Kondratiev, not so much because of his drinking and other wild ways as because of his daughter's governess, who had been showing worrying signs of falling for Tchaikovsky. With this unnerving experience in mind, he sent Anatoly a letter rather more revealing than that he had written von Meck, reflecting more on his own problems than his brother's prospects of happiness.

Although I can never enjoy the same experience, I think I can understand the joy you must now be feeling. Every man has a need for a certain type of tenderness and affection which only a woman can provide. I myself am sometimes gripped by a crazy desire to be stroked by a woman's hand. Sometimes I see attractive women – not young women, though – on whose knees I want to rest my head while smothering their hands with kisses.[20]

It is not only the reference to older women which shows whose love Tchaikovsky was really craving. His recurrent obsession with women's hands recalls the small boy's description of those 'large but beautiful' hands of his mother, hands which 'do not exist nowadays, and never will again'.

The brothers and their young protégés travelled to Naples and Pompeii before Tchaikovsky headed home for Anatoly's wedding. He had managed to complete the All-Night Vigil in Naples, despite the constant hubbub from the street, not to mention a plague of mice (of which he had a morbid terror) in the attic of his rented rooms. But it was financial necessity rather than fraternal affection which drew him back to Russia. He had debated awaiting Anatoly and his bride in Italy, but funds were again low and he could use the trip home to bring his business affairs up to date. He paused for a few days in Sorrento, and then Florence (purely to gratify von Meck, again in residence), before meeting up with the Davidovs in Moscow on 9 April for Anatoly's nuptials a week later.

The groom was a ragbag of nerves, wrongly convinced that he had developed syphilis; Tanya was at her worst, unable to hold down any food; Sasha seemed in a world of her own, fuelled largely by morphine; and Tchaikovsky was horrified to find himself *in loco parentis*, required to deal with an army of Anatoly's new in-laws. To his new sister-in-law, Praskovya Konshina, Tchaikovsky was 'a god'. She had seen him once before, at a concert of his music in St Petersburg, when he had made a surprise appearance in the wake of his marital nightmare. 'We found him cowering in his stall. He seemed quite unaware of the concourse about him and of the enthusiasm which his presence excited. He might not have been there. He looked straight in front of him and seemed a prey to unspeakable suffering.' The Tchaikovsky she met three years later, on the day she married his brother, could not have been more different:

I saw him at the door of the church just before the ceremony began. I could not believe my eyes. I could only think of another Tchaikovsky, pale, thin, bearing every mark of extreme suffering. I now saw an elegant, white-haired gentleman who greeted me with a smile from his magnificent blue eyes . . .[21]

Tchaikovsky warmed to Praskovya, who recalled that 'after the ceremony he came up to me and spoke charmingly and with much affection. There was a great crowd at our wedding and I was amazed at his ease of manner. He spoke to everyone and talked in the most amusing way.' But his stay in Moscow was otherwise ruined partly by abortive negotiations over his next opera, more by the refusal of the military authorities to allow him to see Alexey, then engaged in more exams. At the first available opportunity, in early May, he again escaped to Kamenka.

Each visit to Moscow diminished his appetite for the place, and increased his eagerness to flee to the Ukraine. But the charms of Kamenka were fast beginning to pall. If last summer had proved irksome, this one was to be worse. The Davidov family was back in residence – apart, to Tchaikovsky's relief, from the troublesome Tanya, whom they had left behind in her own apartment in Kiev. With three other daughters at various stages of puberty, and both their parents beset by their own health and money worries, domestic chaos had now become the norm at what had once been an idyllic rural retreat. But Tchaikovsky still regarded Kamenka as his only real home, the one place he could hope to get on with some work. 'If I abandoned ship,' he wrote to Modest with a rare beam of self-knowledge, 'I would miss even that *ennui* which so torments me.'[22] Yet progress on *Mazeppa* was fitful. At times, to judge from his letters, his heart was not in it; at others the domestic disruptions were simply too much even for his powers of concentration.

He was, for once, almost relieved to return to the social round of Moscow, where a concert of his music on 17 August included the first performance in Russia of his Violin Concerto, along with *The Tempest*, the *1812 Overture* and a selection of his songs. Now, at last, Brodsky's performance won his concerto both critical and popular acclaim, and the composer was accorded a standing ovation. The success came hard on the heels of Taneyev's equally successful launch of the Second Piano Concerto, and a rapturous reception for the Serenade for Strings. Within days of the concert, his hectic social schedule was taking its toll on Tchaikovsky, who was further agitated by news that Alexey had fallen ill. Amid the circus of friends and admirers, dinner parties and business appointments, he managed to visit his servant in hospital every day; and he postponed his return to Kamenka, for all his growing claustrophobia in the city, until completely reassured that the initial diagnosis of typhus was a false alarm.

That September in Kamenka proved the worst month yet, the beginning of the end of Tchaikovsky's affection for his happy haven of so many years' standing. From Kiev arrived Tanya, hopelessly reliant on morphine, bringing with her the family's former music tutor, Stanislav Blumenfeld, whom Tchaikovsky himself had introduced into the household some years before. Class prejudice and undisguised anti-semitism were the order of the day on the country estates of late nineteenth-century Russia; Blumenfeld's welcome as a musician and family friend was uncomfortably muted by his social standing as a lower-class Jew. Tchaikovsky's irritation at having Blumenfeld installed next door to him, thus inhibiting his music-making at night, curdled to horror when he quickly perceived, as did everyone except the preoccupied Davidovs themselves, that Blumenfeld and Tanya had become lovers. This scandalous liaison, which had started in Kiev but now blossomed at Kamenka, was the talk of the estate. The composer, a figure of great moral rectitude in all affairs but his own, was not alone in thinking it quite outrageous, not least when the shameless couple engaged in some open dalliance – beneath a rug, during an afternoon carriage ride – before his very eyes. Agonizing over whether to tell Lev and Sasha what was happening, he opted instead to make a rapid exit.

It didn't really matter where, so long as it was outside Russia. After more than a year the sketches for *Mazeppa* were finally complete – the opera, he told von Meck, had caused him 'more difficulty than any other large piece I have written'[23] – and he was now quite accustomed to orchestrating while travelling. 'I'm becoming quite a nomad,' he wrote to Modest. His only regret at leaving was his growing affection for his nephew Bob. 'He's so tender and loving towards me. I find myself constantly moved, sometimes to tears.'[24]

Modest had not been in Kamenka that summer. His life had been dramatically changed by the death in May of Kolya Konradi's father, Herman. As well as leaving him ten thousand roubles, Konradi's will made Modest the boy's legal guardian, responsible for his continued education. Distinctly unamused, Kolya's mother, Alina (now Bryullova), and other members of the family began to make life uncomfortable for Modest, who pleaded with his brother to join him at the Konradi estate, Grankino. Pleased to escape the hothouse of Kamenka, Tchaikovsky arrived for two weeks, and finished up staying for nearly seven. As the Konradi family began litigation to contest the will, blocking not merely Modest's inheritance but the recent salary due to him, Tchaikovsky read *Bleak House* and proceeded with *Mazeppa* while trying to steer his brother through an awkward passage, fraught with irony.

The will had thrown in Modest's lot with his charge at a time when this once inseparable duo had begun to grow apart. At fourteen, for all his physical handicaps, Kolya had matured into an assured young man, who now also happened to be a wealthy landowner, custodian of the Grankino estate. As Modest discerned the truth, that his once dependent pupil had less and less need of him, he grew ill. A painful series of operations for an abscess near his anus may also have been the penalty for other habitual aspects of his life. Even when the legal dispute was satisfactorily settled, with Modest granted an annuity of 6,000 roubles, it was clear that he was *de trop* at Grankino, at least for the present. At the turn of the year he arrived in Moscow just as Tchaikovsky was leaving for Europe, and agreed to catch up with him in Paris. Full of self-pity, both declared themselves in need of a thorough rest.

On his way across Europe, in Berlin, Tchaikovsky heard *Tristan und Isolde* for the first time, which prompted another anti-Wagner diatribe to von Meck. Now, in Paris, he luxuriated in Mozart, enjoying an Opéra Comique production of *Le Nozze de Figaro* so much that he went straight back to hear it a second time – 'and if there are more performances, I shall go again and again and again.' The only problem was that, at his second *Figaro*, he had run into the Grand Duke Konstantin Nikolayevich, to avoid whose social whirl he felt obliged to lie that he was leaving Paris the next day. The mysteries of Mozart, one of the few musical topics on which von Meck summoned the courage to disagree with him, again filled Tchaikovsky with wonder.

> It surprises me, too, that a man as flawed as I am, both mentally and morally, can still take such delight in Mozart, who lacks the depth and force of Beethoven, the warmth and passion of Schumann, the brilliance of Meyerbeer, Berlioz, etc . . . Mozart does not overwhelm me, nor takes my breath away, but he does enslave me, makes me feel good, fills me with warmth. When I listen to his music, it makes me feel virtuous . . . The older I grow, and the better I get to know him, the more I love him.[25]

As Tchaikovsky kicked his heels in Paris, half-heartedly orchestrating *Mazeppa* while awaiting Modest's oft-postponed arrival, impatience for his brother's company led him to write some of the most indiscreet letters of his life.

Presumably to remind Modest what he was missing, he sent vivid descriptions of his evening 'strolls', of the boys he had tempted back to his rooms, of his joy at finding a club catering for homosexuals of all tastes. Filled with longing for Alexey, he again braved the military censors with fulsome declarations of love. When Modest finally arrived, on 28 January, the reason for all the delays became clear. Meeting his brother at the station, Tchaikovsky was appalled to see on his brother's arm the unwelcome sight of their wayward niece, Tanya.

He was soon privy to a secret kept from the rest of the family, even from Tanya's parents: a morphine addict in near-terminal decline, she was also six months pregnant by Blumenfeld, who had disowned her. Tanya had fetched up in St Petersburg and thrown herself on Modest's mercy. Even Pyotr Ilyich agreed that his brother had had no alternative but to take her in, keep her secret safe from her parents, and bring her to Paris in the hope of a cure for her addiction, pending the birth of her child.

Abandoning their plans to move on to Italy together, the brothers installed Tanya in a Paris clinic and watched anxiously as her dependence on morphine was brutally reduced. Tchaikovsky himself wrote to her father, Lev, detailing the treatment she was undergoing, without revealing her pregnancy. This was not the tranquil interlude he had envisaged. To make matters worse, there was news from Anatoly that Alexey was gravely ill in his Moscow barracks with pneumonia; unable to leave Paris, for reasons he could not disclose, Tchaikovsky sent the ever reliable Yurgenson to investigate. By the time he had located Alexey – no easy task – the danger had passed. The relief in Tchaikovsky's subsequent letter to von Meck was soon surpassed by his joy at the news that his servant, as soon as he was fully recovered, would be granted a year's convalescence.

In Paris, meanwhile, there was no such relief from the continuing decline of Tanya. By the end of March, after six expensive weeks in the neurological ward of the Sâlpetrière Hospital, her condition was little improved and Tchaikovsky's finances all but drained. After casting about for another solution, *any* other solution, he had no alternative but to ask von Meck for an advance on his next annual lump sum, not due until June. Her own finances at last having stabilized, to the point where she had bought a new estate at Pleshcheyevo, near Moscow, his patron duly obliged. But this time her reply was tinged with concern about his family's apparent tendency towards drug addiction.[26] She had her reasons – which a long-term conspiracy obliged both of them, as yet, to keep secret – but it was an unusual jarring note in their correspondence, the first sign of ominous developments ahead.

At the time Tchaikovsky was little perturbed, being both grateful for the financial relief and preoccupied with tedious but unavoidable work. Throughout the upheavals of the summer, and the subsequent dramas of the winter and spring, he had struggled on with *Mazeppa*, still awaiting its final touches amid the Tanya crisis. Now he found himself bowed down by two commissions from Russian officialdom, both to mark the coronation in May of the new Tsar, Alexandr III. Already he had fulfilled a request to arrange a chorus from Glinka's *A Life for the Tsar*, linking it to the national anthem, for a choir of no fewer than 7,500 to sing in Red Square during the new Emperor's ceremonial approach to the Kremlin. The organizing committee had since come up with requests for a Festival March and a full-scale Cantata in praise of the city of Moscow, to a text by the poet Apollon Maikov.

Despite the short notice, Tchaikovsky had reasons beyond his natural patriotism to set his opera aside for this work, occasional music of the kind which had always filled him with distaste. Two years before, at the height of von Meck's financial problems, one of his own frequent cash shortages had emboldened him to write to the new Tsar requesting a loan of three thousand roubles, to be repaid as swiftly as possible from his performance royalties. Outlandish though it may sound today, this was not so unorthodox a request; the Tsar's patronage was on permanent offer to state worthies, and Tchaikovsky had reason to believe he could number Alexandr III among his admirers. Instead of granting him the loan, Alexandr had made an outright gift of the money – a handsome personal tribute, which had both surprised and delighted the composer. All his subsequent offers to repay the debt had been regally declined. He therefore felt himself under more than merely a loyal obligation to fulfil every coronation commission, however inconvenient or distasteful, with which the committee chose to land him.

Having this time declined payment, despite his continuing financial straits, Tchaikovsky was delighted to learn that the Tsar had awarded him 1,500 roubles for his coronation music. But his joy was short-lived. To spare the composer embarrassment, Alexandr ordered the payment to be made in the form of a ring, as he had for the Danish Festival Overture nearly two decades before. Frankly, Tchaikovsky admitted to family and friends, he would rather have had the money. There was perhaps some poetic justice in what followed. The day he received the royal ring, so desperate were the composer's finances that he again went straight out and pawned it, for a mere 375 roubles. Later that same day, he lost both the money and the pawn ticket. It was an episode over which he was unable to laugh for some time.

By mid-April the *Moscow* cantata was finished, and Modest felt able to plead Kolya as good reason to return to Russia, leaving Tchaikovsky in sole charge of Tanya. He made the best of a bad job, as was his wont, by sandwiching his hospital visits in between daring excursions into the lively homosexual demi-monde of the French capital. His forty-third birthday, 7 May 1883, was thus a forlorn and solitary combination of more *Mazeppa* and an evening 'stroll' before being summoned to the hospital, shortly after midnight, to greet the latest addition to his family: Tanya's son, his great-nephew, whose destiny lay in his hands.

There was no way that this baby, the product of a scandalous liaison of which few in the family knew, could ever return to Russia with Tanya. His father had disowned him; his mother showed little emotion at the seemingly inevitable prospect of parting with him; his grandparents did not even know of his existence. Taking charge with uncharacteristic efficiency, Tchaikovsky saw to it that the child was baptized (under the name of Georges-Léon), handed over to a wet nurse, and assigned to the care of a French foster family pending his formal adoption by the composer himself.*

This apparently interminable drama now resolved, at least for the present, he was desperate to return to Russia, where the recovered and released Alexey had already been awaiting him for some time. Such was his impatient state of tension that a furious tirade greeted the news that Modest's St Petersburg apartment was crowded with relatives, most of them little more than children: yet more Davidov offspring, entrusted to Modest by their father pending their enrolment at the School of Jurisprudence, with even von Meck offspring paying dutiful daily visits. Alexey would just have to be another burden to him, Tchaikovsky told Modest peremptorily, while he awaited his master's arrival.

Emerging from a long, dark tunnel of a year, the worst since the marriage crisis of five years before, Tchaikovsky was mightily relieved to have seen off the Tanya crisis. Never again would he have anything to do with her, he raged in letters to both Anatoly and von Meck.

> That girl is trouble. I don't believe she will ever be weaned from morphine. Drugs, drink or poison will surely be the end of her . . . I can feel sorry for her, but I cannot love her. Tanya alone will probably see to it that I will never again be a regular visitor to Kamenka. My only wish at this moment is to spend the rest of my life as far away from her as possible. [27]

If he was not to summer at Kamenka, then where? Von Meck had been pressing him to join her at Pleshcheyevo – which had the added advantage of being near Anatoly, who had recently become a father. But proximity to von Meck inevitably involved the oppressive presence of Pakhulsky, whom Tchaikovsky had now come to abhor. His patron's junior protégé had haunted him these last few years. Since his visit to Moscow in August

---

*Three years later, in 1886, the child was in fact adopted by Tchaikovsky's brother Nikolay and his wife.

1882, when Tchaikovsky had managed to avoid him until he was about to leave, Pakhulsky had been pressing his own compositions upon the maestro, who considered them almost as execrable as their creator.

Tchaikovsky found himself in a difficult position. It was easy enough to tell white lies to von Meck about Pakhulsky and his work (which he did constantly); but what to tell the young man himself? At first he contented himself with gentle criticism; but the letters flowing back and forth contain clear hints that each man increasingly resented the other, even if their joint patron remained oblivious. During the previous summer in Paris, when he had been struggling with his Coronation commissions amid the Tanya crisis, Tchaikovsky had barely controlled his rage at being sent another 'indigestible, meaningless' piece of Pakhulsky for detailed comment. This time the criticism, when he finally made time for it, was not so gentle. Tchaikovsky considered the young man completely without talent; but he could not quite say so for fear of alienating his benefactress, who again replied on Pakhulsky's behalf, thanking him for his candour in tones mingling her own dismay with Pakhulsky's brooding resentment.

Straitened though his finances still were, not least because he was helping Lev with Tanya's continuing Paris expenses, Tchaikovsky could not face the oppressive combination of a suffocating von Meck and a seething Pakhulsky. So he begged leave to postpone his début at Pleshcheyevo, pleading Anatoly's greater need of him, and made plans to head for Podushkino. Leaving Tanya in the capable hands of her Russian maid, the only other person in on her secret, he returned on 27 May to an unusually quiet St Petersburg. All the capital's luminaries had decamped to Moscow for the new Tsar's coronation, and Tchaikovsky felt amply compensated for missing his Cantata by the absence of all the people he didn't want to see. So joyous was his reunion with Modest and Kolya, and so relaxed did he feel in a city bereft of its usual irritants, that he stayed almost two weeks before proceeding to Anatoly's new dacha on 11 June.

Immediately he felt he had made the right decision. Marriage and fatherhood had calmed his usually fraught brother, whose choice of summer residence he found idyllic. 'In these surroundings,' according to Anatoly's new wife, Praskovya, 'he became "the real Petya". He was free. He loved his brother, and he saw only his closest friends. He adored nature, and for that reason we always chose a house situated in beautiful countryside.'[28] So relaxed did Tchaikovsky become on a daily routine of rural walks and mushroom-picking that he even braved some trips into Moscow, renewing his lost friendship with Vladimir Shilovsky, wassailing with Kondratiev, even agreeing to see Pakhulsky, who had a new symphony to show him. So appalling did he consider it that he contemplated a terminal showdown. To be rid of Pakhulsky, he was prepared to risk alienating his benefactress. That very week, however, she was devastated by the death of her youngest son, twelve-year-old Mikhail, from a congenital heart condition. Tchaikovsky had no alternative but to stay his hand.

Back at Podushkino, Praskovya noticed that her brother-in-law's moments of exuberance were 'nearly always followed by periods of intense depression. He then seemed completely unaware of his surroundings and became extremely absent-minded':

> One autumn day, when it was very cold and windy, he announced his intention of going to the chemist to buy some cotton-wool to put in his ears. I asked him at the same time to buy me a pound of apples. To my great astonishment he returned with an enormous load of cotton-wool. It appeared that the chemist had asked him whether a pound would be enough. This sufficed to make him forget his commission. He left his umbrella and the apples at the chemist's, and was too shy to go and recover them.[29]

Von Meck was too distraught by her son's death to be upset by his next decision: to postpone again his arrival at her new estate, and instead take himself off to Kamenka. For all the troubles of the previous two summers, and his avowed reluctance to return, the place and his family still exerted a magnetic hold over him. Correcting the proofs of *Mazeppa*, which eventually took him all of three months, was proving almost as arduous a task as composing this troublesome opera; at Kamenka he struggled on, despite all the domestic distractions, thanks to the satisfying incentive of a battle between the main Moscow and St Petersburg opera companies over who should be the first to stage it.

The task was still weighing him down when, somewhat to his surprise, 'the demon of composition' (as he put it to von Meck) returned to take possession of him with 'an irresistible power'.[30] The result was the Second Suite for Orchestra (Op. 53), sketched in a couple of weeks beneath his brother's roof and orchestrated over as many months beneath his sister's. That same autumn, surrounded by children, he also gathered together the Sixteen Songs for Children (Op. 54), of which 'Legend' has proved one of his few short pieces to gain a lasting place in the repertoire.

It was no coincidence that this fruitful end to an otherwise rather fallow year followed Tanya's departure from Kamenka to Paris, torn between proposals of marriage from a Parisian doctor and a local merchant. Tchaikovsky thought neither appropriate, improbably suggesting that she should winter in Italy and headhunt a rich Englishman. If his continuing contempt for the English lurked somewhere beneath this bizarre notion, the turn of 1883–84 saw him teaching himself the language in the hope of reading *David Copperfield* in the original. For neither the first nor the last time in his life, at all levels from the sublime to the ridiculous, Tchaikovsky was content to remain a complex knot of contradictions.

For eighteen months, since the summer of 1882, the pace of Tchaikovsky's correspondence with Nadezhda von Meck had slowed. Through all her financial problems, his patron had become a frail and sickly figure, especially troubled by sharp cramps in her hands – the symbol, ironically, of Tchaikovsky's measure of a woman. 'Nothing seems to help. The pain grows worse all the time,' she told him mournfully. Every line she wrote now caused her considerable pain. Soon it became impossible for von Meck to pen more than a few words at a time, and she feared for the complete loss of the use of her hands.

> What worries me more than anything is being deprived of my conversations with you, my dear, my only friend. In your company I have opened my heart, relaxed, consoled myself for many of the troubles I have been through. To lose this lone consolation would be more than I could bear.[31]

As their exchanges dwindled from one a day to less than one a week, the two were meanwhile growing ever closer to realizing a plot which might provide just the consolation she sought, and act as a symbolic substitute for a union of their own. Since the summer of 1879, five years before, Tchaikovsky and von Meck had been attempting to engineer the marriage of one of her sons to one of his nieces, the Davidov daughters, all of whom were approaching marriageable age. At the time, it was partly Tchaikovsky's way of ducking von Meck's uncomfortable protestations of love; to both, in the longer term, it was also a way of rendering their relationship immortal.

Their letters had always been full of information and enquiries about each other's families. Copious photographs had been exchanged, and Tchaikovsky had eventually agreed to meet and get to know some of her older children. Chief among these was Nikolay von Meck, Nadezhda's second son, who had become a regular visitor to the roving Tchaikovsky ménage, whether at Kamenka or Kiev, Moscow or St Petersburg. Over the last four years, all four of the Davidov daughters had in turn been considered as candidates for his hand by the conspiratorial correspondents, whose own simple aim was to become relations by marriage –

some kind of consummation, to both, of their intimate separateness.

As long ago as October 1879, Tchaikovsky had raised the idea in principle with his sister and her husband, who had responded warmly. It was then eleven-year-old Natalya, the youngest of the four girls, only recently despatched to boarding school in St Petersburg, who was her uncle's unsuspecting long-term victim. Once the idea had been mooted, however, the timetable was naturally accelerated. The subsequent history of the Davidovs' eldest daughter, Tanya, had obviously ruled her *hors de combat*; so by the summer of 1881, it was the next in line, eighteen-year-old Vera, who had become the object of the conspirators' hopes. When Vera became engaged to Rimsky-Korsakov, Tchaikovsky immediately sang the praises of his third niece, Anna, then seventeen.

At her uncle Anatoly's wedding the following spring, Tchaikovsky wasted no time in asking Anna what she thought of Nikolay von Meck, who had recently visited the Davidovs in Kiev. Could she look on him, perhaps, as a potential husband? 'She replied with no hesitation that she certainly could,' he reported to von Meck, 'and that she would be prepared to wait patiently until he had finished his studies.' Anna was about to visit cousins in St Petersburg, and Tchaikovsky suggested that von Meck arrange for her son to visit his niece there. As Nikolay was on the brink of major examinations, his mother hesitated, then demurred, suggesting that he wait to see Anna in the summer at Kamenka. But she was careful to reassure Tchaikovsky that this did not signify any waning of her enthusiasm for their joint enterprise: 'What joy if our dream were to come true!'

Cupid, it seemed, was proving co-operative. As soon as Nikolay had finished his examinations, he wasted no time in calling on Anna in the capital, and accepting an invitation to join the Davidovs at Kamenka, where the couple's love blossomed for all to see. Tchaikovsky reported the joyous news to von Meck (in rather less wistful terms than he told Modest about a spate of marriages among the Davidov servants, including a coachman whose heterosexuality had clearly proved a disappointment to him). So carried away did von Meck become that she even wondered about a second match, between her son Alexandr and the apparently improving Tanya. Having withheld the goriest details of his niece's condition, Tchaikovsky advised caution, causing a nasty moment when von Meck worried aloud about his family's apparent penchant for morphine. Might Anna too succumb? The composer fought a vigorous rearguard action, assuring von Meck that Anna had learnt from her sister's example, and was an altogether 'healthy, wholesome' girl: 'The union of their two souls would be most gratifying.'

Almost five years of matchmaking finally reaped its reward on 23

January 1884, when Tchaikovsky attended the wedding in Moscow of
Anna Davidova and Nikolay von Meck. Most of his family were able to be
there, as was a sizeable contingent of von Mecks – minus, predictably, the
matriarch herself. Outspokenly dismissive of the institution of marriage
von Meck had always wanted to see her children happily settled, then
leave them to get on with their lives without her. So large and demanding
was her own family that she had made it a rule never to get involved
with, even to meet her children's in-laws. It was thus her practice not
to attend her children's weddings.

Much though she rejoiced in this particular match, moreover, it
cemented a bond between herself and Tchaikovsky now wholly
characterized by their continuing agreement not to meet. He sent a
detailed account of the day to her in Cannes, where she revelled in
his warm reports on her offspring and their families. The thought of her
composer mingling with so many von Mecks was as thrilling to her as the
fact that he and she could now consider themselves relations. Thanks to
this match, the bond between them would survive even their deaths.

Tchaikovsky had lingered in Moscow since December, when a triumphant revival of his First Symphony (the first since its première
fifteen years before) had preceded long and tortuous preparations
for the unveiling of *Mazeppa* in February. Already the writing of the
opera had caused him more heart-searching than any previous work;
now its first performances were also to prove highly problematic.

Virtually simultaneous premières in Moscow and St Petersburg were,
as he took it, a sign of the Tsar's growing favour, but the one was
proceeding far more smoothly than the other. By letter he argued
violently with Napravnik over the casting of Marya in the Mariinsky
production, even threatening to withdraw the piece unless a substitute
was found for Wilhelmina Raab, who had disappointed him in the past
(when creating the roles of Oxana in *Vakula the Smith* and Agnes
Sorel in *The Maid of Orleans*). Once he had won the day, Tchaikovsky
decided to leave the St Petersburg preparations to Napravnik and concentrate his own efforts in Moscow, where *Mazeppa* received its first
performance on 15 February 1884.

'It was a success in so far as the performers and I received numerous
ovations,' he reported to von Meck, but followed by a dinner 'at which,
despite being terribly tired, I was obliged to remain past 5 a.m.'[32] His
nerves shattered, as was always the case at major premières, he fled
to Europe the following morning, missing the first performance that
evening of his Second Suite and the St Petersburg début of *Mazeppa*
three days later. Tchaikovsky was already in Berlin when a cable from

Modest informed him of a 'triumph' in the capital; the Tsar had declared himself 'completely satisfied', and had even 'stayed to the end'.

Tchaikovsky was back in his customary rooms in Paris – again keening for Alexey, now back in the Army – before a terse letter from Yurgenson suggested otherwise. Not merely had Erdmannsdörfer, the conductor of the Second Suite, proved furious that the composer had reneged on his promise to attend his concert and *Mazeppa*'s first performance (which 'would have enhanced an already considerable success'). The Tsar himself had expressed disappointment at his mysterious absence from the first night of the opera, which had in truth been poorly received. 'You were right to lie,' Tchaikovsky reassured Modest. 'The truth might have killed me. The most galling aspect of it all is that, if I had been other than I am, and stirred myself to travel to St Petersburg, I would probably have departed crowned with laurels.'

His plans to move on to Rome, where Anna and Nikolay had invited him to join them on their honeymoon, had to be abandoned because Tanya's health was again in decline, and Tchaikovsky himself again short of cash. He took the chance to visit young Georges-Léon, and reassure himself that the boy was being well cared for, between ritual visits to his usual haunts. Then, in a letter from Napravnik, came a dramatic summons. The Tsar wished to see him personally. Tchaikovsky could not think why. But he was aware that His Imperial Majesty had already sanctioned a royal command performance of *Eugene Onegin* for the following season, declaring it his favourite opera. This was a summons he could not ignore.

Entrusting Tanya to the safekeeping of the unfortunate honeymooners, shortly due to arrive in Paris, the composer arrived back in St Petersburg on 15 March to learn that Alexandr had conferred upon him the Order of St Vladimir (fourth class). The formal investiture took place four days later, after a separate audience with the Tsarina, who had also become a great admirer. Both occasions terrified the composer – only liberal doses of bromide, he said, prevented him fainting from nerves – but the warmth of the royal couple quite disarmed him. Merely to meet the Tsar, he told Anatoly, was to become 'his most loyal subject'. The Emperor himself reassured Tchaikovsky that, whatever the critics may say, *Mazeppa* was already proving a success with the public.

Far more important, however, was the composer's sense that this heady moment symbolized the real end of his long marital trauma: that whatever gossip might persist about the apparently scandalous events of seven years before, his acceptance at court betokened a wider acceptance as an utterly respectable figure, untainted by any residual stigma. The relief was enough to see him through three full weeks in Moscow, being fêted by friends and former Conservatoire colleagues, before arriving back in glory at Kamenka. Capping an unusually good month was the presence at his side of Alexey, now at last discharged from military service.

It is a sign of Tchaikovsky's reviving spirits that he now returned to keeping a diary, a habit which had become fitful during the dark events of recent years. He had first started a private journal eleven years before, during his lone summer journey through Switzerland; but nothing survives between those few travel notes and the detailed day-by-day account of the summer of 1884 at Kamenka. If Modest is to be believed, Tchaikovsky wrote regular diaries from the end of the 1870s to the late 1880s, and intermittently in the early 1890s, but burnt most of them two years before his death. The obvious inference is that they contained details of his sexual activities all over the world, of which his growing celebrity made him increasingly nervous.

If so, why would the summer diaries of 1884 survive? Their main themes, apart from the daily social round which punctuated his work on the Third Orchestral Suite (Op. 55), are his self-disgust at his own inward impulses, and his growing adoration of his thirteen-year-old nephew, Bob Davidov.

The explanation seems to be that the most intimate private confessions are in code, lending a marginal ambiguity to their interpretation. On 19 May, for instance, during his habitual evening card game, he grew 'extremely angry, not because of the cards, but more from a general, indeterminate feeling that I will call Z. This Z is less agonizing, if perhaps more powerful, than X, but both are highly unpleasant.' The following day, 'Z is really tormenting me. May God forgive me such despicable feelings!' And the next evening: 'Tormented by Z, all the more troubling because this morning it had virtually subsided.' On 6 June: 'Tormented tonight not by Z itself, but by the torment that it exists within me.' On 15 June: 'Overwhelming attack of Z. God forgive me, and help me conquer it!' And the next evening: 'Very unlucky at cards. For this reason, but mainly because of a thousand other feelings amounting to what I call Z, I was as angry as a vicious snake . . . Returned home besieged by the overpowering, irresistible pressure of Z.'

All that summer Tchaikovsky was drinking and gambling heavily, most of his evenings consumed by a card game called vint, a Russian forerunner of bridge, at which he continually lost money, usually blaming the cards rather than his own apparent ineptitude. 'He played without any great skill,' according to one of his partners, Vladimir Pogozhev, 'but very intensely, with great animation.'[33] For this reason (and others to be examined in the closing chapters), Alexander Poznansky parts company with all previous Tchaikovsky biographers in rejecting any sexual interpretation of the code letters X and Z. David Brown speaks for the consensus by arguing that: 'The symbols X and Z . . . denote homosexual drives.'[34] With a prolix insistence bordering on perversity, Poznansky suggests that the composer himself 'did not fully understand what it was that periodically came over him . . . Insofar as Z possessed any physical aspect, this was a somatic manifestation of Tchaikovsky's nervous condition.'[35] If X and Z symbolize minor physical ailments, as Poznansky attempts at great length to demonstrate, why trouble to disguise them in code? Why do so if they betoken – Poznansky's other suggestion – the composer's shame at his temper tantrums over the card table? If all the references occur in 'the context of card playing', is this not because Tchaikovsky played cards almost every evening, and X and Z seemed to assail him above all by night? To argue that X represents guilt about gambling is as logical as to deduce, from the evidence of the 'X' motif in the composer's ashtray (still to be seen on his desk at Klin), that it symbolized his angst-ridden failure to give up smoking.

It was by night that X and Z haunted Tchaikovsky, and by night that he was assailed by his sexual loneliness – especially uncomfortable in the context of his guilty longings for thirteen-year-old Bob. On his birthday, 7 May, he 'feasted my eyes all day on Bob. How utterly ravishing he looks in his little white suit.' Throughout the summer, he is obsessed with the boy. 'Bob walked with me in the garden, then came to my room. Ah, what a delight this Bob is' (8 May). 'Sat in the window and chatted with [Nata and] Bob . . . Ah, what a perfect being this Bob is!' (9 May). 'A stroll with Bob . . . What a little darling he is!' (10 May). 'After supper (before which, to his great delight, I played piano duets with my darling, incomparable, wonderful, ideal Bob), played vint . . . Between rubbers, went to see my angel Bob' (13 May). 'Lev and Bob were away so long I got really upset . . .' (15 May). 'Wandered about with Bob after dinner' (17 May) . . . 'Went to the market with Bob' (18 May) . . . 'Picked lilies of the valley with Bob' (19 May) . . . 'Bob's ill . . . Bob's better' (21 May) . . . 'Strange dreams last night: wandering around with Bob' (23 May) . . . 'In the end, Bob will drive me mad with his unspeakable charms' (24 May).

This last, candid entry coincides with the first mention of the torments, that evening during cards, of X and Z. Thereafter, they keep recurring in tandem with more breathless longings for Bob: 'After dinner sat in my workroom with Bob' (25 May) . . . 'Read Krylov with Bob' (26 May) . . . 'Sat for hours with Bob on a bench in the conservatory' (28 May) . . . 'Sat on the roof with Bob (only for this angel would I climb up there) . . . [After supper] played with Bob a special, secret, most ridiculous game' (30 May) . . . 'With Bob (the darling!) walked to the cliffs . . . Played children's songs to Bob . . . [An evening of dancing, at which] I played quadrilles on themes Bob gave me, which amused him enormously' (31 May) . . . 'Before lunch I played Bob my songs . . . After tea I was sitting down to work, but Bob tempted me away with his stilts . . . Several times I went out looking for Bob. As soon as I am not working or walking (which to me is also work), I start longing for Bob and missing him. I do love him terribly . . .' (3 June).

And so on – reading Gogol with Bob (4 June), sitting on the balcony steps with Bob (7 June), getting Bob ready for a horseback ride (11 June), 'inseparable from my wonderful, incomparable Bob' (12 June), sitting and talking about school with Bob (14 June) – until on 15 June, five days before he was due to move on, Tchaikovsky is ambushed by apparently unexpected feelings: 'A strange thing. I'm *terribly* reluctant to leave here. I think it's entirely because of Bob.'

In the midst of all this, as well as X and Z, he talks in italics about '*The feeling*' (11 June) . . . 'All day *the feeling*' (12 June) . . . 'After dinner *the feeling* began to pass' (13 June) . . . 'A bit of *the feeling*' (15 June). Alongside the coded passages, and the rest of his mundane daily activities, these cryptic passages can only imply shame at the ebb and flow of his libido, especially when aroused by his pubescent nephew. 'Z' would appear to represent the sex-drive itself, and the far less frequent 'X' his guilt at his methods of relieving it.

If Modest himself in fact destroyed the other diaries, confident that no-one could challenge his bonfire story, it was perhaps through a desire to retain *some* documentary materials for his flagging narrative that he preserved these. Add a dash of wishful thinking, and he could well have deluded himself, like Poznansky almost a century later, that their meaning was ambiguous.

For the third consecutive summer, Tchaikovsky had managed to complete a major piece of work, the Third Suite, despite the domestic torpor of the Davidovs. This year his family further alienated him by making no effort to conceal their dislike of his beloved servant Alexey, and Tchaikovsky's over-indulgence of him. His discomfort was increased by the arrival of Lev's sister Vera (Butakova), recently widowed, who added insult to X and Z with disconcerting displays of affection.

But these were mere subtexts to another new sensation within Tchaikovsky, perhaps long overdue, which first surfaced amid the usual self-recriminations in his diary entry for 6 May, the day before his forty-fourth birthday:

> Soon I'll be forty-four. How long I have lived and in truth, without false modesty, how little have I achieved! Even when it comes to

my real work there is nothing, in all honesty, *perfect, exemplary*. Still I am seeking, hesitating, wandering. And for the rest? I read nothing [of worth], I know nothing. Only on vint do I waste large amounts of precious time. I begin to think it will damage my health. The calm and tranquil life I briefly knew, untroubled by anything, is over. There's too much fuss, too much aggravation, too much that a madman of my age cannot endure with equanimity.

'No!' he concluded. 'It is time I was living *in my own home* and *in my own way*.'[36]

# PART V

---

## *1885–91*
## THE CELEBRITY

*I am living through a very bizarre phase*
*on my journey to the grave.*

# CHAPTER XIII

## 'A home of my own'

TCHAIKOVSKY HAD SPENT MUCH OF HIS ADULT LIFE TRYING TO ESCAPE
Russia – most urgently, as often as not, in the aftermath of the first public
performance of one of his works. These last few years, as his wanderings
of Europe were punctuated by occasional, apparently reluctant trips back,
he had begun to feel more homesick than ever. Whenever he actually
returned home, however, he could not wait to get away again.

Contrary to the last, Tchaikovsky now began to divine why his feelings
for his homeland, while so powerful, were also so ambiguous. His
unequivocal love of the Russian countryside, and his deep affection for
the Russian people and their folk culture, had always been qualified
by the fact that he himself had never laid any real roots there. He had
reached forty-four – to him, a comparatively advanced age – without ever
possessing a home of his own. Only in his Moscow Conservatoire years,
largely spent rooming with Rubinstein and others, had he even briefly
rented one. The few days spent in his marital home, also rented, were
beneath consideration. In Moscow and St Petersburg he had lodged with
his brothers or other friends; in the countryside, around the Ukraine and
elsewhere, he had for years accepted the hospitality of von Meck and the
Davidovs, Shilovsky and Kondratiev. Now that former friendships had
ended, and lifelong ones lost their sheen, he came to see himself as
the parasite which to a large extent – quite apart from his financial
dependence on von Meck – he was.

An incident at Kamenka that summer had intensified this particular gloom. 'All last evening I was in a selfish sulk,' he told Modest, 'because it was chicken for dinner again and some other dish was cancelled and replaced by yoghurt. I have grown too old to be a sponger . . . There have been a thousand other niggling moments which have shown up my sponging nature for what it is. It will become utterly unbearable if I do not settle down in a place of my own.'[1]

This aspiration had first surfaced in the gloomy autumn of 1882, when Tanya had begun to sour the atmosphere at Kamenka. In an effort to cheer up himself as much as Alexey, marooned in the Army in Moscow, Tchaikovsky had painted an idyllic vision of their life together after his servant's eventual discharge: 'I dream that, if I'm still alive when you've finished your military service, I shall stop living in other people's homes and settle for good in some pleasant place in Moscow. The two of us will set up house together in a nice comfortable apartment, with all creature comforts . . . I pray God that these two years will fly by, and that this dream will be fulfilled.'[2] Perhaps hoping to speed up the process, he had also shared his hopes with von Meck. 'I have begun to dream of settling down in some stable and permanent home of my own,' he confided from Paris early the following year. 'I am beginning to find this nomadic life a strain. Whether I will wind up in some place on the edge of Moscow or somewhere even more out-of-the-way I don't yet know. A thousand plans are teeming in my head. One way or another, by hook or by crook, I must eventually live in a place of my own.'[3]

So much had he enjoyed his last visit to Moscow that he had actually begun looking at apartments for rent. He had no luck, but asked Anatoly to keep an eye open for him. Now, from Kamenka, reunited with his beloved 'Alyosha', he issued detailed instructions to, of all people, Pakhulsky, who had offered to help with the search. By transmitting them via von Meck, Tchaikovsky no doubt hoped that she in turn might offer to help with the finance:

Land is quite unnecessary to me, i.e. I want only a modest house with a decent garden, but *established*. A *river* is certainly highly desirable. If there is a wood nearby, so much the better. But I mean, of course, a wood belonging to someone else – for, I repeat, I want to own only a modest house and garden. This dacha or cottage must be completely detached, not in a row of other dachas, and above all must be close to a railway station, so that Moscow is always within easy reach . . . Most important and essential of all these conditions is that the location should be sympathetic, and beautiful. If the house is situated somewhere low down, so that there is no view from the windows, then it does not meet my needs. A factory nearby would also be most undesirable. That, I think, is everything . . .'[4]

As the quest for the right place went on, Tchaikovsky spent the latter part of 1884 as nomadic as ever, sponging off the usual family and friends. From Kamenka he went to join Modest on the Konradi estate at Grankino, where he continued the scoring of the Third Suite and corrected the proofs of a vocal score of Mozart's *The Marriage of Figaro* containing his own Russian translation. Now he embarked upon a new piano concerto, despite continuing mixed feelings about the genre, but soon converted it into an unorthodox two-movement piece of considerable difficulty, eventually to emerge as the *Concert Fantasia* (Op. 56). It was still taking shape at the beginning of August, when he moved on to Skabeyevo, nearer Moscow, where Anatoly and his family had rented a summer villa. In the absence of a piano, Tchaikovsky's six weeks there were spent dealing patiently with other people's problems: helping Modest find the right ending for his new play, refereeing a row between Taneyev and Albrecht, and ministering unto his old friend Laroche, now crippled with syphilis and unable to write. The composer, who had interceded on Laroche's behalf at the Conservatoire more than once these past few years, now sat down to take dictation of his reviews – despite a morbid terror of contracting his friend's disease.

He had planned to return to Kamenka, but swiftly abandoned the idea when he discovered that Lev had brought Tanya back there from Paris. Work would be impossible, so he instead asked von Meck if he might, after all, use her new estate at Pleshcheyevo – once she had left, of course. Arriving on 13 September, with a clear month for uninterrupted work, he punctuated the scoring of the *Concert Fantasia* with one short piano piece, the *Impromptu-Caprice* (commissioned by the French journal *Gaulois* for an anthology in aid of impoverished musicians), and two songs which would eventually form part of the Six Romances (Op. 57). The visit was marred by a furious row with Pakhulsky's father, the estate manager, who was horrified to find Alexey sleeping in von Meck's boudoir, next to Tchaikovsky's room. The composer exploded, insisting that his servant would sleep where he chose, and declared his visit 'thoroughly poisoned'. By 6 October, however, he had at least managed to finish the *Concert Fantasia*. Little more than a showcase for virtuoso pianists, and today heard only rarely, it was first performed with great success by Taneyev in Moscow on 6 March the following year.

Obliged to return to Moscow by 31 October, for the royal command performance of *Eugene Onegin* at the Bolshoi, Tchaikovsky was dismayed to find that the Tsar himself could not attend because of a period of court mourning. There were the usual indifferent reviews, and some criticism from Cui so perverse as to sound almost laughable to late twentieth-century audiences. Tchaikovsky's old nemesis managed to single out all the opera's most memorable passages for savage indictment. Tatyana's Letter Scene, for instance, possessed 'only one or two successful phrases' to relieve 'the monotony, emptiness and vulgarity of the rest'; the duel scene made 'a comic impression', with Lensky's aria 'a mournful diatonic whimper'. Gremin's aria was 'banal' and Onegin's arioso 'commonplace'. To Cui, *Eugene Onegin* was 'stillborn . . . utterly weak and worthless.'[5]

To other Russians from the Tsar to the music-loving public, it was Tchaikovsky's masterpiece – to be repeated and repeated, every performance a sellout. For once, the composer would not allow himself to be put out by his critics. If forced to choose between the two evils of public hostility or press carping, he would 'prefer the latter' every time. The popularity of *Onegin* soon spread throughout Russia, bringing in sufficient revenue to see its composer financially secure for the rest of his life. But it was not merely a financial breakthrough. If Tchaikovsky had hitherto developed a following among fellow musicians and sophisticated concert-goers, *Onegin* saw him develop a mass popular audience. For once, Modest is right to say that it was with *Onegin* that Tchaikovsky became 'famous and beloved among the masses'. We may even accept his brother's judgement that, as of this moment, 'Pyotr Ilyich had achieved the highest degree of popularity ever attained by a Russian composer within his native land.'[6]

Postponing his habitual post-first night flight, Tchaikovsky allowed the Tsar three more chances to attend *Onegin* before giving up on him and heading for Europe, where Kotek had fallen seriously ill. During four days in Berlin he dealt with some outstanding commissions: two Cherubim's Songs (in response to the Tsar's appeal for more church music) and a *Grateful Greeting* for strings, to mark the golden jubilee of the eminent actor, producer and playwright Ivan Samarin, who as Professor of Drama at the Conservatoire had produced the original *Onegin* in 1879. A short but tenderly melancholy piece, it was initially deemed by its composer to be a private gift, too slight to be worthy of publication; in 1890, however, five years after Samarin's death, he changed his mind and reissued it in his friend's memory, still under its original title. There is no known provenance for the name, *Elegy*, under which this haunting piece deserves to have won a lasting place in the string repertoire.

By 19 November Tchaikovsky was in Munich en route to Davos, where he found Kotek in worse shape than he had expected. He spent a week discussing his old friend's case with the doctors, reassuring him, and leaving him sufficient money to cover his costs until he could return. Back in Paris, he was handing out yet more money – for the continuing care of Georges-Léon – when the welcome news arrived from St Petersburg that *Romeo and Juliet* had won the 500-rouble Glinka Award – the first of several to come Tchaikovsky's way over the next few years – prompting him to splash out on an entire new wardrobe. He also took the chance of some solitude to write three more songs, including 'Tell me what in the shade of the branches', to complete the Six Romances (Op. 57), the first set of songs he had published for more than four years.

By mid-December two more nomadic months, so soon after initiating his search for a home, were beginning to take their toll. 'I can't tell you how bored and depressed I've been these last few days,' he wrote to Modest from Paris. 'I feel this deep longing for my native land, a wish to be *at home* which finds no consolation in the fact that tomorrow I leave for Russia. I want to be leaving for *home*. Yet there is still no home for me in Russia. One way or another, I *must* find one.'[7]

Four days later he was back with Modest in St Petersburg, still agonizing whether to look for a city home – 'I must admit a need for society' – or a country one, to provide the solitude he craved most of the time. A series of well-received concerts combined with the continuing popularity of *Onegin* to have success and fame crowding in on him. When news arrived from Davos that Kotek was much worse, he knew he should return, but simply could not face the journey. The world was too much with him. Awaiting him in Moscow, after ten crowded days in the capital, was a letter informing him of Kotek's death. Charged with the responsibility of informing his old friend's parents, he could not face the task for four days.

His long love of Kotek, freely expressed in grief-stricken letters to von Meck, met with a coolly indifferent response. This was the man, after all, who had brought them together, who had once been so popular a member of the von Meck entourage. But the increasingly careworn old lady was unforgiving; even for her beloved Pyotr Ilyich she could not summon more than a few cursory words about his passing. This unspoken disagreement was a measure of the distance growing between Tchaikovsky and his patron, now uncomfortably symbolized by problems surrounding the marriage of Nikolay and Anna, with whom the composer was staying in Moscow. The match itself was happy enough; but the belligerent Anna, who had come to dominate her weak-willed husband, infuriated her mother-in-law by opposing her in sundry family matters, primarily a feud between von Meck's eldest son Vladimir and the rest of the family.

Far from bringing Tchaikovsky and von Meck closer together, the marriage was in danger of driving a wedge between them. Tchaikovsky manfully resisted a falling-out, virtually disowning his niece in letters to his benefactress, bemoaning the fact that their joint dream should have led them into such difficulties. For her part, von Meck hid her true feelings from the composer, trying to make light of matters which had in truth hurt her deeply. Whatever the domestic rights and wrongs, the episode served to illustrate that neither Nadezhda von Meck nor Anna herself was the easiest of women. Despairing of them both, while naturally anxious to preserve his subsidy, Tchaikovsky reached the end of his tether on hearing harsh words from Nikolay, too, about his mother. Such disloyalty was anathema to the composer, who began to fear that his niece really had corrupted her husband's character.

'Every day and in every way,' he raged to Modest, 'Kolya Meck repeats that (1) Nadezhda Filaretovna is at root an unbalanced and insufferable old woman; (2) Vladimir Meck [his brother] is a crook, and his wife a tart; (3) Yulya [von Meck, his sister] is a wicked harpy; (4) Sasha Benningsen [another of his sisters] is a malicious gossip; (5) Sashok [his brother Alexander] is spiteful, vindictive, heartless; (6) Yolshina [his sister Elizaveta] a complete idiot . . .' Etc. 'Do you remember that good-natured fellow Kolya, who used to take loving photographs of his family? What a monster Anna has turned him into!'[8]

If a growing distaste for his family was re-emphasizing his need for a home of his own, such yearnings were ever more accentuated by his popular success. In St Petersburg, on 24 January, Hans von Bülow conducted the first performance of the Third Suite in tandem with a triumphant revival of the First Piano Concerto. Never before, in Modest's judgement, had any Russian symphonic work been greeted with such enthusiasm; never had Tchaikovsky received such wild adulation. Combined with the continuing popularity of *Onegin*, it was the summit of his career so far – one of those moments, as he put it to von Meck, 'which are the best rewards of an artist's life . . . making all the hard work, the hard living worthwhile.'

And yet, as always, success was bitter-sweet. Next day he felt 'sick' with the strain of it all. Four days later the Tsar finally attended the fifteenth performance of *Eugene Onegin*, commanding the composer to join him and the Tsarina, who both showered him with compliments, in the royal box. It was all very gratifying, as Tchaikovsky wrote to all and sundry, yet he longed to get away. Such was his stature now that the Bolshoi, at merely a word from him, laid on a performance of *Mazeppa* purely for the benefit of the visiting von Bülow. Tchaikovsky was also delighted to be elected a director of the Moscow branch of the Russian Musical Society. But above all he was desperate to escape. 'The awareness of my growing success affords me more suffering than pleasure,' as he put it to von Meck. 'A longing to hide myself away somewhere, and a thirst for freedom, peace, solitude prevail over the sense of fulfilled artistic self-esteem.'[9]

If the last few years had been a reaction to the drama of his marriage, and his subsequent fears of scandal, he was now weary of all the wandering. Success and fame had instilled in Tchaikovsky a strongly renewed desire for solitude. His somewhat random, inconsistent musical output these last few years had reflected the uneasy shifting of his soul. Now, as he finally found a *vita nuova* in his first real home, he also found the peace and stability to embark upon his first real masterwork since *Eugene Onegin*.

Before leaving Moscow, Tchaikovsky had placed an advertisement in the classified columns of a local paper: 'Single gentleman seeks country dacha to rent.' Among the replies was the offer of a house at Maidanovo, a mile and a half from the small town of Klin, sixty miles north of Moscow and an hour away by train. 'I am told it stands in a beautiful location, and is fully equipped with furniture, crockery and all that I might need,' he told von Meck. 'The house has plenty of rooms, and the view from the windows is superb.' He had taken 'a heroic decision' and sent Alexey to close the deal. 'I shall take it for a year, and if the upkeep proves beyond my means, I shall meanwhile find something more suitable.' The rent was one thousand roubles a year.[10]

When he arrived there from St Petersburg a week later, Tchaikovsky was at first disappointed. His servant's notions of grandeur did not correspond with his own. 'What Alyosha considered fine and luxurious struck me as pretentious, tasteless, shabby and dingy,' he told Modest. 'I decided at once that Maidanovo won't become my permanent home.' But the position was 'delightful' and the view 'very pleasant'. Above all, the feeling of being in his own home at last was in itself enough to cheer him up. 'It's perfectly possible to live here a year, or at least until winter. In summer it should really be very nice.'[11] Once he had hired a cook, and taken receipt of his piano, his spirits positively bloomed.

> What joy to be in my own home! What bliss to know that no-one will turn up to interrupt my work, my reading, my walks! Now I know for sure that my dream of spending the rest of my days amid the Russian countryside is no passing whim, but a fundamental and deep-seated need.[12]

By the end of his first week, with the arrival of newspapers and journals, his contentment was complete. 'I'm reading a lot, making progress with my English, and working well,' he reported to Modest. 'I eat, walk and sleep whenever and as long as I want. In a word, I am *living!*'[13]

Klin and its environs would be Tchaikovsky's base for the rest of his life. If his years of wandering were not quite over, nor his love-hate relationship with his homeland, settling into a place of his own had answered a profound need. Amid this tranquil if unexceptional countryside he would find within himself at least three more great masterpieces, as well as some of the most popular music ever written. His first, highly ambitious project reflected the darkness of the composer's mood in the wake of Kotek's death, and again owed much to Balakirev, who had re-entered his life after an absence of more than a decade.

Since acting as midwife to *Romeo and Juliet*, Balakirev's fortunes had declined as steadily as Tchaikovsky's had prospered. Driven by penury into deep depression, the once eminent composer had been forced to take employment with a railway company, and had completely withdrawn from musical life for almost five years. It took five more of slow and painful rehabilitation before it was again Shakespeare's lovers who reunited this kindly if often overbearing old man with his sometime protégé, himself by now a composer of international repute.

After finishing his revised and final version of the fantasy overture in 1880, Tchaikovsky had considered it a natural decency to send a copy to the work's dedicatee. No longer knowing even where to find Balakirev, he had sent him a score c/o Bessel, their mutual publisher. Another year passed, probably thanks to the dilatory Bessel, before Tchaikovsky received an exultant reply. 'Your generous letter and dedication suggest that you have not, perhaps, ineradicably wiped me from your heart's memory,' wrote the delighted Balakirev, characteristically pushing his luck by inviting Tchaikovsky to visit him in St Petersburg forthwith (and pointing out an error in the scoring of *Francesca*). He had been following Tchaikovsky's progress with proud admiration, 'rejoicing to see your talent grow stronger and stronger . . . I shall hope to hear news of you, and that soon in St Petersburg you will remember your old friend, who sincerely loves you . . .'[14]

In the same letter, Balakirev could not resist pressing on Tchaikovsky 'the programme for another symphony which you would handle wonderfully well.' Then in the throes of scoring *Mazeppa*, Tchaikovsky had merely made polite noises, which did not deter Balakirev from responding with a detailed plan for a symphony based on Byron's *Manfred*. Originally drafted by Stasov for Berlioz, supposedly as a sequel to his *Harold en Italie*, it had lain fallow in Balakirev's care since the Frenchman had pleaded ill-health and old age. At first Tchaikovsky too had demurred, saying the subject left him cold. Balakirev's characteristically blunt exhortations – 'you must, of course, *make an effort*, take a more self-critical approach, don't hurry things' – seem to have placed Tchaikovsky's tongue firmly in his cheek:

> I could perhaps *make an effort*, as you put it, and wring from myself a series of mildly interesting episodes, in which you would find conventionally gloomy music to reflect Manfred's hopeless disillusionment, and lots of glittering instrumental sparks in the Alpine fairy scherzo, with the sun rising in the high register of the violins, and Manfred dying amid pianissimo trombones. I could dress all this up with piquant harmonic curiosities, and submit it to the world under the portentous title: *Manfred – Symphonie d'après*, etc. I might even win a dash of praise for this child of my musical loins. But such work just doesn't interest me.[15]

But Balakirev refused to give up, and two years later Tchaikovsky changed his mind. This time, it seems, it was God who intervened. In search of solace at the end of his troubled 1884, Tchaikovsky turned with renewed conviction to religion – not least because of Balakirev himself, who was now director of the Imperial Church Choir, based at the Tsar's St Petersburg *capella*. As the two men renewed their friendship, Tchaikovsky in the process renewed his faith. Under Balakirev's kindly influence, he sharpened the rather vague, quasi-superstitious longings he had expressed to von Meck earlier in the year after rereading Tolstoy's *Confession*:

> Enlightenment came for me earlier than for Tolstoy, probably because I am more simple-minded . . . Easily discouraged as I am, with my talent for losing heart to the point where I yearn for *oblivion* at the slightest setback, where would I be without my belief in God, my readiness to accept his will?[16]

To Tchaikovsky, religion was more a prophylactic against his woes than an intellectual conviction. That autumn, however, meeting the reborn Balakirev amid the seductive aesthetics of the Imperial Chapel, he took the chance for long religious discussions, which seem to have deepened his faith. After one such meeting, he wrote to his old mentor: 'I was deeply moved by our conversation yesterday. What a good man you are! And how true a friend to me! How I wish that the enlightenment which has entered your spirit might also invade mine. I tell you in all truth that more than ever I *thirst* for the comfort and support of Christ. I will pray that faith in Him may be confirmed in me.'[17] The wily Balakirev, while keeping up the pressure about *Manfred*, echoed the Tsar in urging Tchaikovsky to write more religious music, undertaking to perform it with the Imperial Chapel Choir.

And so it came to pass that Tchaikovsky, while tending to Kotek in Davos that month, wrote a third Cherubim's Song, sent it off to Balakirev, and began re-reading his Byron. That he did so in the Alps, the very setting of Manfred's adventures, seemed like no less than divine intervention, adding to his conviction that he should now, after all, do Balakirev's bidding. As soon as he returned home, he set about revising his friend's own revision of the original Stasov programme for Berlioz, and began sketching the first movement.

The *Manfred* symphony cost Tchaikovsky as much time, effort and soul-searching as anything he ever wrote, not excluding *Mazeppa* and the *Pathétique*. Towards the end of his labours, in August 1885, he confessed that 'the symphony is emerging on a huge scale, complex, serious, taking up all my time, utterly exhausting me; but an inner voice tells me that I do not labour in vain, that this will turn out to be perhaps the best of my symphonic works.'[18] Not until late September, after four months' uninterrupted work, was he able to report to Balakirev that it was finally finished: 'Never in my life, believe me, have I laboured so long and hard, and felt so drained by my efforts. The symphony is written in four movements, as per your programme, although – forgive me – as much as I wanted to, I have not been able to keep to all the keys and modulations you suggested . . . It is of course dedicated to you.'[19]

Although the symphony owes an obvious debt to Berlioz, Tchaikovsky had made the *Manfred* theme his own, sewing between the staves of Balakirev's programme the distinctive personal resonances which Byron's work held for him. Not least among them was the dangerous theme of incest, never mentioned between the composer and his mentor – but evident in Tchaikovsky's sympathetic response to Byron's love for his half-sister, Augusta, and the composer's suggestion in his B major ending that redemption followed his tragic hero's demise. Coming eight years after his Fourth Symphony, and three years before his Fifth, the *Manfred* proved the perfect interim vehicle for Tchaikovsky's continued broodings about his sexuality. Like Benjamin Britten after him, he seized on a literary portrait of an outsider, rejected by a cruel and conventional world, and made it his own. It was entirely predictable that he would later disown the piece – calling it 'abominable . . . I loathe it deeply'[20] – with the notable exception of the first movement, in which he depicts Manfred bent on self-oblivion, haunted by memories of a dark, forbidden love.

The largest and most complex work he had yet written, the *Manfred* symphony was well enough received when first performed under Erdmannsdörfer in Moscow the following March. True to form, however, Tchaikovsky soon allowed his pride in the piece to evaporate, declaring it 'doomed to fail and to lie forgotten'. As his own distaste for this parade of his innermost feelings grew, so did its public success, the St Petersburg première wringing praise from his old enemy Cui, and a New York performance further increasing his standing in the New World. To this day it remains among the most under-performed of his respected works, with as much to reveal about the man as the composer.

The only sour note echoing from this majestic work lies in Tchaikovsky's subsequent treatment of Balakirev, who had played so indispensable a role in its birth. Understandably reluctant to tolerate the usual interference, Tchaikovsky severed all connections with this almost too willing colleague, writing him off to Yurgenson as a 'madman', and allowing all contact between them to dwindle to a few formal, none too friendly letters, late in his life, on matters merely administrative.

During the seven months devoted to *Manfred*, April to October 1885, Tchaikovsky stayed in one place for the longest period he had managed in a decade, leaving Maidanovo only for occasional forays to Moscow or St Petersburg – to show his director's face at occasional RMS concerts, or to allow himself to get reluctantly involved in the Conservatoire's internal problems.

It was largely through Tchaikovsky's influence, for instance, that Taneyev, though not yet thirty, became the compromise candidate as the Moscow Conservatoire's new director. All the cast of characters in its complex internal politics – Taneyev, Hubert, Laroche, Albrecht, Arensky, Kashkin – were also regular visitors to Maidanovo, where Tchaikovsky enjoyed their musical companionship but shunned all talk of office politics. Other regular visitors included Yurgenson and Modest, who noted his brother's mixed feelings about all these house guests:

> *Manfred* was the last work Tchaikovsky composed in anything but complete isolation, and this is probably the reason why the task proved so difficult, and cost him such moments of depression. The principal advantage of his new surroundings was the enjoyment of complete solitude during his working hours.[21]

At his country retreat, Tchaikovsky had adopted a fixed daily routine upon which visitors intruded at their peril. Not until the evenings, when piano duets and card games were *de rigueur*, would he permit his schedule to be interrupted; he had never worked at night since 1866, when his exertions on the First Symphony had laid him low. For the rest of the day, he maximized his creative output only by maintaining a rigid timetable of which Modest has left a detailed account.

After rising between seven and eight, the composer would take morning tea over a few cigarettes and an hour with a book or the latest journals, followed by a stroll lasting forty-five minutes – no more, no less. From 9.30 a.m. until 1 p.m. he would work, then break for a light lunch followed by a longer walk, often ninety minutes or two hours. To the composer, these strolls were part of his work; he would, as he put it, 'compose in my head' before returning home for afternoon tea at 4 p.m. and another hour's reading. They had also become somewhat obsessive, since he had once read somewhere that two hours' walking a day was 'essential' to good health.

But it was Tchaikovsky himself, during this first year at Maidanovo, who would 'spoil the charm' of these walks (in his brother's words) by over-indulging the local children. Once he had handed out a few charitable kopecks, he found these byways of his outdoor life fraught with unwelcome ambushes. The children, and soon their parents, lurked everywhere in his path, hoping to share the largesse of the new local celebrity. To his dismay, Tchaikovsky was eventually forced to confine his walks to his own grounds.

There followed two more hours' work, from 5 p.m. until 7 p.m., before an evening of relaxation. In summer this would often include another walk before supper at 8 p.m. sharp. If there were no guests – which was rare that summer – Tchaikovsky would play through another composer's work at the piano, or deal with his copious correspondence, writing as many as thirty letters in a day.

Those from this period show the responsible public figure increasingly moving to centre-stage in the composer's fragile psyche. His habitual generosity with money, regardless of his own changing circumstances, now extends to deserving cases beyond his own family. In this, his first year at Maidanovo, he was also the prime mover (and principal benefactor) in setting up a much-needed local school. But the letters also show a concern beyond mere politeness for friends and acquaintances in need of advice or consolation – notably Kondratiev's wife, somewhat brutally abandoned by her husband, and the soprano Emilya Pavlovskaya, for whom he now began writing a new operatic role.

By the autumn of 1885 Tchaikovsky could look back on a productive year. As well as a major symphonic work he had revised *Vakula the Smith*, rechristening it *Cherevichki* (*The Slippers*) and absorbed his three Cherubim's Songs into Nine Sacred Pieces, as much to please the

Tsar as Yurgenson. He had also seen off two commissions which, though unwelcome, he could not duck: a Jurist's March and a song for unaccompanied chorus to mark the golden jubilee of the Imperial School of Jurisprudence, among whose most celebrated alumni he was now numbered. To have declined them would have seemed overly churlish; but Tchaikovsky's nostalgia for his *alma mater* stopped short of attending the jubilee celebrations at which they were performed that December.

During October he finally severed his ties with Kamenka, packing all his books, portraits and other possessions for transportation to Maidanovo during a visit for the Davidovs' silver wedding anniversary. He felt a strong rush of nostalgia for the Ukrainian countryside and its people, but few regrets at finally bidding farewell to a sometime haven which was now as unruly and turbulent as ever. 'The total harmony of old has gone for ever,' he told von Meck. 'Although I love them as much as ever, my relationship with my family has changed completely.'

As he saw in the New Year with Modest and Kolya in St Petersburg, Tchaikovsky succumbed to a bout of nervous exhaustion. Amid a season largely bereft of his own music, his *amour propre* was not helped by an open-ended homage to Anton Rubinstein, fêted between St Petersburg and Moscow in a series of farewell concerts. From the intensity of *Manfred*, whose score he was still polishing, Tchaikovsky had meanwhile moved straight on to another opera, *Charodeika*, or *The Enchantress* (sometimes translated as *The Sorceress*). Yet another portrait of a doomed woman in love, it was based on a recent play by Ippolit Shpazhinsky, from whom the composer had commissioned a libretto.

Nastasya, also known as 'Kuma' ('Gossip'), falls in love with Yuri, a prince above her station, whose parents conspire to thwart the match; the opera ends with 'Kuma' tricked into drinking poison, and the prince going mad. Although the score is entirely worthy of Tchaikovsky, notably the nationalistic opening scene and the love duet of Act III, it was the lameness of the libretto which doomed the project. After a not unsuccessful opening in St Petersburg on 1 November 1887, *The Enchantress* survived only a dozen more performances, and two brief revivals, in the composer's lifetime. It has fared little better with posterity.

While working on his sketches for *The Enchantress*, Tchaikovsky had responded to overtures from his new French publisher, Félix Mackar, with *Dumka (Scène rustique Russe)*, perhaps the most heartfelt work for solo piano he ever wrote. It was the prelude to another extended period of travel. On 23 March, in Moscow, he attended the first performance of the *Manfred* symphony; four days later, in St Petersburg, he took many ovations after another von Bülow performance of the First Piano Concerto; and on 4 April he set out, via two days with his brother Ippolit in Taganrog, on a long-promised visit to Anatoly and his wife in Tiflis (now Tbilisi), where Anatoly had been appointed chief prosecutor.

Much as he enjoyed the spectacular journey across the Caucasus Mountains, of which he sent glowing descriptions to family and friends, Tchaikovsky travelled for more than merely social reasons. In correspondence, and now in person, he had begun what was to prove a lasting friendship with the young conductor of the Tiflis opera company, twenty-six-year-old Mikhail Ippolitov-Ivanov, a great champion of his works under far from easy conditions in this remote Russian outpost. Already this young protégé of Rimsky-Korsakov (who had taught him composition at the St Petersburg Conservatoire) had mounted a production of *Mazeppa*, with his wife Varvara singing Marya, of which Anatoly had sent favourable reports.

Now Ippolitov-Ivanov was planning to revive *The Oprichnik*, so Tchaikovsky saw it as his urgent task to steer him towards *Cherevichki*, even *The Maid of Orleans*. In the long-distance collaboration which followed, and which was to draw the composer back to Tiflis more often than he expected, Ippolitov-Ivanov played a highly significant role in spreading Tchaikovsky's domestic reputation beyond the familiar confines of St Petersburg, Moscow and Kiev.*

In this most remote of Russian provinces, Tchaikovsky found himself pleasantly surprised by the picturesque charms of Tiflis, whose crowded streets and red-tiled roofs reminded him of Naples. Ippolitov-Ivanov's charming welcome was a concert featuring his *Sérénade mélancolique* alongside Beethoven's Eroica Symphony, further evidence of the unlikely 'Europeanization' of this far-flung Asiatic outpost. Fearing that his life would become one long social round, the very thing he had come all this way to escape, Tchaikovsky begged both Anatoly and Ippolitov-Ivanov to discourage all attempts to celebrate his presence in the town – a lost cause while under the roof of so gregarious a social animal as his sister-in-law Praskovya (nicknamed 'Panya' or 'Parasha'). Already she had solicited countless invitations and laid on a charity ball, even an evening of domestic theatricals in which Tchaikovsky and Anatoly were required to join forces in a scene from Turgenev's one-act play, *An Evening in Sorrento*.

Ippolitov-Ivanov, moreover, could scarcely be restrained. As well as *Mazeppa*, he conducted performances of *Romeo and Juliet*, the Serenade for Strings and excerpts from *Eugene Onegin* during Tchaikovsky's month in Tiflis, which saw a gala concert and banquet built around the

*In 1893, the year of Tchaikovsky's death, Ippolitov-Ivanov joined the staff of the Moscow Conservatoire, of which he was director from 1905–22.

composer's forty-sixth birthday that May. Much though he dreaded the occasion, Tchaikovsky felt bound to confess he found himself touched by the warmth and sincerity of such a tribute from the citizens of a provincial town which so strongly put him in mind of his childhood. Nor was he at all unhappy to see how far and how well his reputation had travelled within his homeland. He might even have begun to enjoy himself, were it not for an ugly episode involving Anatoly's wife and a dashing young soldier who had caught his eye.

Soon after his arrival Tchaikovsky had met a young artillery officer named Ivan Verinovsky, who professed to be a great admirer of his music, and soon warmed quite as much to its composer. The feeling was mutual. Within a few days, Tchaikovsky was writing to Modest that he felt he had known Verinovsky 'intimately, for the whole of my life.' In this and other letters to his brother, as usual the only confidant available for these kinds of secrets, he referred to Verinovsky by an affectionate diminutive, *ofitserik*, or 'little officer', which would suggest an erotic element to his feelings. The 'little officer' appears in Tchaikovsky's diary entries for almost every day of his visit. During one of their many evening games of cards, for instance, the composer confesses to feeling 'a sensation . . . of a special kind'. Two weeks later, he notes: 'Dinner on balcony. Verinovsky. Dressed in my clothes.' The following day, again, there is 'a change of clothes'.

But there was an unwelcome complication to what might otherwise have been a Tiflis idyll for Tchaikovsky. His sister-in-law was equally drawn to his little officer; and again the feeling appears to have been mutual. A notorious flirt, well practised in ensnaring impressionable young men, Anatoly's handsome wife appears to have divined the true nature of her brother-in-law's feelings for the young man, and to have used her own charms to torment him. The longer his visit lasts, the more rattled his diary entries become: 'Another exaggerated display of affection on the part of I[van] . . . Verinovsky, and Panya's caprices . . . Panya in carriage with Verin[ovsky] . . . Panya's disgraceful conduct regarding Verinovsky . . . Over breakfast, a quarrel with Panya over Verinovsky . . . An enjoyable evening quite spoilt by Praskovya's shameless tricks . . .' After three weeks he was feeling 'infinitely sorry for Verinovsky and furious with this wretched woman'.

There survives no more detail of these vignettes, so it remains unclear whether Verinovsky was in love with both Tchaikovsky and his sister-in-law, or feigning love for one to remain close to the other (and, if so, which was which). There is also some ambiguity about Praskovya's feelings: had she really fallen for this dashing young man, or was she merely beguiling her dull Tiflis exile with some malicious amusement at the expense of her gullible brother-in-law? All that is certain is Tchaikovsky's devotion to the young man, and his rage at Praskovya's interference – which made it all the more devastating when the composer eventually learnt that, within a few days of his departure, Verinovsky had shot himself.

Tchaikovsky did not hear of the officer's suicide for some weeks, and then only by accident, when the news came in a letter to Alexey from a friend on Anatoly's domestic staff. The composer dashed off a distraught letter to his sister-in-law, demanding an explanation: 'I await details with feverish impatience . . . I have shed many tears over this news and even now, amid the hustle and bustle of my travels, think of him all the time, every moment of every day, wondering whether this would have happened if I had stayed on in Tiflis another week.' To Modest, meanwhile, he laid the blame squarely upon Anatoly's wife: 'She tells me nothing, and I will tell you why: she has a guilty conscience . . . She is very much to blame in this matter.'

Praskovya's eventual letter of explanation is, alas, lost; all we know, from Tchaikovsky's flow of letters to Modest, is that while still in Tiflis he had one last fierce argument with her over Verinovsky, which might even have precipitated his departure. Many years later, by then an émigrée in Paris, Anatoly's widow confessed (to Nina Berberova) that she had 'stolen a lover' from her brother-in-law. In Tiflis, at the time, his suicide was blamed on his failure in the military examinations, a great blow to a man of considerable pride, who had seen them as his passport out of provincial life. But he seems much more likely to have suffered a very different kind of blow to his pride, perhaps his rejection by Praskovya after Tchaikovsky's departure. The composer was inconsolable for many months:

> He was young, happy, adorable, healthy and popular, then suddenly
> he goes and shoots himself. I am quite unable to reconcile myself to
> this thought, which has haunted me persistently, with no mercy . . .

Six months later, in October, he was still recording in his diary: 'Wept uncontrollably over Vanya Verinovsky'.

It was not the first time, of course, that an object of Tchaikovsky's affections had abruptly done away with himself; the composer was irresistibly reminded of the fate of young Eduard Zak thirteen years before. Nor would it be the last time that Anatoly's wife came wilfully between her brother-in-law and a young man he loved.[22]

When Tchaikovsky had finally left Tiflis, after a month, he was escorted to the station by a huge crowd of admirers who bedecked his train with flowers. A cholera scare in Italy forced him to sail via Turkey and Sicily to Marseilles, en route to Paris, where he was to collect Georges-Léon and bring him home to the care of Nikolay and his wife Olga. Through his publisher, Mackar, he enjoyed meetings with Delibes, Lalo and Fauré, all of whom treated him with gratifying deference, though he regretted being unable to see Gounod, Massenet or Saint-Saëns.

Amid visits to his usual sexual hunting-grounds, recorded in code in his diary and letters to Modest, he meanwhile formed a deep attachment to a young cellist, Anatoly Brandukov, whom he introduced to the louche circle of Prince Golitsyn. The death of Golitsyn's longstanding lover, Masalitinov, seems to have softened Tchaikovsky's feelings towards the prince, whose company he now actively sought. But it was through Brandukov that he made the most exciting new acquaintance of this visit: Pauline Viardot, the legendary mezzo-soprano and close companion of Turgenev for the last forty years of his life. In Viardot's possession, purchased many years before by her late husband, was the autograph score of Mozart's *Don Giovanni*, over which Tchaikovsky lingered for hours. 'I cannot express the emotions which overcame me while examining this hallowed musical object,' he told von Meck. 'It was exactly as if I were grasping Mozart himself by the hand, and talking to him.'

By the end of June, having stood godfather at the christening of Georges-Léon in St Petersburg, he was back at Maidanovo after three busy months away, itching to get back to the scoring of *The Enchantress*. Having cleared the horizon of guests, he had just returned to work when an old ghost returned to haunt him in the shape of Antonina, from whom he had heard nothing for five years. She had borne three more children, she announced, all placed in a hospital for foundlings, one of them named Pyotr after her beloved husband. In view of the settlement made five years before, her latest pronouncements were now as irrational as Tchaikovsky himself made out. 'What is to be done', he asked himself in his diary, 'with this madwoman?' Two days later, he wrote: 'Ah, how much I suffer from this Antonina Ivanovna. One day she will be the death of me!'[23]

> The gist of her letters is that she hopes I won't now doubt her love for me, that this love is passionate, and that I should hasten to enjoy its ecstasies with her. *Her letters are completely deranged.* I need hardly describe how much they have upset me. She can't force me to live with her, of course, and there is no real threat in her attempts to get back together – but, all the same, it was so excruciatingly painful for me that I became physically ill. Above

all, despite everything, I still feel sorry for this hapless creature . . . She is so mad that in reply to my first letter, in which I told her to abandon all thoughts of living with me, she sent me a summons to visit her, to confirm with the hotel servant that she had indeed thrown over her last lover (who is still in love with her and might nevertheless turn up at any minute) and then to make passionate love to her. She says she knows how to arouse passion in me . . . She is now ready to be, as she puts it, 'all mine'.[24]

Tchaikovsky took a full two days, he told Modest, over his reply, in which he promised her an allowance of 600 roubles a year if she would leave him in peace. So overwrought was he over Antonina's re-emergence that he developed piles, convinced himself that it was fatal, and began drawing up a will. Again asked to act as intermediary, Yurgenson reported that he found Antonina to have aged; she seemed utterly confused, but prepared to accept the money on offer. She continued to fire off eccentric letters throughout the summer, but Tchaikovsky's loyal publisher managed to keep her disruption of the composer's life to a minimum. By the end of July he was able to tell Modest that he was 'through with Antonina for the time being'.[25] Even another letter five days later, asking him to dedicate some music to her and bring up her children, did not have its usual power to *bouleverse* him.

To a large extent, of course, Antonina's capacity to cause trouble was dependent on Tchaikovsky's own frame of mind. In mid-July he told his diary one day that his attempts to work were still interrupted by 'constant thoughts' of her, the next that she was receding back into history. 'My conscience is clear – but still, despite it all, even the fact that she is the most worthless creature in all the world, I pity her.'[26] When his work on *The Enchantress* was going well, he could put her out of his mind; there are few mentions of her during July and August, when work on his opera proceeded so rapidly that he could declare the sketches complete on 11 September, two days after the arrival of Modest and Kolya.

During their visit, as he embarked upon the opera's instrumentation, he also produced ten of the Twelve Romances, Op. 60 – not as eloquent, perhaps, as Op. 57, but a resonant echo of Tchaikovsky's gloomy year. After completing this 'double' set of songs he dedicated them to the Tsarina, who responded with an inscribed portrait of herself. He had included one waltz to charm the Empress, but the collection otherwise amounts to gloomy reflections upon night-time and darkness, set to a variety of poets. In the most distinctive, 'Last Night', the listener can hear the composer's own attempts that summer to find an escape from his personal darkness into a brighter future.

Tchaikovsky's summer had also been plagued by the presence of the Kondratiev children's young governess, Emma Genton, who appears to have made the awkward mistake of falling in love with the composer. His diary entries are peppered with moments of embarrassed exasperation at her advances, some of which came in the shape of secret love letters with which he scarcely knew how to cope.

Her departure with her employers at the end of the month caused him relief as profound as his dismay at that of Kondratiev's servant, Sasha Legoshin. The counterpoint to Emma in Tchaikovsky's diaries, as larded with praise as she is with scorn, Legoshin had clearly provided some of the highlights of Tchaikovsky's summer. 'What a pleasure to have Legoshin around,' he confided to his diary. 'He is such a wonderful person. And, Good God, there are people who turn up their noses at a valet because he is a valet. Why, I don't know anyone whose soul is purer and nobler than Legoshin's. So he is a valet! He is living proof that all men are equal regardless of their station in life . . .'[27] Cited by Soviet scholars as 'evidence of Tchaikovsky's progressive social views'[28], this passage is clearly, in fact, as sexual as ideological in its sentiments. Tchaikovsky's preference for sexual partners from the lower orders – what would today be called 'rough trade' – was very much the norm in a homosexual subculture still steeped in the old feudal ways.

Another of his regular partners that year was one Ivan, or Vanya, the coachman who used to drive him from Maidanovo to Moscow, but whose role in the composer's diaries goes way beyond the *droshky*. 'Ivan, unexpectedly. Happy. Long walk in the woods . . . In love with V . . . Hesitation. Virtue triumphs,' reads one autumn diary entry.[29] 'I have fallen headlong into Cupid's net,' he wrote to Modest.[30] Through that winter composer and cabbie met frequently, caroused together to the point of ' shameful drunkenness'[31], until Tchaikovsky's sexual obsession began to fade the following April: 'Coolness towards Vanya. Want to get rid of him.' (A year later, however, in the autumn of 1887: 'Met Vanka, the cabman. Happy.'[32]).

Tchaikovsky's generosity to the local urchins, during his strolls through the woods that summer, was also more than mere philanthropy by an artist 'composing in [his] head' as he walked. The diaries contain numerous references to attractive young adolescents, notably one Egor Tabachok, who lived in the nearby village of Praslovo. 'Something keeps drawing me to Praslovo,'[33] he noted cryptically as August turned to September, which sees him tipping Egor twice as much as the other children (who are 'ugly') and teaching the boy to fly a kite. Egor haunts the diaries for a year and more, before disappearing until the spring of 1890, when he emerges from behind some bushes 'quite grown-up and very handsome'.[34]

Sundry nephews and other young relatives earn similarly libidinous diary entries, but none more so than the 'unbelievably wonderful, ideal, infinitely divine' Bob Davidov, still only fifteen but grown to manly stature, and the increasingly obsessive object of his uncle's affections. In Tchaikovsky's diary of a prolonged stay in St Petersburg that autumn, ostensibly to prepare for the opening of *Cherevichki*, not a day goes by without a mention of Bob, his good looks, the composer's fear of earning his disfavour. It was during this tormented trip that the composer took the photograph of his nephew which still stands to this day in the living-room of his last home at Klin, a reminder of the proud adolescent features which inspired such soul-searching in Tchaikovsky's last symphony.

Oblivious to all this, Nadezhda von Meck was still trying to orchestrate his musical career. 'What decision have you reached about conducting your own opera?' she asked during the winter of 1886–87. 'I still don't understand why your so-called friends are trying to push you into it. In my view it is not merely unnecessary, but positively profane to mount the podium and submit yourself to the gaze and criticism of the *hoi polloi*. I consider a composer too *sacred* a figure to exhibit himself like that before the mob.'[35]

Her letter, Tchaikovsky replied, was music to his ears.

> Just think of it, my dear friend: all my life I have been tormented by my *incompetence* as a conductor. I have always felt there was something shameful and disreputable about my inability to prevent myself trembling with fear and horror at the very thought of standing in front of the public, wielding a baton. I suspect that once again, when the time comes, I shall get cold feet and back out at the last minute, even though I have given my word that I will conduct.

For nearly twenty years, since that night at the Bolshoi when he had feared his head would fall off, Tchaikovsky had avoided conducting. On the only occasion he had since attempted it, when in need of the money in 1877, he had struggled through the *Marche Slave* with slightly more reassuring results. But he had since shunned the podium, watching with mixed feelings as nearly all his prominent contemporaries steered their own works through their first and subsequent performances, supplementing their income in the process.

Not merely was the composer-conductor a wealthier and more glamorous figure; he was able to take his music beyond frontiers which might otherwise remain closed to him. Musicians like Rimsky-Korsakov were evangelists for their own works, ensuring that they were not distorted in performance, introducing them to new audiences throughout the length and breadth of Russia, and amplifying their own reputations in the process.

When the illness of the resident Bolshoi conductor, Ippolit Altani, had delayed preparations for his cherished *Cherevichki*, Tchaikovsky himself had rashly offered to fill the breech. Now he was saddled with the consequences of his own impetuosity. As the dread day approached, he swallowed his pride and took some private coaching with Altani. It did little to bolster his confidence, as he confided to Modest and Laroche over a nervous Christmas break at Maidanovo. By the time he had survived the piano rehearsals, however, and faced the gentlemen of the orchestra for the first time, he was beginning to think he might just pull it off. 'Time after time I was on the verge of backing out,' he confided to Modest with the approach of full orchestral rehearsals. 'But in the end I pulled myself together, turned up, was enthusiastically welcomed by the players, was brave enough to give them a speech, and began waving my stick about with supreme confidence.'[36]

Tchaikovsky's self-confidence proved justified. Although he slept badly the night before, and awoke that morning sick with nerves, the first night of *Cherevichki* on 31 January 1887 was an unqualified triumph for its composer-conductor, who was garlanded with laurels before, during and after the performance. Even the critics, for once, were almost unanimously warm, and the two subsequent performances he conducted were both sell-outs, despite inflated ticket prices.

Two more performances, however, were enough for the Bolshoi's director, Apollon Maikov, who made no secret of his dislike of both Tchaikovsky personally and his music, *Cherevichki* in particular. In vain did the composer appeal to Grand Duke Konstantin Konstantinovich, even to the Tsar, to intercede. After only five performances, Maikov cancelled all further performances of *Cherevichki* scheduled for that and the following season. Never again would Tchaikovsky hear the work which, to his dying day, he declared 'well-nigh' his favourite opera.

Posterity, alas, was to side with Maikov. As Tchaikovsky completed the orchestration of *The Enchantress*, however, he could savour a personal triumph which was to prove the launching-pad for a new and lucrative career. A year later, in a diary entry clearly intended for a wider audience, he could look back on that night with a pride which would have astonished the man who had nearly funked it:

> I was already almost forty-seven years old. At that age a genuine, true, born conductor, whatever the degree of his natural talent, already possesses many years of experience. If you remember that I possessed none at all, then my début can be accounted a complete success. I continue to believe that I am not a natural conductor, that I do not possess that combination of mental and physical attributes which go to make up a musician in general and a conductor in particular. But this and all subsequent attempts have proved that I *can* direct a performance of my own music more or less effectively – and this is exactly what was required for my greater well-being . . .

Glinka had given one concert in Paris, and Anton Rubinstein's genius as a virtuoso had long since won him 'citizenship of stages and concert platforms the world over.' Otherwise, it was Tchaikovsky's 'fate', as he put it, 'to be the first Russian composer personally to acquaint foreign audiences with his own works.'[37]

# CHAPTER XIV

## 'A sick joke'

AT THE END OF JANUARY 1887, WHILE DANCING AT A MASKED BALL AT THE Assembly of the Nobility in St Petersburg, Tanya Davidova dropped to the floor dead. She was twenty-five. In Moscow to conduct the first few performances of *Cherevichki*, Tchaikovsky received the news with a mixture of anguish and resignation. Although he had been pleased to learn that his niece had been making regular visits to her son, Georges-Léon, at the home of Nikolay and Olga, he also knew that she had recently returned to her old abandoned ways. Her death, to him, appeared little more than a merciful release from morphine. Unable to travel to the capital for the funeral, Tanya's uncle, who had lived through so much with her, was nevertheless 'bowed down' with a terrible sense of waste. 'A strange mood today,' he reflected in his diary. 'Tanya's death has brought tragedy back into my life, and is haunting me.'[1]

In truth, as he confessed to von Meck, he was more worried about the effect on his beloved Bob. 'From Modest I hear that [Bob], for whom I was very afraid, since he is highly-strung and impressionable, is, thank God, all right.'[2] With each year that passed, as he advanced through his teens, Bob was increasingly becoming the still centre of his uncle's turning world. By March Tchaikovsky was sharing a chaste version of his enthusiasm with von Meck: 'My passionate love for this marvellous boy just keeps on growing. It is hard to convey how generous, how refined, how richly attractive is his nature.'[3] The following month, at

Maidanovo, he was joyously able to record in his diary: 'Bob arrived!!!'
For three days the two were 'inseparable', taking long walks, playing
by the river 'like children', chattering away 'like magpies'. There was
'whist with Bob' and 'duets with *Bob!!!*'.[4] His departure, when it had to
come, was 'a terrible wrench'.

But Tchaikovsky could never sit still for long, and by May he was back
in St Petersburg, spending a few days with the mortally ill Kondratiev,
before returning to Anatoly's Tiflis via the scenic route, aboard a steamship down the Volga. Concealing his identity from the other passengers,
he agreed one evening to accompany an amateur soprano in a romance by Tchaikovsky, only to be told by the singer that he had
no feeling for the piece. 'Allow me to know how this song should
be sung,' she publicly chided her unknown pianist. 'I went through it
with my teacher, who was taught how to perform it by Tchaikovsky
himself.' He bowed respectfully.[5]

There followed a pleasantly idle month exploring the Caucasus with
Anatoly and his family before he felt moved to return to composition:
this time another orchestral suite, in four movements, to be subtitled
*Mozartiana*, Op. 61 – a homage to his musical 'god' in the centenary
year of his masterpiece, *Don Giovanni*. Arriving to take the waters in
Borzhom, a Caucasian spa, Tchaikovsky was devoting an hour or so a
day to adapting these four short pieces by Mozart* when there arrived
a desperate cable from Kondratiev in Germany, begging him to join him
in the spa of Aachen: 'Only your arrival can revive me . . .'

As he had for his dying friends Bochechkarov and Kotek, Tchaikovsky
overcame his reluctance to face the journey, bade a tearful farewell
to Alexey, and was at Kondratiev's side by late July. He stayed five
harrowing weeks, confiding to his diary his mixed emotions about
watching one of his life's more volatile companions prepare to meet
a squalid and painful death by syphilis. So affecting were his old
companion's sufferings, and his agonized contemplation of death, that
Tchaikovsky escaped for a few days' relaxation in Paris with his young
cellist friend, Brandukov. The *Pezzo capriccioso* for solo instrument and
orchestra, Op. 62, which he wrote for him soon afterwards, is some
indication of the composer's confused and tormented mood at this time.
But Tchaikovsky was too firm a friend, for all his other commitments, to
leave Kondratiev's side for long.

Back in Aachen, recalling his own 'annus horribilis' of 1877, exactly

---

*The Gigue in G, K.574; the Minuet in D, K.355; the *Ave verum corpus* for voices,
strings and organ, K.618 (in Liszt's transcription); and the Variations on Gluck's
'Unser dummer Pöbel meint', K.455.

ten years before, he had reason to note that 1887 was also proving a year of mixed fortunes: the euphoria while conducting *Cherevichki* had been dashed by Tanya's death, and now his pleasantly relaxed work on *Mozartiana* was scarred by Kondratiev's rapid decline. The fate of his lustily bisexual old friend prompted a prolonged bout of moody introspection in Tchaikovsky, whose main consolation was the companionship of his former lover Sasha Legoshin. There are moments in his diary when the composer appears more concerned about the servant's health than the master's.

The sheer suffering he was obliged to witness filled him, meanwhile, with morbid reflections on man's ephemeral lot:

> Ten days to go in this hell!!! . . . AND much worse since this morning . . . He is in total despair. I cannot describe the scenes which took place; but I shall never forget them . . . Hours of torment. A strange thing: I was thoroughly weighed down by *horror* and *anguish*, but not by *pity* . . . And yet, God, how he suffers!!! I cannot understand why I have become so hardened. I know I am not wicked and heartless. But it is my nerves and my *self-centredness* which whisper ever more loudly in my ear: 'Get out of here, don't put yourself through this torment, spare yourself!' But I dare not think of leaving . . .[6]

Eventually relieved of his vigil by the dying man's nephew, Tchaikovsky was back in Maidanovo, reunited with Alexey, by the time he heard that Kondratiev had finally succumbed in early October. The news was far from unexpected; and he was by then too busy for morbid reflection, preparing for the public unveiling of *The Enchantress*, whose first four performances he conducted in St Petersburg at the beginning of November. For all his secure public stature, and ever wider following, the new opera was not a success. Audiences offered no more than token ovations, and the critics were back at their coolest. There was by now a respectful consensus about Tchaikovsky's symphonic gifts, reasserted by most before lamenting his apparent lack of dramatic instinct. Cui, of course, said that he had known this all along: 'Tchaikovsky is first and foremost a lyric poet who is gentle, feminine, usually melancholy, while sincere and endearing . . . But his music lacks passionate conviction, vitality, energy, and it was not hard to foresee that the dramatic scenes in his latest opera would be musically unsatisfactory . . .'[7]

He moved on to Moscow in tired and dispirited mood. 'I have been going through a very difficult period in my life,' he sighed to von Meck, 'and find myself too worked up about things to converse as I should like, even with you.' Of *The Enchantress*, he went on: 'On no other opera have I expended so much energy, toiled so long and hard, yet never before have I been subjected to quite such punishment by the press.'[8] Aware that he had been neglecting his patron, Tchaikovsky apologized for writing less frequently of late. Lest she feel he had become 'almost a stranger', he took care to add that she had nevertheless been in his thoughts 'more constantly than ever, these last few days.'

Tchaikovsky was uneasily aware that he had also responded less than sympathetically to her concern about Pakhulsky, who had been suffering from a mysterious nervous disorder. But von Meck, as usual, could not have been more reassuring. 'The more time passes, the more setbacks and disappointments I suffer, the closer and dearer to me you become. In your unfailing friendship and unfailingly divine music I possess the only true pleasures and comforts of my life. From you I have never derived anything but complete happiness and joy.'

Having restabilized this crucial relationship, while still licking his wounds from the reception of his latest work, Tchaikovsky was only too happy to leave Russia behind him again, as he embarked on what amounted to a lucrative new career. Word of his emergence as a conductor had rapidly spread abroad, where his European business partners could now see useful commercial opportunities. Suddenly the composer was inundated with invitations, most of them instigated by wily publishers, to conduct his own music with distinguished orchestras all over Europe. Within a year of that nervous début with *Cherevichki*, he was now in as much demand as any veteran *maestro*. From Kashkin, witness of his early embarrassments, we have one of the few first-hand assessments of the mature Tchaikovsky as conductor. His self-confidence had clearly been boosted by that first performance of *The Enchantress*:

> He has all the essential attributes for conducting an orchestra: total self-control, extreme clarity and definition in his beat . . . His direction of the orchestra is distinctive for its utter simplicity . . . If he had few of the conductor's virtuoso gestures which are acquired only with years of experience, he has instead a quality which cannot be learnt: that inner fire, that animation which communicate themselves to the players, and which irresistibly impress the audience with the integrity and inspiration of the performance.[9]

After a farewell concert in St Petersburg on 24 December 1887, which included a triumphant unveiling of his Fourth Suite, *Mozartiana*, Tchaikovsky left for a ten-week concert tour abroad, travelling for the first time as a conductor of his own work. Despite the high reputation which now preceded him, the composer remained a nervous conductor, aware that he was following in the footsteps of such eminent contemporaries as Brahms and Wagner; and a wrangle over repertoire on his arrival in Berlin, not to mention a surprise public luncheon, nearly had him turning straight round and returning home. After a shaky start, however, the winter of 1887–88 was to turn into a triumphant progress through Leipzig and Berlin, Hamburg and Prague, Paris and London, playing to rapt audiences and respectful critics, building himself an international reputation as secure as any composer-conductor of the day. As if by way of official confirmation, a letter which reached him in Germany on 14 January 1888 brought the news that the Tsar, Alexandr III, had honoured him with a state pension of 3,000 roubles a year for life.

The news did Tchaikovsky no harm at the box office, filling auditoria all over Europe, and obliging him to surrender to the inevitable social whirl he had come to dread. In Leipzig he met Brahms, whose music he had always considered overrated, and whom he now described to Modest as 'blotchy, pot-bellied . . . a terrible boozer'. At the home of Adolf Brodsky, the violinist who had launched his Violin Concerto five years earlier, Tchaikovsky inadvertently walked in on a rehearsal of Brahms's Piano Trio in C minor, with the great man himself at the piano. When Tchaikovsky grew 'uneasy', evidently reluctant to pay Brahms the compliments expected of him, their hostess feared 'a difficult scene' until the day was saved by the arrival of the short, frail figure of Edvard Grieg, to whom Tchaikovsky quickly warmed. At lunch Grieg's wife Nina, finding herself seated between Brahms and Tchaikovsky, sprang from her seat after only a few minutes, exclaiming: 'I can't sit between these two. It makes me too nervous.'

'*I* have the courage,' said Grieg, promptly taking her place. 'So the three composers sat there together, all in high spirits,' recalled Mrs Brodsky. 'Brahms grabbed a dish of strawberry jam, insisting that he wanted to eat it all himself, and that no-one else could have any . . . It was more like a children's party than a gathering of great composers.' So it seems appropriate that her husband, the virtuoso violinist, rounded things off with some conjuring tricks – of each of which Brahms demanded a detailed explanation.[10]

Only on closer acquaintance did Tchaikovsky grudgingly concede that Brahms was 'kind to me . . . and far less self-important than I had expected'. Grieg may have been the lesser composer, but the man and his music held far more charms for Tchaikovsky, who hoped that he sensed the beginnings of a lasting friendship. Amid this coterie he even had a few kind words for the eccentric English composer Ethel Smyth, inseparable from her red setter, Marco, and 'one of the few women composers whom one may take seriously, [despite] an incomprehensible reverence, amounting to a passion, for the enigmatic musical genius of Brahms.'[11] Many years later, grateful for the advice he freely offered her, Smyth repaid the compliment: 'Of all the composers I have known,' she recalled in her memoirs, twenty-five years after his death, 'the most delightful was Tchaikovsky.'

> Accustomed to the uncouth, almost brutal manners affected by many German musicians as part of the make-up and one of the symptoms of genius, it was a relief to find in this Russian, whom even the rough diamonds allowed was a master on his own lines, a polished, cultivated gentleman and man of the world. Even his detestation of Brahms's music failed to check my sympathy – and that, I think, is strong testimony to his charm![12]

In Berlin Tchaikovsky ran into Désirée Artôt, twenty years on, and enjoyed a long and happy conversation of which 'not one word touched on the past'. They met twice that week, but never would again, although a sporadic correspondence eventually resulted in his dedicating to her the Six Romances on French texts (Op. 65), as a middle-aged keepsake of their youthful adventure.

In Berlin he also met the precocious young Richard Strauss, in Leipzig Busoni, in Prague Dvořák, in Paris Massenet, Gounod and Fauré. It was during this tour, in Modest's view, that Tchaikovsky reached 'the highest point of worldly acclaim he was destined to achieve in his lifetime.' Even the ceaseless lionizing, the civic receptions, the press interviews, the official dinners complete with speeches, had begun to beguile his hungry ego. But the longer the tour progressed, the more exhausted and irritable he grew, wearied by constant adjustments in the details of his itinerary, as rehearsal schedules changed, new invitations arrived to challenge old, and rows over repertoire continued. As his habitual homesickness grew, despite the apparent lack of interest in his progress back home in the Russian press, his main consolation was the warm generosity of a succession of hosts: notably, in Germany, the Brodskys and his pianist friend Ziloti.

But Tchaikovsky seems to have derived most pleasure from his travelling companion and fellow performer, a talented young Russian pianist named Vasily Sapelnikov, who was lending welcome companionship as well as giving inspired performances of his piano works. After three weeks, Tchaikovsky told Modest, they were 'inseparable . . . I have grown so fond of him, and he has become so close to me, that he now seems like part of the family. Not since Kotek have I loved anyone as much. You cannot imagine a more attractive, gentle, sweet, delicate and noble individual.'[13] His diary entries, which mount in enthusiasm until Sapelnikov's departure halfway through the tour, make clear the erotic element in Tchaikovsky's feelings – 'I absolutely adore him' – without suggesting that their relationship was anything more than platonic.

Originally undertaken as much for its financial as its professional rewards, the tour was in fact doing a great deal more for Tchaikovsky's renown than for his bank balance. As yet too timid to demand expenses, he found that his travels were costing him increasingly alarming amounts of his own money. In Prague, in the mistaken belief that it was a local tradition, he rashly donated his fee for one of his two concerts to a musicians' charity; in Paris, to his dismay, he discovered that renown was the only reward on offer for his efforts. In England, however, proper contracts were on offer with appropriate fees. For this reason only, he grumbled to Modest, he postponed his return home to visit the country which he had so long held in such low regard, largely because of its intransigence during the Russo-Turkish War.

On 19 March, after an unusually rough Channel crossing, unseasonal snow delayed his onward journey to London, where he finally arrived five hours late, after midnight. What might have proved an inauspicious start was redeemed, however, by the hotel recommended to him by Rubinstein: the Dieudonné, a thoroughly French establishment off St James's in Ryder Street, where Tchaikovsky immediately felt quite at home. A regular haunt of artists and musicians, the hotel was a short walk from the St James's Hall, where on 22 March he conducted his Serenade for Strings and the variations from his Third Suite.

The rehearsals had proved laborious; unable to cope in English, Tchaikovsky had asked his fellow-conductor, Frederic Cowen, to act as interpreter. But the players were excellent, and the audience responsive – especially to the Serenade, after which he was called back to the stage three times. An enthusiastic press also persuaded the organizers, the Philharmonic Society, to boost his fee from the agreed £20 to a handsome £25.

Von Bülow had performed Tchaikovsky's Variations (Op. 19, No. 6) in London in November 1874. But his name was otherwise little known in England at the time 'except among musicians,' according to Cowen, 'although he had already given to the world many of his finest compositions.'[14] To London itself the composer could not warm, professing himself 'bored' with this 'dull and depressing' city for most of his five-day stay, despite two visits to the ballet (*Enchantment* at the Alhambra and *The Sports of England* at the Empire, Leicester Square), one to the theatre (*Tartuffe* at the Royalty), and a dinner hosted in his honour by the secretary of the Philharmonic Society, the pianist Francesco Berger. Perhaps he was jaundiced by some over-indulgence on his last day, when he ate so much of his favourite dish, macaroni, at Gatti's restaurant in The Strand that he developed a stomach-ache severe enough to postpone his departure by twenty-four hours.

As Modest points out, however, this visit was of crucial significance to the growth of Tchaikovsky's reputation in Europe. Before his visit, England had proved more resistant to Tchaikovsky's music than most of mainland Europe; now he had laid the foundations for a popularity in the English-speaking world which would soon see him crossing the Atlantic. 'I shall try to secure an invitation to conduct in America next year or the year after,' he wrote to von Meck on his journey home. 'Isn't it strange that after more than three months of exhausting foreign travel, I am already dreaming of another trip abroad?'[15]

By early April, weary but elated, Tchaikovsky was back in Tiflis with Anatoly and Praskovya, eager to return to composition. After a rest with this newly favourite branch of his family, he completed his homeward journey to Klin, where the recently married Alexey had moved their worldly goods from Maidanovo to a nearby *dacha* in the woods near Frolovskoye. Brimming with self-confidence, yet moved by the events of the past year to broody introspection, Tchaikovsky felt himself on the verge of his first major work for more than twelve months.

At first he was torn between another opera and a symphony. Although he was still haunted by his recent sequence of operatic failures, it was ten years since he had last written a symphony proper, the obvious vehicle for the metaphysical musings stirring within him. His journey home from England had taken him through Aachen, where his mind naturally returned to Kondratiev's reluctant and tortured end. Six months before – on the very day of his old friend's death, though he could not have known it at the time – he had distilled his feelings in his diary:

> How short life is! How much one wants to do, to think about, to say. One puts things off, imagining there is still so much time ahead, yet there around the corner death is already lying in wait . . . My religion has made itself felt much more clearly. During all this year I have thought a great deal about God, about life and death – and especially in Aachen the fateful questions why? how? wherefore? often invaded and hovered disturbingly around my thoughts.[16]

It was also around this time that he was suddenly haunted by dreams of his youthful friend Eduard Zak, 'the man I loved more than anyone', who had committed suicide in 1873 at the age of nineteen: 'How amazingly well I remember him: the sound of his voice, the way he moved, but above all the way he used to look at me . . . The death of this boy, the fact that he no longer exists, is beyond my understanding. I believe I have never loved anyone as much as him . . .' Fifteen years on, Tchaikovsky was still riddled with unexplained guilt about Zak's death: 'My God! No matter what they told me then and how I try to console myself, my guilt before him is terrible! Yet at the same time I loved him – that is, not loved [in the past tense], but love him still. His memory is sacred to me!'[17] If Zak it was who had inspired the love theme in *Romeo and Juliet*, now his ghost joined those of Tanya and Kondratiev to stir in Tchaikovsky the profound emotions at work in his most mature masterpiece to date, the Fifth Symphony in E minor (Op. 64).

Although he had told his friend 'K.R.', the Grand Duke Konstantin Konstantinovich, that the piece had no programme, some of his notes on the first movement ('a wonderful programme, if only it can be pulled off') show that it was very much inspired by those feelings which had been haunting him all year, alongside his perennial preoccupation with Fate:

> Intr[oduction]. Total submission before Fate – or, what is the same thing, the inscrutable designs of Providence.
> Allegro. 1. Murmurs, doubts, laments, reproaches against . . . XXX*[1]
> 2. Shall I cast myself into the embrace of *Faith*?[18]

To clear the summer for uninterrupted work, Tchaikovsky first paid a flying visit to St Petersburg, not least because he had heard that the Tsar wanted to see him again. But Alexandr seemed preoccupied, and Tchaikovsky did not think the atmosphere conducive, as he had hoped, to conveying to his monarch the hard work he had been doing for Russia across Europe.

Back in Frolovskoye on 21 May, he agonized between embarking upon his new symphony and completing some sketches on themes for *Hamlet*, a project which had recently re-suggested itself twelve years after it was first mooted by Modest. After some weeks of indecision, torn between the two, he set *Hamlet* aside and embarked in earnest on the symphony. Single-mindedness proved fruitful, and the sketches were complete by 29 June. He paused for just five days, long enough to finish the draft for the *Hamlet* overture (Op. 67), then set about orchestrating the symphony in a creative frenzy which saw it finished by the end of August.

---

*XXX presumably refers to his homosexuality, as in the diary entries of summer 1884, see pp. 234-6.

The unexpected lull enabled him to pay his first visit in three years to Kamenka, which he now found 'uncommonly disagreeable'. Tchaikovsky was 'rather shocked' by the state of his family; still addicted to morphine, his sister Sasha had aged dramatically, while his beloved Bob had 'put on too much weight'. He soon escaped to Moscow, where he introduced his new symphony with great success to the usual circle of friends – including Taneyev, who had already completed the piano transcription – before returning to Frolovskoye to finish the scoring of *Hamlet* by mid-October. The death that month of Nikolay Hubert, his long-time Conservatoire friend and colleague, compounded the general melancholy which, as so often, followed this remarkable burst of creativity.

Tchaikovsky himself conducted the first performance of his Fifth Symphony in St Petersburg on 17 November, coupling it with the Piano Concerto No. 2, in which the soloist was his new friend Sapelnikov. A week later he repeated the symphony in tandem with the première of his *Hamlet* overture. Both works were received with huge enthusiasm by the audience. At the first concert he was given the rare honour of a triple fanfare from the orchestra, and presented onstage with a scroll admitting him to honorary membership of the St Petersburg Philharmonic Society. But the critics, again, proved hostile, Cui now suggesting that the 'routine' and 'meretricious' new symphony marked a further decline in the composer's powers.

In both these very different works, the Fifth Symphony and the *Hamlet* overture, Tchaikovsky remains conspicuously obsessed with the concept of Fate – hanging 'like the sword of Damocles' over all human life, notably his own. In his Fourth Symphony, ten years before, Fate had been assigned a relentless, battering motif allowing little room for redemption. In the Fifth its presence is evident at the outset, in the sombre foreboding of the low-register clarinets, returning in different guises in each of the four movements. This time, however, Tchaikovsky appears to move from resignation, via despair, to some degree of optimism – symbolized by a quotation from Glinka's *A Life for the Tsar*, singling out the phrase 'Turn not to sorrow'.

But the symphony's predominant mood is profoundly bleak, repeatedly allowing the Fate motif to brush aside brief moments of hope before relapsing into dark introspection. Tchaikovsky's habitual gloom, tinged with self-pity, was again emerging from the 'separateness' inspired by his sexuality. 'If Beethoven's Fifth is Fate knocking at the door,' as one Russian wit observed, 'Tchaikovsky's Fifth is Fate trying to get out.' Even at the symphony's close, at the end of a convoluted finale throughout which the composer has worn his storm-tossed heart on his sleeve, the suggestion of a victory over Fate has a hollow ring, as if the composer could not quite convince himself of his own hopes. As the four closing hammerblows fade, it is chillingly clear that he has again conceded eventual defeat.

At the end of November Tchaikovsky was again off to Europe, to put his latest works on wider display. In Prague, where he conducted his Fifth Symphony and Second Piano Concerto (again with Sapelnikov), he had this time been promised half the takings; but the event was ill publicized, and his share proved so small that he again donated it to a musicians' charity. Whether calculated or not, this gesture ensured him a personal triumph six nights later at the Prague première of *Eugene Onegin*. But his homeward-bound high spirits were dashed in Vienna, where he learnt from a newspaper that his niece, Vera, had died of tuberculosis. The suicide of another friend in Tiflis, a young man named Svinkin whom he had met through the equally tragic Verinovsky, completed a melancholy catalogue of death and disarray throughout 1888. Was it pure coincidence that the year ended with so prodigious a musical coda?

Back in St Petersburg Tchaikovsky paused merely to conduct his symphonic fantasy *The Tempest*, and to hear a student performance of *The Oprichnik* (which he hated as much as ever), before returning to Frolovskoye straight after Christmas and setting about a new ballet, *The Sleeping Beauty* (Op. 66).

A libretto based on Charles Perrault's fairy tale *La belle au bois dormant*, first published in 1697, had originally been the idea of Ivan Vsevolozhsky, the director of the Imperial Theatres, who himself undertook the libretto (and the costume designs). Eager to have any new ballet from Tchaikovsky, Vsevolozhsky had at first suggested *Salammbô*, which the composer had turned down flat, then *Undine* (already, of course, the subject of his second opera), which had briefly tempted him. But Modest's libretto for *Undine* proved inadequate, while Vsevolozhsky's own version of *The Sleeping Beauty* immediately fired the composer's imagination. By the time the two got together with Marius Petipa in November 1888, supposedly to discuss the great choreographer's detailed plans, Tchaikovsky had not been able to resist sketching out the first few scenes. Not until early 1889, however, at Frolovskoye, was he able to get to work in earnest.

He had 'no time for letters', he told Modest that winter, as he raced to complete the sketches of *The Sleeping Beauty* before embarking upon another major European conducting tour. There was time enough, however, to write to von Meck asking yet again for a series of advances on the following year's allowance, pleading the expense of his European tour and the costs of moving house. As always, she complied without a note of complaint. There was also a touching exchange of letters with Dvořák, who wrote to praise the 'warmth' and 'poetry' of *Eugene Onegin*, 'music that draws us to itself and penetrates the soul so deeply that it is unforgettable'. Deeply touched, Tchaikovsky replied with enthusiastic plans to bring the Czech to conduct his own music in Russia the following season.[19]

After the financial difficulties of the last tour, organized by his European publishers, Tchaikovsky had found himself a Russian-based agent, Julius Zet, in an attempt to maximize his earnings. A pianist and musical instrument dealer, Zet had at first come up with some hopelessly grandiose schemes including Scandinavia and the United States, all of which came to naught. Once he had limited his horizons, however, to cover much the same ground as Tchaikovsky's first European tour, a realistic schedule had finally taken shape – this time a three-month progress through six German venues before Geneva, Paris and London again.

On any of his frequent visits to St Petersburg and Moscow, it was by now routine for Tchaikovsky to find concerts of his own music to attend, incognito or otherwise. Dealing with mundane business in the capital before his departure, as well as holding further consultations with Petipa and Vsevolozhsky about *The Sleeping Beauty*, he was also able to hear the tenor Nikolay Figner and his wife Medea in *Eugene Onegin*, his *Sérénade mélancolique* conducted by Rimsky-Korsakov, and his Second String Quartet led by Auer. On 5 February 1889 he set out for Europe.

A week later, on 12 February, he conducted the Third Suite in Cologne, and again three days later in Frankfurt. Although the first orchestra was by far the better, both concerts won him triple fanfares. On 20 February, in Dresden, he was annoyed to find an even worse orchestra laid on for a more ambitious programme; this time the Fourth Symphony and the First Piano Concerto won him only one fanfare. By the 26th, in Berlin, he was winning plaudits for the Serenade for Strings but hisses for *Francesca da Rimini*. Three weeks of social whirl and mixed receptions soon began to take their toll – 'I cannot tell you,' he wrote to the Grand Duke, 'how much *Heimweh*, as the Germans call it, fills me with misery, yearning, homesickness and general suffering' – when the news of the death of his friend Karl Davidov, director of the St Petersburg Conservatoire and dedicatee of the *Capriccio Italien*, deepened his nomadic gloom. Were he not due to meet up with Sapelnikov in London, for another performance of the First Piano Concerto, he swore he would have cancelled the rest of the tour and gone straight home.

But his ego unashamedly enjoyed the role of unofficial ambassador for Russian music, and he was able to enjoy two days' rest with the Brodskys in Leipzig before proceeding to Geneva, where he directed the First Suite, the Serenade for Strings and 'Don Juan's Serenade' to a rapturous reception. His visit was marred only by acute nostalgia for those first few weeks of 1876, more than thirteen years before, when he had enjoyed such happy times here with Sasha, Lev and their children, two of whom were now dead. He was drawn back to the Boulevard Plainpalais, where he had lodged with the Davidovs, and suffused with vivid memories of Tanya and Vera, 'their arms red from running to school in the cold'. And 'you,' he wrote to Bob, 'with your tiny nose, not that trunk you now have instead of a nose, and myself not so grey.' He was again overcome, he confessed, by that particular wistful sadness caught in those favourite lines of Dante: '*Nessun maggior dolore\Che ricordarsi del tempo felice\Nella miseria.*'

Two days later he was in Hamburg, in the next hotel room to Brahms, who had postponed his own departure to attend Tchaikovsky's rehearsals next day for the German première of his Fifth Symphony. The two composers got 'quite drunk' together over lunch. 'I like his directness, and his simplicity,' Tchaikovsky conceded to Modest.[20] But still he could not warm to his music. Brahms was 'an empty chasm . . . His style is always elevated; he never strives for artificial effect, he is never banal, everything he does is serious, noble – but the most important thing, *beauty*, is simply not there.' Unlike the man, his symphonies were 'colourless and boring'. Brahms, in turn, was candid about Tchaikovsky's Fifth, whose last movement he criticized vehemently, renewing the composer's own doubts about a work he himself had come to consider inferior to his Fourth. But a successful performance on 15 March, with a very positive response from orchestra as well as audience, soon had him swinging back in the Fifth's favour.

With a month to kill before his next engagement, Tchaikovsky repaired to Paris, his favourite European city, where he revisited old haunts with Brandukov, with such results as: 'A negro. Back to my place.'[21] When Sapelnikov joined them, Tchaikovsky's delight in his young friends' company was marred only by a sudden spate of letters from Antonina, who soon managed to have him suffering from toothache and fever. She was asking for her allowance of 100 roubles a month – one-fifth of the money he received from von Meck, and perhaps one-tenth of his total income at this time – to be doubled.

'So stupid and worthless a woman, able to surrender several children to foundling hospitals without the slightest compunction, does not deserve a jot of compassion,' he wrote to his long-suffering intermediary, Yurgenson.

> I can't believe that she is hard up, as she should be able to manage easily on 100 roubles. On the other hand, the more I can feel I

am making her happy, the more my conscience is eased, and the better it makes me feel myself. There are even times when I pity this ridiculous woman. Is it her fault that she is stupid, pathetic, devoid of any pride or decency?[22]

After several changes of heart, as more reports arrived from his publisher, he compromised by increasing his wife's monthly allowance to 150 roubles, and authorizing Yurgenson to make 'emergency payments' in moments of special need.

In Paris as a private citizen rather than a performing celebrity, Tchaikovsky steered clear of the 1889 Exhibition – though he did go to inspect the new tower built for the occasion by Alexandre Eiffel, and ascended to the top in its elevator. His one public outing was to hear the variations from his Third Suite performed by Colonne; at the ensuing reception he was delighted to renew his acquaintance with Massenet, whom he also invited to conduct an RMS concert in Moscow the following season. Amid more meetings with Fauré, Delibes and Lalo, Tchaikovsky was enchanted by Paderewski, the Polish pianist and future Prime Minister, whom he also invited to Russia.

On 9 April he arrived back in London to conduct a concert two nights later comprising the First Piano Concerto, again with Sapelnikov, and the First Suite. His original plan had been to introduce the Fifth Symphony to England; but he was still nagged by doubts about its instrumentation – and curiously embarrassed that he had already dedicated it to 'a greatly esteemed German musician, who is a friend of mine', Theodor Avé-Lallemant, rather than the Philharmonic Society, who were now keen to offer him a commission. In an exchange of letters with Francesco Berger, still trying to persuade him to conduct his new symphony, Tchaikovsky had pleaded the cause of the First Suite as 'a novelty' and the First Piano Concerto as 'capable of making a big impression' – letting slip, in the process, that he himself preferred his Second Piano Concerto, which he would hope to bring with him another year.

For all London's warmth towards him, Tchaikovsky still could not warm to London, then shrouded in its own unique blend of fog and damp. 'Drunkenness in private' reads his diary for the morning of his arrival, 9 April, after another rough Channel crossing which had made Sapelnikov violently seasick. The fog in the early mornings Tchaikovsky could understand – it was 'not unlike St Petersburg' – but fog at midday, on emerging from rehearsals in the St James's Hall, was too much. 'It was as dark as a moonless autumn night,' he wrote to Bob. 'I feel like I'm stuck in an underground dungeon.' London's weather had changed little in the hundred years since Haydn called the fog 'so thick that you could spread it on bread'.[23]

After rehearsals he considered laborious and inadequate, not least because he was again obliged to work through Cowen as his interpreter, Tchaikovsky wrote a long letter to Ethel Smyth regretting that he would not have time to accept her invitation to call, then forgot his sorrows by getting drunk again. That evening's concert, none the less, was successful enough for him, and a triumph for Sapelnikov, who subsequently became a particular favourite of British audiences. Tchaikovsky had amply fulfilled his main purpose, to introduce his friend to the London music scene, and could not wait to get back home. Early the morning after the concert, he crept into Sapelnikov's room to kiss the sleeping young pianist goodbye, then checked out of the Hotel Dieudonné and embarked on a two-week journey via Paris and Marseilles to Tiflis, where Anatoly had now been promoted to deputy governor.

The eleven-day voyage to Turkey proved eventful, with volcanoes in full eruption as they sailed past southern Italy, and the composer wildly enamoured of a sickly fourteen-year-old boy called Vladimir Sklifosovsky. Tchaikovsky wept, he confessed, upon taking his leave of him in Constantinople on 19 April, and again nine months later, on hearing of his death; to the memory of this brief travelling companion, four years later, he would dedicate the *Chant élégiaque*, the fourteenth of the Eighteen Piano Pieces, Op. 72.

During the voyage he had sketched the polonaise for *The Sleeping Beauty*, with which he was now anxious to proceed, not least because the première was set for the end of the year. But the obligations of fame kept blocking his way. He could not leave Tiflis until he had attended a concert on 12 May of his music, including the Piano Trio; a week later he arrived in Moscow to find himself drafted as referee of yet another dispute about the Conservatoire's directorship. As so often, Tchaikovsky represented the interests of his old friends, in this instance Albrecht, persuading him to take a lucrative retirement package to clear the way for Vasily Safonov to become director. Five days in St Petersburg, staying with Modest and Kolya, were consumed by business, including more meetings with Vsevolozhsky and Petipa about the sets and costumes for the ballet – on which he was finally able to resume work when he arrived home in Frolovskoye after four months away, on 31 May.

In a ferociously creative burst that January, Tchaikovsky had already written four scenes of *The Sleeping Beauty* before leaving for Europe. Several more had germinated on his travels, and in Tiflis, before he was able to give the piece his undivided attention again that summer.

As in January, a day-by-day diary he kept that June bore eloquent witness to the speed and intensity with which his work advanced: 'I finished the sketches on 7 June 1889 at 8 p.m.,' he noted. 'Praise the Lord! The whole thing has taken me ten days in October, three weeks in January and now a week – so about forty days in all.' The instrumentation proved slower going – he was not, he complained to von Meck, as fast a worker as he used to be – but was nevertheless finished in another two months.

As Tchaikovsky polished some of the greatest music he would ever write, the summer passed as peacefully as any of his summers ever did, with visits from Bob and Modest, Yurgenson and Ziloti, not to mention Hubert's widow and countless other friends for a party on his Name Day. Also in residence that summer was Legoshin and his three-year-old daughter, who afforded Tchaikovsky much delight but were an added strain on his bank balance. With Modest and Laroche almost permanent house guests, the one striving to keep the other from alcoholic excess, Tchaikovsky had to rely on Alexey's ingenuity to keep the household going. By midsummer, as he put it to Anatoly, 'four gentlemen' were 'surviving on credit from a servant.' The situation caused unprecedented strains in the relationship between master and servant, as witnessed by several trivial rows recorded in Tchaikovsky's diary, despite the fact that Alexey's wife was seriously ill all summer.

Again, as always, it was von Meck who came to the rescue. Though distraught over a breech with her youngest daughter Milochka, who had made a match of which she disapproved, Tchaikovsky's patron stumped up next year's allowance in advance, and in full. Perhaps, she suggested, this should become the annual arrangement; as he was usually in Russia in July, it would be easier to hand over all the money then, rather than parcel it around the world all year.

At the end of August, with the orchestration of *The Sleeping Beauty* finished, Tchaikovsky paid a duty visit to a more than usually fraught Kamenka en route to a busy autumn between Moscow and St Petersburg. Weary of being constantly on the move, he hatched plans to rent an apartment in the capital the following year, which he planned to share with Bob: 'To see him, to hear him, and to feel his presence nearby has become, it seems, a *sine qua non* for my well-being.'[24]

Despite minimal press coverage of his overseas tours, musical circles were sufficiently aware of his successes for him to be much in demand as a conductor – not merely, now, of his own music. On 30 September he presided with great success over a lavish production of *Onegin* at the Bolshoi, before tackling Mozart, Glinka and Taneyev as well as his own Violin Concerto (with Brodsky as soloist) in Moscow, where a week later he conducted Ziloti in the First Piano Concerto.

Amid it all he was playing a leading role in the organization of celebrations for Anton Rubinstein's golden jubilee as a pianist. Tchaikovsky composed a Chorus of Greeting for the opening ceremony, and an *Impromptu* in A flat for the presentation volume, as well as conducting the two opening concerts (at the first of which he conducted Rubinstein in his own *Koncertztück* in A flat). Five days later he was back in Moscow, for a charity concert at which he conducted Beethoven's Ninth Symphony as well as Brandukov in the first Russian performance of the *Pezzo capriccioso*. Then it was back to St Petersburg to conduct *Hamlet* and the Concert Fantasia while directing rehearsals of *The Sleeping Beauty*.

For all he had done for Rubinstein, organizing the celebrations and fitting the concerts into his frantic schedule, he appeared to get little thanks from his first mentor. 'I thank you for your love of my brother, not of me' was Rubinstein's response to Tchaikovsky's public homage at a dinner following the first concert. Tchaikovsky was naturally put out; but the remark was probably less cruel than it sounded. Since his brother's death, Anton Rubinstein had been able to develop an uncomplicated admiration for his sometime protégé, in whom, after all, he could take a paternal pride as one of his own pupils. Rubinstein's lifelong crusade, moreover, was primarily for the enhancement of the international reputation of Russian music; and in this Tchaikovsky was fast joining him as its leading worldwide flag-bearer. The older man's gruff manner seems simply to have got in the way of his genuine admiration for the younger man's skills. Rubinstein had no need to envy Tchaikovsky's growing fame, and probably admired his work more than Tchaikovsky ever realized.

At the time, none of this was any consolation for the composer's taut nerves. As if to make amends, it was around this time that he discovered he had an unequivocal admirer in the rising young medical student-turned-writer, Anton Chekhov. Composer and playwright had met briefly the previous winter, *chez* Modest, and Tchaikovsky had taken the chance to express genuine admiration for his young contemporary's work. Now Chekhov reappeared with a pleasant surprise:

This month I am going to begin publishing a small collection of my stories. They are as tedious and boring as the autumn, and their tone is monotonous, with what artistic elements they possess interweaved with medical matter. But none of this inhibits me from being audacious enough to approach you with a very humble request: permit me to dedicate this little collection to you. I very much hope to receive a favourable reply – first, because this dedication would give me enormous pleasure, and secondly because it will

to some small extent express the deep respect which moves me
to think of you every day . . .[25]

A delighted Tchaikovsky took his consent personally round to
Chekhov's house that same day; the two exchanged photographs; and a
touching friendship developed between the established composer and his
young admirer. 'I am sending you a book,' wrote Chekhov, 'and I would
send you the sun, too, if it belonged to me.' Intriguingly, the inscription in
*Gloomy People*, a collection including some of his finest stories, read 'To
Pyotr Ilyich Tchaikovsky, from his future librettist A. Chekhov, 26.x.89.' It
seems that they were discussing the notion of collaborating on an opera
based on *Bela*, the first section of Lermontov's *A Hero of Our Time*. After
early hopes of a lasting friendship, it was Tchaikovsky who let things
slip. As the senior partner in this particular acquaintance, it was up to
him to dictate its pace; but again he allowed himself to be distracted by
a combination of private and professional preoccupations.

The following year saw Chekhov writing to Modest, rather than to the
composer himself, of his admiration for Tchaikovsky: 'I revere him so
much that I would personally stand guard night and day at the porch
of his house . . . To me, he occupies in Russian art the second place
after Tolstoy, who has long monopolized the first (I award the third to
Repin [the painter] and myself the ninety-eighth) . . .'

But by then Tchaikovsky was in Florence, at work on quite a different
opera. When the loyal Vsevolozhsky commissioned another, despite the
failure of *The Enchantress*, he commended to Tchaikovsky a libretto
begun by Modest three years before for the composer Nikolay Klenovsky,
based on Pushkin's novella *Pikovaya Dama (The Queen of Spades)*. Only
three scenes had been written before Klenovsky abandoned the project,
but they excited Tchaikovsky enough to dampen his enthusiasm for
*Bela*.

Re-reading his beloved Pushkin, he could see custom-made leading
roles for his friends Nikolay and Medea Figner, then the stars of St
Petersburg's operatic firmament. For the first time, he could compose
an opera with specific singers in mind. Convinced that he had the
ingredients for his finest work since *Onegin*, Tchaikovsky could not
wait to get on with it. Only the première of *The Sleeping Beauty* stood
in his way as he cancelled discussions about another foreign conducting
tour, and laid plans to go abroad for the winter and spring, preferably to
Italy, to find the solitude he needed to get down to work.

His longing to leave Russia was intensified by another letter from
Antonina, this time containing an implicit reference to his homosexuality,
and a veiled threat to expose him via a friend of a friend in the police. Her

pretext for writing was to announce her return to Moscow, suggest that they move in together again, and complain about Yurgenson's refusal to give her a ticket for one of the Rubinstein concerts. But Tchaikovsky knew full well that, amid her random ramblings, Antonina's threats were the main burden of the letter. Her presence so nearby in Moscow was a direct threat not merely to his powers of concentration, but to his sanity. Were it not for the imminent première of *The Sleeping Beauty*, he would have fled the country at once. Constant delays over décor and costumes detained the increasingly irritated composer in St Petersburg – 'loafing', as he complained, when he could have been working – all through December and into the New Year.

On 14 January 1890, the dress rehearsal of *The Sleeping Beauty* was finally held in the presence of the Tsar himself, who said to the composer of the magnificent production merely the two words: 'Very nice'. A crestfallen Tchaikovsky noted in his diary: 'His Majesty treated me very condescendingly. Well, so be it!' The ballet's first performance the next day wrung much the same response from the audience: a warm but muted reception to a work now widely regarded as one of Tchaikovsky's finest, and the supreme ballet of the romantic era.

Laroche, more than merely loyal, proved as prescient as ever. 'If the production of *The Sleeping Beauty* is one of our theatre's pearls,' he wrote, 'musically, it is one of Tchaikovsky's pearls. Along with *Eugene Onegin* and his symphonies, the First and Third Suites, his (First) Piano Concerto and Fantasia for piano and orchestra, together with some of his songs and many episodes in his operas other than *Onegin*, this represents the highest point yet achieved by the school of Glinka – the point at which the school begins to break loose from Glinka and reveal new horizons, as yet unknown.'[26]

In Vsevolozhsky and Petipa, it was Tchaikovsky's good fortune to come together with an impresario and a choreographer ready to grant the ballet composer – hitherto a mere functionary of the house, often doubling as conductor – an equal if not quite predominant role in the creative process. Vsevolozhsky, already embarked on a wholesale reform of the Imperial Theatres, was proving an especially enlightened friend and patron, who would come to rival either Rubinstein as a benign creative force in Tchaikovsky's life. Even while they were discussing *Undine*, before switching to Perrault's fairy tale, he had readily granted the composer's request for more time, in view of his professed ambition to write 'not just another ballet, but a masterpiece.'

Thanks to Vsevolozhsky's reforms, Tchaikovsky was working in a climate altogether more inspirational than that which had caused a false start for *Swan Lake*. This was St Petersburg, more than ever outranking Moscow in the scale of its resources and the accomplishment of its dancers and musicians; and this was a directorate as lavish and adventurous in its ambitions as any before Diaghilev and Nijinsky. Tchaikovsky seized the chance to show that ballet music could rise above the merely mechanical demands of the choreographer and dancers, taking on symphonic qualities of its own; and in *The Sleeping Beauty* he raised the art form onto an entirely higher plane than the nineteenth century had previously considered possible. Thanks to his majestic score as much as Petipa's historic choreography, what might have been a lacklustre vehicle for passing stars of the dance took on far broader artistic, even philosophical dimensions.

After decades of misunderstanding, it has now been conclusively demonstrated that Tchaikovsky worked well beyond, at times even outside Petipa's guidelines.[27] With Taneyev's strictures still ringing in his ears, perhaps, he was determined to produce a work which would raise the status of ballet music to that of opera in the eyes of his compatriots, of the symphony to the ears of the West. In his hands, as with the greatest fairy tales, the story of Aurora's arousal from her slumbers by a prince's kiss conveys the entire cycle of human life, from childbirth through youth to love and marriage, reflecting also the seasonal cycles of the natural world. To some, it can even be taken as 'metaphysical allegory: birth, death, regeneration, salvation . . . And it is the very absence of the defining, confining force of words that makes this possible.'[28]

Despite another mixed reception from the St Petersburg press, as slow as critics have ever been to recognize a revolutionary moment in the history of their art form, *The Sleeping Beauty* has proved not merely the most substantial of Tchaikovsky's three hugely successful ballets, but the benchmark by which all the world's great companies have measured themselves throughout the ensuing century and beyond. As he prepared to move on again, fleeing the indifference of his contemporaries, Tchaikovsky could never have anticipated that he had achieved all his most cherished goals – and that, to posterity, *The Sleeping Beauty* would remain beyond challenge as the supreme classical ballet in the repertoire.

Within a week of the première, he was on his way from Moscow to Berlin, without knowing where in Europe he intended to settle. All he wanted to do was to flee Russia. By 30 January he had opted for Florence, where he settled into the Hotel Washington in a suite of four small rooms overlooking the Arno.

Alexey had been detained in Frolovskoye by the continuing illness of his wife, Fyokla; so this time Tchaikovsky took along Modest's servant,

Nazar Litrov, who proved a cheerful and willing companion. They had been in Florence barely a month when news came of Fyokla's death, which deeply upset Tchaikovsky, who had been genuinely fond of her. So for now he was stuck with Litrov, to whom he also became very attached; when the servant had a bad fall, the composer interrupted his work to nurse him back to health. This was quite a sacrifice, as we know from a charming diary kept by Litrov (perhaps confirming Tchaikovsky's suspicion that the servant was sneaking looks at his own diary) that the composer's schedule on *The Queen of Spades* had become all but obsessive:

> P.I. in a good mood today. So I can tell that the second scene, which he began yesterday, is going well . . . Each day before he is due to take a break I go into his room and tell him it's time for lunch or supper. Perhaps this disturbs his concentration – it is hard to tell, as he never shows any displeasure. If he had, or had seemed to, I would not of course keep going in . . .
>
> Today I went in at 7. P.I. was not ready to finish. I told him it was time to stop, but he went on writing notes. 'Yes,' say I, 'it will soon be 7 p.m.' 'I'm coming,' says he, and writes yet another note, playing it on the piano as he does so. I stand and wait. He pulls out his watch and takes a look at it. 'There's twenty minutes yet,' [he says], 'so I'll work another ten.' I say something, but he [repeats] 'Let me have just ten more minutes.' I exit. Ten minutes later he appears. 'OK, I've finished,' [says he], and begins asking what I've been up to. (I was writing; he came in as I was closing my notebook.) He goes into his room and begins walking up and down. I stand by the table. He begins talking about Fyokla again . . .

Apart from Fyokla's death, there was yet another interruption from Antonina to disturb Tchaikovsky's Florentine peace. Now she had written an eight-page letter to Rubinstein asking for a job at the St Petersburg Conservatoire. Tchaikovsky was infuriated. 'Tuesday,' reads his diary for 11 February. 'The letter from P.I.Y[urgenson] with the news about A.I. upset me terribly. Like a madman all day. Slept awfully. Did no work at all.' He begged his publisher never again, 'except in an emergency', to write to him about Antonina. 'Any news about her, or some new trick of hers of no benefit to anyone at all, drives me to distraction, kills me!' Something had to be done, he insisted, 'to make that madwoman desist from her scandalous demands.'[29]

He tried to take matters in hand by writing to his wife himself, listing all her recent misdemeanours, telling her that she needed to be punished 'like a naughty schoolgirl' and that he was cutting her allowance by one third. But the letter never reached her. Tchaikovsky left the final decision to Yurgenson, who withheld his letter but implemented his wishes, cutting Antonina's allowance back to 100 roubles. Neither of them could know it, but Tchaikovsky had at last found the most effective sanction for Antonina's continual caprices. Never again would she bother him directly.

At the time, his calm was so shattered that he poured out his heart to a comparative stranger, the young Russian composer Alexandr Glazunov.

> I am living through a very bizarre phase on my journey to the grave. Something is going on deep within me, something I myself do not altogether understand, a distinct weariness with life, a sense of disillusion, at times a crazed anxiety, but not the kind from whose depths emerges a new surge of love for life – no, something more hopeless, final, and, as is the way of finales, anti-climactic . . . At the same time, none the less, I still have a powerful urge to write [music]. The devil alone knows what the matter is with me. One day I seem to feel that my song is sung, the next I wake up with an irresistible impulse to carry on with it – or, even better, write a new song.[30]

The very next day, Tchaikovsky noted in his diary that he had 'worked better; in the evening, with real inspiration.'[31] His enthusiasm for his new opera had evidently got the better of his irritation with Antonina, for after only forty-four days, on 15 March, he could declare the sketches finished. Back in St Petersburg, Modest had been hard pressed to keep up with his brother's progress, rushing him the libretto scene by scene. Pushkin's dark tale of a fatalistic gambler, prepared to kill for the secret which will supposedly win him a fortune, wrung an appropriately obsessive mood from Tchaikovsky, who was moved to some of his darkest, most dramatic music. The scene in which Herman, the gambler, confronts the elderly 'Queen of Spades' in her bedroom, determined to discover her three-card secret at any price, is perhaps the most powerfully gripping he ever wrote – so much so that he himself confessed to being unnerved by it for several days, as if he had been possessed by some alien force while pouring out music beyond his control.

And yet, of course, it is precisely because he was at his most controlled while composing *The Queen of Spades* that the opera sustains such raw dramatic power. He certainly paid conscious homage to several previous works, notably Bizet's *Carmen*, as he humanized the darkly detached characters of Pushkin's bleakly ironic novella. Tchaikovsky himself, for instance, added the scene where Liza, the object of Herman's obsessive love, throws herself into the Winter Canal; in the original Pushkin, once she has served her turn, Liza simply disappears into marital obscurity. Nor does Pushkin kill off Herman, more cruelly consigning him to an asylum, where he sees out his life obsessively muttering the three-card secret: 'Three-seven-ace, three-seven-ace . . .' Tchaikovsky and Modest have Herman stab himself when the trick goes wrong, and the Queen of Spades reappears to trump his ace and ruin him.

In Herman, for the only time in his musical life, the composer found himself more preoccupied by his leading male character than by the women whose doom he precipitates. On the penultimate day of his work on the sketches, according to his own diary, he 'wept copiously' when Herman 'breathed his last . . . Probably from exhaustion, but perhaps because it is really good.' The next day's entry reads: 'Before dinner *finished everything* . . . I thank God that he has given me the strength to finish this opera.'[32] After which, in a fit of post-partum exhaustion, he promptly fell ill for the best part of a month.

Now that his conceptual work on the opera was done, Tchaikovsky realized how bored he was with Florence. Despite the charms of another street singer, this time one Fernando, he had enjoyed neither a social nor an artistic life by night; usually his fixed daily routine had ended with reading or letter-writing. So thin was the musical diet on offer that he even took Litrov to see William 'Buffalo Bill' Cody, then touring Europe with his Wild West roadshow. Plans to move on to Rome had been frequently laid, then abandoned; now, with *The Queen of Spades* finished and the vocal score sent to Yurgenson in Moscow, he and his servant finally moved on, arriving in the Italian capital on 8 April.

So delighted was Tchaikovsky to be back amid Rome's cultural bustle that he began to regret ever going to Florence. Soon, however, he relented, thanking the city in a letter to Modest for midwifing *The Queen of Spades*. Now, as he set about orchestrating the opera, he was in the mood for his usual extra-curricular recreations. As his health improved, amid misty memories of Kondratiev, he took uncomplicated pleasure in the company of Prince Golitsyn and his circle in the evenings, while working by day. But news of his presence spread quickly, and ambitious Romans were soon courting Tchaikovsky's company. Suddenly he found his music being performed around town, and began receiving invitations to attend. By the end of April he had made a precipitate departure from Rome, and by 4 May was back in St Petersburg, in the

bosom of his family for his fiftieth birthday and the wedding of his
niece Natalya to her sister Vera's widower, Nikolay Rimsky-Korsakov.
After Tchaikovsky's exertions on *The Queen of Spades*, and all his other
troubles, Kashkin noticed that his longstanding friend had suddenly
become an old man:

> As his fiftieth birthday approached, the marks of tiredness and old
> age became all too clear . . . His thin hair turned completely
> white; his face became very wrinkled; his teeth began to fall out.
> Pyotr Ilyich had aged drastically.[33]

Ten days later he was back at Frolovskoye. Himself pale and gaunt
in the wake of his wife's death, Alexey had in his master's absence
much enhanced the dacha's interior by accepting the Zilotis' offer of
some spare furniture. Tchaikovsky was as delighted as he was horrified
to find what had happened outside: the almost complete disappearance
of the woods in which he had loved to roam, felled for sale by a new
owner. But his priority remained his work. There was the scoring of
the second half of *The Queen of Spades* to complete while correcting
the proofs of the vocal score. Both tasks, remarkably, were finished by
20 June. Not wishing to visit either Moscow or St Petersburg, in both of
which lay only the prospect of other people confronting him with their
problems, he set about a piece promised four years before to the St
Petersburg Chamber Music Society. A string sextet in D, he entitled it
*Souvenir de Florence*, in fond memory of the creative climate in which
he had worked on his new opera.

Never at his most relaxed with chamber work, Tchaikovsky found it
'incredibly hard work'. The problem, he told Modest, 'is not a lack of
ideas, but the complexity of the form. There must be six independent
yet compatible voices.'[34] He sketched it, none the less, in eighteen
days, by 12 July, and finished the scoring in another twenty-two, by
the first week of August. Unlike the *Capriccio Italien*, the *Souvenir* (Op.
60) is less a programmatic piece, directly inspired by Italian themes,
than a wistful *recherche du temps perdu* – a musical equivalent of
the Romantic poets' 'emotion recollected in tranquillity'. Perhaps the
most personal of Tchaikovsky's medium-sized works, written from inner
urgings rather than to a deadline, this touching piece hints at the
angst driving the last, great symphonies, but in a more gently reflective
and lyrical vein. Once his initial enthusiasm had waned, as so often,
Tchaikovsky set the work aside until early 1892, when he revised it
considerably before its first performance in St Petersburg later that year.
The first section of the slow second movement, *adagio cantabile e con*

*moto*, is particularly cherished by Tchaikovsky connoisseurs; for David Brown, for instance, the composer wrote 'no paragraph that is, by its end, more affecting than this.'[35]

Between November and March there had been the longest break yet, of some four and a half months, in the correspondence between Tchaikovsky and von Meck. There was no hint of any problem between them. He was busy, she was ill, and they anyway received regular news of each other via the egregious Pakhulsky, who now interrupted the composer's work with a visit to Frolovskoye at the end of July.

Undeterred by yet another letter from Tchaikovsky, none too gently criticizing his latest attempts at composition, the ambitious young man continued to seek help and advice from the celebrated older one, who had little time or inclination to offer it. Tchaikovsky knew, however, that too brutal a dismissal of Pakhulsky's efforts, or an outright refusal to see him, would scarcely be in his own interests. Not merely was the young Pole still a von Meck favourite, long her general factotum and *de facto* private secretary; he was now also her son-in-law, having married her daughter Yulya the previous year. At his peril did Tchaikovsky court Pakhulsky's enmity to any greater degree than he already had.

Ten days before this tedious visit, on 13 July, an altogether more welcome emissary from von Meck had arrived in the shape of a servant bearing his subsidy for the whole year ahead. This was an unprecedented way of delivering the funds now discreetly referred to by both patron and protégé as his 'budget', though there had been a series of letters between them that summer in which she had asked if an earlier delivery than usual, in July, would suit him. In the secrecy which suddenly seemed to surround von Meck's financial dealings with him, her reluctance to share any of the details with her family, and her insistence that he bank the full amount as urgently as possible, Tchaikovsky should perhaps have detected warning signs of the hammerblow awaiting him that autumn. But he merely recorded his undying thanks, in terms as lavish as ever, and made plans to rent a stylish apartment in St Petersburg, to share with Bob, the following year.

The *Souvenir de Florence* completed, he felt a sudden pang that he had been neglecting his family all year, and ached for a burst of domestic harmony in its midst. Aware that the omens were mixed, he spent the last week of August in the reliably soothing company of Bob, Modest and Kolya at Grankino. Then he moved on to Kamenka, where things were even worse than he had expected. Now an alcoholic as well as a morphine addict, prone to epileptic-type fits, his sister Sasha was in worse shape than he had ever seen her. Grossly overweight, and a constant cause of concern to her husband and children, she had become the forlorn focus of a dysfunctional family in complete disarray.

Tchaikovsky endured the grim, melancholy scene for a fortnight before escaping to Kopilovo, where Nikolay and Anna were in much better spirits despite mounting financial problems. Two days there, and he moved on to Tiflis, where he rented his own apartment to avoid the social whirl which would inevitably have enveloped him as Praskovya's house guest. He immediately began work on a new orchestral piece, *The Voevoda* (based on a Pushkin ballad, not the Ostrovsky play which had inspired his first opera twenty years before). But he seems already to have been in an apprehensive frame of mind – not least about the attentions Apukhtin was apparently paying Bob in St Petersburg – when at the end of September an unusually long and confessional letter arrived from von Meck.

'My dear, dear friend,' she began – with the same warmth which had characterized their early correspondence, but had been missing from more recent, ritual exchanges – 'I am delighted that you are at last in Tiflis, in that beautiful Caucasus to which I always aspire in my dreams, knowing I could never get there . . .' There followed some inconsequential chat about the weather and her own immediate movements – 'Please reply to me in Moscow' – before the usual family news moved her to a desperate outburst:

> My God, my God, how terrible it all is! You devote your whole life, all your energies and abilities, to providing your children with a good, secure life, only to see, all too soon, the entire edifice which you have constructed with such care and effort collapse like a house of cards. How cruel this is, how pitiless!

Her son Vladimir was in the Crimea, on doctor's orders, following a nervous collapse. Normally her business affairs would have been in his hands, but for the present she would have to manage without him. Her son Alexandr had already lost half his money in the meat business, and now looked like losing the rest. Her youngest daughter Ludmila (alias 'Milochka') was 'heading towards ruin' thanks to her worthless husband, Prince Shirinsky-Shikhmatov, to whose faults she was blinded by misguided devotion.

As for Nikolay and Anna, the couple whose marriage had symbolized their own proxy union: they too were in dire straits, following Nikolay's mismanagement of the Kopilovo estate. How could Lev Davidov have been so wrong about his son-in-law's managerial skills, pushing him against von Meck's better judgement into an investment which would ruin his own daughter? 'I cannot do anything to repair any of this, anywhere,' she concluded bleakly. 'My main fear is that I myself will go mad with all this never-ending worry and heartache.'

Her tirade done, her feelings vented, she ended with an abrupt return to the warmth with which she had begun.

> But forgive me, my dear, for bothering you with all my problems. They are no fun for anyone to listen to. Keep well, my dear, peerless friend, get a good rest, and do not forget one whose love for you knows no bounds . . .[36]

These are the last words from Madame von Meck to Tchaikovsky to have survived. Her next letter, which arrived a few days later on 4 October, would be one of the most crucial documents to a full understanding of the course of their unique relationship, were it not one of the few to have gone missing. But its contents are relatively clear from Tchaikovsky's reply. For whatever reason, apparently near-bankruptcy, Tchaikovsky's benefactress told him that she had decided to discontinue his subsidy. If their financial relationship were to end, she seems to have added, there appeared to be little point in continuing their correspondence.

Tchaikovsky was devastated. Although his own material conditions had vastly improved in recent years – there was his subsidy from the Tsar, on top of his much-increased income as composer and conductor – the letter bore huge symbolic significance to him. The sequence of events lurking between its lines are clearer to posterity than they ever were to him, but it is hard to accept either his immediate reaction or his long-term feelings and suspicions. There were ritual expressions of regret, of course, in a long and elaborate reply to von Meck. But his true feelings were shared, after a few days' reflection, with Yurgenson and Modest, the only two people who knew the full extent of his indebtedness to his patron.

To von Meck, that same day, Tchaikovsky poured out a torrent of self-denying sympathy:

> My dear, dear friend:
> The news brought in your letter, which I have just received, grieves me deeply, *not for my own sake, of course, but for yours*. These are not idle words of mine. Naturally, I would be lying if I said that so radical a reduction in my income will have no effect on my material welfare. But it will have far less impact upon me than perhaps you think. The point is that in recent years my own income has increased

considerably, and I have no reason to doubt that it will continue to grow rapidly. So if you are the slightest bit anxious about me, amid the other endless worries which beset you, I beg you for God's sake to rest assured that I am not experiencing even a passing moment of regret at the prospect of a reduction in my own material circumstances.

Believe me, I beg you, that this is the unvarnished truth. I am not capable of striking poses or telling lies. The point is not that *I*, for a while, will have to trim my sails somewhat; the point is that *you*, with your lavish habits and grand way of life, will have to face suffering and deprivations. The very thought mortifies me; it is too painful. I feel the need to pin the blame for all this on someone (not you, of course, the last person whose fault it is), and yet I don't know where to point the finger. But my anger is futile and pointless. I have no right to pry into the realm of your private family affairs . . .

There follows more in this vein, suggesting that he keeps in touch with her plans and her well-being via Pakhulsky, and repeating his incredulity at the thought of a Nadezhda von Meck without unbounded wealth. Then he gingerly addresses his patron's poignant last request to 'remember' her:

The last words of your letter hurt me somewhat, for I cannot believe that you really mean what you wrote. Do you really consider me capable of remembering you only while I was spending your money? Could I ever forget for one moment all you have done for me, and how much I am in your debt? I can say without exaggeration that you saved me, that I should probably have gone mad and died if you had not come to my rescue and sustained me with your friendship, compassion and material assistance (the anchor, at the time, which rescued me), my energy utterly spent as I still aspired to move forward along my chosen path.

No, my dear friend, rest assured that I shall remember this unto my last breath, and will bless you. I am glad it is in this precise moment, when you can no longer share your resources with me, that I can with my whole heart express my boundless, fervent gratitude which is utterly beyond words. You probably do not yourself appreciate the immeasurable scale of your good deed! Otherwise it could never even have entered your mind that now, when you are poor, I might *for one moment* forget you!!! Without exaggeration I can say that I will always remember you, and will be thinking of you with every moment, for every thought about myself inevitably and invariably leads me to thoughts of you. I kiss your hand warmly, and beg you to know once and for all that no-one sympathizes with you, and shares all your afflictions, more than I.[37]

Tchaikovsky waited six days for a reply that never came. Then he told Yurgenson what he really thought about his patron's abandonment of him:

I have borne this blow philosophically, but I have to say that I was most unpleasantly surprised and hurt. So many times had she written to me that I would receive this allowance until my dying day that I had come to believe it. I really thought that she had arranged matters so that, come what may, I would never be deprived of my main and (as I thought) most reliable source of income. Well, I have now learnt otherwise. Henceforth I suppose I shall have to lead a quite different way of life, perhaps even seek some well-paid employment in St Petersburg . . .

I am very, very *offended*, deeply *offended*. My relations with N.F. von M[eck] were such that I never felt burdened by her lavish gifts. Now, in retrospect, I do feel burdened. My pride is hurt; my trust in her infinite readiness to support me materially, and to make any sacrifice for my benefit, has been betrayed. Now I would like to see her go utterly bankrupt, so that *she* would have to come to *me* for help. But we both know perfectly well that, from our point of view, she is still fabulously wealthy. In short, she has played some kind of sick and silly joke, which leaves me feeling disgusted and ashamed.[38]

After almost fourteen years, and some twelve hundred letters, one of the greatest correspondences and most extraordinary relationships in the modern history of Western culture had ended as abruptly, and as mysteriously, as it had begun.

# CHAPTER XV

# 'I'm a big shot'

TCHAIKOVSKY HAD BEEN AWARE FOR ALMOST A YEAR THAT HIS PATRON was facing financial problems. The previous autumn she had shared with him her fears over government intervention in the railway system, the foundation of her fortune. 'It is particularly distressing,' wrote von Meck, 'because of the threat to my children's financial security, and I am unable to help them, because my security is threatened too . . . At my age, and with my ill-health, it is too painful to contemplate economies. It is this prospect, this threat, which depresses me to the point of exhaustion and despair.'

Tchaikovsky's reply had been surprisingly offhand: 'I can see how difficult life would be for you if your capital diminished. You need wealth; you are one of the few people I know who deserve it, to whom it is essential, and for whom it would be too unjust if fate were to deprive you of it. I will comfort myself with the hope that matters are not quite as bad as they may seem to you at present . . .'[1] Despite his regular protestations of eternal gratitude, he had come to take his patron's generosity – which now accounted for a third of his annual income – somewhat for granted. There was certainly a conspicuous absence of any offer on his part, already in possession of a year's money, to return it, or henceforth to go without any or all of his annual 'budget'. It was at this point, for the first time in thirteen years, that correspondence between the two ceased for several months.

But von Meck did weather the financial storm, at least temporarily, and Tchaikovsky's cavalier attitude to her difficulties was not what lay behind their eventual estrangement. In her increasing frailness, she appears rather to have succumbed to the combined pressures of the jealous Pakhulsky and the rest of her family to staunch any unnecessary drains on their already dwindling inheritance. After all, Tchaikovsky was now well catered for by ever increasing concert fees and performance royalties, not to mention his pension from the Tsar.

All the evidence suggests that von Meck's greedy relatives threatened to expose Tchaikovsky's homosexuality if she kept up her eccentric largesse towards him. And there may even have been an element of blackmail. The abruptness of her withdrawal from his life – without any explanation, after so many years of epistolary intimacy – was completely out of character. All that time, however, she had hidden from him the fact that she too had long carried a guilty secret, which put her completely at her family's mercy. It concerned Milochka, her youngest child, and the one most mentioned in her letters to the composer.

Modest Tchaikovsky again sought to mislead posterity by telling us that von Meck had eleven children who survived infancy. In truth she had twelve. In the early 1870s (as by now her entire family knew) she had become romantically involved with her husband's secretary, one Alexandr Yolshin, to whom she bore a daughter in 1872. For four years, Karl von Meck naturally assumed Milochka to be his own daughter – until 1876, when he was staying with his daughter Alexandra on an otherwise routine visit to the capital. For whatever reason – presumably jealousy of her pampered baby sister – Alexandra took it into her head to tell her father of her mother's infidelity. That very night, Karl von Meck died of a heart attack.

Once Pakhulsky was initiated into this family secret, on his marriage to Yulya, he had a hold over his mother-in-law which would also see off her pet favourite – the composer who had shown him such disdain. According to Anna von Meck, with whom Tchaikovsky remained in touch, his loving patron never bore him any ill will. Whether she tried to communicate with him, using Pakhulsky as an amanuensis once she was no longer able to write, we will never know. The role of her secretary and son-in-law appears at best to have been murky, at worst conspiratorial. This was certainly Alexey's view. 'That Polish friend of yours is behind all this,' servant fearlessly told master. 'He's jealous of you, and your comfortable way of life.'[2]

Tchaikovsky knew nothing of all von Meck's family pressures, though a less self-obsessed man might have worked them out for himself. For the rest of his life, his resentment of her 'abandonment' of him far outweighed any expressions of gratitude for her invaluable role in his rise to fame. At the time, he contented himself with complaints to Yurgenson and Modest, whom he now told to stop looking for that 'luxurious' apartment in the capital. 'The news of your sad material plight has me more depressed than ever,' his brother sympathized. 'Of course, it is not the six thousand roubles that matter here . . . It is the grievous blow to your pride.'[3]

It was primarily this same pride which obliged the composer to attempt to keep in touch with von Meck; he swallowed enough of it, later that month, to write to Pakhulsky enquiring after her health. The news, it seemed, was still bleak. Von Meck's bronchitis was still acute, but it was her nerves which were the real trouble. 'Things are not good at the moment,' was all Pakhulsky would say, while assuring Tchaikovsky that his letters were read to von Meck, and that she dictated her good wishes in reply. For all the indications that his letters never reached her, Tchaikovsky wanted to believe Pakhulsky, largely because of his wounded pride. All that winter he complained to all and sundry about her high-handed treatment of him.

It was supposedly the absence of any response from von Meck, for instance, which dampened his spirits after the triumphant première of *The Queen of Spades* at the Mariinsky on 19 December 1890. Pakhulsky wrote of the family's pleasure at his success; but Tchaikovsky wished to hear this from his friend herself, and could not bear to believe what seems to be the truth: that his letters were now being kept from her. His pleasure in the popular acclaim for his new opera – as always, he said, more important to him than the critics' habitual carping – was diminished by his unwonted inability to share it with von Meck. The same was true of Christmas and New Year at Kamenka, where he braved the continuing claustrophobia to be back at Bob's side, while working on some incidental music for a production of *Hamlet* by his friend Lucien Guitry (for which he reused his 1884 *Elegy* as an entr'acte). Tchaikovsky's resentful bewilderment at von Meck's abrupt disappearance from his life would haunt him for the rest of his days. At the beginning of 1891, it coloured his every decision about the array of options on offer for the year ahead.

His departure from Tiflis the previous month, after seven weeks largely spent avoiding society, had been triumphant. Following an all-Tchaikovsky concert, in which he had conducted his First Suite, Serenade for Strings and *1812 Overture*, he was showered with laurel wreaths and lionized by the local worthies, who conferred honorary membership of the Tiflis Musical Circle and made interminable speeches in his praise at a dinner hosted by the Artistic Circle.

But Tchaikovsky was feeling – and looking – far older than his fifty years. The contralto Alexandra Amfiteatrova-Levitskaya, who had studied with him and later created the part of Olga in *Eugene Onegin*, was 'very struck' by the recent change in his appearance. 'The sternly gloomy aspect of the Conservatoire professor, which had stamped itself on my memory, had completely gone. Before me was a Tchaikovsky unknown to me.'[4] He had gone completely grey, and the bright eyes so beloved of Antonina had grown yellow and rheumy. 'They had quite lost their glitter,' recalled the composer-pianist Leonid Nikolayev. 'Tchaikovsky appeared far older than his years.'[5] His teeth had begun to fall out, cursing these last few years of his life with a pronounced lisp. His eyesight had begun to weaken – as, it seemed, had his memory. On his last visit to Tiflis, he had arrived at the Ippolitov-Ivanov home while Varvara was singing a romance. 'What's that you're singing?' asked Tchaikovsky, to general amusement, as the song was one of his own.[6]

He was certainly in no mood to have his advancing age publicly celebrated. Back in St Petersburg, as preparations for *The Queen of Spades* progressed, he was alarmed to hear of plans to celebrate his silver jubilee as a composer. Nothing he could do, not even an open letter in Suvorin's *Novoe Vremya*, managed to dissuade his Conservatoire colleagues from a commemorative concert four days before the opera première. There followed a similar festival in Kiev, where he was dismayed to find that also taking part was none other than Stanislav Blumenfeld, the father of Georges-Léon, and instigator of so much trouble in the life of his niece Tanya; amid festivities which outdid even Tiflis, he went to some lengths to avoid a face-to-face encounter. Then the holiday season at Kamenka turned out to be more fun than he had expected. Sasha seemed much better – 'not at all like an invalid' – and above all there was Bob, 'as delightful as ever'.

But as soon as Tchaikovsky got back to work in Moscow, all his old neuroses resurfaced, this time in the shape of the delusion that the Tsar had disliked *The Queen of Spades*. After attending the dress rehearsal, Alexandr III had not returned. Now, after only a handful of performances, all of them sold out, the opera had been withdrawn for the rest of the season. Tchaikovsky wrote a long and angry letter of protest to Vsevolozhsky, who took enormous care over his patient, bewildered reply, even going to the trouble of checking with the royal household. The Tsar remained among Tchaikovsky's most fervent admirers. The true reason for the withdrawal of his opera was the intransigence of his friend Nikolay Figner, the tenor singing Herman, who refused to countenance any replacement in the part of Liza for his wife Medea, now forced to withdraw because of pregnancy. Only once this was explained could a placated Tchaikovsky, no longer fearful for his future with the Imperial Theatres, concentrate on where and when to get back to work.

Via his Berlin concert agent, Hermann Wolff, he had received a tantalizing invitation to make a conducting tour of the United States that spring, centred on a performance of his own music at the official opening of a new concert hall in New York, to be named after its founding-father, Andrew Carnegie. Tchaikovsky decided to accept, agreeing to conduct Colonne's orchestra in Paris en route. Countless other European offers he declined, pleading an injured right arm; in truth, he was far more interested in an intriguing commission from Vsevolozhsky for a double-bill comprising a one-act opera, *Iolanta*, and a two-act ballet, *The Nutcracker*.

February saw him pause in St Petersburg for Guitry's *Hamlet*, only to return from Frolovskoye a few days later, somewhat reluctantly, at the urgent insistence of his servant. A year to the day after his wife's death, Alexey had decided to remarry, this time the eighteen-year-old sister-in-law of Modest's valet, Nazar Litrov. So clear did Tchaikovsky make his disapproval, with talk of 'Feklusha [Fyokla] still rotting in the earth only a few yards away', that the servant asked his master to absent himself from the ceremony. A sullen Tchaikovsky duly obliged, consoling himself in the knowledge that 'Alyosha' was deeply distressed by the thought of his prolonged absence abroad again.

On arriving in Paris, he heard from Pakhulsky in Nice that von Meck was making 'a slow recovery' on the French Riviera. The composer's continuing resentment at communing via this intermediary is quite clear from the formality of his reply:

> I rejoice that Nadezhda Filaretovna has survived the journey so well, and hope that the delightful climate of Nice will soon see her restored to complete good health.[7]

On 5 April 1891 Tchaikovsky enjoyed a great triumph in Paris, where he was garlanded in laurels after conducting the Third Suite, *Marche Slave*, *Sérénade mélancolique*, *The Tempest* and the Second Piano Concerto, again with Sapelnikov. With only two weeks before his voyage to America, however, even the knowledge of his growing international reputation could not prevent him sinking back into an acute case of the depression which always preceded prolonged absence from Russia. He found himself back in that familiar gloom about doing one thing while wishing he was doing another – usually, in his case, conducting when he would rather have been composing. So moody did he become that he found himself sniping even at Modest and Sapelnikov. So he took himself off to Rouen, to be alone, and to continue his work on *Iolanta* and *The Nutcracker*. But neither project was progressing well. Tchaikovsky's nervous tension was not eased when Modest, despite his brother's professed wish to be alone, unexpectedly turned up in Rouen.

To Tchaikovsky's surprise, for it was wholly out of character, Modest had come to tell him that he was feeling homesick and planned to return to Russia. This, to Tchaikovsky's relief, he promptly proceeded to do. After a few more days struggling ineffectively with the two new works, and realizing that he would not be able to make much more progress during the formidable tour ahead, he decided to relieve himself of all immediate pressures by suggesting to Vsevolozhsky that plans to perform the double-bill in the 1891–92 season be postponed a year.

With this load off his mind, he returned to Paris for a few last days relaxing before his departure. On his way round to see Sapelnikov, he made a routine detour via the Passage de l'Opéra to the Cabinet de Lecture, a reading-room where he was in the habit of catching up with the latest Russian newspapers and journals. Flicking through a recent edition of *Novoe Vremya*, his eye was caught by an item on the last page. It announced the death of his sister Sasha.

Tchaikovsky ran out of the library 'as if I had been stung'. His immediate instinct was to cancel his American tour. On reflection, he realized that he had already received (and spent) a substantial advance on his $2,500 fee, which he was in no position to refund. On making contact with Modest, he learnt that his brother had in fact received a telegram with the news of their sister's death on 10 April, while still in Paris. Hence his surprise visit to Rouen. Already concerned about Tchaikovsky's nervous condition, and the imminence of his departure for the US, he had decided to withhold the news and invent a reason for returning home so precipitously.

Modest, it gradually transpired, had been almost excessively protective. To prevent his brother hearing the news before his arrival in New York, he had instructed his Paris hotel to forward all mail to the United States (not to Rouen); told all mutual friends in France not to mention the matter to him; even checked out for himself the lack of Russian newspapers in the public libraries of Rouen. The excuse he had invented for his own sudden return to Russia had been particularly ingenious; he knew his brother would ask few questions, having always rather resented the fact that Modest, while abroad, did not get as homesick as he did. The one thing he could not, of course, anticipate was Tchaikovsky's abandonment of his work on the double-bill, and his return to Paris before leaving France.

'I am going through terrible emotional suffering,' he wrote to Modest. 'I am very much afraid for Bob, although I know from experience that such sorrows are met with greater ease at his age.' The composer himself, after his initial shock, had become resigned to his sister's demise. Her long illness and his growing disenchantment with Kamenka had placed between them a distance unthinkable in their youth. Within a week, he was able to conclude that 'Sasha's death and all my tormented thoughts about it seem strangely like memories of a very distant past, which I manage without too much effort to set aside, concentrating instead on the [interests] of the *not-me* that travels in my person to America.'[8]

By then he was in mid-Atlantic. On 17 April Tchaikovsky had boarded the steamship *Le Bretagne* at Le Havre and set sail for New York.

Intending to publish an account of his transatlantic adventure, Tchaikovsky kept a daily log of the ten-day voyage which he sent to Modest for safekeeping.[9] Amid a chronic attack of homesickness, accentuated by the thought of his sister's obsequies, his first disappointment came with the mysterious non-appearance of his scheduled travelling companion, Laroche's wife, Ekaterina. All the first day at sea he lived in hope that she had slept in late, and would eventually appear. When it finally became clear that she was not on board, his spirits collapsed: 'Truly, without exaggeration, I declare that I have never felt so miserable, lonely and bereft. The thought that I must sail for another whole week, that not until New York will I receive any news, makes me utterly wretched. Blast this trip!!!'[10] His morale was not improved by the death that first evening of a fellow-passenger, whom *Le Bretagne* failed to locate after he disappeared overboard. Being the only German speaker in the vicinity, Tchaikovsky was required to translate the apparent suicide note found in his wallet: *'Ich bin unschuldig; der Bursche weiss'* ('I am innocent; that man knows').

Next day, as the weather worsened and the ship began to toss alarmingly, Tchaikovsky sank deeper into gloom, despite winning fifty francs in the ship's sweepstake on how many miles would be travelled by midnight. He was mortified when a fellow-passenger told him that melancholy was 'a natural condition at your age'. He disliked the French woman beside him at dinner, and the *chanteuse* who then rendered some Italian songs 'so abominably that I was surprised no-one booed her.' Vowing that this would be his last trip abroad, he was filled with intimations of mortality: 'At my age it is better to stay at home, close to family and friends. The thought that I am so far away from my loved ones is killing me.'[11]

The beauty of the sea and its sunsets were his only consolation, however rough the weather, as he tried to forget his homesickness amid the society of the second-class passengers, whom he found more congenial than his 'dandified' first-class peers, apart from a Canadian bishop in whose cabin he attended a low mass. With his new second-class

Nadezhda von Meck, Tchaikovsky's patron, confidante and correspondent for nearly fourteen years, with a letter he wrote her from Moscow in July 1877 (*Novosti*).

Von Meck's estate at Brailov, which the composer first visited in 1878 (*Galina von Meck/Robert Harding Picture Library*).

Tchaikovsky in 1879, aged thirty-nine (*Novosti*).

The five Tchaikovsky brothers in 1890. From left: Anatoly, Nikolay, Ippolit, Pyotr, Modest (*Novosti*).

Sasha and Lev Davidov with their seven children, including Vladimir ('Bob', bottom left) and Tanya (standing, centre) (*Novosti*).

Tchaikovsky visits America, 1891; and England, 1893, to receive an honorary degree at Cambridge University (*Novosti*).

# MUSIC CROWNED

## IN ITS NEW HOME.

### Brilliant Inauguration of Music Hall by the First Festival Concert.

## TSCHAIKOWSKY AND BERLIOZ

The Russian Composer and His "Marche Solennelle" Given a Splendid Greeting and the French Master's "Te Deum" Finely Rendered.

## CAMPANINI AND DAMROSCH

About the Programme, the Performance and the Huge Audience Assembled for the Great Event in New York's Musical History.

### BISHOP POTTER'S ORATION.

SPLENDID is the new temple of music that was formally inaugurated last night with the first concert of a largely planned festival, and splendid was the audience assembled for an event which marks a new epoch in the musical history, in which one brilliant page now follows the other, of this metropolis.

The new Music Hall, for which New York is so largely indebted to the public and artistic spirit of Mr. Andrew Carnegie, is the first thoroughly adequate building to be erected here as the special home of orchestral and choral work.

In Music Hall and the Metropolitan Opera House the city now has two temples of music, which in their size and appointments for both performers and public are not surpassed by those of any city in the world.

The programme arranged for four evenings and two afternoon performances of the festival enlist the services of a fine array of soloists, of the Symphony Society orchestra and the chorus of the Oratorio Society, both under the

ANDREW CARNEGIE.

direction of Mr. Walter Damrosch, a feature of musical interest being the first American appearance of the famous Russian composer, Peter Tschaikowsky, as the conductor of his own works.

After the playing of "Old Hundred" the central feature of last evening, which included the first performance in New York of Berlioz's "Te Deum," with Signor Campanini as soloist, was preceded by an oration in dedication of the hall delivered by Bishop Potter. M. Tschaikowsky, who was received with enthusiasm, conducted his "Marche Solennelle," and the other numbers were the singing of the national hymn, "America," by soloist, chorus and audience and the "Leonora No. III" overture.

### THE OPENING OF THE HALL.

The noble building at the corner of Fifty-seventh street and Seventh avenue, which will henceforth be known as Music Hall, was opened last night with hymns and anthems, yea and sermons, and the clash of cymbals.

Bishop Potter read the (it I mean inaugural oration, and proclaimed the hall henceforward

PETER TSCHAIKOWSKY.

### THE DEDICATION.

"The task which, according to the order placed in your hands this evening, has been set for me," began Bishop Potter, "is much larger than any gifts of mine would warrant me in undertaking, or any most generous patience of yours would consent to endure.

"I have no oration to deliver"—(this was the Bishop's fun, of course)—"nor does this occasion demand one. This is a feast of dedication, and as, on the field of historic Gettysburg, Lincoln, with simple but matchless eloquence, declared, in a larger sense, 'We cannot dedicate, we cannot consecrate, we cannot hallow this ground.'

### BETWEEN THE TWO LEADERS.

### CONSIDE  ON HALL.

---

# MRS. BARNABY'S WILL FILED AT PROV

It Will be Contested by Her with Very Good Chances, it is lieved, of Breaking

## SENDING EAST FOR THE W

District Attorney Stevens, of Pro Wants Mother and Son to At Grand Jury Investigation W Was Begun There Yes- terday.

With his beloved nephew, 'Bob' Davidov, in 1892 (*Novosti*).

Tchaikovsky in the garden of his last home, at Klin (above) (*Lebrecht Collection*) in 1893, the year of his death (*Range/Bettmann*).

The room in which Tchaikovsky died, in Modest's apartment, today occupied by squatters (*Andrey Usov*). His funeral was the biggest St Petersburg has ever seen.

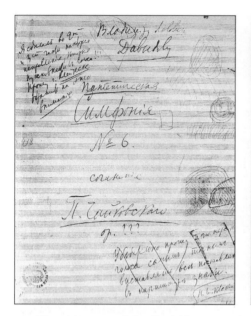 

The title-page of the *Pathétique* symphony, with the dedication to Bob Davidov (*Novosti*); and Tchaikovsky's grave in the cemetery of the Alexandr Nevsky Monastery, St Petersburg (*Novosti*).

One of the last photographs of the composer (*Range/Bettmann*).

friends, meanwhile, he found himself part of a conspiracy to babysit a small child while his mother sold her favours to his first-class 'best friend', the *commis-voyageur* who had joked about his age. The impersonations and bawdy songs performed by this genial Frenchman seem to have endeared him to Tchaikovsky, who was by now warming even to the woman beside him at dinner; she turned out to be married to a member of the Boston Symphony Orchestra, and thus a useful source of American musical gossip.

The fifth day of the voyage, 22 April, brought multiple disasters – above all seasickness, to which Tchaikovsky had begun to think himself immune. Amid this experience of 'hell itself . . . nastier and more upsetting than anything I have ever known', he discovered that his wallet had been stolen from his cabin, complete with 460 francs in gold. There followed an 'abominable' night, 'tossed from side to side so that sleep was impossible', before the ship encountered dense fog off the Newfoundland coast, prompting regular blasts on its foghorn which further frayed the composer's ragged nerves.

On top of it all, word of his identity was spreading among his fellow passengers, with predictably dire consequences. 'Now there is nowhere I can take a peaceful, solitary stroll. Wherever I go, I am shadowed by people who want to talk to me. Then they pester me to play. I decline, of course, but it can only be a matter of time before I have to shut them up [with a recital] on the ship's dreadful piano. Now my one thought is: When will this be over? When will I at last be back home? I rely upon, picture, and dream about the sheer bliss of homecoming . . .'[12]

As the storms increased, so did his torments. 'I suffer terribly . . . My anguish is more emotional than physical. I am desperate and, to put it bluntly, afraid.' The only way to snatch any sleep was to wedge himself between his trunk and the cabin wall. *Le Bretagne* was passing through an unusually ferocious hurricane, which had even the regular passengers rattled. It was Tchaikovsky's bad luck, as he was well aware, to take so rare a battering on his maiden voyage. As the pilot boarded, a sign that the voyage was entering its last twenty-four hours, he heaved a huge sigh of relief: 'Lord, when will this be over? I've already decided to leave New York by German steamer on 12 May. Ten days later, God willing, I should be back in St Petersburg!!!!!!'

This hope was dashed as soon as he finally arrived in New York, on 27 April, to learn that a concert of which he knew nothing had been arranged for 18 May in Philadelphia. As soon as he was left alone in his room at the Hotel Normandie, on Broadway, America's distinguished visitor burst into tears. The delegation which had met him at the quayside, led by the new concert hall's director, Morris Reno, had planned to take him to dinner; but the composer firmly declined, pleading tiredness, and savoured the privacy to give vent to his feelings. Revived by the sheer fascination of his hotel room – which offered such unknown novelties as electric lights, an en-suite bathroom with hot and cold running water, and a voice-tube via which he could contact the hotel desk – he took an evening stroll along Broadway, where he was struck by the number of negroes and, of course, the scale of the buildings: 'A strange street! One- and two-storey houses alternate with nine-storey structures. Highly original!!!!!' Back in his room, he cried himself to sleep, and was still weeping when he woke up next morning.[13]

'Thus, one calm April evening, Tchaikovsky set foot on American soil,' in the words of one wide-eyed historian of the visit. 'He had come from the other end of the earth – an alien with a burden of painful worries. He had not a single friend in America waiting to comfort him. But America was prepared to honour a celebrity and welcomed Tchaikovsky as a superstar, one of the greatest composers of the century.'[14] The lavish nationwide newspaper coverage of his visit got off to a bad start when one of the reception committee – Reno's daughter, Alice – was identified in the next day's *New York Daily Tribune* as Tchaikovsky's wife. But his reception was otherwise splendid enough to rouse him from his shipboard gloom. 'I was greeted with dignity and honour,' he enthused in a letter home. 'My picture is in all the papers, accompanying reports of my arrival. It transpires that I am far more famous in America than in Europe. Here I am a big shot.'[15] This was news he could not wait to tell Bob, whom he was missing most of all:

> Everyone here flatters, honours and celebrates me. It turns out that I am *ten times* better known in America than in Europe. At first, when people told me this, I assumed it was an exaggerated compliment. But now I see it is the truth. Works of mine that are still unknown in Moscow are performed here several times a season, and are the subject of whole reviews and commentaries (*Hamlet*, for example).[16]

On 28 April, Tchaikovsky's first full day in New York, he was taken to meet the prime movers behind his visit: Walter Damrosch, the dynamic twenty-eight-year-old pianist-conductor who had succeeded his father, Leopold, at the helm of the New York Symphony Society; and Andrew Carnegie, the wealthy Scottish-born philanthropist whom Damrosch had convinced of the need for the new concert hall. Tchaikovsky took to them both, particularly appreciating the warmth of an impromptu speech by Damrosch welcoming him to his first rehearsal with the Symphony Orchestra, which went well. Applause from the players before and after the proceedings offered much-needed reassurance to the composer, who was also impressed by the new hall's acoustics. Another ovation greeted his arrival a few days later for the choral rehearsal, though the final pre-concert warm-up was marred by the interruptions of workmen making last-minute preparations.

At the inaugural concert of Carnegie Hall, on 5 May 1891, Tchaikovsky did not make his appearance until the interval. During the first half, in Reno's box, he sat through all the interminable hoopla of any American inaugural: a speech by Reno, a rendition by the Oratorio Society Choir of the 'Old Hundredth', and a long and solemn eulogy from Bishop Henry C. Potter, who performed the formal dedication. The audience then joined in a performance of the national anthem before Damrosch conducted Beethoven's *Leonora* Overture No. 3. Tchaikovsky was received 'with much noise' when he finally emerged to conduct his own Coronation March, then retired to Hyde's box for Berlioz' 'rather dull' *Te Deum*. But his own contribution, he reported, 'went excellently. A great success . . . The Renos took me back to their home for an impromptu supper. Then I slept like a dead man.'[17]

If his contribution to the opening concert had been largely symbolic, he had to wait only two more days, on what happened to be his fifty-first birthday, to take New York by storm. The second inaugural concert, on 6 May, went well enough, with the composer conducting his setting of the Lord's Prayer (from Nine Sacred Pieces) and his orchestral arrangement of his song 'Legend', to another warm reception. But it was a third concert the following day, at which Tchaikovsky conducted his Third Suite, which moved the East Coast press to accolades such as he had never before known.

'Wonderful . . . a power that at once enchains and charms us,' declared the *Morning Journal*. 'Genius!' agreed the *New York Daily Tribune*. 'The best German music is now being written in St Petersburg.' This 'great and unquestioned genius', added *The Press*, 'ranks fairly with Rubinstein, Dvořák, Brahms and Saint-Saëns as one of the half-dozen greatest living musicians.' To the *Evening Post* his Third Suite was 'the climax of the evening . . . imposing . . . original . . . rich . . . majestic.' 'Overwhelming' was the verdict of the *New York World*. For the *Evening Telegram*, the Russian visitor 'roused the audience to a pitch of enthusiasm seldom witnessed.'[18]

The *Evening Telegram* went on to rave about Tchaikovsky the conductor as much as the composer. 'It would be impossible for an orchestra to play badly under such a conductor. Tchaikovsky's leading was a perfect revelation. He inspires his orchestra with his nervous force, and seems to hold every musician at the end of his baton.' Such assessments unsettled

Tchaikovsky. After the inaugural concert, he had declared himself 'acutely uncomfortable' at the verdict of the *New York Herald*:

> He seems a trifle embarrassed, and responds to the applause by a succession of brusque and jerky bows. But as soon as he grasps the baton his self-confidence returns. There is no sign of nervousness about him as he taps for silence. He conducts with the authoritative strength of a master and the band obeys his lead as one man.[19]

'Why must they write not just about my music but about my person too?' he asked. 'It enrages me. I can't stand it when other people notice my embarrassment and are surprised by my "brusque and jerky bows" etc.'[20] More embarrassment was to follow the second concert, of which one critic wrote that the orchestra had played under Tchaikovsky 'with a fire which Mr Damrosch was not able to evoke.'[21]

The *New York Herald* described Tchaikovsky as 'a tall, gray, well-built, interesting man, well on to sixty.' In the week he entered his fifty-second year, he was mortified. According to *The Press*, he was 'a fine-looking man of fifty-five or thereabouts, erect in carriage, and with nearly white hair and beard.' Only the *Evening Post* was more tactful: 'He looks somewhat older than he is, owing to his white hair – but the fire in his eyes, his energetic actions, and still more the creative spontaneity of his latest works, prove that he has only half a century behind him.'[22]

To Damrosch, meanwhile, 'a feeling of sadness seemed never to leave him . . . He was often swept away by uncontrollable waves of melancholia and despondency.'[23] But Tchaikovsky's private grief was eased by the gargantuan hospitality of his hosts, to the point where he granted them the supreme accolade of comparing American hospitality with Russian. On his third evening in New York, for instance, the Renos had hosted a dinner in his honour of such style as to overcome, for once, his distaste for such occasions:

> The ladies arrived decked out in evening gowns, as if for a ball. The table was entirely covered with flowers. Beside every lady's place-setting lay a bouquet; for the men there were buttonholes of lilies of the valley which, upon sitting down, they placed into holders on the lapels of their tailcoats. Beside every lady's place stood a small portrait of me in a delicate frame. The dinner began at 7.30 and ended precisely at 11 . . . Such is the local custom. It would be impossible to spell out all the innumerable dishes. In the middle of dinner ice cream was served in little boxes, to which were attached small writing-slates, each with a pencil and

sponge. Elegantly inscribed on the slates were extracts from my works. Next I was asked to sign my autograph on everyone's slates. The conversation was very animated . . .[24]

Opposite Tchaikovsky that evening 'the little old man Carnegie had deigned to seat himself – Carnegie, admirer of Moscow and possessor of forty million dollars.' The composer warmed to the 'iron master', also a writer and politician, whom he found to bear an uncanny physical resemblance to the playwright Ostrovsky. Before he left New York, Tchaikovsky would be guest of honour at another dinner in Carnegie's own home, which he was surprised to find 'as modest as the next man's'. This 'super-rich man', this 'remarkable original who rose from telegraph boy to become one of America's foremost figures' turned out to be 'a modest and simple man, never one to turn up his nose,' who inspired in Tchaikovsky 'unusually warm feelings, probably because he displays such warmth towards me.' Throughout the evening Carnegie 'demonstrated his affection for me in the most peculiar way. He kept clasping my hands, shouting that I am the uncrowned but true king of music; he embraced me (without kissing me – men never kiss each other here); he stood on tiptoe and raised his arms on high to indicate my great height.' It was quite an achievement on Carnegie's part to have the composer, never too receptive to jokes about himself, leading the laughter as he impersonated his conducting style.

On 9 May, the day before Carnegie's dinner, Tchaikovsky's fourth and final New York concert had proved the most successful of all. As well as some of his songs, including 'Both bitter and sweet', he conducted the First Piano Concerto with the remarkable Adele aus der Ohe as soloist. A pupil of Liszt, who had arrived in New York penniless, aus der Ohe had since grown rich and famous on the strength of sheer virtuosity. Tchaikovsky had been anxious about the lack of rehearsal time, but the concerto 'went off splendidly', largely thanks to her 'perfect' performance. 'There was greater enthusiasm than I have ever before managed to achieve, even in Russia. The audience called for me countless times. They shouted "Upwards [sic!]" and waved their handkerchiefs. In short, it was clear that I am greatly loved by the Americans. But I especially valued the delight which the orchestra appeared to take in my music.'[25]

Carnegie's dinner the following evening was designed to mark the official end of the inauguration festivities for his eponymous concert hall. But already the New York critics had dubbed the celebrations 'Tchaikovsky week'. He had enjoyed as colossal a triumph as he had known anywhere; but the fortnight had exhausted him. As if the musical demands were not enough, his social schedule had been frenetic, and he had of course been subjected to a 'constant stream' of visitors, from journalists seeking his views on Wagner to would-be librettists offering him their manuscripts.

Despite it all, and the dread in which he had arrived, he was eventually sad to leave. Max, a German from Nizhny-Novgorod who serviced his hotel room, had turned it into 'a perfect haven, of a peace and comfort it is impossible to find in any hotel in Europe.' But his hosts had decided he should visit Niagara Falls. All the arrangements had been made for him by Ferdinand Mayer, a genial German who was the New York agent of Knabe, the piano manufacturers. Tchaikovsky seems to have had little say in the matter.

Early on the morning of 10 May, Mayer escorted the composer to the station, reassuring him that there would be two Russian-speaking admirers to help him change trains at Buffalo. Mayer had even organized some German speakers at his Niagara hotel, the Kaltenbach. On 11 May, communicating with his landau-driver largely by sign language, he visited both the American and Canadian sides of the Falls, and even plucked up the courage to don protective clothing and venture beneath them. After a long afternoon walk beside the boiling waters, and a leisurely evening meal, he caught the overnight train back to New York.

Now the entertaining became a real endurance test. With Damrosch leaving for Europe, Tchaikovsky was in the hands of the well-meaning but dull leading lights of the New York music scene: Edwin Hyde, president of the Philharmonic Society, and Mayer, who now wanted the composer to put his name to a testimonial for Knabe pianos. As politely as he could, Tchaikovsky declined, pleading that he had insufficient knowledge of other American pianos (and recording in his diary that he anyway preferred Steinways).[26] By 14 May, which held yet another dinner before his midnight departure for Baltimore, he was 'unconscionably tired'; on the train he slept 'well, but not well enough' before a morning rehearsal for an afternoon concert.

Lost in a world where only English was spoken, he was only too happy to be reunited with Adele aus der Ohe, who was again to be the soloist in his First Piano Concerto. Finding the Boston Festival Orchestra woefully underprepared, he abandoned the Third Suite for the Serenade for Strings, even though they had not rehearsed it as promised. His reception was not as rapturous as in New York, but the critics again wheeled out their superlatives. Knabe, the piano manufacturer, then gave him a hectic thirty-six-hour tour of the city and its musical institutions – not least his own factory – before helping him to pack and putting him on the train to Washington.

Tchaikovsky's one commitment in the US capital was a musical soirée that same evening at the Russian Embassy, one of whose senior diplomats played the piano part in his Trio and a Brahms piano quartet. Amid fellow-Russians he began to enjoy being fêted, and delayed his departure to Philadelphia by twenty-four hours to enjoy a tour of the sights with the Russian ambassador. That evening saw Tchaikovsky as relaxed as at any time on the tour, playing piano duets with the talented diplomat. The next day, 18 May, brought his final appearance in America as a conductor, repeating the Baltimore programme (with the same orchestra and soloist) in Philadelphia.

Again, to his irritation, the reviews concentrated as much on his physical appearance as on his musicianship. Although Tchaikovsky made an 'instantly favourable' impression, declared the *Daily Evening Telegraph*, he did not have 'the professional air which most people possibly expected.'

> He looks like a broker and clubman rather than an artist. He seems to be rising sixty, but is well preserved and active. He is of middle height, slim, erect, with silvery gray hair and beard, florid complexion, and small but piercing and expressive blue eyes – a self-contained and dignified personage, not without grace, but clearly giving no attention to stage niceties – altogether an attractive personality, if somewhat disconcerting to those who expected a more pronounced slavic type, such as Rubinstein. It was agreeable to see the way in which he assumed that a great audience had not assembled to do him personal honor, but to hear certain pieces of music in which he was merely concerned with the interpretation. He conveyed this idea without affectation, nor too much of brusqueness . . .[27]

Pre-empting any Philadelphian attempts at hospitality, Tchaikovsky went straight from the concert to the train back to New York, where one more musical engagement awaited him. Amid more visitors, autograph-signing, and finally agreeing to put his name to Knabe's pre-drafted testimonial, he was the guest of the Composers' Club in the Metropolitan Opera House for a programme of his songs and chamber music. 'I sat in the front row,' he recorded. 'They played the E flat minor quartet, the trio, sang romances (some of which were beautifully performed) etc. The programme was too long. In the middle of the concert, a Mr Smith read an address in my honour, to which I responded briefly in French. There was an ovation, of course.' One lady threw 'a gorgeous bouquet of roses which hit me full in the face.'[28]

Back at his hotel, Tchaikovsky shared two bottles of champagne with Reno and Mayer while packing for his departure. With his ship, the *Fürst Bismarck*, due to leave at 5 a.m., he had to be on board that evening. After saying his farewells to the hotel staff, and then to the 'dear American friends' who saw him to the quayside, he slept as badly as ever, waking early enough to go out on deck as the ship passed the Statue of Liberty. Below, in his cabin, was a model of the statue presented to him by the grateful piano maker, Knabe. One of Tchaikovsky's most cherished souvenirs, it still has pride of place in the Klin museum which was his last home.

As far as America was concerned, a 'genius' had been 'within our gates'. In a retrospective of Tchaikovsky's visit published on 24 May, when the composer was already three days out to sea, the *New York Herald* ranked him alongside Bismarck and Edison, Ibsen and Sarah Bernhardt, Tolstoy and Dvořák in its Top Ten 'men and women of genius now adorning the world.' Fretting that New York had failed to pay him adequate homage, the paper concluded that Tchaikovsky was 'a modest, unassuming man', even though 'no genius is unconscious of his genius'. What impression of New York would the genius be taking back to Europe, 'where his name is both a glory and a power'?[29]

At the time, the genius was more concerned with surviving his journey home. Tchaikovsky's diary entry for that same day is the shortest of his entire journey, reading simply: 'An appalling day! The weather is abysmal. The sea is raging. Seasickness. Vomited. The only thing I ate all day was an orange.'

He had paid handsomely for an upgrade to an officer's cabin; the $300 (1,500 francs) he was 'fleeced' merited three exclamation marks in his diary.[30] But the German liner, though newer and more luxurious than *Le Bretagne*, was 'not as smooth in motion'. After sleeping away most of the first few days, himself surprised to have lost interest in the sight of the sea, he hid himself in his cabin at all but meal-times, when he put up with the company of an affable German who all too clearly knew who he was. Also on board was a celebrated soprano of the day called Antonia Mielke, whom he did his best to avoid, but who usually managed to waylay him 'at least once a day' for a chat about the musical scene in Europe. In the ship's salon he was delighted to find not merely an elegant Steinway, but a decent music library containing some of his own works. Despite his commitment to the postponed double-bill of *Iolanta* and *The Nutcracker*, he makes mention of planning a new symphony during the voyage; but his ten stormy days at sea, passing through the English Channel to Heligoland and Cuxhaven, seem largely to have been spent dodging requests for a recital and vowing never to sail again. After a night in Berlin, Tchaikovsky finally arrived back in St Petersburg on 1 June.

Modest, who hosted his exultant reunion with Bob, reports that his brother was 'tired but elated', even 'radiant' after his triumphant progress through the New World. The composer himself told Ippolit that he was 'happy beyond words' to be back in his beloved homeland. A week later he was back at Maidanovo – 'more than ready', as he wrote to Nikolay, 'to get back to some serious work.'

First, however, there was some unfinished business to deal with. The last three months, during Tchaikovsky's prolonged absence abroad, had been the first time in more than a decade that his letters and diaries lacked any mention at all of his inseparable epistolary companion of fourteen years, Nadezhda von Meck. Internally, however, amid all else that he had been living through, the composer was still seething about the abrupt demise of their relationship. That much is clear from an extraordinary response he now unleashed in reply to a (lost) letter from Pakhulsky, giving full vent to the pent-up feelings he had harboured for the eight months and more during which his last letter to von Meck had gone unanswered.

I quite accept that Nadezhda Filaretovna is ill, weak, upset and still unable to write to me. Not for anything in the world would I wish her to suffer on my behalf. But I am hurt, distressed and, to be frank, deeply offended, not just that she has not written to me, but that she seems to have ceased altogether to take the slightest interest in me . . . Not once has she even used [you] to find out how I am managing, what is going on in my life. Every attempt I have made via you to re-establish regular relations in writing with N.F. has met with a merely polite response, presumably designed to preserve at least a shadow of the past . . . I wanted, I *needed* my relations with her not to change at all as a result of her decision to stop sending me money. Unfortunately, this has proved impossible, because her feelings towards me have obviously cooled. The result is that it looks as if I have stopped writing to her, have severed all relations with her, *because* I have been deprived of her financial support. This turn of events humiliates me in my own eyes, makes it intolerable for me to remember that I once did accept her subsidy, continually torments me and pains me beyond all measure.

The previous autumn, Tchaikovsky continues, he had re-read all von Meck's letters, and found it hard to believe that any illness, misfortune or financial difficulties could have so abruptly changed the powerful feelings contained in them. Yet he could not deny that her feelings did seem to have changed. 'Precisely because I never knew N.F. personally, she took on the form of an ideal person to me. I could never imagine such inconstancy in a demi-goddess. It seemed to me that the earth could crumble to pieces before N.F.'s feelings for me might change.' The fact that they had 'turns upside-down all my impressions of people, my very faith in the best of them. It shatters my peace of mind, poisons what happiness fate has allowed me.'

> Without meaning to, of course, she has treated me very cruelly. Never
> have I felt so humiliated, never has my pride been so wounded. Most
> painful of all is the fact that, because of her ill-health, I cannot share
> with her all these torments, for fear of upsetting her and making her
> worse. I cannot speak out, which might of itself have afforded me
> some relief.[31]

Tchaikovsky confessed that he might regret the letter – 'I just had to get some of this bitterness off my chest' – before enjoining Pakhulsky not to mention a word of it all, 'of course', to von Meck herself.

Despite a postscript asking him not to reply, Pakhulsky swiftly moved to reassure Tchaikovsky that von Meck's feelings towards him had not changed at all; she was simply ill, that was all, and still unable to write. 'So you must not ask why she has changed, because she has not.' Darkly, Pakhulsky hinted that his own relations with his mother-in-law had also changed during the intervening period: 'For this reason, it is not surprising that she does not wish to see me acting as an intermediary between the two of you.' He added further to Tchaikovsky's rage and bewilderment by returning his letter of 6 June, apparently to prevent any other member of the family seeing it and intervening with the matriarch on the composer's behalf. Tchaikovsky thus had no real way of knowing quite how von Meck now felt towards him, nor indeed if she was at all aware of his own bafflement and frustration.

With the return of his letter, all further contact ceased between Pakhulsky and Tchaikovsky, and thus between composer and patron. A remarkable fourteen-year affair, conducted from the safety of correspondence, was finally over; and both parties were to die without healing the wounds caused by the abruptness with which it had ended. More than once Tchaikovsky was to use the word 'betrayal' of his former benefactress, especially when it became clear that she had again, in fact, escaped bankruptcy. On his deathbed, by Modest's account (denied by others present), he was to curse her name. Equally striking (and more reliable) evidence of the strength of his feelings is contained in the postscript to a letter he wrote to Yurgenson some three months before his death, after again re-reading her letters:

Oh Nadezhda Filaretovna, you treacherous woman, why did you betray me?!! I am amazed at the fickleness of female infatuations. One might think, reading these letters, that fire would sooner turn to water than her subsidy cease. One might even wonder that I settled for so paltry a sum when she seemed ready to give me almost anything. Then, suddenly, farewell! Above all, I almost believed, really believed, that she had been ruined. But it turns out to have been something else altogether: merely female inconstancy![32]

Such, at the last, was the level of Tchaikovsky's own constancy – and indeed his gratitude for years of faith, support and encouragement which had not merely made him, in his own words, 'a free man', but had undoubtedly sponsored his rise to fame. It is of course impossible to know what Tchaikovsky might or might not have written without Nadezhda von Meck's support. But it is quite clear that he would have been drastically curtailed, at the height of his powers, in his freedom of choice and movement. She deserved much better of him.

Before leaving America, Tchaikovsky had written to Bob Davidov that the thought of their reunion seemed to him 'a fantastical, unattainable joy . . . I try to think of it as little as possible, so as to endure each day of torture without you.' That summer, as he worked on *Iolanta*, Bob was his regular house guest, along with a young cousin who had caught Tchaikovsky's fancy, Count Alexandr ('Sanya') Litke, and other languid young men who laughingly called themselves Tchaikovsky's 'Fourth Suite'.*

All twenty or thereabouts, they were past the age which most appealed to the composer's sexual inclinations. But Bob was fast becoming more than merely an object of adoration. He was an obsession with Tchaikovsky, and would remain so for the rest of his life. It appears that the pressure occasionally got too much for the young man; after one visit that summer, when Bob had insisted he was overdue elsewhere, his uncle was dismayed to learn via the family that he could in fact have stayed three more days. But Tchaikovsky was certainly a valued friend and mentor to his quixotic nephew. To his prediction that summer that he would eventually become 'either a writer-artist or a writer-philosopher', Bob replied that he felt more like an empty 'container', with no substance of his own. Tchaikovsky was quick to reassure him that he had

---

*Tchaikovsky composed three orchestral suites; the fourth, *Mozartiana*, Op. 61 (1887), was not so designated until after his death.

'a great deal of substance, only the container's contents are still scattered around in disarray . . . Relish your youth and learn to value time. Everything will work out. Farewell, my dear, good, darling beloved! My adorable little container!'[33]

Frolovskoye had been sold at a price Tchaikovsky could not afford; and Maidanovo, now a popular and crowded summer haven, was losing its charm. As Alexey searched for a new *dacha*, Tchaikovsky increasingly travelled to and from St Petersburg for reasons other than the merely professional. His letters to intimates mention frequent visits to the Zoological Gardens, near the Peter and Paul Fortress – a well-known meeting place, along with the garden squares off Nevsky Prospekt, for the capital's homosexual community. Bob, who was developing similar tastes, would often be with him; a 'musical joke' Tchaikovsky sent his nephew that summer, in the form of a winsome love song, includes references to three 'adorable' letters from Bob and 'all the fun we had' in the Zoological Gardens. In Bob's absence, Sanya Litke appears to have taken his place as the composer's escort on these forays. Litke is mentioned in Tchaikovsky's letters to Bob as his *'général de suite'*, which may also translate as procurer.

In the midst of this season of work and play came an incident which soured Tchaikovsky's summer and finally persuaded him to leave Maidanovo. He was in truth less upset than might have been expected by the disappearance from his bedroom table of the Joan of Arc watch given him by von Meck eleven years before, after he had written *The Maid of Orleans*. His natural sense of injustice was perhaps muted by his newly mixed feelings about his former patron. But he confessed himself bewildered by the identity and subsequent behaviour of the apparent culprit.

After an investigation which was the talk of the neighbourhood, the local police arrested the valet of one Novikov, his landlord's son, who confessed to the theft but refused to reveal what he had done with the watch. The youth implicated several other locals, who were questioned and released, then declared that he had given the watch to his master. When Novikov *fils* denied any role in the matter, the servant changed his story again. Persuaded by the police to confront the suspect in person, Tchaikovsky himself fared little better. Left alone with the boy, one Fedya, he was overcome by his 'sweet face' and 'winning smile' and promptly forgave him – at which Fedya rose from his knees and denied stealing the watch in the first place. To the composer's mounting distress, the police tried everything in their power to extract the truth – depriving the youth of food and water, making him drunk, and whipping him. But still his story changed from day to day, creating an impasse.

Tchaikovsky was appalled by the local obsession with the case, which was gaining him unwelcome notoriety – as well as costing him a considerable amount of money, as the person who had brought the charges. So he instructed the police to call off their investigation. The true culprit was never identified, nor was the watch ever found. But the entire episode quite unnerved the composer, who fled to his brother Nikolay's estate at Ukolovo, then moved on to a Kamenka still in mourning for Sasha. After four days in Moscow, he was back at Maidanovo on 14 September. Despite an acute shortage of cash, accentuated by the police investigation and his subsequent travels, he turned down an invitation to return to the United States; the money on offer was barely one-third of his fees that spring. There was no alternative but to stay at home for the foreseeable future, and get back to work.

The invalid Laroche's presence at Maidanovo was a mixed blessing, further draining his resources but providing welcome diversion in the otherwise lonely evenings, which the two old friends passed in piano duets and reading aloud. By day Tchaikovsky corrected the proofs of the full score of *The Queen of Spades*, completed the sketches of *Iolanta*, and began to score a new orchestral ballad.

It was in 1883 that Tchaikovsky had first read the Danish writer Henrik Hertz's one-act play *King René's Daughter*, adapted from a Hans Christian Anderson story about the blind princess Iolanta, daughter of the King of Anjou, whose love for the young Count Vaudemont eventually wins her back the sight she never knew she lacked. Its 'poetical qualities, originality and abundance of lyrical moments', he said in a rare newspaper interview in 1892, had made Tchaikovsky vow that he would one day set it to music – a promise he took almost a decade to keep.[34] In May 1888 he attended a rare performance of the play at the Maly Theatre in Moscow, taking the chance to commend its potential as an operatic vehicle to Vsevolozhsky. But the Director of the Imperial Theatres was more interested, it seems, in a new ballet, *The Nutcracker*, to his own libretto based on Dumas *père*'s version of E.T.A. Hoffmann's *Nussknacker und Mausekönig* (*The Nutcracker and the Mouse-King*).

The resultant agreement on an unusual double-bill – a one-act opera to be followed by a two-act ballet – appears to have been something of a *quid pro quo* for both parties. The subtext of Tchaikovsky's stuttering progress on both projects over the next two years is simple: he was far more interested in the opera. With some justice, he could not see the theatrical appeal of Hoffmann's Christmas fable, which lacked the thematic strength of *The Sleeping Beauty*; as a children's story, moreover, it inevitably gave the better parts to the lesser characters, the adults, thus abandoning even much pretence at narrative drama. His initial design was to write *The Nutcracker* first, to get it out of the way before putting his real energies into the far more interesting task of converting *King René's Daughter* into *Iolanta*.*

Despite constant interruptions, the sketches of *The Nutcracker* begun in France the previous year were completed at Maidanovo in less than a month, during June 1892. But the instrumentation would have to wait another six months. On 22 July Tchaikovsky set *The Nutcracker* aside and began work on *Iolanta*, to a libretto by Modest. But the stream of family visits that summer, punctuated by excursions to the capital, saw him fail to complete the initial sketches until 16 September – slow work by Tchaikovsky's standards, which had him fretting about his hesitant progress and again wondering whether his powers were failing. He was also obliged, throughout that autumn, to keep changing musical horses. Before he could orchestrate either work in the double-bill, he was forced to finish the scoring of his symphonic ballad, *The Voevoda* (Op. 78), due for its first performance in Moscow on 18 November.

Tchaikovsky's turbulent mood that autumn is evident from the dramatic events of that evening, when he attempted to destroy a piece he had disowned even before its first public airing. Based on Pushkin's translation of a ballad by Adam Mickiewicz, *The Voevoda* had been sketched in Tiflis during those three troubled weeks when sundry local inconveniences, aggravated by worries about Bob in St Petersburg, were capped by the receipt of that fateful final letter from von Meck.

The original poem tells of a Polish general who returns home from war to find his young wife in the arms of a former lover; he orders his servant to shoot them both, but the servant chooses instead to shoot his master. Into this grim symphonic programme, Tchaikovsky poured all his gloom and bitterness about his rejection by his once beloved patron. Come its first performance, he had already developed reservations about the piece, which he conducted with little conviction.

On returning backstage, despite an enthusiastic enough response from the audience, he began to tear up his own score and demanded that the

---

*Gilbert and Sullivan's operetta of the same name, a tale of British peers and fairies, is not even a distant relation. Hertz's play had been staged in London in 1880, under the title *Iolanthe*, as a vehicle for Ellen Terry and Henry Irving (who owned the rights to the translation). Fearful of copyright problems, the operetta was called *Perola* (as was its main character) while D'Oyly Carte negotiated with Irving during rehearsals. Only at the final run-through, before the opening at the Savoy Theatre on 25 November 1882, did Sullivan tell the cast that its name would be changed to *Iolanthe*.

orchestral parts be gathered together and brought to him immediately. Seeing that he intended to destroy them, too, Ziloti took his life in his hands and intervened, arguing that his own role of concert organizer prevented him agreeing to the composer's request. In the face of Tchaikovsky's rage, deflected as the first-night visitors began to arrive in his dressing-room, Ziloti had the orchestral parts secretly taken to his own apartment. Tchaikovsky destroyed his own copy of the score the following day; but the argument between them was never resumed. Ziloti held on to the orchestral parts, from which he reconstructed this darkly powerful piece after the composer's death.

This drama came two nights after the first Moscow performance of *The Queen of Spades*, on 16 November 1891, had seen this masterwork begin to receive its due, with the critics far more respectful than at the St Petersburg première twelve months earlier. But nothing could raise Tchaikovsky's spirits as he completed the scoring of *Iolanta* at Maidanovo, then travelled via St Petersburg to Estonia, to visit Anatoly – who had been transferred from Tiflis as deputy governor of Revel, near Nizhny-Novgorod.

Apart from his continuing angst over von Meck, which had clearly soured his feelings for *The Voevoda*, he appears to have embarked around this time on the growing crisis of confidence about Bob which would eventually result in the sublime agonies of the *Pathétique*. 'You are constantly in my thoughts,' he wrote to his nephew from Kamenka, where he spent a subdued Christmas after conducting a concert of his work in Kiev. 'Through every dark sensation, whether grief, melancholy or anguish, whatever the cloud on my mental horizon, comes a piercing ray of light with the thought that you exist, and that I shall soon see you again.'

Amid the myriad tasks attendant on a public figure of international standing, Tchaikovsky now wrote few letters beyond obligatory professional notes. Only for Bob, in von Meck's absence, did he take the time to pour out his inmost feelings. Gradually it became a source of increasing grief to the composer that his nephew did not feel able to reply in similarly effusive terms. Fond though he was of his uncle, Bob was at a different stage of life, with his own interests and enthusiasms, and his own circle of friends his own age.

As a result, though Bob cannot be blamed for it, Tchaikovsky's main preoccupation in the coming months was an acutely painful sense of unrequited love, further darkened by unthinkable sexual feelings for his nephew. As he prepared to boost his funds with yet another European conducting excursion, all his thoughts were for Bob, of whom he now asked 'an enormous favour'. At Kamenka he had long been captivated by a group portrait of the Davidov family, taken in Kiev some ten years before. 'You are divinely enchanting in this photograph . . . It reminds me of one of the most delectable seasons of your bloom. So I want a big print, enlarged twenty times, of you . . . This is my *idée fixe*.'[35]

Within a few days of New Year 1892 Tchaikovsky was in Warsaw, conducting his Violin Concerto, Third Suite, *Capriccio Italien* and *Sérénade mélancolique*, en route via Berlin to Hamburg, where he was due to preside over a first performance of *Eugene Onegin*. With only one rehearsal allocated, and the opera to be sung in German, he soon decided to withdraw – handing over the baton to the local conductor, a man 'of *genius*, with a burning desire to conduct the first performance'. This was the young Gustav Mahler, who gave a 'positively superb' rendering – alas, to an indifferent response.

In a letter to his sister Justine, Mahler described Tchaikovsky as 'an elderly gentleman, very likeable, with elegant manners, who seems quite rich.'[36] If Tchaikovsky would scarcely have recognized himself in this portrait, it is typical of many of the period, which stress his elegant 'French' manners, gentlemanly bearing and prosperous appearance. 'He is a distinguished-looking man,' in one American verdict, 'looking more like a wealthy merchant or a United States senator than a musician.'[37] To his contemporaries, such as Auer, he had 'the personality and manners of a French marquis of the eighteenth century.'[38]

From Warsaw, the 'French marquis' wrote to Kolya Konradi that his longing for his Russian 'homeland' was becoming unbearable. 'But I don't have to suffer too much longer, and besides I should be able to enjoy myself in Paris.' Even this thought proved optimistic. He was in the French capital on the twenty-first, with the reliable Sapelnikov for company, but all the familiar attractions of the Café de la Paix and his other homosexual haunts could not console him. Ziloti too was in town, even staying in the same hotel, but neither of them could dispel Tchaikovsky's pervasive gloom. They took him to the Folies Bergères – not the most obvious way to cheer this particular traveller – and tried to wean him off Zola's new novel, *La Bête humaine*, which was scarcely calculated to raise his spirits. So low did they sink that he abruptly cancelled concert engagements ten days hence in Amsterdam and The Hague, and went straight home. After a restorative week with Bob in St Petersburg, chaperoned by Modest and Kolya, he was back at Maidanovo on 10 February to start orchestrating *The Nutcracker*.

As house guest and companion he was now joined by Vladimir Napravnik, son of the conductor-composer Eduard. Over four weeks sharing Tchaikovsky's rural solitude, Napravnik *fils* formed a vivid portrait of the day-to-day life of the man Kashkin liked to call 'the Hermit of Klin'.

Life at Maidanovo followed a strict daily timetable. At 8 a.m. precisely Alexey awoke me. When I arrived at 8.30 for morning tea my host was already seated at the table, a book in his hand, listening to the daily bulletin of his foreman, Andrey, who would give him a weather report – what the temperature was, whether it was windy, whether the sun was shining, and so on. In fact, the weather always turned out to be the complete opposite of whatever he said. After this [Tchaikovsky] would order lunch and supper. Pyotr Ilyich loved Russian cooking above all else, especially cabbage soup with kasha, bortsch, sauerkraut, and all kinds of fish. Once the cook had been dismissed, he would sink into a 'stubborn' silence and finish his tea while reading his book or that morning's letters.

At 9 a.m. we got dressed, put on felt boots, and left the house together. P[yotr] I[lyich] would go straight over to greet the yard dog, always sitting there on a chain, and smother it in terms of endearment. During our morning walk I always noticed how affectionately he was greeted by everyone we met, for whom he would have a few affectionate words in return. At 10, when we returned home, P.I. at once sat down to work, composing without a break at the piano or his writing table. At 1 p.m. we reconvened in the dining-room for lunch, and told each other what we had managed to achieve that morning . . . From 2 to 3 p.m. P.I. always took a second walk alone, during which he thought through his compositions, noting down on the spot any ideas which came into his head. From 3 to 4 he would read. Tea was taken at 4, in silence, during which my host would continue his reading. After tea until 8.30 p.m. he worked, composing or writing letters. At 8.30 we would have supper.

By day, as the boy revised for his exams, the composer got on with scoring his ballet. In the evenings, after supper, they played piano duets. 'Pyotr Ilyich', recalled the young Napravnik, 'had a large library of piano duets.'

We played the classics, or the most recent contemporary composers: Grieg, Bruckner, Brahms (whose music had little to say to Tchaikovsky's soul). Of Russian composers: Borodin, Rimsky-Korsakov, Glazunov, Rubinstein, Arensky, Konyus (his *Children's Suite*, which Tchaikovsky liked very much), and my father's *The Demon*. Pyotr Ilyich would never allow his own works to be played either as piano solos or duets, and he never played them himself.[39]

The pair got on so well that Tchaikovsky took the boy with him at the end of the month to Moscow, where they 'caroused disgracefully' before proceeding reluctantly on to the capital, where the composer had conducting commitments. On 5 March he led a student orchestra in a programme of his own work. Two days later he conducted his *Romeo and Juliet* overture for the first time under the auspices of the St Petersburg Musical Society, whom he also treated to a sneak preview of his orchestral suite from *The Nutcracker*, although the ballet itself was not due to be premièred until later that year.

In his growing confusion over Bob, Tchaikovsky was drinking harder than ever, as is witnessed by no less a paragon of rectitude than Rimsky-Korsakov, who notes that Tchaikovsky's closer friendship with the publisher Mitrofan Belaev's circle, notably himself, Glazunov and Lyadov, dates from this period. 'Sitting around in restaurants till three in the morning . . . usually put the finishing touches to a day spent together. Tchaikovsky could drink a great deal of wine and yet keep his full powers, both physical and mental. Very few of us could keep up with him in this respect.'

With apparent generosity – strictly for public consumption, for he had already developed a jealous resentment of his rival's greater fame – the elderly Rimsky later acknowledged Tchaikovsky's victory over the 'Mighty Handful':

> At this time there begins to be noticeable a cooling off and even some-what inimical attitude towards the memory of the 'mighty *kuchka*' of Balakirev's period. On the contrary a worship of Tchaikovsky and a tendency towards eclecticism grow ever stronger. Nor could one help noticing the predilection (that sprang up then in our circle) for Italian-French music of the time of wig and farthingale, music introduced by Tchaikovsky in his *Pikovaya Dama* [*The Queen of Spades*] and *Iolanta*. By this time quite an accretion of new elements and young blood had accumulated in Belaev's circle. New times, new birds; new birds, new songs.[40]

After parting with Vladimir Napravnik, Tchaikovsky took Sanya Litke back to Maidanovo with him for the spring. As he continued scoring *The Nutcracker*, both impatiently awaited the arrival of Bob, who eventually turned up for two weeks, mostly spent revising with Litke for their graduation exams from the School of Jurisprudence. 'I am in ecstasies over the Russian spring!' wrote Tchaikovsky to Ziloti. Like all such idylls, however, it could not last long. Sasha's memorial service in St Petersburg in early April proved the prelude to a month between the capital and

Moscow, where Tchaikovsky had more conducting engagements (this time taking on Gounod's *Faust* and Anton Rubinstein's *The Demon* as well as his own *Eugene Onegin* for the private Pryanishnikov Opera). His moral support was also needed to see Modest through the first night of his latest theatrical flop, entitled *Symphony*.

Alexey had finally found them a new home – the best yet, a secluded *dacha* on the edge of Klin, with its own extensive gardens. But his new wife was about to give birth, and he begged his master not to return until he could restore some degree of normality. The composer's first sight of what was to prove his last home – now lovingly preserved as the nucleus of the Tchaikovsky Museum and Archive* – came in mid-May, when he stopped by en route to St Petersburg for the baptism of Alexey's new son. A week later he was ceremoniously installed, dealing with the proofs of *The Nutcracker* piano arrangement and the first published edition of the Festival Overture on the Danish national anthem (Op. 15). But he could never stay still for long. As soon as he had settled into the home he had always wanted, contrary to the last, Tchaikovsky's mind was back on the road.

In the previous two years, amid all his travels and copious woes, Tchaikovsky had composed *The Queen of Spades*, *Souvenir de Florence*, the double-bill of *Iolanta* and *The Nutcracker*, and the symphonic ballad *The Voevoda*. Over the next eighteen months he would manage merely one major symphony, one movement of a piano concerto, a set of eighteen piano pieces and six songs. At last there was some truth in his perennial complaints about 'slowing down'; although only fifty-one, he looked some twenty years older.

For all its gratifications, the strains of international fame were beginning to tell. On top of the steady stream of invitations to conduct (now others' work as much as his own), there were constant requests for his presence at concerts of his music, offers of overseas tributes from mere ovations to national honours, not to mention the interminable correspondence and proof-correcting attendant upon keeping his work before the public. Amid a growing mountain of paperwork – which for years he had relished, but now found merely dispiriting – he was dismayed by unwonted difficulties in transferring his ideas for a new symphony from his head to his manuscript paper. Physically, all these problems resulted in persistent 'catarrh of the stomach'. Never had he felt such an urge to leave it all behind, and allow himself to take an extended break.

*For descriptions of the house at Klin in 1893 and 1993, see pages 347–9 and 403–5 respectively.

For the good of his health, he decided to brave the ardours of Vichy, taking Bob along to sustain his spirits. Leaving Klin via St Petersburg on 9 June, intent on a good time in Paris, both were horrified to learn that Anatoly's wife, Praskovya, was proposing to join them. From his previous experience of her in Tiflis and beyond, the composer's feelings about his sister-in-law were at best equivocal; he had marked her down as a 'flighty', somewhat dangerous woman, impatient with her husband's failure to win a governorship, and bored with a marriage which had slumped beneath the humdrum. Far from supporting Anatoly's slow rise through the ranks of the civil service, regardless of where his duties took them, she now appeared to have walked out on him – at least temporarily – to seek amusement elsewhere.

Tchaikovsky himself was the first and obvious resort for 'Parasha', who had long nursed a soft spot for her brother-in-law – to which he himself remained perhaps wilfully blind. He had never forgiven her for Verinovsky's suicide. Bob, for his part, freely admitted that he had never been able to stand his aunt. 'I am very angry about this, and Bob is close to despair,' Tchaikovsky complained to Modest. 'She has poisoned whatever passing pleasures we had anticipated from the journey ahead. She will inhibit us unthinkably *in all respects.*'[41]

Hoping the family would be able to dissuade her, they proceeded via Berlin to Paris, where they had spent just three days, enjoying *Lohengrin* and *Manon* as well as the city's other familiar diversions, when their European idyll was duly shattered by Praskovya's arrival on 22 June. 'Hateful' was what Tchaikovsky called her in a letter to Modest the next day, on discovering that she proposed to spend the entire month with them, thus depriving him of the rare enough joy of having Bob to himself.[42] Nor did Praskovya help her cause by teasing her brother-in-law about his 'lavish expenditure' on clothes. 'In Paris he ordered far more clothes and hats than I did myself, and he had a special liking for expensive perfume.'[43]

Paris, according to Praskovya, was 'mad about him' at the time. 'His portrait was on display in all the music shops and brochures with a biographical sketch were on sale everywhere.' When she suggested attending a performance of his Fifth Symphony, Tchaikovsky insisted on going incognito. 'We therefore booked seats in the cheapest row, right under the roof, and he bought a huge pair of dark spectacles, in order not to be recognized.' He was still wearing them next day at the Café de Paris, where he insisted on sitting in a corner and talking in hushed tones.

> People at adjoining tables began to stare at us, among them a very well-known French composer with whom Pyotr Ilyich was

closely acquainted. My brother-in-law stared straight at the Frenchman without greeting him. At first the Frenchman seemed to be at a loss as to how to act. In the end he came up to our table, saying, 'Excuse me, are you not Tchaikovsky?'

'No,' said my brother-in-law, 'I am Davidov.'

'What an extraordinary resemblance!'

'I know. We are closely related.'[44]

Within a few days, the jokes began to wear thin as an appalled Tchaikovsky thought he could see Praskovya falling in love with Bob, with whom she flirted outrageously. It was an action replay of their feud, back in Tiflis, over Verinovsky. Praskovya, for all her bubbling effusions about the fun they had in Paris, suddenly goes silent about the events that followed. As far as Tchaikovsky was concerned, there was nothing for it but to put up with her. And so this awkward ménage moved grimly on to Vichy, where they arrived on 24 June. Tchaikovsky, of course, loathed the place as much as he had sixteen years before. He had no time to himself, was depressed by the sight of chronic invalids on all sides, and hated the monotony of the strict health regime.

Soon after their arrival, however, they discovered that Bob too was in poor health, specifically threatened by obesity and diabetes. So the only option was to face three weeks making the best of a bad job, constantly trying to dodge Praskovya, bicycling by day and visiting the casino by night. 'I am very worried about Bob,' Tchaikovsky wrote to Anatoly. 'During this trip I seem, if it is possible, to have come to love him more than ever. All the same, I have begun to look to his future with concern, even alarm. His personality is very morbid, unbalanced, abnormal, reminding me in many respects of Tanya's.'[45]

He made no mention, of course, of Praskovya's misbehaviour, or his true feelings about her. Before the letter winged its way to her husband, however, Tchaikovsky and Bob were busy thwarting her plans to change her schedule and leave with them. With mighty sighs of relief, while still ruing what might have been, they left her behind in Vichy on 15 July and were back in St Petersburg on the 19th.

Four days later Tchaikovsky returned to Klin, in better shape physically if not spiritually. He faced two dull months of correcting proofs, arranging his ballet score, and other drudgery – not least amending an 'inept' four-hand transcription of *The Sleeping Beauty* by a young pianist, a cousin of Ziloti, named Sergey Rachmaninov. Through it all, his mind remained squarely on Bob, apparently the subject of renewed attentions from Apukhtin back in St Petersburg. With no house guests – only Zola's 'disappointing' new novel, *La Débâcle*, for company in the evenings –

Tchaikovsky slid back into almost terminal gloom. It was merely, he lied to Bob, a 'phase of melancholia,' accentuated by the threat of cholera to Modest and Kolya at Grankino, the distance of Anatoly's new posting, and the obsequies for Praskovya's uncle, Sergei Tretyakov.

Whatever his feelings for his sister-in-law, Tchaikovsky had always been laid low by deaths and funerals. His morbid dread of what he called 'death, that snub-nosed monster', whether his own or anyone else's, naturally closed in as more of his friends and colleagues were going to their graves. 'He had an uncommon dread of death and everything to do with it,' according to his friend Laroche, recalling a paranoia dating back to Tchaikovsky's Conservatoire years, when he was appalled to find himself living next door to an undertaker's. 'He feared anything that even hinted at death, so much so that one could not use any words like coffin, grave, funeral or so on in his presence.'[46] As events would soon show, it was around this time that the composer began to sense real premonitions of his own demise.

Nor was his gloom dispelled by the prospect awaiting him at the end of his summer of drudgery at Klin: yet another conducting trip to Europe, for which he left on 11 September. In Vienna, where he sensed 'Russophobia', his travels got off to a worse start than ever. In the adjacent hotel room he could only grind his teeth as the Italian composer Pietro Mascagni, still in his twenties, attracted lines of admirers far longer than his own. Then he found himself expected to perform in a converted restaurant, from which the tables and chairs had not yet been removed. Understandably, for once, Tchaikovsky walked out after two rehearsals. With Sapelnikov he fled to the Tyrolean castle of a close mutual friend, the pianist and composer Sophie Menter, where he spent two very happy weeks before moving on to Prague for the opening of *The Queen of Spades* on 12 October.

The scale of what proved another European triumph, with both press and public, goes unmentioned in his letters – perhaps because, outside Russia, public acclaim had now become the norm. As had his chronic homesickness, which saw him back in St Petersburg three days later, for a brief break with Bob before returning to Klin. The fortnight before he was due back in the capital, to prepare for the opening of the double-bill, was spent continuing to struggle with his new E flat symphony. Bewildered by his apparently failing powers, he returned to St Petersburg in time for the one hundredth performance on 8 November of *Eugene Onegin*.

There followed five weeks of anxiety and euphoria about *Iolanta* and *The Nutcracker* before the dress rehearsal, on 17 December, in the presence of the Tsar. 'His Majesty was delighted, inviting me to his box and showering me with compliments,' reported Tchaikovsky. 'Both the opera and the ballet were superbly staged, the ballet almost *too* magnificently . . . The sheer splendour was literally a sight for sore eyes . . .'[47] Both press and public, however, were not so easily impressed. He might have declared an interest, an opera-ballet of his own having been supplanted from the schedule by Tchaikovsky's, but Rimsky-Korsakov was not alone in considering *Iolanta* 'the weakest of all Tchaikovsky's compositions', with its 'shameless borrowings' and 'haphazard orchestration'. *Novoe Vremya* agreed, adjudging the opera 'well below his normal high standards', while *Birzhevye Vedomosti* spoke for the critical consensus by dismissing *The Nutcracker* as 'completely devoid of creativity'.[48]

He tried to shrug off the criticism, as usual, in letters to his family, but this time Tchaikovsky was mortified. He had endowed *Iolanta* with great charm, going to great pains (divined only by Laroche) to balance it, thematically and harmonically, with *The Nutcracker*; but the opera's qualities were quite lost, then as now, amid a curious fascination with the ballet – at once so musically inventive yet so dramatically empty. As with *The Sleeping Beauty*, Tchaikovsky was making a conscious attempt at raising ballet composition to new heights; and the critical consensus among posterity is that he succeeded – to the point where it is 'a cliché of criticism' that he 'made the ballet symphonic'.[49] Whatever its subsequent choreographic fortunes, *The Nutcracker*'s ceaselessly fertile score has been the main reason behind its survival – without the opera with which Tchaikovsky had so carefully balanced it – as the indestructibly popular Christmas confection it remains to this day.*

The 'Fourth Suite' were very supportive, presenting him with a group photograph taken in an attempt to cheer him up. But Tchaikovsky was inconsolable. As another New Year found him in low spirits, he reneged on promises to attend the German premières of *Iolanta* in Hamburg and Schwerin, pleading the need for 'a rest, probably in Nice' before facing more conducting commitments back in Odessa.

From Berlin, he chose rather to divert via Basle to the nearby French town of Montbéliard, where he had long had an appointment which he now approached 'with dread . . . almost as if I were journeying into the realm of death, of people who have long since made their exit from the stage.'[50]

The previous March, Tchaikovsky had been pleasantly surprised to receive a letter from his old governess, Fanny Dürbach, whom he had long presumed dead. Forty-four years since he had last seen her, he

---

*A rare revival of the double-bill at the 1992 Edinburgh Festival, with Opera North's David Lloyd-Jones policing strict adherence to the composer's original intentions, showed just how far the opera can in fact outshine the ballet.

had promised Fanny that he would try to find time to visit her during his next trip to France.

Amid the ensuing correspondence, Fanny had confessed that it was her present pupils who had encouraged her to write to him after all these years. She had gossiped about bygone days, and chided her former pupil for calling himself 'old': 'Leave that privilege to one who has earned it through length of service.' Addressing him as 'Monsieur Tchaikovsky', she promised that she would not receive him as 'my dear little boy of days long ago', but would be sure to 'address you with all those titles conferred by your renown.' Touchingly, her last letter before his arrival had closed: 'In anticipation of my meeting with the great M. Tchaikovsky, I kiss my dear little Pierre, whom I love and shall always love with all my heart.'

Characteristically, Tchaikovsky had expected the worst: that Fanny would be 'unrecognizably old', a 'shadow' of the woman to whom he had once been so devoted. But he was pleasantly surprised to find her 'remarkably little changed . . .'

> I had very much feared tears, scenes etc – but there was no such thing. She received me with joy, tenderness and perfect simplicity, much as if it was merely a year or so since we had last seen each other. At once I realized why both our parents, and all of us, had loved her so much. She is an unusually sympathetic, down-to-earth and intelligent woman who exudes virtue and probity.[51]

Fanny stunned Tchaikovsky by producing his old exercise books and letters – 'and, most interesting of all, some sweet letters from Mama'. Himself contentedly nostalgia-prone, he evidently let Fanny lead him a merry dance down Memory Lane. 'Words cannot do justice to the sweet and magical feelings which ran through me as I listened to her memories,' he wrote to his brother Nikolay, Fanny's other charge. 'The past returned so clearly, in such perfect detail, that it seemed I was breathing the very air of our home at Votkinsk . . . I grew so carried away that at times it became bitter-sweet, and both of us had to fight long and hard to hold back tears . . .'[52]

Tchaikovsky spent five hours with his former governess that afternoon, and returned for the whole of the following day – apart from the evening, when she sent him back to his hotel for dinner, protesting that the table she shared with her sister was 'too modest' for him. He even agreed to let her show him off to some friends and relatives, without protest, and parted with her very fondly, 'exchanging kisses and promising to return.' For all the delight afforded him by the visit – and Fanny's subsequent urgings that he should retire to Montbéliard, so that she could look after him again – it was a promise Tchaikovsky would not live to keep.

In the first of many subsequent letters to her former charge, complimenting him on his triumph later that month in Brussels, Fanny was bold enough to express disappointment that her 'little Pushkin' had become a composer rather than a poet.

> But I bless God, nevertheless, for your successes, and for granting you the earthly reward your talents deserve. How many gifted people are not recognized in their own lifetime!

Fanny spoke a deeper truth than she could know. Tchaikovsky was indeed at the height of his fame – and, for all his own doubts, at the height of his powers. At the age of only fifty-two, he was on the verge of writing the greatest of all his works. But he had less than a year to live.

# PART VI

---

## *1892–93*
## 'THE SNUB-NOSED MONSTER'

*To be Tchaikovsky, and to die of cholera . . . this
is too cruel a joke of Fate! Many years will go by,
and this case of cholera will be remembered . . .*

*NOVOSTI I BIRZHEVAYA GAZETA,*
St Petersburg, 11 November 1893

# CHAPTER XVI

## 'Let them guess'

IN THE SPRING OF 1892, THE MUSICAL SOCIETY OF CAMBRIDGE UNIVERSITY decided that its fiftieth anniversary the following year was worthy of lavish celebration. Encouraged by its success in attracting Dvořák to Cambridge that year, the society conceived an ambitious plan to invite the two most distinguished composers alive, Brahms and Verdi, to come to Cambridge in June 1893 to receive honorary doctorates and conduct their own work in a commemorative concert.

Cambridge's trump card was Sir Charles Villiers Stanford, Professor of Music at the university, conductor of the CUMS orchestra and himself an eminent composer of the day, on nodding terms with most of his great European contemporaries. To the society's dismay, however, Stanford's informal approach to Brahms proved unpromising. On 23 February 1892 Brahms replied that he was enormously grateful for the great honour done him by the university; at the height of summer, however, he would much prefer to be 'walking beside some lovely Italian lake'. He suggested that Stanford skip the degree ceremony and join him.

If Brahms, at the age of fifty-eight, could not be tempted into the arduous journey to England, what hope was there of Verdi, now almost eighty? By the time he too had refused – 'at my advanced age, I dare not undertake so long a journey' – it was November, and the celebrations were barely six months away. With Dvořák already ticked off their list, the

Society cast around desperately for international musicians distinguished enough to grace their jubilee, yet not too grand to turn up.

The next most popular composer of the day was Charles Gounod, a particular favourite of the public (if almost entirely on the strength of his opera *Faust*) and indeed of Queen Victoria herself. Seven years before, however, Gounod had been unlucky enough to lose an absurd libel suit to a litigious society beauty, Mrs Georgina Weldon, a *chanteuse* for whom he had briefly left his wife in the early 1870s. Upon setting foot in Britain, Gounod would have been liable to Mrs Weldon for the huge sum of £10,000 plus £1,640 costs, on pain of summary imprisonment. To the Frenchman, this was too high a price to pay even for a Cambridge doctorate. So Stanford and his committee were again obliged to look elsewhere.

Having already honoured most of the leading British composers – Sullivan, Parry, Mackenzie and Stanford himself – they thought next of Anton Rubinstein and Edvard Grieg, in that order. Rubinstein's international reputation stood higher than that of the composer of *Peer Gynt*, let alone his rising compatriot Tchaikovsky. Unfortunately, however, Rubinstein had recently published his memoirs, one sentence of which had not gone down at all well in Cambridge:

> The relative knowledge of music among the Germans, French and English, stated arithmetically, would be somewhat as follows: of the German people, at least 50% understand music; of the French, only 16%; while among the English – the least musical of people – not more than 2% can be discovered who have any knowledge of music. Even the Americans have a higher appreciation of music than that.[1]

With Rubinstein self-disqualified, December 1892 found Cambridge with only Grieg's name pencilled in for its festivities the following June. Having failed to keep secret the news of Brahms's and Verdi's refusals, the CUMS felt obliged to add more ballast to its list with the name of Saint-Saëns, the only other living composer whose reputation came within reach of Grieg's. By so doing, however, the Society presented itself with a political dilemma. In an age of intense national consciousness around Europe, Brahms and Verdi might have been thought to transcend their national identities; but the lesser Saint-Saëns was so distinctively French that he would have to be balanced by a German. As the episode's definitive historian, Gerald Norris, summed up: 'Had the choice been, say, Grieg and Dvořák, the problem would not have arisen, for honouring, in effect, Norway and Bohemia would have offended nobody. But France and Germany were major powers, which was a different matter.'[2]

Bruckner and Richard Strauss were as yet unknown in England, and Mahler merely a débutant conductor of opera at Covent Garden. Enter Max Bruch – then placed 'midway between Brahms and the other composers of their country' in J.A. Fuller-Maitland's *Masters of German Music*. With Brahms's Germany accounted for, the committee felt the need to represent Verdi's Italy. None of Puccini's operas having yet been performed in England, the lucky name added to the Cambridge list was that of the composer Arrigo Boito, today better known as Verdi's librettist.

Grieg, Saint-Saëns, Bruch, Boito . . . a fifth name was needed, Cambridge decided, to balance the conspicuously absent weight of Brahms and Verdi. Having chosen German and Italian substitutes, the obvious answer was a Russian to compensate for Rubinstein's unfortunate outspokenness. Though none of his symphonies had yet been performed in England – where the symphony was still regarded as the ultimate criterion of a composer's *gravitas* – there was one other Russian composer who had made two concert visits to London, with reasonably positive results. He was, moreover, a former pupil of Rubinstein's: P.I. Tchaikovsky.

It was sixteen years since the London première of the First Piano Concerto, performed by the (German-born) English pianist Edward Dannreuther, who had since proved a noble champion of Tchaikovsky in Britain. Also something of a musicologist, Dannreuther had written the entry on Tchaikovsky in the first edition of *Grove's Dictionary of Music and Musicians*:

> His compositions, more or less, bear the impress of the Slavonic temperament – fiery exaltation on a basis of languid melancholy. He is fond of huge and fantastic outlines, of bold modulations and strongly marked rhythms, of subtle melodic turns and exuberant figuration, and he delights in gorgeous effects of orchestration. His music everywhere makes the impression of genuine spontaneous originality.[3]

The speed with with Cambridge received replies from its new list of putative graduands is a handsome tribute to the European postal service of the day. The formal invitations having been sent out by the university's vice-chancellor, Dr John Peile, on 12 December, the first reply (from Saint-Saëns in Paris) was dated 13 December, the second (from Bruch in Berlin) 14 December, the third (from Boito in Genoa) 16 December. That same day Tchaikovsky wrote from St Petersburg:

> It would be difficult to put into writing how proud and happy I was to read the letter you were kind enough to send me. The supreme honour that the Academic Council of the University intends bestowing

on me is too great, too flattering for me not to be eager to come, at the time you mentioned, to receive it personally from you. I therefore take pleasure in telling you that, if the good Lord grants me life and health, I shall be coming to Cambridge during the first fortnight in June.[4]

It was proving a heady autumn for Tchaikovsky, who was at the time in St Petersburg, preparing for the première of his double-bill, *Iolanta* and *The Nutcracker*. That month also saw him beat Bruch and the Belgian composer Peter Benoit to election as a corresponding member of the French Académie des Beaux-Arts, taking thirty-two out of the thirty-five votes cast, thus becoming only the second Russian ever to be accorded that honour. His acceptance of the Cambridge invitation arrived in England on 19 December, and Grieg's (from Leipzig, where his invitation had been forwarded from Norway) on Christmas Eve. But still Stanford had problems.

Saint-Saëns wrote that he was due to be in Chicago that week. Could the Cambridge ceremony possibly be brought forward to May? Bruch, meanwhile, was sufficiently forward to ask if he could publicly announce his Cambridge doctorate in Germany.* There remained, moreover, the even more complex politics of getting the five composers to agree on a concert programme of one piece by each, which they would conduct themselves.

Grieg and Bruch proved plain sailing, the former opting for the *Peer Gynt* Suite No. 1, and the latter the Banquet Scene from *Odysseus*. Asked for something from his *Nerone*, Boito preferred to offer the prologue to *Mefistofele*. Having agreed to that, Stanford found himself in difficulties with Saint-Saëns, whose Chicago engagement had conveniently fallen through. Pretending that he had cancelled Chicago, when in fact Chicago had cancelled him, the Frenchman was not best pleased to be told that his setting of Psalm 18 would not be suitable, there being two choral works already scheduled. It was 'unfortunate', he wrote to Stanford, that 'M. Boito has written nothing other than *Mefistofele*, and that I should therefore be . . . forced to let him produce the biggest and most impressive musical effect of the concert.' He proposed his Fourth Piano Concerto, with himself as soloist, for fear that he would otherwise be confined to 'a diminished role' in the proceedings. Poor Stanford was obliged to reply that the concerto would be far too long, after which a protracted

---

*Bruch seems to have gone ahead regardless, as a week later Brahms wrote to their mutual publisher: 'Should we congratulate him? The hat is on another head! Between us, it was also offered to me and Verdi; the latter cannot make the journey because of his great age, and I because of the tawdriness of the honour.'[5]

correspondence finally whittled down Saint-Saëns' contribution to *Africa*, his concert fantasy for piano and orchestra.

Stanford's original letter to Tchaikovsky, sent at the same time as the others, offered him the choice of a piece for choir and orchestra, for soloist and orchestra, or for orchestra alone – perhaps the First Piano Concerto? While liaising with the other four composers, Stanford received no reply from Tchaikovsky, who was by now on his travels again; so he unilaterally announced the piano concerto, informing the composer in a letter sent to him c/o Yurgenson in Moscow.

But by now Tchaikovsky was en route from Europe to Russia, and his mail was not being forwarded. So three more weeks passed without any word from him, during which Stanford was persuaded to add a piece of his own to the programme. Another letter dated 8 February informed Tchaikovsky of the entire programme and rehearsal schedule, adding that Saint-Saëns' final choice ruled out the piano concerto. Could he offer an orchestral work, perhaps the Serenade for Strings?

Two more weeks passed before a reply from Tchaikovsky finally arrived. Postmarked Klin and dated 17 February, it proposed *Francesca da Rimini*. Described by Tchaikovsky as 'the work I prefer above all others I've written in this genre', it had yet to be performed in England. Almost another month elapsed before he replied to a further enquiry from Stanford about the forces required for *Francesca*. Again apologizing for his 'nomadic' way of life, he asked for three extra musicians to play cor anglais, fourth trumpet and tam-tam. The letter arrived in Cambridge on 11 March. In the month between these two letters, the composer had embarked upon his last and, to many, his greatest work: his Sixth Symphony, the *Pathétique*.

Tchaikovsky had seen in the New Year of 1893, the last of his life, alone. After his visit to Fanny Dürbach he had relaxed in Paris for a few days before moving on to Brussels, where on 14 January he conducted his Third Suite, First Piano Concerto, *Nutcracker* suite, *1812 Overture* and two movements from the Serenade for Strings to a wildly enthusiastic reception. There was time for a few more days in Paris before he was due back in Russia, this time at Odessa, the leadership of whose branch of the Russian Musical Society met him off the train on 24 January. Amid the crowd gathered to greet him, the visiting celebrity was relieved to see the friendly faces of Sapelnikov and Sophie Menter, for the next two weeks were to prove frenetic. In Odessa he was fêted and lionized as never before in Russia. 'I've never known anything like it,' he wrote to his cousin, Anna Merkling. 'I am honoured here like some great man, almost like a saviour of my fatherland, and tugged in all directions at once, to the point where I can scarcely breathe.' In those two weeks he 'conducted five concerts, led countless rehearsals, ate a mass of dinners and suppers in my honour. All this has left me utterly exhausted . . .'[6] At the end of his first concert, several of his works had to be repeated four times, after which there was a standing ovation, with ladies waving their handkerchieves and gentlemen their hats, while one by one the orchestra kissed the composer-conductor's hand.

His every move was reported at length in the Odessa newspapers, which raved about his concerts and the production of *The Queen of Spades* mounted to coincide with his presence. His hotel room was besieged not just with autograph hunters, but proud parents keen for him to assess the musical talents of their offspring. There was indeed one potential prodigy, a 'small boy in a velvet suit' named Konstantin Dumchev. 'Pyotr Ilyich was very charming to me,' Dumchev later recalled. 'He made me promise to visit him every day, to take tea with him. And so every morning around 9 a.m. I turned up at the Northern Hotel and enjoyed a long chat with him.'[7] It was also during this stay in Odessa that Tchaikovsky sat for the only portrait ever painted of him from life. In sittings snatched between rehearsals, performances and social commitments he sat for the artist Nikolay Kuznetsov, whose achievement in capturing the mature composer's sheer intensity, both intellectual and emotional, was said by Modest to be a very good likeness, especially capturing his brother's 'tragic streak'. It is now part of the permanent collection of the Tretyakov Gallery in Moscow.

Physically exhausted but spiritually refreshed by his success in Odessa, Tchaikovsky returned to Klin in mid-February in inspirational mood. To Anatoly he wrote of his latest new project in exultant tones: 'It seems that the best of all my works is coming forth from me.'[8] Next day he gave a detailed description of the new symphony to Bob, to whom it was dedicated:

> While on my travels I had an idea for another symphony – a pro-
> gramme work this time, but its programme will remain a conundrum
> to everyone. Let them guess at it. But the symphony will be called
> 'Programme Symphony' (No. 6) . . . This programme is imbued with
> subjectivity. During my journey, while composing it in my thoughts,
> I often wept a great deal. Then, after returning, I began writing drafts,
> and the work was as heated as it was rapid. In less than four days I
> completed the first movement, and the remaining movements were
> clearly outlined in my head. Half of the third movement is already
> finished. There will be much that is new in this symphony where
> form is concerned, one point being that the finale will not be a

loud allegro, but the reverse, a most unhurried adagio. You cannot imagine the bliss I feel after becoming convinced that time has not yet run out and that it is still possible to work. I may of course be wrong here, but I suspect that I am not.[9]

Tchaikovsky's last and greatest symphony seems to have been germinating for more than four years. In 1889, less than a year after completing his Fifth Symphony, he had told his friend 'K.R.', the Grand Duke and poet, that he felt he had one more big symphony in him, which would prove the climacteric of his life and work. On the voyage back from America, he had begun to sketch notes; and it was probably then that he also roughed out a highly distinctive programme:

The underlying essence . . . of the symphony is *Life*. First part – all impulsive passion, confidence, thirst for activity. Must be short (the finale *death* – result of collapse). Second part love: third disappointments; fourth ends dying away (also short).[10]

In this we can recognize the outlines of the programme for what turned out to be the *Pathétique*. But first the composer had to go through a false start.

The previous May, at Klin, while working on the *Iolanta–Nutcracker* double-bill, Tchaikovsky had started sketching the final movement and finale of a Symphony in E flat. It was fully nine months since he had composed any new music; his time had been stolen by instrumentation, proof-reading and transcriptions, as it was again until October. By 4 November, however, the sketches of the entire symphony were finished. Again he had to set it aside, as he supervised the launch of *Iolanta* and *The Nutcracker* in St Petersburg. By the time he returned to his new symphony, his mood had changed, and he found himself disenchanted with it. To Bob he explained that it was written less from any 'creative need' than 'purely for the sake of writing something. There's nothing at all interesting or sympathetic in the entire piece. I've decided to put it aside and forget it.' Was he, he wondered aloud to his nephew, a spent force? Had his inspiration finally dried up? 'Perhaps,' he ventured, '*the subject* still has the potential to stir my inspiration.'

For all this pre-echo of the *Pathétique*, the failure of his new symphony left Tchaikovsky in a state of creative paralysis. But it only took a few words of reassurance from his beloved Bob, who professed himself 'disappointed' at the abandonment of any work by his uncle, for him to reconsider. The following month, he decided to convert his aborted symphony into a piano concerto, completing the first movement between

5 and 13 July. Then, adjudging it 'overlong', he decided the only way to save the piece was to issue it as a one-movement work for piano, an *allegro brillante*. If Taneyev didn't like it, he told Ziloti, he would destroy it.

His fears were well-founded. By the time Taneyev got around to expressing his reservations, however, Tchaikovsky had already promised the piece to the French pianist Louis-Joseph Diémer, head of piano studies at the Paris Conservatoire. So it escaped the flames.

While still ambivalent about the *allegro*, Tchaikovsky proceeded to sketch the remaining movements of a potential Third Piano Concerto from the second and fourth movements of his abandoned E flat symphony. So little conviction did he now feel about the work as a whole – all too obviously a symphony-turned-piano concerto – that he never orchestrated these latter movements. After his death the task was finished by Taneyev, who performed the 'authorized' *Allegro brillante* in St Petersburg on 19 January 1895, and the *ersatz* three-movement concerto in Moscow on 20 February 1896. Faithful to Tchaikovsky's apparent intentions, the works were published separately. That now classified as the Third Piano Concerto (Op. 75) remains the single-movement *Allegro*, while the other two movements took their place in the canon as Andante and Finale (Op. 79). Neither has found a secure niche in the repertoire – as is also true of the so-called Seventh Symphony, reconstructed from these and other sources by a Soviet music scholar, Semyon Bogatyryev, in the 1950s.

Tchaikovsky's visit to Fanny Dürbach had also, meanwhile, stirred memories which inform the Sixth Symphony. 'The past in all its detail was so vividly aroused in my memory that I seemed to be breathing the air of Votkinsk,' as he put it to Nikolay. 'I could hear our mother's voice . . .'[11] He had embarked upon the sketches on 16 February, the day before writing to Stanford in Cambridge and suggesting *Francesca da Rimini* for the degree ceremony that summer. They were finished by 5 April, when he put the work aside, planning to take up the orchestration on his return from Cambridge. Even a work as large and complex as the *Pathétique* had been drafted in just seven weeks, despite constant interruptions.

In late February he had travelled to Moscow to conduct a concert of his own works (including *Hamlet* and the Concert Fantasia, with Taneyev at the piano) and to call on his old friend Vladimir Shilovsky, who was dying of dropsy. After a visit to Anatoly, now deputy governor of Nizhny-Novgorod, he was back in Klin on 3 March to work on the symphony's March. This was completed before he was on the road again six days later, to a series of Moscow concerts via St Petersburg, where he was surprised to discover that his brother-in-law Lev planned to remarry. To the dismay of the entire Tchaikovsky clan, Lev's bride-to-be was a second cousin of Sasha's, Ekaterina Olkhovskaya. Unlike most other members of the family – too swift, in his words, to 'cast the first stone' – the composer quickly overcame his initial sense of shock at Lev's remarrying so soon after Sasha's death, and went out of his way to wish his brother-in-law well.

By 16 March he was back in Moscow to share the podium with Napravnik, himself conducting his *Nutcracker* suite, repeated two nights later, before moving on to Kharkov, to conduct an RMS concert of his own works comprising *The Tempest*, the Violin Concerto, the Second Symphony, the *1812 Overture* and some songs. The orchestra's deputy leader, a violinist named Isaak Bukinik, spoke of 'universal alarm' amid his colleagues at Tchaikovsky's 'eccentric' style of conducting:

> He did not hold the baton in the same way as most conductors: he gripped it not between his fingers but firmly in his fist. He raised it above his head, brought it down sharply on the first beat, raised it to his left shoulder on the second, to his right shoulder on the third, and raised it again on the fourth. The players were not accustomed to such a manner of conducting. Everyone looked around at each other, but the knowledge that the composer himself was conducting the piece we were about to play made us all quickly forget this initial moment of awkwardness . . .[12]

The concert heralded another triumphal progress, with the composer carried shoulder-high from the hall amid countless fanfares. Students from Kharkov University then harnessed themselves to his coach, in place of the horses, and pulled him back to his hotel amid scenes of wild adulation.

Back at Klin by 30 March, anxious to make up for lost time, Tchaikovsky sketched the symphony's finale, then the second movement. Within five days, the task was at last complete. On 5 April 1893, he inscribed at the end of his handwritten score: 'Oh Lord, I thank thee! Today I have completed the sketches in their entirety.'

The Sixth Symphony had thus been composed amid a whirlwind tour of triumphalist music-making. That same afternoon, by way of celebration, he dashed off a robust regimental march as a favour to a cousin, Andrey Petrovich Tchaikovsky, commanding officer of the 98th Yurevsky infantry regiment. And a week later, between 13 and 15 March, he finished a quartet for four solo voices and piano based on Mozart's C minor Fantasia for Piano, K.475.

Amid this furious burst of activity, Tchaikovsky gave himself a week off to see Bob and the 'Fourth Suite' in St Petersburg before getting back to work 'purely to make some money'. Between 19 April and 3 May, he produced the Eighteen Pieces for piano (Op. 72) to a commission from Yurgenson – more than a piece a day, in other words, many dedicated to acquaintances or their children. To Bob he called these his musical 'offspring'; aware that they showed signs of haste, the best he could hope was that these 'musical pancakes' had 'not turned out too badly'. But he moved straight on to writing the Six Romances (Op. 73), to verses sent him by a young Kiev poet, Daniil Rathaus. Their sombre mood seems to reflect the growing isolation he felt, whether alone at Klin or surrounded by too many people on his interminable travels.

In mid-May, after letting his fifty-third birthday pass without celebration, Tchaikovsky paid another brief visit to Anatoly in Nizhny-Novgorod before packing his trunks at Klin and setting off for a week in St Petersburg, en route to England. After this astonishing burst of creativity, he seems to have been in the mood to celebrate; Rimsky-Korsakov, Glazunov and others all testify to some hard drinking in the capital that week. On 25 May he set off for Cambridge.

On this, his last long trip across Europe, Tchaikovsky's ritual professions of homesickness become an index of how much he was missing Bob – so much so, in fact, that he again considered abandoning his journey and returning straight home. From Berlin, he wrote lavishly to Bob of his sufferings: 'This time I have pined away and suffered and wept more than ever, probably because I have been thinking too much about our journey together last year. It is certainly some kind of psychopathy . . .'[13] So distraught did Tchaikovsky become – unable, by his own account, either to eat or sleep – that he arrived in London in a state of virtual collapse. But the flow of letters to Bob carried straight on:

> I write to you with a sense of voluptuousness. The thought that this piece of paper will soon be in your hands, at home, fills me with joy and makes me weep . . . Is it not strange that I have chosen of my own free will to undergo this torture? What curious forces make me subject myself to these agonies? Several times during my journey yesterday I resolved to abandon the whole business and turn back home. But what a disgrace to run away for no good reason . . . I am suffering not only from an anguish beyond mere words (in my new symphony there is a passage that seems to me to express it well) but also from a hatred of strangers, from some vague, ill-defined dread, and heaven knows what else . . .[14]

Being back in London did little, of course, to dispel Tchaikovsky's gloom. He could find nothing to his liking in this 'disagreeable', even 'wretched' city: no *pissoirs* in the streets, nowhere to change money, not even a hat to fit him properly. 'To think that I must kick my heels here another fortnight! It seems like an eternity,' he complained to Bob. 'Never will I go anywhere again except for a large pile of money, and then for a maximum of three days only.'[15] His friend Grieg, he had learnt to his dismay, was too ill to make the journey. So his only consolation was the arrival of Saint-Saëns, his sometime dancing partner, who joined him in conducting a concert of their music with the Philharmonic Society on 1 June.

Before the concert Tchaikovsky was in 'an extremely agitated condition', according to Emile Hatzfeld, the English escort assigned him by Yurgenson's London agent.[16] Sir Alexander Mackenzie, the Scottish composer conjoined in both the London and the Cambridge celebrations, considered Tchaikovsky 'a spent man' whose 'weak voice, intense nervousness and exhaustion after rehearsal plainly indicated failing health.'[17] So worried did Mackenzie grow about his tense Russian colleague that he took him home to Regents Park for tea after the final rehearsal, at which the English conductor Henry Wood was 'staggered' when Tchaikovsky, 'failing to get the reckless Russian spirit he wanted in the *finale* of the Fourth Symphony, eventually obtained it by exclaiming "Vodka – more vodka!"'[18]

That evening – literally, in all likelihood, fortified by vodka – Tchaikovsky failed to find the entrance to the hall in which he had spent most of the day, presenting himself at the box office and asking for directions backstage. Because of his scant English – all he kept saying was 'Tchaikovsky' – there followed a brief charade in which the box-office manager thought this agitated stranger wanted tickets for the concert, and tried to explain that it was sold out. It was little wonder, by the time the composer finally ascended the podium, that the *Daily Chronicle*'s critic felt moved to venture beyond his musical brief: 'M. Tschaikowsky has somewhat altered in appearance since he last visited these shores. His hair is now quite white, but he wields the baton with undiminished spirit.'[19]

Of the Fourth Symphony, sixteen years old but never previously heard in England, the *Daily Telegraph*'s Joseph Bennett noted the 'evanescent excitement and more prolonged plaintiveness of Sclavonic music; the iteration and reiteration of short phrases with the monotonous regularity of an Eastern chant; and the phantastic passages of ornament, having an air of improvisation . . . Though its form be that of a Western classic, in manner and spirit it is of the East and of the race which last began to take its way along the route trodden by the march of empires.' In short, 'Sclavonic' music was not entirely to Bennett's taste, though it had 'lately taken such enormous strides' and 'seems destined to exert the highest influence upon music in general'.[20] Bennett and a consensus of his colleagues preferred Saint-Saëns' *Le Rouet d'Omphale* – which did not stop Tchaikovsky reporting to Modest, with some satisfaction, that his own work had been the better received.

George Bernard Shaw, who also reviewed the concert, was more interested in the chance of an assault on the directors of the Philharmonic, noting that a series of composer-conductors anxious to present their own works in the best possible light had wrung from the orchestra distinguished playing of a standard he had not heard all season. Of Tchaikovsky – that 'Byron de nos jours' – it was merely 'characteristic of him' to play the 'orchestral voluptuary'.

> The notablest merit of the symphony is its freedom from the frightful effeminacy of most modern works of the romantic school. It is worth remarking, too, considering the general prevalence in recent music of restless modulation for modulation's sake, that Tschaikowsky often sticks to the same key rather longer than the freshness of his melodic resources warrants. He also insists upon some of his conceits – for instance, that Kentish Fire interlude in the slow movement – more than they sound worth to me; but perhaps fresh young listeners with healthy appetites would not agree with me.[21]

Not due in Cambridge for ten days, Tchaikovsky found himself subjected to the kind of social whirl which merely accentuated his nervous anxieties. On the day after the concert, 2 June, he and Saint-Saëns were the guests of honour at an 'unbelievably chic and elegant' dinner given by the Philharmonic Society at the St Stephen's Club, Westminster: 'We sat down to table at 7 and rose at 11.30. (I am not exaggerating).'[22] He told the kindly Mackenzie, who walked him back to his hotel, that 'the fight for recognition had been a hard one . . . [everywhere] but in England.' To his new Scottish friend, who roved the streets of London with him until after 1 a.m., the 'amiable' Tchaikovsky, 'without discontent or bitterness . . . appeared melancholy and lonely, devoid of self-assertion.' He certainly gave 'no sign of the passion and force revealed in the music.'

Amid more concert-going – the pianist Diémer and the violinist Sarasate were also in town – Tchaikovsky took tea with the wife of the Russian ambassador, lunched with the Stanfords, and marvelled at the sheer scale of London. 'It makes Paris look like a village,' he told Modest. 'Walking in Regent Street and Hyde Park, one sees so many carriages, with such sumptuous, expensive accoutrements, that the eye is fairly dazzled.'[23] One man invited to most of the same functions, who saw

Tchaikovsky almost daily, was the celebrated baritone (and composer-conductor) Sir George Henschel:

> Though then on the uppermost rung of the ladder of fame, Tchaikovsky was even more inclined to intervals of melancholy than when I had last met him [in Moscow some fifteen years earlier]; indeed, one afternoon, during a talk about the old days in Petrograd and Moscow, and the many friends there who were no more, he suddenly got very depressed and, wondering what this world with all its life and strife was made for, expressed his own readiness at any moment to quit it.[24]

Tchaikovsky also visited Sir George's home (where he autographed Lady Henschel's fan), called on the composer Frederic Cowen, and was the centre of attention at receptions thrown by Francesco Berger, the secretary of the Philharmonic Society; the Stanfords; the painter Alma-Tadema at his fashionable Shepherds Bush salon; and the Italian singing teacher Alberto Visetti. There was scarcely a moment to himself. 'Life here is absolutely frantic,' he told Yurgenson. 'There isn't a minute's peace. The lunches and dinners are especially tedious. It's all so formal and long-drawn-out and dull that I grow almost numb with boredom. I'm so tired and homesick that I feel like running away. But there's nothing for it. I've got to sit out this torture until the end.'[25] 'It's a hideous life' he told Modest. 'There's not one enjoyable moment – only eternal anxiety, melancholy, fear, fatigue, ennui. But the hour of liberation is at hand . . .'[26]

After one rehearsal for the jubilee concert in London, at the Royal College of Music in Kensington Gore (now the Royal College of Organists), Tchaikovsky finally travelled to Cambridge on 12 June. At Liverpool Street station Herman Klein, music critic of *The Sunday Times*, was pleased to have secured an apartment to himself for the sixty-minute journey. Or so he thought. The train 'was actually moving,' Klein recalled, 'when the door opened and an elderly gentleman was unceremoniously lifted in, his luggage being bundled in after him by the porters.' It proved, for Klein at any rate, a happy meeting – 'one of the pleasantest hours I have ever spent in the company of a celebrated musician', during which Tchaikovsky 'chatted freely [in an improvised mélange of English, French and Italian] about music in Russia.'

> He thought the development of the past twenty-five years had been phenomenal. He attributed it, first, to the intense musical feeling of the people which was now coming to the surface; secondly, to the

extraordinary wealth and characteristic beauty of the national melodies or folk-songs; and, thirdly, to the splendid work done by the great teaching institutions of St Petersburg and Moscow . . .[27]

Tchaikovsky confessed himself unsure, according to Klein, whether to consider England an 'unmusical' nation, like his colleague Rubinstein: 'Sometimes I think one thing, sometimes another. But it is certain that you have audiences for music of every class, and it appears to me probable that before long the larger section of your public will support the best class only.' By the time they had discussed the failure of *Eugene Onegin* in England, which the critic explained away in terms of 'the inefficiency of the interpretation and the unsuitability of the locale', they had reached Cambridge. Klein got the carriage-driver to give the composer a conducted tour of the main sights before depositing him at the gates of Downing College, where he had been invited to stay as the guest of Frederic William Maitland, Professor of Law, a Russophile and keen amateur musician.

There was one last rehearsal before, that afternoon, Tchaikovsky conducted the first English performance of *Francesca da Rimini* at the gala concert in the Guildhall. 'Dr Tschaikowsky was rapturously applauded and recalled,' reported Klein the following Sunday.[28] The piece itself evidently caused some consternation among the audience, unaccustomed to such wild and whirling stuff. The *Cambridge Review*, for instance, found it 'hard to believe at certain moments that the composer's treatment of the orchestration can be legitimately styled music.' Saint-Saëns, looking back on the occasion some years later, described *Francesca da Rimini* as 'brimming with pungent flavours and coruscating Catherine Wheels of sound . . .'

> The gentlest and kindest of men has unleashed a terrifying hurricane, with as little pity for his interpreters and listeners as Satan for the damned. Such are his talent and colossal technique, however, that it is damnation and torture in which one can take pleasure.[29]

There was an interval before Stanford completed conducting the concert over whose planning he had taken such pains. The university boat races had even been put back half an hour, to prevent rowing fans leaving the concert at the interval – an 'act of homage', according to the *Daily Graphic*, which 'beautifully illustrated . . . the union of music and gymnastics, as conceived by Plato.'

The concert had proved a triumph for all concerned, notably Stanford, who felt duly relieved as he took Tchaikovsky over to Trinity College for tea. Having once met Turgenev, Stanford was struck by the lack of 'northern roughness' in his guest, who was 'as polished as a Frenchman in his manner, and had something of the Italian in his temperament . . . For all the belief he had in himself, he was to all appearances the acme of modesty.'[30] To the excited Maitland women, who fussed around the composer as he rested back at Downing before that evening's ceremonial dinner, Tchaikovsky was 'rather fat and getting bald . . . [with] blue eyes and a short white beard and moustache – this last curled up like a Prussian's.'*

At the dinner in King's College, he was pleased to find himself sitting between his American friend Walter Damrosch (who happened to be on vacation in England) and one of the most fascinating Cambridge men of the day, the physicist, social reformer and musician Sedley Taylor. He was also mightily relieved not to have to reply to the elegantly witty speech of welcome from the Provost of King's College, also President of the CUMS, Austen Leigh. For once Tchaikovsky was pleased to grant seniority – in age, if nothing else – to Saint-Saëns, who formally thanked their hosts on behalf of all the graduands.

There followed a *Conversazione* (or reception) in the Fitzwilliam Museum, at which the German-born conductor Wilhelm Ganz, who had long since settled in England, enjoyed a long conversation with his compatriot Bruch, then chatted with Saint-Saëns and Boito, before spotting Tchaikovsky standing forlornly alone. 'I went up and spoke to him. He was most affable. On my referring to the frequent performances of his works in London at that time, he said *Je ne demande pas mieux*.'' Among others who spoke to Tchaikovsky at the reception – one of several who considered the moment important enough for their memoirs – was the English composer Sir Frederick Bridge.

> [I] was charmed with his modest, quiet, little manner ('little' seems just to describe my meaning, and does not convey small in dignity or significance). It was difficult to associate this quiet personality, this lined face and thin hair, with the man who produced such a work as the '1812' . . . He disclosed none of his feelings to those who met him

---

*As Gerald Norris points out, this is the only memoir (or indeed photograph) to suggest that Tchaikovsky, even towards the end of his life, was 'fat' – let alone possessed of 'a Brahmsian girth or even a Schubertian *embonpoint*'. To the ten-year-old Stravinsky, who had spotted him six months earlier at the opera in St Petersburg, the composer had 'a corpulent back'. But, as Norris puts it, the 'birdlike' Stravinsky tended to see others 'through Lilliputian eyes'; to him, Aldous Huxley was 'a giant', Rachmaninov 'a six-and-a-half-foot-tall scowl', T.S. Eliot 'big, rather stolid and cumbrous' and Gershwin 'a tall man – taller than I am, anyway.'[3]

at Cambridge on that lovely day in June, and certainly he revealed to me only an engaging courtesy.[32]

Next morning, before the awards ceremony itself in the Senate House, Maitland's wife Florence and her sister Adeline helped Tchaikovsky on with his gown, pinned a rose in his buttonhole and took his photograph. Among other luminaries receiving honorary degrees that day were Lord Roberts of Kandahar, one of Queen Victoria's most decorated generals; Lord Herschell, the Lord Chancellor; Standish Hayes O'Grady and Julius Zupita, two renowned authorities on medieval literature, from Ireland and Germany respectively; and the colourful figure of Sir Takhtsinhji Bhaosinhji, Maharajah of Bhaonagar, who had been excused his doctor's cap to retain his customary head-dress, a ceremonial turban studded with gold, diamonds and precious stones. 'Dare I confess,' wrote Saint-Saëns of the Maharajah, 'that being the enemy of the commonplace, and of the neuter-tints of our modern garb, I was enchanted . . .'[33]

Both the General and the Maharajah were reported to have looked as bemused as all the musicians, Tchaikovsky included, as their praises were sung at length by the Public Orator, Dr John Sandys, in Latin. Still exhausted from the long-drawn-out exertions of the previous day, Tchaikovsky was meanwhile beginning to wilt in the surprise Cambridge heat wave, which saw the temperature climbing into the 80s. Before he could escape back to London, however, there was yet another ceremonial meal to endure: the Chancellor's luncheon, hosted by the vice-chancellor, Dr Peile, in Christ's College, of which he was Master. This time Tchaikovsky sat between his host's daughter, Hester, and the philosopher Henry Sidgwick. The meal ended with the traditional passing-round of a huge silver 'loving cup', from which toasts were drunk to the new Doctors, who were then given a tour of the college gardens before a tea party hosted by Mrs Peile.

Would there be no end to it? For once, Tchaikovsky was not at all put out to be upstaged by Saint-Saëns, who left the tea party to give an organ recital in the chapel of Trinity College. Tchaikovsky happily took the chance to make his excuses, bid the Maitlands a grateful farewell, and leave for London in such a hurry that he forgot the orchestral scores for *Francesca*. That night he had committed himself to hosting a dinner at the Dieudonné, to repay some of the hospitality lavished upon him during a stay which now seemed to have lasted much longer than twelve days. Afterwards, even so, he still had the energy to head with Hatzfeld to the Alhambra Theatre in Leicester Square, to see Georg Jacobi's popular ballet, *Chicago*.

\*     \*     \*

By nightfall the next day, 14 June, Tchaikovsky was in Paris. 'Now it's all over,' he wrote to Kolya, 'I shall enjoy looking back on my success in England, and the amazing kindness shown me everywhere – even though, thanks to my curious temperament, I spent the whole time working myself up into a nervous frenzy.' Because of 'the continual strain on my nerves' his legs had hurt throughout the trip. Now he had started sleeping badly. 'Only here, where at last am I on my own again, have I begun to recover a little.'[34] To Anatoly he sent an amusing account of the Cambridge ceremony, recounting the difficulty of keeping a straight face amid the 'shrieking and screaming' of the students, with 'the biggest stir' being caused by the Maharajah. Now, in Paris, he felt half-dead. Compared to London, with its 'dreadful' traffic, the French capital seemed 'like a desert'. He needed time to recover.[35]

After a fortnight of 'unbelievable exhaustion and nervous tension', a week's relaxation with Sapelnikov and Sophie Menter at her Tyrolean castle was just what he needed. But his rendezvous with Bob was an even more inspiring prospect, and by 30 June the two were reunited at Konradi's Grankino estate. 'Strange as it may sound,' Tchaikovsky wrote to Modest, 'the beauties of the Tyrol gave me barely half as much pleasure as the sight of the interminable steppe through which I rode here yesterday from the railway station. No, absolutely, the Russian countryside is infinitely dearer to my heart than all the [much-vaunted] beauties of Europe.'[36] Yurgenson received very similar greetings: 'From the Tyrol, with its mountains, crags, precipices, ravines etc, I've fetched up on a bare, endless steppe – which I find one hundred times more poetic, more spacious, more beautiful.'[37]

After two weeks at Grankino, and ten days with his brother Nikolay at his Ukolovo estate, Tchaikovsky was back at Klin by the end of the month, 30 July, and immediately set about scoring the Sixth Symphony.

> Only at home can I work properly. I am now right up to my neck in my symphony. The further I progress with the scoring, the harder I find it. Twenty years ago I used to charge ahead without thinking, and it would turn out fine. Now I have become timid, unsure of myself. Today I spent the entire day on two pages, and still it hasn't turned out as I would like. But I'm getting on with it, nevertheless, and nowhere else would I have got so much done as here at home.[38]

Ten days later, he was back in his stride. 'I'm already close to finishing the scoring of the third movement, so in three days I should reach the finale, which should itself take another three days,' he reported to Taneyev.[39] It turned out to take rather longer – but the work was finished by 31 August, to the composer's profound satisfaction. Slowness, he told Anatoly, was 'less the result of failing strength or old age than the fact that I set myself much higher standards . . . I'm *very proud* of this symphony, and I think it's the best piece I've ever written.'[40] To Bob, its dedicatee, he also wrote of his conviction that this would prove his masterpiece:

> I am very pleased with its contents (though not yet totally satisfied with the orchestration) . . . If this symphony is misunderstood, and torn to shreds, I shall think it quite normal, not at all surprising. It will not be the first time. But I myself absolutely believe it to be the best and especially the most *sincere* of all my works. I love it as I have never *loved* any single one of my other musical creations.[41]

At the Cambridge dinner, Tchaikovsky had told Walter Damrosch that he had just finished a new symphony which was 'different in form from anything he had ever written'. Pressed by his American friend for more detail, he replied: 'The last movement is an *adagio* and the whole work has a programme.' When Damrosch asked 'eagerly' to hear the programme, Tchaikovsky said: 'No, that I shall never tell . . .'[42] It was one of many occasions on which he chose to let slip that his Sixth Symphony had a programme, as if begging for the chance to withhold further details. 'Let them guess', as he had put it to Bob, wilfully tantalizing future audiences over the missing programme to the *Pathétique*.

Once it transpired to be his last major work, posterity began to read intimations of mortality into Tchaikovsky's Sixth Symphony, whose brooding agonies, fading at the last into oblivion, were heard as presentiments of his approaching death. Not at all, said his friend Kashkin, who protested that Tchaikovsky was 'busy with plans for the future, and without any premeditation of death.'[43] To their contemporary Vasily Yastrebtsev, an influential critic, Tchaikovsky's last symphony 'depicted ourselves alone . . . with our unresolved doubts, our sorrows and our joys.'[44] But the early twentieth century took a less objective view of the *Pathétique*, which was seen as 'a personal expression, sheerly and absolutely'.

> It is not an objective and a philosophical pessimism; it is one man's individual experience, an experience which, if it had been expressed through the medium of human speech, would have revealed its author as an abject creature crouching beneath the unappeasable winds and havocs of chronic hysteria.[45]

To Anatoly's widow Praskovya, reminiscing about her brother-in-law in 1940, it seemed that Tchaikovsky had 'a dim presentiment of his approaching end . . . in the tragic music of his last symphony.'[46] By the 1970s a leading Tchaikovsky scholar, Edward Garden, could find 'little room for doubt that it was a symphony on the triumph of death over life.'[47] And the 1990s found another, Alexander Poznansky, still arguing that 'the Sixth Symphony was intentionally conceived by the author as autobiographical', the product of 'an irresistible desire to retell in music the story of his life and his soul.' It was dedicated to Bob 'so that his beloved nephew might be able to share and appreciate all that he himself had gone through.'[48]

The subject will recur in later chapters, as Tchaikovsky's last symphony is examined in the context of his mysterious death, barely a week after conducting its first performance. For now, let it suffice to note the symphony's striking presence at the deathbed of another great Russian composer, a lifelong champion of his 'great and beloved' Tchaikovsky, Igor Stravinsky. On 4 April 1971, as Stravinsky lay mortally ill in the next room, his amanuensis Robert Craft found himself listening to the *Pathétique*.

> Strangely, ominously, and for no reason except that the record is on the turntable – I had been listening to it only two days ago with I.S. – I start to play the *Symphony Pathétique*. Two days ago it delighted him; 'Tchaikovsky's best music', he called it . . . Now, at the sound of the first movement, V[era, Stravinsky's wife] runs into the room, begs me to turn it off, says that to Russians it predicts death.[49]

Since his return to Russia, Tchaikovsky had been dealing with a stream of bad news. During his absence in England, his lifelong friends Karl Albrecht and Konstantin Shilovsky had both died, followed a month later by Vladimir Shilovsky. Now, at the end of August, came the news of the death of his oldest (and 'once, my closest') friend, Apukhtin.

Modest tells us that his brother 'would not now travel as far as he once had in order to see a friend before their eternal separation . . .' There had been too many. But the 'moral ordeals he had endured over the last few years' had also led him 'to see death as a deliverance'[50]. At the time, furthermore, he was wholly preoccupied with his symphony, so much so that he absented himself from Apukhtin's burial service in St Petersburg – slightly to his own surprise, as he admitted in a letter to Bob that day. He even declined Grand Duke Konstantin's suggestion that he write a requiem for their mutual friend, a setting of a poem of that name by Apukhtin himself. 'My latest symphony,' he explained, 'just finished and due to be performed on 16 [28] October . . . is steeped in very much the same spirit as [Apukhtin's] poem *Requiem*. I consider the symphony a success, and hesitate to repeat myself so soon by undertaking a work so similar in spirit and character . . .'

> There is another reason why I am little inclined to compose music for any sort of requiem . . . In the requiem there is much talk of *God the Judge, God the Punisher, God the Avenger*(!!!). Forgive me, Your Highness, but I dare to suggest that I do not believe in such a God – or at least that God cannot stir in me those tears, that rapture, that awe before the creator and source of every good which might inspire me.[51]

There was also the simple fact that Tchaikovsky, morbidly super-stitious about anything to do with death, hated funerals. On the day of Apukhtin's, on his way to Europe again, he did in fact pass through St Petersburg – where he stayed with Laroche rather than Kolya Konradi, again at odds with Modest.

After years of supporting his brother with a modest allowance, Tchaikovsky was finding this much more difficult since von Meck had 'cut off' his subsidy. Now Konradi in turn cut off Modest's, which enraged the composer. Modest himself tried to defend his former charge, but Tchaikovsky remained unmoved. 'I consider him a swine of the lowest order, though I'm trying hard not to show him my feelings,' he replied to Modest's assuaging noises. 'And I am very worried about your future. Everything is fine, you say, but what about money, money, money!!! As if on purpose, I now have very little.'[52] Venting his spleen to their cousin, Anna Merkling, he raged: 'Only people like Kolya Konradi . . . live happily on this earth. A callous heart, a mediocre mind, incapable of penetrating the essence of things – these are the prerequisites for a successful vegetative life in this world.'[53] It was during this spate of angry letters that Tchaikovsky delivered to Yurgenson his final denunciation of von Meck as a 'treacherous' woman who had 'betrayed' him.

After a flying visit to Hamburg to hear *Iolanta*, he was back in St Petersburg by 12 September to try to help Modest find a new apartment. A week later, restless again, he paused in Moscow briefly on his way to a few days with Anatoly and his family at their country estate at Mikhailovskoye, near Nizhni-Novgorod. According to Praskovya, 'he enjoyed the beautiful country walks tremendously. He was in perfect health and full of plans for the future.' On the last day of his visit, he went for a long walk in the forest with his sister-in-law, and promised her that he would come to stay for Christmas.[54]

By 29 September he was back in Moscow for the first night of Modest's play, *Prejudices*, at the Maly Theatre; Tchaikovsky, for once, rather admired his brother's work – but the critics, as usual, didn't. There followed ten more days reluctantly (and drunkenly) kicking his heels in Moscow, unable to return to Klin because Alexey's wife was again on the verge of giving birth.

He was back home by early October, as testified by a letter dated the 4th to the director of the Kharkov music school, I.I. Slatin, again enthusing about his Sixth Symphony, which he was 'due to conduct in St Petersburg on 16 [28] October and on 4 [16] December in Moscow . . . It seems to have turned out well, [judging by] how rarely I compose something with passion and enthusiasm.'[55] From Modest in St Petersburg came news that he had found a suitable apartment on the corner of Malaya Morskaya Street. It was available for rent from the 13th. The only problem, as usual, was money. Tchaikovsky duly arranged for his brother to borrow 1,000 roubles from a well-disposed acquaintance, the piano manufacturer Fyodor Mühlbach.

At this critical stage of his narrative, to an unnatural degree, Modest keeps remarking how 'happy' and 'healthy' Tchaikovsky was that September; but all the evidence suggests otherwise. The dramas at Klin continued: Alexey's wife had nearly died in childbirth, and the composer's return coincided with news of the death of yet another old friend, his Conservatoire colleague Nikolay Zverev (to whom he had recently dedicated one of the Eighteen Piano Pieces, *Passé lointain*).

Agitated by the failure of mutual friends to let him know, he again missed the funeral as he worked moodily on the scoring of his abandoned symphony-turned-Third Piano Concerto. To avoid another bout of introspective isolation, he invited Brandukov to bring down another young cellist friend, Yulian Poplavsky – along with a copy of Saint-Saëns' First Cello Concerto, which he wanted to study. When they arrived on 13 October, the wide-eyed Poplavsky was amazed to find that the great man occupied only the upper floor of his stylish *dacha* – just two rooms, leaving the rest of the spacious house to his 'devoted' servant, Alexey. 'Not one of the rooms suggested that this was the abode of the most popular of all Russian composers.'

Tchaikovsky liked to work in his tiny bedroom, at a plain pine table beside the window, which commanded a fine view of the walled garden he had begun to cultivate. Dominating the view were three *beryozy*, silver birch trees, of which he had grown particularly fond while writing the Sixth Symphony. On the composer's work-table, noted Poplavsky, there stood only 'a simple cut-glass inkwell, a suprisingly well-crafted china Pierrot head, and several small items of the crudest primitive workmanship. There was also music paper, pens, and the manuscript of his last piano concerto, which Pyotr Ilyich was looking over when we arrived . . .'

> If you sat in his plain wooden chair and looked straight ahead, there was nothing to distract your gaze except the clouds above, the expanse of fields to the horizon, and the enigmatic smile of Pierrot. Each day Pyotr Ilyich got up at 7 to work at this pine table. Not among the mountains of Switzerland, nor on the shore of the Adriatic, nor in America was Tchaikovsky so inspired to compose as at home here in Klin.

In the adjacent drawing room stood a fine piano, always notoriously out of tune. When the three of them sat down to play the Saint-Saëns, the nervous Poplavsky's hands 'involuntarily jumped from the keys', so surprised was he to discover for himself what had become a joke among the composer's friends. 'So much for all those "well-informed" people who had told me the great Tchaikovsky always composed at the piano!' The only way they managed to stumble their way through the piece was by 'rooting out the most unsuitable keys'.

In the centre of the large drawing room stood a handsome writing desk – strictly for correspondence rather than composition. The walls of the room were crowded with portraits of family and friends, with a huge library of scores (including the complete Leipzig edition of Mozart) and with shelves of books by writers 'of the kind one expects musicians to respect rather than to read': Pushkin, Heine and Hugo, Schopenhauer and Mill, Dante and Shakespeare, Byron and Milton (in English).

By this time of his life, according to Kashkin, Tchaikovsky's failing eyesight 'made reading in the evenings by the fire difficult, depriving him of his chief diversion from his creative life, so that solitude now became distressing for him, especially during the long winter evenings.'[56] Poplavsky may not have noticed them, but Laroche also recalled a large bookshelf of biography and political history: a French translation of Herodotus, Petrushevsky on Suvorov, Bogdanovich on Tsar Alexandr I, several books on Peter the Great – but, above all, volumes of memoirs, 'history of the kind where the fates of the state and of society disappear beneath the minute description of individuality, of the detailed delineation of the psychological and the social.' As an amused Laroche points out, the musician who found 'nothing worthy of his attention' in the history of music, 'loved political history passionately'.[57] And this was the man who all his life, since the Emancipation of the Serfs when he was twenty-one to that very summer in London, at the age of fifty-three, had resolutely declined to discuss politics, saying: 'Music and Art are generally fit subjects for musicians to discuss, not politics.'[58]

As the young Poplavsky marvelled at the signed portraits of the famous, and the framed awards and honours from musical institutions all over the world, his reveries were suddenly interrupted when 'through the almost absolute silence, there sounded a note as pure as a tuning fork, there trembled and echoed through the whole house the chords of silver bells – thirds and minor sixths jauntily widening into octaves . . . and two bells of the purest and deepest timbre angrily arguing in fourths, vibrating long and loud through the empty air . . .' It was one of Tchaikovsky's most prized possessions, a stone clock from Prague, given him for almost nothing by a clockmaker who recognized him as the conductor of the previous evening's concert.

On their afternoon walks, Tchaikovsky spoke of plans to walk the full length of the canal from Klin to the Volga the following spring. And on their last night at Klin together, he talked with great animation about his new symphony, whose première he was due to conduct in St Petersburg in ten days' time. There was also mention of a new opera – at last, perhaps, *Romeo and Juliet*. The next day, 19 October, he took an emotional leave of Alexey.

> Egorka, Alexey's two-year-old son (and the master's godson) appeared. Bidding them both farewell, Pyotr Ilyich exchanged kisses with both father and son. Alexey handed his master sixty roubles, telling him to buy some cloth for a new winter coat while in Moscow . . . Twenty minutes later we were happily climbing aboard the evening train.[59]

Once in Moscow, taking his leave of the two young cellists, Tchaikovsky resumed his busy round. There was Zverev's memorial service to attend, followed by a chance to work with Taneyev on the Third Piano Concerto. It was probably that same evening that Taneyev was also at the piano, with Lev Konyus, for a run-through of the Sixth Symphony for Tchaikovsky's friends at Taneyev's home. The guests included Sergey Rachmaninov – his young admirer, for whom he had predicted 'a great future'.[60] But the evening was not a success. According to Ippolitov-Ivanov, who was also present, 'the symphony did not make much impression on us.' It could have been 'the frequent stops to make corrections of details'; or it could have been 'the nagging interruptions from Pyotr Ilyich, who was especially on edge that evening'; or it could have been the fact that, when Tchaikovsky wanted a cigarette, Taneyev made him retreat to a passageway beside the chimney, to smoke beneath a poster written by Tolstoy about the dangers of tobacco.[61]

The next day, 21 October, he attended a student performance at the Conservatoire of his vocal quartet *Night*, the piece for four voices he had based on Mozart's C minor Piano Fantasia (K.475). Fighting back tears, Tchaikovsky told Kashkin that the beauty of Mozart's music was 'a mystery to him . . . he could not explain the irresistible charm of the quartet's simple melody.'[62] There followed another run-through of the *Pathétique* by the orchestral class at the Conservatoire, supplemented by such teachers as Hřímalý, von Glenn and Sokolovksy under the baton of the director, Safonov. With the composer in almost paranoid mood, security was tight; Hubert's widow had been dragooned into ensuring that no students beyond the orchestral class were allowed to remain in the building. But a fifteen-year-old violinist named Konstantin Saradzhev dodged the security cordon. 'Being both curious and mischievous, I managed to hide myself so that neither the security men nor the supervisors could see me.' For two hours he listened at the door:

> There were many stops: it seems that they were correcting mistakes in the orchestral parts and indeed in the performance. I didn't really understand, of course, the significance of what was going on; but all the same I remember feeling that something out of the ordinary was happening. When the class finished, the students left the hall in great excitement, sensing that this was something unlike anything they had ever heard before. Then I saw Tchaikovsky, Safonov and Hřímalý leaving . . . Tchaikovsky was carrying a very big score. His face was a really deep red, very agitated. Safonov and Hřímalý walked behind him in silence. It was difficult to grasp quite what all these people had just lived through, but it was quite clear to me that something special, exceptional, out of the ordinary, had just taken place.[63]

That evening Tchaikovsky left for St Petersburg. Halfway from Moscow, as the train passed through Frolovskoye, Tchaikovsky pointed out the churchyard and said to his travelling companions: 'That's where I want to be buried – and those who pass by shall point to my grave.' The next morning he was met at the station by Modest and Bob, who took him back to their new apartment.

The next six days were dominated by preparations for the first performance of his Sixth Symphony. By night he relaxed in the company of the 'Fourth Suite', carousing till all hours in 'merry and impish' mood – a veritable 'cornucopia of good humour', according to the circle's newest recruit, Bob Davidov's younger brother Yuri.[64] The latest object of Tchaikovsky's affections, and a frequent visitor to the apartment that week, was the young actor Yuri Yuriev, later to achieve such eminence that even the Soviet authorities turned a blind eye to his flamboyant homosexuality. Yuriev, in his turn, was also smitten; he had first caught sight of the composer at the dress rehearsal of *The Queen of Spades* two years earlier, and had never forgotten his 'captivating inner grace and nobility', and his 'pleasant low bass voice.'[65]

All that week, according to Modest, Tchaikovsky had been 'quite un-concerned' about a virulent epidemic of cholera which had been sweeping through the city, claiming scores of victims daily. His only worry that week was the apparent indifference of the orchestra to his new symphony during its four lengthy rehearsals. The response of the first-night audience was much the same. 'All St Petersburg' turned out for the première of Tchaikovsky's Sixth Symphony on Saturday 28 October. The composer, as usual, was greeted with rapture, his entrance prompting a prolonged standing ovation. But the symphony itself, as its *adagio lamentoso* trailed away into *morendo* oblivion, met a lukewarm reception – not so much disapproval as dismay, even bewilderment.

As he left the Assembly Hall after the concert Tchaikovsky 'com-plained bitterly' to Glazunov, who walked with him. 'Pyotr Ilyich often felt depressed after the first performance of his works. But with this particular offspring he had been especially pleased.'[66] The St Petersburg press proved, like the audience, politely respectful rather than rapturous. Tchaikovsky's Sixth Symphony, of whose power and originality he felt sure, had not proved the public triumph which, for once, its composer had expected. He could only hope, as had happened before, that the anti-climax of this St Petersburg première would be redeemed by a greater success in Moscow three weeks later.

But Tchaikovsky would never conduct that concert. Within a few days of the Sixth Symphony's first performance, St Petersburg was rife with rumour that Russia's beloved 'national composer' had fallen dangerously ill.

# CHAPTER XVII

## 'A classic case of cholera'

EARLY THE FOLLOWING MORNING, SUNDAY 29 OCTOBER, MODEST AROSE
to find his brother already at the breakfast-table, contemplating the
title-page of the manuscript score of his Sixth Symphony, due to go
off to Yurgenson in Moscow the next day. Tchaikovsky had already
decided on the dedication, to his beloved nephew 'Bob' Davidov. But
he was still hesitating, according to his brother, over a title.

Tchaikovsky's original intent had been to call this his 'Programme'
Symphony, to signify that its shifting moods were intended to represent
specific feelings and emotions on the composer's part. Now he had
decided to keep such mysteries to himself. Already, after all, he had said
to Bob: 'Let them guess.' In the intermission of the previous evening's
concert, when Rimsky-Korsakov had asked him whether his symphony
had a programme, Tchaikovsky had again replied: 'Of course, but I do
not wish to disclose it.'[1] Now he told Modest: 'What kind of programme
symphony is this, when I don't want to reveal the programme?' Having
once intended to give it a name, however, the straightforward 'Symphony
No. 6 in B minor' seemed less than adequate to a work of such especial
personal resonance.

Sensitive to the symphony's barely relieved darkness, Modest now
suggested 'Tragic'. But still Tchaikovsky was not satisfied. 'I left the
room,' Modest tells us, 'with Pyotr Ilyich in an agony of indecision.
Suddenly the word "pathetic" occurred to me, and I went back to suggest

it to him.' Modest, in his own words, remembered 'as if it were yesterday' how his brother exclaimed: 'Bravo, Modest, that's it! *Pathétique*!'

'Then and there, in my presence,' writes a proud Modest, 'he added to the score the title by which the symphony has always been known.' Tchaikovsky's brother then goes to some lengths to distance himself from his own boasting: 'I do not relate this incident in order to connect my name with his work.' He would not have mentioned the matter, Modest explains, but for the need to disprove such misguided theories as that of Hugo Riemann, the German musicologist, that Tchaikovsky's choice of title indicates a deliberate thematic reference in the symphony's opening phrase to that of Beethoven's piano sonata of the same name (No. 8 in C minor, Op. 13). 'This serves to illustrate', laughs Modest, 'how far the conjectures of the most enlightened commentators may wander from the truth.'[2]

In a footnote, he adds, 'There was no other witness of this incident apart from myself. But it is clear from the programme of the concert that this title had not then been given to the work. Moreover, anyone can see by a glance at the title-page that this name was written later than the rest.' Doth the brother protest too much? His own limited success as a playwright had lent a love-hate dimension to Modest's intense feelings for his celebrated older brother. From his uneasily defensive tone, it sounds almost as if someone aware of this had accused him of inventing the story – which has passed into Tchaikovsky folklore – that it was he, the otherwise unworthy sibling rival, who had come up with the Sixth Symphony's now celebrated name.

Yurgenson himself, perhaps. For he was the author of a letter preserved in the archive at Klin (and published here for the first time) which shows that Tchaikovsky had thought of the name *Pathétique* at least a month earlier. 'About this *Pathétique* symphony of yours,' Yurgenson had written to him in a letter dated 20 September (old calendar). 'It should be styled *not* Sixth *Pathétique* symphony, but: Symphony No. 6, the *Pathétique*. Do you agree?' The publisher further enquired about the correct transliteration of the name of the dedicatee – 'Davidoff or Davidow?' – indicating that the composer had perhaps suggested both names verbally. There follows another letter with an even more straightforward question: 'How much money do you want for your *Pathétique*?'[3]

At the top of this letter Modest has pencilled the words 'Not received', and the date 19 October (old calendar), suggesting that it took a month to arrive – at a time when letters from Moscow to St Petersburg (or vice versa) often arrived on the day they were sent, certainly the following day. Why Modest went to such clumsy lengths to claim the credit for naming his brother's masterpiece is unclear; nearing the end of his work, perhaps, he was craving a more lasting niche in musical history than his own narrative had hitherto allowed him.

The point of dwelling on the matter here is to reassert how little we can rely on Modest's account of his brother's life, especially as we approach its last days. His version of the following week – the last of Tchaikovsky's life – is so confused and contradictory that it has bequeathed musical history one of its greatest mysteries, almost as vexed as that supposedly surrounding the premature death of his hero, Mozart.

How did Tchaikovsky die?

The next morning, Monday 30 October, found the composer at the Imperial Public Library, the only place in St Petersburg where he could gain ready access to the four-volume score of *The Oprichnik*, which he had promised to revise for a new production by the Kononov company. This involved negotiating retrieval of the rights to the piece from Vasily Bessel, to whom he had sold them almost twenty years earlier; by regaining them and making revisions, Tchaikovsky would also be entitled to full royalties from the forthcoming Kononov performances.

Bessel and Tchaikovsky having long since fallen out, the publisher sent as his emissary for these negotiations a lawyer named Avgust Gerke, a friend of the composer's since their schooldays together at the School of Jurisprudence. Although he disliked meeting up with old schoolfriends – largely because they knew of his 'abnormality' – Tchaikovsky had a soft spot for Gerke, whose father had taught him piano at the Conservatoire, and who was himself an accomplished amateur pianist, a member of the governing board of the Russian Musical Society. Only six months before, Tchaikovsky had dedicated one of his Eighteen Pieces for Piano, *Tendres reproches* (No. 3), to Gerke. The two men were to meet again at least once – perhaps twice, and if so for very different reasons – in the following forty-eight hours.

For now, however, the conversation appears to have been harmonious enough as, on Bessel's behalf, Gerke conceded all Tchaikovsky's contractual demands. That afternoon the composer took the good news over to the Kononov Opera, only a hundred yards from Modest's apartment, where rehearsals were under way for a new production of *Eugene Onegin*. Tchaikovsky promised that the revisions would not take him long, and handed over to the conductor the first volume of the Imperial Library's copy of the score.

That evening he attended a pre-opera dinner in honour of Adele aus der Ohe, the German virtuoso who had played the First Piano Concerto in the previous Saturday's concert (as she had under his baton in the United States two years before). Tchaikovsky then attended another performance of *Onegin*, at the Mariinsky, after which he went backstage and discussed potential amendments to *The Maid of Orleans* with Vladimir Pogozhev, manager of the Office of Imperial Theatres. According to the tenor Nikolay Figner, a close friend whom he also visited backstage, Tchaikovsky was in excellent spirits, 'as cheerful as usual'[4], chatting optimistically about their plans for a series of concerts in Paris together.

His letters show that next morning – presumably early, as was his wont – Tchaikovsky wrote to the Dutch composer-conductor Willem Kes, accepting an invitation to conduct in Amsterdam the following March. The rest of the day, Tuesday 31 October, is a momentous blank. By the evening we find him back at the Kononov, for a performance of Anton Rubinstein's *The Maccabees*; but this time there is no eye-witness account of his mood or his conversation, no word from any Figner that he was 'as cheerful as usual'.

Tchaikovsky had originally planned to return to his home at Klin two days later, on Thursday 2 November, en route to Moscow. Now, for no apparent reason, he told Modest that he had decided to stay on in St Petersburg. Modest later suggested that his brother had yielded to his pleas that he stay for the St Petersburg première of his comedy *Prejudices*, in the hope that it went better than the ill-fated Moscow opening. But that was scheduled for 7 November, a full week ahead. Tchaikovsky had already been in Petersburg ten days, on a visit built around the launch of the Sixth Symphony, which had now proved an anti-climax. He had taken on plenty of work of the kind urgently requiring the tranquillity and solitude of Klin. There were limits to his devotion to his brother, let alone his admiration for him as a playwright. Could something else have changed his mind about leaving?

Next morning, Wednesday 1 November, Tchaikovsky met Gerke to sign the new contract for the revised *Oprichnik*. Later that day, according to his nephew Count ('Sanya') Litke, he was in nostalgic, melancholy mood, reminiscing about the eccentricities of his old friend Bochechkarov as they took a walk together. He dined early with another old friend, Vera Butakova (née Davidova) – Lev's widowed younger sister, who had paid him such unwanted attentions in his youth – before taking his seat in his box at the Alexandrinsky Theatre for a performance of Ostrovsky's *The Ardent Heart*. During the interval he visited the dressing room of the leading actor, Konstantin Varlamov, where the conversation apparently turned via spiritualism to death. 'There'll be time enough for us to meet this repulsive, snub-nosed monster,' Tchaikovsky (by Modest's account) told his actor friend. 'But that's a long way off for both of us.' Modest then has his brother turning back in the doorway, as if himself in a play, to add: 'I know I shall live a long time.'

After the performance Tchaikovsky did not go backstage again, but wandered homeward down Nevsky Prospekt with a clutch of his nephews and cousins – Bob Davidov, Sanya Litke and [Baron] Rudy Buxhövden. Spontaneously he suggested that they stop off for a meal at one of his favourite restaurants, Leiner's. Here his party was soon joined by Glazunov, Fyodor Mühlbach and others – and an hour later by Modest, whose account of the scene now becomes uncannily detailed. Tchaikovsky, he writes, had eaten macaroni, and washed it down, 'as usual', with white wine and mineral water. It was 2 a.m. by the time the two brothers walked home. Modest is at such pains to tell us of Pyotr Ilyich's good spirits – he was 'completely calm and healthy' – that we may be forgiven, in view of what was about to transpire, for questioning his motives.

Later accounts in the St Petersburg newspapers, based on interviews with those present at the dinner at Leiner's, attest that Tchaikovsky impulsively drank a glass of unboiled water, in full knowledge of the cholera epidemic in the city. According to his nephew, Yuri Davidov, 'Pyotr Ilyich summoned a waiter and asked him to bring a glass of water. In a couple of minutes the waiter returned with the news that there was no boiled water. This annoyed Pyotr Ilyich, who said impatiently: "Then bring me some unboiled water. Cold." We all started trying to dissuade him from drinking unboiled water, reminding him of the cholera epidemic then raging in the city, but Pyotr Ilyich dismissed our fears as superstitions . . . As the waiter went to carry out his instructions, the door opened and in came Modest Ilyich, with the actor [Yuri] Yuriev. "Aha, how clever of me!" exclaimed Modest. "On my way past I thought I'd just look in to see if you were here."

'"Where else would we be?" laughed Pyotr Ilyich. Then, just behind Modest Ilyich, the waiter returned with the glass of water on a tray. When Modest found out what was happening, and why we were all arguing, he grew very angry with his brother and shouted: "I strictly forbid you to drink unboiled water!" Still laughing, Pyotr Ilyich jumped up and started to walk toward the waiter. Modest rushed after him, but Pyotr Ilyich got there first, elbowed his brother out of the way, and downed the fatal glass in one gulp.'[5] Modest himself makes no mention of this incident, stressing in fact that his brother drank mineral water. His version of events has Tchaikovsky drinking the fatal glass of water the next day.

Next morning, Thursday 2 November, Modest arose expecting to find his brother taking his morning tea, as usual, in the sitting room. But Tchaikovsky was still in bed. A 'stomach upset', he explained, had caused him 'a bad night'. When Modest offered to call a doctor, Tchaikovsky told him not to fuss. He had suffered many such attacks before; a dose of castor oil usually enabled him to carry on regardless. Modest would have us believe that Tchaikovsky was 'often' subject to such attacks; though 'very violent', they tended to pass 'very quickly'. Besides, Tchaikovsky had a morbid dread of doctors, as we know from two of his lifelong friends. 'Pyotr Ilyich did not like resorting to doctors,' according to Kashkin.[6] 'From his youth through to his mature years,' confirmed Laroche, 'he hated resorting to medical help. He preferred to treat himself, taking medicine most reluctantly and as infrequently as possible.'[7]

So Modest took his brother at his word, and left for rehearsals of his play at the Alexandrinsky. Around 11 a.m. Tchaikovsky left the apartment with the intention of visiting Eduard Napravnik and his wife Olga. Immediately he began to feel much worse. After suffering severe stomach pains in the street, he was forced to take a cab straight back to the apartment. Though he later confessed to feelings of 'great distress', he tried to cover them from all but his intimates, joking with the doorman of the apartment block and smiling cheerfully at other residents. Once back inside, with the solace of a hot flannel, he seems to have made a temporary recovery, for he wrote several letters – the last we possess, and apparently the last he ever wrote. One was to the Napravniks, apologizing for his non-appearance; another to Kolya Konradi, still trying to intercede on Modest's behalf; and the last to the Odessa Opera Theatre, accepting an invitation to visit at the turn of the year.

By the time Sanya Litke arrived, the desperation of his uncle's search for castor oil, for *any* medication, quite frightened him. 'He seemed very upset,' Litke reported, 'by something else.'[8] Modest returned for lunch to find that Fyodor Mühlbach, the piano manufacturer who had advanced him the rent for the apartment, had arrived 'on business'. Tchaikovsky sat with them as they ate, but declined all food, merely sipping the brand of mineral water he favoured, Guniadi. Modest suggests that at this stage Tchaikovsky was not 'averse' to food, rather that he thought eating might exacerbate his condition. But the composer did not last out the lunch; before the other two men had finished, he was overcome by nausea and rushed from the room. 'The mineral water', suggests Modest, 'had probably aggravated the kind of stomach upset to which he was prone.'

It is at this point that Modest's account of his brother's rapidly worsening condition begins to defy all belief. In an apparent attempt to justify his own casual handling of a 'stomach upset' which was to prove fatal, Tchaikovsky's first biographer would have us believe that midway through the lunch, as his two companions were discussing the relative merits of castor oil and mineral water, Tchaikovsky

suddenly poured out a glass of unboiled water and drank it down
– in full knowledge of the virulent epidemic of Asiatic cholera
which had been sweeping St Petersburg. Modest and Mühlbach were
'alarmed'; Tchaikovsky alone was apparently 'indifferent' to the risk
he took in drinking unboiled water – because, Modest would have
us believe, 'of all illnesses, cholera was the one he feared least'. In
view of the trauma of their mother's death from cholera and of the
agonies she suffered from the notorious 'hot bath' treatment – this
statement is so nonsensical as to discredit Modest's entire version
of these events, both before and after what he calls this 'fatal'
moment.

What was a pitcher of unboiled, potentially lethal water doing on the
dining table in the first place? Modest fails to enlighten us. As Tchaikovsky
fled from the room, overcome by nausea and vomiting, Modest insists
that neither he nor his brother himself were at all concerned. 'All this', he
blithely reports, 'had happened before.' He repeats his offer to summon
the doctor, but is again waved away. So back goes Modest to his
rehearsals at the Alexandrinsky.

Now Tchaikovsky stays in his bedroom, lying down with a hot compress on his stomach. He has told Modest he will try to sleep, but
violent diarrhoea begins to punctuate the vomiting. Modest's servant,
that same Nazar Litrov who had nursed him through *The Queen of Spades*
in Florence, tries everything he can think of to ease the composer's
suffering. But when Glazunov arrives in late afternoon, as agreed at
Leiner's the night before, Tchaikovsky is in very bad shape. He asks
to be left alone, complaining that he feels 'extremely ill', even joking
that he has perhaps contracted cholera.

By the time Modest returns at 5 p.m. Tchaikovsky is sinking so fast that
his brother overrules his protests and sends for the doctor – Tchaikovsky's
'favourite' doctor, a family friend named Vasily Bertenson. In his note,
Modest told Bertenson: 'Petya does not feel well. He has continuous
nausea and diarrhoea. For God's sake, come and see what this means.'

Even to those who believe Modest, and accept that Tchaikovsky was
dying of cholera, 'precious time for diagnosis and treatment' had been
'slipping away' during the brother's absence that afternoon.[9] Yet now,
at 6 p.m., having sent his note to the doctor, Modest departs again
– back to the continuing rehearsals of his play. By 8 p.m., there is
still no sign of the doctor. As Tchaikovsky's vomiting and diarrhoea
grow yet worse, Litrov moves his bed into the sitting room, nearer to
the lavatory. At 8 p.m., when Bertenson has still failed to appear, the
servant sends out an SOS for another doctor – *any* doctor – to attend
the composer with the utmost urgency.

At 8.15, soon after Litrov had despaired of him, Vasily Bertenson finally arrived at Modest's apartment. Though he could not make any accurate diagnosis, none of Tchaikovsky's excreta having been preserved for his inspection, the doctor was immediately convinced that the composer was gravely ill. By his own account, it was far worse than an acute 'catarrh of the stomach', the family's own diagnosis. Bertenson was later to admit that he had never before attended, nor even seen, a single case of cholera; but he now concluded that Tchaikovsky's affliction was a 'classic' example.[10] Sending Litrov to fetch Modest back from the theatre, and realizing that he was out of his clinical depth, Bertenson sent for his own more celebrated brother, Lev, the court physician.

As the evening wore on, Tchaikovsky became too weak to move. His vomiting became so painful that it was accompanied by cries of agony. Several times, according to Modest, his brother cried out: 'I think I'm dying. Farewell!' He had sunk back on the bed, exhausted and semi-comatose, by the time Lev Bertenson too arrived, after 10 p.m. By his own subsequent account, though he too had never previously encountered a single case, the senior doctor quickly confirmed his brother's diagnosis of 'severe' cholera, already in the so-called 'algid' stage.[11]

By midnight Tchaikovsky was suffering severe and painful spasms. His head and bodily extremities were so cold that they began to turn blue. A medical attendant, Dr Nikolay Mamonov, was summoned to massage the composer back into life, and to supervise precautions against further infection.

Cholera had arrived in Europe less than a century before. The fifth pandemic of the nineteenth century, which lasted from 1881 to 1895, had crossed Russian borders from Arabia, whither it had been imported by pilgrims from Bombay; the first recorded cases in Russia were in Vladivostok five years earlier, in 1888. By the previous year, 1892, Russia was far the worst of the twenty-one countries plagued by the disease. In 1893 no fewer than seventy regions and provinces were suffering epidemics. According to contemporary Russian medical records, the specific epidemic which supposedly claimed Tchaikovsky's life began on 14 May 1892 and ended on 11 February 1896, during which period 504,924 Russians contracted the disease, of whom 226,940 (44.9 per cent) died.[12]

An authoritative medical textbook of the period, to which Tchaikovsky would have had access that week on his visits to the St Petersburg public library (where it is still to be found), would have informed him that 'fulfilling all the usual sanitary requirements can almost totally prevent the disease' and that 'using only pure water is of the utmost importance . . .

Water should be boiled every day for drinking and other purposes.'[13]

He would also have read that the normal incubation period is 'a minimum of one to three days'. Yet it was now barely twenty-four hours since the dinner at Leiner's, only twelve or so since the lunch at which Modest reports his brother inexplicably drinking a glass of unboiled water. By Modest's and the doctors' accounts, Tchaikovsky had become ill *within hours* of the previous night's dinner, and *before* that day's lunch.

The 'algid' stage is the second and most dangerous phase of cholera, the third being the stage of 'reaction', in which the victim either recovers or dies. Could Dr Bertenson have confused the stages of the disease? Cholera was a disease of the slums, transmitted in unhygienic conditions – and we know, again from Laroche, that Tchaikovsky was scrupulous about his personal hygiene. In the hope of avoiding doctors, Laroche tells us, 'he relied above all on hygiene, of which he seemed (to my layman's view) to be a true master.'[14]

Cholera was rarely encountered in the fashionable, well-to-do circles inhabited by the composer and served by the Bertenson brothers' exclusive practice. This was why neither Bertenson had ever previously seen a case, let alone treated one; all they knew of the disease's symptoms was what they had read in textbooks and medical journals. Was the senior partner, as has been suggested, 'reduced to describing Tchaikovsky's illness not from his observation of the patient, but from what he had once read,' thus using the terminology in the wrong sequence? Or was he 'forced by circumstances to lie'?[15] Was cholera, in fact, a subsequently convenient camouflage for a very different affliction?

Around midnight, Modest would have us believe, Tchaikovsky cried out: 'It's not cholera, is it?' Modest had 'tried to conceal the truth from him,' but Tchaikovsky overheard the doctor's diagnosis and wailed: 'So it *is* cholera!' After 1 a.m. the spasms eased and the bouts of vomiting and diarrhoea grew less intense. Lev Bertenson departed for the night, leaving his brother Vasily in charge.

In the early hours of the Friday morning, 3 November, Tchaikovsky's spasms returned with renewed intensity. The composer's sufferings, according to one of his visitors, the tenor Nikolay Figner, were 'simply horrible . . . It makes me shudder to remember the appalling agonies I witnessed . . . When vomiting, he threw out excretions with such force that they flew halfway across the room.'[16] The next few hours, as described by Modest, were a period of 'uninterrupted struggle', with cramps and numbness which even massage could no longer soothe. To those keeping all-night vigil – Vasily Bertenson, Modest and his servant – there were moments when it seemed that the end was imminent. By dawn the doctor was injecting Tchaikovsky with musk and camphor to keep him from slipping into a coma which might become permanent.

Each time he was revived, according to several accounts, the patient became remarkably lucid, apologizing for all the trouble he was causing, and embarrassed by the spectacle he must make. When Bob Davidov appeared at his bedside, he was even capable of a gentle joke against himself: 'I'm afraid you'll lose your respect for me after all these unpleasant things.' Soon he was calmer again; the upheavals eased, and the spasms came only when he tried to move. Though he complained now merely of depression, Tchaikovsky remained desperately thirsty; but a sip of any liquid would bring back the vomiting and diarrhoea. Early that morning, on the Bertensons' instructions, Modest somewhat tardily fulfilled his legal obligation to report this latest case of cholera to the St Petersburg police.

By 11 a.m., when the senior Bertenson returned, the patient seemed to be entering a period of remission, if not of recovery. All signs of lividity had gone; the black spots on his face were receding, and the spasms had at last eased. The doctor declared himself convinced that the worst was over. Tchaikovsky himself, according to Modest, 'considered himself saved'. He told the doctor he was feeling vastly improved: 'I must thank you. You have snatched me from the jaws of death.' Bertenson handed the case over to one of his assistants, who by nightfall felt confident enough to tell Modest and the others to get some sleep.

By mid-morning next day, Saturday 4 November, the composer's only apparent remaining symptom was an insatiable thirst. His renal artery still appeared to be blocked, preventing urination, but there were no other signs of infection and the critical phase of the illness seemed to have passed. If cholera it was, the third phase of the disease, the so-called 'stage of reaction', appeared to bode well. Friends and relatives were allowed back into the disinfected room, and the composer was even able to greet them with a smile and a weak handshake. The doctors' only concern was that the continuing uraemia would lead to failure of the kidneys.

As the day progressed without dramatic change, a crowd began to gather outside Modest's apartment on Malaya Morskaya Street. The news of Tchaikovsky's illness had finally made the St Petersburg newspapers. By midday the knocks at Modest's door combined with the hubbub outside to prevent the patient resting, so the doctors began to issue regular bulletins on his progress via the apartment block's doorman, who was instructed to let no-one pass. At 2.30 p.m., to keep the crowd at bay, a notice was posted on the door of the apartment:

The dangerous symptoms are still present, and are not responding to treatment. There is complete retention of the urine, together with drowsiness and a marked general weakness.

Eight hours later, at 10.30 p.m., another bulletin – this time in almost illiterate handwriting, presumably that of a servant – was even more pessimistic:

Since 3 p.m. there has been increasing weakness . . . There are very strong signs of uraemia . . . Since 10 p.m. the pulse has been almost undetectable, and there is emphysema.[17]

During the afternoon, as positive evidence of uremic poisoning developed, Lev Bertenson (by his own account) had pleaded with the Tchaikovsky brothers to permit him to attempt the dreaded 'hot bath' treatment. It was necessary, he explained, to restore the circulation and thus aid his patient's failing kidneys.

When later accused of malpractice, Dr Bertenson conceded that he had delayed attempting this last-resort treatment 'because Pyotr Ilyich's mother had died of cholera exactly at the moment she was placed in the bath . . . [which had] instilled in him and all his relatives a superstitious fear of the bath.' By mid-Saturday afternoon, however, with his 'profoundly depressed' patient pleading with him to 'Let me go! Don't torment yourself. I'm not going to recover', Bertenson finally suggested the bath. Tchaikovsky 'readily agreed'. When he had been lowered into it, the doctor asked him: 'Do you find the bath unpleasant?'

'On the contrary,' the composer supposedly replied, 'it's quite pleasant.'

But he soon complained of weakness and asked to be taken out. According to Bertenson, the immediate effect of the bath was 'beneficial: it produced a hot sweat, with which came hope that the effects of the urine poisoning would diminish and the kidneys begin to function again.' By the evening, however, even this hope had evaporated. Tchaikovsky grew 'drowsy', and his heart function weakened to the point where the second of Lev Bertenson's medical assistants, Dr Alexandr Zander, administered another shot of musk and again sent for Bertenson.

I found P.I. in a coma, with a drastically weakened heart action; we could restore him to consciousness for only a very short time. Thus, for example, when he was offered water to drink, he took it quite consciously, saying 'Enough,' 'More,' and so on. But by 10.30 p.m. all hope of a possible change for the better in his general condition had completely disappeared. He sank deeper into a coma, and his pulse became imperceptible, despite frequently repeated injections of stimulants. At 2 a.m. the death throes began.[18]

A priest summoned from nearby St Isaac's Cathedral was unable to administer the Holy Sacraments because the composer remained unconscious. So he simply read the prayers for the dying – of which, said Modest, 'it was obvious my brother did not hear a single word.' Around Tchaikovsky's bed, as the end approached, were his brothers Modest and Nikolay, three of the four doctors, the two Litke brothers, Bob Davidov, Figner and Buxhövden, Nazar Litrov and Alexey Sofronov, Tchaikovsky's devoted servant, who had just arrived from Klin. With so many people in so small a room, Lev Bertenson's last instruction was to open the window. The exhausted doctor then left his other assistant, Dr Nikolay Mamonov, to oversee the inevitable, which took little more than another hour.

Just after 3 a.m., in Modest's description, Tchaikovsky's eyes, until then half-closed and glazed, 'suddenly opened wide, giving an indescribable expression of full consciousness. He rested his gaze in turn upon the three people standing over him, then looked up to the heavens. For a few moments his eyes shone brightly, then faded with his last breath.'

The dead composer was at first laid out on the sofa in Modest's living room – 'as if he were still alive', according to a *Novoe Vremya* journalist, who was allowed in as a photographer from the Imperial Theatres took Tchaikovsky's picture: 'He looks as if he were asleep.'[19] The body was then placed in an open coffin.

Within a few hours, at 11 a.m., the first of five requiem services was held beside Tchaikovsky's open coffin. It was conducted by current and former pupils of the Imperial School of Jurisprudence, led by its director, Lieutenant-General A.I. Panteleyev, and the lawyer-pianist Avgust Gerke. Inside the coffin, just beneath the composer's visible face, Gerke laid a black velvet cushion bearing a silver wreath. A deputation of the school's pupils added an elegant metallic wreath of china roses.

An hour later, at noon, a second requiem was sung by a choir of the Imperial Russian Opera, whose artists were joined by numerous representatives of the music world, business societies, civic leaders – 'all who could squeeze into the apartment', according to the same journalist.[20] The crowd of mourners 'overflowed out into the vestibule and right down the stairs'. At 1 p.m., and again at 6 p.m., St Petersburg choirs led further services. Described by *Novoe Vremya* as 'deeply touching . . . and sublimely sung', the church canticles of the funeral service 'moved to tears almost everyone present beside the open coffin . . . Many people attended these requiems. The small apartment could not accommodate them all. Hundreds stood on the stairs and around the entrance. Visitors kept arriving all day long.'

By the time of the last requiem, at 6 p.m. next day, mourners had begun to arrive from Moscow, including a deputation from the Moscow Conservatoire headed by its director, Vasily Safonov, and the composer's old friend Nikolay Kashkin, who laid an enormous silver wreath of roses, forget-me-nots and olive-branches. Also present by the evening was a delegation from the Moscow-based Imperial Russian Musical Society, whose director laid another huge wreath from Her Imperial Highness the Grand Duchess Alexandra Yosipovna. As delegations from Moscow continued to arrive all evening, wreaths were laid on behalf of the Moscow Philharmonic Society, the Moscow Imperial Opera, from Moscow theatres and many others.

Requiem services for Tchaikovsky had also been held elsewhere around St Petersburg, including a memorial service in the concert hall of the Conservatoire, dominated by a huge portrait of the composer, wreathed in laurels. Senior members of the Conservatoire's teaching staff later visited Modest's apartment to lay their own wreath on their colleague's still open coffin. Among them was Rimsky-Korsakov, who thought it 'odd, that though death was the result of cholera, there was free access to the requiems.' He looked on in horror as the cellist Alexandr Verzhbilovich, 'drunk after some binge', kissed the corpse 'all over the head and face'.[21] If Tchaikovsky had indeed died of cholera, this was, to say the least, unwise.

The latest cholera regulations, revised earlier that year, laid down that: 'The bodies of those who have died from cholera should be wrapped in a shroud moistened with a sublimate solution and in so far as possible placed quickly into a coffin.'[22] Yet 'two streams of visitors', according to *Novoe Vremya*, 'moved continuously up and down the staircase leading to the apartment of the dead composer's brother.' The entrance door was 'continuously open'. Literally 'thousands of people' passed through the apartment those first two days.[23]

The corner room, in which the coffin lay, had a 'special' atmosphere. Its 'tropical setting', with curtains drawn, and wreaths everywhere, was 'permeated with a silent sorrow'. Though crowded to overflowing, the room remained uncannily quiet. 'All visitors have a reverential feeling. Everyone talks in whispers, as if afraid to disturb the eternal sleep of the deceased genius. Occasionally a man with a hissing sprayer [pulverizer] would pass, but otherwise the silence was broken only by the loud voice of some master of ceremonies giving instructions.' The public entered the room 'as if it were a sanctuary, filled with mute sorrow.'

It stands in semi-darkness; two large lamps are lit in the corners, and thick wax candles burn dimly around the coffin. In the adjacent rooms, also filled with people, all the furnishings are turned to the wall, from the mirrors to a piano with a closed keyboard, symbolic of the tragedy which has taken place here. The ottoman on which the deceased died stands in the same place; but no-one would sit on it, and that part of it which was used for sitting is protected by pillows.

After the evening requiem, yet another was held – this time, a 'touching and typical' variation on the theme.

Around 7.30 p.m. a priest wearing a large pectoral cross entered the apartment and asked if a priestly vestment was available. 'Let's have another requiem and pray,' said he. 'Visitors are coming and going all the time and maybe someone would like to pray.' The priest – whom nobody knew – was told that a vestment was available, but there were no singers to form a choir. 'This is no problem,' he said firmly. 'I will perform the requiem for the dead. Maybe there'll be someone who can sing. There are students here. Otherwise I will sing myself. It would be a sin not to pray.' One of those present again indicated some kind of problem. 'Don't worry,' said the priest, 'all will be well.' A moment later his voice could be heard beside the coffin: 'Blessed is our Lord . . .' Someone in the crowd of public shyly sang 'Amen'. Then the priest began to chant the liturgical prayer. That first singer was joined by another, and then another, and finally everyone sang . . .[24]

This requiem became 'quite unique: peculiar, original and moving. Many people wept. As the funeral hymns were sung, everyone went down on their knees.' When the service was finally over the priest took off his vestment, bowed to the coffin, and quietly left the room, without saying a word to anyone. 'He disappeared from the apartment without even giving his name.'

A deathmask of Tchaikovsky, taken by the sculptor Tselinsky, showed an expression of 'complete tranquillity'.* On the second evening the body was wrapped in a sheet soaked in sublimate and placed in the coffin. The inner coffin was made of metal and sealed, then placed in an outer coffin of oak, whose lid was screwed tight. Amid the many

---

*As, of course, it does to this day, as can be testified by the privileged few (including the author) who have been allowed to inspect it in the Tchaikovsky Archive at Klin.

wreaths, which covered most of the coffin, was placed a black velvet cushion bearing the insignia of Tchaikovsky's Order of St Vladimir. At his feet, also on a black velvet cushion, was a silver wreath from the Imperial Russian Musical Society, and another of forget-me-nots, its ribbon bearing the inscription: 'Stricken with great sorrow, the artists of the Imperial Russian Opera mourn the prematurely extinguished light of Russian musical art.' Among the other tributes were wreaths from the teaching staff of the St Petersburg Conservatoire, the Court Chapel of Singers, the orchestra of the Imperial Russian St Petersburg Opera ('To a great symphonist') and many more.

Among the countless telegrams received by Modest was one from Chekhov: 'The news staggered me. It is a terrible anguish. I loved and revered Pyotr Ilyich very much, and I am indebted to him for much. You have my heartfelt sympathy.'[25]

'What do you say about Tchaikovsky's death?' Anton Rubinstein wondered aloud in a letter to his sister. 'Can it possibly be the will of God? What a loss for music in Russia! He was in the prime of life, barely fifty – and all this for a glass of water? What a nonsense are all such tricks – and this life – and creation – and everything, and everything . . .'[26]

There was an elaborate wreath but no telegram, no message of condolence, from Nadezhda von Meck.

It took Modest and the directorate of the Imperial Theatres four days to organize Tchaikovsky's funeral – a state occasion, paid for by the Tsar himself. All that time a stream of visitors continued to flow through the apartment, still in open defiance of the cholera regulations. Small wonder the newspapers began to grow suspicious.

On Saturday 4 November, thirty-six hours before Tchaikovsky's death, St Petersburg's *Novosti i Birzhevaya Gazeta* (*News and Stock Exchange Gazette*) had reported: 'The whole music world is alarmed by the news of P.I. Tchaikovsky's serious illness. Fortunately, according to the latest communiqué, Tchaikovsky's illness (presumed to be typhoid) is expected to have a favourable outcome.'

On Monday 6 November, the same paper solemnly recorded that the 'virulent epidemic [of cholera] has also not spared our famous composer P.I. Tchaikovsky. He was taken ill on Thursday during the day and his illness immediately assumed a dangerous character . . . At 2.30 a.m. this morning the doctors left, having decided that the case was hopeless. At 3.00 a.m. P.I. Tchaikovsky was no more.'

The following day, Tuesday 7 November, the *Peterburgskaya Gazeta* (*St Petersburg Gazette*) was among the first to start asking awkward questions: 'How could Tchaikovsky have contracted cholera when he lived in the most excellent hygienic conditions and arrived in St Petersburg only a few days ago?'

The same edition of the paper printed an interview with Vasily Bertenson – 'the first doctor to attend him' – who testified that Tchaikovsky had begun to feel ill on the Thursday, but 'did not seek medical help all that day and well into the next day.' Not until the Friday evening had Dr Bertenson, by his own account, been summoned, by when 'it was already necessary for the combined strength of six men' to alleviate the patient's suffering. He went on to suggest that the following day, Saturday, had seen 'a significant improvement', leading him to believe that Tchaikovsky had been 'saved from cholera'. Concerned by his growing weakness, said Bertenson, the doctors had begun to suspect 'another infection'.

Why had Vasily Bertenson felt obliged to take the unusual step of discussing the details of a celebrated patient's demise with the press? And in such unusually intimate, at times gruesome detail? The same day saw the *Novosti i Birzhevaya Gazeta* secure an interview with Lev Bertenson's assistant, Dr Mamonov, who aroused further suspicion by saying that Tchaikovsky had begun to feel unwell on the Wednesday, rather than the Thursday. The composer had, nevertheless, 'paid no heed' to his indisposition.[27]

Already, within twenty-four hours of Tchaikovsky's death, St Petersburg was alive with rumour that there was more to this tragedy than met the eye – that Modest and the doctors were at best incompetent, at worst lying. 'The most contradictory rumours are afloat in the city with regard both to the causes of P.I. Tchaikovsky's illness, and to his death,' reported the *Novosti i Birzhevaya Gazeta* by way of preface to its interview with Mamonov. In the words of Rimsky-Korsakov, the very suddenness of Tchaikovsky's end 'occasioned all kinds of gossip and rumour'.[28]

So malicious did the whispers grow that the senior Bertenson, Lev, himself felt obliged to break his silence with an interview to *Novoe Vremya*, which appeared on Wednesday 8 November. Far from quelling the rumours, Bertenson's highly technical (and self-contradictory) account served only to fuel them. By the following day, the distinguished doctor had grown sufficiently concerned about assaults on his reputation to issue a statement:

> Certain papers have, in connection with the illness of P.I. Tchaikovsky, ascribed to me opinions and comments in such distorted form that I am compelled to deny them, especially as I have seen no members of the press except the reporter from *Novoe Vremya*, and therefore could not have spoken with any of them.

The doctor's defensiveness merely inflamed the rumours yet further, to the point where Modest himself would feel obliged to intervene. First, however, he had to bury his brother.

The extraordinary scale of Tchaikovsky's funeral remains a striking index of his fame and popularity in his own lifetime. To this day, according to the present keeper of the cemetery where the composer lies buried, it remains 'the biggest funeral St Petersburg has ever seen', bigger even than those of Turgenev or Dostoevsky.[29]

The previous evening, his fourth lying in state, wreaths had arrived from various members of the royal family. Now, on the morning of Friday 10 November, as the family began to assemble at Modest's apartment, came a floral tribute from the Tsar and Tsarina themselves. Crowds had been gathering in the street outside since dawn. Soon the official delegations began to foregather, almost a hundred of them. By the time the cortège moved off, the line of official mourners was three-quarters of a mile long; two extra hearses and three landau were required to accommodate all the huge, overflowing heaps of wreaths.

All the streets around Malaya Morskaya, including Nevsky Prospekt itself, were closed to traffic by the time the funeral procession was ready to move off at 10 a.m. The coffin was carried out of the apartment by the four Tchaikovsky brothers – Nikolay, Ippolit, Modest and Anatoly – with other friends such as Figner, the actors Melnikov, Yakovlev and others. Six pupils of the School of Jurisprudence stood by the sides of the horse-drawn hearse, holding the tassels of the canopy; three more carried the composer's Order of St Vladimir on its black velvet cushion.

Led by the traditional doorkeeper, the several-thousand-strong procession started off along Bolshaya Morskaya Street in the direction of the black-draped and wreath-bedecked Mariinsky Theatre, where it paused for another requiem. Circling the new Conservatoire building under construction across the road, it then headed for Nevsky Prospekt and the Kazan Cathedral, where it arrived at noon. This, on the Tsar's personal instructions, was to be the setting for the main requiem of the day – the first time in Russian history that a civilian had been so honoured. Two hours later, at 2 p.m., the procession lined up again to proceed down Nevsky Prospekt to the cemetery reserved for great artists in the shadow of the Alexandr Nevsky *lavra* (monastery).

Here, alongside Borodin and Musorgsky, just around the corner from Dostoevsky, Tchaikovsky was buried in a brick-lined grave upholstered with gold brocade. Not until 4 p.m., six hours after the cortège had left Modest's apartment, was the last requiem finally sung, with students from the School of Jurisprudence still playing a prominent role.

Once the clergy had departed, a succession of orators stepped onto the temporary stage of scaffolding beside the grave. Chief among them was Tchaikovsky's old schoolfriend, supposedly the object of his unrequited love, Vladimir Gerard, now an eminent lawyer. 'Everyone who is able to think in Russia,' Gerard began, 'and especially everyone who is able to feel, has been deeply stricken. The music of Tchaikovsky, pre-dominantly music of quiet melancholy and profound sorrow, has resounded in Russian hearts everywhere.'

But an 'even greater' loss had been suffered by the composer's 'family' from the School of Jurisprudence.

> We who grew up with him, we who shared with him both the joys
> and sorrows of childhood, knew what a kind of man he was. I don't
> think that any keen searcher of hearts would be able to determine
> so well the character of the man as did his comrades in boarding
> school; and we all loved him because there was no-one among us
> more generous and warm-hearted, as kind and likeable as Pyotr Ilyich.
> These were the distinctive features of his personality, that attracted him
> to all those who came close to him, and the same distinctive features
> shine brightly in all his creative works . . .

'Fare thee well, kind and dear comrade,' Gerard concluded. 'May the earth rest lightly upon you. I have no doubt about this, as it is always light on him who leaves behind an eternal and good memory. And for Tchaikovsky the eternal memory lies in his works, in the love of those who knew him. Farewell!'[30]

There followed some emotional poems, specially written for the occasion, before the final figure to step up to the grave was Nikolay Figner, who wept as he intoned 'Farewell, dear teacher! Eternal memory for you!' All present then crossed themselves, and threw clods of earth down onto the coffin.

Two hours later, at the Alexandrinsky Theatre, Modest Tchaikovsky attended the postponed première of his new play, *Prejudices*.

On the day Tchaikovsky died, only seven other deaths from cholera were recorded in the St Petersburg area.[31] The epidemic which had raged all year had long since begun to abate. Already it was not only the *Peterburgskaya Gazeta* wondering how Tchaikovsky could possibly have contracted the disease. Alexander Suvorin, the outspoken proprietor and editor-in-chief of *Novoe Vremya*, wrote in his diary for Saturday 11 November: 'Tchaikovsky was buried yesterday. I feel desperately sad for him. The two Bertenson brothers treated him and didn't [even] give him a bath. In my opinion these Bertensons do not deserve their reputations at all.'[32]

Four days later, on 15 November – nine days after Tchaikovsky's death – Suvorin launched a vicious attack on Lev Bertenson and his colleagues in *Novoe Vremya*. He focused on Bertenson's failure to call for second (or third) opinions, especially over the question of the bath, concluding that 'Dr Bertenson did not do everything he ought to have done, considering that he had in his care a patient so dear to all Russia.'[33] Two days later, *Novoe Vremya* was demanding that 'Dr Bertenson ought to present to one of the scientific societies . . . a detailed report on his treatment of P.I. Tchaikovsky . . . so that an objective and public examination of [the doctor's] competence might be held.'[34] Suvorin's campaign prompted yet another contribution from Modest, declaring that 'any reproaches whatsoever directed toward the treatment of Pyotr Ilyich's fatal illness' were 'absolutely unjust'.[35]

St Petersburg remained alive with rumour – the more so since the Bertenson brothers had given their extraordinarily candid, defensive and contradictory interviews, which were raising more questions than they had answered. Even Modest's attempt at damage containment had failed.

The previous weekend – the morning after not only his brother's funeral, but yet another unsuccessful first night for himself – Modest had sat down to write a lengthy letter to all the capital's newspaper editors in an openly acknowledged effort 'to dispel all the conflicting rumours'.[36] While attempting to amplify the doctor's 'brief but thoroughly accurate account', however, Modest's letter only made matters yet worse by appearing to contradict it in significant detail.*

Modest and Bertenson differ, for instance, on the timing of the composer's worst 'spasms' and 'convulsions'. The most striking of many other discrepancies arise in Modest's description of his brother's last hours, which is quite at variance with the doctor's report and the medical bulletins he authorized. While the first bulletin, posted at 2.30 p.m., reports that 'dangerous symptoms are still present, and are not responding to treatment', and the second, posted at 10.30 p.m., that 'since 3 p.m. there has been increasing weakness', Modest reports that after a bath at 2 p.m. and injections at 4 p.m. 'his condition seemed to us to improve' until 8 p.m. Again, Bertenson's evidence suggests that Tchaikovsky was given the dreaded hot-bath

*Both documents, and all the other major contemporary sources relating to Tchaikovsky's death, are reproduced in full in Appendix B.

treatment on the Saturday, while Modest says it was the Sunday. No wonder Suvorin added further to the confusion by suggesting that he had not been given the bath at all – a revisionist thesis maintained by some to this day.

At the time, these two newspaper articles served to forestall further press attacks, if not to staunch public rumours of foul play. To posterity, they serve merely to accentuate doubt and suspicion. So similar in tone are the two men's versions of events that the reader cannot but suspect collusion, as if to conceal a more sinister truth. So contradictory, meanwhile, are a few central details that it is clear we cannot take *both* men at their word. Although St Petersburg remained abuzz with gossip about Tchaikovsky's death, the outside world accepted cholera as the verdict, and remained insulated from the truth for the best part of a century. For decades, the only evidence arousing Western suspicion was the *Pathétique* symphony itself, which to some musicological ears began to sound almost like an extended suicide note.

On Saturday 18 November, two weeks after Tchaikovsky's death, Napravnik took his old friend's place on the podium of St Petersburg's Assembly Hall of the Nobility to conduct the Sixth Symphony a second time, at a memorial concert to its composer. This second public performance of the *Pathétique*, three weeks to the night after the first under the composer's own baton, before much the same audience in the same hall, now dominated by a giant, garlanded portrait of the national hero buried only a week, was a complete contrast with the première which had so disappointed him.

'It is indeed a sort of swan song, a presentiment of impending death,' wrote *Russkaya Muzykalnaya Gazeta*, 'and hence comes its tragic impression.'[37] Now the symphony was hailed as 'prophetic', and interpreted as some sort of formal farewell, written with intimations of mortality. 'The public had simply not fathomed it the first time,' in the judgement (some years later) of Rimsky-Korsakov, who was present at both performances. The very different reception second time around was attributable, in his view, to 'the composer's sudden death (which had given rise to all sorts of rumours), stories about his presentiments of approaching demise (to which mankind is so prone), and a tendency to link these presentiments with the gloomy mood of the last movement of this splendid . . . famed, even fashionable work.'[38]

Relieved that the rumours remained no more than that, with no documentary evidence to support them, Modest repeated his newspaper article almost verbatim in his subsequent three-volume biography of Tchaikovsky, published within a decade of his death – and written in his brother's house at Klin, which soon became (and remains to this day) the central archive on the composer, its files firmly closed to all but approved Russian scholars.

And so the version of his brother's death which Modest sought to convey to posterity – that Tchaikovsky died of cholera, the result of a tragic accident – inevitably became the received wisdom. The basis for most twentieth-century biographies, it was believed by the outside world for the best part of a century.

Within St Petersburg itself, however, rumours of a more sinister truth persisted all that time – gradually hardening, despite seventy years of Soviet censorship, towards common knowledge. It was to take almost ninety years for an alternative, highly dramatic, and far more persuasive version of Tchaikovsky's death to reach the Western world.

# CHAPTER XVIII

# 'The uniform is sacred'

THREE YEARS AFTER TCHAIKOVSKY'S DEATH, A YOUNG SWISS MUSICIAN named Robert Aloys Mooser arrived in St Petersburg to study composition with Balakirev and orchestration with Rimsky-Korsakov. Grandson of the Swiss organ-maker Joseph Mooser, whose standard biography he would later write, the young Mooser subsidized his studies by working as an organist at the Russian capital's French Protestant Church, and writing criticism for the French-language periodical *Journal de St-Pétersbourg*. Within three years of his arrival, at the age of only twenty-three, he had become a member of the directorate of the Imperial Theatres, and a close friend of the Imperial Ballet's resident conductor-composer, Riccardo Drigo. An Italian who had arrived in St Petersburg in 1878, and would make his career there for forty years, Drigo had been a close friend of Tchaikovsky. As chief conductor at the Mariinsky, he had presided over the first performances of *The Sleeping Beauty* and *The Nutcracker*.

Drigo it was who told Mooser, and Mooser who first recorded for posterity, that Tchaikovsky had in fact committed suicide. The favourite version then current on the Petersburg grapevine was that the composer had seduced the son of the caretaker of Modest's apartment block in Malaya Morskaya Street. Upon learning of Tchaikovsky's 'indiscretion', the Tsar had decreed that he must leave the capital forthwith. Realizing that his career was at an end, and that his reputation would be irreparably damaged, Tchaikovsky had poisoned himself.

Astonished by the story, Mooser sought the views of Alexandr Glazunov, whose 'upright moral character, veneration of the composer and friendship with Tchaikovsky' are stressed in Mooser's memoirs (written in the late 1960s, but still awaiting publication) in support of his undoubted reliability as a witness. According to Mooser, Glazunov confirmed that it was true, and wept as he did so.[1] More recently the French Tchaikovsky scholar André Lischke, whose father was a pupil of Glazunov in Petrograd in the 1920s, has also confirmed that Glazunov told his father the same story.[2]

In later life Mooser would become his country's leading music critic, with a reputation in the French-speaking world comparable with that of the conductor Ernest Ansermet. An enthusiastic supporter of Honegger, Frank Martin and Riccardo Malipiero, he was also noted for his constructive opposition to Schoenberg, Messiaen, Boulez and Stockhausen, but most admired for his standard works on Russian music.[3] Since his death in Geneva in 1969, however, at the age of ninety-three, Robert Mooser has been better remembered in the English-speaking world as the first man to produce first-hand evidence that Tchaikovsky killed himself.[4]

At the time Mooser first arrived in St Petersburg – only three years, it should be remembered, after the composer's death – there were many different versions of Tchaikovsky's suicide doing the rounds. One maintained that he had been conducting a homosexual affair with a member of the imperial family – the Tsar's nephew, in some versions, even his son. Ordered by Alexandr III to choose between standing trial for sodomy and committing suicide, the composer had ruefully compared himself with Socrates (the charge against whom was, after all, 'corrupting the youth') and opted for a slightly different version of the same dignified death. The Tsar had given him a revolver for the purpose, or a ring filled with arsenic, or both. Lacking the nerve to use the former, the composer had emptied the poison into a last glass of wine.[5]

Other versions held that Tchaikovsky had been undergoing a severe personal crisis – precipitated, by some accounts, by his infatuation with his nephew, Bob Davidov. Hence the agonies – and the mystery about the programme – in the Sixth Symphony, which he had of course dedicated to Bob. Numerous analysts have since read the *Pathétique* as intensely autobiographical. Realizing the full extent of his feelings for Bob, and the unlikelihood of their physical fulfilment, the theory goes, Tchaikovsky poured his misery into this one last great symphonic work as a conscious prelude to suicide. Unable to find help among his friends, he supposedly began to drink unboiled water in the hope of contracting cholera. In this way, as with his adventure in the Moscow river in 1877, he could commit suicide without bringing the attendant stigma upon his family – perhaps even without their realizing.

Over the century since Tchaikovsky's death, different versions of his demise have abounded, some more outlandish than others. In the St Petersburg of 1993, the present author was even told that Modest had poisoned his brother, for stealing away his lover Lucien Guitry. Back in 1949, the intellectual periodical *Literaturnaya Gazeta* received a letter asserting that Tchaikovsky had been murdered by Lev Bertenson himself. The doctor had apparently admitted his crime over a drink too many. According to family tradition, Bertenson had regularly slipped poison to Tchaikovsky on the orders of the Tsar.[6]

Such rumours persisted throughout the Soviet period, and were familiar in the early 1930s to a musicologist working in the archive at Klin, Georgy Orlov, who was already in possession of dramatic new evidence. While a student of composition at the Leningrad Conservatoire in the 1920s, Orlov had befriended a budding pianist named Nikolay Bertenson, son of Vasily Bertenson, the family doctor who had been the first to attend Tchaikovsky in his final illness. Shortly before his own death in 1933, Dr Bertenson had unburdened himself of a confession to Nikolay, in his friend Georgy Orlov's presence: that in truth Tchaikovsky had poisoned himself.

Another of Orlov's contemporaries at the Conservatoire, as fate would have it, was Yuri Zander, son of Alexandr Zander, one of Lev Bertenson's two medical assistants at Tchaikovsky's deathbed. According to Orlov, the younger Zander also confirmed that his father, too, told him that Tchaikovsky had taken his own life.

Born in Astrakhan in 1900, Orlov had once had ambitions as a composer. After graduating from the Leningrad Conservatoire in the daunting company of Dmitry Shostakovich, however, he had switched to musicology, specializing in librarianship. Orlov too knew Glazunov, by then director of the Conservatoire, who swiftly recognized his talents and appointed him Chief Librarian. Before he was struck down by illness in 1930, Orlov had supervised a wholesale reorganization of the archives of the Conservatoire (which included those of the Russian Musical Society); he it was who, in the process, rediscovered the lost manuscript of Tchaikovsky's graduation cantata, 'To Joy'. After a year's convalescence from major surgery (which was to lead to his premature death ten years later), Orlov became Chief Librarian of the Leningrad Philharmonic Society, which under his stewardship absorbed the archives of several other music libraries in the city.

As word of his skills spread, Orlov was invited in 1937 to do for Moscow what he had for Leningrad: reorganize the Conservatoire library and several of the city's other major musical archives. These included the Tchaikovsky Archive at Klin, sixty miles away, then preparing for the celebrations of the centenary of the composer's birth. Increasingly immersed at Klin, Orlov became one of the leading Tchaikovsky scholars of the day. He undertook an index of all the composer's works, and produced a scientific analysis of his compositional methods and techniques, based on the manuscript scores of *The Queen of Spades* and the Sixth Symphony, the *Pathétique*. Boris Gusman, Klin's equally energetic director, also co-opted him to share the editing of a huge work chronicling Tchaikovsky's activities for every day of his life; but the project was never finished, thanks to Gusman's arrest in 1939 and Orlov's death the following year. What work had been done was lost amid the ensuing chaos of siege, evacuation and war.

In 1935 Orlov had married one of his staff at the library of the Leningrad Philharmonic Society, a twenty-four-year-old scholar named Alexandra Shneyerson, who by 1938 was working alongside him at Klin. Although not on the Museum's permanent staff, Alexandra Orlova's task at Klin was twofold: for the Archive she began a subject-index of Tchaikovsky's correspondence with his brothers, while for a Moscow publishing firm she joined the team compiling the massive official work *Dni i godi P.I. Chaykovskovo: lyetopis zhizni i tvorchestva* (*Days and Years of Tchaikovsky: Annals of His Life and Work*), the first official chronicle of Tchaikovsky's life and work.

Both Jewish-born, the Orlovs were acutely sensitive to the reign of terror in Stalin's Russia throughout their few years together. One side-effect of the secrecy and revisionism in all walks of Soviet life was that Tchaikovsky's death was a taboo subject at Klin, then controlled as much by the composer's family as by the Soviet authorities. Modest's version of events was taken as gospel truth among the staff; none of the familiar rumours were ever discussed, nor did Georgy Orlov feel able to make public the first-hand evidence of Bertenson *père* and Zander *fils*.

Given that her own father, brother and stepfather had been imprisoned since 1937, Alexandra Orlova had especial reason to take care (despite the fact that 'It was not only I that knew Tchaikovsky had poisoned himself. I think that all the old inhabitants of St Petersburg/Leningrad had always known it.'[7]) So when she chanced upon Modest's and Bertenson's newspaper articles, and first grasped the scale on which they differed not merely from each other but from the apparent truth, there was no-one but her husband with whom to discuss her doubts and suspicions.

Only at home, in the rented *dacha* in which their twin sons were born in 1938, did the Orlovs feel able to pool their knowledge and discuss the riddle of Tchaikovsky's death. 'The atmosphere was dreadful,' Orlova recalls. 'We preferred to proceed with our work in secret, and keep it entirely to ourselves.'

They were still puzzling over the relationship between Modest's account and Bertenson's, in some ways so similar yet in various key details so distinct, when Orlov came across two letters among Modest's papers. To this day, a formidable octogenarian still hard at work, his widow still vividly recalls the afternoon in the autumn of 1938 when he came down from Modest's study at Klin, and quietly led her back upstairs to show her a 'staggering' document he had found, a vital discovery in light of the other secrets he had already shared with her.

Together they examined two letters to Modest dated soon after Tchaikovsky's death. Both were from Dr Lev Bertenson, the older brother of Vasily, and senior member of the medical team attending the composer in his final illness. The first read:

> St Petersburg, November 6, 1893
>
> My very dear Modest Ilyich,
>
> I would like to embrace you and to tell you how deeply I am shocked by our common horrible misfortune, but I can hardly stand on my feet, and cannot go out. The dread disease which carried off your cherished brother made me feel at one with him, with you, and with all those to whom he was dear. I cannot recover after this terrible tragedy which I was destined to witness, and cannot tell you all the agonies I am going through now. I can tell you only one thing: that I feel what you feel.
>
> Your faithfully and deeply devoted
>
> Lev Bertenson

The translation is that of the musicologist Nicholas Slonimsky, who also came across the letter in the Klin archive, and passed it to the American writer Herbert Weinstock for publication in a life of Tchaikovsky written during the Second World War. 'It is inconceivable,' he told Weinstock, 'that such a letter, written at such a moment to Tchaikovsky's own brother by a physician and friend, would contain an attempt at concealment of the true circumstances of Tchaikovsky's death.'[8]

Is it? Orlov now showed his wife the second letter from the senior Bertenson which he had found among Modest's correspondence – a document which is today officially declared missing, 'if indeed it ever existed'.[9] It took the form of a detailed medical history of Tchaikovsky's last days: his symptoms, the doctor's conclusions and the resulting treatment, apparently designed to inject some much-needed consistency into public statements by doctor and brother. The Orlovs demonstrated that it bore an uncanny resemblance to Modest's descriptions of his brother's last few days, both in *Novoe Vremya* and subsequently in his biography – and indeed to Vasily Bertenson's recollections in his memoirs, later reprinted in significantly edited form in a volume of reminiscences by Tchaikovsky's friends and colleagues.

'Despite the presence of four doctors at Tchaikovsky's deathbed, there are still people who arrogantly assert that he didn't die of cholera at all, but poisoned himself,' complained Bertenson in the original version of his memoirs, published in 1912. The protest is part of a lengthy passage later censored by Soviet editors, who chose to delete his next sentence: 'Is it worth mentioning the insinuations about the reason for Tchaikovsky's suicide?'[10] Apparently not – and nor, it seems, did the doctor consider it worth mentioning his brother's correspondence with Modest amid the furore over St Petersburg's sudden loss of its beloved Tchaikovsky.*

After Georgy Orlov's death in 1940, his widow passed his papers to his mentor, the musicologist Boris Asafiev, a pupil of Rimsky-Korsakov who had risen to the professorships of musical history, theory and composition at the Leningrad Conservatoire, and who now expressed a wish 'to complete the work of his favourite pupil'. But the blockade of Leningrad intervened, and Orlov's papers were lost.[11] Alexandra Orlova was evacuated with her sons to Novosibirsk, along with the archive of the Leningrad Philharmonic Society, to whose staff she returned for the duration.

After the war, back in Leningrad, Orlova joined the staff of the city's Theatre and Music Research Institute, where she says she heard 'more than once' of Tchaikovsky's suicide from the Institute's director, Professor Alexandr Ossovsky. Another pupil (and close friend) of Rimsky-Korsakov, Ossovsky had been appointed professor of music history, aesthetics and the history of the arts at the Petrograd Conservatoire in 1916, becoming pro-rector in 1922 and rector during Glazunov's subsequent illness and absence abroad. At the time of Tchaikovsky's death, he had been employed at the Ministry of Justice, where the composer had himself worked in his youth, and where, as Ossovsky put it to Orlova, 'the whole truth was known'.[12]

After five years at the Institute, in 1950, at the height of the 'struggle against the Cosmopolites' (or Jews), Orlova was summarily deprived

---

*The contents of this 'phantom' second letter from Bertenson to Modest are now used as a defence of the cholera story even by scholars who deny its existence.[13]

of her post. Over the ensuing twenty years, as an independent writer unattached to any Soviet institutions, she became a renowned musical biographer in her own right, publishing distinguished works on Glinka, Musorgsky and Rimsky-Korsakov.

In 1966, while conducting research into the life of Glinka, she interviewed Alexandr Voitov, senior numismatist at Leningrad's Russian Museum, in his capacity as archivist and unofficial historian of the Imperial School of Jurisprudence. Glinka's friend Vasily Engelhart had been a pupil there – as had Voitov himself, a generation after Tchaikovsky, to whom their conversation naturally turned. Orlova told Voitov that she had 'incontrovertible evidence' that Tchaikovsky had committed suicide, apparently by poison; but her extensive researches into the last few days of his life had as yet revealed neither occasion nor motive. Voitov thought he might be able to help: 'I do not know the precise day on which the incident of which I have information occurred, but most likely it will fill your gap exactly.' Aware that he too was dying, Voitov then passed on to Orlova another confession, vouchsafed to him half a century before by Ekaterina Jacobi, the widow of an eminent St Petersburg lawyer. For years, he had been planning to commit it to paper himself, 'so that it would not be lost to history', but 'all this time I could not bring myself to do it.' He gave her permission to take his evidence down from dictation.

As a boy, Voitov told Orlova, he had spent all his school holidays just outside St Petersburg in Tsarskoye Selo, with the family of Nikolay Borisovich Jacobi, senior prosecutor to the Senate in the 1890s, who had died in 1902. Jacobi's widow, Ekaterina Karlovna, was a family friend of the Voitovs.

> She was very fond of me and welcomed me warmly. In 1913, when I was in the last but one class at the school, the twentieth anniversary of Tchaikovsky's death was widely commemorated. It was then, apparently under the influence of surging recollections, that Mrs Jacobi, in great secrecy, told me the story which, she confessed, had long tormented her. She said that she had decided to reveal it to me because she was now old and felt that she had not the right to take to her grave such an important and terrible secret. 'You,' she said, 'are interested in the history of the school and in the fate of its pupils, and therefore you ought to know the whole truth, the more so since it is such a sad page in the school's history.

During 1893, Voitov told Orlova, Tchaikovsky had embarked on a relationship with a handsome young nobleman, later identified as Alexandr Vladimirovich Stenbok-Fermor, the eighteen-year-old nephew of Count

Alexey Alexandrovich Stenbok-Fermor, a close friend of the Tsar. What follows uncannily mirrors a drama about to unfold in England the following year, when John Sholto Douglas, 8th Marquess of Queensberry, denounced Oscar Wilde over his relationship with his son, Lord Alfred Douglas ('Bosie') – precipitating Wilde's ruin, exile and eventual death.

In St Petersburg, the outraged Count wrote a letter of complaint to the Tsar about Tchaikovsky's conduct, handing it for safe conduct to the most eminent lawyer he knew, Nikolay Jacobi. Jacobi happened to have been a pupil at the School of Jurisprudence at the same time as the composer, even in the same class. Once privy to the contents of the letter, the lawyer was apparently more concerned about the effect of a scandal on the reputation of their *alma mater* than on that of Russia's beloved – and internationally celebrated – 'national composer'.

To Jacobi, in Voitov's words, 'the honour of the school uniform was sacred'. The lawyer promptly convened at his home in Tsarskoye Selo a 'court of honour' of all Tchaikovsky's schoolfriends and contemporaries then in St Petersburg. Eight of them, including the composer, conferred behind closed doors for five hours. Then Tchaikovsky came 'headlong out of the study . . . almost running . . . speechless, very white and agitated' – in the description of Jacobi's wife. The 'court' had told Tchaikovsky that there was only one circumstance in which they could withhold the Count's letter from the Tsar. They required him to kill himself. It was 'a decision by which Tchaikovsky had agreed to abide', and 'a day or two later news of the composer's mortal illness was circulating in St Petersburg.'[14]

A Privy Councillor, then assistant senior public prosecutor, Nikolay Borisovich Jacobi (1839–1902) sounds to have been a thoroughly nasty piece of work. According to the memoirs of his immediate superior, the Chief Public Prosecutor of the Criminal Department of the Senate, Anatoly Fedorovich Koni, the 'slow-witted' Jacobi was 'far from the best' of the public prosecutors on his staff, 'particularly obtuse and bad-tempered', and one of a group who 'considered it a sign of their independence to disagree with their boss.' Sent to observe the judicial investigation of a revolutionary named Avrinsky, and other members of the Mogilev Regional Committee, Jacobi had shown in this 'unfortunate affair' his 'totally servile and shameless diligence . . .'

> Being in a position to influence the case, using downtrodden provincial investigators, Jacobi, like a bloodthirsty wild beast, frenziedly began using the fate of the accused to build his own career. He went to Mogilev, whence he sent me pompous reports, and by any

available means, honourable and dishonourable, using persuasions and threats, wrested a confession of guilt from Avrinsky. Jacobi then began blowing his own trumpet of victory.[15]

To illustrate 'the full extent of Jacobi's unscrupulousness', Koni adds that his assistant had asked for a young clerk called Tseil – 'a hopeless case, but young and very good-looking' – to be sent with him on this mission. 'When I asked why he needed this young man, Jacobi replied that the women in the provinces must know many intimate details about Avrinsky's life, which would be important for the case against him.' Several times, says Koni, he was obliged to 'curb Jacobi's zeal'. When Jacobi subsequently became a fellow Senator, he used to 'turn on me in meetings, green with suppressed rage . . .'

The son of an eminent but hard-up scientist, Boris Semyonovich Jacobi, the young Nikolay had attended the School of Jurisprudence on a state grant.[16] Once a civil servant, according to files in the Russian State Historical Archive, he followed his father's example by applying successfully for state funds for the education of his own three children, Pyotr, Anastasia and Elizaveta, even for the 'treatment of his ailing wife', Ekaterina Karlovna, née Ganzen (once a pupil of Anton Rubinstein). In the early 1890s the authorities granted several requests for state bursaries from Jacobi, 'taking into account his thirty-four years of extremely con-scientious service, and . . . his lack of means to support his family.'[17] In 1893, the Jacobi family was living just outside St Petersburg in the fashionable town of Tsarskoye Selo (now Pushkin), site of the Tsar's sumptuous Summer Palace, at No. 11 Kolpinskaya St (now Pushkin St)[18] – which is where the 'court of honour' would have been convened.

Its other members, former schoolfellows of Tchaikovsky who were in St Petersburg at the time, all now senior lawyers and politicians, would have included two men whom the composer considered his good friends: Vladimir Nikolayevich Gerard (1839–1903), the object of Tchaikovsky's unrequited love during his later years at the school, now a member of the council of advocates of the judicial chamber of the St Petersburg district, and a noted orator who would soon deliver the solemn oration beside the composer's grave; and Avgust Antonovich Gerke (1841–1902), a barrister in the legal advice office at the Ministry of Justice's Department of Civil Appeals, and the amateur musician to whom Tchaikovsky had recently dedicated a piano piece – whose title, *Tendres reproches*, now took on some considerable irony.

Apart from Jacobi, Gerard and Gerke, the other members of the 'court of honour', all of them Privy Councillors, seem likely to have included: Ivan Nikolayevich Turchaninov, legal counsel to the Governor of St

Petersburg (and the author of reminiscences of Tchaikovsky's period at the School of Jurisprudence, written at Modest's request for his biography); Alexey Vasilyevich Belostotsky and Nikolay Nikolayevich Schreiber, both senators in the Department of Criminal Appeal; Boris Alexandrovich Brovtsin, chairman of a department of the judicial chamber; and Vladimir Pavlovich Mordvinov, a senator and barrister in the Synod. Mordvinov was the editor of the jubilee edition of the school's 'Yearbook', a special issue published in 1885 to mark its fiftieth anniversary, in which photographs of Tchaikovsky and all these, his classmates, can be seen to this day in the St Petersburg public library.[19]

Also to be found in that library, but mentioned in no previous biography of Tchaikovsky, is a handwritten letter from the composer to the young nobleman who had so fatefully captured his affections.

> Much respected Alexandr Vladimirovich,
>
> I can come to you tomorrow only at 11 o'clock. It is impossible to come before that. If it is not convenient for you, please let me know.
>
> I am all yours.
>
> P.I. Tchaikovsky

The formal manner in which the note begins may well be a nod from the social snob in Tchaikovsky to his friend's noble birth. But the Russian phrase with which it ends – '*Ya ves vash*' ('I'm all yours') – is strikingly intimate. The letter is undated, and carries no address. Some Soviet archivist has added the surname Adlerberg in an apparent attempt to deflect attention from the document's true significance.

The Russian *Military Encyclopaedia* lists Alexandr Vladimirovich Stenbok-Fermor, the son of Count Vladimir Alexandrovich and nephew of Count Alexey Alexandrovich, as attached to the most prestigious regiment in the country: His Imperial Highness's Life Guard Hussars, whose commander-in-chief was the Tsar himself. From 1904, the Tsarevich, Alexey, was also attached to the same regiment.

In 1901, eight years after Tchaikovsky's death, Alexandr and his cousin Sergey, Count Alexey's son, are both named as cornets in the regiment, though Sergey's subsequent advance through the ranks was the more rapid; by 1906 he had become a lieutenant while Alexandr was still a mere cornet (the fifth commissioned officer in a troop of cavalry, who carries the regimental colours). By 1916 both were staff captains, Sergey directing operations in the Verkhne-Isetian mining and engineering plants, Alexandr still in the Household Cavalry. The following year Alexandr's name disappears from the military records, and indeed all other archives.[20]

Alexandr's uncle, Count Alexey Alexandrovich Stenbok-Fermor, was a Privy Councillor, an Equerry to the Tsar, still listed as a courtier at the time of the 1917 revolution. In *The Russian Book of Genealogy* the Stenbok-Fermors are described as 'an ancient and very distinguished family', with a proud history of public service. In the 1890s Count Alexey's wife, Margarita Sergeyevna, performed good works for the St Isaac's Orthodox Brotherhood; their daughter, Margarita Alexeyevna, was Maid of Honour to the Tsarina. The two Counts, eldest of the six children of Count Alexandr Ivanovich, were the twenty-first generation to have borne the title, tracing their Stenbok ancestry back to a Swedish Reichcouncillor in 1205. It was towards the end of the seventeenth century that Colonel Count Magnus Johann Stenbok had been allowed to join his name and coat of arms with that of his mother, the daughter of Count William Fermor, who had died in England 'as a result of his allegiance to the House of Stuart'. William's son, Governor of Smolensk under Catherine the Great, 'gloriously led the Russian army against Frederick the Great in 1758'; but his Fermor ancestors had fought alongside William the Conqueror.

The Stenbok-Fermor version of Tchaikovsky's death remained Alexandra Orlova's secret for more than a decade after she first heard it from Alexandr Voitov in 1966. Then seventy-four years old, Voitov himself had died only a few months later. Over the next ten years, as Orlova continued her work in Leningrad, there was 'no doubt . . . among the musicians and older residents of the city, that Tchaikovsky had committed suicide, however much Soviet musicology insisted on maintaining the "cholera" version instituted by his brother and the doctors who attended him. The broader public too believes in suicide connected with Tchaikovsky's homosexuality.'[21]

So many and various did the rumours remain that when Orlova's friend Lidya Konniskaya, author of the 'popular but serious' book *Tchaikovsky in St Petersburg*, met some of her readers publicly in Leningrad in 1970, 'the question she was openly asked was not *whether* the composer committed suicide, but only *why*.'[22] Both women thought they now knew why, but felt obliged to hold their peace. It was Konniskaya who had introduced Orlova to Voitov; she too had been present at the 1966 interview. 'We both wrote down what Voitov said,' asserts Orlova, 'and then compared notes.' The only other person in on Voitov's secret, Konniskaya had herself attempted to publish the 'court of honour' story in her own book in 1969, but had fallen foul of its Soviet editor.

Once Konniskaya too died, in 1977, Orlova was the only living repository of Ekaterina Jacobi's evidence. She felt unable to publish it until 1980, a year after fleeing to the West and settling in the United States. 'In the Soviet Union,' she explains, 'I exercised what was known as self-censorship: that is, I knew what I was and was *not* allowed to write about. The idea of promulgating these matters before escaping to the West never entered my head.'[23]

Orlova's role at the Tchaikovsky Archive in the late 1930s is now played down by the current regime at Klin, where she has become regarded at best as a hostile witness, at worst as a fifth columnist. Georgy Orlov's wife, sniffs the current archivist, was merely a 'short-term, part-time member of the staff.'[24] But Alexandra Orlova's name does indeed appear on the title-page of *Dni i godi P.I. Chaykovskovo*, published in the Soviet Union in 1940, as one of four scholars who 'compiled' the work under the editorship of V. Yakovlev.

Also published in Russian in 1940 was Volume One of *Pisma k rodnim* (*Letters to his relatives*), the first instalment of what was to have been a multi-volume collection of Tchaikovsky's voluminous correspondence, edited by Vladimir Zhdanov. It was through this seminal work that the world first received formal documentation, in his own words, of Tchaikovsky's homosexuality – conspicuously unmentioned by Modest in his supposedly definitive three-volume biography, published in 1900–02. Modest's subsequent autobiography is reputedly much more candid about his and his brother's homosexuality. It remains unpublished (although Klin, where the manuscript resides, has now commissioned an approved Russian scholar named Valery Sokolov to edit an 'authorized' edition).[25]

Six years earlier, in his commentary on the first volume of Tchaikovsky's correspondence with his patron, Nadezhda von Meck, Zhdanov had openly mentioned the composer's homosexuality, while feeling obliged to bowdlerize the text of the letters. This time around, however, his editing was far too liberal for the Soviet censors, who ordered the book's immediate withdrawal.

Although he later edited several more specific volumes of Tchaikovsky's letters – to the pianist-composer Sergey Taneyev and his publisher Pyotr Yurgenson – Zhdanov himself was removed from his post, and prevented from further work in the archive for a decade. *Pisma k rodnim* was officially abandoned; Volume Two, already nearing completion, never appeared. Five thousand copies of that first volume had, however, already been printed; rather than destroy them, as the authorities expected, the publishers secretly distributed them to musicologists and other trustworthy recipients. Though hard to find, numerous copies are thus still in existence today.[26]

Orlova managed to smuggle out her own copy of this precious tome when she 'fled Communism' in 1979, escaping from the Soviet Union via Europe to join her sons in America. From her new home in New Jersey, she immediately renewed contact with the English scholar David Brown, Reader in (later Professor of) Musicology at Southampton University, and an international authority on Russian music who had recently embarked on his own study of Tchaikovsky. After several years of censored correspondence with Orlova in the Soviet Union, Brown now encouraged her to publish her new findings. With her agreement, meanwhile, he broadcast their substance on BBC Radio, both domestically via Radio 3 and globally on the World Service. 'They aroused enormous interest on the British musical scene,' he recalls.

America's turn came that autumn, in November 1980, when Orlova chose the relative obscurity of New York's Russian émigré newspaper *Novy Amerikanets* (for which one of her sons works) to make public for the first time the 'court of honour' version of Tchaikovsky's death. In her modest apartment in Jersey City, meanwhile, she worked on a fuller version for academic publication – translated by Brown, then a mere five years and one volume into his fifteen-year, four-volume 'biographical and critical' study of Tchaikovsky and his music,[27] for publication in the April 1981 edition of the leading British musicological journal *Music & Letters*.[28]

At much the same time, in the United States, Orlova's version of events was outlined for American readers by Joel Spiegelman in *High Fidelity* magazine, under the title 'The Trial, Condemnation and Death of Tchaikovsky'.[29] Six months later the same magazine published a rebuttal from an outraged trio comprising two academics, Malcolm H. Brown and Simon Karlinsky, and the Russian émigrée writer Nina Berberova.[30] Orlova's immediate reply, again in *Novy Amerikanets*[31], was noticed by the *New York Times*[32], which now drew the suicide theory to the attention of a far wider audience, prompting another angry reply from the same trio of traditionalists.

The subsequent debate continues to this day, fuelled by the wide credence accorded Orlova's 1981 article. David Brown subsequently recorded the 'court of honour' story in his authoritative entry on Tchaikovsky in *The New Grove Dictionary of Music and Musicians* (1980), moving Edward Garden to follow suit in the 15th edition of *Encyclopaedia Britannica* (1989). Orlova herself enlarged on the theme in several subsequent publications – notably, in 1990, a Tchaikovsky 'autobiography' reconstructed from his letters and diaries.[33] The composer's suicide at the behest of his schoolfriends had become apparent truth, taken as holy writ on record sleeves, in programme notes, and throughout the public domain.

Chief among those 'surprised' (and outraged) by these developments, blaming 'the enthusiastic response of a number of Western musicologists' to Alexandra Orlova's 'sensational theories' was Alexander Poznansky, a Russian-born cultural historian, another émigré living and working in the United States at Yale University – only a hundred miles or so, ironically enough, from Orlova (though the two have never met). In 1988, while working on his own 'psychosexual' biography of the composer, Poznansky mounted a fierce rebuttal of Orlova's article.[34] Granting that rumours about the composer's suicide had existed for almost a century, he proceeded to attempt at great length to demonstrate why 'no serious scholar has ever attached the slightest importance to them'.

The debate between Poznansky, Orlova and other Tchaikovsky scholars has since become very complex – at times heated, even abusive. The cholera and suicide theorists disagree about virtually everything, from the symptoms of cholera poisoning to the nature and extent of the epidemic in St Petersburg that autumn, the cholera regulations in force at the time, and so on. The present author's own extensive researches, while adding considerable flesh to the bones of the 'court of honour' theory, point all but conclusively to a deliberate cover-up by Modest and his medical friends, on the wishes of the composer himself, of the truth: that Tchaikovsky did indeed take his own life.

There can be no dispute, as has been amply demonstrated, that Modest Tchaikovsky's account of his brother's life is wilfully economical with the truth. His version of his brother's death must also be treated with the greatest suspicion, not only because of the contradictions between his and the doctors' accounts, nor even because of the alternative theories which have now persisted in St Petersburg for more than a century. The more the truth of Tchaikovsky's life has emerged, the clearer has become the sheer scale of the extent to which Modest shamelessly hid awkward but vital facts – concerning, above all, the composer's sexuality, and his ambivalence towards it. Even cholera 'traditionalists' like Nicholas Slonimsky blame Modest for 'concealing so crudely the all-explaining factor of Tchaikovsky's emotional aberration that the reader is fully justified in suspecting the objective truth of his biography.'[35]

Nor is it merely Modest's omissions and deceptions which arouse continuing doubts about the cause of the composer's death. There has been a century of evasive protectiveness by his relatives, alongside seventy years of censorship exercised by the Soviet authorities, who blocked full publication of Tchaikovsky's letters and diaries to prevent Russians from knowing that their 'national composer' was a homosexual.

Homosexuality, like suicide, has been a taboo subject in Russia for almost the entire period since Tchaikovsky's death. Even now, in post-Soviet Russia (where homosexuality has been legalized, but is still the butt of ignorance and prejudice), archives are not opening to the extent to which Western scholars had hoped – partly because the secretive Soviet mindset still prevails among post-Communist officialdom, and partly because anti-Western sentiment still has the Russian bureaucracy reluctant to countenance the enquiries of 'outside' biographers into the private lives of their great public figures (except, of course, for large amounts of Western money).

So the hard facts, such as are available, must be set against the propaganda. To return to the Bertenson brothers' diagnosis of cholera, a disease which neither had ever seen before, the records show that the severe summer epidemic in St Petersburg had declined sharply with the arrival of the cold autumn weather. On 13 October 1893, two hundred cases of cholera were reported; by 6 November, the day of Tchaikovsky's death, the figures had more than halved to sixty-eight, with 'a sharp decline in mortality'.[36] The outbreak had been largely confined to the city's slums, where the poor 'lived in crowded, insanitary conditions without observing elementary medical instructions . . . [Cholera] did not usually touch the affluent and more educated families because they observed strict precautions. Medical advice not only forbade the drinking of unboiled water; it recommended that water for washing should also be boiled.'[37]

If Lev Bertenson's narrative is followed closely, moreover (see Appendix B, pages 440–2), the doctor loses a whole day of the composer's agonizing death throes, otherwise so meticulously annotated. By Bertenson's account, Tchaikovsky died not on the morning of 6 November, but on the morning of the day before. Let us make allowances for human error, as Modest watched his brother dying in agony, and deem it understandable that these two witnesses are at odds about the precise phases of the composer's convulsions; even so, how does the Tsar's own personal physician manage to confuse the three textbook stages of the disease, and to telescope the last two days into one, thus managing to get the very date of Tchaikovsky's death wrong? And why is it that his detailed description of the last twenty-four hours does not tally with the two scraps of evidence which we do unequivocally possess: the medical bulletins posted in his name outside the apartment at 2.30 p.m. and 10.30 p.m. on Sunday 5 November? These speak of 'dangerous symptoms . . . not responding to treatment' and 'increasing weakness', apparently preparing St Petersburg for the worst – at a time when Modest says 'the position was not yet hopeless', Dr Vasily Bertenson had felt able to slip away 'to see other patients', and Lev Bertenson says Tchaikovsky had been dead since 3 a.m.

Could it in fact be true that Tchaikovsky died twenty-four hours earlier than was officially announced, during the night of Saturday–Sunday 4–5 November? That Bertenson, in other words, was accurate about the duration of the illness, and that news of the composer's death was withheld, as David Brown has put it, 'for reasons best known to Modest, Bertenson and others'? Why, come to that, were medical bulletins posted only on the fourth and last day of so famous a patient's fatal illness? Could it again be that the composer had *already* died, and the bulletins were 'fabricated to provide further visible evidence to support the following day as the date of his death'?[38] If so, why would Modest, the Bertensons and the four other intimates at Tchaikovsky's deathbed need twenty-four hours' grace before throwing wide the doors, in open defiance of cholera regulations, to admit most of St Petersburg (and, later, Moscow) to pay its homage to a corpse laid out in an open coffin?

Did they in fact spend those twenty-four hours removing all trace of the real cause of the composer's death, literally behind closed doors, and concocting their own private version of the truth? 'Whatever the truth about the composer's end,' concludes Brown, 'it was not what the outside world was meant to believe.'[39]

If Tchaikovsky had really contracted cholera, there was a profoundly irresponsible disregard by these distinguished doctors, both during the composer's illness and after his death, of the most basic – and statutory – sanitary precautions. 'Isolation of cholera patients,' said the latest official regulations, 'should be effected either in the homes where they have fallen ill, or by the removal of the patient from his home to a medical institution . . .'[40] At recent medical conferences to discuss cholera pre-cautions, held in St Petersburg in December 1892 and Moscow in March 1893, special emphasis had been placed on the danger of infection from the patient's excreta. Underwear and bed linen was to be burned, or very carefully disinfected. Yet according to Yuri Davidov's second wife, Tamara Fedorovna, relatives who had lent sheets during Tchaikovsky's last illness (including her mother, Lyubov Pets) received them back unwashed.[41] Assuming that Modest and the doctors would avoid the slightest risk of infecting other family members with the disease of which Tchaikovsky, like his mother, was apparently dying, this would suggest that they had shared with their closest relatives the secret that his complaint was not in fact cholera.

There is now inside evidence to this effect. As the years have passed and the Tchaikovsky and von Meck families proliferated, becoming scattered around the world, they have begun to feel free to reveal other versions of events, as handed down by family tradition. In 1981 Galina von Meck, daughter of the union between Tchaikovsky's niece

Anna and his patron's son Nikolay, was the first to testify that the details of Tchaikovsky's death were 'completely different from the way his brother Modest related them'.[42] Although herself only two when her great-uncle died, the composer's great-niece passed on crucial details she had heard from one of those at the bedside during Tchaikovsky's last hours: his nephew and close friend, Count Alexandr ('Sanya') Litke, a leading member of the 'Fourth Suite'.

Litke's reliability as a witness has since been questioned by supporters of Modest, as his date of birth is recorded in all reference books as 1879, which would make him thirteen years old at the time of the composer's death. Alexander Poznansky, despite himself listing Litke as born in 1879, describes him as 'much sought after as an amateur actor in household theatricals' who spoke 'fluent French' and whose 'title of Count opened all doors for him'. Litke's circle of acquaintance was 'unusually wide'. He knew 'absolutely everyone'. And he performed 'difficult missions' for Tchaikovsky, who chided his religious views as 'heretical'.[43]

All this at the age of thirteen? Like many other biographers, Poznansky goes on to repeat a favourite Tchaikovsky anecdote, first told by a childhood friend of Litke named Alexandr Khessin, who fancied himself as a budding composer: that his classmates Litke and Vladimir Napravnik arranged for Khessin, as a surprise, to meet Tchaikovsky for tea at St Petersburg's Grand Hotel.[44] Both Khessin and Napravnik are known (and acknowledged by all, Poznansky included) to have been born in 1869. If Litke was ten years younger, how could he have been their classmate?

In the St Petersburg Historical Archive, in 1993, the present author found documentary proof that Litke was in fact born on 21 December 1868. At the time of Tchaikovsky's death, therefore, he was almost twenty-five.[45] This adds considerable weight to all Litke's testimony – not least his dramatic eye-witness account of his uncle's return to Modest's apartment on the afternoon of Thursday 2 November 1893, less than three days before his death. Litke was in the room with Modest when Tchaikovsky 'came back home seemingly very upset by something . . . and asked his brother for a glass of water. When told that he would have to wait for the water to be boiled, he ignored his brother's protests, went into the kitchen, filled a glass of water from the tap and drank it, saying something like "Who cares anyway!"'[46]

What had so upset Tchaikovsky? 'We shall never really know,' is all Galina von Meck will say – which Orlova and others now take as a coded reference to the 'court of honour'. In her *Music & Letters* article, Orlova suggested that the court was convened on the Tuesday of that last week of Tchaikovsky's life, 31 October, the day on which Modest's otherwise detailed account of his brother's movements leaves a conspicuous gap. Between the publication of the article in 1981 and her book in 1990, however, she reconsidered this in light of Litke's evidence, as relayed by von Meck in the same breath as accusing Modest of lying.

Von Meck was questioning more than merely the revealing confusion over when Tchaikovsky supposedly drank the fatal glass of water: on the Wednesday evening at Leiner's restaurant, before Modest's arrival, as in the accounts of those present; or in Modest's presence at the apartment at lunchtime the next day, as in Modest's own account. She was primarily concerned to discredit Modest's story that the composer had cursed his patron, her grandmother, on his deathbed. While quoting Litke's 'Who cares, anyway?' story, she actually lends credence to Modest's version that the water was drunk in his apartment – if not, perhaps, from a glass on the lunch table – on the Thursday. The incident, according to Litke, happened 'three days' after Tchaikovsky had sent the manuscript score of the Sixth Symphony to Yurgenson in Moscow. The covering letter to Yurgenson was written, as we have seen, on Sunday 29 October, the day after the *Pathétique* première, and sent with the score on Monday 30th. So 'three days' later would be the Thursday, 2 November, the day on which Modest says his brother first became ill.

Either way, the elapsed time was clearly shorter than the textbook incubation period for cholera. Even Poznansky concedes that the 'notorious' glass of water 'could not have been responsible' for Tchaikovsky's illness – suggesting, *en passant*, that the discrepancies between Modest's and Bertenson's accounts arise from Modest's 'intense remorse for having failed to save his brother's life'.[47] This crucial detail alone is enough to undermine the received wisdom that Tchaikovsky died of cholera – unless of course it had been contracted by other means.

Another recent suggestion is that Tchaikovsky might indeed have caught cholera – but by means entirely other than drinking a glass of unboiled water. The 'faecal-oral route' is the euphemism employed by the cholera specialist Dr Valentin Pokrovsky, President of the Russian Academy of Medical Sciences, to suggest that the composer might have been exposed to the disease as a result of less than hygienic sexual practices with male prostitutes in St Petersburg.[48] This theory has also been separately advanced in *The Times* of London by its veteran medical specialist, Dr Thomas Stuttaford, who believes that Tchaikovsky 'could well' have contracted cholera from one of his sexual partners from 'downtown' St Petersburg.[49*]

---

*The widespread practice of 'rimming' or 'tonguing' (of the consequences of which Dr Stuttaford has long clinical experience) could have led to inadvertent oral ingestion of the cholera bacillus. In this aspect of his life, at least, Tchaikovsky may have been something less than Laroche's 'true master of hygiene'.

There is no further evidence to support this notion, but if Tchaikovsky had indeed caught cholera this way, he and Modest would both have certainly gone to great pains to disguise the fact. By mutual agreement, therefore, they might well have *staged* the drinking of the glass of water for the sake of family, friends, admirers and posterity. In the case of an almost sacred national figure, also an internationally respected 'ambassador' for Russia and its music, the eminent doctors involved might (justifiably) have permitted their medical consciences to go along with such a deception. Performing this service for so celebrated a friend – at his own wish, without committing any medical malpractice, or in any way failing to prevent his already inevitable death – could scarcely amount to a breach of their Hippocratic oath.

So Tchaikovsky may already have been suffering from cholera, and known it, before he drank the legendary glass of unboiled water. Whether he did so at Leiner's on the Wednesday evening or at Modest's apartment the following lunchtime becomes, in the context of the incubation period, quite irrelevant. Perhaps he did both. But the scene at Leiner's appears so stage-managed, in a public place, in front of so many witnesses (and apparently, for once, with no request for discretion), that it begins to take on the ring of truth. Since immortalized in countless books, even films and television documentaries, it has come to carry a certain resonance. If Tchaikovsky wished the world to believe that he had caught cholera by drinking unboiled water, whether deliberately or accidentally, what did he wish the world to think his motive?

At the height of his powers, internationally celebrated, free from money worries, full of plans for the future, the composer had no apparent reason to take his own life, or even endanger it for the sake of slaking his post-theatre thirst (for which there was anyway a plentiful supply of wine, vodka and mineral water, to all of which he was more than partial, on hand at both Leiner's and Modest's). For years he had lived with his angst about his sexuality; for months he had lived with his unrequited sexual feelings for Bob, eloquently expiated in the Sixth Symphony. The only prospect that could possibly have driven Tchaikovsky to suicide – a last resort which he had contemplated more than once before – was the threat of public exposure and disgrace. Which brings us back to the 'court of honour'.

In 1987, six years after Galina von Meck had publicly questioned Modest's veracity, the Tchaikovsky family again broke ranks. From the obscurity of a small town in central Germany, another relative emerged to confirm that the story of the *ad hoc* trial-by-schoolfriends, convened by the odious Jacobi, had passed down to her from one of those beside Tchaikovsky's deathbed, his brother Nikolay.

Natalya Kuznetsova-Vladimova is the granddaughter of Nikolay's sister-in-law, Vera Sergeyevna Kuznetsova (*née* Denisova). A writer on cultural matters, the wife of the eminent Russian author Georgy Vladimov, Mrs Kuznetsova-Vladimova subscribes (and occasionally contributes) to the literary magazine *Kontinent*, which in 1987 published an article by Orlova retelling Voitov's account of the 'court of honour'. In subsequent correspondence with Orlova Mrs Kuznetsova-Vladimova confirmed that, since her childhood, she had known 'for certain' that this was the cause of Tchaikovsky's death. Her grandmother used to tell 'exactly the same version' of the court of honour – 'hissing' Jacobi's name 'very aggressively' as she did so. Vera Sergeyevna had heard the story, according to her grand-daughter, from her sister Olga, wife of Tchaikovsky's oldest brother, Nikolay, who had been with the composer in Modest's apartment throughout those last few days of his life.*

Vera Sergeyevna had died in 1955, 'at a great age, but sound in mind and good in memory'. Three years earlier, at the home she shared with her granddaughter, she had received a visit from Yuri Iosifovich Slonimsky, the authority on Russian ballet. When Slonimsky had said that Tchaikovsky's suicide had been precipitated by his improper attentions to the heir to the throne, Vera Sergeyevna had corrected him. 'No,' she said, 'it was the nephew of Count Stenbok . . .'[50]

In the summer of 1993, in St Petersburg, the present author also tracked down Alexandr Voitov's widow, Inna, the current custodian of his unique archive on the School of Jurisprudence. 'The School was Alexandr's life,' said Mrs Voitova, a sculptress nearly forty years younger than her late husband, who confirmed that he had told her too the details of the 'court of honour' – exactly as relayed by Orlova. Voitov's widow thus refuted the attempts of certain 'cholera theorists' to discredit Orlova's dealings with her husband by alleging (once he was safely dead) that he had refused to sign her version of her conversation with him.[51]

Still wary of the traditionalist atmosphere in the 'new' Russia, Mrs Voitova professed herself reluctant to be drawn further into the controversy. It was, nevertheless, intriguing to hear her use (while the BBC cameras were rolling) exactly the same phrase as Orlova quotes of her husband – 'It was a sad chapter in the school's history' – despite the fact

---

*The author recently traced Mrs Kuznetsova-Vladimova to the German town of Niedernhausen. After two long telephone conversations, in which she again confirmed family talk of a court of honour, she abruptly went back on her agreement to meet. She was hoping to return to Russia, it transpired, to look for documentary evidence, such as her grandmother's diary; if she found anything significant, she would prefer to publish it herself.

that she says she has no knowledge of Orlova's work (which has not, of course, been published in Russia).

During a conducted tour of her husband's archive, from its cocked hats to schoolboy photographs of the composer, Mrs Voitova also quoted him as telling her that pupils at the School of Jurisprudence regularly held 'courts of honour' to resolve schoolboy 'crimes' without bringing them to the attention of the staff.

A striking example can be found in the memoirs of Vladimir Taneyev, older brother of Tchaikovsky's pianist friend Sergey, and a pupil at the School two classes below the composer. In 1860, according to the elder Taneyev, a student named Vladimir Zubov 'waylaid and raped' a younger pupil in a park at Pavlovsk, in the suburbs of St Petersburg. Before the incident could reach the ears of the school authorities, Taneyev himself convened a schoolboy 'court of honour' in which he volunteered to play prosecutor. Several students argued the case for the defence: that the incident had taken place outside the school precincts, even that it was a 'private matter' between assailant and victim. Zubov, it seems, was a popular boy. With student sentiment running in the accused's favour, Taneyev (by his own admission) resorted to some legal 'sleight of hand', and reduced the sentence he was seeking from expulsion to ostracism. This proved a shrewd move, as the trial ended with Zubov being ostracized 'by a vast majority'.[52]

The episode is quoted by Poznansky himself – something of an irony, in view of his almost obsessive mission to discredit Orlova and the 'court of honour' theory, while defending Modest by reasserting that Tchaikovsky died of cholera.[53] For all his considerable scholarship, and the pioneering scale of his research into the composer's sexual habits, Poznansky's central thesis is based on the highly dubious proposition that Tchaikovsky was entirely comfortable with his sexuality. 'In my opinion,' he writes, 'there is no evidence of any sexual qualms during the whole span of his life', although even he excepts the 'brief period' of his marital crisis in 1876–77.[54]

This would plainly appear to disregard Tchaikovsky's own views on the subject, the central theme of his life, as so frequently quoted throughout these pages. To take but a handful of examples: before the 'marital crisis', in January 1875, we have heard him tell Anatoly that it is his homosexuality which has caused 'an unbridgeable gulf' between himself and the rest of society: 'It lends my personality an aloofness, a fear of company, excessive shyness, a mistrust of everyone – in sum, a thousand qualities which make me ever more unsociable . . .' The following year, to his fellow homosexual Modest, Tchaikovsky could not have been more explicit:

> It seems to me that our *inclinations* are the biggest and most insurmountable obstacle to our happiness, and that we must fight against our natures with all our strength . . . not just to silence the gossips [but] for you yourself, for your peace of mind . . . I shall abandon for ever my previous habits, and shall endeavour to be numbered no more among the company [of homosexuals] . . . I think of nothing but ridding myself of all pernicious passions.

This is an attitude which, in Poznansky's scheme of things, Tchaikovsky shed with the years. All the evidence suggests otherwise – from the letters and diaries to the music itself, up to and including the *Pathétique*, while scoring which he wrote in his diary of his obsessive love for his nephew: 'What a monster of a person I am.'[55]

In his attempts to challenge the truth that Tchaikovsky himself articulated time and again – that he was 'a martyr to his homosexuality' – Poznansky goes so far as to argue that the composer 'eventually came to see his sexual peculiarities as an insurmountable and even natural part of his personality . . . [He] gradually succeeded in adjusting his inner circumstances to the societal conditions of his time without experiencing any serious psychological damage.' If this needs any refutation beyond the composer's own words, a more subtle approach can be found in the work of the British musicologist and Tchaikovsky scholar Henry Zajaczkowski, whose research 'along psychoanalytic lines' points rather to 'a severe unconscious inhibition by the composer of his sexual feelings':

> One consequence of it may be sexual overindulgence as a kind of false solution: the individual thereby persuades himself that he does accept his own sexual impulses. Complementing this and, also, as a psychological defence mechanism, would be precisely the idolization by Tchaikovsky of many of the young men of his circle [the self-styled 'Fourth Suite'], to which Poznansky himself draws attention. If the composer's response to possible sexual objects was either to use and discard them or to idolize them, it shows that he was unable to form an integrated, secure relationship with another man. That, surely, was [Tchaikovsky's] tragedy.[56]

In an unpublished reply to Poznansky's assaults on her work, shared with the present author, Alexandra Orlova also reasserts that 'letters over many years as well as Tchaikovsky's diaries sufficiently confirm that he never reconciled himself to his anomaly. He resigned himself to the impossibility of reforming himself, that was all.'[57] Among non-expatriate Russians who emphatically supported this view in conversation with the author, citing the composer's own letters and diaries, were one of the few Tchaikovsky biographers who is also an 'approved' figure at Klin, Boris Nikitin, and the eminent writer Yuri Nagibin, author of a novella on the composer's relationship with von Meck, and of the screenplay of the renowned 1970 MosFilm version of Tchaikovsky's life (which starred the celebrated 'Russian Hamlet', Innokenti Smoktunovsky, as the composer). After reading of Orlova's theory in Nikitin's recent biography of Tchaikovsky[58] – the first public mention of it in Russia – Nagibin was the first to endorse it to a wider audience.[59] Among distinguished Tchaikovsky exponents to accept that he was a 'tortured' figure who almost inevitably died by his own hand are one of the greatest of all twentieth-century interpreters of his music, both as pianist and conductor, Vladimir Ashkenazy, and the British pianist Peter Donohoe, winner of the 1982 International Tchaikovsky Piano Competition.[60]

Unbending enough to discuss the composer's homosexuality – a rare event at Klin – even the senior archivist at the Tchaikovsky Museum, Polina Vaidman, made an intriguing distinction between the young men with whom the composer fell romantically in love, such as his nephew, and those with whom his nature drove him to enjoy what are nowadays called 'one-night-stands'. Citing Tchaikovsky's desperate plea to Modest that he had 'nothing to be ashamed of', Vaidman argued that he was referring to romantic homosexual love, whether Platonic or not. All references to sundry other brief encounters are, she agreed, filled with remorse and self-loathing.[61]*

For all the efforts of the cholera camp, the consensus is that, though many of Tchaikovsky's circle were naturally familiar with his sexual tastes and habits, he lived in a perpetual, morbid dread of any wider circulation of his 'abnormality', most of all among posterity. The *Pathétique* most certainly contains intimations of mortality, but one need not see it as some sort of extended suicide note – a self-evident absurdity, given the timing of its composition – to draw this sad but sympathetic inference. The evidence is everywhere, in and between the lines of his own handwritten words, for all the worst efforts of the Soviet censors and his ever-protective family to hide them.

In the absence of any new documentary evidence – and nothing further now seems likely to emerge from the defensive archives at Klin – the

---

*Vaidman then reverted to type long enough to suggest that the sheer physical effort involved in composing and conducting the *Pathétique* would have weakened Tchaikovsky's immune system to the point where he could have contracted cholera within the normal incubation period.

conclusion that Tchaikovsky committed suicide begins with suspicion of Modest's account, provenly misleading in countless details (above all its wholesale failure to mention his brother's sexuality). It continues with a psychological profile of the composer clear from all the available evidence: his proneness to dramatic fits of melancholy, for instance, and his recurrent thoughts of suicide in his letters and diaries, instanced by the attempt to kill himself in the agonized aftermath of his marriage. And it ends with the conviction that he was ashamed of his sexual inclinations, would rather die than have them revealed to the world, and would go to any lengths to avoid their becoming public after his death.

In this context, the sheer suddenness of Tchaikovsky's death – in stark contrast with the newly optimistic flow of events in his life at that time – lends added credence to the increasingly well-documented drama of the 'court of honour'. David Brown, for one, now admits 'no doubt at all' that Tchaikovsky committed suicide. As to the 'court of honour': 'It sounds bizarre, but no more so than many other well-documented events in the composer's life. It must be taken seriously, though it is no more proven than it has been disproven.'[62]

The final arguments against the 'court of honour' revolve around the late Tsarist attitudes to (and laws about) homosexuality, in principle and in practice. Although illegal, and theoretically punishable by loss of civil rights and exile to Siberia, homosexual acts were widely practised in all classes of society, not least in court circles. Article 995 of the penal code in force in the early 1890s read: 'Any man convicted of the unnatural vice of *muzhelozhstvo* [anal intercourse between men] shall for this be subject to deprivation of all rights of status and exiled to Siberia. If a Christian, moreover, he shall submit to Church penance at the direction of his spiritual adviser.'[63] But the social climate of late nineteenth-century Russia was not unlike that of Victorian England (and indeed contemporary Cabinet government in Britain), where the only real rule was (as it remains) 'Don't get caught'. This is the only social rule that Tchaikovsky appears to have broken. In a climate of such endemic hypocrisy, it scarcely seems relevant to doubt the 'court of honour' on the grounds that several of its members were themselves homosexual. Even if true, which it may well be, this would not seem likely to have proved any impediment to their cynically disowning one of their own number, who had become a potential embarrassment to them all.

Alexander Poznansky goes to great lengths to attempt to prove that Tchaikovsky had nothing to fear from public exposure: 'There is not a single known legal proceeding on homosexual grounds from the entire century in which the principal was a figure of any real prominence.' He further demonstrates that in nineteenth-century Russia, 'individuals widely known as homosexuals' held 'numerous responsible government posts, playing major roles in the political and cultural life of the country.' The homosexual ploclivities of the Tsar's own brother, the Grand Duke Sergey, second son of Alexandr II, were well enough known to be the butt of salon jokes. The poet Apukhtin, the composer's lifelong friend, 'led an openly homosexual life, never fearful or embarrassed, and indeed often making fun of his own conduct.'

> Two circumstances relevant both to Apukhtin and Tchaikovsky helped to make their positions unassailable: first, each belonged to the privileged class and shared with it the proper standards of political outlook . . . and, second, each was judicious in his conduct . . . avoiding real excess and knowing the right measures of discretion, tact and taste.[64]

All this may be true, but Tchaikovsky was a very different character from Apukhtin, always less at ease with his sexuality. It is also debatable whether his conduct was always so 'judicious' – especially, perhaps, in the case of young Alexandr Stenbok-Fermor. Above all, he was aware that high St Petersburg society, however ready to turn a blind eye to the conduct of royalty or other celebrities, nevertheless regarded homosexuality as a 'vice' – the dread word used by Tchaikovsky's contemporary hero, Lev Tolstoy, in his *Resurrection*. Poznansky himself quotes one contemporary commentator, V.P. Obninsky, as saying:

> The shameful vice was indulged in by many well-known people in Petersburg: actors, writers, musicians, grand dukes. Their names were on everyone's lips, and many flaunted their way of life. Countless were the scandals raised by public disclosure of such adventures, but the filthy affairs rarely went to trial.[65]

And this is precisely the point to which Modest's defenders remain blind. Tchaikovsky himself half-believed his sexuality to be a 'vice'; and his real fear was public exposure beyond his intimate circle, not anything as mundane as a court case or exile to Siberia – or indeed the French Riviera. It is irrelevant (as well as wrong) for Poznansky to reject Orlova's inference that Tchaikovsky would have chosen to take his own life rather than face indefinite exile abroad, pointing out that he had travelled abroad fifteen years earlier 'to avert a potential scandal after his disastrous marriage.' It is otiose even to recall that in the last years of his life the composer's letters from overseas had become more homesick than ever, suggesting that he might well have found intolerable the prospect of spending his old age in exile, away from his beloved Russian landscape, his friends and his family. The central psychological point – beyond the apparent comprehension of the cholera apologists – is that it was the exposure itself which Tchaikovsky feared, not its consequences.

To accept or reject the tale of the 'court of honour', it is of course unnecessary to resolve (or even share) Orlova's indecision over the day on which it took place. The Tuesday is tempting because of the conspicuous blank in Modest's narrative, and because it involved a second meeting with Avgust Gerke, ostensibly Bessel's lawyer – but also, it appears, himself a member of the 'court of honour', perhaps the closest personally to Tchaikovsky. Gerke was thus the natural candidate to set up a meeting with the composer, supposedly on behalf of the publisher Bessel, whose real purpose was to deliver the arsenic with which the composer, at Leiner's the following evening, perhaps spiked that very public glass of unboiled water.

Bessel's own memoirs confirm that Tchaikovsky and Gerke met on Monday 30 October 'to renegotiate the agreement made with my firm about *The Oprichnik* [in April 1874].' The following day, he continues, the new agreement was drawn up. After crowing that it all proved a waste of time from Tchaikovsky's point of view, that his company eventually retained 'all the rights to the author's royalties', Bessel goes on to explain why: 'On Wednesday 1 November Gerke took the new agreement round to Tchaikovsky's apartment, *where it remained unsigned.*'[66] The italics are mine, in view of the striking fact that Tchaikovsky did not bother to sign a contract of such financial significance to him that he had interrupted his busy schedule to renegotiate it personally. Could his mind – and indeed his conversation with his old schoolfriend the lawyer – have been on other things? Could this have been the meeting – unmentioned, of course, by Modest, who has his brother busy elsewhere all day – at which its appointed representative concentrated the composer's mind by handing over the poison prescribed by the 'court of honour'?

The symptoms of arsenic poisoning are 'very similar' to those of cholera, as has recently been confirmed by the director of Britain's National Poisons Unit, Dr John Henry of Guy's Hospital, London. The classic pattern is severe diarrhoea, soon followed by vomiting, leading to the patient's collapse, and death 'a few days later' from renal failure. 'In the case of Tchaikovsky,' testifies Dr Henry, 'the symptoms I have read about [in the deathbed accounts] seem to fit very closely with arsenic poisoning.'

At the time, as Dr Henry points out, arsenic was readily available in the form of rat poison, or of certain medications which were 'very toxic if taken in too high a dosage'. So arsenic would have been 'easy to get hold of', and Tchaikovsky himself – or perhaps the members of the 'court of honour', certainly the doctors – would have known of the similarities of its effects with the symptoms of cholera. To Dr Henry, it is entirely plausible that Tchaikovsky died of arsenic poisoning, as 'a complete subterfuge' to 'try to put his death across as cholera'. The only way to solve the riddle for certain, in his view, would be to exhume the body, in which traces of arsenic poison would remain even after a hundred years.[67] The same conclusion was reached by Nikolay Blinov, a microbiologist who presented the case for cholera to the 1988 Glinka Museum Commission of Inquiry into Tchaikovsky's death, which ended inconclusively.

The logical scenario is that it was the 'court of honour' who insisted on suicide within a week, and the doctors who advised Tchaikovsky that counterfeiting cholera by taking arsenic was the way to avoid disgrace and exposure. To accept any or all of this, let alone that Gerke procured and handed over the poison, lends a grotesque irony to the curiously prominent role played in Tchaikovsky's obsequies by people who had not been particularly close friends, from a school to which he felt very little attachment. Those who laid the first wreath and led the first requiem appear to have been the very people who, a few days before, had condemned him to death.

What followed was the dreadful spectacle of any man – let alone a man of such humanity and such gifts, with so many years and so much music left in him – taking four days to die by degrees, inflicting appalling pain upon himself by the self-administration of small, slow doses of poison – having wrung from his brother, his doctors and other intimates a solemn promise to persuade the world he was a victim of cholera.

Later, in some cases, their consciences got the better of them.

There is one final irony, in light of the legal and social niceties of a dilemma to which Tchaikovsky himself saw only this one simple solution. The Tsar, Alexandr III, was not merely a great admirer of his music; he was well aware of the homosexuality rife amid his own courtiers and indeed his close relatives, some of them officials in high public positions. 'And the hair had not yet fallen from his head,' the Tsar is supposed to have said upon hearing of the composer's death. 'We have many dukes and barons, but only one Tchaikovsky.'

If the Tsar *had* received a letter of complaint about his favourite composer's indiscretions, there can be little doubt that he would have consigned it to the nearest waste-paper basket. This would appear to strengthen rather than weaken the case for suicide. It underlines the fundamental assumption behind the 'court of honour': that the composer would have preferred death to exposure, whatever the consequences.

The proudest moment of his life, Tchaikovsky always said, was that evening in late 1876 when he sat next to Tolstoy and watched as the *Andante cantabile* from his First String Quartet moved his great contemporary to tears. The subsequent friendship for which he had hoped never in fact developed, giving Tchaikovsky cause to mutter a few words of dissent about the writer's views on music and other matters. But he remained at heart a fervent admirer, and was immensely proud on leaving America to see his name coupled with Tolstoy's as 'the two greatest living Russian artists'. Tolstoy, to Tchaikovsky, was 'a great connoisseur of the human soul'.

On hearing of the composer's death seventeen years after that 'memorable' evening, Tolstoy in turn was moved. 'Two huge tears rolled down his great cheeks' as he told a friend, encountered by chance on a Moscow street, of the composer's death.[68] 'I am very sorry about Tchaikovsky,' Tolstoy wrote to his wife, 'sorry as for a man about whom something is not quite clear, even more than about him as a musician . . . It's neat and tidy; it's natural and yet unnatural.'[69]

What better epitaph for Tchaikovsky, and how better to summarize the puzzlement of posterity over the mystery surrounding his death? To paraphrase Tolstoy, it is the storm-tossed character of Tchaikovsky's life which makes the 'court of honour' condemning him to premature, self-inflicted death a more than plausible, even grimly appropriate dénouement.

# EPILOGUE

## 'Natural and yet unnatural'

NADEZHDA VON MECK OUTLIVED TCHAIKOVSKY BY BARELY TWO MONTHS, dying in Nice on 13 January 1894. Asked how her mother-in-law had endured Tchaikovsky's death, Anna Davidova von Meck replied simply: 'She did not endure it.'[1]

The composer's adoring patron and confidante never broke her silence, nor asked his family for the return of all those letters into which she had 'put all her heart and unveiled her soul'. Von Meck died apparently believing that her friend had 'behaved like a gentleman' and honoured her request to destroy all her letters, especially the most intimate. In fact he had 'reassured her that her wish had been complied with . . . and carefully stored [that letter] away with the rest.'[2]

In death as in life, Tchaikovsky proved more generous to those in more obvious need. In his will, made in 1891, he left one-seventh of his capital to his servant, Alexey Sofronov, and the rest to Tanya's son, Georges-Léon. Then ten years old, and living contentedly in Nikolay's care, Georges-Léon Tchaikovsky was also to receive 1,200 roubles a year from the composer's royalties, and Alexey 600, as well as all 'moveable property', mostly furniture. To Modest, librettist of *The Queen of Spades* and *Iolanta*, went one-fifth of the royalties from those operas, with the stipulation that he receive not less than 1,800 roubles a year.

The bulk of the royalties and all copyrights were bequeathed to Bob Davidov, on the understanding that he divide all posthumous income among the family as he saw fit. Surprisingly, perhaps, the composer added a codicil awarding his estranged wife, Antonina, an annual pension of 1,200 roubles.

Within three years of her husband's death, Antonina was committed to a lunatic asylum outside St Petersburg, where she spent the remaining twenty years of her life. Four years before her own death in 1917, Tchaikovsky's widow published a rather charming (if unreliable) memoir of her husband, striking such wistful notes as: 'All my life I have never forgotten his extraordinary, wonderful eyes. They glow even when they are far from me . . .'3 Some eighty years later the composer's great-niece, Xenia Davidova, curator of the Tchaikovsky Archive at Klin, told a visitor that she had felt sorry for 'Aunt Tonya'. 'Both her head and her heart were completely empty . . . She was certainly a good woman, but, unfortunately, mentally disturbed.'4

Xenia Davidova herself died two years later, in the autumn of 1992, at last ending an unbroken chain of Tchaikovsky family members to have taken charge of Klin – hereditary 'keepers of the flame' – for little short of a century. After so long, history has forgotten that they nearly missed out on their lucrative legacy – that Modest, in the immediate wake of his brother's death, encountered some unexpected hurdles in assuming what he regarded as his rightful inheritance.

The notion of turning Klin into a permanent monument to his brother, and a central archive for all his scores, letters and other memorabilia, occurred to Modest within days of Tchaikovsky's demise. But he had reckoned without the wily Alexey Sofronov, who promptly demanded an outrageous 5,000 roubles for the furniture and other effects he had inherited in his master's will. By the time Modest had managed to meet the sometime servant's exorbitant demands, Alexey had secretly negotiated the purchase of the house itself – which even Tchaikovsky had merely rented, never owned – for a mere 8,500 roubles. Alexey was prepared to let Modest live there, he announced, for the not inconsiderable rent of fifty roubles a month.

It took Modest three years to buy the house back from Alexey, using funds disbursed by Bob from the composer's posthumous royalties. Modest and Bob then moved in together, adding a new wing which today houses photographs, awards and other memorabilia available for inspection (unlike the archive itself, now housed in an adjacent modern building) by the few who brave the journey from Moscow.

In 1897, the year he moved into Klin with Modest, Bob Davidov gave up his military career to help his uncle create a shrine worthy of their beloved Pyotr Ilyich. Within a decade, far from carving out the brilliant career Tchaikovsky had predicted for him, Bob was dead by his own hand at the age of thirty-four. An acute depressive, he seems never to have recovered from his poignant role in the last few years of his uncle's life, apparently remaining traumatized by the deathbed agonies he had witnessed. After dabbling awhile in music and poetry – while turning for consolation, like his sister before him, to morphine and other drugs – he shot himself at Klin in 1906.

Modest, to whom Bob left the house, had by then earned his own modicum of celebrity as his brother's biographer. The voluminous chronicle which so doggedly concealed the truth of Tchaikovsky's private life was handsomely published by Yurgenson, in three volumes, between 1900 and 1902. While laying the foundations of the archive, Modest went on to write his own (unpublished) memoirs, several more plays and some literary translations, notably of the Sonnets of Shakespeare. In the last few years of his life, otherwise blighted by cancer, he was consoled by the companionship at Klin of a young violinist whom he had sponsored at the Moscow Conservatoire. Modest Tchaikovsky died in January 1916, at the age of sixty-five.

His twin brother Anatoly, who had risen to the rank of senator, had died the previous year, and their oldest brother, Nikolay, in 1910. Now Ippolit, the last surviving Tchaikovsky sibling, took over the stewardship of Klin, publishing an edition of the composer's diaries six years before his own death in 1927, at the age of eighty-three. As the Davidov clan took over command of the archive, in close co-operation with their Soviet paymasters, the last surviving member of Tchaikovsky's generation, Anatoly's widow Praskovya, took up exile in the West, where she reminisced contentedly about her celebrated brother-in-law until her death in Paris in 1956 at the age of ninety-two. Praskovya had outlived even Georges-Léon Tchaikovsky by sixteen years.

Within a year of Georges-Léon's death in 1940 aged fifty-seven, Klin had to weather the storm of Nazi occupation. The 1941 offensive against Moscow saw Tchaikovsky's dining-room become a motor-cycle garage, his sitting-room and bedroom (where he wrote the *Pathétique*) a military barracks. Thanks to the foresight of the Soviet authorities, who had evacuated the composer's effects to his birthplace at Votkinsk for the duration, no permanent damage was done.[5]

So the contemporary visitor to Klin, an unprepossessing chemicals and glass-making town on the main Moscow–St Petersburg road, can see

Tchaikovsky's last home lovingly preserved almost exactly as it was at the time of his death. Still screwed to the front door (spared, amazingly, by the Nazis) is a brass plaque redolent of the composer's paranoia:

PYOTR ILYICH TCHAIKOVSKY
Reception on Mondays and Thursdays
From 3 to 5.
Not at home. Please do not ring.

Next to 'Not at home' was a brass panel which Alexey would slide across the word 'Not' when his master was receiving. Having fled the city to this rural retreat, Tchaikovsky was determined to keep at bay the constant stream of casual visitors who had so disrupted his work. In Klin, to his dismay, they turned out to be very few.

Through the door, donning overshoes to protect the sacred floorboards, the latter-day visitor climbs the stairs to Tchaikovsky's two-room, first-floor apartment, past his hat, cane and travelling trunks into the sitting-room which amounts to an illustrated history of his life. Crowding the wall are photographs of his family, his musical colleagues and contemporaries, and other major *dramatis personae* from Apukhtin via Artôt to von Meck. In the bookcases are his editions of Dickens and Thackeray, Shakespeare and Pushkin, volumes of history and philosophy, the Leipzig edition of Mozart, the complete works of Glinka and countless other scores.

Among the books in the library is a small octavo Latin volume, whose title-page bears the inscription, in Tchaikovsky's handwriting: 'Stolen by Pyotr Ilyich Tchaikovsky, Court Counsellor and Conservatory Professor, from the Library of the Palace of the Doges, at Venice, on 3 December 1877.'[6]

The many trophies and mementoes displayed in glass-fronted cupboards include the replica of the Statue of Liberty presented him on leaving New York. On the mantelpiece stands the marble clock from Prague which so startled Poplavsky, still chiming every half-hour. On the composer's desk sit a deck of cards, a cigarette-holder and the ashtray with the X motif. In the centre of the room stands the piano presented him by the firm of J. Becker, still notoriously out of tune – apart from one celebratory day every four years, when the winner of the International Tchaikovsky Piano Competition comes to Klin to play the master's works on his own instrument.

To one side is a small glassed-in balcony, where the composer sat in the morning sun to take tea and read the papers. To the other, separated only by a curtain, is the bedroom where he worked at a small wooden desk by the window. Above his narrow bed hangs a grim, night-time seascape called *Mélancolie*, a gift from a Berlin admirer of which he was particularly fond. Opposite, behind his wash-basin and dressing-table (laden with perfumes), hangs a silver-framed icon of the Virgin, entitled 'Our Lady of Kazan'. Through the window, only one of the three silver birch trees which sustained his last work still stands. The other two fell in the storms of 1991.[7]

Sixty miles south of Klin, in Moscow's Gertsena Street, an imposing statue of Tchaikovsky stands guard at the entrance to the Moscow Conservatoire, which today bears his name. Nearby is the McDonald's fast-food restaurant on the site of 17 Ogaryok Street (then Gazetny Street), the house where he first met Antonina. Not far away, in the shadow of the Kremlin, is the Kamenny Bridge, the scene of his suicide attempt in 1877. The only other traces of the composer in the modern capital are two crumbling houses marked by plaques to show that he lived in them, however briefly, in his youth.

In the imperial capital, another plaque marks the building in which he died. The apartment once rented by Modest is today occupied by squatters (who are inevitably shouldered with the blame for the city's continuing failure to convert it into a museum). The staircase stinks of urine, and the Tchaikovsky devotee who climbs it in search of access is likely to meet a brusque rebuff. In contemporary St Petersburg, however, a $20 bill works wonders, cheap enough as the price of admission to the corner room where Tchaikovsky breathed his last. With its peeling wallpaper, random rubbish piled high in the corners, furnished only by a broken stove, it wears an appropriately forlorn air. In the next room, unreplaced in a century, is the tap into which treated water now flows from the River Neva.

It is but a short walk to 8 Nevsky Prospekt and Leiner's Restaurant, now the Literary Café, where little more than water was on offer during the food shortages of mid-1992. A string quartet played melancholy airs in a corner as most visitors remembered Tchaikovsky less than Pushkin, who called here in 1837 to collect the gun with which he went forth to fight his fatal duel.

The School of Jurisprudence, at 6 Fontanka Naberezhnaya, is now the Town Planning Institute, the Ministry of Justice at 25 Italyanskaya Street the headquarters of the International Red Cross. In the St Petersburg Conservatoire, named for Rimsky-Korsakov, a statue of Tchaikovsky can be found only by those who penetrate beyond its teeming corridors to a corner off a disused staircase. Outside, flanking the Conservatoire building, stand statues of Rimsky-Korsakov and Glinka.

It took four years after Tchaikovsky's death for a fund established by

the government to raise enough money, largely from memorial concerts and private donations, to erect the elaborate monument to the
composer which today constitutes the composer's grave in the cemetery
of the Alexandr Nevsky monastery. Personally designed by his friend
Vsevolozhsky, the director of the Imperial Theatres, the tomb consists
of a bust of the composer guarded by a weeping Muse and an angel
bearing a cross in its outstretched wings; at the time of its erection, in
1897, it was widely criticized for an 'over-theatrical vulgarity'.

Until 1990, and the 150th anniversary of the composer's birth, when a
Tchaikovsky statue was placed in an obscure children's park in St Petersburg, the composer's tomb remained the only public monument to him
in the city so closely associated with his name. Even today the celebrated
Russian sculptor Mikhail Annikushin, whose model won a competition
for a public statue of Tchaikovsky in the 1980s, is denied the public funds
needed to complete the work, supposedly to stand in the square outside
the Mariinsky Theatre, looking across to the Conservatoire.[8]

When the contemporary visitor asks why there is no major public statue
of Tchaikovsky in a city littered with monuments, many of them to lesser
figures, fingers are placed to lips in a silent gesture to the continuing
machinations of the rumour-mill.

'We musicians do like to talk about Musorgsky,' wrote Dmitry Shostakovich in 1979. 'In fact, I think it's the second favourite topic after
Tchaikovsky's love life.'[9] Tchaikovsky's death may since have overtaken
his love life as a favourite talking-point among musicians – the two are, of
course, inextricably intertwined – but both will always remain in crucial
counterpoint to his creative output.

It is the autobiographical element in Tchaikovsky's work which has,
at root, been responsible for the fluctuations in his twentieth-century
fortunes. Securely established on both sides of the Atlantic within a
decade of his death – by 1902 there was already a weekly 'Tchaikovsky
Night' at the Queen's Hall, London – the composer's reputation soon went
into a long decline among academic musicologists, if not with the lay
music-lover. For most of four decades, the 1920s through the 1950s, the
predominant school of critical thought derided Tchaikovsky's 'huge and
splashy'[10] compositions, too gushingly Romantic, too redolent of specific
moods and emotions. For structure and manipulation of form, the master
musicians remained Bach and Mozart, Beethoven, Wagner and Brahms.

This lofty school of cold critical analysis, exemplified by the influential
Sir Donald Tovey, Professor of Music at Edinburgh University from 1914
to 1940, relished its conflict with popular opinion. Tchaikovsky, in short,
was too popular for his own good. 'Since Tchaikovsky was beloved of

the "man in the street", who simply relied on his ears and his heart,' in the summary of one historian, 'he was more frequently abused than any other composer. And critics were confident that the "man in the street" could never find the arguments with which adequately to fight back.'[11]

By the 1960s a determined resistance movement, long led by scholars like Edwin Evans and Herbert Weinstock, finally began to regain the upper hand. Tchaikovsky's academic rehabilitation by such Sixties figures as Hans Keller coincided with his popular apotheosis in the lyrics of a Chuck Berry rhythm-and-blues classic made famous by the Beatles: 'Roll over Beethoven, and tell Tchaikovsky the news.' But still this very status as a public icon, a handful of whose 'greatest hits' could fill the Royal Albert Hall for Tchaikovsky Gala Nights, prevented the musical establishment granting him a place in the very first rank. Only towards the end of the twentieth century, thanks to the work of such musicologists as John Warrack, Edward Garden and particularly David Brown, has Tchaikovsky's technical mastery at last been accorded the same respect as his undoubted command of melody and musical passion.

In his native Russia, the composer's posthumous reputation has lain more in the hands of politicians than musicologists – both, as throughout the rest of the world, consistently gainsaid by the music-loving public. Detested by the Bolsheviks as a reactionary Romantic, and banned briefly in the 1920s, Tchaikovsky's music was gradually reinstated under Stalin, who confessed simply to 'liking' it. During the Second World War he became the 'People's Composer' – as much an emblem of patriotism, at times jingoism, as Elgar for the English. And so he has since remained, through the collapse of the Soviet Union and beyond. Today, in the dry words of the deputy director of the St Petersburg Conservatoire, Tchaikovsky is 'a dead classical composer: to be respected, and highly prized, but no more.'[12]; in the words of one of his Conservatoire students, however, reflecting the view of the post-Communist-in-the-street: 'Tchaikovsky speaks as much for Russia as for himself, and always will.'

Still, whether in Russia or the West, it is the autobiographical self-reference which niggles. Even to Richard Taruskin, a leading current authority on Russian music (and scourge of the British 'suicide squadron', whom he denounces as 'colonialist' homophobes): 'Biographical fallacies only cheapen artistic response.'[13] Tchaikovsky himself would beg to disagree. 'You ask if I've ever been in love,' he wrote to Nadezhda von Meck from Florence during the long, hard winter of 1878. 'Non-Platonic love, I take you to mean. The answer is *yes* and *no . . .*'

If we rephrase the question slightly, and ask whether I've ever known complete happiness in love, the answer is *no, no and no again.*

I think, in fact, that I answer that question in my music. But if you ask me whether I appreciate the full power, the invincible force of this emotion, then I'll answer *yes, yes and yes again*. And I would say that I have repeatedly tried to express in my music the torments and bliss of love . . .[14]

Throughout his life, whatever his vacillations over passing works-in-progress, Tchaikovsky's confidence in his own worth was ultimately vindicated by the concert-going public. The same has proved true, at the expense of high-minded critics, over the century since his death. As on the mystery surrounding that death, so on the music it silenced, let the last word go to Tolstoy, whose words to his wife on the day Tchaikovsky died have proved so poignantly prophetic:

Gossip has not ceased. It hasn't ceased for one day, for one year. But despite this Tchaikovsky's fame has grown from decade to decade. The tastes and directions of art have changed, fashion has changed, but Tchaikovsky's music has continued, and is continuing to move the hearts of listeners throughout the whole world.[15]

# APPENDICES

# APPENDIX A

# List of Works
## and Recommended Recordings

### (in chronological order, by date of composition)

(1) ORCHESTRAL WORKS     (2) SOLO INSTRUMENT AND ORCHESTRA
(3) CHAMBER MUSIC        (4) PIANO WORKS         (5) SONGS
(6) STAGE WORKS          (7) CHORAL WORKS        (8) MISCELLANEA

*The author is grateful to Professor David Brown for verification of dates of composition and to* The Gramophone *Classical Catalogue for confirmation of recordings available on compact disc at the time of publication. All the listed recordings are recommended, but a critical guide follows each section.*

## (1) Orchestral Works

**Juvenilia and other minor, lost or unfinished works (*unrecorded*)**

Allegro non tanto in G, for strings (1863–4)
Largo and Allegro in D, for 2 flutes and strings (1863–4)
Andante ma non troppo in A (1863–4)
Agitato and Allegro in E minor, for small orchestra (1863–4)
Allegro vivo in C minor (1863–4)
*The Romans at the Coliseum* (1863–4) [lost]
*Characteristic Dances* [used in the opera, *The Voevoda*] (1865)
Overture in F (1865 rev 1866)

Overture in C minor (1865–6)
Jurists' March (1885)
Symphony [No. 7] in E flat (unfinished, sketches used for Piano Concerto No. 3 in E flat, Op. 75)

*The Storm* , **overture** [to Ostrovsky's play] (Op. 76:1864 op. posth.)
Gennady Rozhdestvensky/London SO (*Pickwick PCD 878*)

**Symphony No. 1 in G minor ('Winter Daydreams')** (Op. 13: 1866, rev 1874)
Bernard Haitink/Concertgebouw (*Philips 420 751-2*)
Mariss Jansons/Oslo PO (*Chandos CHAN 8402*)
Herbert von Karajan/Berlin PO (*DG 429 675-2*)
Andrew Litton/Bournemouth SO (*Virgin VC7 91119-2*)
Lorin Maazel/Vienna Phil (*Decca 430 787-2*)
Igor Markevich/London SO (*SAL 3578*)
Kurt Masur/Leipzig GO (*Teldec 2292 44939-2*)

**Festival Overture on the Danish national anthem in D** (Op. 15: 1866)
Geoffrey Simon/LSO (*Chandos CHAN 8310/11*)

*Fatum* **[Fate], symphonic poem** (Op. 77: 1868)
[*destroyed by Tchaikovsky; reconstructed, 1869*]
Leonard Slatkin/St Louis SO (*RCA RD60432*)

**Romeo and Juliet, fantasy overture** (1869, rev 1870, 1880)
Yuri Ahronovitch/LSO (*Pickwick PCD 801*)
Vladimir Ashkenazy/RPO (*Decca 421 715-2*)
Leonard Bernstein/NYPO (*DG 429 234-2*)
Sian Edwards/Royal Liverpool PO (*EMI Eminence EMX 2152*)
Herbert von Karajan/Berlin PO (*DG 410 873-2*)
Lorin Maazel/Vienna Phil (*Decca 430 787-2*)
Kurt Masur/Leipzig GO (*Teldec 9031-76456-2*)
Seiji Ozawa/Boston SO (*DG 413 135-2*)
André Previn/LA PO (*Philips 416 382-2*)
Georg Solti/Chicago SO (*Decca 430 152-2*)
[*1869 version*] Geoffrey Simon/LSO (*Chan 8310/11*)

**Symphony No. 2 in C minor ('Little Russian')** (Op. 17: 1872 rev 1879–80)
Claudio Abbado/New Philharmonia (*DG 431 604-2*)
Bernard Haitink/Concertgebouw (*Philips 420 751-2*)
Mariss Jansons/Oslo PO (*Chandos CHAN 8460*)
Herbert von Karajan/Berlin PO (*DG 429 606-2*)
Andrew Litton/Bournemouth SO (*Virgin VC7 91119-2*)
Lorin Maazel/Vienna Phil (*Decca 430 787-2*)
Igor Markevich/London SO (*SAL 3601*)
Geoffrey Simon/LSO (*Chan 8304*)

**Serenade for Nikolay Rubinstein's Saint's Day** (1872)
Geoffrey Simon/LSO (*Chan 8310/11*)

***The Tempest***, **symphonic fantasia in F minor** [after Shakespeare] (Op. 18: 1873)
Claudio Abbado/Chicago SO (*Sony SK47179*)
Andrew Litton/Bournemouth SO (*Virgin VMT7 59701-2/59598-2*)
Vyacheslav Ovchinnikov/USSR RSO (*Olympia OCD 180*)
Leonard Slatkin/St Louis SO (*RCA RD60425*)

**Symphony No. 3 in D major ('Polish')** (Op. 29: 1875)
Bernard Haitink/Concertgebouw (*Philips 420 751-2*)
Mariss Jansons/Oslo PO (*Chandos CHAN 8463*)
Herbert von Karajan/Berlin PO (*DG 419 178-2/Galleria 431 605-2*)
Andrew Litton/Bournemouth SO (*Virgin VC7 90761-2*)
Lorin Maazel/Vienna Phil (*Decca 430 787-2*)
Igor Markevich/London SO (*SAL 3549*)
Leonard Slatkin/St Louis SO (*RCA RD60433*)

***Marche Slave*** (Op. 31: 1876)
Yuri Ahronovitch/LSO (*Pickwick PCD 801*)
Charles Dutoit/Montreal SO (*Decca 430 152-2*)
Sian Edwards/Royal Liverpool PO (*EMI Eminence EMX 2152*)
Neeme Jarvi/Gothenburg SO (*DG 429 984-2*)
Herbert von Karajan/Berlin PO (*DG 413 135-2*)
Mikhail Pletnev/Russian Nat Orch (*VC 7 91487-2*)
Gennady Rozhdestvensky/London SO (*Pickwick PCD 867*)
Leopold Stokowski/London SO (*Decca 433 625-2*)

***Francesca da Rimini***: **symphonic fantasia** [after Dante] (Op. 32: 1876)
Vladimir Ashkenazy/RPO (*Decca 421 715-2*)
Leonard Bernstein/NY Phil (*DG 429 778-2*)
Sian Edwards/Royal Liverpool PO (*EMI Eminence EMX 2152*)
Kurt Masur/Leipzig GO (*Teldec 9031-76456-2*)
Leopold Stokowski/NY Stadium Orch (*Dell'Arte CDDA 9006*)

**Symphony No 4 in F minor** (Op. 36: 1877–8)
Claudio Abbado/New Philharmonia (*DG 431 604-2*)
Leonard Bernstein/NY PO (*DG 429 778-2*)
Christoph von Dohnanyi/Vienna (*Decca 475 792-2*)
Bernard Haitink/Concertgebouw (*Philips 426 797-2*)
Mariss Jansons/Oslo PO (*Chandos CHAN 8361*)
Herbert von Karajan/Berlin PO (*DG 419 872-2*)
Andrew Litton/Bournemouth SO (*Virgin VMTZ 59699-2*)
Lorin Maazel/Vienna Phil (*Decca 430 787-2*)
Igor Markevich/London SO (*SAL 3481*)
Evgeny Mravinsky/Leningrad PO (*DG 419 745-2*)

Gennady Rozhdestvensky/London SO (*Pickwick PCD 867*)
Leonard Slatkin/St Louis SO (*RCA RD60432*)

**Suite No. 1 in D** (Op. 43: 1878–9)
Evgeny Svetlanov/USSR SO (*LDC 278 825/26*)

*Capriccio Italien* (Op. 45: 1880)
Vladimir Ashkenazy/RPO (*Decca 421 715-2*)
Charles Dutoit/Montreal SO (*Decca 430 152-2*)
Bernard Haitink/Concertgebouw (*Philips 422 469-2*)
Herbert von Karajan/Berlin PO (*DG 423 225-2*)
Erich Kunzel/Cincinnati SO (*Telarc 80041*)
Andrew Litton/Bournemouth SO (*Virgin VC7 90761-2*)
Eduardo Mata/Dallas SO (*RCA VD 87727*)
Leonard Slatkin/St Louis SO (*RCA RD60433*)

**Serenade in C major for string orchestra** (Op. 48: 1880)
William Boughton/English String Orchestra (*Nimbus 5016*)
Philippe Entremont/Vienna CO (*Naxos 8 550404*)
Richard Hickox/City of London Sinfonia (*Virgo 7567-91568-2*)
Herbert von Karajan/Berlin PO (*DG 400 038-2*)
Raymond Leppard/ECO (*Philips 420 883-2*)
Neville Marriner/Academy St-Martins-in-the-Fields) (*Decca 430 155-2*)
José Sebrier/Scottish CO (*ASV DCA 719*)

*1812* : **a festival overture** (Op. 49: 1880)
Yuri Ahronovitch/LSO (*Pickwick PCD 801*)
Christoph von Dohnanyi/Vienna (*Decca 475 792-2*)
Sian Edwards/Royal Liverpool PO (*EMI Eminence EMX 2152*)
Arthur Fiedler/Boston Pops (*DG 413 135-2*)
Neeme Järvi/Gothenburg SO (*DG 429 984-2*)
Erich Kunzel/Cincinnati SO (*Telarc 80041*)
Georg Solti/Chicago SO (*Decca 430 152-2*)
Leopold Stokowski/Band of the Grenadier Guards (*Decca 433 625-2*)

**Festival Coronation March in D major** (1883)
Neeme Järvi/Scottish NO (*CHAN 8476*)
Kurt Masur/Leipzig GO (*Teldec 9031-76456-2*)
Gennady Rozhdestvensky/USSR Ministry of Culture SO (*Erato 2292 45970-2*)

**Suite No. 2 in C** (Op. 53: 1883)
Michel Tilson Thomas/Philharmonia (*MDK 46503*)
Evgeny Svetlanov/USSR SO (*LDC 278825/26*) [w/o Valse]

**Suite No. 3 in G** (Op. 55: 1884)
Gennady Rozhdestvensky/USSR Ministry of Culture SO (*Erato 2292 45970-2*)
Evgeny Svetlanov/USSR SO (*LDC 278825/26*)

**A *Grateful Greeting*, Elegy in G (in honour of Ivan Samarin), for strings**
(1884) [*used as Act 4 entr'acte in* Hamlet]
Vladimir Ashkenazy/RPO (*Decca 421 715-2*)
José Sebrier/Scottish CO (*ASV DCA 719*)

***Manfred* Symphony** [after Byron] (Op. 58: 1885)
Riccardo Chailly/Concertgebouw (*Decca 421 441-2*)
Bernard Haitink/Concertgebouw (*Philips 442 061-2*)
Mariss Jansons/Oslo PO (*CHAN 8535*)
Ondrej Lenard/Bratislava (*Naxos 8-550224*)
Andrew Litton/Bournemouth SO (*Virgin VC7 59230-2*)
Riccardo Muti/Philharmonia (*EMI CDC7 47412-2*)

**Andante cantabile for cello and strings** (Op. 11: 1886–8)
(*arr. by Tchaikovsky from String Quartet No. 1, 2nd mvmt*)
Ofra Harnoy (Paul Freeman/Victoria SO) (*RCA 71003*)
Steven Isserlis (John Eliot Gardiner/Europe CO) (*Virgin VC7 59595-2*)
Yo-Yo Ma (Lorin Maazel/Pittsburgh SO) (*Sony SK 48382*)
Raphael Wallfisch (Geoffrey Simon/ECO) (*CHAN 8347*)

**Suite No. 4 in G major (*'Mozartiana'*)** (Op. 61: 1887)
Michael Tilson Thomas/Philharmonia (*MDK 46503*)
José Sebrier/Scottish CO (*ASV DCA 719*)
Evgeny Svetlanov/USSR SO (*LDC 278825/26*)

**Symphony No. 5 in E minor** (Op. 64: 1888)
Leonard Bernstein/NYPO (*DG 429 234-2*)
Charles Dutoit/Montreal SO (*Decca 425 503-2*)
Sian Edwards/London PO (*EMI EMX2187*)
Rafael Fruhbeck de Burgos/LSO (*Nimbus NI5194*)
Bernard Haitink/Concertgebouw (*Philips 426 797-2*)
Mariss Jansons/Oslo PO (*Chandos CHAN 8351*)
Herbert von Karajan/Vienna PO (*DG 439 019-2*)
Andrew Litton/Bournemouth SO (*Virgin VC7 59598-2*)
Lorin Maazel/Vienna Phil (*Decca 430 787-2*)
Igor Markevich/London SO (*SAL 3579*)
Evgeny Mravinsky/Leningrad PO (*DG 419 745-2*)

***Hamlet*, fantasy overture** [after Shakespeare] (Op. 67: 1888)
Akulov/USSR TV&RSO (*MFSL MFCD 870*)
Dutoit/Montreal SO (*Decca 425 503-2*)
Leopold Stokowski/NY Stadium Orch (*Dell'Arte CDDA 9006*)
[+ *incidental music*]
Kovaleva/Vladimirov/Ziuratis/USSR TV&Radio SO (*Melodia 1577-51870-2*)
Kelly/Hammond-Stroud/Simon/LSO (*Chan 8310/11*)

**Voevoda, symphonic ballad in A minor** (Op. 78: 1890–1)
Ondrej Lenard/Bratislava (*Naxos 8-550224*)
Leonard Slatkin/St Louis SO (*RCA RD60432*)
Vyacheslav Ovchinnikov/USSR RSO (*Olympia OCD 180*)

**The Nutcracker: suite from ballet** (Op. 71a: 1892)
Herbert von Karajan/Berlin PO (*DG 410 873-2*)
André Previn/London SO (*EMI CZS7 62816-2*)
Mstislav Rostropovich/Berlin PO (*DG Galleria 429 097-2*)

**Symphony No 6 in B minor ('Pathétique')** (Op. 74: 1893)
Vladimir Ashkenazy/Philharmonia (*Decca 430 154-2*)
Bernard Haitink/Concertgebouw (*Philips 426 797-2*)
Mariss Jansons/Oslo PO (*Chandos CHAN 8446*)
Herbert von Karajan/Vienna (*DG 415 095-2*)
Lorin Maazel/Vienna Phil (*Decca 430 787-2*)
Andrew Litton/Bournemouth SO (*Virgin VC7 59239-2*)
Igor Markevich/London SO (*835126 AY*)
Evgeny Mravinsky/Leningrad PO (*DG 419 745-2*)
Mikhail Pletnev/Russian Nat Orch (*VC 7 59661-2*)
Gennady Rozhdestvensky/LSO (*PCD 878*)

Mariss Jansons' outstanding recordings with the Oslo Philharmonic Orchestra of all six **Symphonies**, plus the **Manfred**, are available either individually or as a boxed set. The same is true of von Karajan's cycle with the Berlin Philharmonic (though Karajan, surprisingly, never recorded the *Manfred*). Other excellent versions are available from Haitink (with the Concertgebouw), Andrew Litton (with the Bournemouth Symphony), Lorin Maazel (with the Vienna Philharmonic), Leonard Bernstein (with the New York Philharmonic) and many others. The recent recording of the **Pathétique** by pianist-turned-conductor Mikhail Pletnev, with his own Russian National Orchestra, has attracted wide critical praise, while Jansons' blend of true romantic feeling combines with the crystalline playing of his orchestra to make his the most consistently distinguished complete set available. For the three major symphonies, however, the **4th**, **5th** and **6th** (*Pathétique*) symphonies, there is no-one to match the late Yevgeny Mravinsky conducting the Leningrad Symphony Orchestra, a truly Russian reading of Tchaikovsky, which no Westerner can hope to approach.

As to the **Serenade for Strings**: one of the finest of all Tchaikovsky records is Herbert von Karajan's scintillating Serenade with the Berlin Philharmonic on Deutsche Grammophon. Other fine versions have been made by Raymond Leppard with the English Chamber Orchestra (Philips) and Neville Marriner with the Academy of St Martins (Decca).

## (2) Works for Solo Instrument and Orchestra

**Piano Concerto No. 1 in B flat minor** (Op. 23: 1874–5)
Martha Argerich (Kondrashin/Bavarian RSO) (*Philips 411 057-2*)
Vladimir Ashkenazy (Maazel/London SO) (*Decca Ovation 417 750-2*)
Michele Campanella (Renzetti/Italia) (*Nuova Era 6735*)
Peter Donohoe (Barshai/Bournemouth) (*EMI 7 49939 2*)
Andrey Gavrilov (Muti/Philharmonia) (*EMI 7 6915 2*)
Emil Gilels (Mehta/NYPO) (*CBS Masterworks CD44643*)
Gary Graffman (Szell/Cleveland) (*CBS Maestro M2YK 46460*)
Vladimir Horowitz (Toscanini/NCB SO) (*RCA GD 60449/87992*)
Mikhail Pletnev (Fedoseyev/Philharmonia) (*Virgin VC7 59612-2*)
Ivo Pogorelich (Abbado/London SO) (*DG 415 122-2*)
Artur Rubinstein (Wallenstein/Boston SO) (*RCA Gold Seal 09026-61262-2*)
Andras Schiff (Solti/Chicago SO) (*Decca 430 153-2*)

**Sérénade mélancolique, for violin and orchestra, in B minor** (Op. 26: 1875)
Ofra Harnoy (Paul Freeman/Victoria SO) (*RCA 71003*)
Jascha Heifetz (Wallenstein/LA PO) (*RCA GD 60927*)
Itzhak Perlman (Temirkanov/Leningrad PO) (*RCA RD 60739*)
Itzhak Perlman (Ormandy/Philadelphia) (*EMI 7 47106-2*)
Xue-Wei (Accardo/Philharmonia) (*ASV DCA 713*)
Pinchas Zukerman (Mehta/Israel PO) (*CBS CD 46503*)
[*piano reduction*] Lidya Mordkovitch (violin) (*Chandos CHAN 8500*)
[*orch*] Michael Tilson Thomas/Philharmonia (*MDK 46503*)

**Variations on a Rococo Theme in A, for cello and small orchestra** (Op. 33: 1876)
Ofra Harnoy (Paul Freeman/Victoria SO) (*RCA 71003*)
Lynn Harrell (Lorin Maazel/Cleveland SO) (*Decca 430 155-2*)
Steven Isserlis (John Eliot Gardiner/Europe CO) (*Virgin VC7 59595-2*)
Julian Lloyd Webber (M. Shostakovich/London SO) (*Philips 434 106-2*)
Yo-Yo Ma (Lorin Maazel/Pittsburgh SO) (*Sony SK 48382*)
Leonard Rose (Ormandy/Philharmonia) (*CBS M2YK 46460*)
Mstislav Rostropovich (von Karajan/Berlin PO) (*DG 413 819-2*)
Paul Tortelier (Y. Tortelier/Northern Sinfonia) (*EMI CMS7 64069-2*)
Raphael Wallfisch (Geoffrey Simon/ECO) (*CHAN 8347*)

**Valse-scherzo in C, for violin and orchestra** (Op. 34: 1877)
Nathan Milstein (Irving, orch.) (*EMI CMS7 64830-2*)
Istzhak Perlman (Temirkanov/Leningrad PO) (*RCA RD 60739*)
Xue-Wei (Accardo/Philharmonia) (*ASV DCA 713*)
[*piano reduction*] Lidya Mordkovitch (*Chandos CHAN 8500*)

**Violin Concerto in D major** (Op. 35: 1878)
Joshua Bell (Ashkenazy/Cleveland) (*Decca 421 716-2*)

Kyung Wha Chung (Dutoit/Montreal) (*Decca 410 011-2*)
Kyung Wha Chung (Previn/LSO) (*Decca 417 707-2*)
Arthur Grumiaux (Krenz/NPO) (*Philips 422 473-2*)
Nigel Kennedy (Kamu/LPO) (*EMI CDC7 47623-2*)
Nathan Milstein (Abbado/Vienna) (*DG 419 067-2*)
Viktoria Mullova (Ozawa/Boston) (*Philips 416 821-2*)
David Oistrakh (Szell/Cleveland) (*CBS Maestro M2YK 46460*)
Itzhak Perlman (Ormandy/Philadelphia) (*EMI 7 47106-2*)
Ruggiero Ricci (Fournet/Netherlands) (*Decca 417 687-2*)
Viktor Tretyakov (Ovchinnikov/USSR RSO) (*Olympia OCD 180*)
Xue-Wei (Accardo/Philharmonia) (*ASV DCA 713*)
David Oistrakh (Ormandy/Philharmonia) (*CBS M2YK 46460*)
Itzhak Perlman (Mehta/Israel) (*EMI CDC7 54108-2*)
Isaac Stern (Ormandy/Philadelphia) (*CBS 42537*)
Pinchas Zukerman (Mehta/Israel) (*CBS Masterworks CD44643*)

**Piano Concerto No. 2 in G** (Op. 44: 1879–80)
Peter Donohoe (Barshai/Bournemouth) (*EMI 7 49940-2*)
Andrey Gavrilov (Ashkenazy/Berlin PO) (*EMI 7 49632-2*)
Emil Gilels (Svetlanov/USSR) (*Olympia OCD 229*)
Jerome Lowenthal (Comissiona/LSO) (*Ara Z 6583*)
Mikhail Pletnev (Fedoseyev/Philharmonia) (*Virgin VC7 59631-2*)

***Concert Fantasia* in G for piano and orchestra** (Op. 56: 1884)
Peter Donohoe (Barshai/Bournemouth) (*EMI 7 49939 2*)
Gary Graffman (Szell/Cleveland) (*CBS Maestro M2YK 46460*)
I. Zhukov (Kitaenko/USSR) (*Olympia OCD 229*)

***Pezzo capriccioso* in B minor for cello and orchestra** (Op. 62: 1887)
Ofra Harnoy (Paul Freeman/Victoria SO) (*RCA 71003*)
Steven Isserlis (John Eliot Gardiner/Europe CO) (*Virgin VC7 59595-2*)
Paul Tortelier (Y. Tortelier/Northern Sinfonia) (*EMI CMS7 64069-2*)
Raphael Wallfisch (Simon/ECO) (*Chan 8347*)

**Piano Concerto No. 3 in E flat** (Op. 75: 1893) [*unfinished; one movement only*]
Peter Donohoe (Barshai/Bournemouth) (*EMI 7 49940 2*)
Emil Gilels (Maazel/NPO) (*EMI CD-EMX2001*)
Gary Graffman (Szell/Cleveland) (*CBS Maestro M2YK 46460*)
Jerome Lowenthal (Comissiona/LSO) (*Ara Z 6583*)
Mikhail Pletnev (Fedoseyev/Philharmonia) (*Virgin VC7 59631-2*)

**Andante in B flat and Finale in E flat, for piano and orchestra** (Op. 79: 1893)
[*unfinished; completed & orchestrated by Taneyev*]
Werner Haas (Imbal/Monte Carlo) (*Philips 438 329-2*)

Tchaikovsky's **Piano Concerto No. 1** in B flat min (Op. 23) is, of course, one of the most recorded works in all music, with more than seventy versions currently listed in the CD catalogues. For sheer exuberance and virtuosity, it is hard to beat one of the earliest ever made – Vladimir Horowitz's celebrated 1943 account at a live concert in New York's Carnegie Hall with his father-in-law, Toscanini, conducting the NBC Symphony Orchestra. Although the orchestral sound suffers from the limited recording standards of the day, Horowitz's piano shimmers gloriously through the decades (though available in mono only). Fine recordings have also been made by Martha Argerich (with Dutoit and the RPO), Vladimir Ashkenazy (with Maazel and the LSO) and Andras Schiff (with Solti and the Chicago Symphony). Though now hard to find, historic recordings were also made by Van Cliburn (with Kondrashin and the RCA Symphony) and Clifford Curzon (with Solti and the Vienna PO).

Peter Donohoe's stunning recording of the **Piano Concerto No. 2** in G (Op. 44) with the Bournemouth Symphony under Rudolf Barshai naturally draws the listener to his performance of the First, available in a boxed set with the **Concert Fantasy** (Op. 56). He is joined by a fine, pre-punk Nigel Kennedy (violin) and the superb Steven Isserlis (cello) for the second movement of the second concerto, rightly restored to its original version, sounding like a triple concerto with all three performers at their most lyrical. And Donohoe's sparkling account of the third movement must rank as one of the most exciting pieces of piano-playing recently recorded. The disc has deservedly won several prizes. Completed by the less well-known **Piano Concerto No. 3** in E flat (Op. 75), the Donohoe cycle is a major achievement without which no Tchaikovsky collection is complete. Joshua Bell's recording of the **Violin Concerto** in D major (Op. 35) with Ashkenazy and the Cleveland is outstanding amid a huge selection. Also superb are either of Kyung Wha Chung's two versions, both equally spirited, with Previn/LSO or Dutoit/Montreal. Best among many other distinguished recordings are Heifetz with Reiner/Chicago, Grumiaux with Krenz/NPO, Perlman with Ormandy/Philadelphia, Oistrakh with Ormandy/Philadelphia (CBS), and Viktoria Mullova with Ozawa/Boston.

Of several excellent recordings of the **Variations on a Rococo Theme**, notably that by the much-hyped Ofra Harnoy (with Paul Freeman and the Victoria Symphony), the best buy is undoubtedly the superb version by Raphael Wallfisch with Geoffrey Simon and the English Chamber Orchestra on a Chandos disc which also offers the **Andante Cantabile** (Op. 11), **Nocturne** (Op. 19/4), **Pezzo capriccioso** (Op. 62), and two of Tchaikovsky's own song transcriptions, *Legend* and *Was I Not a Blade of Grass*. Other fine versions have been recorded by Lynn Harrell (Lorin Maazel/Cleveland), Steven Isserlis (John Eliot Gardiner/Chamber Orchestra of Europe) and Leonard Rose (Ormandy/Philharmonia).

## (3) Chamber Music

### Minor, lost or unfinished works (*unrecorded*)
Adagio in C, for 4 horns (1863–4)
Adagio in F, for 2 flutes, 2 oboes, 2 clarinets, cor anglais and bass clarinet (1863–4)
Allegretto moderato in D, for string trio (1863–4)
Allegro in C minor, for piano sextet (1863–4)

**Allegretto in E, for string quartet** (1863–4)
**Allegro vivace in B flat, for string quartet** (1863–4)
**Andante ma non troppo in E minor, for string quartet** (1863–4)
**Andante molto in G, for string quartet** (1863–4)
**String Quartet in B flat [one movement only]** (1865)
Shostakovich Quartet (*Olympia OCD521*)

**Adagio molto in E flat, for string quartet and harp** (1863–4)
Shostakovich Quartet/E. Moskvitina (*Olympia OCD522*)

**String Quartet No. 1 in D major** (Op. 11: 1871)
Borodin String Quartet (*EMI CDS 7 49775 2*)
Emerson String Quartet (*DG 427 618-2*)

**Serenade for Nikolay Rubinstein's Name Day** (1872)
Geoffrey Simon/London SO (*Chan 9190*)

**String Quartet No. 2 in F** (Op. 22: 1874)
Borodin String Quartet (*EMI CDS 7 49775 2*)

**String Quartet No. 3 in E flat minor** (Op. 30: 1876)
Borodin String Quartet (*EMI CDS 7 49775 2*)
Leningrad Quartet (*Vogue 651009*)
Shostakovich Quartet/E. Moskvitina (*Olympia OCD522*)

**Album for the Young** (Op. 39: 1878) [*string transcription* ]
Borodin Trio & friends (*Chan 8365*)

***Souvenir d'un lieu cher,* for violin and piano** (Op. 42: 1878)
Lidya Mordkovitch (*Chandos CHAN 8500*)
Hideko Udagawa (Klein/London PO) (*Pickwick PCD 966*)
*3. Mélodie in E flat major* [*orchestral version*]
Xue-Wei (Accardo/Philharmonia) (*ASV DCA 713*)
Pinchas Zukerman (Zubin Mehta/Israel PO) (*CBS MDK 46503*)

**Piano Trio in A minor 'To the Memory of a Great Artist'** (Op. 50: 1881–2)
Pierre Amoyal/Pascal Rogé/Frédéric Lodéon (*Erato 2292-45972-2*)
Itzhak Perlman/Vladimir Ashkenazy/Lynn Harrell (*EMI CMS7 64789-2*)
Artur Rubinstein/Jascha Heifetz/Gregor Piatigorsky (*RCA GD 87768*)

***Nocturne* for cello and small orchestra** (Op. 19/4: 1888)
[*transcribed by composer from 1873 piece for solo piano, Op. 19, No. 4*]
Ofra Harnoy (Paul Freeman/Victoria SO) (*RCA 71003*)
Steven Isserlis (John Eliot Gardiner/Europe CO) (*Virgin VC7 59595-2*)
Julian Lloyd Webber (M. Shostakovich/London SO) (*Philips 434 106-2*)
Raphael Wallfisch (Simon/ECO) (*Chan 8347*)

***Souvenir de Florence*, string sextet in D minor** (Op. 70: 1890 rev 1891–2)
Borodin String Quartet (*EMI CDS 7 49775 2*)
Camerata Lysy (*Claves 50-8507*)
Leningrad Quartet (*Vogue 651009*)
[*orchestral version*]
Philippe Entremont/Vienna CO (*Naxos 8 550404*)
Richard Hickox/City of London Sinfonia (*Virgo 7567-91568-2*)

The Borodin Quartet's boxed set is the most highly recommended recording available, coupled with the string sextet **Souvenir de Florence** (Op. 70). There is a historic recording of the **Piano Trio in A minor** (Op. 50) by Rubinstein, Heifetz and Piatigorsky, and a more recent one by Itzhak Perlman, Vladimir Ashkenazy and Lynn Harrell.

## (4) Works for Piano

**Minor, lost or unfinished works (unrecorded)**
Anastasia valse, in F (1854)
Allegro in F minor (1863–4) [incomplete]
Funeral march on themes from *The Oprichnik* (1877) [lost]

**Theme and Variations in A minor** (Op. 19, No. 6: 1863–4)
Andrey Gavrilov (*EMI 7 6915 2*)
Michele Campanella (*Nuova Era 6735*)

**Sonata in C sharp minor** (Op. 80: 1865)
Emil Gilels (*Russ RDCD 11170*)
Victoria Postnikova (*Erato 2292-45512-2*)

***Deux morceaux*** (Op. 1: 1867)
1. *Scherzo à la russe*, in B flat (1867) 2. *Impromptu*, in E flat minor (1863–4)
Victoria Postnikova (*Erato 2292-45966-2*)

***Souvenir de Hapsal*** (Op. 2: 1867)
1. *Ruines d'un château*, in E minor  2. *Scherzo*, in F 3. *Chant sans paroles*, in F
Victoria Postnikova (*Erato 2292-45966-2*)
2. *Scherzo*, in F/Ilona Prunyi (*Naxos 8-550504*)

**Potpourri on themes from the opera, *The Voevoda*** (1868)
Victoria Postnikova (*Erato 2292-45968-2*)

***Valse caprice***, in D (Op. 4: 1868)
Victoria Postnikova (*Erato 2292-45966-2*)

***Romance*, in F minor** (Op. 5: 1868)
Victoria Postnikova (*Erato 2292-45966-2*)
Ilona Prunyi (*Naxos 8-550504*)
Sviatoslav Richter (*Melodia SUCD 10-00252*)

**Fifty Russian folk songs** [arranged for piano duet] (1868–9)
Duo Crommelynck (*Claves CD50-8805*)
Victoria Postnikova/Gennady Rozhdestvensky (*Erato 2292-45968-2*)

**Valse-scherzo [No. 1] in A** (Op. 7: 1870)
Victoria Postnikova (*Erato 2292-45966-2*)
Sviatoslav Richter (*Melodia SUCD 10-00252*)

**Capriccio, in G flat** (Op. 8: 1870)
Victoria Postnikova (*Erato 2292-45966-2*)

**Trois morceaux** (Op. 9: 1870)
1. *Rêverie*, in D   2. *Polka de salon*, in B flat   3. *Mazurka de salon*, in D minor
Mikhail Pletnev (*Chante du Monde LDC 278 953*)
Victoria Postnikova (*Erato 2292-45966-2*)
1. *Rêverie* Ilona Prunyi (*Naxos 8-550504*)

**Deux morceaux** (Op. 10: 1871)
1. *Nocturne*, in F   2. *Humoresque*, in E minor
Victoria Postnikova (*Erato 2292-45966-2*)
Ilona Prunyi (*Naxos 8-550504*)
Sviatoslav Richter (*Melodia SUCD 10-00252*)
2. *Humoresque* S. Rachmaninov (*RCA 09026 6 1265-2*)

**3 romances** [trans Op. 16: 1872–3]
1. *Berceuse* (Op. 16, No. 1)   2. *On chante encore* (Op. 16, No. 4)   3. *Qu'importe* (Op. 16, No. 5)
Victoria Postnikova (*Erato 2292-45968-2*)

**Six morceaux** (Op. 19: 1873)
1. *Rêverie du soir*, in G minor   2. *Scherzo humoristique*, in D
3. *Feuillet d'album*, in D   4. *Nocturne*, in C sharp minor
5. *Capriccioso*, in B flat   6. *Thème original et variations*, in F
Victoria Postnikova (*Erato 2292-45967-2*)
1. *Rêverie du soir*/5. *Capriccioso* Ilona Prunyi (*Naxos 8-550504*)
1. *Rêverie du soir*/5. *Capriccioso* Sviatoslav Richter (*Melodia SUCD 10-00252*)

**Six morceaux composés sur un seul thème** (Op. 21: 1873)
1. *Prélude*, in B   2. *Fugue à 4 voix*, in G sharp minor   3. *Impromptu*, in C sharp minor   4. *Marche funèbre*, in A flat minor   5. *Mazurque*, in A flat minor   6. *Scherzo*, in A flat
Victoria Postnikova (*Erato 2292-45967-2*)

**The Seasons** (Op. 37b: 1875–6)
1. January: *Au coin de feu*, in A   2. February: *Carnaval*, in D
3. March: *Chant de l'alouette*, in G minor   4. April: *Perce-neige*, in B flat
5. May: *Les nuits de mai*, in G   6. June: *Barcarolle*, in G minor
7. July: *Chant du faucheur*, in E flat   8. August: *La moisson*, in B minor
9. September: *La chasse*, in G   10. October: *Chant d'automne*, in D minor

11. November: *Troika*, in E   12. December: *Noël*, in A flat
Lidya Artymiw (*CHAN 8349*)
Peter Katin (*Olympia OCD 192*)
Mikhail Pletnev (*Chante du Monde LDC 278 952*)
Victoria Postnikova (*Erato 2292-45512-2*)
[*May–Oct only*] Barry Douglas (*RCA RD87887*)
[*orch arr*] Mikhail Parkhomovsky/Siberian Ensemble (*Melodia SUCD 10-00201*)

**Album for the Young: 24 easy pieces** (Op. 39: 1878)
1. *Prière de matin*, in G   2. *Le matin en hiver*, in D   3. *Maman*, in G 4. *Le petit cavalier*, in D   5. *Marche des soldats de bois*, in D   6. *La nouvelle poupée*, in B flat   7. *La poupée malade*, in G minor   8. *Enterrement de la poupée*, in C minor   9. *Valse*, in E flat   10. *Polka*, in B flat   11. *Mazurka*, in D minor   12. *Chanson russe*, in F   13. *Le paysan prélude*, in B flat   14. *Chanson populaire (Kamarinskaya)*, in D   15. *Chanson italienne*, in D   16. *Mélodie antique française*, in G minor   17. *Chanson allemande*, in E flat   18. *Chanson napolitaine*, in E flat   19. *Conte de la vieille bonne*, in C   20. *La sorcière (Baba Yaga)*, in E minor   21. *Douce rêverie*, in C   22. *Chant de l'alouette*, in G   23. *A l'église*, in E minor   24. *L'orgue de barberie*, in G
Luba Edlina (*Chan 8365*)
Victoria Postnikova (*Erato 4509-91843-2*)

**Douze morceaux de difficulté moyen** (Op. 40: 1878)
1. *Etude*, in G   2. *Chanson triste*, in G minor   3. *Marche funèbre*, in C minor   4. *Mazurka*, in C   5. *Mazurka*, in D   6. *Chant sans paroles*, in A minor   7. *Au village*, in A minor   8. *Valse*, in A flat   9. *Valse*, in F sharp minor   10. *Danse russe*, in A minor   11. *Scherzo*, in D minor   12. *Rêverie interrompue*, in F minor
Victoria Postnikova (*Erato 2292-4595-2*)
5. *Mazurka*/10. *Danse russe* Ilona Prunyi (*Naxos 8-550504*)
2. *Chanson triste*/8. *Valse* Sviatoslav Richter (*Melodia SUCD 10-00252*)
8. *Valse* S. Rachmaninov (*RCA 09026 6 1265-2*)

**Piano Sonata in G (Grand Sonata)** (Op. 37: 1878)
Barry Douglas (*RCA RD87887*)
Peter Katin (*Olympia OCD 192*)
Victoria Postnikova (*Erato 4509-91843-2*)

**March for the Volunteer Fleet, in C** (1878) [pseudonymous]
Victoria Postnikova (*Erato 2292-45967-2*)

**Six Morceaux** (Op. 51: 1882)
1. *Valse de salon*, in A flat   2. *Polka peu dansante*, in B minor
3. *Menuetto scherzoso*, in E flat   4. *Natha-valse*, in A
5. *Romance*, in F   6. *Valse sentimentale*, in F minor
Victoria Postnikova (*Erato 2292-45995-2*)
5. *Romance* Barry Douglas (*RCA RD87887*)
2. *Polka*/5. *Romance* Ilona Prunyi (*Naxos 8-550504*)
1. *Valse de salon*/3. *Menuetto scherzoso*
Sviatoslav Richter (*Melodia SUCD 10-00252*)

**Dumka (Scène rustique Russe) in C minor** (Op. 59: 1886)
Michele Campanella (*Nuova Era 6735*)
Vladimir Horowitz (*RCA GD 60526*)
Victoria Postnikova (*Erato 4509-91843-2*)
Ilona Prunyi (*Naxos 8-550504*)

*Trois morceaux* (1889)
1. *Impromptu*, in A flat (1889)   2. *Valse scherzo*, in A (1889)
3. *Impromptu caprice*, in G (1884)
Victoria Postnikova (*Erato 2292-45967-2*)

*Impromptu (Momento lirico)*, **in A flat** (1892–3)
Victoria Postnikova (*Erato 2292-45996-2*)

*Aveu passioné,* **in E minor** (1892)
Victoria Postnikova (*Erato 2292-45967-2*)

**Military march [for the 98th Yurevsky infantry regiment], in B flat** (1893)
Victoria Postnikova (*Erato 2292-45967-2*)

*18 morceaux* (Op. 72: 1893)
1. *Impromptu*, in F minor   2. *Berceuse*, in A flat   3. *Tendres reproches*, in C sharp
minor   4. *Danse caractéristique*, in D   5. *Méditation*, in D   6. *Mazurque pour
danser*, in B flat   7. *Polacca de concert*, in E flat   8. *Dialogue*, in B   9. *Un poco
di Schumann*, in D flat   10. *Scherzo-fantasie*, in E flat minor   11. *Valse Bluette*,
in E flat   12. *L'Espiègle*, in E   13. *Echo rustique*, in E flat   14. *Chant élégiaque*,
in D flat   15. *Un poco di Chopin*, in C sharp minor   16. *Valse à cinq temps*, in
D 17. *Passé lointain*, in E flat 18. *Scène dansante (Invitation au Trépak)*, in C
Angela Brownridge (*Helios CDH88029*)
Mikhail Pletnev (*Chante du Monde LDC 278 952/3*)
Victoria Postnikova (*Erato 2292-45996-2*)
3. *Tendres reproches*/7. *Polacca de concert*/8. *Dialogue*/12. *L'Espiègle*
Ilona Prunyi (*Naxos 8-550504*)
5. *Méditation*/12. *L'Espiègle*/15. *Un poco di Chopin*
Sviatoslav Richter (*Melodia SUCD 10-00252*)

Victoria Postnikova's name appears so frequently because she is the only pianist to have
recorded a complete cycle of Tchaikovsky's works for solo piano, on seven compact
discs available in a boxed set (*Erato*). In many cases, hers is the only available recording.
Among other readily available recordings of individual pieces for solo piano, sadly
few, the obvious exception is **The Seasons** (Op. 37b), charmingly played by Lydia
Artymiw; in part (May–October) by Barry Douglas, whose version also includes the
**Grand Sonata** (Op. 37) and the *Romance* from **Six morceaux** (Op. 51, No. 5: 1882);
and in full by Mikhail Pletnev, winner of the 1978 Tchaikovsky Piano Competition (now
turned conductor, see *Symphonies*), who adds the **18 morceaux** (Op. 72) and **Trois
morceaux** (Op. 9) on an expensive, imported two-disc set. Other single discs worth
a hearing include Angela Brownridge's 18 Pieces and Luba Edlina's version of **Album
for the Young** (Op. 39) on an enterprising disc which adds a string transcription of the

same pieces played by the Borodin Trio. Highly recommended is a new, low-price CD on which Ilona Prunyi plays a wide selection including *Rêverie du Soir*, *Tendres reproches*, *Danse russe* and *Dumka*. Andre Gavrilov and Michele Campanella have both recorded *Theme and Variations* (Op. 19, No. 6).

## (5) Songs

**'My genius, my angel, my friend'** (Fet) (c. 1854)

**'Zemfira's Song'** (Pushkin) (c. 1855–60)

**'Mezza notte'** (c. 1860–1)

**Six Romances** (Op. 6: 1869)
1. 'Do not believe, my friend' (A. Tolstoy)
2. 'Not a word, O my friend' (Pleshcheyev, after Hartmann)
3. 'It's both bitter and sweet' (Rostopchina)
4. 'A tear trembles' (A. Tolstoy)
5. 'Why?' (Mey, after Heine)
6. 'None but the lonely heart' (Mey, after Goethe)

**'To forget so soon'** (Apukhtin) (1870)

**Six Romances** (Op. 16: 1872)
1. 'Cradle song' (Maikov)
2. 'Wait a while' (Grekov)
3. 'Accept but once' (Fet)
4. 'O sing that song' (Plescheyev, after Hemans)
5. 'Thy radiant image' (Tchaikovsky)
6. 'Modern Greek song' (Maikov)

**'Take my heart away'** (Fet) (1873)

**'Blue eyes of Spring'** (Mikhailov, after Heine) (1873)

**Six Romances** (Op. 25: 1874–5)
1. 'Reconciliation' (Shcherbina)
2. 'As o'er the burning ashes' (Tyutchev)
3. 'Mignon's song' (Tyutchev, after Goethe)
4. 'The canary' (Mey)
5. 'I never spoke to her' (Mey)
6. 'As they reiterated: "Fool!"' (Mey)

**Six Romances** (Op. 27: 1875)
1. 'At bedtime' (Ogaryov)
2. 'Look, yonder cloud' (Grekov)
3. 'Do not leave me' (Fet)
4. 'Evening' (Mey, after Shevchenko)
5. 'Was it the mother who bore me?' (Mey, after Mickiewicz)
6. 'My spoiled darling' (Mey, after Mickiewicz)

**Six Romances** (Op. 28: 1875)
1. 'No, I shall never tell' (Grekov, after de Musset)
2. 'The corals' (Mey, after Kondratowicz)
3. 'Why did I dream of you?' (Mey)
4. 'He loved me so much' (Apukhtin)
5. 'No response, or word, or greeting' (Apukhtin)
6. 'The fearful minute' (Tchaikovsky)

**'I should like in a single word'** (Mey, after Heine) (1875)

**'We have not far to walk'** (Grekov) (1875)

**Six Romances** (Op. 38: 1878)
1. 'Don Juan's serenade' (A. Tolstoy)
2. 'It was in the early spring' (A. Tolstoy)
3. 'Amid the din of the ball' (A. Tolstoy)
4. 'O, if only you could for one moment' (A. Tolstoy)
5. 'The love of a dead man' (Lermontov)
6. 'Pimpinella' (Tchaikovsky, after a popular Neapolitan song)

**Six duets** (Op. 46: 1880)
1. 'Evening' (Surikov)
2. 'Scottish Ballad' (A. Tolstoy)
3. 'Tears' (Tyutchev)
4. 'In the garden, near the ford' (Surikov)
5. 'Passion spent' (A. Tolstoy)
6. 'Dawn' (Surikov)

**Seven Romances** (Op. 47: 1880)
1. 'If only I had known' (A. Tolstoy)
2. 'Softly the spirit flew up to heaven' (A. Tolstoy)
3. 'Dusk fell on the earth' (Berg)
4. 'Sleep, poor friend' (A. Tolstoy)
5. 'I bless you, forests' (A. Tolstoy)
6. 'Does the day reign?' (Apukhtin)
7. 'Was I not a little blade of grass?' (Surikov)

**Sixteen Children's Songs** (Op. 54: 1883)
1. 'Granny and grandson'
2. 'The little bird'
3. 'Spring'
4. 'My little garden'
5. 'Legend'
6. 'On the bank'
7. 'Winter evening'
8. 'The cuckoo'
9. 'Spring'
10. 'Lullaby in a storm'
11. 'The flower'
12. 'Winter'

13. 'Spring song'
14. 'Autumn'
15. 'The swallow'
16. 'Child's song'

**Six Romances** (Op. 57: 1884)
1. 'Tell me what in the shade of the branches' (Sollogub)
2. 'On the golden cornfields' (A. Tolstoy)
3. 'Do not ask' (Strugovshchikov)
4. 'Sleep' (Merezhkovsky)
5. 'Death' (Merezhkovsky)
6. 'Only thou alone' (Pleshcheyev)

**Twelve Romances** (Op. 60: 1886)
1. 'Last night' (Khomyakov)
2. 'I'll tell you nothing' (Fet)
3. 'O, if only you knew' (Pleshcheyev)
4. 'The nightingale' (Pushkin)
5. 'Simple words' (Tchaikovsky)
6. 'Frenzied nights' (Apukhtin)
7. 'Gipsy's song' (Polonsky)
8. 'Forgive' (Nekrasov)
9. 'Night' (Polonsky)
10. 'Behind the window in the shadow' (Polonsky)
11. 'Exploit' (Khomyakov)
12. 'The mild stars shone for us' (Pleshcheyev)

**Six Romances** (Op. 63: 1887) (Grand Duke Konstantin Konstantinovich Romanov)
1. 'I did not love you at first'
2. 'I opened the window'
3. 'I do not please you'
4. 'The first meeting'
5. 'The fires in the rooms were already out'
6. 'Serenade (O child, beneath thy window)'

**Six Romances** [on French texts] (Op. 65: 1888)
1. 'Sérénade (Où vas-tu, souffle d'aurore?)' (Turquéty)
2. 'Déception' (Collin)
3. 'Sérénade (J'aime dans le rayon de la limpide aurore)' (Collin)
4. 'Qu'importe que l'hiver?' (Collin)
5. 'Les larmes' (Blanchecotte)
6. 'Rondel' (Collin)

**Six Romances** (Op. 73: 1893) (Rathaus)
1. 'We sat together'
2. 'Night'
3. 'In this moonlight'
4. 'The sun has set'
5. 'Mid sombre days'
6. 'Again, as before, alone'

## Recommended songs and song collections on compact disc
[Titles are reproduced as on sleeve notes]

My Protector, My Angel, My Friend/None But the Lonely Heart/Why?
Not a Word, Beloved/Heed Not, My Love/Spirit My Heart Away/Lullaby
Acquiescence/The Frightening Moment/It Happened in the Early Spring
Nights of Delirium/Gipsy Girl's Song/The Stars Looked Tenderly Upon Us
This, Our First Reunion/Indoors, the Lights Were Being Put Out/Serenade
The Sun Has Slipped From Sight/Night/Once Again, Alone
**Olga Borodina** soprano/Larissa Gergieva, piano (*Philips 442 013-2*)

Once again before I am alone (Op. 73, No. 6) Nightingale (Op 60, No. 4) Heroism
(Op. 60, No. 11) I threw open the window (Op. 63, No. 2) Don Juan's Serenade
'Darkness is unfolding' (Op. 38 No. 1) Reconciliation: 'O heart of mine, sleep deeply!'
(Op. 25, No. 1) A tear trembles in your jealous gaze (Op. 6, No. 4) None but the lonely
heart ('No, only to those who have longed') (Op. 6, No. 6) The Fearful Minute: 'You
listen, your sweet head bowed' (Op. 28, No. 6)
**Dmitri Hvorostovsky baritone**/Oleg Boshniakovich, piano (*Philips 432 119-
2*)

Speak Not, O Beloved (Op. 6, No. 2) Do Not Ask (Op. 57, No. 3) The Gentle
Stars (Op. 60, No. 12) Forget So Soon/Frenzied Nights (Op. 60, No. 6) So What?
(Op. 16, No. 5) If I Had Known (Op. 47, No. 1) At the Ball (Op. 38, No. 3)
Why Did I Dream Of You? (Op. 28, No. 3) Whether By Day (Op. 47, No. 6)
Tell Me, What in the Shade of the Branches (Op. 57, No. 1) In This Moonlit
Night (Op. 73, No. 3) The Fearful Moment (Op. 28, No. 6) Green Grass (Op. 47,
No. 7) Night (Op. 73, No. 2) Solitude (Op. 73, No. 6) It was Early in Spring
(Op. 38, No. 2)
**Makvala Kasrashvili** soprano/Liya Mogilevskaya, piano (*Melodia SUCD 10-00264*)

A Summer Love (Op. 6) Warum (Op. 6) L'oublié (Op. 6) Attends! (Op. 16) What
Matter! (Op. 16) Je voudrais méttre dans une seule parole (w/o op. no.) No,
Whom I Love I Will Not Name (Op. 28) Don Juan's Serenade (Op. 38) The
Dawn of Spring (Op. 38) The Tapers Were Flashing (Op. 38) Unsatisfied (Op. 47)
Le Soir et le Matin (Op. 47) Cradle Song During a Storm (Op. 54) Absence
(Op. 60) Ah! Si vous saviez (Op. 60) Le Rossignol (Op. 60) La Nuit (Op. 60)
La Tête blanche (Op. 60) New Hopes (Op. 63) A Serenade (Op. 63) An dem
schlum-ernden Strom (Op. 73) Nacht (Op. 73) O du mondhelle Nacht (Op. 73)
Sonne ging zur Ruhe (Op. 73) In trüber Stund (Op. 73) Weil ich wie einstmals
allein (Op. 73)
**Alexei Martynov** tenor/Aristotel Konstantinidi, piano (*MK 417054*)

'Do you not hear the nightingale?' (*Romeo and Juliet*: duet)
**Suzanne Murphy/Keith Lewis (Jarvi/SNO)** (*CHAN 8476*)

Last Night (Op. 60, No. 1) To forget so soon (w/o op. no.) The Nightingale
(Op. 60, No. 4) It was in the early spring (Op. 38, No. 2) Amid the din of
the ball (Op. 38, No. 3) The Fearful Minute (Op. 28, No. 6) Do not believe
my friend (Op. 6, No. 1) The Cuckoo (Op. 54, No. 8) Was I Not a Little Blade

of Grass? (Op. 47, No. 7) Cradle Song (Op. 16, No. 1) Behind the window (Op. 60, No. 10) Serenade (Op. 63, No. 6) The Canary (Op. 25, No. 4) Not a word, O my friend (Op. 6, No. 2) Lullaby in a storm (Op. 54, No. 10) Spring (Op. 54, No. 9) Why did I dream of you? (Op. 28, No. 3) None but the lonely heart (Op. 6, No. 6) Does the day reign (Op. 47, No. 6) If only I had known (Op. 47, No. 1) Why? (Op. 6, No. 5)
**Joan Rodgers** soprano/Roger Vignoles, piano (*Hyperion CDA 66617*)

The Cuckoo (Op. 54, No. 8) Evening (Op. 27, No. 4) The Nightingale (Op. 60, No. 4) Last Night (Op. 60, No. 1) None but the weary heart (Op. 6, No. 6) Cradle Song (Op. 16, No. 1) Why? (Op. 6, No. 5) The Fearful Minute (Op. 28, No. 6) Whether day reigns (Op. 47, No. 6) Spring (Op. 54, No. 9) Simple Words (Op. 60, No. 5) Mezza notte (no op. no.) Serenade (Aurore) (Op. 65, No. 1) Deception (Op. 65, No. 2) Poème d'octobre (Op. 65, No. 4) Les Larmes (Op. 65, No. 5) The sun has set (Op. 73, No. 4) As over burning ashes (Op. 25, No. 2) My guiding spirit, my angel, my friend/Zemfira's song (no opus nos) Do not believe it my friend (Op. 6, No. 1) To forget so soon/O do sing that song (Op. 16, No. 4) Take my heart away/Why did I dream of you? (Op. 28, No. 3) It was in the early spring (Op. 38, No. 2) Amid the noise of the ball (Op. 38, No. 3) If only I'd known (Op. 47, No. 1)
**Elisabeth Söderström** soprano/Vladimir Ashkenazy, piano (*Decca 436 204-2*)

Why? (Op. 6, No. 5) Mid the Din of the Ball (Op. 38, No. 3) It Was in the Early Spring (Op. 38, No. 2) Whether By Day (Op. 47, No. 6)
**Anatoli Solovyanenko** tenor/Parkhomovsky-Siberia (*Melodia SUCD 10-00201*)

Ich wollt' meine Schmerzen ergossen sich all' (w/o op. no.) Glaube nicht, mein Freund (Op. 6, No. 1) Warum sind denn die Rosen so blaß (Op. 6, No. 5) Warum? (Op. 28, No. 3) Wenn ich das gewußt hatte (Op. 47, No. 1) Die Seele schwebt langsam gen Himmel (Op. 47, No. 2)
Six French Songs (Desirée Artôt de Padilla) (Op. 65: 1888)
Sechs Lieder nach Gedichten von Daniel Rathaus (Op. 73)
**Julia Varady** soprano/Aribert Reimann, piano (*Orfeo C 053 851 A*)


**Two Songs** (*orchestrated by cpsr*)
(a) Legend: Christ had a garden (Op. 54, No. 5) (b) Was I Not a Blade of Grass? (Op. 47, No. 7)
**Raphael Wallfisch (Geoffrey Simon/ECO)** (*CHAN 8347*)

Until recently there was little to challenge **Galina Vishnevskya**'s 1991 selection of Tchaikovsky songs, accompanied by Rostropovich. Of late, however, a clutch of collections has appeared, all of high quality. Outstanding are the three recitals now available from the dashing young Russian baritone **Dmitri Hvorostovsky**. *Russian Romances* combines songs by Tchaikovsky and Rachmaninov (including the celebrated 'None but the Lonely Heart'), and *My Restless Soul* three numbers from the magical Opus 38 (above all, 'Amid the Din of the Ball'), while *Tchaikovsky and Verdi Arias* includes arias from *Eugene Onegin*, *The Queen of Spades*, *Charodeika* ('The

Sorceress'), *Mazeppa* and *Iolanta*. One of the few English sopranos to boast a Russian degree, **Joan Rodgers** is as eloquent as **Olga Borodina** and as lyrical as **Elisabeth Söderström**. *Aficionados* should also check out **Julia Varady**'s Orfeo recording of eighteen Tchaikovsky lieder (Op. 6, 47, 65 and 73). Tchaikovsky's most popular song, 'None but the Lonely Heart', has been recorded by **Fritz Wunderlich**, **Nikolay Ghiaurov**, **Boris Christoff**, **Richard Tauber** and, of current luminaries, **Placido Domingo** (on 'Domingo and Perlman – Together' *EMI CDC7 54266-2*). Caruso and Tauber are also among the throng to have recorded 'Don Juan's Serenade'. Jessye Norman performs the 'Sérénade' and 'Rondel' from Op. 65 in the live recording of a 1990 gala concert in Leningrad to celebrate the 150th anniversary of the composer's birth. But my personal favourite of all Tchaikovsky's songs remains 'Amid the Din of the Ball', from Opus 38, passionately sung by the Russian tenor **Anatoli Solovyanenko** in a rare orchestral version picked up during my Russian travels, and played with remarkable warmth by the Siberian Violinists Ensemble under Mikhail Parkhomovsky (*Melodia SUCD 10-00201*). Purists will quite rightly prefer **Robert Tear**'s haunting 1972 version for Decca, and should fight to find a copy of his now sadly deleted LP, *Tchaikovsky Songs (ZRG 707)*.

## (6) Works for the Stage

### Minor, lost or unfinished works [*unrecorded*]
*Hyperbole*: opera in one scene (1854) [incomplete; lost]
Music for the fountain scene in *Boris Godunov* (1863–4) [lost]
Introduction and Mazurka for *Dmitry the Pretender and Vasily Shuisky* (1867)
Couplets for a vaudeville, *The Tangle* (1867) [lost]
Recitatives and a chorus for Auber's *Le domino noir* (1868) [lost]
'Chorus of flowers and insects' for an opera, *Mandragora* (Rachinsky) (1870)
Cradle song for a play, *La Fée* (Feuillet) (1879)
Music for a tableau, *Montenegrins receiving the news of Russia's declaration of war on Turkey* (1880) [lost]
Domovoy's monologue: melodrama for the play *The Voyevoda* (Ostrovsky) (1886)

**Voevoda**, opera in 3 acts (Op. 3) (1867–8)

**Undine**, opera in 3 acts (1869)

### Couplets for tenor and two violins for Beaumarchais' *The Barber of Seville* (1872)
*Vous l'ordonnez* E. Raikov (Akulov/USSR) (*Melodia 1577-51870-2*)

### *The Oprichnik* (1870-2)
[*Natalia's arias from Acts 1 & 3*]
Carole Farley (Serebrier/Sicilian SO) (*Pickwick MCD 64*)
[*Danses*] Colin Davis/ROH (*Philips 422 845-2*)

### *The Snow Maiden* (Op. 12: 1873)
Simonova/Martinov/Elnikov/Lomonossov/Provatorov–USSR Radio & TV Ch/Orch (*Chant du Monde LDC 278 904*)
[*Overture*] Alexander Gauk/USSR RSO (*Melodia 1577-51870-2*)

**Vakula the Smith** (1874) (rev 1885 as **Cherevichki**, a.k.a.: **Les Caprices d'Oxane**
[*Oxana's aria*]
Carole Farley (Serebrier/Melbourne) (*Pickwick MCD 64*)
[*Polonaise*]
Evgeny Svetlanov/USSR Academy SO (*Olympia OCD 136*)
[*Introduction/Danse russe/Danse des cosaques*]
Colin Davis/ROH (*Philips 422 845-2*)

**Swan Lake** (Op. 20: 1875–6)
Richard Bonynge/National PO (*Decca 425 413-2*)
Charles Dutoit/Montreal SO (*Decca 436 212-2*)
Mark Ermler/Royal Opera House (Covent Garden) Orchestra (*ROH 301/33*)
John Lanchberry/Philharmonia (*CD-CFPD 4727*)
André Previn/LSO (*EMI CZS7 49531-2*)
Leonard Slatkin/St Louis SO (*RCA RD 87804*)
Georg Solti/Chicago SO (*Decca 430 151-2*)
[*Excerpts*] André Previn/London SO (*EMI 7 69044 2*)
Mstislav Rostropovich/Berlin PO (*DG Galleria 429 097-2*)
Georg Solti/Chicago SO (*Decca 430 707-2*)

**Eugene Onegin** (Op. 24: 1877-8)
Hvorostovksy/Focile/Shichoff/Bychkov–Paris (*Philips 438 235-2*)
Allen/Freni/von Otter/Shichoff/Levine–Dresden (*DG 423 959-2*)
Weikl/Kubiak/Burrows/Hamari/Ghiaurov/Solti–ROH (*Decca 417 413-2*)
Bolshoi soloists/Khaikin–Bolshoi (*Legato LCD 163-2*)
Sofia soloists/Tchakarov–Sofia (*Sony S2K 45539*)
[*Polonaise/Valse/Ecossaise*] Davis/ROH (*Philips 422 845-2*)

**The Maid of Orleans** (1878-9, rev 1882)
[*Joan's arias from Acts 2 & 4*]
Carole Farley (Serebrier/Melbourne) (*Pickwick MCD 64*)
Jessye Norman (Temirkanov/Leningrad) (*RCA RD 60739*)
[*Entracte/Danse des bohémiens/Danses des polchinelles et des histrons*]
Davis/ROH (*Philips 422 845-2*)

**Mazeppa** (1881-3)
Leiferkus/Gorchakova/Kotscherga/Dyadkova/Larin/Järvi–Gothenburg (*DG 439 906-2*)
[*Arioso, Mazeppa, Act II: O Maria, Maria!*]
Dmitri Hvorostovsky (Valery Gergiev/Rotterdam) (*Philips 426 740-2*)
[*Maria's arias from Acts 2 & 3*]
Carole Farley (Serebrier/Sicilian SO) (*Pickwick MCD 64*)
[*Cossack Dance*]
Erich Kunzel/Cincinnati SO (*Telarc 80041*)
Kurt Masur/Leipzig GO (*Teldec 9031-76456-2*)
Geoffrey Simon/LSO (*Chan 8310/11*)
[*Battle of Poltava*] Geoffrey Simon/LSO (*Chan 8310/11*)

***The Sorceress/The Enchantress (Charodeika)*** (1885-7)
[*Scene & Arioso, Kurtyatev, Act II*]
Dmitri Hvorostovsky (Gergiev/Rotterdam) (*Philips 426 740-2*)
[*Polya's arias, Act IV*]
Carole Farley (Serebrier/Sicilian SO) (*Pickwick MCD64*)
[*Introduction/Danse des histrions et scène*]
Colin Davis/ROH (*Philips 422 845-2*)

***The Sleeping Beauty*** (Op. 66: 1888–9)
Richard Bonynge/National PO (*Decca 425 468-2*)
Mark Ermler/Royal Opera House (Covent Garden) Orchestra (*ROH 306/8*)
John Lanchberry/Philharmonia (*EMI CDS7 49216-2*)
André Previn/London SO (*EMI CZS7 62816-2*)
Richard Bonynge/NPO (*Decca 430 151-2*)
[*Excerpts*]
Mark Ermler/Royal Opera House (Covent Garden) Orchestra (*ROH 003*)
André Previn/LSO (*EMI 7 69044-2*)
Mstislav Rostropovich/Berlin PO (*DG Galleria 429 097-2*)
[*piano arr.*] Mikhail Pletnev (*Virgin 7567-91169-2*)

***The Queen of Spades*** (Op. 68: 1890)
Atlantov/Valaitis/Fedoseyev/Milaskina/Levo/Ermler–Bolshoi (*Philips 420 375-2*)
Ochman/Evstatieva/Konsulov/Mazurok/Tchakarov–Sofia (*Sony S3K 45720*)
Atlantov/Freni/Leiferkus/Forrester/Hvorostovsky/Ozawa–Tanglewood-Boston (*RCA 09026-60992-2*)

***Iolanta*** (Op. 69: 1891)
Vishnevskaya/Gedda/Groenroos/Petkov/Krause/Rostropovich–Orch. Paris (*Erato 2292-45973-2*)
[*Scene & Aria, Robert*]
Dmitri Hvorostovsky (Gergiev/Rotterdam) (*Philips 426 740-2*)
[*Iolanta's arioso*]
Carole Farley (Serebrier/Melbourne) (*Pickwick MCD 64*)

***The Nutcracker*** (Op. 71: 1891–2)
Vladimir Ashkenazy/RPO (*Decca 433 000-2DH2*)
Richard Bonynge/National PO (*Decca 425 450-2*)
Antal Dorati/London SO (*Mercury 432 750-2*)
Mark Ermler/Royal Opera House (*ROH 304/5*)
John Lanchberry/Philharmonia (*EMI CDS7 49399-2*)
Charles Mackerras/London SO (*Telarc CD 80137*)
André Previn/RPO (*EMI CDS7 47267-8*)
Michael Tilson Thomas/Philharmonia (*CBS 42173*)

**Duet for an opera based on *Romeo and Juliet*** (?1893) [incomplete]
'Do you not hear the nightingale?' [completed and orch by Taneyev]
Suzanne Murphy *soprano* Keith Lewis *tenor*/Järvi–Scottish NO (*Chandos 8476*)

Until recently joined by Järvi's pioneering **Mazeppa**, *Eugene Onegin* and *The Queen of Spades* were the only Tchaikovsky operas available in complete recordings. For all Hvorostovsky's resonant appeal (more so, all too often, on record than in the concert hall), Thomas Allen's **Eugene Onegin** for Levine is far more accomplished, with the bonus of a superb Tatyana in Mirella Freni. Hvorostovsky fans would be better off savouring his Yeletsky in **The Queen of Spades** to Vladimir Atlantov's legendary Herman, with Freni again superb as Lisa and Margaret Forrester a noble Countess, in what has been described as 'Ozawa's finest achievement on record'. Opinions on the ballets are almost as numerous as the versions available. But bargain-hunters cannot go wrong with the ballet specialist John Lanchberry's budget **Swan Lake** with the Philharmonia, quite as compelling as Bonynge, Ermler or Dutoit. For both **The Sleeping Beauty** and **The Nutcracker**, the critical consensus favours Antal Dorati with the Concertgebouw and the LSO respectively. Tchaikovsky loyalists will wish to preface whatever *Nutcracker* they choose with the wonderful Rostropovich–Vishnevskaya **Iolanta**, to hear all the parallels in his carefully wrought double-bill so rarely available to live audiences. The Murphy–Lewis version of the duet from **Romeo and Juliet**, based on the famous love theme from the overture, is a tantalizing taste (thanks to Taneyev) of the opera Tchaikovsky always wanted to write, but never quite got around to.

## (7) Choral Works

**Invocation to Sleep ['At bedtime'] (Ogaryov) for unaccompanied chorus** (1863–4)
Valeri Polyansky/USSR Ministry of Culture Chamber Choir (*Melodia SUCD 10-00015*)

**Cantata: 'An die Freude' (Schiller) for SATB soloists, chorus and orchestra** (1865)

**'Nature and Love' (Tchaikovsky) for SSA and piano** (1870)

**Cantata in commemoration of the bicentenary of the birth of Peter the Great for tenor, chorus and orchestra** (1872)

**Cantata (Hymn, or Chorus) in celebration of the golden jubilee of Osip Petrov for tenor, chorus and orchestra** (1875)

**Liturgy of St John Chrysostom** (Op. 41: 1878)
1. Lord have mercy 2. Glory be to the Father 3. O Come, let us worship 4. Alleluja 5. Glory be to thee 6. Cherubical Hymn 7. Lord, have mercy 8. The Creed 9. The mercy of peace 10. We sing thee 11. It is meet 12. Amen, and with thy spirit 13. Our Father 14. Praise ye the Lord 15. Blessed be he that cometh in the name of the Lord
Bulgarian Choir/Svyatolsav Obretenov (*AVM 1020*)
USSR Ministry of Culture Chamber Choir/Polyansky (*Melodia SUCD 10-00014*)
Leningrad Glinka Academy/Vladislav Tchernouchenko (*Melodia LDC 278 728*)

**'Evening', for unaccompanied men's chorus** (1881)

**All-Night Vigil [Vespers], for unaccompanied chorus, Op. 52** (1881–2)
Leningrad Glinka Academy/Chernoshenko (*Chant du Monde LDC 278 749*)

***Moscow*: coronation cantata for soloists, chorus and orchestra** (1883)
[unrecorded]

**Nine sacred pieces, for unaccompanied chorus** (1884–5)
1. Cherubim's song in F 2. Cherubim's song in D 3. Cherubim's song in C 4. *Thee we hymn* 5. *Meet it is indeed* 6. Lord's Prayer 7. *Bliss I chose* 8. *Let my prayer be set forth* 9. *Today the heavenly powers*
Moscow Chamber Choir/Yuri Oukhov (*Chant du Monde LDC 278 728*)
3. *Cherubim's song in C*/5. *Meet it is indeed*/7. *Bliss I chose*
Polyansky/USSR Ministry of Culture Chamber Choir (*Melodia SUCD 10-00015*)

**Hymn in honour of SS Cyril and Methodius, for unaccompanied chorus** (1885)
Gloriae Dei Cantores/E.C. Patterson (*Gloriae GDCD007*)

**Jurists' song for the golden jubilee of the School of Jurisprudence, for unaccompanied chorus (Tchaikovsky)** (1885)

**'An angel weeping', for unaccompanied chorus** (1887)
Gloriae Dei Cantores/E.C. Patterson (*Gloriae GDCD007*)

**'Sleeping golden cloud' (Lermontov) for unaccompanied chorus** (1887)
Polyansky/USSR Ministry of Culture Chamber Choir (*Melodia SUCD 10-00015*)

**'Blessed is he who smiles' (Grand Duke Konstantin Konstantinovich Romanov) for unaccompanied men's chorus** (1887)

**'The Nightingale' (Tchaikovsky) for unaccompanied chorus** (1889)
Polyansky/USSR Ministry of Culture Chamber Choir (*Melodia SUCD 10-00015*)

**A greeting to Anton Rubinstein for his golden jubilee as an artist (Polonsky), for unaccompanied chorus** (1889)

**'Legend' (Pleshcheyev) for unaccompanied chorus** (Op. 54, No. 5: 1889)
Morris/Ambrosian Singers (*Decca 433 673-2DSP*)
Polyansky/USSR Ministry of Culture Chamber Choir (*Melodia SUCD 10-00015*)

**'The cuckoo' (Tsyganov) for unaccompanied chorus** (1891)
Polyansky/USSR Ministry of Culture Chamber Choir (*Melodia SUCD 10-00015*)

**'Before your time comes' (Tsyganov) for unaccompanied women's chorus** (1891)
Polyansky/USSR Ministry of Culture Chamber Choir (*Melodia SUCD 10-00015*)

**'The voice of mirth grew silent' (Pushkin) for unaccompanied men's chorus** (1891)

'Night' (Tchaikovsky) for SATB and piano [after Mozart] (1893)

'Spring' for unaccompanied women's chorus [lost]

## (8) Miscellaneous

Weber, Scherzo of piano sonata, Op. 39. Orchestrated (1863)

Beethoven, 1st movement of piano sonata, Op. 31, No. 2. Orchestrated (1863)

Beethoven, 1st movement of violin sonata, Op. 47 ('Kreutzer'). Orchestrated (1863–4)

Gung'l, *Le retour* (valse) for piano. Orchestrated (1863–4)

Schumann, Adagio and Allegro brillante from *Etudes symphoniques*, Op. 13. Orchestrated (1864)

K. Kral, Festival march for piano. Orchestrated (1867)

Dargomyzhsky, *Little Russian kazachok*, fantasia. Arranged for piano (1868)

E. Tarnovskaya, 'I remember all', song, arranged for piano duet (1868)

A. Rubinstein, *Ivan the Terrible*, musical picture for orchestra. Arranged for piano duet (1869)

A. Dubuque, *Maria-Dagmar*, polka for piano. Orchestrated (1869)

Dargomyzhsky, 'The golden cloud has slept', for 3 voices and piano. Piano part orchestrated (1870)

Stradella, 'O del mio dolce', aria. Piano part orchestrated (1870)

A. Rubinstein, *Don Quixote*, musical piece for orchestra. Arranged for piano duet (1871)

Cimarosa, 'Le faccio un inchino', trio from *Il matrimonio segreto*. Piano part in vocal score orchestrated (1871)

Weber, Finale (perpetuum mobile) from Piano Sonata, Op. 24. Transcribed for piano, left hand (1871)

V. Prokunin, 66 Russian folk songs. Edition (1872)

M.A. Mamontova, A collection of children's songs on Russian and Ukrainian melodies. Harmonized (1872, 1877)

Anon, 'Gaudeamus igitur'. Arranged for men's chorus and piano (1874)

Haydn, 'Gott erhalte' (Austrian national anthem). Orchestrated (1874)

Schumann, *Ballade vom Haideknaben*, Op. 122, No. 1. Piano part orchestrated (1874)

Liszt, 'Der König in Thule', song. Piano part orchestrated (1874)

Bortnyansky, Complete church music. Edited (1881)

Couplets on a theme from Glinka's *A Life for the Tsar*, linked with the Russian national anthem of A. Lvov. Arranged for chorus and string orch (1883)

Laroche, *Karmozina*: overture. Orchestrated (1888)

S. Menter, *Ungarische Zigeunerwiesen*, for piano. Arranged for piano and orchestra (1893)

### OTHER RECOMMENDED RECORDINGS

One of the most distinctive of all available Tchaikovsky recordings is a fine double album entitled 'World Première' (*CHANDOS 8310/1*) in which Geoffrey Simon conducts the LSO in the first recording of the **Festival Overture on the Danish national anthem in D** (Op. 15: 1866), the first complete recording of the *Hamlet*

**overture** together with the rest of the incidental music, the original 1869 version of the fantasy overture **Romeo and Juliet**, the Battle of Poltava and Cossack Dance from **Mazeppa**, and the rarely heard **Serenade for Nikolay Rubinstein's Saint's Day**, also in its first and only appearance on disc. An obvious must for all collectors. **The Storm** overture (Op. 76: 1864) is available on a Gennady Rozhdestvensky recording with the LSO, coupled with the Sixth Symphony (*Pathétique*). The symphonic poem **Fatum** (Op. 77: 1868) is played by the St Louis Symphony under Leonard Slatkin on a CD which also offers a fine reading of the Fourth Symphony and a rare recording of the symphonic ballade **The Voevoda** (Op. 78, 1890–1). The symphonic fantasy **The Tempest** (Op. 18: 1873) is coupled with the Fifth Symphony by Litton and the Bournemouth, and Slatkin and the St Louis. But the best value for Tchaikovsky collectors is perhaps the Russian version by Vyacheslav Ovchinnikov and the USSR SO, coupled with the Violin Concerto (Fedoseyev) and another of the few other recorded versions of **The Voevoda**.

Another superb Russian recording is the Glinka Academy's rendition of the austere **Liturgy of St John Chrysostom** (Op. 41). All that is available on record of **The Oprichnik** is a selection of dances on a Royal Ballet recording of Tchaikovsky ballet music conducted by Colin Davis on Philips (which also includes samples of the rarely heard **Maid of Orleans**, **The Sorceress** and **Les Caprices d'Oxane**).

Finally, three curiosities. Tchaikovsky's four-hand piano arrangement of the Sixth Symphony, *Pathétique*, is energetically committed to disc by the Duo Crommelynck, along with the 50 Russian Folk Songs. And the ever enterprising Chandos label, responsible for liberating much little-known Tchaikovsky, offers Bogatyryev's completion of the unfinished 7th Symphony, by the London Philharmonic under Neeme Järvi, coupled with a spirited performance of its *alter ego*, the Third Piano Concerto, by Geoffrey Tozler (*CHAN 9130*). If you've ever wanted to sing along with the love theme from the *Romeo and Juliet* fantasy overture, Chandos give you a chance as Suzanne Murphy and Keith Lewis give us a mouth-watering taste of the opera Tchaikovsky never wrote.

# APPENDIX B

# Tchaikovsky's Death:
# Primary Sources

## November 1893: Dr Vasily Bertenson
*Peterburgskaya Gazeta [St Petersburg Gazette] no. 293, 25 Oct/6 Nov 1893*

It is the opinion of Dr Bertenson, the first doctor called to Tchaikovsky, that if the patient on first feeling cramps in his stomach had taken castor oil instead of Guniadi-Yanos water, he probably could have been saved – even though his case, as this very experienced physician points out, was an Asiatic cholera of a rare intensity.

Besides, medical assistance was summoned too late. On Wednesday night Pyotr Ilyich dropped into Leiner's Restaurant after the theatre, with several of his friends, his brothers and nephews, and ate macaroni. He did not wash it down with anything. After returning home, however, he asked for a glass of water to be placed on his bedside-table – which he drank, all of it, during the night. In the morning, feeling unwell, he sent for some mineral water, and treated himself with this throughout Thursday – without realizing that Guniadi water only produces the excretion of mucus, and does not expel the solid excremental elements containing the lethal bacteria. By the time Dr Bertenson was summoned, the patient had already been suffering vomiting and diarrhoea; it took the efforts of six men to rub the patient in an attempt to ease his affliction. During the critical period of the illness, the patient had some seventy-five attacks of vomiting and diarrhoea . . . But the deceased had such a robust and healthy constitution that the strength of his resistance to the illness surprised the doctors, and gave hope for recovery.

By Saturday morning all cholera symptoms had actually disappeared; and he was, technically speaking, saved from cholera. So much so that, after disinfection, it was possible to let his friends enter the room. They came and offered him handshakes which he returned all too feebly . . . The doctors made his visitors wash their hands in a sublimate solution when they left the room – really for the sake of form, for they were absolutely certain that the infection had already left the patient and been completely eliminated.

By Sunday morning, however, they were alarmed by a new and dangerous symptom: the patient's continuing failure to be able to urinate. They began to grow apprehensive about blood poisoning, as the blood absorbed the bacteria retained by the urine, and made every effort to encourage urination. But none of the diuretics prescribed proved effective, and the blood soon became infected; as the blood poisoning grew worse, all hope of recovery vanished . . .

Dr Bertenson, an old and intimate friend of the deceased, accomplished an incredible feat of self-control in hiding his own despair from his patient, who had not yet lost consciousness, and his relatives. In the morning and briefly in the afternoon he managed to get away to see others of his patients, but only for a short time; from 5 p.m. to 1.30 a.m. he stayed at Tchaikovsky's bedside, leaving only when it was clear that there was nothing more he could do . . .

'Those who were present at that moment would never forget the indescribable sorrow in the face and voice of this respected doctor when he pronounced the dread words: 'He's dying . . .'[1]

## November 1893: Dr N.N. Mamonov
*Novosti i Birzhevaya Gazeta [News and Stock Exchange Gazette] no. 295, 26 Oct/7 Nov 1893*

Wishing to learn more about the course of the illness and the last moments of our deceased composer, P.I. Tchaikovsky, we approached the young Dr N.N. Mamonov, assistant to the famous physician-in-ordinary, L.B. Bertenson, who stayed permanently with his patient, P.I. Tchaikovsky, and witnessed his demise.

'P.I. Tchaikovsky,' Dr Mamonov told us, 'was generally disposed to suffer gastric disorders, and had a cholerine last summer. I should tell you that Pyotr Ilyich was very sceptical about the cholera epidemic, and this was one of the reasons for the illness which has taken him prematurely to his grave.'

'*When did Tchaikovsky fall ill?*'

'On Wednesday morning he was already complaining of a loss of appetite and of general indisposition, but he didn't pay much attention to it. By 9 a.m. Thursday morning he had a severe stomach upset, which grew more serious after he drank two glasses of water. On that day it became clear to us doctors how grave his condition was. Towards the evening of the same day choleric spasms appeared. What worried us most of all was the absence of urine. His relatives tried to warm him up by rubbing him, and this made him feel somewhat better. That night, Thursday–Friday, was a quiet one for Pyotr Ilyich, and his convulsions ceased. Saturday passed reasonably well, but the absence of urine continued to worry us. On Sunday morning signs of urine poisoning became clearly apparent, and we gave him a hot bath, which resulted in heavy perspiration. After that the patient seemed to feel better. At 8 p.m. uraemia developed and by midnight he was in agony.'

'*Was Tchaikovsky unconscious during his final illness?*'

'Not at all. Pyotr Ilyich was fully conscious, but he was certainly depressed. He often fell into a doze, but as soon as one asked him: "Are you thirsty?" or some such question, he would immediately recognize the person speaking to him and would indicate his wishes. He lost consciousness completely only some seven hours before his death.'

'*Was the dying man aware of the gravity of his condition?*'

'Yes, he was. The day before he died, he said that he felt death approaching, and declared: "I am not afraid to die, but I would still like to live a little longer."'

'*Was he in great pain?*'

'The pain was not too acute, but it lasted a long time, from midnight to 3 a.m.'

'*Did you hear Pyotr Ilyich express any last wishes or say any last words?*'

'He spoke little, and his consciousness was generally low.'

'*At what stage was artificial respiration applied?*'

'From 10 p.m., for two hours, we had to change the oxygen bags every five minutes. For the duration of Tchaikovsky's illness we got 14 cubic feet of oxygen from the pharmacy.'[2]

## November 1893: Nikolay Figner

*Peterburgskaya Gazeta [St Petersburg Gazette] no. 293, 25 Oct/6 Nov 1893*

Among the intimate friends who witnessed Tchaikovsky's last moments was N.N. Figner, who was especially impressed by the energy with which he resisted his horrible fatal illness. 'Until almost the very last minute he would turn in bed and even raise himself slightly, without any help. When vomiting, he threw out excretions with such force that they flew halfway across the room.

'He had lost his voice a few hours before his death, and his hearing had been considerably impaired, but when someone whispered gently in his ear, he showed by gestures, and with his eyes, that he understood. Just before the actual moment of his death, Tchaikovsky opened his eyes, which had been closed for a very long time, glanced over to his nephew [Bob Davidov] whom he loved so very much, then moved his eyes on to his brother Modest, and, giving off a hardly noticeable sigh, passed away . . .'[3]

*Novosti i Birzhevaya Gazeta [News and Stock Exchange Gazette] no. 295, 26 Oct/7 Nov 1893*

Various contradictory rumours are circulating the town about the causes of P.I. Tchaikovsky's illness, as well as the precise nature of his illness. To put an end to all the gossip, which to a large extent is not based on factual evidence, we interviewed the distinguished lead singer of our opera company, N.N. Figner, who knew the deceased intimately and was at his side during his final moments.

'The only truth in all the rumours,' he told us, 'is that P.I. Tchaikovsky had had supper at Leiner's restaurant on the ill-fated night of Wednesday 20 October [1 November]. He ate macaroni. At night he placed a bottle of water on his bedside table, as he usually did, since he tended to sleep with his mouth open. The night proved alarming because he developed a severely upset stomach. Without paying any attention to this, since he had often experienced such attacks, Pyotr Ilyich the next morning (without telling anyone) took some Guniadi-Yanos [mineral] water instead of castor oil, which was his usual remedy. The result was a strong attack of diarrhoea, soon followed by vomiting. Dr L.B. Bertenson, a very close friend of Tchaikovsky, was sent for. The doctor came as quickly as possible, and without hesitation diagnosed an acute and critical case of cholera. He observed that he had never before come across this type of cholera.

'It goes without saying that all possible measures were taken immediately. Two more doctors were summoned, so that the patient enjoyed constant medical attention. And indeed, thanks to the heroic efforts of the doctors, it proved possible to overcome the cholera. The patient was fully conscious throughout; he himself pointed to the areas affected by spasms and convulsions, and when the critical phase was over he even managed to joke with those around him. By Friday night the symptoms of cholera had eased, which raised hopes for our friend's recovery. Unfortunately, however, the worst fears of Dr Bertenson were realized, as he had foreseen. By Saturday night the cholera was over, but it gave way to kidney malfunction, which in turn caused the blood poisoning and . . . death.

'The last hours of Pyotr Ilyich's life were simply horrible. It makes me shudder to remember the appalling agonies I witnessed. The dying man retained consciousness until virtually the last minute. I cannot describe the suffering of those around him, especially that of his brother Modest, and L.B. Bertenson, who both remained beside the dying man until the very minute of his death . . .'

'*Did Pyotr Ilyich complain before 20 October [1 November] of feeling unwell? Wasn't his illness a direct consequence of a previous indisposition?*'

'The last time I saw Pyotr Ilyich was before he fell ill, on Monday, in the Mariinsky Theatre. He was as cheerful as ever. He spoke of his latest symphony concert, and of our planned trip to Paris. Pyotr Ilyich was due to go there with myself and my wife to give some concerts.'

'*Did he speak of any further plans?*'

'Pyotr Ilyich had intended to leave for his estate at Klin on Thursday 21 October [2 November] to do some work (he never worked here in Petersburg). He generally didn't like to talk, even to his friends, of work either projected or unfinished. I know only that he was planning to compose a new opera, and if it were not for his tragic fate he would doubtless have blessed us with many more compositions. [*According to another informant Tchaikovsky was planning to compose a semi-comic or semi-lyrical opera, something in the style of Bizet's* Carmen – *Editor.*]

'*Presumably Pyotr Ilyich has left a last Will?*'

'As far as I know, he hadn't made a last Will. And he had nothing much to leave. Pyotr Ilyich died with nothing to leave behind but his music. He earned as much as 40,000 rubles a year, but he never refused anyone any help he could give. He gave away almost everything that he earned. But he didn't like to talk about it.'[4]

## November 1893: Dr Lev Bertenson
'P.I. Tchaikovsky's Illness', *Novoe Vremya* [*New Times*] *no. 6345, 27 Oct/8 Nov 1893*

The diversity of the evidence appearing in the press in connection with the illness of the late P.I. Tchaikovsky led us to make inquiries of Dr L. B. Bertenson, who was in charge of the treatment of the deceased composer. This is what he told us in response to our urgent enquiries:

I was called to see Pyotr Ilyich on the Thursday evening, 21 October [2 November], by my brother Dr V.B. [Vasily] Bertenson, who was a close friend of the Tchaikovsky family and their longstanding family physician. When I arrived, at about 10 p.m., at the apartment of M.I. Tchaikovsky, where P.I. was, I found the deceased in the so-called algid phase of cholera. His symptoms were completely typical, and from the very start I could not but recognize a very severe case of cholera. We began to apply all the various methods scientifically prescribed for this condition. By 2 a.m. we had almost managed to stem the convulsions which, before my arrival, had been so strong as to make the patient cry out loud. The fits of diarrhoea and vomiting became less frequent and less severe. I left before morning, asking my brother to stay with the patient. Early on Friday morning, while I was still absent, the patient's condition deteriorated further; the convulsions returned, and the functioning of the heart became so weak that my brother had to give a hypodermic injection of musk and camphor. Early that morning, Friday, my brother was replaced by an assistant, Dr Mamonov, and at 11 a.m. I returned. The patient's condition was such that I was convinced that the convulsions which had threatened his life through the night had passed.

'How are you feeling?' I asked Pyotr Ilyich.

'Much better,' he replied. 'Thank you. You have snatched me from the jaws of death.'

The convulsive phase of cholera could be considered over. Unfortunately, however, the second (or 'reaction') phase had not begun. I should say that, in a case of cholera as severe as this, the kidneys usually cease to function, so rapid is their deterioration. Since the very beginning of the illness, P.I.'s kidneys had completely ceased to function. This is a highly dangerous phenomenon, resulting in the poisoning of the blood by constituents of the urine. On the Friday, however, there were as yet no very marked signs of such poisoning. All possible measures were taken to stimulate kidney function, but all proved vain. Still I did not attempt one of these methods – a bath – because the mother of the late Pyotr Ilyich had died of cholera, and she died exactly at the moment she was placed in the bath. This was known to P.I., and it had instilled in him and all his relatives a superstitious fear of the bath. By Saturday, however, the symptoms of poisoning by urine became clear, along with a new and very severe fit of diarrhoea, indicating paralysis of the intestines. The deceased found the attacks of diarrhoea profoundly depressing, and he began to plead with me: 'Let me go! Don't torment yourself. I'm not going to recover.'

I suggested that we tried the bath, and he readily agreed. When he had been placed in it, I asked 'Do you find the bath unpleasant?'

'On the contrary,' he replied, 'it's pleasant.' But after some time he complained of weakness and asked to be taken out.

The immediate effect of the bath was beneficial. It produced a hot sweat, with which came hope that the effects of the urine poisoning would diminish and the kidneys begin to function again. By the evening, alas, this hope had disappeared. Pyotr Ilyich became drowsy, and the functioning of the heart suddenly weakened to such a degree that my assistant Dr Zander, who had stayed with the patient, injected musk and sent for me. I found P.I. in a coma, with a drastically weakened heart action; we could restore him to consciousness for only a very short time. Thus, for example, when he was offered water to drink, he took it quite consciously, saying 'enough,' 'more,' and so on. But by 10.30 p.m. all hope of a possible change for the better in his general condition had completely disappeared. He sank deeper into a coma, and his pulse became imperceptible, despite frequently repeated injections of stimulants. At 2 a.m. the death throes began, and by 3 a.m. Pyotr Ilyich was no more.[5]

## November 1893: Modest Tchaikovsky
'P.I. Tchaikovsky's Illness', *Novoe Vremya* [*New Times*] no. 6350, p. 3, 1/13 November 1893

As a supplement to the brief but thoroughly accurate account by Lev Bertenson of the last days of my brother's life, I feel it necessary, in order to dispel all the conflicting rumours, to give you for publication as full an account as possible of everything I witnessed.

On Wednesday evening [20 October/1 November] my brother attended a performance of *The Passionate Heart*. From the theatre he proceeded with our nephews, the Counts Litke and Baron Buxhövden to Leiner's restaurant. I was to join them later. When I arrived, after an hour or so, I found all the above mentioned in the company of I.F. Gorbunov, A.K. Glazunov and F.F. Mühlbach. The meal was already over, but I learned that my brother had eaten macaroni and washed it down, as usual, with white wine and mineral water. Supper did not last long, and after 1 a.m. the two of us returned home together on foot. My brother was absolutely calm and healthy.

When I came out of my bedroom the next morning, Thursday 21 October [2 November], my brother was not taking tea in the sitting room as usual, but was still in his own room, where he complained that he had passed a bad night because of a stomach upset. I was not particularly worried by this, as he had often had such disorders in the past; though acute, they always passed quickly. At 11 a.m. he got dressed and went out to see Napravnik; but he was back in half an hour, without having made it. Now he decided to take certain measures in addition to the flannel shirt which he had already put on. I offered to send for Vasily Bernardovich Bertenson, his favourite doctor, but he firmly refused. I did not insist, knowing that he was accustomed to illnesses of this sort and that he always managed to get over them without assistance. Usually he found that castor oil would bring him relief. Convinced that he would resort to it on this occasion, and knowing that it could anyway do him no harm, I was quite unconcerned about his condition and went about my own business until 1 p.m. without seeing him further. After lunch he had a business appointment with F.F. Mühlbach. In any case, between 11 a.m. and 1 p.m. the deceased was cheerful enough to write two business letters, but had no patience to write a third letter in full and confined himself to a short note.

At lunch he was not without appetite; he sat with us but did not eat anything – only, it seems, because he thought it might upset his stomach. It was then that he told me that instead of castor oil he had taken Guniadi water. I suspect that this meal had a fatal significance, for it was during the conversation about his medicine that he poured out a glass of water and took a sip of it. The water was unboiled. We were all alarmed; he alone showed indifference and told us not to worry. Of all illnesses, he had always been afraid of cholera. Soon after this he had to leave as he began to feel sick. He did not return to the sitting-room, but lay down in his own room in order to warm up his stomach. None the less, neither he nor those of us present were at all concerned. All this had happened before quite often. Although his indisposition grew worse, we put this down to the effect of the mineral water. I again suggested sending for Vasily Bernardovich, but again received a firm refusal; besides, he soon began to feel better, and asked to be allowed to go to sleep. He remained alone in his room and, as I thought, fell asleep. Having checked that all was quiet in his bedroom, I went out on my own affairs, and was away from home until 5 p.m. When I returned his illness had worsened so much that, despite my brother's protests, I sent for Dr Vasily Bertenson. At that stage, none the less, there were still no alarming symptoms of a mortal illness.

At about 6 p.m. I again left my brother after applying a hot compress to his stomach. By the time I returned, at 8 p.m., my servant was looking after him, and had moved him from his bedroom into the room in which, later, his coffin stood. During this time, i.e. from 6 p.m. to 8 p.m., the vomiting and diarrhoea had become so severe that my servant, without waiting for Vasily Bernardovich to arrive, had sent for the first doctor that could be found. But still nobody was thinking in terms of cholera.

Vasily Bertenson arrived at 8.15 p.m. The diarrhoea and vomiting were growing progressively more frequent, but the patient was still strong enough to get up whenever he needed to. Since no specimens of his excreta had been preserved the doctor could not at first determine that it was cholera, but he was at once convinced of the extremely grave and severe character of the illness. Having prescribed all the necessary treatment for such a condition, the doctor thought it imperative to call his brother, Lev B. Bertenson. The situation was growing more disturbing all the time. The motions were becoming more frequent and very abundant. The patient grew so weak that he was unable to move without help. He found the vomiting especially unbearable; while it was happening, and for some moments afterwards, he became quite frenzied and cried out at the top of his voice, not once complaining about the pain in his abdomen, but only of intolerable spasms in the area of his chest. In the midst of this, at one point he turned to me and said: 'It seems I am dying. Farewell!' He later repeated these words several times. After every bout he would sink back on the bed in a state of complete exhaustion. As yet, however, there were neither livid spots nor convulsions.

Lev Bertenson and his brother arrived at 11 p.m. and, after examining the patient and excreta, diagnosed cholera. A medical attendant was immediately sent for. Including the doctors there were eight of us at the patient's bedside: the three [in fact, two] Counts Litke, our nephew [Vladimir] Davidov, my servant Nazar Litrov, the medical attendant and myself. Between 11 and midnight my brother began complaining of spasms and crying out loud. Together we all began to massage him. He was fully conscious. The spasms appeared simultaneously in various parts of his body, and my brother asked us to massage now this part, now that. His head and bodily extremities began to turn very blue and grew completely cold. Shortly before the first spasms began, the deceased asked me: 'It's not cholera, is it?'

I tried to conceal the truth from him. But when he heard the doctors giving orders to take precautions against infection, he cried out: 'So it is cholera!'

It is difficult to give more details of this stage of the illness. Right up to 5 a.m., it was one long continuous struggle with his numbness and his spasms, which became gradually less amenable to our energetic rubbing and warming of his body. There were several moments when it seemed that death had come, but injections of musk and a tannin enema revived the patient.

By 5 a.m. the illness began to abate and my brother became calmer, complaining only of his depressed state of mind. Up to this point the most alarming moments had been those when my brother complained of the pain around his heart, and of his difficulty in breathing, being suffocated. Now this eased. Three-quarters of an hour of complete calm went by. The vomiting and motions continued quite frequently, but lost their alarming appearance. Cramps occurred whenever he tried to move. He had developed a thirst, but said that water seemed incomparably more pleasant in his imagination than in reality; on being offered a teaspoonful of something to drink, he would turn away from it with revulsion, yet a few minutes later would be begging for it again. In general what exercised him most was the inconvenience which the unpleasant effects of his illness was causing those around him. During the most severe attacks he virtually apologized for the trouble he was causing others. He feared that some aspects would provoke their revulsion, and remained sufficiently alert to make occasional jokes. Thus he turned to our favourite nephew [Vladimir Davidov] with the words: 'I'm afraid you'll lose all respect for me after seeing all these unpleasant things.'

All the time he was trying to persuade everyone to go to bed, and thanked us for the smallest service. Early in the morning, as soon as the patient no longer needed our full attention, Vasily Bertenson sent me to report the matter to the police.

On Friday 22 October [3 November], at 9 a.m., Vasily Bertenson, who had not left my brother for a single moment, was replaced by Dr N.N. Mamonov. At this time his relatively calm condition lasted for about an hour. Vasily Bernardovich gave the case history to Dr Mamonov and left without waiting for my brother to wake. By this time the blue [livid] spots had gone, but there were darker spots on his face. These quickly disappeared: the first remission. We all breathed more easily. But the attacks continued, accompanied by convulsions, though significantly less frequently. In any case, he felt so much better that he believed he was saved; his general state was sufficiently improved for him to feel he was out of danger. Thus when Lev Bernardovich returned at about 11 a.m., he said: 'Thank you. You have snatched me from the jaws of death. I feel immeasurably better than during the first night.'

These words he repeated several times that day and the following one. The fits of convulsions finally ceased by midday. At 3 p.m. Dr Mamonov was replaced by Dr A.L. Zander. It seemed that the illness had yielded to the impeccably careful treatment. The doctor already feared the onset of the second phase of cholera – nephritis [inflammation of the kidneys] and typhoid, though as yet there were still no signs of either illness. His only discomfort was an unquenchable thirst. This condition continued until evening, but improved so much by night that Dr Mamonov, who came to replace Dr Zander, insisted that we all go to bed, since he expected no life-threatening symptoms that night.

On the morning of Saturday 23 October [4 November], there was no improvement in the morale of the patient, who in fact seemed more depressed than the previous evening. His hopes of recovery had ebbed. 'Let me go!' he said to the doctors. 'You can't do anything for me. I shan't recover.'

Now some irritability began to show itself in his treatment of those around him. The previous evening he had still been joking with the doctors, arguing with them over that glass of water – but now he just meekly obeyed their instructions. The doctors began concentrating their efforts on stimulating the kidneys, but all to no avail. We all pinned our hopes on the hot bath which Lev Bertenson was planning to give him that evening. I should say that our mother had died of cholera in 1854, and had died at the very moment they placed her in the bath. My elder brother and I instinctively had a superstitious fear of this necessary measure. Our fear grew on hearing my brother say, when asked by the doctor whether he wished to take the bath: 'I'm quite ready to try the bath. But I shall probably die, like my mother, as soon as you put me in it.'

That evening, however, his diarrhoea again grew worse, and we were forced to abandon the bath. The diarrhoea became uncontrollable, and the patient grew weaker. Lev Bernardovich left after 2 a.m., deeply concerned about the situation. Nevertheless the night passed quite quietly. After two enemas the diarrhoea decreased significantly, but still his kidneys did not function.

By the morning of Sunday 24 October [5 November], the position was not yet hopeless, but the anxiety of the doctors about his kidney failure increased. My brother's general condition was very bad. Every time he was asked how he was feeling, he repeatedly replied: 'Awful!' To Lev Bernardovich, he said: 'All your kindness and patience is wasted on me! I can't be cured!'

After sleep he returned to full consciousness with more difficulty than on the previous days. Thus he did not immediately recognize his servant Sofronov, who arrived that morning from Klin; but he was nevertheless pleased to see him. Until 1 p.m. there was no visible change in his condition. There was not a single drop of urine, so it was impossible to examine it even once. Lev Bernardovich arrived at 1 p.m. and at once deemed it necessary to resort to the extreme (as it seemed to us) measure for stimulating kidney function: the bath. At 2 p.m. the bath was ready. My brother was only semi-conscious while it was being prepared in the same room. At last we had to rouse him. It seems that at first he did not grasp what we were going to do with him, but he then gave his consent to the bath, and when he was put into it was fully conscious of everything that was happening. When the doctor asked him whether he found the hot water unpleasant, he replied: 'On the contrary, it's quite pleasant.'

But very soon he asked to be taken out, saying he felt weak. And, indeed, as soon as he was taken out of the bath his drowsiness and his sleep took on a rather peculiar character. The bath did not produce the results we had hoped for, though it did cause a heavy perspiration; at the same time, according to the doctors, it reduced for a while the signs of the blood poisoning [uraemia]. The sweating continued; but at the same time the pulse, which up to this point had been relatively regular and strong, again weakened. Another injection of musk was required to restore its strength. This proved successful; despite the sweating, the pulse quickened and the patient grew calmer. Until 8 p.m. his condition seemed to us to improve. But soon after Dr Mamonov had left, at 8.15 p.m., his replacement, Dr Zander, again detected a sharp weakening of the pulse, and was sufficiently alarmed to deem it necessary to inform Lev Bernardovich immediately. According to the doctors, the patient was at this time in a comatose condition, so that when I went into his room, the doctor advised me that I should no longer leave him even for a moment. His head was cold, his breathing laboured and accompanied by moans. But it was still possible to bring him instantly into consciousness by asking 'Do you want a drink?' He would reply 'Yes' or 'Certainly'; afterwards he would say 'Enough', 'I don't want any', 'I don't feel like it'. Just after 10 p.m. Dr Zander diagnosed the onset of emphysema, soon after which Lev Bernardovich arrived. At the request of those present, a priest from St Isaak's Cathedral was sent for. Only by increased injections of heart stimulant could the condition of the dying man be kept stable. All hope of any improvement vanished. The father who came with the Holy Sacraments was unable to administer them because my brother remained unconscious, so he simply read in a loud and clear voice the prayers for the dying, of which it was obvious my brother did not hear a single word. Soon after this the fingers of the dying man began to move in a curious way, as if he felt an itch in various parts of his body.

Tirelessly the doctors continued to apply all possible measures to maintain the action of the heart as though they still anticipated a miracle of recovery. At the dying man's bedside at this time were the following: three doctors, the two Litke brothers, Buxhövden, Nikolay Figner, Bzul, our nephew Davidov, my brother's servant Sofronov, Litrov, the medical attendant, our brother Nikolay, and I. Lev Bernardovich thought there were too many people for the small room. The window was opened. Figner and Bzul left. Bertenson, having abandoned all hope, departed in complete exhaustion, entrusting Dr Mamonov to watch my brother's last moments. His breathing became more irregular, though it was still possible to bring him back to consciousness by asking if he wanted a drink. He was no longer able to answer in words, but only by affirmative or negative noises.

Suddenly his eyes, until then half-closed and glazed, opened wide, giving an indescribable expression of full consciousness. He rested his gaze in turn upon the three people standing over him, then looked up to the heavens. For a few moments his eyes shone brightly, then faded with his last breath. It was a little after 3 a.m.[6]

## 1943: Yuri Davidov

'And so the fateful day of 20 October [1 November] arrived. Free after classes, I went to visit my Uncle Modest and found out that Pyotr Ilyich was going to dinner at the home of Vera Vasilievna Butakova, my father's younger sister. Her son, Grigory, was my closest childhood friend, so I went over there. Uncle Pyotr arrived soon after me. He was in a very good mood: cheerful, hale and hearty. In his youth, Pyotr Ilyich had fancied Vera Vasilievna, and dedicated to her the series of piano pieces known as *Souvenir de Hapsal* [Op. 2, 1867]. They remained friends right to the end of his life. The dinner was very intimate, with no strangers present, and it passed in a warm and friendly atmosphere, as Pyotr Ilyich always had interesting things to talk about . . .

'Suddenly Pyotr Ilyich looked at his watch, turned to me and said, "Well, get ready, or we'll be late." When Vera Vasilievna asked where he was going, he told her that he had taken a box in the Alexandrinsky Theatre to amuse us, his nephews . . .

'After the performance (which was brilliant) we all left the theatre together, apart from my Uncle Modest, who stayed behind to talk to Maria Gavrilovna Savina. He promised that, if we went on foot, he would catch up with us. On our way out we met the very talented actor/story-teller Gorbunov, and soon we were all trooping down Nevsky Prospekt in the direction of the Admiralty. En route Pyotr Ilyich offered to take us to Leiner's Restaurant, which we often visited with him, because it was one of the few restaurants where we students were allowed in – but via the back door, of course, and by no means free of charge. That evening there were several of us who were not really allowed into the restaurant: my brother, Buxhövden and Alexandr Litke were 'Short-term volunteers'[*1] in military uniform; Konstantin Litke and I were cadets; and for all of us admission was illegal. So we all went into the restaurant's back yard and waited for Pyotr Ilyich to sort things out with the management. We had not been waiting long when we were escorted inside to a big suite, all of us, plus Fyodor Fyodorovich Mühlbach, a close friend of the Tchaikovsky brothers. As we arrived Pyotr Ilyich was busy ordering dinner for all of us.

*A "volunteer" was "a person in secondary education who is not a conscript but who volunteers under privileged conditions". Volunteers wore army uniform for only one year, [and] had the right to live not in barracks but in a private apartment. After taking the exam at the end of the first year they were promoted to the rank of reserve ensign.' [Ushakov Dictionary, vol. i, p. 353]

'Once that was done, Pyotr Ilyich summoned a waiter and asked him to bring a glass of water. In a couple of minutes the waiter returned with the news that there was no boiled water. This annoyed Pyotr Ilyich, who said impatiently: "Then bring me some unboiled water. Cold." We all started trying to dissuade him from drinking unboiled water, reminding him of the cholera epidemic then raging in the city, but Pyotr Ilyich dismissed our fears as superstitions, in which he didn't believe. As the waiter went to carry out his instructions, the door opened and in came Modest Ilyich, with the actor [Yuri] Yuriev. "Aha, how clever of me!" exclaimed Modest. "On my way past I thought I'd just look in to see if you were here."

'"Where else would we be?" laughed Pyotr Ilyich. Then, just behind Modest Ilyich, the waiter returned with the glass of water on a tray. When Modest found out what was happening, and why we were all arguing, he grew very angry with his brother and shouted: "I strictly forbid you to drink unboiled water!"

'Still laughing, Pyotr Ilyich jumped up and started to walk toward the waiter. Modest rushed after him, but Pyotr Ilyich got there first, elbowed his brother out of the way, and downed the fatal glass in one gulp. Modest swore at him again, and then the fun started. It was always fun with Pyotr Ilyich. Fun radiated out of him like a sunbeam. But I should stress that this happened only in his own chosen company – that is, in the company of close friends and relatives, with whom he never felt shy. The presence of even one stranger was enough to spoil his merry mood.

'So we sat there until 2 a.m., chatting and drinking wine and beer. I walked my uncles and my brother home and then went back to college, in high spirits, going over the last few hours in my mind, and not worrying how I was going to get back into my dormitory without being noticed by a watchman . . .

'[Two mornings later], during a mathematics lesson, the teacher (Company Commander Ivan Sergeyevich Diomin, who was not very respected by the class) was trying to explain something to us when the duty officer came into the classroom. After whispering something to the teacher, he asked me to come out with him. I assumed that, being a sergeant-major, I was about to be assigned some task; but it transpired that my brother's cook, Vasya Kharchenko, had come to see me. My heart missed a beat. I knew at once that it was no accident that he had been sent to me at that inappropriate time of day. There was no note. Vasya told me only that Pyotr Ilyich had been taken ill, and that I had been summoned. All I could discover from him was that Uncle Petya had stomach ache. As he often had stomach problems, I tried to calm myself down; but the memory of that ill-fated incident with the glass of water put the idea of cholera in my head, and it just wouldn't go away . . .

'I went straight to the director's room . . . and had no problem obtaining his permission to go into town. While I was putting on the full-dress uniform and greatcoat, my anxiety increased, and once out of the school it seemed to me that I was not walking but flying. I ran straight upstairs to the fourth floor, rang the doorbell and waited impatiently for the door to open. Two or three minutes later, which seemed an eternity, Uncle Modest opened the door. When he saw it was me, he flapped his hands and said "You can't come in, you can't come in!" Then he came out onto the staircase, sank down on a step, quite exhausted, and started to tell me what had happened. His story went roughly as follows.

'After returning from Leiner's everybody had gone their separate ways to bed. The night had passed completely uneventfully. In the morning Modest heard my uncle's door creak, but didn't pay much attention to it. When Modest got up, Pyotr Ilyich complained of a stomach ache. Nazar Litrov, Uncle Modest's servant, was sent to a drug-store to fetch castor oil – the usual precaution used by Pyotr Ilyich for his constant stomach disorders. But Nazar fetched Guniadi purgative salt instead of oil. Pyotr Ilyich immediately took it anyway. Soon he started feeling better, and he played a joke on Modest, saying "Well, look, all your cholera flew away!" Then he sat down and wrote some letters. During lunch he was at the table but refused to eat, talking business to F.F. Mühlbach. Then he decided to go to see [Edward] Napravnik, but on the way the stomach ache returned and he had to go back to the apartment.

'He started having diarrhoea, but refused to call a doctor. Uncle Modest was not at home. Only towards evening, when he returned home from the theatre and saw the condition Pyotr Ilyich was in, did he immediately – over his brother's protests – call the doctor: Vasily Bernardovich Bertenson, known to the family as "Vasya". The latter hesitated to make a firm diagnosis, but eventually pronounced the dread word "cholera". He decided to call in his brother Lev Bernardovich, one of the most respected and fashionable doctors in St Petersburg, who confirmed Vasya's suspicion: Pyotr Ilyich had contracted cholera.

'Next day I again got permission to leave school and ran to the sacred flat. I called Uncle Modest out to the staircase and asked him about the course of Pyotr Ilyich's illness and the state of his morale. Modest Ilyich looked incredibly tired, but he didn't seem unduly worried. He told me he thought the worst was past; in the doctor's opinion Pyotr Ilyich had overcome the cholera, but the problem now was that his kidneys had not functioned for some seven or eight hours. Too young to realize just how serious this was, I was nevertheless worried by Uncle Modest's anxiety.

'The school administration had learnt from the newspapers what Pyotr Ilyich was suffering from, and refused to let me go round any more. Through the Litke brothers, however, I could get news of the patient. On 24 October [5 November] Alexandr Nikolayevich Litke called round. He was in a very tired and agitated state; in something of a frenzy he told me that the kidneys had totally stopped functioning, and that the doctors now wanted to put my uncle in a hot bath, hoping to improve his kidney function and to induce heavy perspiration to stop uraemia developing. The doctors, he said, had grown very worried about the patient's condition . . . Apparently Pyotr Ilyich had been drifting in and out of a coma, and talking in a delirious way – about our walk in Klin, among other things, and his fear that the express train would overtake him. He had been saying that he had so many plans and projects in his head, already part formulated . . . He remembered his mother and father, his childhood, all of us and many more of his friends, including Nadezhda Filaretovna von Meck, his "best friend". He expressed resentment that she had turned away from him. But what figured most in his delirium was "that damn snub-nose"; this is what he called death, and he was trying to see her off. When Pyotr Ilyich came to his senses, he was distressed by the amount of trouble he was causing everybody. He apologized, and thanked them all profusely.

'That night, around 11 p.m., I managed to slip out of school to Malaya Morskaya Street, where I discovered that Uncle Nikolay Ilyich had moved in to help take care of his brother. From him I learnt that Pyotr Ilyich was very weak, that the bath hadn't helped, that there was little hope. I walked back down the staircase feeling deeply depressed. Before going out into the street I sat on a window-sill and collapsed in floods of tears, which almost choked me . . .

'The next morning's papers carried the news of Pyotr Ilyich's death. Although I had been prepared for it, I was devastated by the news. The sun had set; my uncle, the musical genius, had passed away. A wonderful man, full of feeling, was no more . . .'[7]

## 1966: Alexandr Voitov

'In the list of students who graduated from the Imperial School of Jurisprudence at the same time as Tchaikovsky there appears the surname Jacobi. When I was a student at the School of Jurisprudence I spent all my holidays with the family of Nikolay Borisovich Jacobi, who died in 1902. His wife was a friend and distant relative of my parents, was very fond of me and always welcomed me. In 1913, when I was in my last year at the School of Jurisprudence, the twentieth anniversary of Tchaikovsky's death was widely marked. And then, evidently under the influence of memories which came flooding back, Ekaterina [Orlova wrongly says 'Elizaveta'] Jacobi told me, under oath of secrecy, the story which, as she admitted, had long tormented her. She told me that she had decided that this was the moment to reveal it to me, because she was getting old and felt that she did not have the right to carry this important and terrible secret with her to the grave. She said, "You are interested in the history of the School and the fate of its students. This is why you must know the whole truth, all the more so because it is so sad."

'. . .The story begins in the autumn of 1893. Tchaikovsky was threatened with a serious catastrophe. Count Stenbok-Fermor had become concerned by the attentions which the composer was paying to his young nephew, and had written an indignant letter addressed to the Tsar and had handed this official letter for presentation to Alexandr III to Jacobi, who was at that time Deputy Chief Procurator for the Department of Criminal Appeal in the Senate. Exposure would inevitably have threatened Tchaikovsky with unavoidable disgrace.

'Exposure would also have threatened with disgrace the School of Jurisprudence and all graduates who had been fellow students of Tchaikovsky. But the honour of the uniform of the School was held sacred by all its graduates.

'In order to prevent the matter from becoming public knowledge, Jacobi decided to act: he invited all the former fellow students of Tchaikovsky to his house, including the composer himself, and arranged a court of honour. In all there were eight men [the number cited by Mrs Jacobi exactly corresponds with the number of surviving fellow students who were living in St Petersburg at the time]. Mrs Jacobi herself sat with her needlework in her usual place in the drawing room, which adjoined her husband's study. Voices could be heard coming from it from time to time, sometimes loud and emotional and sometimes dropping to a whisper. This went on for a very long time, almost five hours. Then Tchaikovsky came bursting out of the study. He was very pale and upset, almost ran straight past but made a sort of sideways bow and left without saying a word. All the others remained for a long time after that in the study and talked in low voices.

'But when the visitors had left, after swearing his wife to secrecy, Jacobi told her that they had discussed Stenbok-Fermor's letter to the Tsar. Jacobi had no right to impede the progress of the letter. And so the fellow students had taken a decision which Tchaikovsky had promised to observe. The letter could be suppressed only in the event of his death . . . A day or two later the news of his fatal illness was spreading throughout St Petersburg.'[8]

449

## 1981: Galina von Meck

'. . . On 10 [22] October he came to Petersburg for the rehearsals [for the first performance of the 6th Symphony] and stayed at his brother Modest's flat. On 16 [28] October the 6th Symphony was given for the first time, conducted by the composer.

'"I am prouder of this Symphony than any of my other compositions," wrote Tchaikovsky to P.I. Yurgenson on 18 [30] October. Three days later the composer came back home seemingly very upset by something – we shall never really know what – and not feeling very well. He asked his brother for a glass of water. When told that he would have to wait for the water to be boiled (Petersburg water not being fit to drink unboiled as the town stood on boggy ground) he ignored his brother's protests, went into the kitchen, filled a glass of water from the tap and drank it, saying something like "Who cares anyway!"

'That same evening he felt quite ill; the doctor who was sent for the next morning diagnosed cholera, which was then ever-present in Petersburg. Three days later the composer died in great agony.

'. . .There were, besides his brother Modest and the doctor, several other people present and the interpretation of some of the things said by the dying man in his agony, according to what I know from the composer's nephew, young Count Alexandr Litke (Sanya Litke) who was present, was completely different from the way his brother Modest related them. Anyway, the curse which Modest said was meant for my grandmother, Nadezhda von Meck, could not possibly have been directed towards her as Modest wanted it to be thought . . .'[9]

## 1987: Natalya Kuznetsova-Vladimova

'From my childhood I knew for certain of Pyotr Ilyich Tchaikovsky's suicide through my paternal grandmother, Vera Sergeyevna Kuznetsova (*née* Denisova). Her elder sister, Olga Sergeyevna, was married to Tchaikovsky's brother, Nikolay Ilyich. Vera Sergeyevna told the same version that you [Orlova] do. She lived in Leningrad . . . dying at the beginning of 1955 at a great age, but sound in mind and good in memory. [She had heard it] probably from Olga Sergeyevna, but in fact spoke of it most reluctantly, seeing in this court a kind of besmirching of a gentleman's honour for Tchaikovsky. But more than once she referred to Jacobi very aggressively . . . While writing to you I can hear how she pronounced that name . . . Vera Sergeyevna said that Alexandr III knew of the letter *after* Tchaikovsky's death. I well remember that at our home in 1952 my grandmother talked with Yuri Iosifovich Slonimsky, the author of books on ballet, and when he said that the cause of Tchaikovsky's suicide was that he had paid improper attention to the heir [to the throne], she had corrected him. "No, it was the nephew of Count Stenbok and not to the heir . . ."'[10]

# APPENDIX C

# Bibliography

## Books

Abraham, Gerald (ed): *Romanticism 1830–1890* Vol IX, *The New Oxford History of Music* (Oxford: Oxford University Press, 1990)

Abraham, Gerald (ed): *Tchaikovsky, A Symposium* (London: L. Drummond, 1945)

Abraham, Gerald: *Tchaikovsky* (London: Duckworth, 1949)

Berberova, Nina: *Tchaikovsky* (Berlin, 1936, republished St Petersburg, 1993)

Biancolli, Louis: *Tchaikovsky and His Orchestral Work* (New York: Grosset and Dunlap, 1950)

Blom, Eric: *Tchaikovsky's Orchestral Works* (London: Oxford University Press, 1927)

Bowen, Catherine Drinker, & von Meck, Barbara: *Beloved Friend* (New York: Random House, 1937)

Bowen, Catherine Drinker: *Free Artist: The Story of Anton and Nicholas Rubinstein* (New York: Random House, 1939)

Brown, David: *Tchaikovsky: A Biographical and Critical Study*
  vol 1 *The Early Years (1840–74)* (London: Gollancz, 1978)
  vol 2 *The Crisis Years (1874–78)* (London: Gollancz, 1982)
  vol 3 *The Years of Wandering (1878–85)* (London: Gollancz, 1986)
  vol 4 *The Final Years (1885–93)* (London: Gollancz, 1991)

Brown, David: 'Tchaikovsky' in *The New Grove: Russian Masters 1* (London: Macmillan, 1986)

Brown, David: *Tchaikovsky Remembered* (London: Faber & Faber, 1993)

Brown, Malcolm, & Wiley, R.J. (eds): *Slavonic and Western Music: Essays for Gerald Abraham* (Ann Arbor, Michigan, 1985)

Calvocoressi, M.D., & Abraham, Gerald: *Masters of Russian Music* (New York: Knopf, 1946)

Carpenter, Humphrey: *Benjamin Britten* (London: Faber & Faber, 1992)

Craft, Robert: *Stravinsky: Glimpses of a Life* (London: Lime Tree Books, 1992)

Davidov, Yuri: *Zapiski o P.I. Chaykovskom* [*Notes on Tchaikovsky*] (Moscow, 1962)

Dombayev, Grigory: *Tvorchestvo P. I. Chaykovskovo* (*The Works of P. I. Tchaikovsky*) (Moscow, 1958)

Evans, Edwin: *Tchaikovsky* (London: Dent, 1906 rev 1935)

Frid, E. (ed.): *M.A. Balakirev: Vospominanya i Pisma* [M. A. Balakirev: Recollections and Letters] [incl. *Perepiska s P.I. Chaykovskim* [Correspondence with P.I. Tchaikovsky] (Leningrad, 1962)

Garden, Edward: *Tchaikovsky* (London: Dent, 1973, rev 1993)

Garden, Edward, & Gotteri, Nigel (eds): 'To My Best Friend': Correspondence between Tchaikovsky and Nadezhda von Meck [translated by Galina von Meck] (Oxford: Clarendon Press, 1993)

Gee, John, & Selby, Elliott: *The Triumph of Tchaikovsky* (New York: Vanguard, 1960)

Hoffman, Michel: *Tchaikovsky* (London: Calder, 1962)

Huneker, James: *Mezzotints in Modern Music* (New York: Scribner, 1899)

John, Nicholas (ed): *Eugene Onegin: Opera Guide 38* (London: English National Opera/The Royal Opera; John Calder, 1988)

Kendall, Alan: *Tchaikovsky* (London: Bodley Head, 1988)

Kashkin, Nikolay: *Vospominanya o P.I. Chaykovskom* [*Reminiscences of Tchaikovsky*] (Moscow, 1896)

Kolodin, I. (ed): *The Critical Composer: the Musical Writings of Berlioz, Wagner, Schumann, Tchaikovsky & Others* (New York, 1940)

Konniskaya, Lidya: *Chaykovsky v Peterburge* [*Tchaikovsky in St Petersburg*] (Leningrad, 1969)

Mann, Klaus: *Pathetic Symphony: A Novel about Tchaikovsky* (New York: Allen Towne and Heath, 1948)

Mayo, Waldo: *Tchaikovsky: His Life Told in Anecdotal Form* (New York: Hyperion Press, 1945)

Newmarch, Rosa: *Tchaikovsky, His Life and Works* (London: William Reeves, 1900)

Norris, Gerald: *Stanford, the Cambridge Jubilee and Tchaikovsky* (London: David & Charles, 1980)

Orlova, Alexandra: *Tchaikovsky: A Self-Portrait* (New York: Oxford University Press, 1990)

Poznansky, Alexander: *Tchaikovsky: The Quest for the Inner Man* (New York: Schirmer Books, 1991)

Prokofiev, Sergei: *Soviet Diary 1927 and Other Writings* [translated and edited by Olga Prokofiev] (London: Faber & Faber, 1991)

Protopopov, V. (ed): *Vospominanya o P.I. Chaykovskom* [*Reminiscences of Tchaikovsky*] (Moscow, 1962, 4th edition, 1980)

Ridenour, Robert C.: *Nationalism, Modernism and Personal Rivalry in Nineteenth-Century Russian Music* (Ann Arbor, Michigan: UMI Research Press, 1977/1981)

Rimsky-Korsakov, Nikolay: *My Musical Life* (New York: Knopf, 1923; 3rd edn 1942)

Ringer, Alexander (ed): *The Early Romantic Era* [Vol. VI, *Man and Music*, ed. Stanley Sadie] (London: Macmillan, 1990)

Ronald, Landon: *Tchaikovsky* (New York: Frederick A. Stokes, 1912)

Schonberg, Harold C: *The Lives of the Great Composers* (London: Futura, 1980)

Shaw, George Bernard: *The Great Composers* [edited by Louis Crompton] (Berkeley: University of California, 1978)

Shaw, George Bernard: *Shaw's Music* Vols I-III (London: Bodley Head, 1981)

Shostakovich, Dmitri: *Testimony (The Memoirs of Dmitri Shostakovich)* (New York: Harper & Row, 1979)

Shostakovich, Dmitri & others: *Russian Symphony: Thoughts About Tchaikovsky* (New York: Philosophical Library, 1947)

Stasov, Vladimir: *Selected Essays on Music* [translated by Florence Jonas; Introduction by Gerald Abraham] (New York: Praeger, 1968)

Suvorin, A.S.: *Diaries* (reprinted Moscow, 1992)

Tchaikovsky, Modest Ilyich: *Zhizn P.I. Chaykovskovo (The Life of P.I. Tchaikovsky)* (3 vols, Moscow, 1900–02; English trans, London, 1906; abridged English version by Rosa Newmarch, London, 1906)

Tchaikovsky, Pyotr Ilyich: *Perepiska s N.F. von Meck* [Correspondence with N.F. von Meck], ed. Vladimir Zhdanov and Nikolay Zhegin, 3 vols, (Moscow/Leningrad, 1934–6)

Tchaikovsky, Pyotr Ilyich: *Perepiska s P.I. Yurgensonom* [Correspondence with P.I. Yurgenson], ed. Vladimir Zhdanov and Nikolay Zhegin, 2 vols, (Moscow, 1938–52)

Tchaikovsky, Pyotr Ilyich: *Pisma k rodnym (1840–79)* [Letters to Relatives] ed. Vladimir Zhdanov (Moscow, 1940)

Tchaikovsky, Pyotr Ilyich: *Dnevniki (1873–91) (Diaries)* ed. I.I. Tchaikovsky (Moscow/Petrograd, 1923) [English version translated and edited by Vladimir Lakond (New York: Norton, 1945)]

Tchaikovsky, Pyotr Ilyich: *P. I. Chaykovsky: S.I. Taneyev, Pisma* [Tchaikovsky-Taneyev Letters] (Moscow, 1951)

Tchaikovsky, Pyotr Ilyich: *Muzykalno-kriticheskie stati* [Music criticism] (Moscow, 1953)

Tchaikovsky, Pyotr Ilyich: *Polnoe Sobranie Sochineny: literaturnie proizvedenya i perepiska (Complete Collected Edition: Literary works and correspondence)*, 17 vols (Moscow, 1953–)

Tchaikovsky, Pyotr Illyich: *Pisma k blizkim* [Letters to his Family] (Moscow, 1955)

Volkoff, Vladimir: *Tchaikovsky; A Self-Portrait* (London: Robert Hale, 1975)

Volkov, Solomon: *Balanchine's Tchaikovsky* (New York: Simon & Schuster, 1985)

von Meck, Galina (ed): *Tchaikovsky: Letters to His Family* (London: Dennis Dobson, 1981)

Warrack, John: *Tchaikovsky* (London: Hamish Hamilton, 1973)

Warrack, John: *Tchaikovsky's Ballet Music* (London: BBC, 1979)

Warrack, John: *Tchaikovsky's Symphonies and Concertos* (London: BBC, 1969; rev edn 1974)

Weinstock, Herbert: *Tchaikovsky* (London: Cassell, 1946)

Wiley, R.J.: *Tchaikovsky's Ballets* (Oxford: Oxford University Press, 1985)

Wood, Sir Henry: *My Life of Music* (London: Gollancz, 1938)

Yakovlev, Vasily (ed): *Dni i Godi P.I. Chaykovskovo: Letopis zhizni i tvorchestva* (*Days and Years of P.I. Tchaikovsky: Annals of Life and Works*) (Moscow-Leningrad, 1940)

Yoffe, Elkhonon: *Tchaikovsky in America: The Composer's Visit in 1891* (New York: Oxford University Press, 1986)

Zajaczkowski, Henry: *Tchaikovsky's Musical Style* (Ann Arbor: UMI Research Press, 1987)

## Articles

Abraham, Gerald: 'Tchaikovsky: Some Centennial Reflections', *Music & Letters*, xxi, 1940, pp. 110–119.

Bennigsen, Olga: 'More Tchaikovsky–von Meck Correspondence', *The Musical Quarterly*, xxiv No. 2, April 1938, pp. 129–138.

Berberova, Nina; Brown, Malcolm H; and Karlinsky, Simon: 'Tchaikovsky's Suicide Reconsidered: A Rebuttal', *High Fidelity* 31, no. 8 (1981)

Berlin, Isaiah: 'Tchaikovsky, Pushkin and Onegin', *The Musical Times*, cxxi, 1980.

Bertenson, Sergey: 'The Tchaikovsky Museum at Klin', *The Musical Quarterly*, 3 July 1944, pp. 329–335.

Bessel, Vasily: 'Memories of Tchaikovsky', *Russkaya Muzykalnaya Gazeta*, xii, 1897.

Brown, David: 'Balakirev, Tchaikovsky and Nationalism', *Music & Letters*, xlii, 1961, pp. 227–241.

Brown, David: 'Tchaikovsky and Chekhov', in *Slavonic and Western Music: Essays for Gerald Abraham* (ed. Brown, M. & Wiley, R.J., Ann Arbor, 1985)

Brown, David: 'Tchaikovsky's Marriage', *The Musical Times*, cxxiii, 1982, pp. 754–756.

Brown, David: 'Tchaikovsky's *Mazeppa*', *The Musical Times*, cxxv, 1984, pp. 696–698.

Buchanan, Charles L: 'The Unvanquishable Tchaikovsky', *The Musical Quarterly*, vol. v, 3 July 1919, pp. 364–389.

Clapham, John: 'Dvořák's Visit to Russia'. *Musical Quarterly* vol. li, 1965, 493–506.

Felber, Rudolf: 'Tchaikovsky and Tolstoy', *The Chesterian*, vol. xii no. 91, December 1930, pp. 65–69.

Fiske, Roger: 'Tchaikovsky's Later Piano Concertos', *Musical Opinion*, lxii, October [pp. 17–18], November [pp. 114–115] and December [pp. 209–210] 1938.

Friskin, James: 'The Text of Tchaikovsky's B flat minor concerto', *Music & Letters*, l, 1969, pp. 246–251.

Garden, Edward: 'Tchaikovsky and Tolstoy', *Music & Letters*, lv, 1974, pp. 307–316.

Garden, Edward: 'Three Russian piano concertos', *Music & Letters*, lx, 1979, pp. 166–179.

Garden, Edward: 'The Influence of Balakirev on Tchaikovsky', *Proceedings of the Royal Musical Association*, cvii, 1980–81, pp. 86–99.

Garden, Edward: 'A Note on Tchaikovsky's first piano concerto', *The Musical Times*, cxxii, 1981, pp. 238–239.

Henahan, Donal: 'Did Tchaikovsky Really Commit Suicide?', *The New York Times*, 26 July 1981 [reprinted *International Herald Tribune*, 28 July 1981].

Holden, Anthony: 'The death of Tchaikovsky: Cholera or Suicide?', International Tchaikovsky Conference, University of Tübingen, Germany, 24 October 1993. Published in Čajkovskij-Studien, Schott, Mainz, 1995.

Holden, Anthony: 'Who killed Tchaikovsky?', *The Sunday Express*, London, 24 October 1993 [reprinted in *Hot Air*, August 1994].

Lloyd-Jones, David: 'A background to *Iolanta*', *The Musical Times*, cix, 1968, pp. 225–226.

Macdonald, Hugh: 'Tchaikovsky: Crises and Contortions', *The Musical Times*, cxxiv, 1983, pp. 609–612.

Malev, Evgeny: 'Exchanging Jurisprudence for a Hooter', *Vedomosti*, St Petersburg, 1 May 1992.

Mitchell, Donald: 'A Note on Tchaikovsky's *Queen of Spades*, *The Chesterian*, April 1951, pp. 86–89.

Nagibin, Yuri: 'How did Tchaikovsky die?', *24 Hours*, Moscow, no. xlii, 1992.

Newmarch, Rosa: 'Tchaikovsky's last visit to England', *The Musical Times*, 1 February 1904, pp. 95–97.

Newman, Ernest: 'The Essential Tchaikovsky', *Contemporary Review*, lxxix, 1901.

Norris, Geoffrey: 'Tchaikovsky and the 18th Century', *The Musical Times*, cxviii, 1977, pp. 715–716.

Orlova, Alexandra: 'Taina zhizni Chaykovskovo' ['The secret of Tchaikovsky's life'] . . . 'Taina smerti Chaykovskovo' ['The secret of Tchaikovsky's death'], *Novy Amerikanets*, New York, 5–11 November, pp. 20–21, and 12–18 November, pp. 22–23, 1980.

Orlova, Alexandra: 'Tchaikovsky: The Last Chapter' [translated by David Brown], *Music & Letters*, lxii, April 1981, pp. 125–145.

Orlova, Alexandra: 'Kholera ili samoubiistvo?' ['Cholera or suicide?'], *Novy Amerikanets*, 19–25 July 1981, pp. 38–42.

Orlova, Alexandra: 'Poslednie dni Chaykovskovo' ['Tchaikovsky's Last Days'] in *Sem Dnei* [*Seven Days*], 1983, no. 7.

Orlova, Alexandra: 'Taina zhizni i smerti Chaykovskovo' ['The secret of Tchaikovsky's life and death'], *Kontinent*, Paris, no. 53, 1987, pp. 311–316.

Orlova, Alexandra: 'Despite the Facts: Once Again Concerning Tchaikovsky's Death', 1989, *unpublished*.

Poznansky, Alexander: 'Tchaikovsky's Suicide: Myth and Reality' [translated by Ralph C. Burr, Jr], *19th Century Music*, xi, 1988, pp. 199–220.

Sabaneev, Leonid: 'Tchaikovsky', *The Musical Times*, lxx, 1 January 1929, pp. 20–23.

Sabaneev, Leonid: 'Tchaikovsky', *The Musical Times*, lxxxi, 1940, pp. 201–202.

Slonimsky, Nicholas: 'Further light on Tchaikovsky', *Musical Quarterly*, xxiv, 1938, pp. 139–146.

Spiegelman, Joel: 'The Trial, Condemnation and Death of Tchaikovsky', *High Fidelity* 31, no. 2 (1981), 49–51.

Taruskin, Richard: 'Pathetic Symphonist', *The New Republic*, 6 February 1995, pp. 26–40.

Tchaikovskaya, Antonina: 'Vospominaniya vdovy P.I. Chaykovskovo' ['Reminiscences of Tchaikovsky's widow'], *Russkaya Muzykalnaya Gazeta*, 1913.

Tchaikovskaya, Olga: '*Pikovaya dama*', *Novy mir*, Moscow, x, 1986.

Tchaikovsky, Mme. Anatol: 'Recollections of Tchaikovsky', *Music & Letters*, xxi no. 2, April 1940, pp. 103–109.

Tovey, D.F.: 'Tchaikovsky: Pathetic Symphony No. 6', *Essays in Musical Analysis*, ii, 1935, pp. 84–89.

Tovey, D.F.: 'Tchaikovsky: Symphony No. 5', *Essays in Musical Analysis*, vi, 1939, pp. 58–65.

Westrup, J.A.: 'Tchaikovsky and the Symphony', *The Musical Times*, lxxxi, June 1940, pp. 249–252.

Wiley, Roland John: 'The Symphonic Element in Nutcracker', *The Musical Times*, cxxv, 1984, pp. 693–695.

Wiley, Roland John: 'Dramatic time and music in Tchaikovsky's ballets', in *Slavonic and Western Music: Essays for Gerald Abraham* (ed. Brown, M. & Wiley, R.J., Ann Arbor, Michigan, 1985)

Woodside, Dr Mary: 'Comment and Chronicle', *19th Century Music*, xiii, no. 3, Spring 1990, pp. 273–274.

Zajaczkowski, Henry: 'The Function of Obsessive Elements in Tchaikovsky's Style', *The Music Review*, xliii, 1982, pp. 24–30.

Zajaczkowski, Henry: 'Tchaikovsky's Fourth Symphony', *The Music Review*, xlv, 1984, pp. 265–276.

Zajaczkowski, Henry: 'Tchaikovsky: The Missing Piece of the Jigsaw Puzzle', *The Musical Times*, cxxxi, 1990, pp. 238–242.

Zajaczkowski, Henry: 'Not To Be Born Were Best' [an analysis of the *Pathétique* Symphony], *The Musical Times*, cxxxiv, October 1993, pp. 561–566.

# APPENDIX D

# Source Notes

*All dates, including those of letters originally dated in the Russian [Julian] calendar have been updated to the Western [Gregorian] calendar, with the exception of Russian newspaper articles, which are given old/new references.*

## Prologue: 'The most Russian of us all'

1   Letter to Yurgenson, 29 October 1893.
2   Modest Tchaikovsky, *The Life & Letters of Peter Ilich Tchaikovsky*, abridged and translated by Rosa Newmarch (1906).
3   Humphrey Carpenter, *Benjamin Britten* (1992), p. 585.
4   Vladimir Ashkenazy, interview with the author, October 1993.
5   Letter to Nadezhda von Meck, 22 August 1880. P.I. Tchaikovsky, *Polnoye Sobranie Sochineny*, (Moscow, 1953–81), ix, 233–4.
6   John Warrack, *Tchaikovsky* (1973), p. 5.

## Chapter I: 'A Child of Glass'

1   Peter Pringle, 'Secrecy lingers in home of the SS-20', *The Independent*, London, 16 March 1992.
2   Modest Tchaikovsky (Newmarch), *op. cit.*
3   To Nadezhda von Meck, 21 February 1878.
4   Modest Tchaikovsky, *op. cit.*
5   This theme is exhaustively explored in Christoper Nupen's television biography of the composer, *Tchaikovsky's Women*, Channel 4, London, 1989.

6   Fanny Dürbach's reminiscences of Tchaikovsky were first published by Modest
    Tchaikovsky in *Russkaya Muzykalnaya Gazeta* (*Russian Musical Gazette*), nos.
    3–5, in 1896, and selectively in his subsequent biography, *op. cit.*
7   *ibid.*
8   Modest Tchaikovsky, *op. cit.*
9   *ibid.*
10  *ibid.*
11  *ibid.*
12  Letters v.48, in R.M. Davison's translation, from Orlova, *Tchaikovsky, A Self-
    Portrait* (1990), p. 5.
13  Modest Tchaikovsky, *op. cit.*
14  *ibid.*

## Chapter II: 'Respice finem'

1   Dominic Lieven and Allen A. Sinel, 'The Socialisation of the Russian Bureaucratic
    Elite', *Russian History* 3, 1976, pp. 1–31.
2   Evgeny Malev, 'Exchanging Jurisprudence for a Hooter', *Vedomosti*, St Peters-
    burg, 1 May 1992.
3   V.I. Sobolevsky, quoted in Poznansky, *The Quest for the Inner Man* (1991), p.
    19, also the source (quoting Richard S. Wortman, *The Development of Russian
    Legal Consciousness*, Chicago, 1976) for the details of the curriculum.
4   Lieven and Sinel, *op. cit.*
5   Ippolit Tchaikovsky, 'Epizody iz moei zhizni', *Istoricheskii vestnik*, 1913.
6   Vladimir Taneyev, *Detstvo, Yunost, Mysli o Budushchem*, 1959.
7   *The Music Lovers* (UA/Rossfilms, 1970), directed by Ken Russell, screenplay by
    Melvyn Bragg, based on Bowen & von Meck's *Beloved Friend*.
8   To Nadezhda von Meck, from Vienna 5 December 1877, & Kamenka 25 June
    1879.
9   *Vospominanya o P.I. Chaykovskom* ['Recollections of Tchaikovsky'] (Moscow,
    1962/Leningrad, 1980). This collection of reminiscences of the composer by
    various hands, the most valuable single source book on him (apart, perhaps,
    from Modest's biography), has been through many different editions in several
    different Russian eras. The two main editions are cited here.
10  Gerard, *Vospominanya*.
11  Maslov, *ibid.*
12  Poznansky, *op. cit.*, pp. 33–34.
13  Stasov, *Uchilishche Pravovedeniya sorok let nazad*, quoted by Poznansky, *op.
    cit.*, p. 35.
14  Poznansky, *op. cit.*, p. 5.
15  Seen among the composer's letters in the Tchaikovsky Archive at Klin by a
    Russian scholar who was refused permission to publish it, and wishes to remain
    anonymous.

## Chapter III: 'I can be somebody'

1     Soviet censors have deleted the reason for Tchaikovsky's mixed feelings, but Poznansky, *op. cit.* pp. 47–8 is surely right that this is the unprintable explanation.
2     Modest Tchaikovsky, *op. cit.*
3     Laroche's recollections of Tchaikovsky, some of which appear in Modest Tchaikovsky, *op. cit.*, were collected in *Izbrannye stati, vypusk ii: P.I. Chaykovsky* [*Selected Articles, ii: P.I. Tchaikovsky*] (Leningrad, 1975).
4     Evgeny Malev, 'Exchanging Jurisprudence for a Hooter', *Vedomosti*, St Petersburg, 1 May 1992.
5     To Sasha, 22 March 1861.
6     To Sasha, 4 November 1861.
7     David Brown, *Tchaikovsky: A Biographical and Critical Study* (London, 1978–1991), vol i, pp. 56–7, & many others.
8     Poznansky, *op. cit.*, p. 59.
9     To Sasha, 4 November 1861.
10    To Sasha, 16 December 1861.
11    Rubinstein's memoirs, quoted in Bowen and von Meck, *Beloved Friend*, p. 21.
12    *Pervaya Russkaya Konservatorya* ['The First Russian Conservatoire'], Leningrad, 1987.
13    Laroche, *op. cit.*
14    Author's visits to Klin, October 1992 & July 1993.
15    To Sasha, 22 September 1862.
16    Modest Tchaikovsky, *op. cit.*
17    To Sasha, 22 September 1862.
18    Poznansky, *op. cit.*, p. 78.
19    *Vospominanya*; cf Brown, i, 69.
20    Laroche, *op. cit.*
21    Alexander Suvorin, *Dnevnik* [*Diary*] for 14/26 March 1893 (Moscow, 1923).
22    N.D. Kashkin, *Vospominanya o P.I. Chaykovskom* ['Recollections of P.I. Tchaikovsky'] (*Russian Review*, Moscow, 1896), an English version of which appeared in *The Musical Times*, London, 1 July 1897, pp. 449–452.
23    Author's interview with Georgy Abramovsky, Professor of the History of Russian Music, St Petersburg Conservatoire, July 1993.
24    Cui's article appeared three months after the concert, in *Sankt-Peterburgskie Vedomosti*, 24 March/5 April 1865.
25    Modest Tchaikovsky, *op. cit.*

## Chapter IV: 'You are needed here'

1     Stravinsky, 'An Open Letter to Diaghilev', *The Times*, London, 18 October 1921.
2     Kashkin, *Vospominanya. See also* Wiley, *Tchaikovsky's Ballets*, p. 26.
3     Modest Tchaikovsky, *op. cit. See also* Poznansky, *op. cit.*, p. 92.
4     Laroche, *op. cit.*

5   Dombayev, *Tvorchestvo*, p. 278, quoting Alina Brullyova.
6   To Anatoly, 18 March 1866.
7   Kashkin, *op. cit.*
8   Modest Tchaikovsky, *op. cit.*
9   To Sasha, 28 April 1868.
10  To Sasha, 6 October 1868.
11  To Anatoly, 12 November 1867.
12  See also David Brown, 'Balakirev, Tchaikovsky and Nationalism', *Music & Letters*, xlii, 1961, pp. 227–241; and Edward Garden 'The Influence of Balakirev on Tchaikovsky', *Proceedings of the Royal Musical Association*, cvii, 1980–81, pp. 86–99.
13  Kashkin, *op. cit.*
14  Rimsky-Korsakov, *Letopis Moyey Muzykalnoy Zhizni* (St Petersburg, 1909), published in English as *My Musical Life* (Knopf, New York, 1923, 3rd edn 1942), p. 75.
15  Brown, *op. cit.* i, p. 132.
16  Modest Tchaikovsky, *op. cit.*
17  *ibid.*
18  Mrs Anatoly Tchaikovskaya, 'Recollections of Tchaikovsky', *Music & Letters*, xxi no. 2, April 1940, p. 108.
19  To his father, 7 January 1869.
20  From his father, quoted by Modest, *op. cit.*
21  Kashkin, *op. cit.*
22  Poznansky, *op. cit.*, p. 115.
23  Kashkin, *op. cit.*
24  Poznansky, *op. cit.*, p. 115.
25  From Balakirev, 30 March 1869.
26  Brown, i, p. 172.

## Chapter V: 'What is the point?'

1   Episode reconstructed from differing accounts in *Vospominanya* (1962/1980) and Sokolova, *Istorichesky Vestnik*, 119 (1910).
2   Diary entries for 16–17 September 1887.
3   Alexandra Orlova, 'Tchaikovsky, The Last Chapter', *Music & Letters*, lxii, 1981.
4   Author's interviews, October 1992 and July 1992, with Polina Vaidman, senior archivist at Klin, where plans are afoot to publish an edition of Modest's memoirs edited by an 'approved' Russian musicologist, Valery Sokholov.
5   To Anatoly, 15 August 1869.
6   From Balakirev, 16 October 1869.
7   The phrase is John Warrack's (*Tchaikovsky*, 1973, p. 47), as are the essential elements of this reading of the piece.
8   Yuri Davidov, *Zapiski o P.I. Chaykovskom* [*Notes on P.I. Tchaikovsky*] (Moscow, 1962, 1977).
9   'Even Soviet commentators, who have had unlimited access to the composer's archive in Klin, do not dispute this fact,' writes Poznansky, *op. cit.*, p. 133.

10   *ibid.*
11   Klimenko's memoirs, quoted by Poznansky, *op. cit.*, p. 139.
12   Translation by Poznansky, *op. cit.*, p. 139, whose Chapter 8 ('The Petrolina Letters') examines these matters in much greater detail.
13   Poznansky, *op. cit.*, p. 148.
14   To Lev Davidov, 22–30 April 1870.
15   To Anatoly, quoted by Orlova, *op. cit.* p.24.
16   Balakirev, *Vospominanya* (ed. E. Frid, 1962), p. 162.
17   To Anatoly, 13 January 1872.
18   Brown, *op. cit.*, i, pp. 250–1.
19   To Sasha, 21 January 1873.
20   'Our Music During the Last Twenty-Five Years', first published in *Vestnik Evropy*, October 1883, reprinted in *Selected Essays on Music* (NY, 1968), p. 112.
21   Modest Tchaikovsky, *op. cit.*
22   To von Meck, 4 May 1878.
23   Stasov, quoted in Dombayev, 356–7, & Modest.
24   Brown, *op. cit.* i, p. 295.
25   Rimsky-Korsakov, *op. cit.*, p. 197.
26   Kashkin, *op. cit.*
27   Brown, *op. cit.* i, p. 305.
28   *Sankt-Peterburgskie Vedomosti*, 12/24 March 1874.
29   Modest Tchaikovsky, *op. cit.*
30   Brown, *op. cit.* i, p. 228.
31   Warrack, *op. cit.*, pp. 57–8.
32   To Modest, 9 May 1874.
33   To Napravnik, 31 October 1874.
34   To Taneyev, 13 December 1876.

## Chapter VI: 'I'm all written out'

1    To von Meck, 2[–3] February 1878.
2    To Anatoly, 21 January 1875.
3    To Rimsky-Korsakov, *op. cit.*, p. 157 fn.
4    To von Meck, 5 January 1878 and 30 July 1880.
5    Brown, *op. cit.*, ii, pp. 61–2.
6    Stasov, *Selected Essays on Music*, p. 181.
7    Kashkin, *op. cit.*
8    To Modest, 5 April 1876.
9    Modest Tchaikovsky, *op. cit.*
10   *Sovremennye Izvestia*, 26 Feb/10 March 1877, quoted in Wiley, *op. cit.*, p. 51.
11   *The Russian Gazette*, March 1877.
12   To Anatoly, 15 July 1876.
13   To Modest, 13–14 July 1876.
14   To Anatoly, 15 July 1876.
15   *Inferno*, Canto V, 121–3.
16   To Modest, 20 August 1876.

17  Poznansky, *op. cit.*, pp. 179–80.
18  To Modest, 14 August 1876.
19  To Modest, 20 August 1876.
20  Modest Tchaikovsky, *op. cit.*
21  To Modest, 31 August 1876.
22  To Modest, 22 September 1876.
23  To Modest, 29 September & 10 October 1876.
24  To Lev Davidov, 24 September 1876.
25  To Sasha, 31 September 1876.
26  Brown, *op. cit.*, ii, p. 100.
27  *ibid*, 101.

## Chapter VII: 'To silence the gossips'

1   Modest Tchaikovsky, *op. cit.*, & letter to his sister, 23 December 1876. *See also* Rudolf Felber, 'Tchaikovsky and Tolstoy', *The Chesterian*, xii, 91, December 1930, pp. 65–69; and Edward Garden, 'Tchaikovsky and Tolstoy', *Music & Letters* 55 [1974] pp. 307–16.
2   To Modest, 30 May 1877.
3   Ivan Klimenko, *Moi Vospominanya*, quoted in Poznansky, *op. cit.*, pp. 208–9.
4   The most detailed account of Tchaikovsky's wedding and marriage comes from Nikolay Kashkin, in *Iz Vospominany o P.I. Chaykovskom* ['From recollections of Tchaikovsky'], published in *Proshloye Russkoy Muzyki: materialy i issledovaniya. i: P.I. Chaykovsky* [*The Past of Russian Music: Materials and Researches. i: P.I. Tchaikovsky*] (Petrograd, 1920), pp. 105–28. Kashkin felt unable to publish it until after Antonina's death in 1917.
5   Antonina Milyukova's letters to Tchaikovsky are preserved in the archive at Klin.
6   Further extracts from Antonina's letters are most easily accessible in an Appendix to Garden/Gottieri (ed.), *To My Best Friend*, pp. 425–7.
7   Kashkin, *op. cit.*
8   To von Meck, 15 July 1877.
9   *ibid*.
10  *ibid*.
11  *ibid*.
12  *ibid*.
13  Kashkin, *op. cit.*
14  Author's interview, Moscow, July 1993, with Valery Sokolov, who is working on a biography of Antonina Tchaikovskaya authorized (and to be published) by the Tchaikovsky Archive at Klin.
15  Antonina Tchaikovskaya, 'Vospominany vdovy P.I. Chaykovskovo', *Russkaya Muzykalnaya Gazeta* 42 (1913).
16  Poznansky, *op. cit.*, p. 206.
17  Antonina Tchaikovskaya, *op. cit.*
18  Poznansky, *op. cit.*, p. 216.
19  To Ilya Petrovich Tchaikovsky, 5 July 1877.

20  To Sasha, 17 July 1877.
21  From Sasha, 24 July 1877.
22  To Anatoly, 5 July 1877.
23  Kashkin, *op. cit.*
24  Antonina Tchaikovskaya, *op. cit.*
25  To Anatoly, 20 July 1877.
26  *ibid.*
27  Kashkin, *op. cit.*
28  Antonina Tchaikovskaya, *op. cit.*
29  To Anatoly, 23 July 1877.
30  *ibid.*
31  To Sasha, 1 August 1877.
32  To von Meck, 9 August 1877.
33  *ibid.*

## Chapter VIII: 'My beloved friend'

1  *Beloved Friend*, by Catherine Drinker Bowen and Barbara von Meck, pp. 29–30. This novelized account of the Tchaikovsky–von Meck relationship, published in 1937, amounted to the first publication in English of their correspondence. Barbara von Meck was Nadezhda's granddaughter-in-law; she had married Vladimir II, known as Volichka, oldest son of Nadzehda's oldest and favourite son, Vladimir I; the couple had inherited the letters [see *op. cit.* p. 38 fn].
2  *ibid.* p. 30.
3  Letter to Sasha, 6 March, 1877.
4  *ibid.*
5  From von Meck, 27 February 1877.
6  To von Meck, 28 February 1877.
7  From von Meck, 19 March 1877.
8  To von Meck, 28 March 1877.
9  From von Meck, 30 March 1877.
10  From von Meck, 12 May 1877.
11  To von Meck, 13 May 1877.
12  *Ibid.*
13  From von Meck, 14 May 1877.
14  From von Meck, 30 March 1877.
15  From von Meck, 18 July 1877.
16  To von Meck, 27 July 1877.
17  From von Meck, 31 July 1877.
18  To von Meck, 7 August 1877.
19  To von Meck, 9 August 1877.
20  To von Meck, 14 August 1877.
21  From von Meck, 20 August 1877.
22  To von Meck, 23 August 1877.
23  To von Meck, 24 August 1877.
24  To Anatoly, 26 September 1877.

25 To Anatoly, 6 October 1877.
26 To von Meck, 24 September 1877.
27 Kashkin, *op. cit.*
28 Antonina Tchaikovskaya, *op. cit.*
29 Kashkin, *op. cit.* This is the only account of Tchaikovsky's suicide attempt, and has been disputed by some scholars. But Kashkin is in all other respects a reliable witness, and I see no reason to doubt his word about an incident quite in keeping with Tchaikovsky's frame of mind. 'I fell into despair,' he wrote to von Meck from Clarens on 23 October, 'and sought death.'
30 Andrey Budyakovsky in Chapter Six of the (unpublished) biographical volume of his five-volume *Tchaikovsky: Life, Musical Activity, Works* (1935–42).
31 Kashkin, *op. cit.*
32 To von Meck, 6 November 1877.

## Chapter IX: 'I must hide for a year'

1 Antonina Tchaikovskaya, *op. cit.*
2 To von Meck, 23 October 1877.
3 From von Meck, 29 October 1877.
4 To von Meck, 6 November 1877.
5 *ibid.*
6 *ibid.*
7 To von Meck, 14 August 1877.
8 To von Meck, 23 August 1877.
9 To von Meck, 11 September 1877.
10 To von Meck, 24 September 1877.
11 To Anatoly, 13 December 1877.
12 To von Meck, 19 November 1877.
13 To von Meck, 21 November 1877.
14 From von Meck, 11–12 December 1877.
15 To von Meck, 17 December 1877.
16 From von Meck, 22 January 1878.
17 From von Meck, 24 January 1878.
18 From von Meck, 3 February 1878.
19 To von Meck, 21 January 1878.
20 To von Meck, 30 November 1877.
21 To Anatoly, 14 December 1877.
22 To von Meck, 5 January 1878.
23 To von Meck, 28 December 1877.
24 To Anatoly, 25 February 1878.

## Chapter X: 'A free man'

1 From von Meck, 24 February 1878.
2 To von Meck, 1 March 1878.

3   From Taneyev, 30 March 1878.
4   To Taneyev, 8 April 1878.
5   Edward Garden, *Tchaikovsky* (London, 1973, 1993), pp. 75–6.
6   To Anatoly, 18 February 1878.
7   From von Meck, 11 March 1878.
8   To Anatoly, 25 February 1878.
9   Eduard Hanslick, 'Concerts, Composers and Virtuosi of the Last Fifteen Years' (Berlin, 1896), reprinted in *Musik Konkret 7, Tschaikowsky aus der Nähe* (Berlin: Verlag ernst kuhn, 1994) pp. 197–198.
10  Brown, *op. cit.* ii, p. 274.
11  To von Meck, 18 July 1878.
12  To Anatoly, 15 August 1878.
13  'Moskovsky feleton', *Novoe Vremya*, 285; 14/26 August 1878.
14  To von Meck, 16–28 September 1878.
15  From von Meck, 2 October 1878.
16  To von Meck, 19 October 1878.

## Chapter XI: 'Things can't get worse'

1   To Modest, 18 December 1878.
2   To Modest, 7 January 1879.
3   To Anatoly, 7 January 1879.
4   To Modest, 6 March 1879.
5   David Brown, *The Viking Opera Guide* (London, 1994), pp. 1087–8.
6   To von Meck, 5 April 1879.
7   To Anatoly, 27 August 1879.
8   From von Meck, 26 September 1879.
9   To Anatoly, 7 December 1879.
10  Brown, *op. cit.*, iii, p. 96.
11  *ibid*, p. 97.
12  To Modest, 11 March 1880.
13  To von Meck, 20 March 1880.
14  From Antonina, 7 July 1880.
15  From Yurgenson, 10 June 1880.

## Chapter XII: 'I hate to be abroad'

1   To Taneyev, 13 August 1880.
2   *Golos*, 19 Feb/3 March 1881.
3   To Anatoly, 15 March 1881.
4   To von Meck, 7 March 1881.
5   From von Meck, 18 March 1881.
6   To von Meck, 28 March 1881.
7   To Alexey, 14 & 23 May 1881.
8   To Yurgenson, 31 August 1881.

9    See also David Brown, 'Tchaikovsky's *Mazeppa*', *The Musical Times*, cxxv, 1984,
     pp. 696–8.
10   To von Meck, 5 June 1881.
11   To Yurgenson, 18 June 1881.
12   To Anatoly, 30 June 1881.
13   Episode reconstructed from T's letters to von Meck, Modest and Tkachenko.
14   To Modest, 24 October 1881.
15   Brown, *op. cit.*, iii, p. 149.
16   To von Meck, 8 December 1881.
17   To von Meck, 13 December 1881.
18   To von Meck, 27 December 1881.
19   To Yurgenson, 11 February 1882.
20   To Anatoly, 20 February 1882.
21   Mrs Anatoly Tchaikovskaya, 'Recollections of Tchaikovsky', *Music & Letters*, xxi
     no. 2, April 1940, pp. 103–4.
22   To Modest, 27 May 1882.
23   To von Meck, 26 September 1882.
24   To Modest, 23 October 1882.
25   To von Meck, 23 January 1883.
26   From von Meck, 30 March 1883.
27   To Anatoly and von Meck, 13 April and 20 May 1883.
28   Mrs Anatoly Tchaikovskaya, *op. cit.*, p. 104.
29   *ibid.*, pp. 105–6.
30   To von Meck, 13 September 1883.
31   From von Meck, 17 July 1882.
32   To von Meck, 19 February 1884.
33   Vladimir Pogozhev, *Vospominanya*.
34   Brown, *op. cit.*, iii, p. 257.
35   Poznansky, *op. cit.*, pp. 438–9.
36   From Tchaikovsky's diary for 6 May 1884. *Dnevniki 1873–91*, a new edition
     of his diaries, was published in paperback in St Petersburg in 1993.

## Chapter XIII: 'A home of my own'

1    To Modest, 14 May 1884.
2    To Alexey, 30 September 1882.
3    To von Meck, 10 March 1883.
4    To von Meck, 21 May 1884.
5    Dombayev & Modest *op. cit.*, quoted by Brown, *op. cit.* iii, p. 283.
6    Modest Tchaikovsky, *op. cit.*
7    To Modest, 15 December 1884.
8    To Modest, 14 January 1885.
9    To von Meck, 30 January 1885.
10   To von Meck, 15 February 1885.
11   To Modest, 15 February 1885.

12 To von Meck, 16 February 1885.
13 To Modest, 19 February 1885.
14 From Balakirev, 10 October 1882.
15 To Balakirev, 24 November 1882.
16 To von Meck, 25 March 1884.
17 To Balakirev, 12 November 1884.
18 To Emilia Pavlovskaya, 1 August 1885.
19 To Balakirev, 25 September 1885.
20 To Grand Duke Konstantin Konstantinovich, October 1888, quoted by Modest.
21 Modest Tchaikovsky, *op. cit.*
22 Episode reconstructed from letters to Modest and diary entries for April–October 1886.
23 Diary entries for 10 & 12 July 1886.
24 To Modest, 16 July 1886.
25 To Modest, 30 July 1886.
26 Diary entries for 14 & 15 July 1886.
27 Diary entry for 5 July 1886.
28 Poznansky, *op. cit.*, p. 464.
29 Diary entry for 14 September 1886.
30 To Modest, 30 September 1886.
31 Diary entry for 26 September 1886.
32 Diary entry for 6 October 1887.
33 Diary entry for 4 September 1886.
34 To Modest, 17 May 1890.
35 From von Meck, 27 October 1886.
36 To Modest, 16 December 1886.
37 Dombayev, quoted by Brown, *op. cit.*, iv, 100.

## Chapter XIV: 'A sick joke'

1 Diary entry for 2 February 1887.
2 To von Meck, 3 February 1887.
3 To von Meck, 22 March 1887.
4 Diary entries for 14–15 April 1887.
5 Tatyana Shchepkina-Kupernik, *Vospominanya.*
6 Diary entries for 27–28 August 1887.
7 *Muzykalnoye Obozreniiye*, 5/17 November 1887.
8 To von Meck, 25 November 1887.
9 Kashkin, *op. cit.*
10 Mrs A. Brodsky, *Recollections of a Russian Home* (Manchester/London, 1904), pp. 153–167, quoted in Brown, *Tchaikovsky Remembered*, pp. 138–142.
11 *Autobiographical Account of a Foreign Tour in 1888*, written at Tiflis in April 1888, and originally intended by the composer for publication.
12 Ethel Smyth, *Impressions that Remained* (London, 1919), pp. 167–8.
13 To Modest, 24 January 1888.

14 Sir Frederic Cowen, *My Art and My Friends* (London, 1913), pp. 148–9.
15 To von Meck, 3 April 1888.
16 Diary entry for 3 October 1887.
17 Diary entries for 16–17 September 1887.
18 *Muzykalnoye Naslediye Chaykovskovo*, ed. K.Y. Davidova & others, Moscow (1958), p. 239. Quoted in Brown, *op. cit.*, iv, p. 148.
19 From Dvořák, 14 January 1889. For an account of Dvořák's eventual visit (in which Tchaikovsky played little or no part), see John Clapham, 'Dvořák's Visit to Russia', *Music Quarterly*, vol. li, 1965, 493–506.
20 To Modest, 12 March 1889.
21 Diary entry for 3 April 1889.
22 To Yurgenson, 2 April 1889.
23 Quoted by Gerald Norris, *Stanford, The Cambridge Jubilee and Tchaikovsky*, an Aladdin's Cave of colourful detail on Tchaikovsky's visits to England.
24 To Modest, 12 September 1889.
25 A.P. Chekhov, *Pisma [Letters]* (Moscow, 1974–), iii, 259–262.
26 *Izbrannye Stati*, ii (Leningrad, 1975)
27 See R.J. Wiley, *op. cit.*, pp. 106–112.
28 David Brown, *BBC Music Magazine*, vol II no. 3, November 1993.
29 To Yurgenson, 11 February 1890.
30 To Glazunov, 11 February 1890.
31 Diary entry for 12 February 1890.
32 Diary entry for 15 March 1890.
33 Kashkin, *op. cit.* [cf. *The Musical Times*, London, 1 July 1897, p. 452].
34 To Modest, 25 June 1890.
35 Brown, *op. cit.*, iv, p. 284.
36 From von Meck, 25 September 1890.
37 To von Meck, 4 October 1890.
38 To Yurgenson, 10 October 1890.

## Chapter XV: 'I'm a big shot'

1 Exchange of letters, 26 November & 4 December 1889.
2 From Alexey, 25 October 1890.
3 From Modest, 22 October 1890.
4 Alexandra Amfiteatrova-Levitskaya, *Vospominanya*.
5 Leonid Nikolayev, *Vospominanya*.
6 Mikhail Ippolitov-Ivanov, *Vospominanya*.
7 To Pakhulsky, 6 April 1891.
8 Transatlantic diary, 20 April 1891.
9 Published (in Russian and English) as *25 Dney v Amerike [25 Days in America]* ('Muzyka', Moscow, 1991), to mark the centenary of the visit, as part of Klin's contribution to a commemorative exhibition at Carnegie Hall.
10 Transatlantic diary, 18 April 1891.
11 *ibid.*, 19–21 April 1891.
12 *ibid.*, 22–23 April 1891.

13  Transatlantic diary, 24–27 April 1891.
14  In *Tchaikovsky in America* (OUP, 1986), the head librarian of the Detroit Symphony Orchestra, Elkhonon Yoffe, devotes a 216-page book to his fellow Russian's 25-day visit.
15  To Anatoly, from New York, 27 April 1891. The final phrase, also chosen as the title of this chapter, is Yoffe's rather endearing translation.
16  To Vladimir ['Bob'] Davidov, 30 April 1891.
17  Diary entry, 5 May 1891.
18  All newspaper quotations from the issues of 8 May 1891.
19  Newspaper issues of 6 May 1891.
20  Diary entry, 6 May 1891.
21  *Brooklyn Daily Eagle*, 8 May 1891.
22  Newspaper issues of 6 May 1891.
23  Walter Damrosch, *My Musical Life* (New York, 1923), pp. 143–4.
24  Diary entry, 10 May 1891.
25  Diary entry, 9 May 1891.
26  Diary entry, 14 May 1891.
27  *Daily Evening Telegraph*, Philadelphia, 19 May 1891.
28  Diary entry, 20 May 1891.
29  *New York Herald*, New York, 24 May 1891.
30  Diary entry, 20 May 1891.
31  To Pakhulsky, 18 June 1891.
32  To Yurgenson, 15 August 1893.
33  To Bob Davidov, 23 July & 3 August 1891.
34  *St Petersburg Life*, November 1892. See also: David Lloyd-Jones, 'A Background to *Iolanta*', *The Musical Times*, cix, 1968, pp. 225–6.
35  To Bob Davidov, 23 July & 3 August 1891.
36  Gustav Mahler, quoted in Henry-Louis de La Grange, *Gustav Mahler*, i (New York, 1973), p. 248.
37  *North American*, Philadelphia, 19 May 1891.
38  Leopold Auer, *My Long Life in Music* (London, 1924), pp. 139–40.
39  Vladimir Napravnik, *Vospominanya*.
40  Rimsky-Korsakov, *op. cit.*, pp. 308–9.
41  To Modest, 12 June 1892.
42  To Modest, 23 June 1892.
43  Mrs Anatoly Tchaikovskaya, 'Recollections of Tchaikovsky', *Music & Letters*, xxi no. 2, April 1940, p. 106.
44  *ibid.*, p. 106.
45  To Anatoly, 28 July 1892.
46  Laroche, *op. cit.*
47  To Anatoly, 18 December 1892.
48  Newspaper issues of 12/24 & 13/25 December 1892.
49  Roland John Wiley, 'The Symphonic Element in Nutcracker', *The Musical Times*, cxxv, 1984, p. 693.
50  To Modest, 30 December 1892.
51  To Nikolay, 15 January 1893.
52  *ibid.*

## Chapter XVI: 'Let them guess'

1  The translation is that of Gerald Norris, on whose uniquely fascinating book *Stanford, the Cambridge Jubilee and Tchaikovsky* (London, 1980), this account gratefully draws. (Rubinstein letter, p. 213.)

2  Norris, *op. cit.*, p. 232.

3  Dannreuther, 'Tschaikowsky', in Sir George Grove (ed.), *A Dictionary of Music and Musicians*, iv (London, 1890).

4  To Dr John Peile, 16 December 1882 [trans. Norris, *op. cit.*, p. 267].

5  Norris, *op. cit.*, p. 267.

6  Modest Tchaikovsky, *op. cit.* & cf. letter to Modest, 9 February 1893.

7  Konstantin Dumchev, *Vospominanya*.

8  To Anatoly, 22 February 1893.

9  To Vladimir 'Bob' Davidov, 23 February 1893.

10  *Muzykalnoye Nasledie Chaykovskovo*, ed. Davidova, K.Y. & others (Moscow, 1958), p. 245.

11  To Nikolay, 15 January 1893.

12  Isaak Bukinik, *Vospominanya*.

13  To 'Bob' Davidov, 27 May 1893.

14  To 'Bob' Davidov, 29 May 1893.

15  *ibid*.

16  Recollections of Hatzfeld's daughter, Maude, in Norris, *op. cit.*, p. 351.

17  Mackenzie, Sir Alexander: *A Musician's Narrative* (London, 1927).

18  Wood, Sir Henry: *My Life of Music* (London, 1938).

19  *Daily Chronicle*, London, 2 June 1893.

20  *Daily Telegraph*, London, 2 June 1893.

21  Shaw, G.B., *Shaw's Music* (Bodley Head, London, 1981), ii, 905.

22  To Modest, 3 June 1893.

23  *ibid*.

24  Henschel, Sir George, *Musings and Memories of a Musician* (London, 1918), p. 365.

25  To Yurgenson, 5 June 1893.

26  To Modest, 10 June 1893.

27  *The Sunday Times*, London, 12 November 1893, reprinted in Herman Klein, *Thirty Years of Musical Life in London, 1870–1900* (London, 1903), pp. 343–8.

28  *The Sunday Times*, London, 18 June 1893.

29  Saint-Saëns, 'Docteur à Cambridge', *Portraits et Souvenirs* (1899).

30  Stanford, C.V., *Pages from an Unwritten Diary* (London: Arnold, 1914), p. 280.

31  Norris, *op. cit.*, p. 399

32  Ganz & Bridge, quoted in Norris, *op. cit.*, p. 417.

33  Saint-Saëns, *op. cit.*

34  To Kolya Konradi, 15 June 1893.

35  To Anatoly, 15 June 1893.

36  To Modest, 1 July 1893.

37  To Yurgenson, 5 July 1993.

38  To Modest, 3 August 1893.

39  To Taneyev, 13 August 1893.

40  To Anatoly, 31 August 1893.

41  To 'Bob' Davidov, 15 August 1893.

42  Damrosch, *op. cit.*, pp. 144–145.

43  N.D. Kashkin, 'Vospominanya o P.I. Chaykovskom' ['Recollections of P.I. Tchaikovsky'] (*Russian Review*, Moscow, 1896), an English version of which appeared in *The Musical Times*, London, 1 July 1897, pp. 449–452.

44  Vasily Yestrebtsev, *Vospominanya* (1980).

45  Charles L. Buchanan, 'The Unvanquishable Tchaikovsky', *Musical Quarterly* v, 3 July 1919, pp. 364–389.

46  Mrs Anatoly Tchaikovskaya, 'Recollections of Tchaikovsky', *Music & Letters*, xxi no. 2, April 1940, p. 109.

47  Edward Garden, 'Tchaikovsky and Tolstoy', *Music & Letters*, lv, 1974, p. 315.

48  Poznansky, *The Quest for the Inner Man*, p. 559.

49  Robert Craft, *Chronicle of a Friendship 1948–71* (London: Gollancz, 1972), p. 408.

50  Modest Tchaikovsky, *op. cit.*

51  To Grand Duke Konstantin Konstantinovich, 7 October 1893.

52  To Modest, 1 September 1893.

53  To Anna Merkling, 9 October 1893.

54  Mrs Anatoly Tchaikovskaya, *op. cit.*, p. 109.

55  *Novoe Vremya*, no. 6348, 18/30 October 1893.

56  Kashkin, *op. cit.*

57  Laroche, *op. cit.*

58  Francesco Berger, *Reminiscences, Impressions, Anecdotes* (London, n.d.), p. 87.

59  Yulian Poplavsky, 'Recollections', first published in *Artist* (1894), no. 42, reprinted in *Vospominanya*.

60  Mrs Anatoly Tchaikovskaya, *op. cit.*, p. 104.

61  Ippolitov-Ivanov, *op. cit.*

62  *ibid.*

63  Konstantin Saradzhev, Recollections (1938), first published in *Stati, Vospominanya* [*Articles, Recollections*] (Moscow, 1962), reprinted in *Vospominanya*.

64  Yuri Davidov, *op. cit.*

65  Yuri Yuriev, *Zapiski* [*Notes*] (Leningrad/Moscow, 1948), reprinted in *Vospominanya*.

66  Glazunov, *Vospominanya*.

## Chapter XVII: 'A classic case of cholera'

1   Rimsky-Korsakov, *Letopis Moyey Muzykalnoy Zhizni* (St Petersburg, 1909), published in English as *My Musical Life* (Knopf, NY, 1923, 3rd edn 1942), pp. 339–40.

2 Modest Tchaikovsky (Newmarch), *op. cit.* pp. 720–1.
3 Letters shown to the author by the senior archivist at Klin, Polina Vaidman, in October 1992 & July 1993. Photocopying was not permitted, as Vaidman proposes to publish the letters herself in a new edition of the 6th Symphony.
4 N.N. Figner interviewed in *Novosti i Birzhevaya Gazeta*, 26 October/7 November & *Peterburgskaya Gazeta* 25 October/6 November 1893.
5 Yuri Davidov, *Poslednie dni P.I. Chaykovskovo* [*Tchaikovsky's Last Days*] (1943), reprinted in *Vospominanya*.
6 Kashkin, *op. cit.*
7 Laroche, *op. cit.*
8 Epilogue to Galina von Meck (trans.): *Letters to his Family* (1981), pp. 555–6.
9 Alexander Poznansky, *Tchaikovsky: The Quest for the Inner Man* (1991), p. 581.
10 *Novosti i Birzhevaya Gazeta*, St Petersburg, 26 October/7 November 1893.
11 *Novoe Vremya*, St Petersburg, 27 October/8 November 1893.
12 'Asiatic Cholera', *Encyclopaedia of Brogkauz & Efron*, St Petersburg, 1903, vol. 37a, pp. 507–515.
13 *ibid.*
14 Laroche, *op. cit.*
15 Alexandra Orlova, *Tchaikovsky, A Self-Portrait* (1990), p. 408.
16 N.N. Figner interviewed in *Novosti i Birzhevaya Gazeta*, 26 October/7 November & *Peterburgskaya Gazeta* 25 October/6 November 1893.
17 Seen by the author in the archive at Klin.
18 Dr Lev Bertenson interview, '*Bolezn P.I. Chaykovskovo*' [*'Tchaikovsky's illness'*], *Novoe Vremya*, St Petersburg, 27 October/8 November 1893.
19 'At the coffin of P.I. Tchaikovsky', *Novoe Vremya*, no. 6345, St Petersburg, 27 October/8 November 1893.
20 *ibid.*
21 Rimsky-Korsakov, *op. cit.*, p. 340.
22 Government bulletin: *Directions concerning measures of personal protection against cholera*, 2/14 July 1893.
23 *Novoe Vremya*, no. 6345, 27 October/8 November 1893.
24 *ibid.*
25 Anton Chekhov, telegram to Modest Tchaikovsky, 8 November 1893: Chekhov, *Pisma v 12 tomakh* [*Letters in 12 vols*] (Moscow, 1974–), v, p. 240.
26 Letter from Anton Rubinstein to his sister Sofya, in Odessa: A. Rubinstein, *Literaturnoye Nasledie* [*Literary Legacy*], vol. 3 (Moscow, 1986), p. 140.
27 *Novosti i Birzhevaya Gazeta*, No. 294, 26 October/7 November 1893.
28 Rimsky-Korsakov, *op. cit.*, p.340.
29 Author's interview with Yuri Piryutko, curator, Alexandr Nevsky Lavra cemetery, St Petersburg, July 1993.
30 *Novoe Vremya*, no. 6347: 29 October/10 November 1893 (reprinted in *Pamyatnaya Knizhka Pravovedov*, No. 20, St Petersburg, 1894).
31 *Novosti i Birzhevaya Gazeta*, Saturday 30 October/11 November 1893.
32 A.S. Suvorin: *Diaries*, reprinted Moscow 1992.
33 *Novoe Vremya*, 3/15 November 1893.
34 *Novoe Vremya*, 5/17 November 1893.

35  *Novoe Vremya*, 7/19 November 1893.
36  '*Bolezn P.I. Chaykovskovo*' ['*Tchaikovsky's illness*'], *Novoe Vremya*, 1/13 November 1893.
37  *Russkaya Muzykalnaya Gazeta*, November 1893.
38  Rimsky-Korsakov, *op. cit.*, p. 340.

## Chapter XVIII: 'The uniform is sacred'

1   Dr Mary Woodside, 'Comment and Chronicle', *19th Century Music*, xiii, no. 3 (Spring 1990), pp. 273–4.
2   Letter to David Brown from M. Lischke, quoted in *Tchaikovsky Remembered* (1993), p. 223.
3   Jürg Stenzl, *The New Grove Dictionary of Music and Musicians* (1980), xii, 552.
4   See also Berberova, Brown & Karlinsky: 'Tchaikovsky's Suicide Reconsidered: A Rebuttal', *High Fidelity* 31, no. 8 (1981), in which Mooser's evidence is challenged by Berberova, who maintained that Glazunov made no mention of suicide when she met him in Paris in the 1930s. First published in France in 1936, Berberova's 'novelized' biography did not appear in Russia until 1993.
5   Oral tradition in St Petersburg, still alive during the author's three visits in 1992–93.
6   Olga Tchaikovskaya, 'Queen of Spades', *Novy Mir*, x, 1986.
7   Alexandra Orlova, letter to the author, 1 April 1994.
8   Herbert Weinstock, *Tchaikovsky* (NY, 1943; Cassell, London, 1946), p. 350 fn.
9   The author asked to see the letter when visiting Klin in October 1992 and July 1993, and was told it was 'a figment of Orlova's imagination'.
10  Bertenson's memoirs were published in 1912 under the title 'Thirty Years On: Pages from the memoirs of V.V. Bertenson' in *Istorichesky Vestnik* [*Historical Bulletin*] *1912*. vol. cxxviii. The edited version appeared sixty years later in *Vospominanya o P.I. Chaykovskom* (Moscow, 1973).
11  Orlova, letter to the author, 1 April 1994.
12  Orlova, 'Tchaikovsky: The Last Chapter', *Music & Letters*, lxii, 1981, pp. 125–145.
13  Alexander Poznansky, 'Tchaikovsky's Suicide: Myth and Reality', *19th Century Music*, vol xi (1988) p. 220 note 147.
14  Orlova, 'Tchaikovsky: A Self-Portrait', pp. 411–12.
15  Koni, A.F.: *Collected Works* [in 8 Volumes], vol. ii (Moscow, 1906).
16  File 355/1/3716 in the St Petersburg Central State Historical Archive (TsGIA).
17  File 1363/8/831 ['Concerning the work of Senator N.B. Jacobi (1878–1902)'] in the Russian State Historical Archive (RGIA).
18  *Ves Peterburg* [*All St Petersburg*], and interviews in St Petersburg in 1992–3 with L.A. Baranova, neighbour of the Jacobi family; Olga Armaderova, wife of Jacobi's grandson; and Jacobi's great-granddaughter Marina Armaderova.
19  *Pamyatnaya Knizhka Uchilishcha Pravovedenya* (St Petersburg, 1885).
20  *Military Encyclopaedia* 1912, St Petersburg, vol vii p. 204.
21  Orlova, 'Tchaikovsky: The Last Chapter', p. 125.
22  *ibid*, p. 125.

23 Author's (filmed) interview with Orlova: Jersey City, New Jersey, USA, 6 August 1992; and Orlova, letter to the author, 30 November 1993.

24 Polina Vaidman, senior archivist at Klin, interviewed by the author, July 1993.

25 *ibid*.

26 Author's interview with Boris Nikitin, author of a 1990 monograph on Tchaikovsky, Moscow, 8 October 1992.

27 *Tchaikovsky: A Biographical and Critical Study*: vol. 1 The Early Years (1840–74) (London: Gollancz, 1978), vol. 2 The Crisis Years (1982), vol. 3 The Years of Wandering (1986), vol. 4 The Final Years (1991).

28 'Tchaikovsky: The Last Chapter' (translated by David Brown), *Music & Letters*, lxii, 1981, pp. 125–145.

29 *High Fidelity* 31, no. 2 (1981), 49–51.

30 'Tchaikovsky's Suicide Reconsidered: A Rebuttal', *High Fidelity* 31, no. 8 (1981).

31 'Kholera ili samoubiystvo?' in *Novy Amerikanets*, 19–25 July 1981, pp. 38–42.

32 Donal Henahan, 'Did Tchaikovsky Really Commit Suicide?', *New York Times*, 26 July 1981. Following the letter from Berberova, Brown (M) and Karlinsky, some final comments from Henahan appeared on 9 August.

33 Orlova, Alexandra: *Tchaikovsky: A Self-Portrait* (Oxford University Press, 1990).

34 'Tchaikovsky's Suicide: Myth and Reality', *19th Century Music*, vol xi, 1988, pp. 199–220.

35 'Further Light on Tchaikovsky', *Musical Quarterly* xxiv, 1938, p. 139.

36 Orlova, 'Tchaikovsky: The Last Chapter', p. 128 fn 12. Although these figures are drawn from *Novosti i Birzhevaya Gazeta*, Poznansky challenges them as 'inaccurate' ('Tchaikovsky's Suicide: Myth and Reality', p. 217 note 81).

37 Orlova, *ibid.*, p. 128.

38 David Brown, *Tchaikovsky Remembered* (Faber & Faber, London, 1993), p. xv.

39 *ibid.*, p. xv.

40 *Regulations Concerning the Executive Sanitary Commissions*, June 1892 rev March 1893.

41 Lyubov Pets' evidence reported by Lidya Konniskaya to Orlova.

42 Galina von Meck: *Tchaikovsky: Letters to His Family* (London: Dennis Dobson, 1981), pp. 555–6.

43 Poznansky, *The Quest for the Inner Man*, p. 537.

44 *Vospominanya* (1962/1980), & Poznansky, *Quest for the Inner Man*, pp. 549–550.

45 Private archive of TsGIA St Petersburg: 14/3/26668. The file includes Litke's entrance pass to the university, valid until Spring 1892, and his certificate of graduation from the Imperial Philanthropic Society. The directory *Ves Peterburg* [*All St Petersburg*] for 1917 shows that he was a State Councillor, an official in the Ministry of Communications. He was married to Ekaterina Sergeyevna, with whom he lived at 25 Torgovy Street, St Petersburg.

46 Galina von Meck, *op. cit.*, p. 555.

47 'Tchaikovsky's Suicide: Myth and Reality', *op. cit.*, p. 208.

48 Author's (filmed) interview, Moscow, July 1993.

49 'How did the Great Composer Die?', *The Times*, London, 4 November 1993, & telephone interview with the author, London, November 1993.

50  Private letter to Alexandra Orlova, 1987. See also Appendix B, pp. 437–50, and Brown's footnote, iv, pp. 484–5.

51  In 'Queen of Spades', *Novy Mir*, x, p. 246, Olga Tchaikovskaya, a distant relative of the composer, waxes abusive about Orlova, charging (with no supporting evidence) that Voitov 'refused to sign her notes' of their interview.

52  V.I. Taneyev, *Detstvo, Yunost, mysli o budushchem* (Moscow, 1959), p. 399.

53  Poznansky, *The Quest for the Inner Man*, p. 36.

54  Poznansky, 'Tchaikovsky's Suicide: Myth and Reality', p. 215 fn 13, col 2.

55  Edward Garden's translation in 'Tchaikovsky and Tolstoy', *Music & Letters*, lv, 1974, p. 316.

56  Henry Zajaczkowski, *The Musical Times*, cxxxiii, no. 1797, November 1992, p. 574.

57  Alexandra Orlova, 'Despite the Facts: Once Again Concerning Tchaikovsky's Death', 1989, *unpublished* (but shared with the present author).

58  *Tchaikovsky* (Moscow, 1990) by Boris Nikitin, interviewed by the author, Moscow, 8 October 1992.

59  'Tchaikovsky, the Final Tragedy', *24 Hours*, Moscow, 1992, by Yuri Nagibin, interviewed by the author, July 1993.

60  Ashkenazy and Donohoe in conversation with the author, and (filmed) interviews for BBC Television's *Omnibus*, 'Who killed Tchaikovsky?', BBC1, 4 December 1993.

61  Polina Vaidman, senior archivist at Klin, interviewed by the author, July 1993.

62  David Brown, *Tchaikovsky Remembered* (Faber & Faber, London, 1993), p. xv, & interviews with the author, including a filmed interview in BBC TV's *Omnibus*, 'Who killed Tchaikovsky?', 4 December 1993.

63  *Svod Zakonov Rossiskoy Impery*, St Petersburg, 1857, xv, pt 1, ch. 4.

64  Poznansky, 'Tchaikovsky's Suicide: Myth and Reality', p. 204.

65  *ibid.*, pp. 202–3.

66  Vasily Bessel, 'Memories of Tchaikovsky', *Russkaya Muzykalnaya Gazeta*, xii, 1897.

67  Dr John Henry, 'Pride or Prejudice?', BBC Radio 3, 5 November 1993.

68  Marie Scheikevich, *Souvenirs d'un temps perdu*, quoted in Paul Morand, *Journal d'un attaché d'ambassade, 1916–17* (Paris, 1963), p. 65.

69  Tolstoy, letter to his wife, 6 November 1893, quoted in Orlova, *The Last Chapter*, p. 125.

## Epilogue: 'Natural and yet unnatural'

1  *Vospominanya* (1980).

2  Olga Bennigsen, *The Musical Quarterly*, xxiv no. 2, April 1938, pp. 129–138.

3  Antonina Milyukova Tchaikovskaya, *op. cit.*

4  T. Slyusarenko, 'Meeting in Klin', *Muzykalnaya Zhizn*, ix, 1990.

5  A description of Klin before and during the evacuation has been left by Sergey Bertenson (son of Lev) in 'The Tchaikovsky Museum at Klin', *Musical Quarterly*, xxx, 3 July 1944, pp. 329–35.

6  'Tchaikovsky's brother Ippolit tore up the title-page with the inscription when he

came across the volume, but the director of the Klin Museum retrieved the fragments from the waste-paper basket and pasted them together again, so that the self-accusing document is restored for posterity to behold' – Nicholas Slonimsky, 'Further Light on Tchaikovsky', *Musical Quarterly*, xxiv, 1938, p. 145.

7   Author's visits to Klin, June 1992 and July 1993.

8   Mikhail Annikushin, interview with author, St Petersburg, July 1993.

9   *Testimony*, The Memoirs of Dmitri Shostakovich (1979), p. 235.

10   Donald Tovey, quoted in Gerald Norris, *op. cit.*, p. 517.

11   Gerald Norris, *op. cit.*, p. 514.

12   Alexandr Belonenko, interview with the author, St Petersburg, July 1993.

13   Richard Taruksin, 'Pathetic Symphonist', *The New Republic*, 6 Feb 1995, p. 40.

14   Letter to von Meck, from Florence, 21 February 1878.

15   Lev Tolstoy, letter to his wife, 6 November 1893.

## Appendix B: Tchaikovsky's Death: Primary Sources

1   Dr Vasily Bertenson interviewed *Peterburgskaya Gazeta*, no. 293, 25 October/6 November 1893.

2   Dr Mamonov interviewed *Novosti i Birzhevaya Gazeta*, 26 October/7 November 1893.

3   N.N. Figner interviewed *Peterburgskaya Gazeta*, no. 293, 25 October/6 November 1893.

4   N.N. Figner interviewed *Novosti i Birzhevaya Gazeta*, 26 October/7 November 1893.

5   Dr Lev Bertenson interview, '*Bolezn P.I. Chaykovskovo*' ['*Tchaikovsky's illness*'], *Novoe Vremya*, no. 6345, 27 October/8 November 1893.

6   Modest Tchaikovsky, '*Bolezn P.I. Chaykovskovo*' ['*Tchaikovsky's illness*'], *Novoe Vremya*, St Petersburg, no. 6350, 12/24 November 1893.

7   First published in Moscow in 1943, as *Posledniye dni P.I. Chaykovskovo* [*Tchaikovsky's Last Days*], Yuri Davidov's memoirs of his uncle were not published in full until much later, in part posthumously, as *Zapiski o P.I. Chaykovskom* [*Notes on Tchaikovsky*] (Moscow, 1962; and 1977, eight years after Davidov's death).

8   First published in *Music & Letters*, 1981, republished in *Tchaikovsky: A Self-Portrait* (OUP, 1990), pp. 411–12.

9   From Galina von Meck's epilogue to her edition of Tchaikovsky's *Letters to His Family* (London, 1981), p. 555.

10   Private letter to Alexandra Orlova after reading her article in *Kontinent*, 1987 [David Brown's translation and summary in his *Tchaikovsky*, vol. iv *The Final Years*, 1990, pp. 484–5 fn].

# INDEX